CLARK McGINN was born in Ayr and talked so much as an infant his granny claimed he'd been vaccinated with a gramophone needle. Educated at Ayr Academy and University of Glasgow, he clocked up enough exams (in between speeches and debates) to embark on a banking career that would take him to London and New York and establish him as a specialist advisor to the global mission-critical helicopter industry. Burns has been a key joy since addressing his first Haggis in 1975 and he has toasted the 'Immortal Memory' every year since 1977, with nearly 250 speeches performed in 35 towns and cities across 16 countries, travelling the equivalent of 12 times around the globe. He was awarded a PhD by the University of Glasgow for his research on the history of the Burns Supper and is an honorary research fellow in its award-winning Centre for Robert Burns Studies. He is a Past President of the Burns Club of London (No 1) and of the Dublin Burns Club. In 2009, he gave the Eulogy at Burns's 250th Anniversary service in Westminster Abbey. He is an honorary fellow of the University of Glasgow, a Fellow of the Chartered Banking Institute and an Arkansas Traveler (Honorary Ambassador of Arkansas). He and his wife Ann live in Harrow-on-the-Hill, near their three daughters and two grandchildren, and in Fowey in Cornwall.

By the same author:

The Burns Supper: A Comprehensive History, Luath Press, 2019
The Burns Supper: A Concise History, 2019
Out of Pocket: How Collective Amnesia Lost the World its Wealth, Again, Luath Press, 2009
The Ultimate Burns Supper Book, Luath Press, 2006, 2024
The Ultimate Guide to Being Scottish, Luath Press, 2008, 2024

Burns and Black Lives

CLARK McGINN

Luath Press Limited
EDINBURGH
www.luath.co.uk

First published 2025

ISBN: 978-1-804251-69-0

The author's right to be identified as author of this book
under the Copyright, Designs and Patents Act 1988
has been asserted.

This book is made of materials from well-managed,
FSC®-certified forests and other controlled sources.

Printed and bound by
Ashford Colour Ltd, Gosport

Typeset in 11.5 point Sabon by
Main Point Books, Edinburgh

© Clark McGinn 2025

*Everything I do or have is thanks to Ann,
and this is no exception.*

If she doesn't mind sharing a bit on this one occasion, I hope this book can be seen as part of my *alma mater*'s, University of Glasgow's, courageous and vital process of reparation. And I sincerely hope that by the continued efforts of us all to understand and to change, our grandchildren, Lucy and Alfred, will grow in a world where 'man's inhumanity to man' has declined to the point that we can hope to see 'man to man, the world o'er' as our brothers and sisters regardless of skin colour, or any other accident of our humanity, as hoped for, prayed for and prophesied by Robert Burns.

'That man to man, the world o'er
Shall brothers be, for a' that.'

'Man's inhumanity to Man,
Makes countless thousands mourn.'

[Burns] was the first white man I read who seemed to understand that a human being was a human being and that we are more alike than unalike.—Nobel Prizewinner, Dr Maya Angelou[1]

Burns has also been described as a poet of the poor, an advocate of social and political change, and an opponent of slavery, pomposity and greed. —Former United Nations Secretary General, Kofi Annan[2]

Burns […] was a great outsider who […] made it fun to look through and poke at the veneer of white skin and have our day laughing at their wrong and distorted assumptions and perceptions of us. Like him, and with him, we craved to be most human.—Former High Commissioner, Republic of South Africa, Dr Lindiwe Mabuza[3]

[Burns is] the first national poet of people's hearts, and still arguably our national bard in many ways, […] Interestingly, Burns, like Shakespeare, is a poet that still speaks to our times – his work rings across the centuries, fresh as anything.—Former Scots Makar, Jackie Kay[4]

I locate myself near Robbie Burns – the Scottish vernacular and the folk qualities of his verse in particular.—poet and activist, Linton Kwesi Johnson[5]

---

1 Dr Maya Angelou in *Angelou on Burns*, BBC documentary directed/produced by Elly M Taylor, transmitted 21 August 1996.
2 Kofi Annan, 'Inaugural Robert Burns Memorial Lecture', United Nations Building, New York, 13 January 2004. Text from UN Information services: www.unis.unvienna.org/unis/pressrels/2004/sgsm9112.html (accessed 1 September 2024).
3 Dr Lindiwe Mabuza, in Andy Hall, ed, *Touched by Burns: Images and Insights* (Edinburgh: Birlinn, 2008), p.136.
4 Jackie Kay, 'Let Poetry Raise Our Spirits, Let Poetry Give Us Hope,' *Sunday Post*, 22 March 2020.
5 Yasmin Alibhai-Brown, 'LKJ: As Good as His Words,' *The Independent* [London], 19 June 2003.

Contents

	Contextual Notes	13
INTRODUCTION	Would Burns 'Take the Knee' Today?	15
CHAPTER ONE	Slavery in Burns's Ayrshire and in the Wider Scotland of His Time	23
CHAPTER TWO	Slavery in Burns's Life	64
CHAPTER THREE	Slavery in Burns's 'Annus Horribilis,' of 1786	83
CHAPTER FOUR	Slavery in Burns's Writings	109
CHAPTER FIVE	Slavery in Burns's Reading	235
CHAPTER SIX	Slavery in Burns's Counterfactual Caribbean	318
CHAPTER SEVEN	Slavery in Burns's Afterlife	349
CHAPTER EIGHT	Conclusion: Should Burns 'Fall'?	404
APPENDIX I	Original Article: 'Burns and Slavery' [2006]	416
APPENDIX II	Frederick Douglass	
A)	Burns Anniversary Festival [1849]	421
B)	A Fugitive Slave visiting the Birthplace of Robert Burns [1846]	422
C)	Self-made Men [1859]	425
	Bibliography	431
	Index	457

Tables

Table 1:	Arguments of the 12 Judges in *Knight v Wedderburn*	58
Table 2:	Burns's Life and the British Abolition Movement: Key Timelines	62
Table 3:	Burns and Jamaica – Timeline	88
Table 4:	Incomes From the Jamaican Economy, Around 1774	101
Table 5:	Burns's Uses of the Word 'Slavery'	109
Table 5a:	'Metaphorical Slavery'	111
Table 5b:	'Political Slavery'	115
Table 5c:	'Coward Slavery'	120
Table 6:	Comparison of Sentiments: 'The Slave's Lament' and 'The Farewell'	195
Table 7:	Transcription of the Dumfries Menagerie Handbill	227
Table 8:	Burns's Writings on Slavery – Summary	232
Table 8a:	Burns's Writings on Slavery – Evaluation By Period	233
Table 8b:	Burns's Writings on Slavery – Adjusted Evaluation by Period	234

Table 9:	Burns in a Counterfactual Caribbean – Process Chart	345
Table 9a:	Percentage Evaluation of Counterfactual Outcomes	346
Table 9b:	Ranked Evaluation of Counterfactual Outcomes	347
Table 10:	'A Man's a Man' in the Rhetorical Lexicon of Abolition, 1836–1866	358
Table 11:	Burns Centenary Celebrations Across the Antebellum USA, 1859	373
Table 12:	Further Rhetorical Use of 'A Man's a Man', 1871–1920	384
Table 13:	Frequency of Use of 'Man's Inhumanity to Man' by Dr Martin Luther King, Jr	397

CONTEXTUAL NOTES

It is easy, childish even, to judge yesterday with the wisdom of today when the wisdom of today will become tomorrow's ignorance.—Andrea Marcolongo (2024)[1]

CONTEXTUAL NOTE ONE: Language

ONE OF THE consequences of increased interest and objective research into the question of Scottish participation in the industrial complex of chattel enslavement has been an appropriate move to humanise the terms used in academic discussion to reflect that those who had been enslaved were in fact people and not chattels as claimed. In this study of Robert Burns, I have endeavoured to use language which accords due respect to the memories of those who endured that repression, avoiding the euphemisms mainly employed by pro-enslavement participants. In this work 'enslaved' is used as the adjective denoting the victim of slavery. Many now use 'enslaver' instead of 'slave owner' or 'slave master', but I believe this not to be granular enough, and so here 'enslaver' will be used for those who make the initial enslavement on the African continent, 'trafficker' for those involved in the 'triangular trade' and the 'auctions', 'slave-holder' for the owner of the plantation which relied on forced enslaved labour, and 'enforcer' for the 'overseers' and 'gang masters.'

There are several compound words that are not easily or simply modernised, such as 'slave trade', 'slave-driver', 'slave economy', 'slave ship', 'slave surgeon', 'slave code', 'slave market' and 'slave plantation'. These are used here without intending disrespect.

Please note and be aware that racialist epithets, including 'the N-word' (and variants), are not elided in quotations from contemporary documents and that use does not reflect my language, or that of the publisher.

However, the language around race and slavery continues to evolve and develop: the introduction and later removal of the term 'BAME' being a good example of that lexical and political process. If, by chance today, or in future readings, a word or phrase of mine appears infelicitous, I ask the Reader to excuse my failing, recognising the honest intent behind my choice of words today.

---

1 From Andrea Marcolongo, trans Will Schutt, *Shifting the Moon from its Orbit: A Night at the Acropolis Museum* (London: Europa Editions UK, 2024), p.120.

CONTEXTUAL NOTE TWO: Colonialism

This study focuses on Burns and Black chattel enslavement. Believing that it is a category error to combine 'slavery' and 'colonialism' as a single study, this study focuses on the 'plantocrats' of the West Indies and their maintenance of the enforced/enslaved model of production, and not the 'nabobs' of the East Indies who adopted a colonising economic model without needing industrial levels of enslavement. Similarly, there is no space to debate extirpation policies in regard to native inhabitants. (Also Burns had relatively little engagement with those nabobs, though, of course, his two younger sons rose to field officer positions in India in the service of the monopoly coloniser, The Honourable East India Company.)

CONTEXTUAL NOTE THREE: Personal Historical Responsibility

It must be remembered that enslavement was condoned by law and practice for many centuries before the 18th-century Abolition movement (and after). In reviewing that past, one must be careful not to judge everyone there by the moral and social conventions we expect as standard today. This is particularly true of the period of Burns's later life when the Abolition movement was gaining traction (say 1787–1793) but did not yet hold a sufficient majority to change the law. While there are historical figures who gloried and gained in the traffic and exploitation of Black chattel slaves, it is also true that virtually all of that society used commodities produced through enslaved labour, be it sugar, rum or cotton, or provided goods and services to the owners of enslaved plantations. This is summed up by Vincent P Gillen, the noted Greenock museum curator and local historian:

> Virtually every person named in this book has some connection to slavery through their genealogy or direct involvement. It is pointless to pick names out and mak[e] examples of them purely because their names are more historically visible. Let us remember the times they lived in.[2]

---

2 Vincent P Gillen, *Sugar, Ships & Slavery: An Illustrated History of Georgian & Victorian Greenock*, 2 vols (Greenock: Cartsburn Publishing, 2022), vol.I, p.497.

INTRODUCTION

Would Burns 'Take the Knee' Today?

ROBERT BURNS, SCOTLAND'S national poet, is loved the world over as the bard of freedom, of liberty and of the common good of humankind. Through performing and hearing his poems and songs we share his understanding of mankind, of nature and ecology and of society; we feel his passion, his love and his loss; we become aware of our national pride and the need to fight for our rights; and we come to appreciate the unity of humanity: politically, economically and, above all, convivially.

Almost 20 years ago, in late 2006, I was asked by the Scottish Executive to write a blog essay on 'Robert Burns and Slavery' to launch its bicentennial celebrations marking the abolition of the Slave Trade in Britain in 1807. I had known, of course, that Burns had accepted a job as a 'bookkeeper' in Jamaica, a plan which was set aside following his successful first publication, and I also recalled that his poems like 'Scots Wha Hae', 'Honest Poverty' and 'The Slave's Lament' railed against slavery and stood up for individual human rights. However, when I started to explore this part of Burns's life and legacy in depth, while watching the growing understanding of the much more prominent role that Scots in general played in the Black chattel slave trade, I found a significantly darker story, and a less than rosy picture of our Bard's feelings, actions and, most importantly, writings when it comes to his interface with slavery.

It was no secret that Burns had accepted a job on a Jamaican slave plantation in 1786 – in fact, James Currie's 1800 biography *Life and Works of Burns*, opens with the fact:

> Robert Burns was, as is well known, the son of a farmer in Ayrshire, and afterwards himself a farmer there; but having been unsuccessful, he was about to emigrate to Jamaica.[1]

---

1 [Dr James Currie, ed], *The Works of Burns. With an Account of His Life, and a Criticism of His Writings, To Which Are Prefixed, Some Observations on the Character and Conditions of Scottish Peasantry*, 4 vols (Liverpool, London and Edinburgh: McCreedy, Cadell and Davies, Creech, 1800), vol.I, p.1. [*Currie Edition*.] It is notable that Currie, a sincerely committed Abolitionist, makes no criticism of his subject on this score.

However, of all the complexities of Burns's life, this episode had received comparatively little critical interest. Since those celebrations in 2007, a number of writers have sought to explore Burns's attitudes to, and engagement with, what Burns had once called 'the infernal traffic'.[2] It is not a straightforward task (candidly, little is straightforward when it comes to analysing such a complex man and skilful wordsmith as Robert Burns). Black slavery and its abolition is hardly touched on except in one of his letters and is the direct subject of but a single poem: 'The Slave's Lament', a song which many commentators place at the weaker end of his creative output, although there are other references in his prose and poetry which will be teased out in these pages. Despite Burns's friendships with leading Abolitionists and the Abolitionist prose and verse found on his bookcase, his near silence raises questions about whether the poet who was famed for his humanity failed to register the human cost of chattel slavery and, therefore, its fundamental immorality.

It is a contentious topic (at least for some people). Gerry Carruthers writes of being called 'nae freend' for 'questioning Burns and slavery', and this strength of feeling can be seen in this formal complaint to the UK's Press Complaints Commission (PCC): *Mr Andrew Morgan v The Sun (2012)*:

> Mr Andrew Morgan complained [...] that an article reporting on Burns Night inaccurately reported that the poet Robert Burns lived and worked in the West Indies in breach of Clause 1 (Accuracy) of the Editors' Code.
>
> Resolution: The complaint was resolved when the PCC negotiated the publication of the following correction: Rod Liddle's column of January 25 claimed that Robert Burns had lived and worked in the West Indies. In fact, this was not the case as Mr Burns accepted a post in Jamaica but changed his mind after successfully publishing his poetry. We are happy to set the record straight.[3]

---

2 J De Lancey Ferguson and G Ross Roy, eds, *The Letters of Robert Burns* (Second Edition), 2 vols (Oxford: OUP, 1985) ['*Letters*']: to Helen Maria Williams, dated [late July or early August] 1789, [L.353B].

3 Gerry Carruthers, 'Robert Burns and Slavery', in *Fickle Man: Robert Burns in the 21st Century*, ed by Johnny Rodger and Gerard Carruthers (Dingwall: Sandstone Press, 2009), p.172; *Morgan v The Sun*: www.pcc.org.uk/cases/adjudicated.html (accessed 1 September 2024). Rod Liddell had written 'The Scots like Burns because he was a champion of social equality and human rights — overlooking

INTRODUCTION: WOULD BURNS TAKE THE KNEE TODAY?

Changing literary tone and century, one wants to remind these critics that for every hard-working, respectable Dr Jekyll in the Scottish national tale, there is an equal and darker Mr Hyde lurking just out of view. As the umquhile Scots Makar Jackie Kay tells us:

> Most British people think of slavery as something that happened in America and perhaps the Caribbean. [...]. Being African and Scottish, I'd taken comfort in the notion that Scotland was not nearly as implicated in the horrors of the slave trade as England. Scotland's self image is one of a hard-done-to wee nation, yet bonny and blithe. I once heard a Scottish woman proudly say: 'We don't have racism up here, that's an English thing, that's down south.' Scotland is a canny nation when it comes to remembering and forgetting. The plantation owner is never wearing a kilt.[4]

This is seen time and again in the 'ya-boo' world of Burns legend which was famously captured by Byron's summation of Burns's 'antithetical mind! – tenderness, roughness, delicacy, coarseness – sentiment, sensuality – soaring and groveling [sic], dirt and deity – all mixed up in that one compound of inspired clay!'[5] The temptation is, on one hand, to gild 'THE BARD'S' icon (hoping that further gold leaf will distract the critical eye from some of the darker or shabbier corners of that portrait) or, on the other, to add another dollop of January 'click-bait' demonising 'RABBIE' specifically to create a wave of dyspepsia through the serried ranks of haggis-eaters and a consequent rise in readership. The first of those approaches can be seen in the Scottish Executive's larger work commemorating Britain's Abolition of the Slave Trade in 1807: Burns features prominently in the narrative and is described as one of the 'Leading Abolitionists' in the following exaggerated terms:

---

the fact that he worked as a bookkeeper on a slave plantation.' *The Sun*, 25 January 2012. On the other side of the political press, Roy Greenslade said 'Liddle [...] wrote an anti-Burns diatribe about the "joke poet" [...] but its good to see that the P[ress] C[omplaints] C[ommission] entertained a third-party complaint about a man who has been dead for over 200 years.' *The Guardian*, 30 March 2012.

4 Jackie Kay, *The Guardian*, 24 March 2007.

5 Lord Byron, *Works of Lord Byron*, 6 vols, ed by RE Protheroe (London, John Murray; 1898), 'Journal, 13 December 1813,' vol.II, p.357.

Robert Burns, the celebrated Scottish poet, was born into humble beginnings. In 1783 [sic] he was almost penniless and decided to accept an offer to go to Jamaica as a bookkeeper on an estate. To raise the fare to get from Greenock to Jamaica on the Nancy he was persuaded to raise a subscription to publish some of his poems. The publication and success of the Kilmarnock edition changed his mind about leaving.

He became affected by the abolitionist cause. The circles he mixed in, especially after the publication of his first book of poetry, would have opened him to abolitionist messages. A number of writers refer to Burns' personal dislike of anyone being treated in a servile manner, and his interest in social injustice issues. In 1792 he published 'The Slave's Lament', based on the stories he heard coming from the Scottish estates in Virginia.[6]

The poor grasp of chronology in the first paragraph – it was 1786, not 1783 – should warn the reader of the significant weaknesses of interpretation in the second, which will be looked at in depth in the following chapters, but this passage serves as a 'stock' description of that period of Burns's life, seen through the rose-tinted lens of the typical positive reader.

On the other hand, as January comes round, we find the annual dose of 'knock 'em down' tabloid journalese attacks on some aspect or other of Burns's colourful life. In 2008, Gerry Carruthers's sober investigation was introduced in one newspaper as '[n]otorious for fornication and exploiting women, Burns had a fantasy to emigrate to Jamaica and become a slave driver before making his fortune and returning to Scotland.'[7] Michael Fry went much further in the attack the following year, denouncing the choice of Burns as the icon of the 2009 'Homecoming' on his thesis that the great poet was 'a racist, misogynist drunk,' so while marking 'Burns' 250th anniversary in

---

6 Paula Kitching, *Scotland and the Slave Trade: 2007 Bicentenary of the Abolition of the Slave Trade Act* (Edinburgh: Scottish Executive, 2007), p.32 [the 'The Slave's Lament' text is at p.56]. The original researchers/authors (Iain Whyte and Eric J Graham, who are heavily quoted in this book) had their contracts terminated for refusing to adopt editorial changes which they believed 'compromised historical accuracy and our professional integrity'. See TM Devine, 'Lost to History', in *Recovering Scotland's Slavery Past: The Caribbean Connection*, ed by TM Devine (Edinburgh: EUP, 2015), pp.21–40, at p.26. Please note that the author's commission (see Appendix 1) was not subject to editorial pressure.
7 *The Herald* [Glasgow], 19 January 2008.

a literary sense,' was understandable, 'in 2009, his example, in a practical sense, could well send Scotland straight down the tubes.'[8] The negative view of Burns's morality was echoed in a review of Robert Crawford's *The Bard* that same year:

> Throughout this book, we do not see a single example of Robert Burns acting with moral courage when his character was tested.[9]

Similarly, in 2018 the noted poet and former Scots Makar Liz Lochhead drew a post-#MeToo comparison of Burns to a 'Weinsteinian sex pest', generating much heat (but little light) in the press for a fortnight.[10] Or in 2022 when the Scottish Poetry Library commissioned a group of four Scots female poets ('The Trysting Thorns') to write new poems on Burns and reflect on his legacy (both poetic and social). Their output was driven by a common perception that Burns was a misogynist:

- 'a guid poet but an awfy man for the women' (Susi Briggs).
- 'I struggle to understand the ongoing appetite for Burns' (Morag Anderson).
- 'Maybe it's time for another poet to take the throne' (Janette Ayachi).
- 'There are aspects of Burns' life and his personal behaviours that I'm uncomfortable celebrating' (Victoria McNulty).

(Although McNulty tempered her remarks saying that '[d]espite all my reservations about his work and his legacy I was surprised how connected I became to the humanity of his writing.')[11]

Neither approach, the co-optive nor the dismissive, gets us close to understanding the complexity of Robert Burns's thought. I have continued to plough this field since writing that first article over 15 years ago, as have others who have contributed to a new paradigm understanding of Scotland and slavery, and while I was (fractionally) too kind to Burns in 2006, it is still a shock to ask ourselves the key questions: (a) how could *our* Burns, the people's poet, look to become

---

8 'Robert Burns: A Racist, Sexist Drunk?' *The Scotsman*, 4 January 2009.
9 Daniel Ritchie, '[Review] "The Bard: Robert Burns a Biography," by Robert Crawford, *Christianity and Literature* (Summer 2011), p.668.
10 'Robert Burns', *The Guardian*, 24 January 2018.
11 www.scottishpoetrylibrary.org.uk/the-trysting-thorns/ (accessed 1 September 2024).

an instrument in what many now call 'The Black Holocaust'? and (b) in the last decade of his life, as the debate for Abolition grew louder in Scotland, to what extent did this campaigning tide of information change his mindset?

This book follows the various threads that slavery wove in the warp and weft of Burns's checkered life. In Chapter One, the economic, legal and social position of slavery in Burns's Scotland is set out, with Chapter Two looking closer at slavery's direct (and indirect) touchpoints in Burns's short life. Chapter Three starts by defining some of the confusion over how Burns used the word 'slave' and then uses that to analyse the 27 (or potentially 28) of his poems, songs and letters that have some connection with Black chattel slavery. Chapter Four performs a similar task by going through Burns's library to capture what he read from others (in fiction, non-fiction and in verse) about the increasingly contested space around Abolition and Slavery. This is a comprehensive list of passages, and the Reader might well be excused from reading each quotation in this chapter line-by-line. Next, Chapter Five performs a slight digression by seeking to answer the oft-posited question, 'what would Burns have done had he actually gone?' It does this in four counterfactual approaches: assessing the risk of death through tropical disease, looking at Andrew O Lindsay's novel *Illustrious Exile,* then Shara McCallum's poem cycle *No Ruined Stone* and lastly using the near-contemporary Scots slaver-turned-Abolitionist Zachary Macaulay's experiences and awakening. Chapter Six presents how Burns was used after his death in the fights for Abolition and Emancipation, particularly in the United States of America, and its Civil War and its Civil Rights movement (with some thought on his poetic influence and legacy in Black poetry and the Harlem Renaissance.)

Unfortunately, the detailed research that will be laid out in this book, and which leads to its final 'verdict', does not support an entirely positive 'spin'. On the negative side of this new history, it will be seen that the 'bookkeeper' was a role that used the lash more than the pen, that Burns did intend to travel knowing he would become a slave-driver (and broadly what that meant in terms of imposing suffering on others) and that this knowledge did not actively change his mind on emigrating to Jamaica. It also shows that – with some important exceptions – he was relatively unaffected by the Abolitionist cause until it was in full swing and, even then, was but tangentially engaged with one of the biggest moral, social and political movements of his lifetime. While he was no active supporter of slavery, he evinced hardly any activity (in words or deeds) for Abolition, although it should be remembered that the progressive decline in his health occurred at the very same time that the Abolitionist movement picked up its stride. Had he another decade to live, it seems a fair assumption that we would, in all likelihood, have seen this branch of his poetry produce greater fruit.

That being said, his 'redemption' comes from how his poetry and its philosophy were used posthumously as a core part of the rhetoric of Abolition, Emancipation and Civil Rights: truly inching our way forward to that day when, as Burns had prayed for, 'man to man, the world o'er, shall brothers be for a' that.' Today, where at long last there is a greater awareness across the board of the issues around race and society, Burns's innate humanity has an important place in teaching us about our relationships with others.

Yes, Burns could have done more in his lifetime to advance the emancipation of enslaved people: but then, could each of us not say that of ourselves? As William Wilberforce said in his first great speech on Abolition to the House of Commons: 'We are all guilty – we ought all to plead guilty, and not seek to exculpate ourselves by throwing the blame on others.'[12] So be it with Burns, whose words have stood as a beacon of humanity, equality and freedom, and that absolves his all-too-human frailties.

---

12 William Wilberforce, Speech 12 May 1789, *Cobbett's Parliamentary History of England*, Volume XXVIII, [1789–1791] (London: Longman, Hurst, Rees, Orme & Brown [and others], 1816), p.42.

CHAPTER ONE

Slavery in Burns's Ayrshire and in the Wider Scotland of His Time

Town and County

THE AYRSHIRE OF Burns's day was a county engaged in social and economic development. Agricultural improvements had started in the county some years before and that process, plus an increase in trade and the first steps of industrialisation, accelerated after the notorious collapse in 1772 of Messrs Douglas, Heron & Co (known widely as the 'Ayr Bank'). This debacle ruined many of the old landed lairds and so created opportunities for the nouveau wealth arising from the colonialism of the East Indies ('the nabobs') and from the Black chattel slave economy of the West Indies ('the plantocrats') to repatriate.[1] This 'county interest' was exemplified by both the number of local peers whose estates led the county's social and political life and by the number of parliamentary electors for Ayrshire. Although the number of them seems embarrassingly low by our standards, with 205 voters, the county of Ayrshire had the largest electorate in Scotland at the time, as an anonymous commentator said in 1786: '[t]he county of Ayr is perhaps superior to any in Scotland in the number of its Peers, Nabobs, and wealthy Commoners.'[2]

It was also a period of change within the Royal Burgh of Ayr. The economic shock caused by the loss of the town's Virginia trade on the back of American independence, following on from the depression caused by the Ayr Bank's failure, had hit the town hard. Daniel Defoe, on his national tour, described it as follows:

> Over the River *Aire* is a Bridge of Four Arches, [...]; and South

---

[1] This book concerns only the Black chattel slavery of the West Indies. It is a category error of some proportion to join colonialism with slavery (for example the confused report of the National Trust in England and Wales).
[2] 'Alan Ramsay' [pseudonym], 'To the Editor,' *Edinburgh Evening Courant*, 13 November 1786. Electoral Rolls can be found in John Strawhorn, *Ayrshire in the Time of Burns* (Ayr: Ayrshire Archaeological and Natural History Society [AANHS], 1959).

of the Bridge stands the old Town of *Aire* or *Erigena*, famous for its Antiquity and Privileges [...] It is now like an old Beauty, and shews the ruins of a good Face, but is still decaying every Day [...] from having been the fifth best town in *Scotland*.[3]

The burgh's oligarchic merchant families supported Provost John Ballantine's introduction of urban enlightenment into the 'old Beauty.'[4] The money raised by feuing (selling on long leaseholds) the burgh lands of Alloway was channelled through private acts of Parliament allowing major redesign of the town harbour and the building of his New Bridge over the River Ayr. This benefited the town through improved trading patterns to Ireland and to Glasgow respectively, while the trading businesses which had operated into Virginia (and other ports on the Chesapeake) pivoted to the Caribbean instead.[5] Not every plan reached fruition: an attempt to capture a percentage of the refining capacity for Caribbean sugar from the Clyde ports came to nothing, despite significant investment.[6] Socially, Ballantine's reconstitution of the ancient burgh or grammar school into Ayr Academy, his support for the burgeoning Air Library Society and the building of the Ayr Racecourse under his sponsorship would lead, in time, to his successors laying out the new Georgian Streets around what would become Wellington Square with its imposing County Buildings. The town's redevelopment was continued after Ballantine's death and was completed in 1827 by the town hall and its impressive 225ft steeple.[7]

---

3 [Daniel Defoe], *A Tour thro' the Whole Island of Great Britain, Third Edition*, 4 vols (London: J Osborn [and others], 1742), vol.IV, p.109.

4 John Ballantine of Castlehill (1743–1812): Town Councillor, 1781; Dean of Guild, 1781–1787; Provost 1787–1788, 1793–1794 and 1796–1797. Partner, latterly Managing Partner, of Messrs Hunter & Co, Bankers. Preses, Air Library Society, Master, Ayr Operative Lodge, Preses, The Allowa' Club (the first established Burns Club) and of 'The Sunday School' dining club.

5 Eric J Graham, *The Shipping Trade of Ayrshire 1689–1791* (Ayr: AANHS [1993]), pp.33–34. ['Graham, *Shipping*.']

6 'Enterprise and Refinement: James Hunter and the Ayr Sugar House,' southayrshirehistory.wordpress.com/2013/08/05/enterprise-and-refinement-james-hunter-and-the-ayr-sugar-house/ (accessed 1 September 2024). The bank's capital invested in the project was recovered when Ballantine sold the buildings to the British Army as a barracks.

7 Bob Harris and Charles McKean, *The Scottish Town in the Age of the Enlightenment 1740–1820* (Edinburgh: Edinburgh University Press, 2014), pp.[510]–[511]; Rob Close and Ann Riches, *The Buildings of Scotland: Ayrshire and Arran* (New Haven/London: Yale University Press, 2012), pp.120–121, ['Pevsner']. *25 Geo III, c.37* 'Bridge of Ayr Act, 1785' and *34 Geo III, c.59,* 'Ayr Harbour Act 1794.' Ballantine was an astute man. The wording of the *Bridge of Ayr Act* allowed

In terms of religion, the burgh was appreciably more liberal than the rest of the county. For most of Burns's life, the ministers of Ayr's Auld Kirk (Ayr and Alloway being a single parish with two ministers) were Revd Dr William Dalrymple (1723–1814) from 1746 and Revd Dr William McGill (1732–1807) from 1760. Both divines were leading 'New Lichts' in the Church of Scotland, the theological school which sought to moderate the traditional severity of strict Calvinism, as promoted by the conservative school of 'Auld Lichts.' They experienced rather different careers, with Dalrymple serving as Moderator of the General Assembly in 1781 while McGill suffered under the shadow of a formal interrogation over potential heresy in his writings by his rural Auld Licht antagonists a few years later.[8] As Burns described it, 'one of the worthiest as well as one of the ablest, of the whole priesthood of the Kirk of Scotland,' was on trial 'for the blasphemous heresies of squaring Religion by the rules of Common Sense, and attempting to give a decent character to Almighty God and a rational account of his proceedings with the Sons of Men.'[9] Thanks in part to robust support from the Ayr Town Council (led by Provost David Kennedy, Ballantine's brother-in-law) an armistice was brokered following a carefully constructed apology by McGill. However, we know from Burns's continuing clerical satires that there had been no resolution of the underlying, doctrinal differences.

Slavery in the Ayrshire Economy and the Supply Chain for the Plantations

The understanding of how Scotland participated in the slave trade has developed in the last decade from a *bien pensant* belief that it was an English problem, to remembering individual invidious Scots who were personally active in buying and selling slaves on the coast of Africa

---

the Burgh to raise debt to build the bridge and to charge a toll ('pontage') to repay the lenders and to meet necessary ancillary expenses. Ballantine (and his successors as provost) took a very liberal view of what was 'necessary' and 'ancillary', and additionally through 'custom' milked the bridge tolls to regenerate Ayr. This was only discovered in 1835, when the County Commissioners of Supply found that, of the £4,000 borrowed to build the bridge, only £1,000 had been repaid in 30 years of operation. See 'Corporations (Scotland): General Report and Local Reports,' *Parliamentary Papers Session 19 February – 10 September 1835*, vol.XXIX, pp.87–88.

8 James Kinsley, ed, *The Poems and Songs of Robert Burns*, 3 vols (Oxford: Clarendon Press, 1968), vol.III, pp.1306–1308. ['*Poems*.']

9 *Letters*: To Robert Graham of Fintry, 9 December 1781 [L.373] at vol.I, p.454.

or in Western slave markets, to a wider class of those who profited through developing the economic system dependent on enslaved labour on Britain's sugar islands in the Caribbean.[10] Recent research has disproved that idyllic misremembrance:

> There was no single 'Scottish' response to enslavement. A strong sense of abolitionism belied a national ambivalence: although many Scots at home denounced enslavement, there were plenty more who happily profited from it in the colonies. There was no major difference between Scottish planters and those of other nationalities in their dealings with the enslaved.[11]

However, that needs to be taken further, for while the number of direct actors might be relatively small and there was no visible trade in enslaved people in Scottish ports, the chain of supply and demand reached right into the core of Scottish and Ayrshire society. The National Trust for Scotland's commendable 2021 interim report, *Facing Our Past*, uses a helpful model to categorise connection with slavery:

> DIRECT: consisting of the traffickers in, managers of, medics to, and holders of enslaved people (and in the latter case including absentee plantation owners and those with Black domestic servants);[12]

---

10 Stephen Mullen, *It Wisnae Us: The Truth About Glasgow and Slavery* (Edinburgh: The Royal Incorporation of Architects in Scotland, 2009).
11 Douglas J Hamilton, *Scotland, the Caribbean and the Atlantic World, 1750–1820* (Manchester: Manchester University Press, 2005), p.76.
12 There is an additional subset of investors in incorporated companies such as The Company of Royal Adventurers Trading into Africa. Founded by Royal Charter in 1660 it expanded its trading in 1663 to cover enslaved people, holding the monopoly in 'redwood, elephants' teeth, negroes, slaves, hides, wax, guinea grains, or other commodities of [Africa]' [emphasis added]. This corporation collapsed during the Anglo-Dutch wars and was reformed as the Royal African Company of England in 1672, maintain a slaving monopoly until 1698, and abandoning the slave trade in 1731 to concentrate on gold and ivory. The company was dissolved in 1752 with its assets transferred to the new Merchant Company of Africa, who then resumed slave trading until 1807. Here the individual investors were deliberately financing the slave trade and fall in the 'Direct' category. See William A Pettigrew, *Freedom's Debt: The Royal African Company and the Politics of the Atlantic Slave Trade, 1652–1752* (Chapel Hill, NC: Omohundro Institute of Early American History and Culture, 2013). The problem arises where 'paper' investors buy shares in these companies on the stock price for pure speculation rather than as an investment in the business model; these persons are more 'indirect.' The paradigm example would be the South Sea Bubble which had little or nothing to do with the assiento slave contract, but more with the financial manipulations of the promoters, or the case of the composer George Frideric Handel (1685-1759) who was paid as court musician in South Sea scrip which he immediately encashed. Guilt is granular.

INDIRECT: the merchants who traded in the commodities imported from the West Indies and who manufactured and exported goods and services to those colonies, along with the financiers of those trades (and of West Indian plantations, properties and businesses), and the services underpinning them (such as shipping, legal work and insurance);[13]

INTERGENERATIONAL: the wives, families, heirs and descendants of the above two classes, who were not personally managing enslaving businesses, but whose financial privilege was based on the historical profits earned from the labour of the enslaved workers and typically re-invested in British land or enterprise;[14] and

ABOLITIONIST: those men and women active (to a greater or lesser extent) in the long movement to secure freedom for the enslaved. (Noting that several Abolitionists could, earlier in their lives, have been classified in one of the three previous categories.)

To which should be added a final class (not in the NTS model): that of the retail consumers of West Indian produce: obviously sugar, but also rum, cotton, dyestuffs and other produce, being a much larger group of people ranging across all ranks of British society.[15]

It is easy to condemn the wealthy plantocrats, or their heirs, or their enforcing minions whose income was wrung from the labour of enslaved workers. However, those direct investors, managers and agents could not function alone, as each of the island economies in the Caribbean needed most of the necessities of life to be shipped in – tea, teapots and teaspoons, guns, bullets and gunpowder, bibles, books and writing paper – as British policy was to limit manufacture in its colonies, imposing two monopolies: the colonies' trade of raw materials into the British Isles, and a reciprocal flow of finished goods and luxuries from Britain

---

13 There is a particular subset here of financial creditors who foreclosed on the assets of a plantation (including its enslaved workforce) due to non-payment of debt, who edge into the 'Direct' category to an extent.

14 Some slavery reviews include persons whose siblings, cousins or in-laws were invested in enslavement, even if the person named had no other linkage, which seems inappropriate, in certain specific cases.

15 Jennifer Melville, ed, *Facing Our Past: Interim Report on the Connections between the Properties now in the care of the National Trust for Scotland and Historical Enslavement* (Edinburgh: National Trust for Scotland, 2011), p.6. And this is the context of what the report rightly calls '[t]he complex, changing position of Robert Burns, who moved from intending to work on a Jamaica plantation in 1786 to being remembered as a champion of the anti-slavery movement.' (p.6.)

back across the Atlantic.[16] These colonies were as dependent on British exports for their day-to-day living as they were on the patrols of the Royal Navy for their independence from foreign powers. This became particularly true after trade from the closer North American ports was interrupted by the struggle for independence. Whyte calculates that, for the Caribbean overall, '[a]fter the American War, imports more than doubled by 1790, exports rose by 60%.'[17]

Exporters shipped their goods not knowing to whom or how they would be used, but without those exports, Caribbean society would collapse. With the growing home demand for sugar and cotton in particular, the plantocrats were wealthy customers and many British merchants made a fortune on this side of the Atlantic by shipping mundane goods which nevertheless propped up the plantations. The nail manufacturer has no idea whether his product is for the church or school roof, or to build the gallows or nail the ear of an enslaved person to a tree. Yet, upon closer thought, many product lines such as these could be clearly seen to contribute to the efficiency of chattel slavery, as abolitionist William Dickson showed on his 1792 tours, where he presented shackles, whips and instruments of torture to the gaze of his audiences.[18] It was (and to an extent remains) easy to forget to condemn the ironmasters in Britain, such as at the Muirkirk Ironworks in Ayrshire, who manufactured manacles, leg-irons, thumbscrews and chains, or the leather workers crafting ruthless bullwhips, belts and straps. The community of investors in and owners of Caribbean plantations (known as the 'West Indian Interest') was not slow to remind people of this. A pamphlet of 1789 is a good example: 'There is not a manufacturing town in Britain which does not furnish articles to the islands [of the Caribbean]. Shall these industrious workmen and their families be left to starve?'[19]

Similarly, while Ayrshire ports (and those in the wider Scotland) were not physically involved in the 'middle passage', the county earned good money by supporting both of the other legs of the 'triangular trade,'

---

16 This, of course, was one of the *casus belli* of the 13 Colonies of America. The policy is often sloganised as 'not a nail is to be made in the colonies' but I can find no contemporary quotation.
17 Iain Whyte, *Scotland and the Abolition of Black Slavery, 1756–1838* (Edinburgh: EUP, 2006), p.43.
18 Michael Morris, *Scotland and the Caribbean, c.1740–1833: Atlantic Archipelagos* (Abingdon/New York: Routledge, 2015), p.109.
19 William Innes, *The Slave Trade Indispensable: In Answer to the Speech of William Wilberforce Esq on 13 March*, 1789 (London: np, 1789), p.9.

providing the trading stock (cloth, spirits and manufactured goods) that were the currency of exchange in the slave markets of West Africa, as well as the necessities of plantation life in the West Indies.[20] Similarly, Ayrshire homes (of all classes) and businesses happily bought up the inward passage's exports of sugar, rum and other commodities with never a thought on their method of production (until late in the century).

The slave economy, therefore, surreptitiously reached into the heart of British industry and the industry of the British hearth, with Scotland being no exception. A good example is in cloth and clothing. Plainly, the plantocrat and his wife ordering fine fashionable garments were paying their costumier in cash generated by enslaved labour, so the costumier's business is but one step removed from the physical cruelty of chattel slavery. Similarly at the other end of the market, there was a need for robust but cheap fabric to clothe the slaves. A number of Scottish communities, including Irvine to the north of Ayr, experimented in raising flax and then 'heckling' it to weave linen. These growth opportunities arose from the increasing demand for Osnaburgh cloth, a coarse linen specifically developed for sale to plantation owners to clothe their enslaved workers.[21] Another example was the cotton mill at Catrine in Ayrshire, built by Claude Alexander of Ballochmyle (1752–1809) in partnership with the famous industrialist David Dale (1739–1806).[22] Here raw cotton shipped from the West Indies was picked at home by women and then sent to the mill for carding and spinning. By 1796, their 445 employees were producing

---

20 Long cites the following key imports from the Scottish market into Jamaica: 'Wrought iron, linens, osnabrigs [sic], checks, bonnets, tobacco-pipes, herrings, stockings, shoes, boots, &c.' [Edward Long], *History of Jamaica*, 3 vols (London: T Lowndes, 1774), vol.I, p.505.
21 It was called osnaburg(h) (occasionally 'oznaburg' or 'osnabrig') cloth as the first examples were shipped to Britain from Osnabrück in Westphalia earlier in the century: William Guthrie, *A New Geographical, Historical, and Commercial Grammar, and Present State of the Several Kingdoms of the World* (London: Charles Dilley and George Robinson, 1772), p.658.
22 Claude Alexander of Southbar made his fortune as paymaster general of the East India Company and, on returning from India as a wealthy 'nabob', bought Ballochmyle House and Estate in 1786 from Sir John Whitfoord, who was forced to sell to cover his losses in the Ayr Bank crash. To mark the acquisition he had Johan Zoffany paint his portrait, showing him reading a letter about the purchase to his brother Boyd, an Indian servant and a spaniel in attendance. It stood on the grand staircase of Ballochmyle House until it was requisitioned as a hospital in 1939. Burns wrote 'The Bonnie Lass o' Ballochmyle' [K.89] to his sister Miss Wilhelmina Alexander (1753–1843) and described the brothers (whom he had met at Edinburgh) thus: 'When Fate swore that their purses should be full, Nature was equally positive that their heads should be empty [...] Ye canna mak a silk-purse o' a sow's lug.' Robert Burns, *The Glenriddell Manuscript* ['Glenriddell Ms'], vol.II, p.28 in *The Oxford Edition of the Works of Robert Burns* ['Oxford Burns'], vol.I, p.256. There is no record of Burns seeing the portrait.

2,660lbs of spun cotton from raw material grown on plantations by enslaved labourers.[23] To stress the point, without this trade, the plantation economy could not maintain itself, and while that must have become increasingly apparent during the 20 years leading up to Abolition in 1807, a modern phrase comes to mind: 'don't ask and don't tell.'

Given that the plantations (and hence the enslaved population) grew on the back of home demand for West Indian exports, it can truthfully be said that, at one level, slavery was embedded in the ordinary working and family lives of almost everyone in Burns's Ayrshire: partly invisible and partly simply not mentioned.[24] It was only as the Abolition movement achieved momentum from 1788 that silence became increasingly difficult in the midst of polarised debate. Over time, particularly from 1792, the wider society became aware of the human cost of their consumer goods, one indicator of that being the campaign of sugar abstinence amongst '[t]he heaven-born daughters of our isle' who declined to 'enjoy those sweets, which they supposed to be the price of blood.'[25] Such that the leading Abolitionist Thomas Clarkson reported (in a modest exaggeration) that:

> there was no town, through which I passed, in which there was not some one individual who had left off the use of sugar. In the smaller towns there were from ten to fifty by estimation, and in the larger from two to five hundred, who made this sacrifice to virtue. These were of all ranks and parties. Rich and poor, churchmen and dissenters, had adopted the measure. Even grocers had left off trading in the article, in some places. In gentlemen's families, where the master had set the example, the servants had often voluntarily followed it; and even children, who were capable of understanding the history of the sufferings of the Africans, excluded, with the most virtuous resolution,

---

23 Strawhorn, *Ayrshire*, pp.51–52. See also Michael Morris, 'The Problem of Slavery in the Age of Improvement: David Dale, Robert Owen and New Lanark Cotton,' in *Cultures of Improvement in Scottish Romanticism, 1707–1840*, ed by Alex Benchimol and Gerard Lee McKeever (New York: Routledge, 2018), pp.111–131.
24 See Michael Morris, '*Yonder Awa*: Slavery and Distancing Strategies in Scottish Literature,' in *Recovering Scotland's Slavery Past. The Caribbean Connection*, ed by TM Devine (Edinburgh: EUP, 2015), pp.41–61. In particular the distancing euphemism used by Bailie Nicol Jarvie (in Sir Walter Scott's 1817 novel, *Rob Roy*) who does not name the West Indies but calls it 'yonder awa'.'
25 Anon, *Strictures on an Address to the People of Great Britain on the Propriety of Abstaining from West Indies Sugar and Rum* (London: T Boosey, 1792), p.4.

the sweets, to which they had been accustomed, from their lips.[26]

However, while some few disavowed sugars, the overall consumption of sugar and rum continued to grow, for as Walter Scott's character, the Glaswegian Bailie Nicol Jarvie, put it, 'good ware has aften come frae a wicked market.'[27] In 1704 the average British sugar consumption per head per annum was 4lbs (or 1.8kg); by 1800 it had jumped to 18lbs (8.2kg), while in 2020 the United Kingdom's per capita consumption stood at 96lbs (or 43.3kg) leading poet Kate Tough to mark the history and present use of sugar and tobacco in her poem, 'People made Glasgow': 'What we murdered them for/ We kill ourselves with.'[28] It now appears ironic that the early Burns Suppers would toast 'a man's a man for a' that' while consuming punch made from sugar, rum, citrus fruits and spices all harvested by enslaved labour. The more sugar consumed, the greater the number of enslaved labourers were needed to be bought in and it may be that growth in the enslaved population helped bring the cause of Abolition to the fore of other minds.

The Ayrshire plantocrats and the wider British 'West Indian Interest' were equally dogged in holding to what they saw as their constitutionally guaranteed property rights.[29] They constructed a political lobby which fought a consistent (and one must say with grudging respect, effective) rear-guard action, playing both to public ignorance and to a governmental fearful of losing the wealth of the

---

26 Thomas Clarkson, *The History of the Rise, Progress and Accomplishment of the Abolition of the African Slave-Trade by the British Parliament*, 2 vols (London: Longman, Hurst, Rees, and Orme, 1808), vol.II, pp.349–350.
27 Morris, 'Yonder Awa', pp.42–43. I think that Carla Sassi tries to push this argument too far in her 'Sir Walter Scott and the Caribbean: Unravelling the Silences,' *The Yearbook of English Studies*, 47 (2017), pp. 224–240, where she reads an anti-slavery message in Scott's *The Antiquary* (of 1816) where Captain Hector McIntyre is bored by the Antiquary's ruminations and 'would exchange for the West Indies' to escape his uncles ruminations. The awfulness of a military posting to the Caribbean has little to do with its widespread use of enslavement and everything to do with the extraordinary scale of death from tropical disease amongst Britain's soldiers and sailors in that theatre. Burnard reports that '[d]uring the American Revolution, an estimated 11 per cent of troops *en route* to Jamaica died in passage and a further 30 per cent of newcomers died on arrival.' While '[e]ven as late as the 1830s a soldier in the West Indies stood a 450–700 per cent greater chance of death than a soldier in Britain.' Trevor Burnard, "The Countrie Continues Sicklie': White Mortality in Jamaica, 1655–1780,' *Social History of Medicine* 12.1 (1999), p.54.
28 Sidney W Mintz, *Sweetness and Power: The Place of Sugar in Modern History* (New York: Viking Penguin, 1985), p.67. Kate Tough, 'People made Glasgow,' *tilt-shift* (Tarland: Tapsalteerie, 2016), ll.16–17.
29 Similar 'proprietorship' rights which were defended against reform included Church Patronage, the Parliamentary Franchise and the rights of Burghs to regulate trade within their boundaries.

Caribbean islands in the same way as the 13 American colonies were lost to the Crown. The 19-year gap between the first anti-slavery legislation ('Dolben's Act') in 1788 and Abolition of the Trade in 1807 was appalling, but can be partly explained by the eruption of the first phases of the Revolutionary and Napoleonic Wars in April 1792. As Nigel Leask rightly says:

> In the 1790s Tory abolitionists had to work hard to disassociate their humanitarian cause from French revolutionary politics, a move which inevitably alienated more radical abolitionists, for whom the end of slavery was inseparable from the cause of political reform.[30]

When Abolition was debated in the Lords in 1793, the case against was led by the Earl of Abingdon who was explicit about this purported connection:

> What does the abolition of the slave trade mean more or less in effect than liberty and equality? what, more or less than the rights of man? and what is liberty and equality, and what are the rights of man, but the foolish fundamentals of this new [French Revolutionary] philosophy.[31]

This effectively boxed in the Abolitionists, for while Admiral Rodney's 1782 naval victory over the fleets of France and Spain at 'The Battle of the Saintes' had given Britain superiority in European waters, in the Atlantic and Caribbean it was not unchallenged by the French and Spanish navies seeking to blockade or capture Britain's West Indian colonies. It was only after Nelson defeated the combined French and Spanish navies at Trafalgar in 1805 that Britain's mastery of the seas effectively removed that risk, allowing Abolition to follow close behind in 1807. However, even then, the West Indian Interest had sufficient power to delay full Emancipation for a further quarter of a

---

30 Nigel Leask, 'Burns and the Poetics of Abolition', in *The Edinburgh Companion to Robert Burns*, ed by Gerard Carruthers (Edinburgh: Edinburgh University Press, 2009), pp. 50–51.
31 Willoughby Bertie, 4th Earl of Abingdon (1740–1799): Speech, House of Lords 11 April 1793, *Cobbett's Parliamentary History of England*, Volume XXX, [1792–1794] (London: Longman, Hurst, Rees, Orme & Brown [and others], 1817), p.635. Reprised in his speech on 2 March 1794 (*Cobbett's Parliamentary History*, vol.XXXI, p.468). In other ways Lord Abingdon was a polite and cultured man, who patronised Haydn during his London sojourn.

century (and then to garner the benefits of 'Apprenticeship' and cash compensation, as will be discussed later).

Master and Servant

There is also an argument that can be made that most people at home failed to differentiate between the oppression of Black enslaved people (across the Atlantic and out of sight) and the grinding lot of the poor peasantry and workers of Scotland (across the road and in plain view). There were many in Ayrshire suffering from what we would certainly call injustice today in the relations between employer and employed, or landlord and tenant (or even husband and wife, or parent and child). Poorer folk felt tied to the meagre land they worked, or the trade they plied: those families bore the risk of a poor crop or a trade depression personally, with no 'social safety net' to protect them (in fact, the limited poor relief that existed was widely seen as a final degradation rather than any social last resort).[32] 'The factor's snash' in Burns's 'The Twa Dogs' is both painfully autobiographical and depressingly general at the same time. The slave-holders often used this argument: that economic self-interest naturally led them to care for their enslaved workforce as that 'stock' was their mechanism of production. Just as one maintains a piece of machinery – a gun, a steam-engine, a blade – so the slave-holder (they claimed) provided food, clothing and health-care to maintain their investment in these human 'machines' – all staples which the free poor at home could not count upon.

Of course, the lot of the cottar or the mill-worker or the coal miner was in no way as harsh as the death sentence of enslavement. It is important, however, to remember that the legal structures of what was then known as the 'Law of Master and Servant' (now called 'Employment Law') gave the employee basic rights, but was heavily weighted in the employer's economic favour (although the standard hiring was typically for a twelvemonth, giving the servant an option to leave freely at the anniversary). Aitcheson summarises it:

> Seventeenth century legislation gave the justices of the peace the power at their quarter sessions in August and February, 'to fix the

---
[32] TC Smout, *A History of the Scottish People 1560–1830* (Glasgow: William Collins, 1969), p.303.

ordinary wages of workmen, labourers and servants, to imprison such as refuse to serve for the appointed hire, and to compel payment by the masters.'[33]

She gives a 1767 example of John Hamilton of Sundrum (1731–1829), one of Ayr's leading plantocrats, obtaining a sheriff's warrant to incarcerate his cook, David Kaithness (dates unknown), who had attempted to break his contract: but that was a matter of enforcing a contract entered into without coercion (albeit one struck with unequal economic bargaining power – remembering that 'combination' or trades unionism was at that time explicitly illegal).[34] The servant under a Scots Law contract was 'free', unlike the slave, unless he (or she) was 'indentured' under a stricter form of voluntary contract (or one imposed by a judicial sentence) which committed the servant to working for a fixed period of years for a fixed annual payment. (As Scots Law developed, the notion that bonded service for life without payment, even if entered into 'voluntarily', was equivalent to enslavement and so became impermissible). This was not chattel slavery, for the servant retained his/her legal *persona* but his/her individual rights were prescribed by the specific terms of the indenture contract enforceable to the letter by the master, with a lesser degree of legal protection for the servant. As the Court of Session ruled in 1747: 'There is no state of slavery with us; and a man's dependence as a servant, will not take from him a right otherwise compliant.'[35]

Apprenticeship was an analogous contract, where a young person would be indentured to a 'master' in the field for a period of sufficient duration (typically seven years) for him/her to become fully trained as a 'journeyman' in the trade, craft or profession. Here, too, the master was firmly in charge of the apprentice (as employer, skill-teacher and

---

[33] Jean Aitcheson, 'Servants in Ayrshire 1750–1914', in *Ayrshire Monographs* No 26 (Ayr: AANHS, 2001), p.15 summarising *Acts of the Parliament of Scotland, APS*, iv, 535, [1617], c.8, 'Regarding the Justices for Keeping of the King's Majesty's Peace and their Constables.'
[34] Aitcheson, p.12.
[35] *The Burgesses of Rutherglen v Andrew Leitch* [1747] MOR 1841. Some commentators erroneously try to equate the Scots prisoners of war transported to the Americas after Cromwell's victory at Dunbar (1650) or the Jacobites after the '15 and '45 Rebellions with the lot of the Black chattel slave. While those White men were forced into seven-year debentures and, like prisoners in jail, had their rights curtailed, they retained a legal personality and some protection over treatment. See: Stephen Mullen, 'The Myth of Scottish Slaves,' *The Sceptical Scot*, sceptical.scot/2016/03/the-myth-of-scottish-slaves/ (accessed 1 September 2024).

substitute parent). However, in all these forms of employment, no master could maim any servant, let alone kill them, a protection not extended to the enslaved.[36]

The most extreme form of employment contract covered workmen in Scotland's salt and coal industries whose workers (men, women and children) from 1606 to 1798 suffered under an effective form of serfdom which TC Smout has characterised as:

> a degradation without parallel in the history of labour in Scotland. [...] a man accepting employment in a colliery or saltpans thereby made himself a serf for life: he became a piece of mining equipment that could be bought, sold and inherited by his master, with the sole proviso that he might not be separated from the works at which he started his bondage.[37]

The initial act of 1606 (ratified and amended in 1641 and 1661) gave the masters certain rights of physical chastisement, while in 1701 – when the concept of *Habeus Corpus* was introduced into Scots Law by statute – that right was 'not to be extended to colliers or salters.'[38]

To make matters worse, this servitude was inter-generational. The custom of 'arling' allowed the coal- or salt-master to give a gift to his miners' children at their Christening which was deemed to tie that child into its father's servitude during its own life. (Although this process was not enshrined in the legislation, it was habitually enforced as if it were.) Oddly, despite the legal oppression of their servitude, colliers during this period commanded wages 'two or three times as high as farm servants [...] [at] fifteen shillings or more by 1790.'[39] However,

---

36 TC Smout, *A History of the Scottish People 1560–1830* (Glasgow: William Collins, 1969), pp.162–164. Remembering Stair's dictum: '[T]hough *Slavery* be against the Natural Law of Liberty, yet it is received for conveniency by the Nations, being more willing to lose Liberty than Life.' Stair, *Institutions*, Lib.I, §1,11, at p.6.
37 TC Smout, p.168. Christopher A Whatley posits a less bleak view, based on how the 'collier serfs, their bearers and families' maintained resilience within the legal regime. Unlike chattel slaves, they maintained an (admittedly circumscribed) legal persona and rights and were prepared to go to court to defend them. See Whatley, '"The Fettering Bonds of Brotherhood:" Combination and Labour Relations in the Scottish Coal-Mining Industry c. 1690–1775,' *Social History* (May, 1987), pp.139–154.
38 The relevant Acts were: APS IV, 286 [1606], c.10: 'An Act anent Coalyers and Salters'; APS VIII, 218 [1641] 'Act anent Coal-Hewers'; APS VII, 304 [1661] 'Act anent Coal-Hewers' and *The Criminal Procedure Act* 1701.
39 TC Smout, p.404.

the salters' wages were much less, at around six shillings a week.⁴⁰

These men and women were not legally 'slaves' although occasionally so denominated in legal contexts. For example the Ayrshire colliers' lot was described as 'the only remaining vestige of slavery amongst us,' by the Court of Session in 1708, or in the wording of the first relatively feeble *Emancipation Act*, 1775 which described its subjects as 'colliers, coal-bearers and salters [who] are in a state of slavery and bondage,' inasmuch as they retained legal personality, including the rights to receive due wages, to own chattels, to marry and bear children and to worship.⁴¹ Their final emancipation, which commenced in 1799, was brought about as much by a shortage of mineworkers, as the coal industry grew to fuel the furnaces of the Industrial Revolution, as by any humanitarianism.⁴²

There appears to have been very little concern over this particular tyranny in wider Scots society. The coal miners working Ayrshire's pits (such as Mungo Smith's at Drongan, or Newton-on-Ayr's) or the salters around Saltcoats, Ardrossan and Kilburnie toiled in their antediluvian contracts without attracting popular distress.⁴³ It is not absolution, but the fact that these inequalities inflicted locally on Ayrshire men and women were not called out partially explains the

---

40 John Strawhorn, *The Scotland of Robert Burns* (Darvel: Alloway Publishing, 1995), p.45.
41 *Sir William Wallace of Craigie v William Cunningham of Brownhill*, [1708] MOR 2349. *15 Geo III, c.58* [1775], 'An Act [...] respecting Colliers, Coal-bearers, and Salters.' See the dicta of Lord President Dundas in the Court of Session, 'Joseph Clark and Others *against* Mr Archibald Hope (1769)': 'I must observe that it is wrong to talk of coalliers as slaves. A coallier is not a slave, though bound to work at a particular work. No man can sell his coallier any more than he can sell his bound servant.' MP Brown, ed, *Decisions of the Lords of Council and Session, Reported by Sir David Dalrymple, Bart, Lord Hailes*, 2 vols (Edinburgh: Wm Tait, 1826), vol.I, pp.278–279.
42 *39 Geo III, c.55*, [1799] 'An Act to Explain and Amend the Laws Relative to Colliers in that Part of Great Britain called Scotland.' Even this Act was necessarily gradualist: 'And whereas the emancipating or setting free the Colliers, Coal-bearers, and Salters in Scotland, who are now in a state of servitude, gradually and upon reasonable conditions, and the preventing others from coming into such a state of servitude, would be the means of increasing the number of Colliers, Coal-bearers, and Salters to the great benefit of the Publick, without doing any injury to the present Masters, and would remove the reproach of allowing such a State of Servitude to exist in a free Country.' Emancipation was not immediate: workers under 21 had to serve ten further years, those between 21 and 35 could reduce that period by three years by training an apprentice and those over 45 had to serve three years. Their families achieved freedom when their husbands did. While the masters received no government compensation, the additional enforced period is very similar to the 'apprenticeships' mandated under the *3 & 4 Will IV c.73*, Slavery Abolition Act [1833].
43 Impressment in the Royal Navy during the Revolutionary and Napoleonic Wars is a further example of a legal deprivation of liberty and obligation to obey/work, but within regulations which respected the persona of the impressed man, although imperilled him with serious corporal, or even capital, punishment upon transgression of 'The Articles of War'.

absence of criticism over Black chattel slavery across the seas from Scotland before the Abolition movement gained traction in the 1780s.

White Emigration From Ayrshire to the Colonies

The growing British Empire provided billets for many young Scotsmen in the West Indies, both in wealthy multi-generational family businesses, such as Ayrshire's prosperous Hamiltons (or the struggling Douglas brothers), and with younger, poorer men taking their chance of rising up the hierarchy of slave-driving (through merit or mere survival) to become manager for an absentee plantocrat. As AM Kinghorn (who was teaching at the University of the West Indies at the time) described the idea: '[t]he lure of a tropical island as a means of avoiding responsibilities piling up at home is not an unusual manifestation of "cultural primitivism."'[44]

The importance of those Scottish emigrants in the Caribbean cannot be underestimated. Writing in 1774, Edward Long estimated that nearly one third of the White residents of Jamaica were Scots or of Scottish heritage.

> Jamaica, indeed, is greatly indebted to North Britain [sc: Scotland], as very nearly one third of the inhabitants are either natives of that country, or descendants from those who were. Many have come from the same quarter every year, less in quest of fame, than of fortunes; and such is their industry and address, that few of them have been disappointed in their aim. To say the truth, they are so clever and prudent in general, as, by an obliging behaviour, good sense, and zealous services to gain esteem, and make their way through every obstacle.[45]

This percentage was validated by the research of Alan Karras in 1992 through identifying Scottish names of owners on several maps of Jamaican parishes, and extrapolating that to the whole island. The maps from (a) 1763, gave a figure of 19.0 per cent and (b) from 1804, gave 29.6 per cent.[46]

---

44 AM Kinghorn, 'Robert Burns and Jamaica,' *A Review of English Literature* (July 1967), p.78.
45 Long, vol.II, pp.286–287.
46 Allan L Karras, *Sojourners in the Sun: Scottish Migrants in Jamaica and the Chesapeake, 1740–1800*

Recently, Mullen and Newman have challenged those numbers as too high given that '[t]he six parishes identified by Karras remained the most heavily Scottish ones on the island' and that, in the compensation records at abolition, by their calculation some 11 per cent of claims were paid to 'residents of Scotland.'[47] This analysis appears to suffer from two defects. The first (also a problem for Karras) is that the resident Scottish population was greater than just plantation owners; the 'clannishness' described elsewhere meant that for every Douglas there was a Burns beneath him. The second, as admitted by Mullen and Newman, is that 'resident in Scotland' does not define being a Scot (who could be living in and operating out of, say, Liverpool or London) and, in other research, Draper estimates the total paid to Scots (wherever resident) was 15–16 per cent of the total pool.[48] While there is insufficient hard data to be conclusive, Karras's calculations chime with Long's contemporary, albeit broad-brush, number.

Certainly, the philosophy of Scottish self-advancement in the colonies was widespread: Gilbert Burns later recalled a story told by John Murdoch, who taught him and Robert:

> When Mr Murdoch left Alloway, he went to teach and reside in the family of an opulent farmer capable of observation, who had a number of sons. A neighbour coming on a visit, in the course of conversation, asked the father how he meant to dispose of his sons. The father replied that he had not determined. The visitor said that were he in his place he would give them all good education and send them abroad, without, perhaps, having a precise idea where. The father objected that many young men lost their health in foreign countries, and many their lives. True, replied the visitor, but, as you have a number of sons, it will be strange if some one of them does not live and make a fortune.
>
> Let any person who has the feelings of a father comment on this story; but though few will avow, even to themselves, that such views

---

(Ithaca, NY: Cornell University Press, 1992), pp.126–129.

47 Stephen Mullen and Simon P Newman, 'Scotland and Jamaican Slavery: the Problem with Numbers,' *Centre for the Study of the Legacies of British Slavery Blog*, posted 12 November 2021, lbsatucl.wordpress.com/2021/11/12/scotland-and-jamaican-slavery-the-problem-with-numbers/ (accessed 1 September 2024).

48 These problems are discussed in Nicholas Draper, 'Scotland and Colonial Slave Ownership: The Evidence of the Slave Compensation Records,' in *Recovering Scotland's Slavery Past* ed Devine, pp.173–174.

govern their conduct, yet do we not daily see people shipping off their sons (and who would their daughters also, if there were any demand for them), that they may be rich or perish?[49]

The climate and conditions of the Caribbean were harsh for the uninitiated White Scot. Unlike the colonies and former colonies in North America, few men came to the West Indies with the intent of spending the rest of their lives there (though many did, by dying of tropical diseases). This was a sojourner community: programmed for the lucky minority to prosper and return home in wealth, or die sooner or later from tropical disease. Yellow Fever, or the *vomito negro*, constituted the greatest health risk. Ironically brought from West Africa by immune enslaved people, the deforestation and water pools arising out of the sugar business proved an ideal habitat for the *Aedes aegypti* mosquito. In creating the economic conditions for the sugar economy, the planter community created its nemesis, too. Trevor Burnard points out the physical risk:

> white susceptibility to disease, especially yellow fever, led to appalling white mortality [which] accentuated whites' penchant for fast living, for fatalism, and contributed to slaveowners' callous disregard for the welfare of their slaves. White life chances were not helped by inappropriate medical attention. Although Jamaican doctors' explanations of high white mortality were occasionally correct, their adherence to humoral and miasmic theories of medicine led them to promote remedies that were at best ineffectual, at worst detrimental.[50]

Dr Jonathan Troup (ca 1770–1800), an Aberdonian physician, described the commercial risks in his West Indian journal in 1789:

> One man only makes a fortune in the W[est] Indies out of 500 — It

---

49 'Letter from Gilbert Burns to Dr James Currie,' *The Works of Robert Burns. With an Account of his Life, and a Criticism on His Writings, to which are Prefixed, Some Observations on the Character and Conditions of Scottish Peasantry* [Second Edition], 4 vols, ed by James Currie (London/Edinburgh: Cadell & Davies/Creech, 1801), vol.I., pp.382-383.
50 Burnard, *Countrie Continues Sicklie*, p.45. The 'Humoral Theory' is the Ancient Greek medical principle around the balancing of the four humours (blood, phlegm, black bile, yellow bile) while 'Miasmic theory' held that disease was spread by inhaling air exposed to 'corruption.'

is long before he gets into business & when he is in business he risques much by bad pay[men]ts [and] loss of Negroes — that in space of 20 years he will not be able w[ithou]t great frugality to make more than £3–4,000. [...] Doctors and managers of estates die more than any set of people.[51]

Yet, despite those odds, Burnard calculates that around 1774 across the British West Indies the 'average wealth was £1,000 per white person, over ten times as much as' at Home or in the 13 American Colonies, and of that pool of wealth Devine uses the statistic that 'in the period 1771–[177]5 Scots accounted for nearly 45% of all inventories at death above £1,000.'[52] So for every scion of a family like the Ayrshire Hamiltons, there were multiple adventurers, but all participating in the economy of cruelty. Many felt convinced that their lot was not much worse than that of the Black enslaved, and studies certainly show that White mortality rates were higher than Black rates in the first two years after landing in Jamaica. As Burnard stated above, this fact effectively defined the whole structure of Jamaican society.

There were some plantations where the slave-holders believed themselves 'kind masters' in a form of self-delusion. Even the noted Scottish philosopher and poet James Beattie (1735–1803), who was a renowned and early Abolitionist, could say (in 1789) that 'many of my pupils have gone to the West Indies; and, I trust, have carried my principles along with them, and exemplified those principles in their conduct to their unfortunate Brethren [sc: the enslaved]'.[53] However, the view of even many of those ameliorists was that the 'stock' of enslaved people, if they were not a different (and lower) species of the genus *homo*, were at least socially and culturally inferior and incapable of rational self-government at a personal, social or national level. West Indian society was not only morally bankrupt, but socially too.

---

51 'Journal of Dr Jonathan Troup. 30 July 1789,' in *Scotland and the Americas, c 1650–c 1939: A Documentary Source Book,* ed by Linda G Fryer, Marjory Harper, Allan I Macinnes (Edinburgh: Scottish History Society, 2002), p.216.
52 Trevor Burnard, 'Plantation Slavery in the British Caribbean,' in *The Palgrave Handbook of Global Slavery Throughout History,* ed by Damien A Pargas and Juliane Schiel (London: Palgrave Macmillan, 2023), p.396. TM Devine, *Scotland's Empire* (London: Penguin, 2004), p.231.
53 Sir William Forbes, ed, *Life and Writings of James Beattie LLD,* 2 Vols (London: E Roper, 1824), vol.II, pp.441–442.

> Those whites set in immediate authority [over the enslaved] were an isolated and beleaguered minority, non-gentlemen of limited education, dissolute and shiftless for the most part, outnumbered fifty to one by their charges, tied by contract and the requirement to make a profit, with only the parlous rewards of power to offset unpleasant work in a harsh climate, the ever-present threat of lethal or crippling disease, and the perils of insurrection.[54]

This milieu was felt to be completely unsuited for the European female and, as the economy grew, the number of White women present in the colonies declined, with that trend being greater in Scots-owned estates.[55] Through the White chain of command this led to the extravagant 'fast living' exhibited in vast alcohol consumption and (often coerced) inter-racial sexual activity.

> Bookkeepers were not expected to marry, and were often forbidden to do so, but were encouraged to take 'housekeepers' from amongst the slave women.[56]

With a daily cycle of cruelty, danger, death and rape, it is in no way surprising that the veneers of Enlightenment Scotland cracked in Jamaican life. As the century progressed, the 'West India Interest' gained a reputation for wealth and a coarseness of manners. Zachary Macaulay, a bookkeeper who became a leading Abolitionist, described how, on returning home after two years of Jamaican life, he 'had contracted a boorishness of manner, arising doubtless from the nature of my employment and associations.'[57] This character was captured sarcastically by John Galt later in his *Annals of the Parish* where 'Mr Cayenne,' his wealth and his Black enslaved servant return to Ayrshire from the West Indies and have difficulty in fitting

---

54 Michael Craton, *Empire, Enslavement and Freedom in the Caribbean* (Kingston: Ian Randle, 1997), p.153.
55 Hamilton, p.210.
56 Anon, 'Burns' Jamaica Connexions' (attributed to a descendent of Patrick Douglas of Garallan), *Burns Chronicle* (1903), p.81. *Greenock Telegraph*, 14 July 1902, identifies the author as Bailie Grierson Macara of Greenock (1868–1933), a past-president of the Greenock Burns Club, but this has not been verified.
57 Lady Knutsford, *Life and Letters of Zachary Macaulay* (London: E Arnold, 1900), p.10. See x below for a detailed discussion of Macaulay's life.

into genteel society due to his peppery temperament.[58]

The significant community of sojourning Scots in the Caribbean, notably in Jamaica, exemplified an almost *Punch* cartoon display of Scottishness, being clannish, 'canny' and fond of the bottle. In the 1850s, the Abolitionist Samuel Ringgold Ward, a fugitive slave himself, praised his Abolitionist hosts in Scotland, but recalled that

> Scotchmen, in the West Indies, became slave-holders. They were severely exacting and oppressive. It was just like them to demand, and, if possible to receive, the last *'baubee'* [sic] from the unpaid toil of their slaves. They required the exhibition of Scottish energy from their bondmen; if they did not receive it, they were prepared to exhibit Scotch energy in forcing it out of them. Instances of this sort are to be remembered of many Scotch slaveholders (and alas! by many Negroes who were their slaves) to this day. The record of them, and the names of their perpetrators would be the largest, blackest roll and record of infamy that ever disgraced the Scottish name or blighted Scotch character.[59]

However, in the 1780s, the rewards were more obviously discussed than the risks, while the underlying cruelty was rarely discussed, if at all. To an extent the adventurers were correct, as the law of compound interest favoured the surviving risk takers; at the Final Emancipation, while Scotland represented around ten percent of the UK population, Scots slave-holders garnered 15–16 per cent of the compensation fund.[60]

Black Immigration From the Colonies to Ayrshire

As Gerry Carruthers rightly says, while Ayrshire made good money out of the enslaved economy, 'Scotland had no such notorious port as Liverpool or Bristol where African slaves [...] were chained in the most appalling captivity', so while there were some few slave ventures out of Scottish ports in the earlier part of the century, this part of the trade was not at a visible, let alone industrial, level, so

---

58 [John Galt], *Annals of the Parish or, The Chronicles of Dalmailing* (Edinburgh: William Blackwood, 1821), pp.227–230.
59 Samuel Ringgold Ward, *Autobiography of a Fugitive Negro* (London: John Snow, 1855), pp.349–350.
60 Draper, pp.166–186.

the stay-at-home Scot strolling through Glasgow, Leith or Ayr would not have seen (or smelled) this leg of the trade.[61]

However, it is easy to forget that there has been a Black community living in British society throughout the modern period of history. As Norma Myers reminds us:

> Although black people have sustained a continuous presence in Britain for at least four centuries, they remain almost invisible in historical writing. This is partly a reflection of the ephemerality of evidence, but also serves to indicate [their] economic and legal position.[62]

Correspondingly, Whyte reminds us of the sheer difference in scale of the population of enslaved people across Great Britain: while there were an estimated 15,000 Black enslaved men and women working across England and Wales in the later decades of the 18th century, there were only around 70 Black enslaved people resident in Scotland.[63] Mostly, these people were in personal service. Cairns suggests that

> [s]uch [Black] enslaved domestic servants in many ways were probably not outwardly in so different a position from that of free [White] servants. Except that always held over them was the threat of forced return to the colonies for sale.[64]

The other way that enslaved Black men came to Scotland was by being sent over to be apprenticed to a master craftsman to learn his trade and then return to the plantation as a valued (and valuable) journeyman. Cairns also studies this pathway:

> There was always a demand in the British colonies for skilled tradesmen, who were often in short supply. This will have made it

---

[61] Carruthers, 'Robert Burns and Slavery', p.163. The myth of Burns seeing a slave ship at Dundee in 1787 is discussed below at pp.192.

[62] Norma Myers, *Reconstructing the Black Past: Blacks in Britain 1780–1830* (London/Portland OR: Frank Cass & Co, 1996/2006), p.1.

[63] Whyte, *Scotland and the Abolition*, p.11. That is having been enslaved under the laws of a foreign country, or an overseas colony. The population in the latter decades of the 18th century was around eight million in England & Wales and just under one-and-a-half million in Scotland.

[64] John Cairns, 'Enforced Sojourners: Enslaved Apprentices in Eighteenth-Century Scotland,' in *Ad Fontes: Liber Amicorum Prof Beatrix van Erp-Jacobs*, ed by EJMFC Broers & RMH Kubben (Oisterwijk [NL]: Wolf Legal Publishers, 2014), p.71.

tempting for masters to have slaves who showed aptitude trained: acquisition of skills as an artisan also greatly increased the value of a slave. [...] One advantage to the master of a black slave being apprenticed was that the law was unambiguous in the authority that it gave masters over apprentices: runaways could be retrieved and controlled without any possibility of question of the legitimacy of the power exercised over them.[65]

So many of these people would have been invisible to ordinary Scots folk, rarely competing in trade with them or moving in the same social sphere. Thus, it can be argued, Black people appeared unthreatening, resulting in

Scotland's treatment of those of African descent in her midst [being] as yet untainted by [racism] – not perhaps out of any virtue, for Scots in the Empire were to exhibit some of the worst examples of racism, but simple because the comparatively few [B]lack people of Scotland at that time were not seen as a challenge to the livelihoods of the communities amongst whom they lived.[66]

Ayrshire was home to some dozen of those 70 people in the second half of the century so, while certainly uncommon, Black people were not invisible in Ayrshire society. The most cited Black Ayrshireman of the period is Scipio Kennedy of the Culzean estate in Carrick (the southern division of the county), the seat of the head of the Kennedys which is now managed by the National Trust for Scotland.[67] Scipio was born in 'Guinea' but, as is typical in the history of enslaved people, neither his birth date (later assumed to be ca 1695) or his birth-name are known. He was enslaved at the age of about six and after surviving his 'middle passage,' he was bought in the Caribbean by Captain Andrew Douglas (?–1725), a Scottish officer in the Royal Navy who returned to Scotland in 1702 accompanied by his 'boy,' under the appellation 'Scipio Douglas.' Three years later, when the Captain's daughter, Jean (?–1767), married John Kennedy (?–1744), the heir to Culzean, Scipio accompanied her to Ayrshire and like her,

---
65 Ibid, pp.71, 79.
66 Whyte, *Scotland and the Abolition*, p.100.
67 Melville, *Facing our Past*, pp.17–18.

his name changed to 'Kennedy.' After 20 years' service, John Kennedy, now Sir John Kennedy Bart, agreed to formalise his employment of Scipio Kennedy (now baptised) in a 19-years indenture contract to serve the family for an annual wage of £12 Scots and a proportion of the servants' 'drink money.'[68] Later, it would seem that he took up weaving on the estate and the respect that Sir John had for the old servant can be seen as he had a house built on the estate for Scipio and his family.[69]

It appears that Scipio was also accepted as a member of the village community, if only from reading the Kirk Session minutes of 1727 where:

> Margaret Gray [...] was compeared and owned that she was with child to ye Blackamoor at Cullean [...] [having sinned] at Cullean House last August [...] The accused man was not yet recorded a member of ye church, tho' it be said that he was probably baptized by an episcopalian minister [....] [70]

Just as with Robert Burns and Jean Armour, Scipio was summoned to appear before the Minister and the Session to confirm that 'he did adhere to the Christian faith and professed his great satisfaction his now being a Christian', but he only admitted his antenuptial fornication at a subsequent meeting.[71] Over the coming months, Margaret and Scipio received three public rebukes in Church for their sin, but it is interesting to note that none of the six Session minutes makes comment on the inter-racial aspect of this affair, only concerned that two members of the parish were acting shamelessly.[72] They were married in 1728, after she had borne him a daughter, and they would raise eight children together in their house

---

68 NRS, *Ailsa Muniments*, GD25/9/72/9, 'Contract Betwixt Sir John Kennedy & Scipio Kennedy his servant for 19 years, 6 February 1725.' The document is not, strictly, a manumission as often described as it skates over Scipio's actual status before and at the date of the contract, implying (rather than granting) his freedom to enter into a bond of service. Note: 'drink money' (more often called 'vails') were customary cash gifts to the servants given by house guests, and not (as some commentators suggest) a share in smuggling profits.
69 Michael Moss, The 'Magnificent Castle' of Culzean and the Kennedy Family (Edinburgh: EUP, 2002), pp.25–26.
70 NRS, *Kirkoswald Kirk Session Minutes* (1617–1660,1694–1758), CH2/562/1, 10 December 1727, pp.183–184.
71 Ibid, 7 January 1728, p.184: 14 January 1728, p.185. Noting that the Kennedys were Scots Episcopalian, and Scipio would have been baptised into that church in a private ceremony.
72 Ibid, 10 March 1728, p.187; 26 May 1728. p.188.

near the old Culzean Castle.[73] On Lady Kennedy's death in 1767, she remembered 'my old servant' (who, by then, had been with her nigh on 50 years) by leaving the sum of £10 Sterling to him, which pretty much equal to the £40 bequest she left to be shared by her three grandchildren.[74] On Scipio's death in 1774, his eldest son Douglas (1732–1781), who had been named after Lady Kennedy's maiden name and who was now body servant to Sir Thomas Kennedy Bart (later Earl of Cassillis) (?–1775), buried his father in the old churchyard with a gravestone which still stands to his memory: 'This stone is erected by Douglas Kennedy in Memory of his father Scipio Kennedy who died June 24, 1774. Aged 80 years.'[75] Alan Rice rightly says:

> Scipio Kennedy's memorial stone at Culzean attests to a full life despite the debilitating, exploitative practices of the middle passage. […] Memorials like that of Scipio Kennedy cut across such collective amnesia and as such should be highlighted exhibitions of Scottish history in general they are no longer marginalized and posited as peripheral to the national story.[76]

Scipio was not the only enslaved Black person in Ayrshire in the second half of the 18th century, and not many of the others appear to have had such a comfortable later life.

Another case in the burgh was that of the elderly Lady Dunduff (?–1775), the widow of Basil Whitefoord of Dunduff, who kept a Black servant (whom she called Othello) at her Ayr home at some point between 1767 and her death in 1775.[77] There are also a pair of interesting stories around Black servants in misfortune in Ayr. Edward Young 'a Negroe from Virginia [who had] landed at Ayr in the Month of June 1783 with one Mr McAdam,' had become mentally deranged and by 1785 was incarcerated in Irvine's Tolbooth at the heritors' cost. They unsuccessfully appealed for financial help from the Ayrshire Commissioners of Supply to have him transferred to the 'Glasgow Madhouse' (which would accept him on payment

---

73 NRS, *Kirkoswald OPR*, Births 601/20.84 (Elisabeth Kennedy); NRS, *Kirkoswald OPR*, Marriages, 31 October 1728, 601/20.40.
74 Moss, *Culzean*, p.36.
75 Photograph in Melville, *Facing our Past*, p.17.
76 Alan Rice, *Radical Narratives of the Black Atlantic* (London/New York: Continuum, 2003), p.213.
77 James Paterson, *History of the County of Ayr*, 2 vols (Ayr: James Dick, 1847), vol.I. p.177.

of £15 per annum) but such a large commitment was refused. There is no record of the fate of that poor man.[78] Another case which concerned the Ayr Kirk Session was in April 1784, when

> Milly, a Negro Woman appeared before the Session with a child in her arms which she had born in uncleanliness [the father being] Charles McGowan, a Soldier and former servant to Cap[tai]n Shaw lately gone to Ireland [...] who would have nothing to do with her or the Child.'[79]

Private McGowan was sought and the lack of progress in bringing him to account is noted in the minutes and he was not found. While nothing is known about Milly, it is a safe assumption that she had been in service and would have been turned out of her position, and losing her 'character' due to her 'immorality.' Heartlessly, Milly and her child, too, drift out of White history.

Beyond the burgh and in the county, Mungo Smith of Drongan (1737–1814) (an East Indies nabob rather than West Indies plantocrat) was an innovative agricultural improver and an industrialist who commissioned the pioneering engineer William Symington (1764–1831) to build a steam engine to power his colliery.[80] His tax returns show him as having kept a 'Black boy called Jack Scott' between 1777 and 1779. Similarly, these registers show that surgeon David Wardrope employed 'Richard a black chaise driver', while Major Brown, the tenant of Treesmills near Kilmarnock, had 'Prince, a Negro house servant.'[81] In the late 1780s in Kilmarnock, a millwright known as 'Black Prince' worked for George Tannahill (the poet's uncle) but it is unknown if he is same man as the major's former servant or another.[82] In Mauchline in 1784, a Black servant of Sir John Whitefoord (1734–1803) (who had been brought to the county from the West Indies by

---

78 David McClure, 'Records and Functions of the Ayrshire Commissioners of Supply', *Scottish Local History Journal* (1997). McClure suggests that this may have been John Loudoun McAdam (1756-1836), the great road engineer, who returned to Ayrshire in 1783 from the USA.
79 NRS, *Ayr Kirk Session Minutes, (1781–1793)*, CH2/751/14, 5 April 1784, p.86.
80 It was Symington who built the engine for Patrick Miller's prototype steamboat on Dalswinton Loch and the engine at the Wanlockhead lead mines.
81 NRS, *Male Servant Tax Rolls*, volume 1 (1777-1778, counties) E326/5/1/20; volume 2 (1778–1779, counties) E326/5/3/20.
82 John Parkhill, *Sketch of the Life of Peter Burnet, a Negro, Who came to Paisley Sixty Years ago, where He still lives, a very Old and Respectable Man* (Paisley: J Neilson, 1841), p.14.

'Sandy Bell' of Burns's 'The Mauchline Wedding,' [K.74]) was baptised as 'John Cartwright' in the parish church, as recorded in its register:

> A Black Boy servant to Sir John Whitefoord of Whitefoorde Bar[one]t having given Satisfaction to the Session of his knowledge was Baptized 5 Sept[embe]r [1784] called JOHN CARTWRIGHT.[83]

While, in the early 1790s, there is anecdotal reference to an unnamed young woman living in Beith in the north of Ayrshire who is described as 'a young Mulatto girl' with 'a fortune at her own disposal of £2,000', nothing else is known of her.[84]

The other group of Black people who may have lived in Ayrshire at this time were linked to the powerful Hamilton family who owned several estates on both sides of the Atlantic, in Jamaica and Ayrshire. The elder brother, Robert (II) Hamilton (1698–1754), was based at Bourtreehill near Irvine and in 1754 he bought another estate in Ayr, which he renamed Rozelle after one of his Jamaican properties.[85] A nephew of his, John Hamilton (1739–1821), was orphaned when his father died at sea, and his trustees bought the Ayrshire estate of Sundrum for him. John was a classmate of James Boswell's at Glasgow University and, after studying, he personally managed the family's Jamaican interests from 1755.[86] After six years on the island, and after being in considerable personal danger through the time of Tacky's Rebellion (1760–1761), he retired to Sundrum and became a leading figure in the affairs of the county, serving as the Convenor

---

83 NRS, *Old Parish Registers Births* 604/20 p.24, Mauchline, 5 September 1784: Cartwright, John. He chose the Christian name in honour of his patron, and the surname was Lady Whitefoord's maiden name. (See further discussion of 'The Mauchline Wedding' at p.124 below). Sir John, due to his losses in the Ayr Bank, was forced to sell his estates at Whitefoord to Sir James Hunter Blair (who renamed it Blairquhan) and Ballochmyle to Claude Alexander. From 1785 he lived at Whitefoord House on the Canongate, meeting Burns again, and even seconding Glencairn's motion for the Caledonian Hunt's subscription to the Edinburgh Edition. While John Cartwright's subsequent history is unknown, there is an entry in Canongate Kirk's burial registers of 'John Cartwright, vintner of Barrington's Close' who died on 29 December 1815 aged 54, of 'Decay' which could, perhaps, be the same person. National Registers of Scotland, *Old Parish Registers Deaths*, 685/3 310, 2 January 1816, Canongate.
84 Parkhill, p.22. As will be discussed below, Beith was the home of Robert Sheddan, who went to court in 1757 to assert his 'rights' over James Montgomery, an enslaved Black servant. Perhaps this young woman was his illegitimate child or grandchild.
85 Eric J Graham, *Burns & the Sugar Plantocracy of Ayrshire* (Ayr: AANHS, 2009).
86 This friendship must have been influential in confirming Boswell's pro-slavery stance, as evidenced in his anonymous 1791 'No Abolition of Slavery or The Universal Empire of Love': Whyte, *Scotland and the Abolition*, p.57.

of the county's Commissioners of Supply from 1786 to 1820.[87] There is an interesting tale about how Sundrum worked his Scottish estate:

> In the village of Joppa on the main road from Ayr to Cumnock there were at one time a number of Negroes brought from the plantations in West Indies, belonging to John Hamilton of Sundrum. They intermarried with the local inhabitants, and traces of Negro in the hair and countenance could be observed for some generations.[88]

As late as 1894 a Black stonemason worked on the Hamilton's Sundrum estate: Alexander Waters (ca 1830–1894) had been born in Jamaica on the Pemberton plantation and was shipped to Sundrum as a child to be apprenticed to an Ayrshire stonemason. As a journeyman he did not return to Jamaica, but maintained the estate until his death, when his obituary called him 'a worthy and faithful servant to the Hamilton family'.[89]

Another nephew of Bourtreehill's was Hugh Hamilton (1746–1829) who replaced Sundrum as the family agent on the island and spent several years managing the Jamaican concerns, working with John Ballantine as his banker in Ayr and Ballantine's brother Patrick (?–1810) as Hunter's bank's Jamaican agent at Kingston. Hugh returned to Ayr (worth an estimated £3,000 on his own account, around £400,000 in 2024 values) in 1783, purchasing firstly the Pinmore estate near Girvan, then the Belleisle property on the road between Ayr and Burns Cottage.[90] When his friend John Ballantine became the managing partner of Hunter's Bank, he brought Hugh into the partnership.[91] Records show that his daughter Jane sailed from Jamaica to Scotland in 1785, accompanied by her Black servant called Gammetta, presumably to live at Belleisle.[92]

Hugh was succeeded in Jamaica by Sundrum's second son Alexander ('Sandy') West Hamilton (1764–1837) who remained there for two

---

87 Graham, *Plantocracy*, pp.31–37.
88 Aitcheson, p.15 quoting from JE Shaw, *Ayrshire, 1745–1950, A Social and Industrial History* (Edinburgh & London: Oliver & Boyd, 1953), p.23; Strawhorn, *Ayrshire*, p.314.
89 *Ayr Advertiser*, 6 September 1894.
90 Graham, *Plantocracy*, pp.47–48.
91 Robert S Rait, *The History of the Union Bank of Scotland* (Glasgow: John Smith, 1930), pp.164–165.
92 NRS GD/142/2/24, quoted in Graham, *Plantocracy*, p.59.

decades before his cousin Hugh made him his heir to the Pinmore and Bellisle estates in 1816. On entering into his inheritance as Colonel Hamilton, it was noted that he always employed a Black butler at the house.[93]

Over and above these Black residents who leave some trace in the county and family records, it is probable that there were other transient Black servants seen in Ayrshire, whether accompanying visiting Glasgow 'Tobacco Lords,' or on duty at the other plantocrat estates in the county such as the Oswalds at Auchincruive, so the sight of a Black person in Ayrshire, while not common, was in no way unknown.

Questioning how or why Black people were there would have been difficult. These Black servants were employed by men and women at the top of Ayrshire society, who brought capital and cash into its economy, and consequently expected a level of unquestioning deference in return. Remembering that there was little debate at all on Abolition before 1787, that silence is probably explained as

> most Scots [in the West Indies] considered themselves temporary residents, they elected to keep quiet about [the brutal regime] until they could return home. At home, a combination of ignorance of the facts, respect for the sanctity of property, and fear of revolution combined to 'keep the lid' on any challenge to slavery.[94]

Slavery and the Law of Scotland

Scots Law, unlike the common law jurisdictions of England and Wales, is a civil law tradition which is based on the principles of Roman Law. In Burns's day (and many might still believe today), it was seen as conservative with both a large and a small 'c'. That Roman society accepted enslavement as a normal part of social and economic life and regulated it accordingly was recognised by historians and jurisprudents, and so was broadly unquestioned as a part of Scottish society in the 18th century, partly through that conservatism, but also because of the very small cadre of chattel slaves within its borders.

There were, however, already cracks in the legal façade of enslavement. As early as 1681, Dalrymple of Stair's influential legal textbook *The*

---

93 James Paterson, *History of the Counties of Ayr and Wigton* (Edinburgh: James Stille, 1863), vol.I, p.133.
94 Whyte, *Scotland and the Abolition*, pp.5–6.

Institutes recognised that 'though Slavery be against the Natural Law of Liberty, yet it is received for conveniency by the Nations, being more willing to lose Liberty than Life,' and baldly states the legal maxim that in Scots Law '[s]lavery is abolished.'[95] Thus, should a case come to the courts, such as 'the Tumbling Lassie Case' of 1687, the law was plain. That particular judgement clearly states 'we have no slaves in Scotland, and mothers cannot sell their bairns.'[96]

These ideas were bolstered by the beginnings of the Scottish Enlightenment, where Glasgow's professor Francis Hutcheson set the basis of the philosophical opposition to chattel slavery in his lectures in the late 1730s and early 1740s:

> [N]o endowments, natural or acquired, can give a perfect right to assume power over others, without their consent. This is intended against the doctrine of Aristotle, and some others of the ancients, 'that some men are naturally slaves [...]' [...] The natural sense of justice and humanity abhors the thought.[97]

> As to the notions of slavery which obtained among the Grecians and Romans, and other nations of old, they are horridly unjust. No damage done or crime committed can change a rational creature into a piece of goods void of all right, and incapable of acquiring any, or of receiving any injury from the proprietor.[98]

That being said, in the century after 'The Tumbling Lassie' case, Scotland hosted a population (albeit small) of Black servants, along with several Black men sent to Scotland to sojourn as apprentices before returning as tradesmen to the colonies, whose legal status went unquestioned.

Though just under one hundred people who were of African, Indian

---

95 In Scots jurisprudence, several authors of texts are known as 'Institutional Writers' whose philosophical and legal codifications are held to be persuasive before the Law. The first of these was James Dalrymple, 1st Viscount Stair with his *Institutions* (1691). These passages are at Lib.1, §1,11, at p.6 and Lib.4, §45,17, at p.707.
96 *Reid against Scot[t] of Harden and his Lady*, MOR 9505; Fountainhalls, I.439.
97 Francis Hutcheson, *A System of Moral Philosophy in Three Books*, 2 vols, ed by Francis Hutcheson MD (Glasgow/London: R and A Foulis/A Miller, T Longman, 1755), vol.I. pp.301–303.
98 Ibid, vol.II, pp.202–203.

or (in one case) Native American origin can be documented between 1701 and 1780 as apprentices, servants, or journeymen, the actual number will have been considerably greater. [...] Indeed, it is fair to suppose that, certainly by the 1760s and 1770s, the presence of such a person, perhaps held as enslaved, would not have been a matter of surprise in any part of Scotland.[99]

These were, in the main, enslaved people although (save in a few cases) their actual status was rarely mentioned in the community and certainly not in the courts, with the 'masters' relying on the claim that the 'slave' had been duly and legally enslaved under the independent laws of one or other of Britain's colonies.[100] The exceptions to this silence occur in newspaper adverts which were published around Burns's lifetime: a few involved with the sale of enslaved people, and several more appeared when the slave-holder's control was broken through the enslaved person's flight for freedom. There are seven newspaper advertisements in the period 1766 to 1771 where people are openly advertised for sale, all in Edinburgh.[101] There are slightly more notices of 'runaways' (as freedom-seeking slaves were often called by their oppressors) where the purported 'masters' sought the return of their 'property' in 13 instances which are more dispersed across Scotland.[102] The tone of these appeals makes it clear that the

---

[99] JW Cairns, 'After Somerset: The Scottish Experience,' *Journal of Legal History*, 33.3 (2012), pp.313–314; Whyte, *Scotland and the Abolition*, p.70. Whyte records the cases of servants of the Earl of Perth (or Jacobite Duke of Perth) and of the Duchess of Buccleuch with 'accompanying slaves hav[ing] silver collars,' and a runaway slave 'Ann' having 'a brass collar on her neck, on which is engraved "Gustavus Brown in Dalkeith, his negro,"' Whyte, ibid, p.15.

[100] Stephen Mullen makes the statement that '[s]lavery could not be abolished in Scotland since it was never codified' in his *Glasgow, Slavery and Atlantic Commerce: An Audit of Historic Connections and Modern Legacies* (Glasgow: City of Glasgow, 2022), p.26. This is not entirely exact: for while Stair confirmed that slavery was abolished in Scotland (as discussed above) it was codified in the Roman Law from whence Scots jurisprudence flowed. The important point here is more the principle of 'Comity' or recognition of the effect of laws of other nations within one's own, particularly in relation to Diasporan Scots who had 'bought' a enslaved person in accordance with the statutes of the Caribbean or the USA.

[101] Advertisements prior to Burns's birth in 1759 are not included. Of those after that date, six relate to young men under 16, and one to a 19-year-old woman with her one-year-old infant. Data for this and the fugitive slaves is taken from the project 'Runaway Slaves in Britain: Bondage, Freedom and Race in the Eighteenth Century,' whose database can be found at www.runaways.gla.ac.uk/ (accessed 1 September 2024).

[102] Again, adverts prior to Burns's birth in 1759 are not included. All of the subsequent fugitives were male (eight boys or youths, four young men and a man of 35). Five records are from Glasgow/Greenock, four from Edinburgh and one each from Alloa, Atholl, Arbroath and Stranraer.

fugitive is a chattel slave and that the 'master' is seeking to enforce his ownership rights against them, and this would be the ground on which three important enslavement law suits hinged. The first, coincidentally arising in Ayrshire, though before Burns's birth, was the case of *Robert Sheddan v James Montgomerie, a Negro*, of 1757. This came about, as the advertisement for his recapture recounts, when 'One Negroe Man, [...] a Virginia born Slave [...] with him a Certificate, which calls him James Montgomerie, signed, John Witherspoone Minister' ran away from 'his Master' Robert Sheddan of Beith in April 1756.[103]

At first sight, the Court of Session was 'generally inclined to find that the negro was not manumitted by his being brought to Scotland' but felt that a full hearing should be held, however, this case failed to be judged as the allegedly enslaved Montgomerie died before a judgement was handed down.[104] One of the judges, the Ayrshireman Lord Kilkerran (1688–1759), expressed his doubts with a note on his case bundle:

Mors ultima linea rerum. There the servant shall be free from his master. The poor young man is dead, and so has put an end to the question, what influence Christian charity or love to our neighbour, whatever his colour is, ought to have.[105]

A second, similar case *Dalrymple v Spens* in 1769 was also abandoned, this time on the death of the slave-holder.[106]

---

103 *Edinburgh Evening Courant*, 4 May 1756. Revd John Witherspoon (1723-1794): Scots Presbyterian minister and later president of the College of New Jersey (now Princeton University) who signed the Declaration of Independence for New Jersey. He was a believer in gradual emancipation, yet at his death he still owned two enslaved people, which has become a question of considerable controversy at Princeton.

104 *Robert Sheddan against a Negro*, (1757), MOR, 14545. 'A Negro, who had been bought in Virginia, and brought to Britain to be taught a trade, and who had been baptized in Britain, having claimed his liberty, against his master Robert Sheddan, who had put him on board a ship, to carry him back to Virginia, the Lords appointed counsel for the negro, and ordered memorials, and afterwards a hearing in presence, upon the respective claims of liberty and servitude by the master and the negro. But, during the hearing in presence, the negro died; so the point was not determined.' See also, NRS, CS234, Court of Session: Unextracted processes, 1st arrangement, Innes-Durie office 1757.

105 'Death, the final boundary of things.' Quoting Horace, *Epistles*, I, xvi, 79. *Robert Sheddan v James Montgomery Sheddan, a Negro*, (1757), 5 Brn 324. Note that the judge's eldest son, Sir Adam Fergusson of Kilkerran (1733–1813), was joint owner of large slave plantations in Jamaica. See Alex Renton, *Blood Legacy: Reckoning with a Family's Story of Slavery* (Edinburgh: Canongate, 2021).

106 *David Dalrymple against David Spens [Spence], a Negro*, (1769), Court of Session: Unextracted processes, 1st arrangement, McNeill office (1574–1861), NRS, CS236/D/4/3 box 104 and NRS, CS236/S/3/13.

It would be the third of these lawsuits, *Knight v Wedderburn* in 1774 which would clarify the law in favour of the enslaved person, however, many commentators miss one other important Scots Law case, a scandalous divorce entitled *Mrs Margaret Porterfield v Houston Stewart Nicolson of Carnock* (1770, affirmed on appeal to the House of Lords in 1771). Here the question was raised as to whether 'a Negro Slave, not a Christian, may be received as a witness' to a wife's adulterous behaviour. The judgement was that the 'slave' Latchemo's evidence was admissible. Lord Hailes ruled that:

> there are no slaves among us, in the Roman sense of the word. Latchemo is indeed bound to perform service for life, but he is capable of acquiring property. His master, were he to beat him, would be liable to an action of battery. Were he to murder him, he would suffer no less punishment than if he were to murder the first peer of Great Britain.[107]

At the appeal before the House of Lords in 1771, Latchemo is clearly designated as 'a slave,' with neither discussion nor judgement on the legality of his particular status.[108]

In effect, an enslaved person being brought to Scotland became, not fully free, but rather a species of bonded servant for life, not unlike the colliers and salters, retaining an independent legal persona and such rights appertaining to it (however, strictly bounded by the terms of the servitude bond.)[109] The other keynote case, this time in England (although the judge was Scots-born), was *Somerset's Case* of 1772. Here, the Lord Chief Justice of England, Lord Mansfield (1705–1793), denied that an English Virginian trader could punish a slave resident

---

107 *Hailes Decisions*, vol.I, pp, 371–378, at p.374. For Hailes, true slavery ('in the Roman sense of the word') had to include the *jus vitæ et necis* (the power of life and death) which was a part of a Roman slave-holder's *patria potestas* ('paternal power or authority').

108 House of Lords, Upon Appeal from The Courts of Scotland, 1771, No. 121: *Mrs. Margaret Houston Stewart Nicolson v Houston Stewart Nicolson, Esq*, 18 February 1771, (1771) 3 Paton 655. Note that, by 1778, Sir William Maxwell had dispensed with Latchemo's services. See NRS: *Male Servant Tax Rolls*, Counties: Kirkcudbrightshire, 1777–1778, E326/5/1/116 (9/10).

109 Additionally, there is one criminal case. *HM Advocate v Bel[l] alias Belinda* [1771]. Here, 'a girl or woman from Bengal in the East Indies, the Slave or Servant of John Johnston,' was accused of the capital crime of infanticide. In effect she 'plea bargained' and avoided trial by agreeing to transportation for life to 'one or other of His Majesty's plantations [sc: colonies] in America during all the days of her life [...] to be sold as a Slave for Life [with payment to John Johnston Esq] of the price she shall yield after deducting the Expence of here Transportation.' NRS, JC26/193 and NRS, JC11/28.

in England by sending him forcibly from England to be re-sold onto a Jamaican plantation.[110]

Mansfield's ruling was carefully crafted and was significantly narrower than was (and is) popularly assessed. While slavery, he ruled, 'is so odious, that nothing can be suffered to support it, but positive law [in England],' he repeated established case law 'that there was no foundation in law [for the belief that] if a slave came into England, or became a Christian, he thereby became emancipated.' However, 'the power of a master over his servant [...] must always be regulated by the laws of the place where exercised' and it was good law that 'no master was ever allowed here to take a slave by force to be sold abroad.'[111] Mansfield's judgement was not against slavery itself, but was carefully (almost gnomically) crafted around the *habeus corpus* issue which did give enslaved people a degree of protection, but did not give them freedom.[112] However, popular opinion held that the judgement went wider in effect, as Brycchan Carey suggests, the 'Mansfield ruling [...] made slavery, if not actually illegal in England, then certainly unenforceable by law.'[113]

It is the later case of Joseph Knight, however, which is seen as the Scottish touchstone.[114] The facts of the case are recorded in most of the critical literature, but for ease, this is a brief summary: Joseph Knight (dates uncertain) appeared before the Justices of the Peace in Perth in 1774 seeking their confirmation that, despite being in an enslaved state, having been bought in Jamaica by John Wedderburn of Ballindean (1729–1803), by his being brought to Scotland he had become a free man and could therefore leave Wedderburn's service, as Wedderburn was intending to return him to Jamaica.[115] The Justices

---

110 *Somerset v Stewart* (1772) *English Reports* vol.98, p.510.
111 Ibid.
112 Lord and Lady Mansfield cared for the illegitimate daughter of his nephew and a Black woman whom he had rescued from slavery (in rather obscure circumstances). That daughter, Dido Elizabeth Belle (1761–1804), was treated as a family member and acted as amanuensis for the judge at Kenwood House. Mansfield's will in 1793 left Dido a bequest of £500, an annuity of £100 and confirmation of her status as a free woman. Gretchen H Gerzina, 'Georgian Life and Modern Afterlife of Dido Elisabeth Belle,' in *Britain's Black Past*, ed by Gretchen H Gerzina (Liverpool: Liverpool University Press, 2020), pp.161–178.
113 Brycchan Carey, 'Slavery and Romanticism,' *Literature Compass* (May, 2006), p.405.
114 As exemplified by two modern works: a novel by James Robertson, *Joseph Knight* (London/New York: Fourth Estate, 2003) and a radio play written by May Sumbwanyambe, *The Trial of Joseph Knight*, broadcast by BBC Radio 4 on 12 July 2018.
115 Wedderburn's father, Sir John Wedderburn of Blackness, Bart, fought for the Young Pretender,

initially ruled for Wedderburn, and Knight appealed to the Sherrifdepute of Perthshire, John Swinton (1723–1799) who found in his favour, making the robust judgement:

> That the state of slavery is not recognised in this kingdom, and is inconsistent with the principles thereof: and found that the regulations in Jamaica, concerning slaves, do not extend to this kingdom; and repelled [sc: dismissed] the defender's claim to perpetual service.[116]

Naturally, Wedderburn further appealed to Scotland's highest court, the Court of Session in Edinburgh, where his suit was heard *en banc* in January 1778. After complex discussions, the Senators divided eight for Knight (to a greater or lesser extent) and four for Wedderburn, and '[t]he Lords remitted to the Sherrif *simpliciter*,' (ie, they upheld his precise judgement). One of the leading case law books summed up the ruling:

> the dominion assumed over this Negro, under the law of Jamaica, being unjust, could not be supported in this country to any extent: That, therefore, the defender had no right to the Negro's service for any space of time, nor to send him out of the country against his consent: That the Negro was likewise protected under the act 1701, c.6. from being sent out of the country against his consent.[117]

Although Lord Hailes (one of the senators) concluded his own detailed report with a caveat: 'NB The judgement of the Court ought not to have adopted the whole of the Sherrif's judgement; and probably it did not.' On reading the full minute of each judge's interpretation Hailes's point becomes clear, as there an incredible disparity of views between the judges on the actual question of the legality of slavery within the bounds of Scotland:

---

and was attainted of treason and executed in 1746. Notwithstanding that, Wedderburn, younger (who also fought at Culloden, but fled to Jamaica), often claimed to be styled as Sir John, the *de jure sixth* baronet.

116 'Joseph Knight, a Negro, against John Wedderburn, Esq.' *Hailes Decisions*, vol.I, p.776. John Swinton of Swinton (1723 – 1799): admitted advocate (1743), appointed Sheriff of Perth (1754), raised to the Bench as Lord Swinton (1782).

117 *Hailes Decisions*, vol.I, pp.776–780. 12 William II, c.6, The Criminal Procedure Act, (1701), (APSX 272 c6) remains on the UK statute book, and provides *habeus corpus* remedies within Scots Law.

- Slavery is mandated in the Bible, so is God's Law [Covington, Monboddo];
- Slavery is against the teachings of Christ, so is against God's Law. [Auchinleck].

- Slavery is permitted by Natural Law [Monboddo];
- Slavery is against Natural Law [Kames].

- Slavery is permissible if enacted by a specific law [Braxfield, Westhall];
- Slavery is abolished [Barskimming, Gardenstone].

- Slavery is not part of Scots Law, but other countries' laws must be respected [Dundas];
- Slavery laws abroad cannot conflict with Scots laws at home [Elliock, Hailes, Kennet].[118]

Reading the report, it appears that Lord Hailes was correct with (roughly speaking) four supporting slavery worldwide, four recognising slavery beyond Scotland only, and four for adjudging its abolition. The majority of 8:4 divided on the same effective question as Lord Mansfield: was any person (free, indentured or enslaved) not subject to the laws of *habeus corpus* (or the 1701 act in Scotland)? So, remitting the case '*simpliciter*' and thus abolishing slavery had but four votes. That being said, that is what happened. It is important to recognise that the breadth of opinion on the bench in 1778 reflected the division of opinion in the country.[119]

Whatever the precise jurisprudence, again popular and political opinion took this as an end of formal, legal enslavement in Scotland.

---

118 The Judges' dicta are analysed in more detail in Table 1 below.
119 As a footnote, in the case *Lieutenant William Stewart v James Graham* (1782) the Court of Session overturned the impressment of James Graham of Glasgow into the Royal Navy, as although he had served as a mariner on a West Indiaman, he did so as an enslaved man and, having not made a free choice to ply the seas, he was not subject to the Press. scos.law.virginia.edu/node/54751 (accessed 1 September 2024).

Table 1: Arguments of the 12 Judges in *Knight v Wedderburn*

ANALYSIS					JUDGE
DISSENT	SLAVERY IS PART OF INTERNATIONAL LAW	CHATTEL	SLAVE	NOT SUBJECT TO THE ACT OF 1701	COVINGTON
					MONBODDO
		LEGAL PERSON	LIFE BONDSMAN	SUBJECT TO THE ACT OF 1701	DUNDAS (President)
MAJORITY					ELLIOCK
					HAILES
					BRAXFIELD
	SLAVERY AGAINST NATURAL LAW		REMUNERATED SERVANT		WESTHALL
					BARSKIMMING (Justice-Clerk)
					GARDENSTONE
					KENNET
					KAMES
					AUCHINLECK

DICTA

'It is [...] sacrilege and blasphemy to say that [Slavery] is against the law of morality, or the law of God.' 'Slavery has gone into disuse with us, and I do not suppose that a native of this country can be a slave.' 'A slave coming into this country is not made free.'

It has not been 'proved that slavery is contrary to the *jus gentium*, [there] is no turpitude in it.' St Paul gives rules for slaves.

'By the laws of the West Indies [he is] a bonded servant [...] what hinders a man to become bound as a servant for life?'

He is 'a servant bound for life; there is no moral turpitude in this; but the powers [exercisable] in Jamica cannot be exercised here'

'[T]he right of his master is not determined or varied [if a slave is brought into Scotland], but the exercise of his master's right is suspended while the negro continues in Scotland.' However, no person can be forced to leave Scotland against their will.

He 'was a slave by the laws of Jamaica [...] by violence: for he was not of an age either to suffer slavery for offences, or as a prisoner of war, or through consent.'

'Declare my opinion for liberty in full extent' [Would be different fact pattern had Knight been born into slavery in Jamaica]

'Slavery [...] is contrary to the spirit, if not the enactments of our religion.' 'The law of our land does not allow [...] a servant to serve during life without wages.'

'Slavery is abolished by the law, or at least by the manners of this country [...] colliers [taken by their master to England] would not be obliged, by English judges, to return back to Scotland.'

He 'is a slave in Jamaica, but not here [...] there is no equity in [Jamaican] law concerning negroes; it is founded on mere expediency.'

'Slavery is a forced state, – for we are all naturally equal.' 'We cannot enforce [the laws of Jamaica], for we sit here to enforce right, not enforce wrong.'

'Although, in the plantations, they have laid hold of the poor blacks, and made slaves of them, yet I do not think that is agreeable to humanity, [nor] to the Christian religion. Is a man a slave because he is black? No. He is our brother, and he is a man, although not of our colour; he is in a land of liberty [...] let him remain there.'

The Abolition Movement in Scotland in the Decade After 1786

Notwithstanding the verdict in *Knight v Wedderburn*, public debate over the slave-trade itself was not in the public eye for almost a decade. Whyte describes the catalyst:

> it was to be the founding of the London-based Society for the abolition of the Slave Trade in May 1787 that marked the start of an organised mobilization of public opinion throughout Britain.[120]

By June the following year, some 16 petitions to Parliament had been delivered out of Scotland (out of a total of 101 across Great Britain), mainly through presbyteries and synods of the Kirk, but also from universities, town councils and the Edinburgh Chamber of Commerce.[121] But it was some years later, in 1792 after an Abolitionist tour of Scotland by William Dickson, that the floodgates broke, with the Commons receiving 184 Scottish petitions (around 35 per cent of the total), with a further 67 anti-slavery declarations in the Scottish press. This surge of activity prompted significant backlash from the West Indian interest:

> Even in North Britain [*sc*: Scotland], where they are in general so totally ignorant in the business [*sc*: the slave-trade], the frenzie [of Abolition] spreads amazingly, for which great pains are taken by some individuals and religious motives are of course introduced.[122]

However, external events would come to the support of the status quo, as the French executed their King and Queen the following January, changing the political agenda at a stroke. As the latest biographer of Wilberforce assesses:

---

120 Whyte, Scotland and the Abolition, p.70.
121 Ibid, pp.70–71, 84–85
122 Letter: James Stothert of Cargen to David Hood in Jamaica, 29 January 1792, quoted in Frances Wilkins, *Dumfries and Galloway and the Transatlantic Slave Trade* (Kidderminster: Wyre Forest Press, 2007), p.85. Stothert (?–1800) built a fortune from the Dundee Castle Estate, Jamaica returning to Scotland in the 1770s with the estate under management, including David Hood (dates unknown) from 1791. The University of Michigan, William L Clements Library, *James Stothert Papers (1784–1807)*: Acquisition 1974. M-1650. His son, Captain William Stothert (1791–1863) received compensation for 175 enslaved people on Dundee Castle totalling £3,616 19s 9d. 'William Stothert', *UCL Legacy Database* (accessed 1 September 2024).

> By the end of 1792, all other questions in British politics had been overtaken by a very simple one: war or peace [...] It was the beginning of the darkest and most dispiriting time of all for the abolitionist campaign.[123]

By 1796, little progress had been achieved, and what little traction had accrued was lost in Wilberforce's defeat on the Third Reading of his latest Abolition Bill on 15 March 1796, effectively closing the question until Nelson cleared the seas of Napoleon's allied fleets in 1805.[124]

Conclusion

In the history of slavery, the Scots were in no wise spotless; as Sir Tom Devine sums it up: 'few aspects of Scottish society at the time were insulated from the impact of the enslaved-based economies.'[125] Whether through direct participation, marriage or repatriation of plantocrat wealth, whether functioning as a key part of the supply chain, or in being one of millions of end-users of its produce, slavery's reach was deep into the fabric of Scotland. As Enlightenment thought developed from its beginnings in the writings of Francis Hutcheson, the morality of enslavement and its legality began to be questioned by some and ardently defended by others. Iain Whyte captures this antisyzygy by contrasting the two most famous Ayrshiremen of the day:

> Boswell and Burns illustrate two aspects of the phenomenon of Scottish involvement in slavery – the first demonstrating that Enlightenment thought was no automatic ally in the anti-slavery cause, and the second that despite educated and enlightened Scots having a distaste for slavery, social and economic factors could outweigh this and enable many of them to accept a living from its fruits.[126]

Before taking the decision to emigrate to the West Indies on a combination of 'economic factors' and his personal circumstances,

---

123 William Hague, *William Wilberforce* (London: Harper Collins, 2007), pp.240–241.
124 Ibid, p.260.
125 TM Devine, 'Conclusion: History, Scotland and Slavery,' in *Recovering Scotland's Slavery Past*, ed Devine, p.247.
126 Whyte, *Scotland and the Abolition*, p.57.

Burns, like so many, had the effects of slavery around him. The next chapter looks at how close to him those factors came, the better to judge his own understanding of Black chattel slavery.

Table 2: Burns's Life and the British Abolition Movement: Key Timelines

YEAR	ABOLITION TIMELINE	AGE	BURNS'S TIMELINE	POEMS/SONGS LINKED TO CHATTEL SLAVERY
1757	*Montgomery v Sheddan*	-	William Burness builds Burns Cottage and marries Agnes	
1758	PA Quakers renounce slavery	-		
1759	Birth of Wilberforce	0	Birth of Burns	
1760	Tacky's Rebellion (Jamaica)	1		
1761	London Quakers adopt Abolition	2		
[...]		3–5		
1765		6	Murdoch's School (to '68)	
1766		7	Move to Mount Oliphant	
1767		8		
1768		9		
1769	*Dalrymple v Spens*	10		
1770	Beattie's 'Essay'	11		
1771		12		
1772	Somerset Case	13	Summer at Dalrymple School	
1773		14	Weeks at Ayr Grammar	
1774	Death of Scipio Kennedy	15		
1775		16	Roger's School at Kirkoswald First Poems	
1776	US Declaration of Independence	17		
1777		18	Move to Lochlie	
1778	*Knight v Wedderburn*	19		
1779		20		
1780		21	Tarbolton Bachelors' Club	
1781	British Surrender at Yorktown Zong Incident	22	Joins the Freemasons Befriends Richard Brown	
1782	Sancho's 'Letters'	23	Irvine flax-dressing ends	

YEAR	ABOLITION TIMELINE	AGE	BURNS'S TIMELINE	POEMS/SONGS LINKED TO CHATTEL SLAVERY
1783	Treaty of Paris London Quakers Petition	24	Prize for flax-seed Starts his Commonplace Book	
1784	Baptism of John Cartwright at Mauchline	25	Father wins at Court and dies soon after	Epistle to JR
1785		26	Birth of Bess Meets Jean	Mauchline Wedding
1786	Clarkson's 'Essay'	27	His crisis year: including Jamaica *Kilmarnock Edition*	The Ordination Farewell poems
1787	London Abolition Society founded: Wedgwood medallion	28	Tours Birth of Twins (Jean†,Robert) *First Edinburgh Edition*	Castle Gordon
1788	101 (16 Scots) Petitions to Parliament: Dolben's Act passed General Assembly condemns slavery (annually to '92)	29	Clarinda Marries, takes on Ellisland Birth of Twins (unnamed girls††)	Ode to Mrs O Critiques Miss Williams
1789	Wilberforce's first speech Bastille Falls	30	Birth of Francis Wallace Joins Excise/Illness	Election Ballads
1790	Commons Committee reviews slavery Abolition Societies (Edinburgh, Aberdeen, Perth, Glasgow, Paisley)	31	Leaves Ellisland/Promotion list	
1791	First Abolition Bill falls 163:88 Saint-Domingue rebellion Sugar boycott across UK	32	Dumfries Births of Betty, William Nicol	Glenriddell's Fox
1792	Dickson's Abolition tour of Scotland 519 (185 Scots) Petitions to Parliament Second Abolition Bill (gradual) passes 230:85. Stuck in Lords	33	Birth of Elizabeth Riddell Loyalty queried by Excise	Slave's Lament
1793	Revolutionary France: War Third Abolition Bill falls 61:53	34	Mill Vennel move *Second Edinburgh Edition*	
1794	France abolishes slavery Fourth Abolition Bill passes 56:38 Blocked in Lords 45:4	35	Breach with Riddells Birth of James Glencairn	Epitaph on WR Washington Ode Kemble/Yarico
1795	War continues Fifth Abolition Bill falls 79:61 Maroons rebel on Jamaica	36	Death of Elizabeth Riddell Breach with Mrs Dunlop Dumfries Volunteers/Ill health	Honest Poverty Poetic Inscription
1796	War continues Sixth Abolition Bill falls by 74:70	37	Final illness and Death Birth of Maxwell	Groves o' Sweet Myrtle; Menagerie

CHAPTER TWO

Slavery in Burns's Life

IN THE LAST CHAPTER, the complexities of Black chattel slavery in the laws, customs, politics and, above all, the economics of Scotland were discussed. How, if at all, did those complexities actually affect Burns himself? This question can conveniently be broken down into three parts: what Burns saw of slavery (directly or indirectly) in his early life up to his year of crisis in 1786; a more detailed examination of what happened in that fateful year to propel him towards the enforcer's job in the West Indies; and finally, a review of Burns's last decade of life in the light of the growth in the Abolition movement in Scotland.

Town and County

As discussed in the last chapter, Burns's Ayrshire was a rich and influential county which had seen a significant level of economic stress created by the Ayr Bank's collapse and the consequences of losing the American War of Independence. An influx of West Indian or Virginian plantocrats and East Indian nabobs and their (often ill-gotten) capital filled that void, buying estates from the landed families and professional men who needed to liquidate real estate to cover their extensive losses. While regrets were expressed over the loss of some ancient lairds, there was considerable relief that the county maintained its net stock of wealth, allowing both agricultural innovation and the first signs of industrialisation, which clearly partly explains the silence in the rural west of Scotland generally in the years leading to Abolition. As Sally Beattie, the Curator of the Robert Burns Birthplace Museum, has said:

> Burns's decision to accept a post as a slave overseer in Jamaica in 1786 has become an important aspect of Burns scholarship in recent years. Although anachronistic [sic] to the egalitarian views expressed in his poetry, it is an important example of the prevalence and paradox of transatlantic trade and slavery within Scottish

society during the Enlightenment era. Burns grew up in a region where transatlantic trade and slavery were deeply engrained in the economy.[1]

These changes were apparent to Burns: his gardener father, William Burnes (1721–1784), first worked in Ayrshire at Fairlie under the noted agriculturalist Alexander Fairlie of Fairlie (1723–1803) and then in landscaping two of the new Alloway estates, but that agricultural shift was very much work-in-progress in the 1770s and '80s. William Burnes had seen the possibilities of the new agriculture, and took up Mount Oliphant farm just outside Alloway in 1766 to improve the land and his family's future. However, the soil and luck were against him both here and on his next farm, Lochlie, where he transferred in 1777. Burns wrote to his cousin James Burness with William Burnes 'in a dying condition' updating him on the 'wretched state' of Ayrshire in June 1783:

> Our m[arkets] are exceedingly high: oatmeal 17 & 18d p[e]r peck, & [not to] be got at even that price [...] & what will become of us, particularly the very poorest sort, Heaven only knows. — This country, till of late was flourishing incredibly in the Manufactures of Silk, Lawn [*sc*: linen] & Carpet Weaving and we are still carrying on a good deal in that way but much reduced from what it was; we also had a fine trade in the Shoe w[ay], but now entirely ruined & hundreds driven to a starving condition on account of it. — Farming is also at a very low ebb with us [...] We are also much at a loss for want of proper methods in our improvements of farming [...] In short, my d[ea]r Sir, since the unfortunate beginning of this American war, & its unfortunate conclusion, this country has been, & is decaying very Fast.
>
> Even in higher life, a couple of our Ayrshire Noblemen, and the major part of our Knights & squires, are all insolvent. A miserable job of a Douglas, Heron, & Co's Bank, which no doubt you have heard, has undone numbers of them; and imitating English, and French, [and] other foreign luxuries and fripperies, has ruined many more. —[2]

---

1 Melville, *Facing Our Past*, p.50.
2 *Letters*: To [James Burness], [L.14], 21 June 1783, at vol.I, pp.18–19. Note: an Ayrshire Barley

Fairlie's system of crop rotation ('three course farming') along with enclosure to make larger, more viable farms was progressing unevenly through the county as Burns was writing this. It would be uniformly adopted by 1800, but as can be seen from William Burnes's experiences and after his death when Gilbert and Robert leased a farm at Mossgiel, many farms remained (through lack of initiative, or lack of capital) wedded to the old and inefficient school. This is clearly seen in the 'Autobiographical Letter' to Dr Moore where Burns described his own life on the farm as 'the unceasing moil of a galley slave'.[3]

In the urban environment, Burns witnessed Ballantine's modernisation of the burgh's infrastructure, celebrating his patron's progress in his poem 'The Brigs of Ayr,' [K.120]. At one point, the vexed mediaeval Auld Brig bemoans all this urban modernisation:

Nae langer Rev'rend Men, their country's glory,
In plain braid Scots hold forth a plain, braid story:
Nae langer thrifty Citizens, an' douce,
Meet owre a pint, or in the Council-house;
But staumrel, corky-headed, graceless Gentry,
The herryment and ruin of the country;
Men, three-parts made by Taylors and by Barbers,
Wha waste your weel-hain'd gear on d[amn']d *new Brigs* and *Harbours*!
(ll.166–173)

But the Enlightenment-designed New Brig counters that 'Nae mair the Council waddles down the street, / In all the pomp of ignorant conceit;' (ll.184–5) as Burns applauds the new burgher civility where ignorance has been trumped by 'common-sense' instilling a common respect between inhabitants and magistrates within the community, promoting both individual and civic advancement.

When it comes to the religious changes occurring, Burns is a strident supporter of 'D'rymple mild' and 'Doctor Mac' in the civility of Ayr and its Auld Kirk, and famed for mocking the clerical hardliners (typically found in the rural parishes) in his satires.[4]

---

peck was equivalent to just under 8 lbs, or just over 3.5 kg, Strawhorn, *Ayrshire*, p.135.
3 *Letters:* To Dr John Moore, 2 August 1787 [L.125], commonly called 'The Autobiographical Letter.'
4 *Poems*, 'The Kirk's Alarm,' [K.264], ll.1–4, 14–17.

Slavery in the Ayrshire Economy and the Supply Chain for the Plantations

The realignment of trade from the Chesapeake to the Caribbean, while hurting many established merchants, opened up new business ventures including the growing of flax and its processing into linen cloth, not the finer quality, known as 'Lawn', but coarser 'Osnaburg' weaves. Gilbert later remembered that he and his brother

> had for several years taken land of my father for the purpose of raising flax on our own account. In the course of selling it, Robert began to think of turning flax-dresser, both as being suitable to his grand view of settling in life, and as subservient to the flax raising. He accordingly wrought at the business of a flax-dresser in Irvine for six months, but abandoned it at that period, as neither agreeing with his health nor inclination.[5]

In July 1781, Burns wrote to a friend reporting that 'I have three good acres of flax this season,' which would win him a three pound premium from the Commissioners of Fisheries, Manufactures and Improvements in Scotland for the quality of his 'lintseed saved for sowing.'[6] Keen to escape farm life, he engaged with a lint-dresser in Irvine to learn the trade of 'heckling' the flax ready for spinning, however that plan ended on Hogmanay 1791/92 when the drunken dresser accidentally set fire to his shed.[7] Commentators have seen this as Burns's first attempt to create an independent life, as it was, but it is also his first direct link with the slave-trade, for the growth in the linen industry arose from the need for coarse cloth for sale to slave-holders to clothe their enslaved workers.[8]

Burns appears well-aware of this, making a sly crack on the quality of osnaburg fabric in his 1786 poem 'A Dream,' [K.113]. Prince Frederick (1763–1827) was elected by his father, King George III (1738 – reg 1760 – 1820), to the Prince-Bishopric of Osnabrück when he was six months old. He enjoyed the substantial episcopal income until

---

5 'Gilbert's Narrative' at p.74.
6 *Letters*: to William Niven, July 1780, [L.1], at vol.1, p.4; *Glasgow Mercury*, 16–23 January 1783.
7 'Autobiographical Letter.'
8 Hamilton, p.15.

the city-statelet was absorbed into his Father's Hanoverian Crown in 1803. In 1784 he became Duke of York and of Albany. Burns contrasts the cheap quality of osnaburg against the fine linen lawn-sleeves which are part of Anglican episcopal vestments:

> For you, right rev'rend O[snaburg],
> Nane sets the lawn-sleeve sweeter.'9

Burns would have been well aware of the end market for his linens when he considered that as a career.

Master and Servant

Burns displays some of his sharpest words in depicting the unequal relationship between the rural poor and their masters, or landlords. We have the semi-autobiographical depiction of the stress of rent day in 'The Twa Dogs' [K.71]:

> I've notic'd, on our Laird's court-day,
> (An' monie a time my heart's been wae),
> Poor *tenant-bodies*, scant o' cash,
> How they maun thole a *factor's* snash (ll.93–96).

Or, in the impressive satire 'The Address of Beelzebub' [K.108] of 1786, he prefaces the poem with a denunciation of the Highland landlords:

> To the R[igh]t Hon[oura]ble John, EARL OF BREADALBANE, President of the R[igh]t Hon[oura]ble the HIGHLAND SOCIETY, which met, on the 23d of May last, at the Shakespeare, Covent garden, to concert ways and means to frustrate the designs OF FIVE HUNDRED HIGHLANDERS, who, as the Society were informed by Mr McKenzie of Applecross, were so audacious as to attempt an escape from their lawful lords and masters whose property they were, by emigrating from the lands of Mr Macdonald of Glengary to the wilds of CANADA, in search of that fantastic thing — LIBERTY —[144]

---

9 *Poems*, 'The Dream,' [K.113], ll.100–101.

Here, granting these Highland families the right to travel freely to the United States of America would not only reduce the landlords' rentals, but might convert them to the beliefs of that newly independent republic:

Till, God knows what may be effected,
When by such HEADS an' HEARTS directed:
Poor dunghill sons of dirt an' mire,
May to PATRICIAN RIGHTS ASPIRE.[10]

Yet, he calls out no injustice over the multitude of local restrictions that lie on the workers closer to him in Ayrshire. While Burns is openly critical of actual unfairness under canon law or leasehold practices, he is silent on the inherent inequality in employment. Certainly, Burns makes no mention of the folk in Ayrshire who laboured under the old and onerous bondsmanship as salters around Saltcoats and Kilburnie or those indentured at the growing collieries in the county at Kilwinning, Irvine, Drongan and at Newton-upon-Ayr.[11]

Equally, Burns seems generally unengaged with the industrial changes happening around him and with how this new economy affected the lives of workers being drawn to the large-capital industrial projects such as the Carron Ironworks and the Wanlockhead/Leadhills lead mines, both of which he visited to satisfy his curiosity, with neither drawing any social commentary from the poet. Burns first attempted to visit the Carron Works with Willie Nicol on a Sunday in August 1787 and was piqued that the ironworks was closed for the Sabbath. His irritation found poetic spleen, which was riposted by a Carron employee reminding the poet that the workingman deserved his day of rest.

---

10 *Poems*, '[Address to Beelzebub],' [K.108], preamble, and ll.17–20. Within a generation, committing a *volte face*, Applecross's son Thomas (1789–1822) had started forcibly to clear his estate of the tenants in the name of 'improvement.' However, on his Highland Tour, Burns commented favourably of the beauty of Breadalbane's estate in his poem 'Written with a Pencil over the Chimneypiece, in the Parlour of the Inn at Kenmore, Taymouth,' [K.169].
11 CA Whatley, *The Finest Place for a Lasting Colliery. Coal Mining Enterprise in Ayrshire c.1600–1840* ([Ayr]: AANHS, 1983), p.59.

VERSES WRITTEN ON A WINDOW OF THE INN AT CARRON[12]	REPLY TO BURNS[13]
We cam' na here to view your warks, / In hopes to be mair wise, / But only, lest we gang to hell, / It may be nae surprise: / But when we tirl'd at your door / Your porter dought na bear us; / Sae may, shou'd we to hell's yetts come, / Your billy Satan sair us!	If you came here to see our works / You should have been more civil / Than to give a fictitious name / In hopes to cheat the Devil. / / Six days a week to you and all / We think it very well; / The other, if you go to church, / May keep you out of Hell.

Burns eventually succeeded in touring the industrial complex in October 1787 with medic (and later Abolitionist) Dr James McKittrick Adair (1765–1802) who recalled visiting

> the iron-works at Carron, with which the poet was forcibly struck. The resemblance between that place, and its inhabitants, to the cave of the Cyclops, which must have occurred to any classical visitor, presented itself to Burns.[14]

It appears that Burns was impressed by the spectacle of the furnaces, without being depressed by the underlying conditions of the working men.

Similarly, when he visited the lead mines at Wanlockhead in 1792 as one of a party including his friend Maria Riddell, neither of them takes issue with the hard life the skilled lead miners faced. Although these specialist miners were free of the servitude of the colliers and were even more highly paid, it was still dangerous, unhealthy work. We hear of no words of empathy for those workers, even when Burns experienced the appalling conditions underground. Maria Riddell recorded that the party had 'proceeded about a mile in the cavern, [when] the damp and confined air affected our fellow adventurer Burns so much, that we resolved to turn back.'[15] Burns makes no comment

---

12 *Poems*, K.165.
13 *Poems*, vol.III, p.1242. Written by William Benson (dates unknown) then clerk of the blast furnace. He was promoted to blast furnace manager and invested in shares of the company.
14 *Oxford Burns*, vol.I, p.157.
15 Hugh S Gladstone, 'Maria Riddell; Friend of Burns,' in *Dumfriesshire and Galloway Natural History & Antiquarian Society Transactions and Journal of Proceedings, 1914–15*, ed by GW Shirley (Dumfries: By the Council of the Society, 1915), p.27.

on how others had to endure such harsh conditions six days a week.

Here is the problem that we face in analysing Burns's views on slavery. At this level, Burns seems to have a heart-felt sympathy for the poor rural working class – that all poor workers share in his lived experience of 'galley slavery.' He writes out against oppression of the agrarian poor, even on behalf of highlanders seeking a free life abroad, yet not for the traditional forms of life servitude of colliers and salters – both industries active in Ayrshire – nor of labourers in the new huge industrial plants (like Catrine Cotton Mills or the Muirkirk Ironworks in Ayrshire) which would soon absorb increasing percentages of the unskilled population. Those working lives are beyond his experience, and apparently beyond his sympathy.

White Emigration to the Colonies

In his 'Autobiographical Letter' Burns notes that lads whom he knew in the town and environs of Ayr regularly 'dropped off for the west- or east Indies' which confirms the assumption that (to an extent at least) Burns had been aware of that potential career path, were the right patronage in place to secure a situation in the colonies. It is apparent that Burns appreciates the potential rapacity of those imperial adventurers (in the East Indies at least), by citing the case of 'Munny Begum' (1720–1813) the puppet regent of Bengal, appointed by Warren Hastings (1732–1818) and a major contributor to, and conduit for, his extensive infrastructure for financial bribery. However, Burns was more familiar with the young men who sailed west, rather than east.[16]

At his social level, he knew of people like Sandy Bell of Mauchline who had returned from Jamaica blinded by disease but £500 the richer for it, while one of Burns's closest friends of that period, Richard Brown (1753–1833), served on a Westindiaman – one of the cargo ships which specialised in the import/export of goods between Scotland and the Caribbean colonies but not part of the 'Triangular Trade' – although it is a safe assumption that Brown would have been

---

16 An exception being Revd Dr William Tennant (1758–1813), the eldest son of John Tennant of Glenconner (1725–1810), 'my father's friend and my own' as Burns called him. William, or 'my auld school-fellow Preacher Willie' in 'Letter to J[ame]s T[ennan]t of Gl[e]nc[onne]r,' [K.90, l.39] who studied with him under John Murdoch and, after taking a degree at the University of Glasgow, became a chaplain in the Honourable East India Company. His evangelistic ministry and writings on India earned him an LLD *honoris causa* from Glasgow. He retired, unmarried, to Glenconner.

well aware of it.[17] Another of his close friends was fellow Bachelors' Club member and poet David Sillar (1760–1830) who struggled (and failed) to set up his own grocer's business. While 'Dainty Davie' was, like Burns, 'scant of cash', his elder brothers Robert and John (dates uncertain) were active in enslaved trafficking, the former in Liverpool and the latter on the coast of Africa and who 'gained colossal wealth in trading between Liverpool and Africa' and the West Indies.[18] While it is likely that they were directly involved earlier, *The Slave Voyages Database* records some nine voyages connected to John as a principal between 1796 and 1807, trafficking some 2,500 enslaved people to the Caribbean and to Demerara.[19] Both brothers died unmarried, John in Africa and Robert at Liverpool, and David inherited some £12,000 from the former around 1811 and a larger, unspecified amount from the latter not long afterwards, changing David's ramshackle life into that of a man of property and a respected magistrate and councillor in Irvine.[20] In an attempt to stave off imprisonment for debt in 1791, having failed to borrow from his brothers, Sillar was turned down by Burns who claimed to be but 'five shillings rich at present'; it is fair to assume that Burns was aware of the Sillar family's financial condition as Burns expressed the opinion that Sillar's 'many rich and powerful friends will enable you to get clear.'[21]

Gilbert Burns added some interesting thoughts a few years after his brother's death, which may have been influenced by Robert's own views on these expatriate sojourners:

> When I have seen a fortunate adventurer of the lower ranks returned from the East or West Indies, with all the hauteur of a vulgar mind accustomed to be served by slaves, assuming a character which, from early habits of life, he is ill fitted to support — displaying magnificence which raises the envy of some, and the contempt of others in[ward]ly pining at the precedence of the hereditary gentry — maddened by the polished insolence of some of the unworthy part of them — seeking pleasure in the society of men who can

---

17 See a discussion of a word which Brown may have introduced to Burns at p.132 below.
18 Robert D Thornton, *James Currie: The Entire Stranger and Robert Burns* (Edinburgh/London: Oliver & Boyd, 1963), p.230.
19 Slave Voyages Database (accessed 1 September 2024).
20 James L Hempstead, 'David Sillar,' *Burns Chronicle* (May 1994), p.116.
21 *Letters*, To David Sillars [sic], [early Summer 1791], [L.461].

condescend to flatter him, and listen to his absurdity for the sake of a good dinner and good wine — I cannot avoid concluding that his brother, or companion, who, by a diligent application to the labours of agriculture, or some useful mechanic employment, and the careful husbanding of his gains, has acquired a competence in his station, is a much happier, and, in the eye of a person who can take an enlarged view of mankind, a much more respectable, man.[22]

Above him in the social strata, Burns would have known several of the successful plantocrats and nabobs. John Hamilton of Sundrum, for example, would have been known obliquely to Robert Burns at a number of levels, starting when he was a young boy and William Burness borrowed books from Hamilton's uncle's gardener at Bourtreehill.[23] Sundrum was one of the founders of the Tarbolton Masonic Lodge which Burns joined, serving as its Master in 1777.[24] He was directly known to the Burns family when he acted as the oversman or arbitrator in the painful and protracted legal dispute which William Burnes fell into with his Lochlie landlord. Sundrum's *Decreet Arbitral* of 17 August 1782 found that Burns's father only owed 30 per cent of the landlord's inflated claim of £775 (which was an amount just within William Burnes's powers to pay) and which set the scene for old Burnes's pyrrhic victory at the Court of Session.[25] Of his Ayrshire poetical patrons, Robert Aiken collected taxes from and, with Gavin Hamilton, acted for, various slave-holders and/or their businesses. John Ballantine's bank was a major facilitator of debt capital invested in, and payments to and from, Jamaica. These men, while not personally or directly responsible, were enabling the slaving activities of others.

In the run up to 1786, it is fair to say that there was little if any open questioning of colonial slavery and no social or moral obloquy attached to those in Ayrshire who were active in the slave economy.

---

22 'Letter from Gilbert Burns to Dr James Currie,' *The Works of Robert Burns. With an Account of his Life, and a Criticism on His Writings, to which are Prefixed, Some Observations on the Character and Conditions of Scottish Peasantry* [Second Edition], 4 vols, ed by James Currie (London/Edinburgh: Cadell & Davies/Creech, 1801), vol.1, pp.383-384.
23 'Gilbert's Narrative,' p.66.
24 'Burns and the Tarbolton Freemasons,' *Irvine Herald*, 29 November 1889.
25 John McVie, 'The Lochlie Litigation and the Sequestration of William Burnes,' *Burns Chronicle* (1935), pp.69-87.

In fact, those who swaggered home carrying fortunes were welcomed and envied as they bought up estates with their Indian or Caribbean gains. These White *arrivistes,* however, were not the sole connection between Ayrshire and slavery.

Black Immigration from the Colonies to Ayrshire[26]

The returning plantocrats did not just bring wealth back into Ayrshire – sometimes they brought Black enslaved people 'home' as servants (and as status symbols). In the last chapter, ten specific Black people in that category (plus, perhaps, an unspecified number of workers at Sundrum) were identified as living in Ayrshire for some time period during Burns's life there – around 15 per cent of the estimated Black population in the whole of Scotland, based on Whyte's estimates. While that is a small number of individuals compared to the population of Ayr in the mid-1780s, which stood at just under four thousand people in the burgh proper (or twice that including the suburbs that make modern Ayr) or in the county (around 75,000 souls), it raises the very interesting question of whether Burns ever met a Black person.[27]

One year after Scipio Kennedy's death at Culzean, the 16-year-old Robert Burns came to Kirkoswald to Hugh Rodgers's 'noted school, to learn mensuration, surveying, dialling, &c.'[28] He lived with his mother's relatives, the Brouns, and would have seen Scipio and Margaret's children, and probably some of their grandchildren, around the village and at worship on Sundays. So Burns, in all likelihood, met some of Scipio's mixed-race family and would have heard the tale of the boy who had been kidnapped in Guinea, but who was buried in Ayrshire.

Of the servants in the town of Ayr, Alexander Scotland disappears from view after his baptism at the Auld Kirk in Ayr in 1754, so the possibility of Burns meeting him must be discounted. Lady Dundaff's Othello (in service ca 1767–1775) lived across the road from John Murdoch when Burns made a short stay with him in 1773, so it is possible that he might have seen him. Similarly, the unfortunate Milly

---

26 An early version of this part was published as Clark McGinn, 'Robert Burns's Black Neighbours in Ayrshire,' *Burns Chronicle* (March 2024), pp.1–18.
27 Strawhorn, *Ayrshire*, p.168.
28 *Currie Edition*, vol.I, p.47.

and her child (1784) and Miss Hamilton and Gammetta of Belleisle (from 1785) could well have been seen by him in the street or some public venue, or even poor Edward Young when he arrived in Ayr in 1783. Young's incarceration at Irvine in 1785 was after Burns's unlucky sojourn there, but the fracas did make the newspapers and no doubt entertained local gossip, so again it is not impossible that this newsworthy event came to Burns's attention.

Turning to the other servants in the county, Burns did have a connection with Mungo Smith of Drongan who served as the grand master of Lodge Tarbolton (Kilwinning) St James in 1780–1781 during its merger with its fellow lodge and when Burns was 'entered apprentice' (on 4 July 1781) and 'passed and raised' (on 1 October 1781), although Smith was not present on those two occasions.[29] In 1787, Smith subscribed to Burns's second volume of poems (known as the *First Edinburgh Edition*), so he may well have met the poet though there is no record of that, and certainly no evidence that Burns met young 'Jack Scott' as nothing is known of his whereabouts after 1779, though it is not outwith the bounds of possibility.[30] Burns had no connection with Major Brown at Treesmills or the surgeon Wardrope (who employed Black servants, Prince and Richard respectively), nor is there any record of him passing through the village of Joppa (and in any case, the report of Black workers there could be hearsay).[31] It is possible that he saw 'Black Prince,' the Kilmarnock millwright, on his visits to that town or possibly he saw Prince's friend 'Black Peter' Burnet, a Paisley weaver who dressed in a dandified fashion, when visiting Paisley to promote his poems or when 'Black Peter' moved to Edinburgh for a period as a servant in 1788.[32]

There is one Black person, however, whom it is highly likely that Burns met. Alexander ('Sandy') Bell made his money in the West

---

29 John Weir, Lodge St James Tarbolton, Kilwinning No 135 (the Lodge of Robert Burns): A Historical Review 1771–1976 (Cumnock, Ayrshire: A Guthrie & Sons, Ltd, [1976]).
30 *First Edinburgh Edition*, p.xxxix.
31 There may have been one further Black servant: the Servant Tax Rolls for 1778–1779 show one John McMicken, a 'riding servant' to John McMicken Esquire of Kilsaintninians. That master and servant shared the same name could well be an indicator of an enslaved (or formerly enslaved) person. NRS: *Male Servant Tax Rolls*, Counties: Ayrshire, 1787–1788, E326/5/1/19 (60).
32 Peter Burnet (1764–1847) was a free Black man from Virginia who came to Scotland as valet to a Glasgow trader returning home during the War of Independence. He was introduced to James Tannahill, the poet's father, and took up weaving. Burnet rescued Robert Tannahill's corpse from the water in 1810. See Parkhill.

Indies, and would have been richer had he not caught a tropical disease which affected his eyes.[33] He returned to Ayrshire after losing his sight, accompanied by 'a native of that far distant country – a real, live [B]lack boy from the Indies.'[34] Once at home, and cared for by his family, Sandy Bell had no need of his servant, and so 'made a present of him to Sir John Whitefoord,' which indicates his enslaved status. To his credit, Sir John paid for the boy to study at the local school, including the elements of religion of the Kirk, which he demonstrated to the minister and elders of Mauchline Kirk in preparation for his Baptism.[35]

The Burns brothers had taken a tack of Mossgiel farm the previous March, and so Robert and his family would have been attending Divine Service that September Sunday morning in 1784 which saw 'the old church [...] crowded to the door by earnest on-lookers eager to see the [B]lack man baptized.'[36] Burns, despite his connection with Sir John, made no record of the event, so it is not known whether he did more than look on, or whether his curiosity and human interest would have impelled him to converse with young Cartwright. However, it is clear that (at least once) Burns was in the same room as a Black person in Ayrshire.[37]

Possibly, Burns saw servants in a different light: so perhaps Black or White mattered not, they as a class were 'othered' to the working man. As he has Caesar report in 'The Twa Dogs,'

> An' tho' the gentry first are steghan,
> Yet ev'n the *ha' folk* fill their peghan
> Wi' sauce, ragouts, an' sic like trashtrie,
> That's little short o' downright wastrie.
> Our *Whipper-in*, wee, blasted wonner,
> Poor, worthless elf, it eats a dinner,

---

33 Probably ophthalmia, which was prevalent on slave ships. The Abolitionist poet Edward Rushton of Liverpool contracted this disease and was blinded aged 19.
34 John Strawhorn, *Mauchline Memories of Robert Burns* (Darvel, Ayrshire: AANHS, 1985), p.255, quoting *Ardrossan and Saltcoats Herald*, 31 July 1858. The story is rather garbled and has been corrected in line with 'The Mauchline Wedding' discussed below.
35 Ibid, p.225.
36 Ibid, p.226. Burns had previously written to Sir John in his capacity of Grand Master of Lodge St James ([Nov 1782?], [L.12]) and had recently been elected its Deputy Master under his Sir John's successor, Captain Montgomerie of Coilsfield. Burns would pick up the baronet's acquaintance in Edinburgh.
37 It was Bell's bequest of £500 to his sister which resulted in Burns's burlesque 'The Mauchline Wedding,' [K.74] discussed below.

> Better than ony *Tenant-man*
> His Honor has in a' the lan':
> An' what poor *Cot-folk* pit their painch in,
> I own it's past my comprehension. —[38]

Does Burns see the Black servants, then, fortunate as 'ha' folk' compared to the hard-worn Cottar's family rather than as involuntary, unpaid labour? This is a possible explanation for his apparent distance at this period.

As discussed previously, the relative wealth of Ayrshire and the prominent place in the county's social hierarchy of returning sojourners (be they plantocrats or nabobs) saw some of these families bringing back Black servants as much as status symbols as for service.[39] Therefore, enslaved people, although a rarity, were not invisible to Ayrshire sensibilities and at the time Burns considered throwing over Scotland to seek a new life in the Caribbean, there were several Black people resident in his home county whom he might have met (or at least seen or heard of). Given that it is likely Burns was present in the congregation at John Cartwright's Baptism, that he would have known Scipio Kennedy's offspring and may well have seen other Black servants in Ayr, it is safe to say that the concept of a Black person could not have been completely alien to him.

Burns's Last Decade

Fêted in the Edinburgh salons of 1787, Burns consorted with many men who would be influential on both sides of the Abolition debate. From the bench of *Knight v Wedderburn*, he met Lord Monboddo on many occasions (who, through jurisprudence and practice, upheld slavery and is recorded as having a Black enslaved servant called Gory), as well as Lord President Dundas (in the middle of the argument) and Lord Barskimming (resoundingly against).[40] His

---
38 *Poems*, 'The Twa Dogs,' [K.71], ll.61–70.
39 In the last months of Charles Douglas's life, in 1815, a transaction is recorded: 'Laetitia Cosser, a Quadroon girl bought by Mr [Charles] Douglas to send home: [Paid] £100/-/-; Paid her Passage: £32/10/-; Cloathes £20/-/-.' She was the illegitimate daughter of a deceased friend and fellow planter, John Cosser, and was intended for service at Garallan. See 'Inventories of the Estate of Charles Douglas, with Copies of His Will,' Beinecke Library, Yale: Boswell Collection, GEN MSS 150: Box 21/Folder 621.
40 'Gory, my lord's black servant, was sent as our guide so far. [...] Johnson observed how curious

friends, patrons and patronisers included the ministers of the High Kirk, Blair and Greenfield and, from the book trade, Creech and Smellie; these men would become leaders of the Edinburgh Abolition movement supported by Principal Robertson and Professor Dugald Stewart, and also by Revd Dr William Dalrymple of Ayr. Each of these men was well-known to the poet.[41] Agnes ('Nancy') McLehose, his correspondent 'Clarinda', was the deserted wife of a rake who found success in Jamaica, and would later and briefly (without result) seek a marital reconciliation on the island where her husband, now Chief Clerk to the Court of Common Pleas of Jamaica, preferred the company of his Black concubine and their illegitimate daughter.[42] Nancy recommended that Burns read *Sancho's Letters*, though there is no evidence that he did so.[43]

While these prominent Abolitionists were Burns's friends, yet there were many slave-holders and advocates of slavery in his coterie, too: in the autumn of 1787, Dr James McKittrick Adair (junior) (1765–1802) was his cicerone around Stirlingshire and Clackmannan. His father, Dr James McKittrick Adair (senior) (1728–1801), was an Ayrshire doctor (and friend of Mrs Dunlop's) who, following a period as a medic in Antigua, had become a committed anti-Abolitionist and pamphleteer.[44] The plantocrat Robert Cunningham Graham of Gartmore (1735–1797), whom Burns met at Edinburgh, had returned to Scotland with a Jamaican fortune, with 'his consumptive Creole wife, his little daughter and his black servant Tom [...] afterwards buried at Gartmore in the family burial-ground.'[45] After moving to Dumfries, Burns met slave-holders, such as Walter Riddell (1762–1802) (whom he disliked), and

---

it was to see an African in the north of Scotland, with little or no difference of manners from those of the natives. [...] When Gory was about to part from us, Dr Johnson called to him, "Mr Gory, give me leave to ask you a question? Are you baptised?" Gory told him he was — and confirmed by the Bishop of Durham. He then gave him a shilling.' James Boswell, *The Journal of a Tour to the Hebrides, with Samuel Johnson, LLD* (London: Charles Dilly, 1785), pp.83–84.

41 Whyte, Scotland and the Abolition, pp.60, 77.
42 WC McLehose, ed, *The Correspondence Between Burns and Clarinda* (Edinburgh: William Tait, 1843), pp.37–42.
43 Ibid, 'Letter, Clarinda to Sylvander, 10 January 1788,' at p.137. *Letters of the late Ignatius Sancho, an African*, 2 vols, ed by Miss Crewe and J Jekyll (London: J Dodsley J Robson, J Walter, R Baldwin, and J Sewell, 1782).
44 Oxford Burns, vol.I, p.375. James M Adair, Unanswerable Arguments Against the Abolition of the Slave Trade, With a Defence of the Proprietors of the British Sugar Colonies (London: J P Bateman, [1790]).
45 RB Cunninghame Graham, *Doughty Deeds, An Account of the Life of Robert Graham of Gartmore, Poet & Politician, 1735–1797* (London: W. Heinemann, Ltd, 1925), p.85.

their supporters, notably Patrick Heron of Heron MP (ca 1736–1803) (whom he admired). Six months before Burns's death he attended his Mason Lodge to propose 'James Georgeson, a Merchant in Liverpool' be admitted as a Freemason, but it is not known if he was part of the Triangular Trade or an Abolitionist friend of William Roscoe.[46]

There is no record of Burns meeting a Black person in Edinburgh or on his tours, although it is interesting to note that his good friend Peter Hill (1754–1837), the bookseller, married Elisabeth Palmer Lindsay (1766–1842), the Jamaican-born illegitimate half-sister of Dido Belle, Lord Mansfield's ward, in 1783. Nothing is known of her mother, described only as 'Martha G' in the Port Royal baptismal registers, so her racial ancestry is unclear.[47] Interestingly, and perhaps due to the effect of Knight's case, Black servants are mentioned as being employed at Edinburgh in the years before 1788 and in the decades after 1807, but not in the intervening period.[48]

In the first year of petitions against the slave-trade, 1788, the synod of Glasgow and Ayr considered 'the interesting subject of the African Slave trade' at its sederunt of 8 April. The synod was invited to consider an 'overture' from the presbytery of Glasgow:

> The Sufferings of human Nature claim the sympathy of men. When these unite with the interests of Religion they are peculiarly worthy of the Attention of the Ministers of Jesus Christ. The present state of the African Slave Trade, in both these respects, & the Desire now prevalent thro' this Nation of obtaining some mitigation of the sufferings of that unhappy part of our Species loudly call for the immediate & earnest Interposition of all Ranks, & especially of Christian Ministers. [...] It is therefore humbly Overtured, That the very Rever[en]d the Synod of Glasgow & Air may petition Parliament on behalf of their African Brethren.[49]

---

46 *Minute Books of St Andrew's Lodge, Dumfries No 179*, Meeting of 28 January 1796: transcribed in RT Halliday, 'Burns and Freemasonry in Dumfriesshire', *Burns Chronicle* 1947, pp.26–31, at p.29.
47 Author's correspondence with Dr Jennifer Melville, Project Leader, 'Facing our Past,' The National Trust for Scotland in June 2021. Burns refers to her as 'my fair friend,' but not much should be read into that passing compliment. *Letters:* To Peter Hill, 29 January 1796 [L.686]. 'Peter Hill,' in Maurice Lindsay, *The Burns Encyclopaedia*, rev and ed by David Purdie, Kirsteen McCue and Gerard Carruthers (London: Robert Hale, 2013), p.164. For Dido Belle, see footnote 104 above.
48 See, Lisa Williams, 'African Caribbean Residents of Edinburgh in the Eighteenth and Nineteenth Centuries', *Kalfou*, Spring 2020, pp.42–49.
49 National Records of Scotland, *Minutes of the Synod of Glasgow and Ayr (1761–1802)*, 8 April

The Synod 'adopted heartily, and with universal satisfaction' the proposition and accordingly petitioned the Commons (through Henry Dundas).[50] It is impossible to imagine that Burns was not aware of these stirrings in the West of Scotland and at Edinburgh. However, there is no record of his meeting any Black servants in the great houses and salons he visited, nor can be seen any activity or commentary on his part.

When Burns left Ellisland for Dumfries in November 1791, he was settling his family in the town during the busy year for Abolitionists of 1792. The campaign does seem to have made some impression on the poet as he wrote 'The Slave's Lament' during the year which saw both the Presbytery of Dumfries and the 'Freeholders, Justices of the Peace, and Commissioners of Supply for the County of Dumfries' petition parliament for Abolition.[51] That being said, the argument was not one-sided, as Devine reckons '[a]round one in ten of all [London's] African traders were Scots in the 1750s, a figure which increased in subsequent decades.'[52] Closer to home for Burns, Hancock asserts that 'some documentary evidence survives to suggest that men in smaller towns like Dumfries and Kirkcudbright were occasionally involved in the [slave] trade.'[53] While Frances Watkins reminds us that, although Dumfries was not a functioning enslaving port, a number of prominent Liverpool and Whitehaven slaving operations were owned by Dumfries and Kirkcudbright families, in fact the very last legal slave trading ship to sail was the *Kitty & Amelia* from Liverpool in 1807, whose owners hailed from Moffat.[54]

These connections appear to have subdued the Abolitionist leaders

---

1788, CH2/464/4, p.226–227.

50 Ibid, p.227.

51 Whyte, *Scotland and the Abolition*, p.79. Note that both of these petitions were not public, but official, so it is slightly unfair of Morris to say '[t]he name of Robert Burns has not been found on any of the petitions.' Morris, *Scotland and the Caribbean*, p.109.

52 Devine, *Scotland's Empire*, p.245. One of the most prominent being Robert Milligan (1746–1809) whose statue outside his West India Docks in London was removed in June 2020 'on the grounds of its historical links to colonial violence and exploitation.' www.museumoflondon.org.uk/news-room/press-releases/robert-milligan-statue-statement (accessed 1 September 2024). See Alex von Tunzelmann, *Fallen Idols: Twelve Statues that made History* (London: Headline Publishing Group, 2021), p.3.

53 David Hancock, 'Scots in the Slave Trade', in *Nation and Province in the First British Empire: Scotland and the Americas, 1600–1800*, ed by Ned C Landsman (Lewisburg, PA: Bucknell University Press, 2001), p.76. ['Hancock, *SST*.']

54 Wilkins, pp.19–22.

in south-west Scotland. When the Moffat-born Abolitionist William Dickson visited Dumfries from 15 to 17 March 1792, he found that Revd William Burnside, surgeon Copeland and writer Ramsay were sympathetic to his cause, but were equally nervous of backlash if they appeared personally too prominent in the agitation.[55] This caused Dickson to lament in his journal, 'Find little hopes in Dumfries.'[56] His diary does not mention Burns, but Dickson's 'little hope' again could explain some of the poet's lack of interest as part of a wider disengagement across the town.

Beyond the confines of Dumfries, Burns maintained correspondence with friends in Edinburgh and beyond. Notably, though none of the letters survive, with the leading abolitionist William Roscoe (1753–1831) the Liverpool lawyer, banker, writer and bibliophile and, latterly, briefly its MP. Roscoe was a close friend of Dr James Currie (1756–1805) who met Burns briefly in 1792 in Dumfries and, in sharing Roscoe's politics, may have introduced Roscoe as a correspondent, although his well-known anti-slavery poem of 1787, *The Wrongs of Africa*, does not appear on Burns's shelves.[57]

A final point to consider is Burns's official position in the Excise service. A number of incidents reported about the poet in 1792 resulted in a formal order from the Board of Excise for Collector Mitchell, his superior officer in Dumfries, 'to enquire into [Burns's] political conduct [...] as a person disaffected to the Government.'[58] Burns escaped formal censure (through a combination of florid, patriotic

---

55 Revd William Burnside (1751–1806) then minister of the New Church, Dumfries. He translated to St Michael's in 1794, and he conducted Burns's funeral in 1796; the other two gentlemen are untraced.
56 William Dickson, 'Diary of a Visit to Scotland for the Abolition Committee, January – March 1792,' Friends' Library, London TEMP MSS 10/14/2. [With sincere thanks to Lucy Saint-Smith for sourcing the quotation during COVID lockdown.]
57 An early, vocal and active Abolitionist from 1787, Roscoe recognised that the entrenched West Indian interest (particularly in his home of Liverpool) needed financial encouragement to accept Abolition. Pragmatically, to secure his aims, he advanced the concepts of financial compensation (for the slave-holders) and was the first to propose an 'apprenticeship' scheme to provide a transition (following the precedent in Scotland for the emancipation of the colliers and salters). On returning to Liverpool in May 1807, a mob of pro-slavers attacked him, forcing him to decline to stand for the seat again. His banking house suspended payment in 1816, forcing Roscoe to sell his extensive library and art collection. When he fell into bankruptcy in 1820, a group of friends created a fund to support him in his later life. He greatly admired Burns (and would write two elegies after the poet's death) and had invited Burns to visit him in Liverpool in 1796, a plan which foundered on Burns's death. RD Thornton, *James Currie the Entire Stranger and Robert Burns* (Edinburgh/London: Oliver & Boyd, 1963), pp.286–287. [William Roscoe], *The Wrongs of Africa*, 2 vols (London: R Faulder, 1787).
58 *Letters*, To Robert Graham of Fintry, 31 December 1792 [L.528] at vol.II, p.168.

prose and the weighty influence solicited from his patron-friends) but he explained the admonishment he did receive to a correspondent: 'my business was to act, not to think; & whatever might be Men or Measures, it was my business to be silent & obedient.'[59] So it is not unbelievable to think that he would avoid any questions which appeared to indulge in public political controversy, which could easily include the topic of Abolition in a Dumfries which appeared generally against it. However, other members of the Excise were open and public in support of the Abolition movement: the treasurer and his hard-working deputy in the Edinburgh Committee, Alexander Alison and Campbell Haliburton, were prominent in their efforts, though they too were both more senior officers, and so were less vulnerable to criticism when compared to a 'common Gauger.'[60] As Burns versified on a window-pane around that time:

> In politics if thou would'st mix,
>   And mean thy fortunes be;
> Bear this in mind, be deaf and blind,
>   Let great folks hear and see.[61]   ll.1–4.

The chilling effect of that Excise investigation, no doubt combined with the threats arising out of the Revolutionary and Napoleonic wars which impinged on the wider anti-slavery movement and (in some eyes) positioned Abolition as dangerous and 'radical', could explain why the bright sparks of Burns's interest in 1792 failed to kindle a stronger, sustained commitment from the poet.

This will be reviewed through his prose and verse below.

---

59 *Letters*, to [John Francis Erskine of Mar], 13 April 1793, [L.538].
60 Whyte, *Scotland and the Abolition*, p.88.
61 *Poems*, '[Lines Written on Windows of the Globe Tavern, Dumfries]', [K.536D], ll. 1–4.

CHAPTER THREE

Slavery in Burns's 'Annus Horribilis' of 1786[1]

IT IS WORTH repeating how difficult the concept of imagining Robert Burns as an actual tyrant over enslaved Black men and women has been, and remains, for those who admire the 'Bard', whom Robert Crawford, in the most recent biography of Burns, called 'the master poet of democracy.'[2] When addressing his Jamaica plan, early biographers hid behind the bland job description of 'book-keeper' (or effectively ignored the detail of the scheme, as it did not come to fruition).[3] Recent commentators, in their anguish, have resorted to theorising that this plan was not a real attempt to establish a new life across the Atlantic, but a 'cri de cœur', or even 'a suicide threat,' with even Gerry Carruthers 'tend[ing] to side with those commentators who see Burns as never seriously intending to emigrate.'[4] A few make vague, generalised assertions that it simply was not going to happen, such as Maurice Lindsay who claimed (with limited evidence) that '[f]rom the very beginning the Jamaican plan was utterly repugnant to him.'[5] The question remains

> [h]ow the great humanist Burns [...] would have coped with entering [Jamaica's] degenerate and unjust society at the lowest social level for whites, will no doubt remain a matter for debate

---

1 The argument in this chapter was first developed by the author in a panel session at the First World Conference of Scottish Literatures at Glasgow University, 4 July 2014 and then expanded in Clark McGinn, 'The Scotch Bard and "The Planting Line": New Documents on Burns and Jamaica,' *Studies in Scottish Literature*, 43:2 (2017), pp.255–266. With sincere thanks to Professor Patrick Scott for his kind encouragement.
2 Robert Crawford, *The Bard* (London: Jonathan Cape, 2009), p.3.
3 JG Lockhart, *Life of Robert Burns* (Edinburgh/London: Constable & Co/Hurst, Chance, and Co, 1828), 'Jamaica was now his mark [...] the situation of assistant-overseer on the estate of Dr Douglas, in that colony, was procured for him [...]' p.114. 'Burns's prospects of life were so extremely gloomy, he had seriously formed the plan of going out to Jamaica in a very humble position.' p.124 (the latter slightly misquoting Dugald Stewart in *Currie Edition*, vol.I, pp.133–134).
4 Thom Cross, 'Robert Burns's planned journey to Jamaica may have been merely a cri de coeur,' *Herald* [Glasgow], 30th April 2013; Carruthers, *Slavery*, p.166.
5 Maurice Lindsay, *Robert Burns* (London: MacGibbon & Key, 1954), p.76, likely based on Stewart's comments in Currie.

ad [in]finitum [...] In his defence, it must be emphasised that his plan had all the hallmarks of desperation.⁶

Unfortunately, sifting through the limited evidence, it is plain that Burns *did* intent to take up the job. This was, as Carruthers describes it, 'a failure in sympathy, a failure in imagination,' but it was a plan that Burns fully intended to implement (and arguably, as will be shown, one he did not purposefully relinquish).⁷

Robert Burns's life had many turns of fate, and in many ways the year 1786 saw him at the lowest of them. Financially, he faced ruin as a combination of his father's death and the poor soil on the farm he worked with Gilbert had reduced the wider Burns family to near starvation.

His love life was even more troubled: his irregular marriage to Jean Armour had horrified her parents and incensed the Kirk. It was under this combined pressure that Jean had agreed to separate (without knowing that she was pregnant with his twins); then Robert had fallen in love with another girl, Mary Campbell, whom we now call 'Highland Mary,' with whom some kind of (again) irregular 'betrothal' (perhaps) took place, however, she died unexpectedly while waiting for him to come to her. Jean's vindictive father commenced court proceedings to force Robert to support his illegitimate child so, like a fox with the hounds snapping at his heels, the poet needed an escape from Ayrshire.

Some years before, Richard Brown (1753–1833), the transatlantic seaman, had introduced Burns both to the joys of houghmagandie and to the prospects for a young man in the Atlantic trade (thus bringing Burns to the crisis point while equally suggesting an escape from its consequences). As the poet said in his epistle to John Rankin, paying a 'gowd Guinea,' the standard fine 'for the behoof of the poor', for introducing a 'bastart wean' into the congregation was sufficient absolution of all further paternal obligations, allowing the forgiven fornicator to join the flow of young Scots crossing the Atlantic 'to herd the buckskin kye.'⁸ Thanks to the American War of Independence, the specific sea bridge to Virginia was presently closed, but Scotland's sweet tooth opened up a Caribbean vista, and the chance to make his own

---

6 Graham, *Plantocracy*, pp.19–20.
7 Carruthers, *Robert Burns and* Slavery, p.166; McGinn, 'Planting Line', expanded below.
8 *Poems*, 'Epistle to John Rankine,' [K.47], l.64.

pot of 'Jamaica siller' beyond the reach of the Scots courts, the ire of the Armours, or the censorious chatter of 'The Unco Guid' of Ayrshire.

So, in the midst of flying writs and burning accusations, the poet sought an escape from his troubles. Through the poetical patronage network he had been building, he was introduced, by Provost Ballantine, to Doctor Patrick Douglas of Garrallan. The doctor was able to offer Burns a fresh start by way of emigration to his Jamaican plantation to work under his brother, Charles, the resident manager. Burns may well have been inspired by the not-impossible dream of a return to Ayr (like Sandy Bell) at some future date with a fortune in his pocket to prove the clacking tongues (especially Jean's obdurate father) wrong about 'the whim-inspired fool.' So a deal was struck between the men and Burns accepted a salaried role in enforcing the slave economy.

The Douglases of Garallan were an old Ayrshire family from Carrick who, like many others, had switched their extensive trading and family links from Virginia to the Caribbean. The older sibling, Patrick (1728–1819), as a second son had been trained as a 'chyrurgeon apothecary' in the late 1740s. As his elder brother had predeceased their father, on the latter's death in 1776 Patrick inherited the family estate and, with it, one of the few parliamentary votes for Ayrshire which he used to support the Tory interest. His family's fortunes had been overshadowed by the failure of the Ayr Bank in 1772, where he was kin to its Douglas partners, and he personally held one £500 share in the enterprise which cost him around £2,600 (the equivalent of £350,000 today). However, Patrick managed to hold onto both his Ayrshire and Jamaican properties through the financial accommodation of Burns's patron, the powerful burgh politician and banker John Ballantine who helped him avoid financial cataclysm. Doctor Patrick appears to have been a gregarious man, being both a Freemason (serving as Master of Ayr Kilwinning Operative Lodge, No 123) and a member of the wicked Beggar's Benison society. He served for four years as surgeon to the West Lowland Fencible regiment and was promoted lieutenant in the corps in 1796. He is remembered fondly in Burnsian circles as a guest at the first Burns Supper in Burns Cottage, Alloway in 1801. He died at Garallan in 1819.[9]

His younger brother, Charles Douglas (1735–1815), left Scotland as a young man to become the resident manager of the family's Jamaican

---

9 McGinn, *Comprehensive*, p.391.

investments on the northeast of the island a few miles inland of Port Antonio. The main plantation was Ayr Mount, centred on its mansion house called Springbank, with its complement of 65 enslaved people and a smaller animal pen called Nightingale Grove. During the 1780s, this estate seems to have been under some financial pressure due to its debts to Messrs Hunter & Co, the banking house in Ayr, however, it seems that they traded through the downturn as Charles, who never returned to Scotland, died in Jamaica leaving a sizeable legacy (after providing for what looks like his Black concubine and their grandchildren) in cash, goods and enslaved people to his niece, Mrs Jane Douglas Boswell (1779–1862), the only child of his brother.[10] None of Jane, her husband Hamilton Douglas Boswell (1768–1824), or Dr Patrick ever visited the West Indies and it appears that the Douglas Jamaica interests were sold in 1817 to one John Donnan.[11]

The Traditionally Accepted Story of Burns and Jamaica

The traditionally accepted story of Burns and Jamaica has been almost uniformly recorded by the poet's biographers from the very first, Dr James Currie in 1800, to Professor Robert Crawford's *The Bard* of 2009.[12] The evidence cited is principally found in two documents written after the episode: his 'Autobiographical Letter' (of 1787) and 'Gilbert's Narrative' (of 1797).[13] Both of these were key planks in the

---

10 See 'Inventories of the Estate of Charles Douglas, with Copies of His Will,' Beinecke Library, Yale: Boswell Collection, GEN MSS 150: Box 21/Folder 621. Charles died worth some £15,000 (around £1.1M in 2024 values) which he left entirely to his niece Jane, in Ayrshire. Within the inventory, the following enslaved people are itemised and 'valued': Charles (£170), Adam (£160), O'Meally (£156), Joe, Bob and Stephen (£150), Kitty, Molly (£140), John, Jack, Nancy Draper, Belinda (£130), Nancy (£120), Thomas (£110), William (£100), Jakes (£70), George 'a boy' (£40) and [illegible] (£10). Folder 622 is a Power of Attorney from Jane Douglas Boswell to Robert Hamilton and John Steel (2 March 1816) in connection with the sale (to the latter) of 'whatsoever Negroes and other Slaves or Stock of any kind.' Interestingly, his will allowed for the manumission of his 'old servant' Mary Douglas with a J£5 annuity and the right to buy her son Patrick (for £140) and his sons, the boys Richard and Charles (for £370 each), 'as I do not like to divide a family of good people.'. A final codicil implies that Patrick has died, increases Mary's annuity to J£40 and manumits her two grandsons with annuities of J5 each. The combination of first names and the manumissions strongly suggests that Patrick was the illegitimate son of Mary and Charles Douglas.
11 Graham, *Plantocracy*, p.12.
12 The most recent, succinct summary of the 'Core Story' can be found in Carol McGuirk, *Reading Robert Burns: Texts, Contexts, Transformations* (London: Pickering & Chatto, 2014), pp.xv–xvi (although this following analysis disagrees with some of McGuirk's conclusions).
13 'Gilbert's Narrative' is the title given to a letter from the poet's brother Gilbert Burns, to Mrs Dunlop of Dunlop, which is found in the *Currie Edition* at vol 1, pp.58–79.

biography written by Dr Currie (who was a committed Abolitionist), but both need to be marked against the fragmentary correspondence of Burns. This received history consists of five elements:

1. Burns accepted a job offer from Dr Douglas as an 'assistant overseer' or 'book-keeper' on his slave plantation, Ayr Mount near Port Antonio in north-east Jamaica, under the management of his younger brother, Charles;
2. Burns's annual salary was to be £30 (Sterling);
3. Burns had to arrange his own passage from Scotland to the Caribbean, but did not possess the nine guineas needed for his ticket, nor any funds to supply himself with the necessities of tropical life. His earliest patron, the Mauchline lawyer Gavin Hamilton (1751–1805), suggested that Burns publish his poems by subscription and use such profits as arose to pay for his journey along with some additional provisions and comforts (and thus avoid indenturing himself in return for a berth paid for by Charles Douglas);
4. While he was making these arrangements, and during his estrangement from Jean Armour, Burns fell in love with 'Highland Mary' Campbell (1766–1786). They would appear to have undertaken some personal betrothal ceremony between them, with Mary returning to her family in Greenock to prepare for marriage (and, as some commentators erroneously believe, emigration), however, she contracted a fever while nursing her sick brother and died without seeing Burns again;
5. Burns had booked a berth on the brig *Nancy*, departing from Greenock and destined for Savanna-la-Mar on the south coast of Jamaica, but the success of the *Kilmarnock Edition* upset his timing and he was further advised to sail to a port closer to the plantation. He re-booked on the *Bell* from the same port but again missed her departure having gone to Edinburgh to arrange his second edition. At the turn of the New Year, 1787, he finally decided to let the third boat he had booked, the *Roselle,* sail from Leith without him. His poetic success and new patronage in terms of leasing another farm, with additional income within the Excise service, gave him the opportunity of reuniting with Jean and raising their family together in Scotland.

However, in 2010, the author discovered some letters between the Douglas brothers within the Boswell Papers at Yale which throw additional light on this episode, casting some doubts on the accuracy of the 'traditional story.'[14] To assess the timeline of events, here are all the relevant quotations from contemporary sources available to scholarship today in chronological order.

Table 3: Burns and Jamaica – Timeline			
Date	Between [15]	Text	Q#[16]
29 November 1785	Charles to Dr Patrick Boswell 111	I wrote to Mr McWilliam to tell you to send me an active young lad to look after my Cattle & Negroes with a Dog or a Bitch. I hope you will send him By Capt[ai]n Ramsey or Capt[ai]n Bowie as they both come here or much any other that comes to this side.[17]	1*
23 February 1786	Dr Patrick to Charles	[Letter missing, its receipt was acknowledged in Q4 below.]	[2]*
17 April	Burns to John Arnot L.29	[...] by & bye, I intend to earth among the mountains of Jamaica. —	3

---

14 On Doctor Patrick's death, his heiress was his only child, Jane. She had married Hamilton Boswell, a cadet of Auchinleck, assuming the surname of Douglas Boswell. After the death of Sir Alexander Boswell in a duel in 1822, the two branches became financially intertwined and the Garrallan papers were joined with the Auchinleck muniments, which came to Yale via Castle Malahide near Dublin. Frederick A Pottle, *Pride and Negligence: The History of the Boswell Papers* (New York: McGraw-Hill, 1981).
15 Sources in this table: Burns's letters by L number; Boswell Papers, Beinecke, BCA, GEN MSS 150, Box 3 by folder number; RBBM by object number. In-line text referenced by the 'Q' number in the table. The documents which were newly discovered in my 'Scotch Bard' paper of 2017 are marked *.
16 References in this section will be in-line, using the Q[uotation] Number allocated in the table.
17 Captain J Bowie of the *Glasgow* which shipped between Greenock and Jamaica and Captain J Ramsey of the ship *Ruby*. *Lloyds Register of Shipping*, 1786, at G:83 and R:198 respectively.

Date	Between [18]	Text	Q#
29 May 1786	Charles to Dr Patrick Boswell 112	I have been very much disappointed in your not sending me the young Lade I wrote for I promoted the Man I had thinking he would have been here by now & I have no body attending my place which is a great loss to me as I cannot be often at home; I suppose you can get a young Lade that can write a little & would be glad to get ten or Twelve pounds; perhaps Less; what I meant is a young Active Lade that can read & write that he may be able to read any the Letters I send to him & write me Answers of what he is doing; if I should be kept away from Home I would not wish him too young I could get enough here at 16 years old would bond for Seven years for their Cloths and for five pounds and Anon but I do not like their Connections, Send one by the first ship that comes to Manchioneal, Port Antonio or Annatto Bay, Kingston or, Port Morant.	4*
12 June	Burns to David Brice L.31	[...] and now for a grand cure, the Ship is on her way home that is to take me out to Jamaica, and then, farewel dear old Scotland, and farewel dear, ungrateful Jean, for never, never will I see you more! [...] You will have heard that I am going to commence Poet in print; and tomorrow, my works go to the press. — I expect it will be a Volume about two hundred pages. — It [is ju]st the last foolish action I in[tend] to do; and then turn a wise man as fast as possible. —	5
19 June	Charles to Dr Patrick RBBM 3.6138	[...] by the by I never heard of the News Papers you gave him to send, if you want to send me any then give it to Capt[ai]n Bowie, Ramsay, or any other coming to this side of the Country. [...] The young fellow I want is one that can write & read and be able to answer a letter, if I wrote to him whether I am abroad. A post boy or hind lad; may get enough for 10 or 12 pounds a year or less.	6

---

18 Sources in this table: Burns's letters by L number; Boswell Papers, Beinecke, BCA, GEN MSS 150, Box 3 by folder number; RBBM by object number. In-line text referenced by the 'Q' number in the table. The documents which were newly discovered in my 'Scotch Bard' paper of 2017 are marked *.

Table 3: Burns and Jamaica – Timeline (cont.)			
Date	Between [19]	Text	Q#
10 July [Received 23 September] 1786	John Hutchison to Burns L/App.2[20]	Has rec'd one from Burns dated D [xxxx] Will be glad to return the kindness [xxxx] B in the planting line, tho' he must [xxxx] good advice. — Thanks for the account of h[xxxx]	7
17 July	Burns to David Brice L.34	I am now fixed to go for the west Indies in October. — [...] I m[ust certainly] see y[ou] before I leave the country [. —]	8
22 July	Burns to Gilbert Burns L.35	[...] I Robert Burns in Mossgiel: whereas I intend to leave Scotland and go abroad.	9
30 July	Burns to John Richmond L.36	[...] My hour is now come. — You and I will never meet in Britain more. — I have orders within three weeks at farthest to repair aboard the Nancy, Cap[tai]n Smith, from Clyde, to Jamaica, and to call at Antigua. — [...]. I write it in a moment of rage, reflecting on my miserable situation, — exil'd, abandon'd, forlorn —	10
10 August	Burns to John Arnot L.39	[...] I am in such a bustle at present, preparing for my West-India voyage, as I expect a letter every day from the Master of the vessel, to repair directly to Greenock: [...] If orders from Greenock do not hinder, I intend doing myself the honour of waiting on you, Wednesday the 16th Inst.	12
10 August (or shortly after)	*Glasgow Mercury*, 6–13 July	The *Nancy* departs from Greenock for Savanna-la-Mar, without Burns.[21]	13

---

19 Sources in this table: Burns's letters by L number; Boswell Papers, Beinecke, BCA, GEN MSS 150, Box 3 by folder number; RBBM by object number. In-line text referenced by the 'Q' number in the table. The documents which were newly discovered in my 'Scotch Bard' paper of 2017 are marked *.
20 Currie catalogued the various papers he received from the Burns family and others. This letter is lost but recorded in the damaged volume listing inward letters to Burns which can be found as an appendix to *Letters*, vol.II.
21 The brig *Nancy* under Captain A Smith, *Lloyd's Register of Shipping*, 1786 at, N:430.

Date	Between[22]	Text	Q#
13 August 1786	Dr Patrick's *Journal* Boswell 2474/4	Sunday a wet forenoon & Very Wet afternoon & [indecipherable] at night, Mr & Mrs White dined with me.	14*
14 August	Dr Patrick's *Journal* Boswell 2474/4	Monday […] paid 9 sh[illings] for Burns's poems [i.e., three copies]	15*
14 August	Burns to James Smith L.40	[…] I went to Dr Douglas yesterday fully resolved to take the opport[uni]ty of Capt Smith; but I found the Doctor with a M^r and Mrs White, both Jamaicans, and they have derang'd my plans altogether. — They assure him that to send me from Savanna la Mar to Port Antonio will cost my Master, Charles Douglas, upwards of fifty pounds; besides running the risk of throwing myself into a pleuratic fever in consequence of hard travelling in the sun.— On these accounts, he refuses sending me with Smith for pas[sage]; but a vessel sails from Greenock the first of Sept:, right for the place of my destination; the Capⁿ of her is an intimate of Mr Gavin Hamilton's, and as good a fellow as heart could wish: with him I am destined to go. —	16
19 August	Burns to Thomas Campbell L.41	[…] Having an opportunity of sending you a line, I joyfully embraced it. — It is perhaps the last mark of our friendship you can receive from me this side of the Atlantic. - Farewel!	17
1 September	Burns to John Richmond L.43	[…] I am still here in statu quo, tho I well expected to have been on my way over the Atlantic by this time. — The Nancy, in which I was to have gone, did not give me warning enough. — Two days notice was too little for me to wind up my affairs and go for Greenock. I am now to be a passenger aboard the Bell, Capt[ai]n Cathca[rt], who sails the end of this month.	18

---

22 Sources in this table: Burns's letters by L number; Boswell Papers, Beinecke, BCA, GEN MSS 150, Box 3 by folder number; RBBM by object number. In-line text referenced by the 'Q' number in the table. The documents which were newly discovered in my 'Scotch Bard' paper of 2017 are marked *.

Table 3: Burns and Jamaica – Timeline (cont.)			
Date	Between [23]	Text	Q#
5 September 1786	Mauchline Kirk Register of Births [24]	Burns, Robert, Tenant in Mossgiel, and Jean Armour had Twin Children Born 3d and Baptized 5th Sept[embe]r called Robert and Jean.	19
8 September	Burns to Robert Muir L.46	[...] I believe all hopes of staying at home will be abortive, but more of this when, in the latter end of next week, you shall be troubled with a visit from [me].	20
[?] September	Burns to Mrs Stewart L.47	[dated] on the eve of my going to Jamaica — [...] The hurry of my preparations for going abroad, has hindered me from performing my promise as soon as I intended. — I have sent here a parcel of Songs, &c, [...]	21
8 September	Dr Blacklock to Revd George Lawrie [25]	It were therefore much to be wished, for the sake of a young man, that a second edition, more numerous than the former, could immediately be printed [...]	22
26 September	Burns to John Kennedy L.48	[...] My departure is uncertain, but I do not think it will be till after harvest. —	23
[27 September]	Burns to John Richmond L.49	[...] I am going perhaps to try a second edition of my book — If I do, it will detain me a little longer in the country; if not, I shall be gone as soon as harvest is over. —	24
[end September]	Burns to John Ballantine L.51C	[...] I have seen a Print of the old Cross of Ayr — 'tis not to be bought — could you send me one just now that I might take it with me [to Jamaica.]	25

---

23 Sources in this table: Burns's letters by L number; Boswell Papers, Beinecke, BCA, GEN MSS 150, Box 3 by folder number; RBBM by object number. In-line text referenced by the 'Q' number in the table. The documents which were newly discovered in my 'Scotch Bard' paper of 2017 are marked *.
24 NRS: *Old Parish Birth Records* Mauchline, 604/20/43.
25 Donald A Low, ed, *Robert Burns: The Critical Heritage* (London: Routledge & Kegan Paul, 1974), p.62.

Date	Between [26]	Text	Q#
7 October 1786	*Caledonian Mercury* 25 September	The *Bell* departs from Greenock for Port Morant, without Burns.[27]	26
[8 October]	Burns to Robert Aiken L.53	[...] I have been feeling all the various rotations and movements within, respecting the excise. There are many things that plead strongly against it [...] which may perhaps make it impracticable to stay at home; and besides I have for some time been pining under secret wretchedness [...] All of these reasons urge me to go abroad; and to all these reasons I have only one answer — the feelings of a father. This, in the present mood I am in, overbalances everything that can be laid in the scale against it.	27
26 October	Dr Patrick to Charles RBBM 3.6139l	I intended to have sent out your man you wanted by Captain Cathcart but have delayed by your hand or till Capt[ain] Bowie sails.	28
30 October	Burns to William Logan K.53B	'Ance tae the Indies I were wonted' (When I am acclimatised to the Caribbean.... [the final of Burns's 'farewell poems']	29
27 November	Burns to John Ballantine K.59	I am thinking to set out beginning of next week, for [Edinburgh] myself. —	30
9 December	[Henry Mackenzie], *The Lounger*.[28]	Burns possesses the spirit as well as the fancy of a Poet. That honest pride and independence of soul which are sometimes the Muse's only dower, break forth on every occasion in his works. It may be, then, I shall wrong his feelings, while I indulge my own, in calling the attention of the public to his situation and circumstances.	31

---

26 Sources in this table: Burns's letters by L number; Boswell Papers, Beinecke, BCA, GEN MSS 150, Box 3 by folder number; RBBM by object number. In-line text referenced by the 'Q' number in the table. The documents which were newly discovered in my 'Scotch Bard' paper of 2017 are marked *.
27 The brig *Bell*, under Captain J Cathcart, *Lloyds Register of Shipping*, 1786, at B:76.
28 [Henry Mackenzie], 'Surprising Effects of Original Genius, Exemplified in the Poetical Productions of *Robert Burns*, an Ayrshire Ploughman,' *Lounger*, No 97, 9 December 1786, pp.385-388 (and reprinted, with minor variations in *Scots Magazine*, December 1786, pp.591-593).

Table 3: Burns and Jamaica – Timeline (cont.)			
Date	Between [29]	Text	Q#
9 December 1786 (cont.)	[Henry Mackenzie], *The Lounger*.[30]	That condition, humble as it was, in which he found content, and wooed the Muse, might not have been deemed uncomfortable; but grief and misfortunes have reached him there; and one or two of his poems hint, what I have learnt from some of his countrymen, that he has been obliged to form the resolution of leaving his native land, to seek under a West-Indian clime that shelter and support which Scotland has denied him. But I trust means may be found to prevent this resolution from taking place; and that I do my country no more than justice, when I suppose her ready to stretch out her hand to cherish and retain this native Poet, whose 'wood-notes wild' possess so much excellence. To repair the wrongs of suffering or neglected merit; to call forth genius from the obscurity in which it had pined indignant, and place it where it may profit or delight the world; these are exertions which give to wealth an enviable superiority, to greatness and to patronage a laudable pride.	31
15 December	Burns to Robert Muir L.64	[...] I am still undetermined as to the future; and, as usual [ne]ver think of it [...]	32
23 December	*Caledonian Mercury* 23 December	The *Roselle* departs from Leith for Kingston, without Burns.[31]	33
30 December	Dr Patrick to Charles n/a	[Letter missing, its receipt was acknowledged in Q36 below.]	[34]*
2 January 1787	Burns to John Hutchison [n/a]	[Letter missing, its receipt was acknowledged in Q38 below and probably was not sent until 24 February see Letter to Captain Richard Brown, L.211]	[35]

---

29 Sources in this table: Burns's letters by L number; Boswell Papers, Beinecke, BCA, GEN MSS 150, Box 3 by folder number; RBBM by object number. In-line text referenced by the 'Q' number in the table. The documents which were newly discovered in my 'Scotch Bard' paper of 2017 are marked *.
30 [Henry Mackenzie], 'Surprising Effects of Original Genius, Exemplified in the Poetical Productions of *Robert Burns*, an Ayrshire Ploughman,' *Lounger*, No 97, 9 December 1786, pp.385–388 (and reprinted, with minor variations in *Scots Magazine*, December 1786, pp.591–593).
31 The ship *Roselle*, under Captain T Liddell, *Lloyds Register of Shipping*, 1787, at R:183.

Date	Between [32]	Text	Q#
4 March 1787	Charles to Dr Patrick Boswell 113	I am very well Satisfyd that you have Changed my Man, I want no warm heads & Poets must have them; the other Lad will do for me.	36*
11 June	Burns to James Smith L.113	I cannot settle my mind. [...] I cannot, dare not risk on farms as they are. If I do not fix, I will go for Jamaica.	37
14 June	John Hutchison to Burns Currie Edition, vol.II, pp.92–93	you acquaint me you were engaged with Mr Douglas of Port Antonio, for three years, at thirty pounds sterling a year; and I am happy some unexpected accidents intervened that prevented your sailing with the vessel, as I have great reason to think Mr Douglas's employ would by no means have answered your expectations. [...] I am very confident that you can do far better in Great Britain, than in Jamaica.	38
Later Commentary			
2 August 1788	Burns to Dr Moore L.125	[Around 1776] This kind of life — the cheerless gloom of a hermit, with the unceasing moil of a galley-slave, brought me to my sixteenth year [...] [In 1786] I gave up my part of the farm to my brother; in truth it was only nominally mine; and made what little preparation was in my power for Jamaica. But, before leaving my native country for ever, I resolved to publish my poems [...] and it was a delicious idea that I should be called a clever fellow, even though it should never reach my ears — a poor negro-driver — or perhaps a victim to that inhospitable clime, and gone to the world of spirits! [...]	39

---

32 Sources in this table: Burns's letters by L number; Boswell Papers, Beinecke, BCA, GEN MSS 150, Box 3 by folder number; RBBM by object number. In-line text referenced by the 'Q' number in the table. The documents which were newly discovered in my 'Scotch Bard' paper of 2017 are marked *.

Table 3: Burns and Jamaica – Timeline (cont.)

Date	Between[33]	Text	Q#
2 August 1788 (cont.)	Burns to Dr Moore L.125	I was pretty confident my poems would meet with some applause; but at the worst, the roar of the Atlantic would deafen the voice of censure, and the novelty of West-Indian scenes make me forget neglect. My vanity was highly gratified by the reception I met with from the public; and besides, I pocketed, all expenses deducted, nearly twenty pounds. This sum came very seasonably, as I was thinking of indenting myself, for want of money to procure my passage. As soon as I was master of nine guineas, the price of wafting me to the torrid zone, I took a steerage passage in the first ship that was to sail from the Clyde, [...] I had been for some days skulking from covert to covert, under all the terrors of a jail; as some ill-advised people had uncoupled the merciless pack of the law at my heels. I had taken the last farewell of my few friends; my chest was on the road to Greenock, I had composed the last song I should ever measure in Caledonia, 'The gloomy night is gathering fast,' when a letter from Dr Blacklock to a friend of mine, overthrew all my schemes, by opening new prospects to my poetic ambition [...] The baneful star that had so long shed its blasting influence in my zenith, for once made a revolution to the nadir [...]	39
10 August	Burns to Mrs Dunlop L.254	[...] my rumoured West Indian voyage [...]	40

---

33 Sources in this table: Burns's letters by L number; Boswell Papers, Beinecke, BCA, GEN MSS 150, Box 3 by folder number; RBBM by object number. In-line text referenced by the 'Q' number in the table. The documents which were newly discovered in my 'Scotch Bard' paper of 2017 are marked *.

Date	Between [34]	Text	Q#
Late 1792	*The Interleaved Scots Musical Museum* RBBM Collection [35]	My Highland lassie was a warm-hearted, charming young creature as ever blessed a man with generous love. After a pretty long tract of the most ardent reciprocal attachment, we met by appointment, on the second Sunday of May, in a sequestered spot by the Banks of Ayr, where we spent the day in taking a farewell[l], before she should embark for the West-Highlands, to arrange matters among her friends for our projected change of life. At the close of Autumn following, she crossed the sea to meet me at Greenock, where she had scarce landed when she was seized with a malignant fever, which hurried my dear girl to the grave in a few days, before I could even hear of her illness.	41
26/27 October 1792	Burns to George Thomson L.511	In my very early years, when I was thinking of going to the West Indies, I took the following farewell of a dear girl	42
1797	'Gilbert's Narrative' Currie Edition, vol.I, p.76	In the state of mind which this separation [from Jean Armour] produced, he wished to leave the country as soon as possible, and agreed with Dr Douglas to go out to Jamaica, as an assistant overseer, or as I believe it is called, a book-keeper, on his estate. As he had not sufficient money to pay his passage, and the vessel in which Dr Douglas was to procure a passage for him was not expected to sail for some time, Mr Hamilton advised him to publish his poems in the meantime by subscription, as a likely way of getting a little money to provide him more liberally in necessaries for Jamaica.	

---

34 Sources in this table: Burns's letters by L number; Boswell Papers, Beinecke, BCA, GEN MSS 150, Box 3 by folder number; RBBM by object number. In-line text referenced by the 'Q' number in the table. The documents which were newly discovered in my 'Scotch Bard' paper of 2017 are marked *.
35 R[obert] H[artley] Cromek, *Reliques of Robert Burns* (London: T Cadell, and W Davies, 1808), pp.237–238. See also: Gerard Carruthers *et al*, 'Some Recent Discoveries in Robert Burns Studies', *Scottish Literary Review*, 2.1 (2010), pp.143–147.

Table 3: Burns and Jamaica – Timeline (cont.)			
Date	Between [36]	Text	Q#
1797 (cont.)	'Gilbert's Narrative' Currie Edition, vol.I, p.76	Agreeably to this advice, subscription bills were printed immediately, and the printing was commenced at Kilmarnock, his preparations going on at the same time for his voyage. The reception however which his poems met with in the world, and the friends they procured him, made him change his resolution of going to Jamaica, and he was advised to go to Edinburgh to publish a second edition.	43
[1798]	Dugald Steward to James Currie Currie Edition, vol.I, pp.133–147	At this time Burns' prospects in life were so extremely gloomy, that he had seriously formed a plan of going out to Jamaica in a very humble situation, not however, without lamenting, that his want of patronage should force him to think of a project so repugnant to his feelings, when his ambition aimed at no higher an object than the station of an exciseman or gauger in his own country.	45

Reconciling the 'Traditional Story' of Burns and Jamaica with the Evidence

1: His Job as a Book-keeper: Was That a Clerical Position?

Gilbert described his brother's duties as 'an assistant overseer, or as I believe it is called, a book-keeper' [Q.43]. This description contains a euphemism bordering on sanitisation as previous research has clearly shown that the 'bookie' was not insulated from the crimes of slavery. As Iain Whyte observes:

> Those with fewer professional skills formed a substantial part of the Scottish community in the Caribbean. [...] Those who had the basic educational background became administrative secretaries, clerks or bookkeepers on the sugar estates, the latter post often deceptively named and frequently entailing the oversight of slave labour.[37]

---

[36] Sources in this table: Burns's letters by L number; Boswell Papers, Beinecke, BCA, GEN MSS 150, Box 3 by folder number; RBBM by object number. In-line text referenced by the 'Q' number in the table. The documents which were newly discovered in my 'Scotch Bard' paper of 2017 are marked *.
[37] Whyte, *Scotland and the Abolition*, p.49.

Furthermore, the job for Burns was even lower (socially and morally) down the scale; Charles Douglas's needs were for someone inferior to a book-keeper, someone whose daily life would have involved his personal activity of 'herding buckskin kye' (as Burns had foreseen in his *Epistle to John Rankine*) in the capacity of a 'poor negro Driver' (as he accurately described the role in the *Autobiographical Letter*). Burns was not destined to an indoor life on a high stool in the counting-house, but to daily life in the fields or the boiling house. Many commentators have assumed that he would not have known what the specific role entailed, as Kinghorn (for example) puts it:

> The poet was, of course, quite ignorant of the duties which 'book-keeping' involved. He knew nothing about sugar or about the life of a White hired man in Jamaica, an innocence shared by nearly all would-be estate employees brought to the colony from the British Isles.[38]

However, that cannot be true, for Charles Douglas is perfectly clear about the role [Q.1], and Burns would have read about the way Jamaican plantations were worked in his copy of Salmon's *Geographical Grammar*:

> It were to be wished also, that the *English* would forbear to treat their Negroes with that Cruelty they have formerly done, [...] for though Torture be abolished in *England*, it was exercised upon the Negroes [in Jamaica] with the greatest Barbarity [...][39]

Or in Guthrie's similar work:

> The misery and hardships of the negroes is truly moving [...] the ill treatment they receive so shortens their lives, [...] [they] pine and die by the hardships they receive. They are indeed, stubborn and untradable for the most part, and they must be ruled with a rod of iron; but they ought not to be crushed with it, or to be thought

---

38 AM Kinghorn, 'Robert Burns and Jamaica,' *A Review of English Literature,* July 1967, p.70.
39 Thomas Salmon, *A New Geographical and Historical Grammar* (London: W Johnston, 1766), p.581. Burns deprecated the careless use of 'England' or 'English' being extended to the whole United Kingdom (see *Letters*, To Mrs Dunlop, [L.397, at p.24]) and so would not have thought that the reference to 'English' and 'England' meant that this statement was not applicable to Scots and Scotland.

a sort of beasts without souls, as some of their overseers do at present, though some of these tyrants are themselves the dregs of this nation, and the refuse of the jails of Europe.[40]

Burns clearly knew that his salary was reward for personally inflicting human suffering by managing the enslaved workforce as a 'tyrant' using a dog and, doubtless, a whip [Q.1].

2: How Much Did the Job Pay?

In 'Gilbert's Narrative' [Q.43] no salary is mentioned and the only contemporary evidence that the salary was set at £30 annually comes from a letter from John Hutchison of Jamaica replying to a lost letter from Burns. Hutcheson's identity and dates are uncertain, and it is not known how Burns was introduced to him (perhaps by Captain Richard Brown), however, this letter is part of a wider correspondence which commenced in early 1786 when Burns was seeking initial advice on starting for Jamaica 'in the planting line' [Q.7].[41] The only letter between them which survives in full transcription is dated 14 June 1787 in response to Burns's missing letter of 2 January 1787. Here Hutchinson mentions that Burns was 'engaged with Mr Douglas of Port Antonio, for three years, at thirty pounds sterling a year' and that he could do better elsewhere [Q.38].

It can be seen from the Douglas correspondence, however, that the job did not pay £30 sterling per annum. How does Burns's pay compare to wages in across the slave plantation economy? Burnard, Panza and Williamson completed a detailed study of income distribution (and inequality) in Jamaica around 1774, a decade before Burns.[42] Using their research, the hierarchy of incomes in Jamaica can be seen in the table below.

---

40 William Guthrie, *A New Geographical, Historical, and Commercial Grammar [etc]*, (London: Charles Dilley and George Robinson, 1772), pp.659–660.
41 'B. on the planting line.' Contrary to Carol McGuirk's suggestion that 'the phrase "in the planting line" need not refer to the poet's emigration [... and] could even be referring to Burns's farming activities in Scotland' (McGuirk, *Reading RB*, p.200, FN25), 'the planting line' is a clearly established euphemism for the Jamaican sugar trade. See multiple contemporary sources, eg, JB Moreton, *West India Manners and Customs* (London: J Parsons, 1793), pp.55, 64, 79, 80.
42 Trevor Burnard, Laura Panza, Jeffrey G Williamson, *The Social Implications of Sugar: Living Costs, Real Incomes and Inequality in Jamaica c. 1744* (Cambridge, MA: National Bureau of Economic Research, 2017).

Table 4: Incomes from the Jamaican Economy around 1774[43]

Averages	£ Jamaican					£ Sterling[a]
ROLE	NUMBER	INCOME	BED/ BOARD	EXTRAS[b]	TOTAL	TOTAL
Owner (Average)	875	£3,960	n/a	n/a	£3,960	£5,544
Douglas Brothers[c]	1	£923	n/a	n/a	£923	£1,292
Overseer	1,035	£250	£117	£28	£455	£637
Surgeon	564	£100	£105	£14	£219	£307
Bookkeeper	875	£55	£101	£0	£156	£218
White Labourer	299	£25	£0	£0	£25	£35
Burns's story[d]	1	?	?	£0	£22	£30
Douglas's offer[e]	1	£7–8	£22[f]	£0	£30	£45–48

Table Notes

a) The exchange rate between local currency and Sterling was relatively constant at £1/8/- [equal to decimalised £1.40] Sterling to £1 Pound Jamaican (ie, an FX rate of 1.40:1.00).

b) Income derived from the higher employees being permitted to own one or two enslaved people themselves.

c) Burnard *et al* estimate that 100 slaves produced a net income of £(J)1,420. The Douglas brothers employed 65 enslaved persons [Graham, *Plantocracys*, p.11]. The decline of the estate meant that by Charles's death in 1815 he employed only 20 enslaved men and women, inventoried in his will at £2,300. Boswell Mss GEN MSS 150 Box 21/621.

d) As described by Burns to John Hutchinson. NB, he does not specify which currency.

e) As described in Charles's letters, £10–12 Sterling (currency assumed).

f) Taken from Burnard *et al*, Table 6: 'bare bones' living costs around 1779 was 442 Jamaican shillings per annum.

---

43 Ibid.

The data above shows that the Douglas plantation was much smaller than average, while the correspondence between the brothers clearly shows that Charles Douglas had little time, less patience and scant cash. His letters to Dr Patrick are full of the woes of a man trying to make the business earn enough to keep afloat: the references are unclear, but Patrick Ballantine ('Provost John's' brother and his bank's legal agent on the island) is often mentioned as a creditor.[44] Charles was patently looking for one of the myriad Scotch lads ready to gamble health against wealth, and so was looking for a youngster costing a meagre annual payment of only £10 or £12 to work on his small, encumbered estate. [QQ.4,6].[45]

So Burns's statement that his salary was to be £30 per annum in Sterling is a gross overstatement: Charles Douglas was offering an annual Jamaican £30 of which two-thirds was in kind, giving him a bed (in a bunkhouse), his board (no doubt including rum *ad libitum*) with only the local equivalent of £10 Sterling in cash. While this is almost half as much again as his imputed wages of £7 on the family farm, it is less than the £12 to £18 (over and above his bed-and-board) he could have earned given his skill as a ploughman had he left Ayrshire but remained in another part of Scotland.[46] When describing his prospects in Jamaica (whether to Hutchison, or to brother Gilbert) it appears that Burns is playing with ambiguity. As is not uncommon even today, on his résumé Burns appears to have clearly exaggerated not only his job scope and title, but the basis of his salary, too. There is little chance of emulating Sandy Bell, let alone a cadet Ayrshire Hamilton, on less than one pound a month in cash, without climbing the ladder of 'efficient' management of the enslaved.

It is also noteworthy that Burns wrote to Hutchinson the same week as Patrick wrote to Charles about the change of plan [QQ.34,35] – it is interesting to speculate: was Burns attempting to get a sympathetic story out in Jamaica before Charles heard the news?

---

44 It would seem a fair supposition that the mortgages on Jamaica underpinned loans made by Hunter & Co's bank to rescue Dr Patrick from the Ayr Bank fiasco.
45 As Charles is looking to hire a Scot, it is assumed that the £10–12 is Sterling.
46 Strawhorn, *Scotland*, p.45.

3: How Could He Pay for the Passage to Jamaica?

While Charles is fairly explicit on the mechanics of how the candidate should travel out to the plantation [QQ.4,6], there is no mention of his paying for the new employee's travel. It would seem to have been the convention that new employees were responsible for paying their own travel and if they could not afford that, they could agree an indenture (or bond of service) with the employer who, in return for a binding contract to serve for a fixed period and receive little or no wage alongside their clothing, bed and board, would take the responsibility for payment of the travelling out from (and sometimes back to) Scotland. Along these lines, Burns affirmed that he was 'about to indent myself for want of money to pay my freight' [Q.39] and Gilbert remembers that 'as [Burns] had not sufficient money to pay his passage [...] Mr [Gavin] Hamilton advised him to publish his poems in the meantime by subscription, as a likely way of getting a little money to provide him more liberally in necessities for Jamaica' [Q.43].

That plan being agreed, Burns set in motion the subscription lists in April with the firm plan that, as 'soon as I was master of nine guineas, the price of wafting me to the torrid zone,' he would book 'a passage in the very first ship that was to sail' [Q.39]. Nine guineas equates to 63 subscriptions paid in hand, but he would need to clear sufficient copies to meet John Wilson's costs of paper, printing and binding (in the final account, £35 17s 0d, less the 70 copies he subscribed for) which needed 169 sales to break even.[47] Combining those two sums, Burns exceeded his target through the underwriting of two patrons: Robert Aiken, who signed for 145 copies, and Gavin Hamilton, for 40.[48]

There is little concrete evidence on his travel plans as there are no receipts or other evidence of any of the tickets on any of the proposed crossings and Burns's comments are inconsistent (eg, compare Q.16 with Q.18).

---

47 Allan Young and Patrick Scott, *The Kilmarnock Burns: A Census* (Columbia, SC: University of South Carolina Libraries, 2017), p.xxvi.

48 The remaining primary subscribers were friends of the poet: Robert Muir (70), John Kennedy (20), John Logan (20) and David McWhinnie (20). His brother Gilbert subscribed for 70 copies but was reliant on finding 70 people to buy his copies, as he was as impoverished as his brother.

4: How Did Mary Campbell Feature in His Plans?

Many commentators have said that Mary Campbell had agreed to be both Burns's wife and his travelling companion to Jamaica. Again, the little hard evidence we have seems to discount that, despite the thrust of Burns's highly popular song 'Will ye go to the Indies, My Mary,' [K.387]:

> Will ye go to the Indies, my Mary,
>   And leave auld Scotia's shore;
> Will ye go to the Indies, my Mary,
>   Across th' Atlantic roar.   ll.1–4

Leaving aside the constant danger of assuming that any writer's œuvre is entirely and truthfully autobiographical, there is no documentary evidence that Mary was planning 'to leave auld Scotia's shore.' There is nothing discussed in the letters between the Douglases about the candidate bringing a wife, unsurprisingly, as it was not the custom. As Eric J Graham says: '[t]hirty years earlier bringing out a supportive 'wife' might have been condoned. But by the 1780s a single profit-driven manager and overseer was the norm.'[49] And we know that Burns was budgeting for a single berth on the boat at nine Guineas, not two at 18 [Q.39].

The partner song to 'Will ye go…' is 'Highland Lassie, O —' [K.107] which has a different story, one which reflects the more likely reality of the lovers separated by the Atlantic, hoping that the man will make his fortune on the ocean's far side enabling him return, with pockets full of gold, to his true (and faithful) love on its nearside:

> For her I'll brave the billow's roar;
> For her I'll trace a distant shore;
> That Indian wealth may lustre throw
> Around my Highland Lassie, O. —   ll.21–24

This second song ties in more with the broad pattern of expatriate life. In general, the Scot's approach to the Caribbean was as a sojourner rather than a long-term settler: his clear plan was to go alone, and

---

49 Graham, *Plantocracy*, p.13.

in that inhospitable environment seek to garner as much money as possible in as brief a spell as necessary, then return, if still alive. Douglas Hamilton's research shows that plantations owned by non-Scots were three times more likely to have female residents; '[c]learly, Scots tended to travel to the West Indies alone. These were not the lands in which they intended to make new lives for themselves and their families, if they had dependents at all.'[50]

So, it seems clear that any belief about Mary Campbell going to the West Indies with the poet is totally false.[51] It certainly not impossible that Burns lied outright to her, as he had to others over the nature of the job and its emoluments and it would not be the first – or the last – time that his strict truthfulness to women could be questioned. So perhaps Mary did believe that she might go, but that would have been a highly unusual arrangement and one unsanctioned by his potential employer, and so must be completely discounted as something that could occur in practice.[52]

5: What Were Burns's Plans for His Voyage to Jamaica?
Finally, looking at Burns's description of the various passages booked, but not taken, to his new employment also throws up several inconsistencies.

Charles was insistent that his 'boy' take passage to one of the north-eastern or eastern ports of Jamaica [QQ.1,4,6]. As Burns tells the story, he (on his own initiative) booked a ticket with Captain Smith on the *Nancy* departing the Clyde to Savanna-la-Mar (on the wrong side of Jamaica) and was subsequently encouraged to take a more direct route by some Jamaican friends of Doctor Patrick, Mr

---

50 Hamilton, pp.44, 45. Leask tentatively suggests that 'possibly the match [with Mary Campbell] would have been of material benefit to R[obert] B[urns] in Jamaica, given the power of Campbell privilege on the island.' (*Oxford Burns*, vol.I, p. 336 at n.94) but even if she were to emigrate, it is hard to imagine what clannish benefits a poor serving lass could claim for herself or her 'bookie' husband. As will be seen below, Zachary Macaulay arrived with what seemed like a 'gold-plated' clan introduction that led to nothing, see p.336.
51 *Poems*, 'My Highland Lassie O,' [K.107]. The SMM interleaved copy, *Poems*, vol III, pp.1182-3, talks of 'our projected change of life' that must mean marriage, for the poem clearly shows the poet 'on a distant shore' while his love remains 'within the glen.' Similarly, much later, he described the inspiration of his song, 'Will Ye Go to the Indies My Mary,' *Poems*, K.387, vol.II, pp.656-657, as a 'farewell of a dear girl [...] when I was thinking of going to the West Indies.' While marriage (of some sort) may have been contemplated, her travel furth of Scotland was certainly not.
52 Graham, *Plantocracy*, p.13, see also, Anon, 'Burns' Jamaica Connections,' *Burns Chronicle* (1903), pp.79-83.

& Mrs White, when he visited Garallan on 13th August [Q.16]. Dr Patrick's manuscript journal confirms the gist of the story [Q.14] and also shows he subscribed for three copies of the *Kilmarnock Edition* [Q.15] at that visit.[53]

However, Burns's explanation is odd, being against Charles's express instructions to sail to the north coast and not to the south. In any case, the *Nancy* had been scheduled to sail by 10 August, days *before* he met Dr Patrick [Q.13].[54] Burns then says he rebooked a voyage with Captain Cathcart on the brigantine *Bell* which was scheduled to depart by the end of September out of Greenock for Port Morant. This was a much more sensible route, as he would land about 20 miles south of the Douglas's Ayr Mount plantation [QQ.16,18]. Yet, even that is not a simple fact, for it was Doctor Patrick [Q28] who had delayed Burns's travel arrangements until Captain Bowie sailed unless Charles expressly agreed to the passage on the *Bell*, which did not happen prior to its sailing on 7 October [Q.28].[55] That letter does confirm that Burns was still committed to the journey in late October, even after (or perhaps because of) Jean Armour being delivered of the poet's twins. Burns wrote at the end of September 'my departure is uncertain, but I do not think it will be till after harvest' [Q.23]. This timing clearly contradicts Burns's statement that his emigration schemes were 'overthrown' upon receiving a letter sent to his friend Revd George Lawrie from Doctor Blacklock (dated 4 September) advising him to pursue a second edition [Q.22]. This faulty timeline was echoed by Gilbert to Mrs Dunlop:

> The reception however which his poems met with in the world, and the friends they procured him, made him change his resolution of going to Jamaica, and he was advised to go to Edinburgh to publish a second edition. [Q.43]

The documents, however, do not show that; they show that he had merely *postponed* his emigration, not that he had cancelled his plans entirely at this stage. His revised plan was to supervise the *First*

---

53 Beinecke Rare Book & Manuscript Library, Yale Library General Collection of Rare Books and Manuscripts, *Patrick Charles Douglas Boswell Family Papers 1653–1807*, MS GEN 972, Box 1, Folder 2474/4, 'Patrick Douglas, Journals and Day Books, 1785/1786.'
54 *The Glasgow Mercury*, 6–13 July 1786, quoted in Carruthers, *Slavery*, p.164.
55 *Caledonian Mercury*, 25 September 1786.

Edinburgh Edition and when that was complete to embark for Jamaica at the neighbouring port of Leith. It is probably fair to assume that, in the upswing of his lionisation in the salons (and inns) of Edinburgh, men of status expressed surprise that he was committed to Jamaica, partly on Abolitionist principles, partly due to the enormous risks to health and partly at losing a literary talent and boon-companion. In Henry Mackenzie's generous article in *The Lounger* of 9 December, which made Burns's fame, he concluded with the observation that Burns

> has been obliged to form the resolution of leaving his native land, to seek under a West-Indian clime that shelter and support which Scotland has denied him. But I trust means may be found to prevent this resolution from taking place [...] [Q.31]

Finally, his biographers say that Burns booked passage on the *Roselle* from Leith to Kingston, under Captain Liddell, a plan closer, but still not absolutely following Charles Douglas's instructions. Be that as it may, this third – and final – ship departed on 23 December without Burns on board [Q.33]. It would seem that Doctor Patrick was not aware of Burns's change of plans as he wrote only on 30 December to his brother [Q.34] to advise him that Burns was not on board (had he been aware earlier, he would have sent the letter by the *Roselle* itself). That letter is missing, but Charles's reply [Q.36] gives the gist of it ('I want no warm heads & Poets must have them'), with the Doctor describing the dropping of the poet as a potential employee as *his* idea, not Burns's. The change of candidates sounds more like the exasperation of an employer over a ditherer rather than the poet choosing to relinquish the job offer having found (belatedly) some scruples, or a better offer of a job at home. (The odd, outlying Jamaica mention to James Smith [Q.37] nearly six months after the literal and figurative ship had sailed seems to support that thesis.)[56]

The Douglas brothers moved from transporting Burns to employing an orphan boy from a family acquaintance and for Burns the rest is history, or at least myth. The Douglas letters and journals are tantalisingly vague but it seems clear that the traditional biographical narrative is not the whole story. Burns's few comments are clearly at

---

[56] After the failure of his partnership in Linlithgow, Smith emigrated to the West Indies himself, and was presumed dead by 1808. Cromek, *Reliques*, p.2.

odds with the letters between the Douglas brothers and often appear less than straightforward. The truth is the job offered to the poet was more vile than we had imagined and was to be undertaken for paltry sums. This was destined to be a lonely and dangerous existence and Burns certainly represented it as a better outcome than that to his friends.

Conclusion

Charles Douglas made the job description clear, so it is definite that Burns knew that the job he accepted was not a clerical position but was an active role oppressing Black enslaved people, which was confirmed by two books in his possession at that time, Guthrie's and Salmon's *Geographical Grammars*. By taking all these documents in the round, it looks as if Burns kept his options open to the last moment and only turned down the offer (possibly in a formal written resignation or probably more likely simply by not taking up his berth on the boat) in late December 1786.

Much as it hurts to recognise, these letters can easily be read to show Robert Burns sought to prosper from chattel slavery and only dropped the opportunity because a better offer came along, not because of any moral scruples over him personally inflicting human suffering on enslaved men, women and children.

CHAPTER FOUR

Slavery in Burns's Writings

Introduction

OUR UNDERSTANDING OF a poet's world view, by definition, must be defined through his or her works (without the automatic assumption that everything written is honest autobiography). The well-spring of poetic creation opens our eyes to both the poet's outward theme, but also to the poet's inner thoughts. This chapter will first address the knotty question of Burns's wider use of 'slave' and associative words and phrases across his poems and songs, then, secondly, look at each of his works which has a specific reference to Black chattel slavery.

What does Burns mean when using the word 'slave'? In examining Burns's own writings to establish his true held beliefs on Black chattel slavery, there is an initial problem which needs to be addressed: Burns uses the words 'slave' and 'slavery' in four broad meanings. This first part of the chapter will look at three uses Burns makes of a broad concept of slavery, in what might be called 'metaphorical slavery,' in 'political slavery' and finally in 'coward slavery.' The second part of this section will look at where Burns writes (directly or indirectly) about the enslavement of Black people.

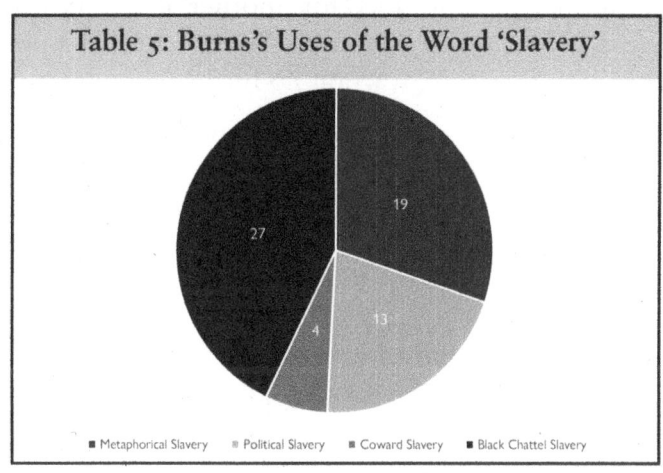

Table 5: Burns's Uses of the Word 'Slavery'

Metaphorical Slavery

First, there are a raft of references where Burns uses the traditional literary trope of a man (typically) being a 'slave' to his Passions (usually Love, but Wealth, his Belly, or his Bottle would be equally valid in this usage). While this is a trope which verges on cliché, several commentators feel that by 1788–1792 a wordsmith should have been more aware of the increasingly difficult connotations of the word 'slave' and therefore should have used it more carefully: as Carruthers puts it '[p]eople can indeed be slaves to the wrong thing, but to use this metaphor at a time of real, appalling, miserable actual slavery is rather insensitive.'[1] This point would be hammered home in 1846 by Frederick Douglass on his speaking tour of Scotland:

> It is common in this country to distinguish every bad thing by the name slavery. Intemperance is slavery; to be deprived of the right to vote is slavery [...] I am here to say that I think the term slavery is sometimes abused by identifying it with that which it is not.[2]

This was a construction that went beyond the purely poetical, as one of the most famous quotations out of the Scottish Enlightenment is David Hume's 'Reason is, and ought only to be the slave of the passions, and can never pretend to any other office than to serve and obey them,' an adage to which Burns would clearly adhere.[3]

In these following examples, Burns is dealing in pure metaphor (often around one person's love for another, in a very traditional trope). These lines bear no relation to 'slavery' in either a political or a legal sense and, therefore, warrant no further consideration here.[4]

---

1 Carruthers, *Robert Burns and Slavery*, p.172.
2 Alasdair Pettinger, *Frederick Douglass and Scotland, 1846: Living an Antislavery Life* (Edinburgh: EUP, 2019), p.147.
3 David Hume, *A Treatise on Human Nature* (London: John Noon, 1739), p.417.
4 Poems are identified with their number in Kinsley's *Poems and Songs* [K.xx] and Letters with their number as in Ferguson and Roy's *Letters* [L.xx].

Table 5a: Metaphorical 'Slavery'				
DATE	K/L #	TITLE	QUOTATION	LINES
1784	K.30	'Mary Morison'	How blithely wad I bide the stour, / A weary slave frae sun to sun	5–6
1785	K.84	'The Jolly Beggars'	Great love I bear to all the Fair, / Their humble slave an' a' that;	220–221
1787	L.145A	[To Margaret Chalmers]	I look on the [female] sex with something like the admiration with which I regard the starry sky in a frosty December night. [...] I mean this with respect to a certain passion don't j'ai eu l'honneur d'être un miserable esclave [trs: I have the honour to be a miserable slave.]	
	L.166	To Agnes McLehose	I believe there is no holding converse, or carrying on correspondence, with an amiable woman, much less a gloriously amiable, fine woman, without some mixture of that delicious passion, whose most devoted slave I have more than once had the honour of being: but why be hurt or offended on that account?	
	L.170	To Agnes McLehose	What art thou, Love? whence are those charms, / That thus thou bear'st an universal rule? / For thee the soldier quits his arms, / The king turns slave, the wise man fool.5	
1789	L.360	To David Blair	Know you anything of a worse than Galley-bondage, a slavery where the soul with all her powers is laden w[i]t[h] weary fetters of ever increasing weight; a Slavery which involves the mind in dreary darkness and almost a total eclipse of every ray of God's image; and all this the work the baneful doings of that arch-fiend known among mortals as Indolence?	

---

5 *Letters* FN: quoting an 'Anonymous song in *The Hive*, 1724, p.33.' 'Philomusus', *Mirth diverts all Care: Being Excellent New Songs, Compos'd by the Most Elegant Wits of the Period, On Diverse Subjects* (London: J Morphew, 1708), p.92 by Jacob Allestry (1653–1686), an Oxford poet.

Table 5a: Metaphorical 'Slavery' (cont.)

DATE	K/L #	TITLE	QUOTATION	LINES

1790	K.288	'Beware o' Bonie Ann'	The captive bands may chain the hands,
			   But loove enslaves the man:
			Ye gallants braw, I rede you a',
			   Beware o' bonie Ann!
				13–16

	K.305	'Merry Hae I been Teethin a Heckle [Kissing My Katie]'	Bitter in dool I lickit my winnins O' marrying Bess, to gie her a slave: Blest be the hour she cool'd in her linnens, And blythe be the bird that sings on her grave!	9–12

	K.312	'[Tho' Women's Minds]'	Great love I bear to all the Fair,
			   Their humble slave an' a' that;
			But lordly WILL, I hold it still
			   A mortal sin to thraw that.
				9–12

1791	K.333	'Lovely Davies'	The man in arms 'gainst female charms,
			   Even he her willing slave is;
			He hugs his chain, and owns the reign
			   Of conquering lovely Davies.
				21–24

	K.600	'O Lay Thy Loof in Mine, Lass'	A slave to love's unbounded sway,
			   He aft has wrought me meikle wae;
			But now he is my deadly fae,
			   Unless thou be my ain.
				5–8

	K.598	'Sweetest May'	Sweetest May let love inspire thee; Take a heart which he designs thee; As thy constant slave regard it; For its faith and truth reward it.	1–4

1793	K.398	'Song — [O Poortith Cauld]'	This warld's wealth when I think on,
			   Its pride, and a' the lave o't;
			My curse on silly coward man,
			   That he should be the slave o't.
				9–12

	L.537	Burns to William Nicol	[...] How infinitely is thy puddle-headed, rattle-headed, wrong-headed, round-headed slave indebted to they super-eminent goodness [...]. Thy devoted slave, Robt Burns.	

DATE	K/L #	TITLE	QUOTATION	LINES

1793 cont.	K.441	'English Song'	Husband, husband, cease your strife,
			  Nor longer idly rave, Sir:
			Tho' I am your wedded wife,
			  Yet I am not your slave, Sir.
				1–4

1794	L.608	To Mrs Riddell	Forgive the offences, and pity the perdition of, Madam, your humble slave [...]	
	K.457	'She says She lo'es Me best of a' —'	Hers are the willing chains o' love By conquering beauty's sovereign law,	21–22
1796	K.496	'Song, [Their Groves o' Sweet Myrtle]'	In LOVE'S willing fetters, the chains o' his JEAN.	16
	K.499	'Song, [Mark Yonder Pomp]'	In Love's delightful fetters she chains the willing soul!	19

Political Slavery

Significantly more complex is his use of 'slavery' in a political, religious or social sense: here is another context where Burns aligns 'slavery' with cowardice, weakness or infirmness of purpose. This comes from a long-standing philosophical belief from Aristotle that 'people who are unable to face danger courageously are the slaves of their attackers.'[6] In Scottish history it finds an echo in the Declaration of Arbroath's ringing vow: 'It is in truth not for glory, nor riches, nor honours that we are fighting, but for freedom alone, which no honest man gives up but with life itself.' Equally, in Scots Law, as discussed above, Stair recognised that slavery existed in previous ages and was still found beyond the boundaries of Scotland, for although it was 'against the Natural Law of Liberty, yet it is received for conveniency by the Nations, being more willing to lose Liberty than Life.'[7]

---

6 Aristotle, *Politics*, Loeb Classical Library 264, trans H Rackham (Cambridge, MA: Harvard University Press, 1932), at VII, 15, 1334a21.
7 Stair, *Institutions*, Lib.I, §1,11, at p.6.

Therefore, for Burns who had been inspired from youth by the tales of Sir William Wallace, the tragic early hero of Scots Independence, this Patrick Henry principle of 'give me Liberty or give me death' is a crucial part of his worldview. Just as Wallace was betrayed and cruelly executed without losing his virtue, so many of his countrymen fell in honour at Bannockburn, as expressed in the song that most captures this belief of the Bard. Who, of free spirit would not 'drain his dearest veins' to avoid the ultimate oppression, the loss of country, status and liberty, existing thereafter as a tyrant's mere slave? This was not just a view of Scotland: for the free-born, constitutional Briton should, by these lights, scorn the poor subjects of the absolute monarchies across the Channel (including, not least, the temporal and spiritual autocracy of the Pope).[8] The *locus classicus* of that thought being the song 'Rule, Britannia!', whose lyrics, by the Scot James Thomson, carry the repeated defiance that 'Britons never will be slaves.'[9]

For Burns, in this sense, the living survivor after the tyrant's victory is a lesser person (a coward) than he who sacrificed all, albeit in vain, to maintain his liberty and that of his family and his nation. It is important to remember that, as Murray Pittock argues persuasively, the language of Burns's day around slavery was echoing Stair, being

> slippery and problematic, because it was inherited from an earlier language unconcerned with [B]lack slavery, but seeing the condition as one brought about by tyranny and voluntary subjection to it.[10]

Burns tends to see that survivor as effectively a 'volunteer' slave, and not a 'victim' slave: one who chose an inglorious life over a glorious death, echoing Stair's dictum on slavery, in what might be called 'political slavery' as opposed to the growing industrialisation of Black chattel slavery.[11]

---

8 Murray Pittock, 'Slavery as a Political Metaphor in Scotland and Ireland in the Age of Burns', in *Robert Burns and Transatlantic Culture*, ed by Sharon Alker, Leith Davis and Holly Faith Nelson (Farnham: Ashgate, 2012), pp.19–31.
9 James Thomson, *The Works of James Thomson, with His last Corrections and Improvements*, 4 vols (London: John Donaldson, 1775), from 'Alfred, An Ode,' vol.III, pp.220–221. [NB: This volume was in Burns's library.] The ritual, annual controversy over this song at the Last Night of the Proms is a perfect illustration of the conflation of the differing uses of the word 'slave' being discussed in this chapter.
10 Pittock, *Slavery*, p.20.
11 Similarly, the words of the National Anthem of the USA, 'The Star Spangled Banner' by Francis

Table 5B shows the set of quotations from Burns where slavery is shown in the 'political slavery' sense (sometimes with a degree of irony).[12]

Table 5b: 'Political Slavery'				
DATE	K/L #	TITLE	QUOTATION	LINES
1784	K.64	'Man was made to Mourn'	If I'm design'd yon lordling's slave, By Nature's law design'd, Why was an independent wish E'er planted in my mind? If not, why am I subject to His cruelty, or scorn? Or why has man the will and pow'r To make his fellow mourn?	65–72
	K.81	'The Author's Earnest Cry and Prayer'	Let half-starv'd slaves in warmer skies, See future wines, rich-clust'ring, rise; Their lot auld Scotland ne'er envies, But blythe an' frisky, She eyes her freeborn, martial boys, Tak aff their Whisky. What tho' their Phebus kinder warms, While Fragrance blooms and Beauty charms, When wretches range, in famish'd swarms, The scented groves; Or hounded forth, dishonour arms, In hungry droves.	151–162

Scott Key (1779–1843) has engendered a similar controversy over lines in its third verse:
No refuge could save the hireling and slave
From the terror of flight or the gloom of the grave,
And the star-spangled banner in triumph doth wave
O'er the land of the free and the home of the brave.

12 Leask uses the term 'a negative relationship of feudal dependence' to cover this context, Leask, *Poetics*, p.48. I strongly believe that 'The Tree of Liberty' is spurious and so it is excluded from this study.

| \multicolumn{5}{c}{Table 5b: 'Political Slavery' (cont.)} |
DATE	K/L #	TITLE	QUOTATION	LINES
1787	K.151	'Prologue, Spoken by Mr Woods'	O thou, dread Power! Whose empire-giving hand Has oft been stretch'd to shield the honour'd land! Strong may she glow with all her ancient fire; May every son be worthy of his sire; Firm may she rise with generous disdain At Tyranny's, or direr Pleasure's chain; Still self-dependent in her native shore, Bold may she brave grim Danger's loudest roar, Till Fate the curtain drop on worlds to be no more.	35–43
	K.172	'The Humble Petition of Bruar Water'	My lord, I know your noble ear Woe ne'er assails in vain; Embolden'd thus, I beg you'll hear Your humble slave complain, How saucy Phoebus' scorching beams, In flaming summer-pride, Dry-withering, waste my foamy streams, And drink my crystal tide.	1–8
1787 cont.	K.180	'On Scaring Some Water-Fowl on Loch Turit'	Or, if man's superior might Dare invade your native right, On the lofty ether borne, Man with all his pow'rs you scorn; Swiftly seek, on clanging wings, Other lakes and other springs; And the foe you cannot brave, Scorn at least to be his slave.	33–40
1788	L.261	To Miss Rachel Dunlop	I am in perpetual warfare with the doctrine of our Reverend Priesthood that 'we are born into this world bond slaves of iniquity & heirs of perdition, wholly inclined to that which is evil and wholly disinclined to that which is good' [...]	
	L.284	To Bruce Campbell, for James Boswell	To crouch in the train of meer, stupid Wealth & Greatness, except where the commercial interests of worldly Prudence find their account in it, I hold to be Prostitution in anyone that is not born a Slave [...]	

DATE	K/L #	TITLE	QUOTATION	LINES
1789	K.264	'The Kirk of Scotland's Garland — a New Song [The Kirk's Alarm]'	Poet Willie! poet Willie, gie the Doctor a volley, Wi' your 'Liberty's Chain' and your wit;* * William Peebles in Newton upon Ayr, a Poetaster who, among many other things, published an Ode on the Centenary of the Revolution in which was this line — 'And bound in Liberty's endearing chain'	34–35

	K.272A	'[Answer to an Invitation]'	The king's blackguard slave am I
			   And scarcely dow spare a minute;
			But I'll be wi' you by an' bye,
			   Or else the devil's in it.
				1–4

1792	K.361	'I hae a Wife o' My ain'	I am naebody's lord,
			   I'll be slave to naebody;
			I hae a gude braid sword,
			   I'll tak dunts frae naebody.
				9–12

1793	L.558	To John Frances Erskine of Mar	BURNS was a poor man, from birth; & an Exciseman, by necessity: but — I will say it — the sterling of his honest worth, no poverty could debase; and his independent British mind, Oppression might bend, but could not subdue! — Have not I, to me, a more precious stake in my Country's welfare than the richest Dukedom in it? — I have a large family of children, & the probability of more. — I have three sons, whom, I see already, have brought with them into the world souls ill qualified to inhabit the bodies of Slaves. — Can I look tamely on, and see any machination to wrest from them, the birthright of my boys, the little independent Britons in whose veins runs my own blood? — I will not! — should my heart stream around my attempt to defend it! —	p.209

Table 5b: 'Political Slavery' (cont.)					
DATE	K/L #	TITLE	QUOTATION	LINES
1793 cont.	K.412(B)	'[Annotations in Verse]'	Grant me, indulgent Heaven, that I may live To see the miscreants feel the pains they give: Deal Freedom's sacred treasures free as air, Till SLAVE and DESPOT be *but things that were!*	1–4
1795	K.512	'[The Solemn League and Covenant]'	The Solemn League and Covenant Now brings a smile, now brings a tear. But sacred Freedom, too, was theirs; If thou'rt a slave, indulge thy sneer.	1–4

Coward Slavery

The fame and genius of Burns's 'Honest Poverty' [K.492] elevates this question with the usage 'the coward-slave, we pass him by/ We daur be poor for a' that' (lines 3–4). Following Leask, this study believes that there may just well be a link between this particular poem and Burns's view of Black chattel slavery, but the first verse is clearly talking of 'political slavery,' with an important caveat: just as 'poverty' can be dissected into 'honest poverty' and (one supposes) 'dishonest poverty,' (say, a farmer ruined by bad weather and failing crops on the one hand compared to an idle drunkard on the other) so too can slavery be classified as 'coward slavery' (or 'volunteerism', in Pittock's construction, a reprehensible status of surrender) as contrasted with 'chattel slavery' or 'victim slavery' (which is either innocent or passive, but always coerced).[13]

Again, an understanding of this juxtaposition, which seems harsh to the liberal ear, of an essential linkage between the state of slavery and the condemnation of cowardice can be gleaned from the writings of Frederick Douglass. Douglass was born into slavery, so had no choice in the Stair sense. However, his bestselling autobiography contains a harrowing chapter called 'The Last Flogging' and this is his summary of the turning point of his own life as a human being, when he turned on his slaver-holder and beat *him*:

---

13 Some advocates have sought (with no textual authority) to reread 'coward' as 'cowered', 'cow'rd' or perhaps 'cowed' to avoid the juxtaposition. See Ian MacMillan, 'The Coward Slave,' *Burns Chronicle* (Autumn, 2009), p.22.

> Covey [his slave-master] was a tyrant and a cowardly one withal. After resisting him, I felt as I had never felt before. It was a resurrection from the dark and pestiferous tomb of slavery, to the heaven of comparative freedom. I was no longer a servile coward, trembling under the frown of a brother worm of the dust, but my long-cowed spirit was roused to an attitude of manly independence. I had reached the point, at which I was not afraid to die. The spirit had made me a freeman in fact, while I remained a slave in form.[14]

Douglass saw the point that Burns had made in his poem 'Honest Poverty' [K.482] because he had lived through it.

The leaders of the great movements for Abolition and Emancipation, and many of the Black population, saw Burns as accurately describing their plight: Burns was not calumniating the enslaved as people, but was telling them that, as with Douglass, it is internal fortitude and character which defines a person – not the branded mark on the forearm, or the whip scars on the back and especially not the colour of the skin. Douglass clearly saw that emancipation came in two steps: first, no more coward slaves through internal personal resolve, then no more slaves at all through external societal change. Dare to be true to yourself even under the slave owner's tyranny, then dare to be free when the time came for emancipation, escape or rebellion. Or, as Bob Marley (1945–1981) sings in 'Redemption Song,' channelling a 1937 quotation from Marcus Garvey (1887–1940): 'Emancipate yourself from mental slavery/ None but ourselves can free our minds.'[15] Burns uses this conceit of 'coward slavery' only four times, but two are in some of his most important works:

---

14 Frederick Douglass, *My Bondage and My Freedom* (New York/Auburn: Miller, Orton & Co, 1857), p.247. Which also chimes with the Stair Dictum.
15 Bob Marley, 'Redemption Song,' final track on Bob Marley & the Wailers, *Uprising* (Island Records, 1980), from Marcus Garvey, 'Menelik Hall in Sydney, Nova Scotia, October 1937': 'We are going to emancipate ourselves from mental slavery because whilst others might free the body, none but ourselves can free the mind. Mind is your only ruler, sovereign. The man who is not able to develop and use his mind is bound to be the slave of the other man who uses his mind.' Marcus Garvey, Robert A Hill and Barbara Bair, eds, *The Marcus Garvey and Universal Negro Improvement Association Papers, Vol. VII: November 1927–August 1940* (Berkeley: University of California Press, 1991), p.791.

Table 5c: 'Coward Slavery'

DATE	K/L #	TITLE	QUOTATION	LINES

1788	K.196	'McPherson's Farewell'	Now farewell, light, thou sunshine bright,
			   And all beneath the sky!
			May coward shame distain his name,
			   The wretch that dares not die!
				21–24

1791	K.330	'Orananaoig, or, The Song of Death'	Thou grim king of terrors, thou life's gloomy foe,
			   Go frighten the coward and slave!
			Go teach them to tremble, fell tyrant! but know,
			   No terrors hast thou to the Brave!
				5–8

1792	K.425	'Scots wha hae'	Scots, wha hae wi' WALLACE bled,
			Scots, wham BRUCE has aften led;
			Welcome to your gory bed, —
			   Or to victory, —
			
			Now's the day, and now's the hour;
			See the front o' battle lour;
			See approach proud EDWARD'S power—
			   Chains and Slaverie. —
			
			Wha will be a traitor-knave?
			Wha can fill a coward's grave?
			Wha sae base as be a Slave?
			   — Let him turn and flie. —
			
			Wha for SCOTLAND's king and law
			Freedom's sword will strongly draw,
			FREE-MAN stand, or FREE-MAN fa',
			   Let him follow me. —
			
			By Oppression's woes and pains!
			By your Sons in servile chains!
			We will drain our dearest veins,
			   But they *shall* be free!
			
			Lay the proud Usurpers low!
			Tyrants fall in every foe!
			LIBERTY's in every blow! —
			   Let us DO — OR DIE!!!
				1–24

DATE	K/L #	TITLE	QUOTATION	LINES
1795	K.482	'Honest Poverty' [16]	Is there for honest Poverty That hings his head, and a' that; The coward-slave, we pass him by, We dare be poor for a' that! For a' that, an' a' that. Our toils obscure and a' that, The rank is but the guinea's stamp, The Man's the gowd for a' that. —	1–8

Black Chattel Slavery

This, the principal part of the analysis of Burns's poems and songs, will look at around two dozen works which directly or indirectly contain reference to Black chattel slavery. The works range in date from 1784 until 1796, the last being written as he lay dying in Dumfries, bookending his writing career and so allowing an overarching view of the extent to which his views and understanding of Slavery and Abolition changed.

These will be reviewed in order of their composition, with each being ranked towards 'POSITIVE' if aligned with Abolition or 'NEGATIVE' if not.

No 1: [1784] [K.47] 'Epistle to J[ohn] R[ankine], Enclosing Some Poems.'

In this early poetic epistle, Burns writes to his friend about his affair with Elizabeth ('Betsy') Paton, his parents' servant, which resulted in her pregnancy with the poet's first child, Elizabeth ('Bess') Burns, who would be born in May 1785. The reference to enslavement occurs towards the end of the poem:

> As soon's the *clockin-time* is by,   61
> An' the *wee pouts* begun to cry,
> L[or]d, I'se hae sporting by an' by,
>   For my *gowd guinea*;
> Tho' I should herd the *buckskin* kye
>   For't, in Virginia!   66

---

16   The possibility of this being a reference to chattel slavery will be discussed below, at p.212

ANALYSIS

This is the first mention of what would be Burns's 'plan B' in the case of any potential 'disgrace': a resolution to flee the confines of Ayrshire and seek a new life across the Atlantic (as many Ayrshire men had done before, and many were still doing, although there were now few opportunities in the new, independent USA). Andrew Noble is surely right in suggesting that '[l]ike all of the early Ayrshire epistles, it is preoccupied with the poet's own reputation, or more often, his lack of it.'[17]

Here, he envisages no easy life in the colonies and assumes that he will have to start at the bottom of their society as a slave-driver, the 'buckskins' being a metonym for the American colonists, and 'kye' or 'cattle' metaphorically referring to the human beings they held in enslavement. In 18th- and 19th-century slang, 'cattle' meant not only cows, but coach-horses or plough-horses – as in Burns's 'The Inventory' where he indites '*Imprimis* then, for carriage cattle/ I have four brutes o' gallant mettle,' [K.86, ll.5–6] – or a riding horse, such as the 'sma' droop-rumpl't, hunter cattle' that 'Auld Mare Meg' could outdistance in K.75, l.55 or poor 'Peg Nicholson' who was 'much opress'd [...]/ As priest-rid cattle are,' in K.283, l.16. It could be used to refer to other agglomerations of beasts, such as in Burns's 'To a Louse': 'There ye may creep, and sprawl, and sprattle,/ Wi' ither kindred, jumping cattle,' [K.83, ll.14–15].[18] By extension, 'herds' of a 'lower type' of person could be so called, too: for example, boys, prostitutes or women in general. Burns used it in this sense when he talks of '*delvers, ditchers* an' sic cattle' in 'The Twa Dogs,' [K.71, l.90]. The phrase 'kittle cattle' for a group of quixotic or hard to manage folk is still (occasionally) heard today.[19]

It is no coincidence that the etymology of 'cattle' and 'chattel' is

---

17 Andrew Noble, 'Burns, Scotland, and the American Revolution,' in *Burns and Transatlantic Culture*, ed Alker et al, p.38.
18 Nigel Leask sees that '[i]n the 1780s, this conceit possessed a specific geographical connotation. Namely the North American "plantations," originally populated by the outcasts of Britain and Ireland, but recently transformed into an independent republic.' Nigel Leask, *Robert Burns and Pastoral, Poetry and Improvement in Eighteenth Century Scotland* (Oxford: Oxford University Press, 2010), p.172. This is probably pushing the conceit too far, as, while certainly Jamaican and Caribbean emigrants from Scotland were often 'outcasts', the previous generations of merchants and traders into the East coast of what would become the USA were more heterogenous.
19 *Poems*, 'The Twa Dogs,' [K.71], l.90.

interlinked.[20] So, the use of 'Kye' or 'cattle' is genuinely de-humanising for the Black enslaved people and its use here directly aligns with the jargon of the slave-holder and of the plantation: the 'stock' of enslaved labourers 'driven' by 'drivers', the same phraseology being used for humans as for cows. Perhaps Captain Richard Brown brought this metaphor to Burns, possibly with the 'N-word' (which Burns will use in 'The Ordination' as discussed below)?

The absence of humanity in the phrase is slightly distanced by using Virginia as the *locus* (which had been Ayrshire's primary trading market, but which was now, following the surrender of the British Army at Yorktown in 1782, closed to a poor Scot) rather than the Caribbean. (Burns uses this distraction in 'The Slave's Lament', too, as will be seen below.)

In some ways, this seems a throwaway line where Burns seeks sympathy for his own plight rather than expressing any care about the oppression of chattel slaves. But of course, it prefigures his concrete steps the following year in accepting the 'negro-driver' position on the Douglas plantation. It, therefore, cannot therefore be easily glossed otherwise than as a recognition of the role as a potentially viable career option which was likely unpleasant and uncongenial, but not unacceptable. One counter-argument is given by Andrew Noble who considers that, here and in the 'Autobiographical Letter,'

> Burns is in neither case belittling the slaves but seeing in the mirror a hellish image of what those positions would reduce him to, and by implication, the reality of the institution of slavery.[21]

While this is an argument which appears to fit 'The Ordination' (see below), the attitude to slavery which is generally maintained through the poems written prior to the *First Edinburgh Edition* makes it impossible to sustain, and appears more as special pleading on the Bard's behalf.

Interestingly, when Revd Dr Hugh Blair examined Burns's poems for the *First Edinburgh Edition*, he remarked on the sexual indecency of the extended 'shooting the hen' metaphor in this poem (that it referred to Burns's fornication with Elisabeth Paton, the mother of

---

20 See the *Oxford English Dictionary*: 'ME, catel — A Fr, O N Fr, catel, var. of chattel, whence CHATTEL'.
21 Noble, p.39.

his first child, had to be drawn to his innocent attention) but made no adverse comment on the slave-driving. It would take a further year or so before Blair would be sermonising against the slave trade, which mitigates (to an extent) Burns's own position on chattel slavery when writing in 1784.[22]

EVALUATION: VERY NEGATIVE
In this particular poem, Burns sees slave-driving as an unfortunate or unlucky chance for him personally, but adds no moral reprehension to the task, nor any recognition of the greater misfortunes of the enslaved. While the tone of these verses is jocular and adopts a 'boys-will-be-boys' attitude for an audience of his 'ram-stam friends', he appears to accept the fact of Black chattel slavery without a qualm, even deploying de-humanised language in respect to the enslaved peoples. It is, or course, written before the rising popular opinion in favour of Abolition, as evidenced by Blair's comments, so Burns's acceptance of it as a potential career is quite within accepted societal norms at that date of writing, although repugnant to our understanding today.

No 2 [1785] [K.74] ['The Mauchline Wedding.']
As mentioned above, Alexander 'Sandy' Bell of Mauchline made a small fortune in the West Indies, returning home to Ayrshire in poor health. At his death, he bequeathed a considerable sum to his sister, Agnes, who subsequently married William Miller, son of the landlord of the Sun Inn and brother of two of the 'Belles of Mauchline'.[23] Burns had been 'walking out' with Elizabeth ('Miss Betty') and claimed that her rejection of his suit was down to her prospective sister-in-law's wealth giving her a presumptuous feeling of her own importance. As the poet explained to Mrs Dunlop on sending her the manuscript of this burlesque of Will and Agnes's wedding-day, on 29 August 1785:

> You would know an Ayr-shire lad, Sandy Bell, who made a Jamaica fortune. And died some time ago — A William Miller, formerly a Mason, and now a merchant in this place, married a sister german

---

22 J De Lancey Ferguson, 'Burns and Hugh Blair,' *Modern Language Notes*, 45.7 (1930), p.441; Whyte, *Scotland and the Abolition*, p.71.
23 *Poems*, 'Song —' ['The Belles of Mauchline,'] [K.42]: 'Miss Miller is fine [...]/ [...] Miss Betty is braw;' (ll.5–6).

of Bell's for the sake of the 500£ her brother had left her. — A sister of Miller's who was then Tenant of my heart for the time being, huffed my Bardship in the pride of her new Connection; and I, in the heat of my resentment resolved to burlesque the whole business.[24]

The opening of the poem alludes to the source of wealth thus:

> WHEN Eighty-five was seven month auld,
>   And wearing thro the aught,
> When rotting rains and Boreas bauld
>   Gied farmer-folks a faught;
> Ae morning quondam Mason Will,   5
>   Now Merchant Master Miller,
> Gaed down to meet wi' Nansie Bell
>   And her Jamaica siller,
>   To wed, that day. —

ANALYSIS
In this stage of his writing career, Burns has (and generates) a lot of fun in his satires on real events and on the heads of real people, here at the expense of Elizabeth ('Bess') and Helen ('Nell') in their vicarious joy at their brother marrying into £500.[25] However, despite the clear description of Miss Bell's fortune as 'Jamaica siller' in line 8, there is no direct criticism of how that was earned and at what human cost to the enslaved people. This is particularly of interest inasmuch as Burns must have now met, or at least seen, John Cartwright, Sir John Whitefoord's Black servant, who had been brought from the West Indies by Sandy Bell.[26]

EVALUATION: NEGATIVE
It is fair to assume that Burns merely accepted this Jamaican bounty as a not untypical story in Ayrshire, perhaps even (grudgingly) respecting

---

24 *Letters*: to Mrs Dunlop, 21 August 1788 [L.265], at vol.1, p.308. Elizabeth Miller (1768–1795) married John Templeton, a merchant in Mauchline, but died in childbirth. Her elder sister, Helen Miller (?1765–1827), 'Miss Miller' or 'Nell' had been an early friend of Burns, and married his friend Dr John Mackenzie (?–1827).
25 Five hundred pounds invested in Government gilt-edged securities at that time would yield £15 annually. In context, Robert's attributable wage on the family farm was £7 a year.
26 See above at p.48.

the 'rags-to riches' element behind it, without associating it with the human story of John Cartwright (or his less fortunate peers). While the poem was written seven years after *Knight v Wedderburn*, it was written before the Abolition debate gained traction in 1788, but remains a 'negative', as Burns, in line with most public opinion, was indifferent to the source of (and perhaps even approving and/ or envious of) Caribbean fortunes. Burns would have written the same poem if the 'siller' had come from some windfall other than the Jamaican plantations, as the poem attacks the presumptions of the wealthy, not how their 'siller' was made.

No 3 [1786] [K.85] 'The Ordination'
The context of this poem is the religious factionalism found in the Church of Scotland of Burns's day between the 'New Lights' (or 'Moderates') and the 'Auld Lights' (or 'Evangelicals') who contested many areas of the Kirk's teaching and its constitutions. One flashpoint was the contentious subject of Church patronage.[27] Here Burns imagines the joy amongst the Auld Lichts when the normally liberal patron of the parish, Lord Glencairn (1749–1791), choses an Evangelical minister for the Laigh Kirk in Kilmarnock.[28] In stanza IV of this long

---

27 10 *Ann, c.13,* 'The Church Patronage (Scotland) Act, 1711.' Since patronage was restored by this Act, the right to present a qualified minister to a vacant parish was transferred from the heritors (the local propertied class) jointly with the elders of the kirk to the local patron (who might be the Crown, a corporation such as a town council or university, or mostly, a local landowner). The Auld Lights were vehemently opposed to this, and often orchestrated protests and riots to disturb or prevent a Moderate becoming shepherd to a traditional, evangelical flock. As well as Burns's poetic poke at these shenanigans, see John Galt's *Annals of the Parish*. The Moderates were at first passive, and then accepting of the increasingly enlightenment tenor of the corps of patrons (particularly in the light of grass-roots objections). As Revd Hamilton Paul remarks in his preface to his edition of Burns: No curse can befall a nation with regard to the civil administration of its affairs more pregnant with calamity than universal suffrage; and consequently if that mode of election be perilous in politics, it must be terribly fatal in matters of religion. It is a kind of anomaly in ecclesiastical economy, that the most ignorant of mankind should sit in judgement on the qualifications of those who are to be their teachers. Revd Hamilton Paul, ed, *The Poems & Songs of Robert Burns, With a Life of the Author* (Air: Wilson and McCormick, 1819), p.xxxviii.
So, amongst all the ironies that Scottish ecclesiastical history throws us, we find the Moderates in favour of abolishing slavery, but against widening the suffrage at home, while the Evangelicals accept Black chattel slavery, yet value the vote of every communicant man. In 1843 it was this question of patronage which led to 'the Great Disruption,' and the schism between the 'Church of Scotland' and the 'Free Church of Scotland', the latter walking out, leaving manses and salaries behind. It was that financial need which took several prominent ministers to the USA where the Southern states were especially generous in sending donations, leading to the 'Send the Money Back' campaign by Abolitionists the following year. See Chapter 7 below.
28 The Revd James Mackinlay (1756–1841), who was not chosen by Glencairn for his theology but

satirical poem, Burns envisages which Bible readings might be suitable for a 'hellfire and brimstone' minister on ascending his new pulpit to preach at his ordination and induction:

> Come, let a proper text be read,
>   An' touch it aff wi' vigour,
> How graceless *Ham** leugh at his Dad,   30
>   Which made *Canaan* a niger;
> Or *Phineas*† drove the murdering blade,
>   Wi' wh[o]re-abhorring rigour;
> Or *Zipporah*,‡ the scauldin jad,
>   Was like a bluidy tiger   35
>   I' th' inn that day.
>
> [Burns's Footnotes] * Genesis, ch. ix, vers. 22;
> † Numbers, ch. xxv, vers. 8; ‡ Exodus, ch. iv, vers. 25.

Interestingly, each of those three Bible stories reflect on inter-racial relationships.

ANALYSIS

Burns, of course, was aligned to the New Lichts, and so this poem is a mirror image of his own thoughts and beliefs, exaggerated for comic and satirical effect.

The fundamental hypocrisy of the Auld Lichts is that they are celebrating the 'call' of one of their brethren through the patronage that they opposed in other parishes when a 'New Licht' minister was presented. Rather than having any reading from the New Testament, the Auld Lichts glory in the more vengeful parts of the Old Testament. So, after years of Moderate sniping, now is the time to 'let a proper [ie, Auld Lichtish] text be read.' [line 28]. The three selected bible passages are the stories of Ham, of Phineas and of Zipporah from the Pentateuch.

---

as an act of political patronage to reward Sir William Cunningham of Windyhill, in whose house Mackinlay had tutored. *Poems*, vol.III, p.1164. The Cunninghams of Windyhill were related to the Cunninghams of Glencairn. Sir William (11th Baronet) (?–1790) died while managing the Grandvale Estate in Westmoreland, Jamaica, of 3,500 acres and around 300 enslaved people. His heirs would receive Government compensation for 185 enslaved people amounting to £3,278/5/-. *University College London Legacies of British Slave Ownership*: www.ucl.ac.uk/lbs (accessed 1 September 2024) [UCL Legacies Database].

Burns's satire is deft, and it is easy to forget that he had a sound knowledge of the Bible, so why choose these three texts? Taking the second text first, as Burns refers to this story in other places: Phineas (or Phinehas) was the grandson of Aaron, and the son of Eleazar (the brother and the nephew of Moses) who became the third High Priest of Israel in succession to his grandfather and father. When the Israelites committed one of their periodic strays from the ways of God, they started to intermarry with the Midianites and then to worship their deities. Phineas saw an Israelite man (Zimri the Simeonite) and a Midianite princess (Kosbi, daughter of Zur) set up a tent together and he took a spear and killed them both in the act of coitus, by which act he halted the plague that God had sent to punish the apostates, as told in Numbers, chapter xxv:

> 1 And Israel abode in Shittim, and the people began to commit whoredom with the daughters of Moab.
> 2 And they called the people unto the sacrifices of their gods: and the people did eat, and bowed down to their gods. [...]
> 6 And, behold, one of the children of Israel came and brought unto his brethren a Midianitish woman in the sight of Moses, and in the sight of all the congregation of the children of Israel, who were weeping before the door of the tabernacle of the congregation.
> 7 And when Phinehas, the son of Eleazar, the son of Aaron the priest, saw it, he rose up from among the congregation, and took a javelin in his hand;
> 8 And he went after the man of Israel into the chamber, and thrust both of them through, the man of Israel, and the woman through her belly. So the plague was stayed from the children of Israel. [...]

In reward, God marked Phineas' faithfulness, granting him 'and to his seed after him, the covenant of an everlasting priesthood; because he was jealous for his God, and made atonement for the children of Israel.' [verses 12,13]. [29] From this text comes two strictures: the first against 'miscegenation' (sexual congress across racial groups) and the second the covenant of priesthood, which is related to the core Calvinist dogma of the predestination of 'the Elect'.

---

29 See also: *Psalms* cvi, 30–31: 'Then stood up Phinehas, and executed judgment: and so the plague was stayed. And that was counted unto him for righteousness unto all generations for evermore.'

Burns returned to this story later in another poem, that underscores his stance in 'The Ordination' and shows his own view of the story of Phineas, which he scratched on a window of the Globe in Dumfries in 1795:

> I MURDER hate by flood or field,
>   Tho' glory's name may screen us;
> In wars at home I'll spend my blood,
>   Life-giving wars of Venus:
> The deities that I adore   5
>   Are social Peace and Plenty;
> I'm better pleased to *make one more*,
>   Than be the death of twenty. —
> I would not die like Socrates,
>   For all the fuss of Plato;   10
> Nor would I with Leonidas,
>   Nor yet would I with Cato:
> The Zealots of the Church, or State
>   Shall ne'er my mortal foes be,
> But let me have bold * ZIMRI'S fate,   15
>   Within the arms of COZBI![30]

[Burns's footnote] * Vide Numbers Chap 25th Verse 8th–15th.

Burns's view is well summarised by Leask:

> The chauvinistic persecution of love crossing ethnic boundaries at the behest of a cruel Deity. [Burns] prefers to identify with the lovers 'thrust through' by Phinehas's javelin in the act of love.[31]

So, Burns clearly sees no 'colour bar' on 'true' love. Again, does that have a direct bearing on what Burns thought or felt about chattel slavery? Certainly, the avoidance of inter-marriage between Black and White is a key thread around the pro-slavery argument, based (to an

---

30 *Poems*, 'Song —' [K.534(B)] and a version of this also appears in *Glenriddell Ms*, vol.I, p.20, *Oxford Burns*, vol.I, p.185.
31 *Oxford Burns*, vol.I, p.381.

extent) on these specific Bible passages. As discussed previously, Burns would, in all likelihood, have met the mixed-race children of Scipio Kennedy at Kirkoswald so, while the Preacher in 'The Ordination' extols (and relishes) Phineas's vengeance, Burns concentrates on the underlying love in the tragic story.

The second text, about Zipporah the wife of Moses, is by any standards a complicated piece of theological exegesis. After fleeing from Egypt, young Moses rescued the daughters of the Midianite priest, Jethro, and married (outwith the Israelites) his extraordinary, talented and beautiful daughter Zipporah. They had two sons: the first was circumcised according to the rite of Abraham and the Hebrews, while the second was not, following the customs of Midian. This resulted in such disfavour in God's eyes that He resolved to kill Moses during a rest-stop at an inn with his family while returning to Egypt to free the Israelites (in obedience to God's orders to him). God's wrath is turned aside as Zipporah circumcises the younger son, throwing the foreskin at her 'bloody husband.' The text, Exodus, chapter IV, runs:

> 24 And it came to pass by the way in the inn, that the Lord met him, and sought to kill him.
> 25 Then Zipporah took a sharp stone, and cut off the foreskin of her son, and cast it at his feet, and said, Surely a bloody husband art thou to me.
> 26 So he let him go: then she said, A bloody husband thou art, because of the circumcision.

Burns's imagined Preacher's lesson from the text is likely to be stressing the return to Orthodoxy, cleaving to the old covenants to dispel the wrath of God and his Kirk, but again, other lessons could be drawn here: it was the chosen priest of God who was targeted for destruction, and was saved by his religiously – and racially – impure wife who (literally) took matters in her own hand and performed a form of *bris,* which in holy law could only be performed by an adult male Israelite. Honouring God, therefore, need not be patriarchal or hierarchical. There is a second string to this alternative analysis, as the beautiful Zipporah is elsewhere referred to as 'the Cushite' or 'the Ethiopian woman' (Numbers, xii, 1), and so was perceived by some scholars as a Black woman, which adds to the emphasis of this analysis.

In terms of Burns and slavery, however, it is the first of these texts (the story of Ham) that is most significant. After the Flood, Noah's three sons Shem, Ham and Japeth are commanded by God to replenish the earth with people and each branch of the Noahic family is granted a specific region of the Earth to populate, as outlined in Genesis chapter x – traditionally described as Europe for Japeth, Africa for Ham and the Middle East and Asia for Shem. However, before that could take place, an incident occurred:

> 20 And Noah began to be an husbandman, and he planted a vineyard:
> 21 And he drank of the wine, and was drunken; and he was uncovered within his tent.
> 22 And Ham, the father of Canaan, saw the nakedness of his father, and told his two brethren without.
> 23 And Shem and Japheth took a garment, and laid it upon both their shoulders, and went backward, and covered the nakedness of their father; and their faces were backward, and they saw not their father's nakedness.
> 24 And Noah awoke from his wine, and knew what his younger son had done unto him.
> 25 And he said, Cursed be Canaan; a servant of servants shall he be unto his brethren.
> 26 And he said, Blessed be the Lord God of Shem; and Canaan shall be his servant.
> 27 God shall enlarge Japheth, and he shall dwell in the tents of Shem; and Canaan shall be his servant.

This ordering of the sons of Noah, although specifically pointed at his grandson Canaan, became known as 'the Curse of Ham,' expanding the curse (or, as some would see it, covenant) of servitude from the specific Canaanite enemies of early Israel to the wider Hamitic portion of humankind. Beyond the Bible, Milton relates the 'Curse' and its effect in *Paradise Lost* (remembering that this was a favourite and influential book for Burns):

> Yet sometimes nations will decline so low
> From virtue, which is reason, that no wrong,
> But justice, and some fatal curse annexed,

> Deprives them of their outward liberty;
> Their inward lost: Witness the irreverent son
> Of him who built the ark; who, for the shame
> Done to his father, heard this heavy curse,
> Servant of servants, on his vicious race.[32]

Over time this text and its exegesis became even more generalised in attaching the 'Curse' to all Black people. As Stephen R Haynes summarises 'the biblical justification of slavery':

> In western Europe, prior to the modern period, the curse [of Ham] was invoked to explain the origins of slavery, the provenance of black skin, and the exile of the Hamites to the less wholesome regions of the earth. But these aspects of malediction were not integrated in an explicit justification for racial slavery until the fifteenth-century, when dark-skinned peoples were enslaved by the Spanish and Portuguese, and the European slave stereotype was stabilised.[33]

Burns had any number of harsh or vengeful stories in the Bible to choose from to illustrate the Auld Licht Preacher's desire to keep his parish under close discipline (or face the consequences). To choose the text that became known as 'the *vade mecum* of slave-holders' – ie the text they carried with them – cannot be a coincidence and so must, therefore, hold a meaning for Burns. [34] The verse is also brought into sharp relief (for the modern reader, at least) by the earliest use of a Scots variant of the taboo N-word.[35] It is likely that he picked up this new word from his sailor friend of the time, Captain Richard Brown, who plied the transatlantic shipping routes. We have no knowledge of what cargoes Brown carried in his career and the addition of the

---

32 Milton, *Paradise Lost*, Book XII, ll.83–104. This was regularly glossed by commentators: see James Paterson, *A Complete Commentary [...] on 'Paradise Lost'* (London: R Walker, 1744), p.483: '[Africa] was Peopled by the Posterity of Ham, who bear his Curse to this Day, for they have always been Slaves to other Nations.'
33 Stephen R Haynes, *Noah's Curse: The Biblical Justification of American Slavery* (Oxford: OUP, 2002), p.8.
34 'This prophecy of Noah is the *vade mecum* of slaveholders, and they never venture abroad without it.' Theodore Weld, *The Bible Against Slavery* (New York: American Anti-Slavery Society, 1838), p.46.
35 The word 'niger' is glossed in the *First Edinburgh Edition* as 'a negro' (at p.357). See also: John Jamieson, *Etymological Dictionary of the Scottish Language*, 4 vols (Edinburgh: W Creech [and others], 1808), vol.IV, p.158.

N-word to his vocabulary, and thence to Burns's, could simply be through its day-to-day use in the Southern states and the West Indies. That word (however spelled) was not at that point considered the toxic slur it now is (at least in White usage of the English language then), however, it was not uniformly or meekly accepted by all the Black Community. As Ignatius Sancho said in 1766, 'I am one of those people whom the vulgar and illiberal call "Negurs".'[36]

Has this been selected to ridicule the orthodoxy of slavery? It would be possible to make an argument for that, but it appears more as a general slap against the core belief in salvation through election: the belief in a small clan of 'us' set against the myriad forms of lesser 'thems'. That reading is supported by a passage in Burns's 'A Dedication to G[avin] H[amilton] Esq,' [K.103]:

> As Master, Landlord, Husband, Father,   35
> He does na fail his part in either.
> But then, nae thanks to him for a' that;
> Nae *godly symptom* ye can ca' that;
> It's naething but a milder feature
> Of our poor, sinfu', corrupt Nature: 40
> Ye'll get the best o' moral works,
> 'Mang black *Gentoos*, and pagan *Turks*,[37]
> Or hunters wild on *Ponotaxi*,
> Wha never heard of Orth[o]d[o]xy.
> That he's the poor man's friend in need,   45
> The GENTLEMAN in word and deed,
> It's no thro' terror of D[a]mn[a]t[io]n;
> It's just a carnal inclination.

This chimes with the Enlightenment philosophies of Smith and Beattie, which we know Burns read and understood, and it constitutes a rejection of the Auld Licht view which could be parodied as 'it's not

---

36 Laurence Sterne, *The Works of Laurence Sterne, With a Life of the Author, Written by Himself*, 10 vols (London: W Strahan, J Rivington and Sons, J Dodsley, G Kearsley, T Lowndes, G Robinson, T Cadell, J Murray, T Becket, P Baldwin and T Evans, 1780), 'Letters of the Late Laurence Sterne to His intimate Friends,' 'LETTER LXXV. From Ignatius Sancho, to Mr Sterne (1766),' vol.IX, p.196. See below, p.291.

37 Gentoos = Indian Hindus. See also: *Letters*: to Robert Aiken, [about 8 October] 1786, [L.53] 'to use a Gentoo phrase the *hallachores* of the human race.'

enough that the few like us are saved unless the many who are unlike us are damned.' However, that is a step away from being an open criticism of what was then a legal trade in Black chattel slaves as essentially immoral, although it is a good first step towards it.

The relevance of these three chosen Bible lessons has not been fully explored before. Burns's later explicit approval of Zimri and Cosbi shows the reader how he inverts the moral of the text to add an 'honest' inverse to the vengeful rigour sought to be promulgated from the pulpit, and so Burns uses the other two readings in the same vein, pointing to a kinder message across the three texts embracing a common humanity rather than an isolating election.

EVALUATION: POSITIVE
In attacking the strict Calvinist love of 'hellfire and damnation' by voicing Auld Licht theology in a burlesque of its own words, Burns obliquely challenges the division of humanity into racial strata as an act of God, and therefore the natural order of the world, the 'Law of Nations.'

Burns knew his Bible, so the choice of these three texts is not at all accidental. While, at face value, each is concerned with the vengeance of the righteous, Burns here also defends the concept of a common humanity, the right to love across socially imposed barriers and the agency of women. The Auld Licht Preacher has chosen his texts, but Burns draws a different message from them, upending the sermon and so echoing another Biblical passage: 'Your own mouth condemns you, and not I; Yes, your own lips testify against you.' (Job, xv, 6). This is sufficient to be deemed 'positive', particularly in the pre-1788 period, even allowing for the early print use of a variant of the N-word, which at that point would have been deemed 'vulgar' or 'slang' rather than a 'hate' word.

No 4: [1786] [K.99] 'Extempore — to Mr Gavin Hamilton.'
Burns's first mention of his emigration plans in verse occurs in a tangential reference in this poem on 'naething' which shows that he had discussed the plan with his mentor and landlord, Gavin Hamilton, probably in February or March 1786.

And now I must mount on the wave,   45

My voyage perhaps there is death in;
But what of a watery grave!
The drowning a Poet is naething — [38]

ANALYSIS

In the poems and songs Burns wrote between accepting Dr Douglas's job offer and his (postponed then ultimately abandoned) embarkation there are nine 'farewell' poems showing the poet's state of mind over those complex months in his life. None of them mentions, let alone makes any apology for, his chosen future as a plantation enforcer (even cloaked in the euphemistic title of 'book-keeper').

This verse, unpublished in the poet's lifetime, is unusually pessimistic when it reflects on his probable emigration, as he foresees his death on the Atlantic passage. Given Burns's existing health problems (particularly considering his mental and physical breakdown in Irvine in 1781) it is not an entirely unreasonable fear that he may not even have made landfall in Jamaica. The Scottish Abolitionist and former slave surgeon Revd James Ramsay (1733–1789) estimated that the average White mortality risk on a conventional transatlantic crossing was in the order of 5 per cent.[39] More modern research on datasets of transporting British convicts from England to the American colonies between 1768 and 1775, or general German immigration into Philadelphia between 1727 and 1805 show average death rates on board at 2.5 and 3.4 per cent respectively.[40] It would be safe to assume that the generic risk for a traveller in 1786 was in that 3 per cent plus-or-minus range. In Burns's specific case, he had underlying health issues, but at that age they were not so severe that he could not work the plough, so a modest premium would be warranted, taking his risk of death, say, to 5 per cent: so of, say, 20 passengers, one dies *en route*.

In other circumstances the mortality rate could be much higher: transport statistics for the period of the American War of Independence

---

38 Also Second Commonplace Book, p.31 at *Oxford Burns*, vol.1, p.100, *Glenriddell Ms*, vol.1, p.112, at *Oxford Burns*, vol.1, p.223.
39 James Ramsay, Essay on the Treatment and Conversion of African Slaves in the British Sugar Colonies (London: James Phillips, 1784), p.79.
40 Herbert S Klein, Stanley L Engerman, Robin Haines and Ralph Shlomowitz, 'Transoceanic Mortality: The Slave Trade in Comparative Perspective,' *William & Mary Quarterly* (January 2001), pp. 93–118.

show that some 11 per cent of soldiers died on the troop ships carrying them to the conflict.⁴¹ Even this does not come close to the mortality rates of the enslaved people being trafficked at that period. There are different ways of calculating how many deaths occurred, but a good benchmark comes from statistics quoted by William Wilberforce in the early days of his campaign. His estimate was that 12.5 per cent of the enslaved being trafficked died at sea in the foul and cramped conditions of the Middle Passage, with a further 4.5 per cent of them dying in port at Jamaica, meaning that, on average, 17 per cent failed to reach the 'Slave Market.' Then, within the following year, up to one third succumbed to Yellow Fever or Malaria.⁴²

These bald statistics rather put Burns's self-pity to shame, as those being trafficked endured five or more times the risk of death compared to a commercial White passenger.

EVALUATION: NEUTRAL
While fearing the personal risks to the poet, nothing in these verses recognises that the Black enslaved people faced those risks involuntarily, with over 15 per cent of those transported in the 'Middle Passage' ending their lives 'beneath th' Atlantic roar.' However, this is a tangential reference, from which it would be wrong to draw too much inference.

No 5: [1786] [K.100] 'On a Scotch Bard, Gone to the West Indies.'
Burns wrote to several friends between April and October 1786 about his proposed emigration. Most of the letters and verses were gloomy and resigned in tone, but here he adopts an attitude of considerable (perhaps over-compensating) bravado:

---

41 Burnard, 'Countrie Continues Sicklie,' p.54.
42 William Wilberforce, Speech 12 May 1789, in *Cobbett's Parliamentary History of England*, Volume XXVIII, [1789–1791] (London: Longman, Hurst, Rees, Orme & Brown [and others], 1816), at column 47. There were various other calculations (Ramsay and Thomas Cooper of note) which had varying percentages ascribed to the various stages of enslavement/trafficking, but all in the range of the death of half the population corralled at the 'Slave Factories' of Africa. Taking that analysis one step backwards, a later leading Abolitionist, Thomas Fowell Buxton (1786–1845), estimated that the 'Slave Factories' received only half the persons captured by enslavers and marched to captivity, the other half dying of wounds, disease, malnutrition or exhaustion. Thomas Fowell Buxton, *The African Slave Trade and its Remedy* (London: John Murray, 1840), p.196.

A' YE wha live by sowps o' drink,
A' ye wha live by crambo-clink,
A' ye wha live and never think,
   Come, mourn wi' me!
Our *billie's* gien us a' a jink, 5
   An' owre the Sea!

Lament him a' ye rantan core,
Wha dearly like a random-splore;
Nae mair he'll join the *merry roar,*
   In social key; 10
For now he's taen anither shore,
   An' owre the Sea!

The bonie lasses weel may wiss him,
And in their dear *petitions* place him:
The widows, wives, an' a' may bless him, 15
   Wi' tearfu' e'e;
For weel I wat they'll sairly miss him
   That's owre the Sea!

O Fortune, they hae room to grumble!
Hadst thou taen aff some drowsy bummle, 20
Wha can do nought but fyke an' fumble,
   'Twad been nae plea;
But he was gleg as onie wumble,
   That's owre the Sea!

Auld, cantie KYLE may weepers wear, 25
An' stain them wi' the saut, saut tear:
'Twill mak her poor, auld heart, I fear,
   In flinders flee:
He was her *Laureat* mony a year,
   That's owre the Sea! 30

He saw Misfortune's cauld *Nor-west*
Lang-mustering up a bitter blast;
A Jillet brak his heart at last,

> Ill may she be!
> So, took a birth afore the mast,　　　　　　　　　　35
> 　　An' owre the Sea.
>
> To tremble under Fortune's cummock,
> On a scarce a bellyfu' o' *drummock*,
> Wi' his proud, independent stomach,
> 　　Could ill agree;　　　　　　　　　　　　　　40
> So, row't his hurdies in a *hammock*,
> 　　An' owre the Sea.
>
> He ne'er was gien to great misguidin,
> Yet coin his pouches wad na bide in;
> Wi' him it ne'er was under *hidin*;　　　　　　　45
> 　　He dealt it free:
> The *Muse* was a' that he took pride in,
> 　　That's owre the Sea.
>
> *Jamaica bodies*, use him weel,
> An' hap him in cozie biel:　　　　　　　　　　　50
> Ye'll find him ay a dainty chiel,
> 　　An' fou o' glee:
> He wad na wrang'd the vera *Deil*,
> 　　That's owre the Sea.
>
> Farewell, my *rhyme-composing billie*!　　　　　55
> Your native soil was right ill-willie;
> But may ye flourish like a lily,
> 　　Now bonilie!
> I'll toast you in my hindmost *gillie*,
> 　　Tho' owre the Sea!　　　　　　　　　　　　60

ANALYSIS

Kinsley's assessment is apposite: Burns 'was capable of representing his misfortunes as tragic or comic, as occasions for despondency or for a display of swaggering courage.'[43] This poem is certainly in the

---
43 *Poems*, vol.III, p.1176.

latter camp, with much Burnsian verve, as one of his 'Farewells' to Scotland, to his friends and (hopefully) to his travails.

The first observation is that there is no mention of the type of work – or society – that he is going to. His Ayrshire friends well knew (as did Burns, at least in broad detail, from reading the two *Geographical Grammars*) that Jamaica was worked by a huge number of Black men, women and children 'overseen' by young White men who were very often Scots: Iain Whyte records a remark by Samuel Taylor Coleridge 'that three out of four overseers in the West Indies were Scots.'[44] The importance of those Scottish sojourners in the Caribbean cannot be underestimated. Burns had worked out that a jolly, self-deprecating 'Standard Habbie' in Scots would find a receptive audience in Jamaica, without a doubt, from that fraternal group of 'Jamaica bodies' exhorted in the penultimate stanza. Albeit they operated more as a clan than an associative body, as Hamilton says, '[i]t is also striking that there were no Scottish societies in the [Caribbean] islands, despite their proliferation on the [North American] mainland.'[45] Jamaican society was fast-and loose, 'boorish' as Zachary Macaulay coloured it, and so the civility of associationalism was not particularly valued. AM Kinghorn, probably correctly, suggests that Burns would have found this society less 'cosie' than imagined, and therefore hard to adapt to:

> Rigid class-distinctions such as he would never have encountered in Scotland and a purblind philistinism were features of the Jamaica landscape which a man having Burns's ideals could never have endured, even for a short time.[46]

The second thought is that the poem is all about Burns, and while we do sympathise with his lot, the Black enslaved gang workers under his oversight will do more than 'tremble under Fortune's cummock'

---

44 Whyte, *Scotland and the Abolition*, p.49. In popular culture, too, there are dissonant echoes of old Scotland resonant in the representation of enslavement: the harrowing film *Twelve Years a Slave* (2013, director Steve McQueen) opens with its hero, Solomon Northup, freely and cheerfully fiddling away to the Scottish tune 'Diel Amang the Tailors' and it finds one of its deepest abysses when, as an enslaved man, Solomon returns to his plantation to be welcomed by his vicious and near-deranged master with the greeting 'for auld lang syne.'
45 Hamilton, p.49.
46 Kinghorn, p.79.

(or 'cromack', not Harry Lauder's kitsch walking-stick, but a heavy, knobbly club to deliver beatings). The enslaved labourers whom Burns would have managed faced much worse in what the Abolitionist Revd James Ramsay called '[t]he ordinary punishments of slaves, [...] cart whipping, beating with a stick, sometimes to the breaking of bones, [...] [which] shortens the life of many a poor wretch' who could not expect to be 'well or plentifully fed.'[47]

Their diet was much less than his 'scarce a bellyfu' o' drummock' (which was oatmeal mixed with cold water). The enslaved person's diet in Jamaica consisted of a daily ration of around one pint of corn or grain (568 g) and around some small portion of protein (45 g), being typically the offal of pigs or salted fish, both often rancid and close to inedible. Additionally, time was given on Sundays for the cultivation of foodstuffs in 'slave gardens'. These food supplies could be interrupted either by hurricanes or other bad weather, while imports were at risk of embargoes such as during the American War of Independence. Any diminution in supply would result in greater hardship and higher mortality amongst the enslaved population.

The data on the calorific consumption of the enslaved workers in Jamaica is patchy, however it is estimated that the average enslaved man would have a daily ration equivalent to 1,500 to 2,000 calories, with women receiving less (and little of the small ration of protein). With a broad-brush estimate of typical working days being eight hours of hard labour in the Winter, an enslaved man would expend some 2,500 calories daily, and with 12 even harder hours in the Summer, around 3,650. For female outdoor workers, the numbers would be in the order of 2,300 and 2,750. (Of course, the diet of the enslaved population was also imbalanced in terms of vitamins and minerals, which compounded their health issues.)[48] It is no surprise, therefore

---

47 Ramsay, pp.85–86. The apogee of cruelty in Jamaica is generally considered to be Thomas Thistlewood (1721–1786) who catalogued his diurnal tortures and rapes in his diary. Beinecke Rare Book & Manuscript Library, Yale Library General Collection of Rare Books and Manuscripts, Thomas Thistlewood Papers, OSB MSS 176, Series I. Diaries. *Diaries of Thomas Thistlewood*. Long deprecates the prevalence of venereal diseases throughout the colonists, but remarks: 'It is probable, that, the, Scotch and Irish, who come over, with sounder constitutions, less impaired perhaps by scorbutic and venereal taints are, for this reason, more healthy than the English. Besides, the Scotch, in particular, if not more chaste, are at least in, general more circumspect in their amours.' *Long*, vol.II, p.536, a comment which seems over-generous.

48 Robert Dirks, 'Resource Fluctuations and Competitive Transformation in West Indian Slave Societies', in *Extinction and Survival in Human Populations*, ed by Charles D Laughlin and Ivan A Brady (New York: 1978), p.146.

(even if the exact numbers are uncertain), that '[a]t the middle of the eighteenth century the symptoms of chronic malnourishment showed through almost every aspect of estate life.'[49] The results were seen in excess mortality (both in adults and infants) and a steep decline in female fertility, resulting in a cycle of additional inbound enslaved people being trafficked to keep the enslaved population at a constant.

True, Burns's life was uncertain as it was well known that more young Scotsmen died of tropical disease than returned home with a fortune (and possibly he was scared of the sea voyage, too), but the lot of the enslaved had an unforgiving certainty, absent (even by inference) throughout the poem, of hard life, perpetual terror and, ultimately, an inexorable early death.[50] As Leask trenchantly puts it, 'we look in vain for any glimmer of ethical doubt concerning slavery in Burns's valedictory poem.'[51]

Finally, while Burns maintains that he will be found to be a 'dainty chiel' who 'wad na wrang'd the vera deil/ That's ore the sea,' he will daily 'wrang' the poor Black enslaved people enclosed in their own Hell on earth. As Burnard describes it, 'the plantation system of the eighteenth-century British Caribbean was brutal even for an age very used to brutality.'[52] Commentators, in his defence, posit that the sheer cruelty of the punishments inflicted on enslaved people was hardly widely known at that date, but it is mentioned in books read by Burns. Salmond's *Geographical Grammar* was most outspoken on the 'torture' faced by enslaved men and women, who

> were almost whipped to Death without any Trial, by the arbitrary Commands of a private Planter, for the smallest offences; and for greater Crimes were fastened to the ground and burnt by inches, till they expired in Torment.[53]

---

49 JR Ward, *British West Indian Slavery, 1750–1834* (Oxford/New York: Clarendon Press, 1988), p.105. This is also evidenced in the severity of punishments meted out to enslaved workers caught eating the sugar cane.

50 In her biography of Burns, Catherine Carswell asserts 'The inhuman expanse of the sea rather saddened and repelled [the young Burns].' There is no primary source to vouch this statement, which has been copied into other biographies. Perhaps it is drawing an inference from 'The Gloomy Night is Gath'ring Fast,' [K.122], see below, p.145. Catherine Carswell, *The Life of Robert Burns* (Glasgow: William Collins, 1930), p.44.

51 Leask, *Poetics*, p.51.

52 Burnard, 'Plantation Slavery', p.396.

53 Salmon, p.591.

If Burns had believed this to be an English problem and not an accusation against the Scots, his fellow-countryman William Guthrie's *Geographical Grammar* laid a broader condemnation of the life of the enslaved of Jamaica 'who must be ruled with a rod of iron; but they ought not to be crushed with it.'[54] Guthrie does go on to tell of 'many' of enslaved people who

> fall into the hands of gentlemen of humanity, find their situations easy and comfortable; and it has been observed, [...] that those nations which have behaved with the greatest humanity to their slaves, were always well served, and run the least hazard from their rebellions.[242]

Could Burns have latched onto that caveat seeing himself as an example of a 'gentleman of humanity'? Did he imagine that he could have touched the pitch and not be defiled? It is hard to believe that, as Charles Douglas's letters clearly flagged that the role would be for 'an active young lad to look after my Cattle & Negroes with a Dog or a Bitch,' so Burns cannot be said to have been entirely in the dark as to the scope of his duties. This leads Robert Crawford to the opinion that:

> His knowledge of the West Indies was not extensive, but he knew about the slave trade. His readiness to become involved in slave management may have been a sign of desperation; it is still shocking, and contradicts the ideology implicit and explicit in much of his poetry. That Scotland's bard should have been so ready to become part of the system of slavery is one of the most striking indications of how complicit Scotland was in the slave trade.[55]

EVALUATION: VERY NEGATIVE

The jollity of the poem is chilling; when seen in the context of his leaving Scotland to become a slave-driver is at least thoughtless, and likely careless. While accepting that there was little to no debate in Ayrshire around the situation of the enslaved and their treatment (particularly in terms of inhuman punishment), Burns was an intelligent

---

54 Guthrie [1772], p.658.
55 Crawford, *The Bard*, p.223.

man and, through his reading of Guthrie and Salmon and from the detail of Charles Douglas's job description, he must have been well aware of what he was getting himself into, yet he can write a cheeky, cheerful 'adieu'.

No 6. [1786] [K.106] '[Lines Written on a Bank-note.]'
Contemplating all his woes: his precarious finances, his complex love-life and the formulation of his plan to emigrate, Burns wrote this verse on the obverse of a Bank of Scotland One Guinea note:

> WAE worth thy pow'r, thou cursed leaf!
> Fell source of all my woe and grief!
> For lake o' thee I've lost my lass!
> For lake o' thee I scrimp my glass!
> I see the children of Affliction 5
> Unaided, thro' thy curst restriction;
> I've seen th' Oppressor's cruel smile
> Amid his hapless victim's spoil;
> And for thy potence vainly wish'd,
> To crush the Villain in the dust: 10
> For lake o' thee, I leave this much-lov'd shore,
> Never perhaps to greet old Scotland more!
>   R B — Kyle.

ANALYSIS
In this poem, Burns is focused on his significant financial problems, maybe wondering how he could raise the nine guineas of passage-money to reach Jamaica, or whether he would have to voluntarily indenture himself to work for virtually an entire year to repay the debt to his employer for financing his ticket.

That being said, if Burns had thought he had seen 'children of Affliction,' 'Oppressor[s'] cruel smile[s]' and 'hapless victim[s]' in Kyle, what did he expect on the far side of the Atlantic? While in 1786 the brutality of the slave plantation economy was hardly bruited in British conversation or debate, as discussed in the last poem's analysis, Burns had read about the harsh realities of plantation life in Guthrie and in Salmon, yet he seems to ignore that inhumanity in this and his other 'farewell' poems.

EVALUATION: NEGATIVE

Although this verse is a slight, occasional work, and while the theme of oppressive poverty is common in Burns, the implication that he is leaving 'Oppression' and 'Affliction' behind in Scotland, incredibly suggests that he will find none of this in Jamaica, despite having read of the 'greatest Barbarity' he would be expected to inflict upon his own 'hapless victims' on the Douglas plantation.

No 7: [1786] [K.121] 'Wrote on the Blank Leaf of a Copy of My First Edition, Which I sent to an Old Sweetheart, then Married.'
Peggy Thompson or Neilson (?–1830) was the 'charming Fillette' who distracted Burns from his studies at Kirkoswald in 1775. When taking leave of his mother's relations *en route* for Jamaica he visited his 'old sweetheart' and her husband, leaving her with the gift of an inscribed *Kilmarnock Edition*.

> ONCE fondly lov'd, and still remember'd dear,
>   Sweet early Object of my youthful vows!
> Accept this mark of friendship, warm, sincere,
>   Friendship — 'tis all cold duty now allows.
> And while you read the simple, artless rhymes,
>   One friendly sigh for him — he asks no more,
> Who, distant, burns in flaming torrid climes,
>   Or haply lies beneath th' Atlantic roar.[56]

ANALYSIS
Leaving aside the wistful, 'it might have been' undertone, in this farewell poem Burns positions himself to his old flame as the focus of the tragedy unfolding (at least in his own mind), meeting death either by drowning or from overwork in the heat of the tropical sun. Once again, nothing in these verses recognises that the Black enslaved faced those risks involuntarily and, if they were to survive the inhumanity of the 'middle passage', all but a handful would be guaranteed to

---

56 *Oxford Burns*, vol.I, p.205, version in GRM1, pp.63–64 (with minor orthographic differences, and the following footnote: 'Poor Peggy! Her husband is an old acquaintance & a most worthy fellow. — When I was taking leave of my Carrick relations intending to go to the West Indies, when I took farewell of her, neither she nor I could speak a syllable. Her husband escorted me three miles on my road, and we both parted with tears. —')

die, enslaved, in those 'flaming torrid climes.'⁵⁷ Those people do not get the sympathy Burns seeks from his friends on his own account.

EVALUATION: NEGATIVE
A brief, occasional piece formulaically suggesting that the pain of her loss will be greater than the sorrows he faces. It has an inconsequential feel which almost makes it a 'neutral' rather than 'negative.'

No 8: [1786] [K.122] Song. [The Gloomy Night is gath'ring Fast]/ ['The Farewell'], Tune: 'Roslin Castle'.⁵⁸

With his Jamaica assignment agreed, and while preparing his departure, Burns wrote that 'I composed this song as I conveyed my chest so far on my road to Greenock, where I was to embark in a few days for Jamaica. I meant it as my farewel[l] Dirge to my native land.'⁵⁹

I.

The gloomy night is gath'ring fast,
Loud roars the wild, inconstant blast,
Yon murky cloud is foul with rain,
I see it driving o'er the plain;
The Hunter now has left the moor,   5
The scatt'red coveys meet secure,
While here I wander, prest with care,
Along the lonely banks of *Ayr*.

II.

The Autumn mourns her rip'ning corn
By early Winter's ravage torn;   10
Across her placid, azure sky,
She sees the scowling tempest fly:
Chill runs my blood to hear it rave,
I think upon the stormy wave,
Where many a danger I must dare,   15
Far from the bonie banks of *Ayr*.

---

57 Whyte, Scotland and the Abolition, pp.8–9.
58 *Oxford* Burns, 'The Bonie Banks of Ayr,' III.284, vol.ii, p.354; vol.III, p.92: 'The Gloomy Night is Gathering Fast' 'Air — Farewell to Ayr.', ST58 (T85), pp.106–107 and pp.437–440.
59 Cromek, *Reliques*, p.279. ('The Bonie Banks o' Ayr) expanding with Cromekian licence, a line from the *ABL*.

III.

'Tis not the surging billow's roar,
'Tis not that fatal, deadly shore;
Tho' Death in ev'ry shape appear,
The Wretched have no more to fear: 20
But round my heart the ties are bound,
That heart transpierc'd with many a wound;
These bleed afresh, those ties I tear,
To leave the bonie banks of *Ayr*.

IV.

Farewell, old *Coila's* hills and dales,   25
Her heathy moors and winding vales;
The scenes where wretched Fancy roves,
Pursuing past, unhappy loves!
Farewell, my friends! farewell, my foes!
My peace with these, my love with those —   30
The bursting tears my heart declare,
Farewell, the bonie banks of *Ayr!*

ANALYSIS

Here, stanza III stands out as particularly self-centred. Pittock suggests that comparing the earlier *Stair Ms* version's lines 13–4 show a variant reading:

[*Stair*: 1786]	[*First Edinburgh*: 1787]
The whistling storm affrightens me;	Chill runs my blood to hear it rave,
I think upon the raging sea,	I think upon the stormy wave,

Which he posits as a 'distancing' in the *First Edinburgh Edition*, 'perhaps reflecting the receding possibility of exile to Jamaica'. It is interesting, though, that this is one of the few emendations for the 1787 printing, which would be published after Dr Douglas let him go following the third missed berth.

It is noteworthy that the 'realistic' biography of Burns by Catherine Carswell in 1930 (which alone mentions a putative dread of the sea) sympathises most with Burns's self-pity in the farewell poems, as can be seen in this passage (with its unbelievable final sentence):

But he was beset with nightmares. He had accepted the Jamaica offer, but the post — bookkeeper on a plantation at £30 a year for three years — was neither well-paid nor congenial. It was a terrifying prospect, alleviated only by the fact that his master would be an Ayrshire man. There was the question too of passage money. To travel to Port Antonio at his master's charges on terms of indenture meant working for a year and more after his arrival without pay **and in conditions far worse for the unacclimatised white overseer than for the negro slaves he must drive.**[60]   [*emphasis added*]

Yes, transatlantic travel was not without its discomforts and risks for Scots passengers, but bore no equivalency to the horrors of the 'Middle Passage' (even if, *pace* Carswell, Burns did have some fear of sailing). To appreciate this contrast, read this poem first, followed by 'The Slave's Lament.'[61]

EVALUATION: NEGATIVE
These farewell verses are characterised by a heightened level of self-pity, and its content gets no closer to Jamaica than being on the stormy seas *en route* to the island. Burns shows no concern about the nature of his work on his arrival, and, while he shows no enthusiasm either, his failure to imagine the significantly greater horror of the 'Middle Passage' faced by the enslaved tips this poem into 'negative' territory. It seems amazing that, less than a century ago, Carswell (a noted modernist, socialist and feminist) shared Burns's belief that he, not the enslaved, was the victim here.

---

60 Carswell, p.161.
61 The similarities between the two are shown in Table 6 below.

No 9 and No 10:[1786/1792] [K.387] 'Will Ye Go to the Indies, My Mary?' Tune: 'Will Ye go to the Ewe-Bughts, Marion'[62] and [1786] [K.107] 'Highland Lassie, O —' To its own tune — 'McLauchlin's Scots Measure.'[63]

K.387

1
WILL ye go to the Indies, my Mary,
And leave auld Scotia's shore;
Will ye go to the Indies, my Mary,
Across th' Atlantic roar?

2
O sweet grows the lime and the orange   5
And the apple on the pine;
But a' the charms o' the Indies
Can never equal thine.

3
I hae sworn by the Heavens to my Mary,
I hae sworn by the Heavens to be true;   10
And sae may the Heavens forget me,
When I forget my vow!

4
O plight me your faith, my Mary,
And plight me your lily-white hand;
O plight me your faith, my Mary,   15
Before I leave Scotia's strand.

5
We hae plighted our truth, my Mary,
In mutual affection to join:
And curst be the cause that shall part us,
The hour, and the moment o' time!!!   20

K.107

NAE gentle dames tho' ne'er sae fair
Shall ever be my Muse's care;
Their titles a' are empty show,
Gie me my Highland Lassie, O. —
[...]

But fickle Fortune frowns on me,
And I maun cross the raging sea;
But while my crimson currents flow,   15
I love my Highland Lassie, O. —
    Within the glen &c.

Altho' thro' foreign climes I range,
I know her heart will never change;
For her bosom burns with honor's glow,
My faithful Highland Lassie, O —   20
    Within the glen &c.

For her I'll dare the billow's roar;
For her I'll trace a distant shore;
That Indian wealth may lustre throw
Around my Highland Lassie, O. —
    Within the glen &c.

She has my heart, she has my hand,   25
By secret Truth and Honor's band:
Till the mortal stroke shall lay me low,
I'm thine, my Highland Lassie, O. —

Farewel, the glen sae bushy! O
    Farewel, the plain sae rashy! O   30
To other lands I now must go
To sing my Highland Lassie, O. —

In the midst of his disputed marriage to Jean Armour, his plans to publish his poems by subscription and arranging his leaving for Jamaica, Burns famously became involved with Mary Campbell, the 'Highland Mary' of far too much embroidered Burns legend. He wrote two songs

---

62 *Oxford Burns*, ST127 (T8), vol.IV, p.228 and pp.562–564.
63 *Second Commonplace Book*, p.34, in *Oxford Burns* vol.I, pp.101–102 and p.336; SMM II.117 'The Highland Lassie O,' in *Oxford Burns* vol.II, p.173, vol.III, pp.36–37; ST18 (T37), 'Nae Gentle Dames, Tho' E'er So Fair, Air — The Deuks Dang O'er My Daddy,' *Oxford Burns* vol.IV, pp.34–35, pp.374–375.

about her in this period ('To Mary in Heaven' [K.274] is a later work, and outside the scope of this study) which are interesting as they show two opposite scenarios. As he described 'Will Ye Go' to his publisher, Thomson, 'In my very early years, when I was thinking of going to the West Indies, I took the following farewell of a dear girl [...]'

ANALYSIS
Here is another pair of farewell songs. If 'On a Scotch Bard' cried *'vale'* in jollity, then this pair cries its goodbyes in one of his most memorable love songs ('Will Ye go to the Indies, my Mary?'), an opinion not initially shared by George Thomson who called it 'a very poor song,' but who would eventually publish it and its companion, the simpler 'Highland Lassie, O'.[64]

'Will Ye Go' has spawned a myriad myths of Burns intending to take Mary with him to Jamaica. As has been said, it would have been unheard of for a man in a subordinate position such as his, is unmentioned by the Douglas brothers in discussing the job and is contradicted in 'Highland Lassie, O' where the pair are clearly sundered by the Atlantic. It is the latter song which reflects the reality of Burns's situation, as the Douglases were hiring a single man, not a married couple. In fact, Hamilton, in his study of 'the scarcity of White women in the Caribbean,' makes it plain that even landowners rarely had a spouse living with them on the island.[65] The marital history of Agnes Craig or McLehose ('Clarinda') gives support to this argument that wives were not welcome on the plantations.[66] This is a topic on which Revd James Ramsey felt strongly:

> Though married managers [...] have numberless other advantages over single men, in point of character, faithfulness, and application; yet planters have determined it to be better to employ perhaps a dissipated, careless, unfeeling young man, or a grovelling, lascivious, old batchelor [sic] (each with his half score of black or mulattoe [sic] pilfering harlots [...]) rather than allow a married woman to be entertained on the plantation.[67]

---

64 *Poems*, vol.III, p.1409.
65 Hamilton, p.43.
66 WC McLehose, ed, *The Correspondence Between Burns and Clarinda* (Edinburgh: William Tait, 1843), pp.37–42. ['*Clarinda's Letters.*']
67 *Ramsay*, pp.83–84 (specifically on St Kitts, but applicable to the wider West Indies).

Again, we hear Burns look forward to 'the charms o' the Indies' and its 'wealth' (supposing he can survive 'th' Atlantic's roar'/'the raging sea' and the island miasmata). Again, this is mentioned without the least acknowledgement of the dark truth of the underpinning of chattel slavery that awaits him as an actor. An argument could be made that it would have been wrong to frighten Mary (staying at home to wait for his return) with either a true assessment of the job, or of the high risk of his never returning, and while that is rather paternalistic, it may have some traction.

EVALUATIONS: NEGATIVE
Both songs totally ignore the slavery question. In the romanticised 'Will Ye Go,' Burns could be inviting his paramour to join him on a pleasure cruise, while in the more realistic 'Highland Lassie' she sits and waits patiently while he amasses his fortune (by unnarrated means), allowing his return which will change their joint lives into a simulacrum of 'John and Jean Anderson,' living out a happy retirement on his pot of 'Jamaica siller.' Both of these fantasies disregard the immoral squalor of the job.

No 11: [K.115] [1786] 'The Farewell, To the Brethren of St James's Lodge, Tarbolton.'[68]

Freemasonry was, and would remain, an important part of Burns's life. Here is another farewell piece, this time to mark the breaking of the pattern of Burns's attendance at the meetings of his 'mother lodge.'

> ADIEU! a heart-warm, fond adieu!
>   Dear brothers of the *mystic tye*!
> Ye favour'd, ye enlighten'd Few,
>   Companions of my social joy!
> Tho' I to foreign lands must hie,   5
>   Pursuing Fortune's slidd'ry ba',

---

[68] *SMM* VI,600, 'Good Night, and Joy be wi' You All,' *Oxford Burns*, vol.II, p.700 [with an opening traditional verse], 'Burns's Farewell to the Brethren of St James's Lodge, Tarbolton; At the Time when He had Resolved on Going to the West Indies. The Same Air [Good Night and Joy be with You All']', ST137 (T200), p.284 and pp.595–597. The tune is important, as (before 'Auld Lang Syne,' [K.240]) this was the traditional parting song sung at the end of convivial occasions and anniversaries, see McGinn, *Comprehensive*, p.342.

> With melting heart, and brimful eye,
>   I'll mind you still, tho' far awa'.
> [...]
>
> A last request, permit me here,
>   When yearly ye assemble a',   30
> One *round,* I ask it with a tear,
>   To him, *the Bard, that's far awa'.*

ANALYSIS

The sentiments of this song are delivered generically, his leaving for unspecified 'foreign lands' to '[p]ursu[e]', in an excellent metaphor, 'Fortune's slidd'ry ba.' No doubt other Masons had made similar choices in the past and would do so again. Burns is keen to be remembered, not just in the generic toast to the cadre of absent brothers, but specifically in a 'round' or toast to himself. This has an interesting masonic connotation: the final toast at any lodge dinner was, and is, 'The Tyler's Toast:'

> To all poor and distressed Masons, wherever dispersed over the face of Earth and Water, wishing them a speedy relief from all their sufferings, and a safe return to their native country; should they so desire it.[69]

In asking for his own toast, Burns is distancing himself from his 'poor, distressed' and 'dispersed' brethren, maintaining his independence, just like former masters of the Lodge, John Hamilton of Sundrum and Mungo Smith, who had returned with western and eastern fortunes respectively.

In the context of this work, does Burns's affiliation to, and respect for, the tenets of Freemasonry add any evidence to his views on slavery?[70] The question of racism within the Craft is a complex one (and merits different analyses in terms of the differing Grand Lodges or traditions in each of Scotland, England and Ireland, let alone the very different traditions of non-Anglophone masons). Given the tiny scale

---

69 George Draffen of Newington, 'Masonic Etiquette and Scottish Usage,' *Grand Lodge of Scotland Year Book 1966.*
70 David Stevenson, *The Origins of Freemasonry: Scotland's Century 1590–1710* (Cambridge: Cambridge University Press, 1988) and *The First Freemasons: Scotland's Early Lodges and their Members* (Aberdeen: Aberdeen University Press, 1988).

of the Black population of Scotland in Burns's masonic lifetime and the patterns of lodge membership (moving from a generally 'operative' body of working stonemasons to a primarily 'speculative' one) there are neither contemporary records of any Black journeymen or master stonemasons (though there are cases of carpenters, a trade sometime included within the wider ambit of 'squaremen'), nor is there any mention of Black geometrical, or speculative, freemasons at that time in Scotland. However, that is not to say that there were no Black Masons. In New England, a minister and free Black man, Prince Hall (1735[?]–1807), and several Black friends, after being rejected by the local lodge (Boston St John's, an English charter), were 'made' in 1775 by one of the British Boston garrison's Military Lodges (under the Irish constitution) and, some time after the regiment's return to England, Hall and his fellows successfully petitioned the United Grand Lodge of England for a charter to set up their own lodge in 1784, with an 'AFRICAN' provincial grand lodge being created in 1791.[71] Similarly, French Freemasonry was active in Saint-Domingue and the Haitian Republic and was inclusive with Touissant L'Ouverture (1743–1803) and several of his generals being brethren.[72]

The fundamental principles of the Craft assume the equality and fraternity of man, however, the eligibility of a candidate to become an 'Entered Apprentice' was traditionally expressed that:

> he which shall be made a Masson [sic] be able in all manner of degrees: that is to say, free-born, come of good kindred, true, and no bond man. And also, that he have his right limbs, as a man ought to have.[73]

Could this concept of 'free-born' (which Burns would have heard in the ritual of the Lodge) have influenced the poet's views on Black enslaved people? Dr Douglas, the plantation owner, was past-master of Ayr Kilwinning Lodge, so he had no qualms and was certainly not the

---

71 Peter P Hinks, Stephen David Kantrowitz, eds, *All Men Free and Brethren: Essays on the History of African American Freemasonry* (Ithaca, NY: Cornell University Press, 2013).
72 Cécile Révanger, 'Freemasonry and Blacks,' in *Handbook of Freemasonry*, ed by Henrik Bogdan and JAM Snoek (Netherlands: Brill, 2014), pp.422–438.
73 'The Kilwinning "Auld Charges"' as inscribed in the minute book of Lodge Atcheson in 1666, quoted in David Murray Lyon, *History of the Lodge of Edinburgh (Mary's Chapel) No 1* (Edinburgh: William Blackwood and Sons, 1873), p.115.

only slave-holder to be a practicing Freemason – think also of Smith of Drongan and Hamilton of Sundrum, as masters of Tarbolton.[74] Racism within the history of Freemasonry requires analysis at the philosophical and the practical level. The philosophical principle is that any man beyond the legal age of maturity who believes in a 'Supreme Deity' is eligible as a candidate for apprenticeship. That 'Supreme Deity' need not be the Christian God, and there are many records of men of the Jewish and Muslim faiths being 'entered, passed and raised.'[75] The practical element, however, is that all of the existing members of the Lodge had to vote affirmatively to accept that candidate. With a secret ballot, and no requirement for explanation, individual Masons with racist inclinations could easily keep the lodge 'White' without having to make an overtly racist statement in public.

Had Burns arrived in Jamaica in late 1786, amongst the 'Jamaica bodies' he would have found a cadre of fellow Masons to welcome him fraternally (remembering that there would have been virtually no Lodge member not active in the slave economy). The first masonic lodge on the island was founded in 1739 under the English constitution, with 'Scotch Lodge St Andrew's, No 102' following in 1757 under warrant from the Grand Lodge of Scotland, which august body went on to establish the Provincial Grand Lodge of Jamaica at Kingston (which largely overlapped with the officers of St Andrew's). Burns would have been welcomed to meetings of St Andrew's Lodge if he could travel to Port Morant and may well have anticipated singing this song (or an updated version) at the Lodge Harmony. At that date, the Provincial Grand Master was Brother Alexander Edgar (?–1794/5), who owned the coffee plantation of Gloster Mount and who was succeeded in 1788 by Revd Middletown Howard (?–1791), the Anglican rector of St Thomas's, when the Right Worshipful Master of No 102 was William Smellie, owner of Hatfield (or 'Platfield') Plantation.[76] While enthusiasm for the Craft was evident, 'the organization was hampered by high rates of mortality, causing leadership crises and the collapse of most lodges.'[265] Firstly the Irish lodges failed, then in 1788 the Scots fell dark: the addition of other home nation brethren to the remaining English lodges allowed many of them

---

74 McGinn, *Comprehensive*, p.391.
75 Murray Lyon, p.261.
76 FW Seal-Coon, *An Historical Account of Jamaican Freemasonry* (Kingston: Goulding Print, 1976), p.48.

to continue until the reduction in the Royal Navy's Caribbean fleet and the British Army units stationed in Jamaica following Waterloo in 1815 caused most of the remaining lodges to close, though Royal Lodge, No 207, has met continuously from 1789 (under an English charter) until today: perhaps Burns might have been its Poet Laureate.[77]

EVALUATION: NEGATIVE
Consistent with the other 'farewell poems,' the route to Burns's 'fortune' in 'foreign lands' is glossed over (although many of the Ayrshire brethren were well aware of the implications). Burns was a true and faithful supporter of Masonry all his adult life (Ayrshire, as he would have seen it, being the cradle of Masonry) and he no doubt anticipated a suitable masonic welcome on his arrival, providing both a helpful network and convivial company. The paradox (which has only been addressed in the last decades) is that Masons like Dr Patrick Douglas – or Burns himself – could subscribe to a philosophy exemplified in the song 'A Man's a Man,' yet, at exactly the same time, profit from an economy build on enslaved labour.

No 12: [1786] [K.129] 'Epistle to Capt[ai]n Will[ia]m Logan at Park —'
William Logan of Park (?–1819) was a volunteer officer who had served in America and was a noted fiddler, freemason and wit (or at least a prolific punster). He lived in Ayr with his spinster sister and shared convivial evenings with the poet. Burns's epistle takes leave of his friends.

> My loss I mourn, but not repent it:
> I'll seek my pursie whare I tint it;
> Ance to the Indies I were wonted,
>   Some cantraip hour,   70
> By some sweet Elf I'll yet be dinted;
>   Then, VIVE L'AMOUR!

ANALYSIS
This cheerful, rhyming epistle to Captain Logan is another of the suite of farewells. While regretting Jean Armour's repudiation of their

---

[77] Samuel Biagetti, '"What Virtue Unites, Death Cannot Separate": The Trials of Early Freemasonry in Jamaica, 1739–1800,' *The Journal of Caribbean History*, 51.1 (2017), p.1.

marriage contract (referred to obliquely as '[m]y loss' at line 67), Burns cheerily forecasts that there will be other fish in the sea, or in this case, across 'the herring-pond.' As discussed above alongside 'Will Ye Go to the Indies, My Mary,' there were few White female inhabitants of Jamaica at that time, so in all likelihood any 'sweet Elf' who might 'dint' him would be an enslaved woman, with little to no choice in the matter.

> Inter-racial relationships, whether consensual or otherwise, took place throughout the islands. For planters, the possession of the enslaved implied ownership, not just of their labour, but of their bodies.[78]

The enslaved female population was prey to the sex-drive of their oppressors, with unnumbered women subjected to opportunistic rape. A generation earlier, Robert Cunningham Graham of Gartmore (1735–1797), a man whom Burns described as 'the noblest instance of great talents, great fortune and great worth that I ever saw in conjunction' had built not only a career and a fortune on Jamaican plantations, but offspring, too:

> I was not remarkable for that cold Virtue, Chastity, but indiscriminately found my sentiments agreeable to my desires and gave rather too great a latitude to a dissipated train of whoring, the consequence of which I now dayly [sic] see before me in a motely variegated race of different complexions.[79]

This was both socially acceptable and legally permissible, as Alex Renton starkly points out:

> It was not until 1826 that rape of an enslaved woman became a crime in Jamaica. At the same time sex with a girl under ten was, for the first time outlawed. Nonetheless it appears no white man was punished for rape in Jamaica during the entire slavery period.[80]

---

78 Hamilton, p.46.
79 *Letters*, to Peter Hill, 2 February 1790, [L387]; Letter, Cunningham Graham to Samuel Bean Esq, 24 March 1760, quoted in Cunningham Graham, *Doughty Deeds*, p.71.
80 Renton, p.152.

A smaller proportion of women formed some unofficial familial bond (or 'concubinage') with a White plantation man and, on occasion, these relationships appear to show vestiges of human kindness. In any case the 'mulatto' offspring conceived in any of the variant conjugations were the legal property of the plantation owner (not the father, and certainly not of the mother) and, while contemporary records show that a few of the men bought their concubine and children out of enslavement, most of them, through insufficient funds or even less inclination, abandoned the women and children to their fate on the plantation.[81]

One of the threads in Andrew O Lindsay's interesting counterfactual novel, *Illustrious Exile*, grapples with how Burns's love of the lassies would work in practice in Jamaica. However sensitively portrayed by Lindsay, Burns's plantation rencontres would be more like his affair with Meg Cameron or Jenny Clow, rather than his life with Jean Armour.[82]

EVALUATION: NEGATIVE
Although this epistle is much further-ranging, its brief mention of the possibility of love (or at least sex) on the other side of the ocean is boastful and dismissive, failing entirely to recognise the realities of sexual life ahead of him were he to fulfil his contract to the Douglases.

No 13: [1787] [L.125]: 'The Autobiographical Letter,' To Dr John Moore, London, 2 August 1787.[83]

The famous 'Autobiographical Letter' [the 'ABL'] of 1787 had Burns outline his life to Dr John Moore (1729–1802), an author and physician friend of Mrs Dunlop, whose successful novel *Zeluco* (1789), later presented a picture of a truly vicious man, and slave-holder, in line with its author's Abolitionist sympathies.[84] Dr James Currie endorsed the original manuscript letter as 'Burns' life addressed to Dr Moore — The Original Material for the biography.'[85] In an obviously crafted piece of writing,

---

81 A good example is shown in Graham, *Plantocracy*, pp.56–57.
82 Andrew O Lindsay, *Illustrious Exile* (see below, pp.321).
83 *Oxford Burns*, vol.I, pp.188–198: 'Copy of a Letter from Mr Burns to Doctor Moor [sic],' *Glenriddell Ms*, vol.I, pp.27–48.
84 Burns was gifted a copy by Mrs Dunlop, 'Letter: Mrs Dunlop to Burns, 27 June 1789,' in William Wallace, ed, *Robert Burns and Mrs Dunlop* (London: Hodder & Stoughton, 1896), p.180. An analysis of the anti-slavery message contained in *Zeluco* will be found below at pp.284.
85 *Letters*, L.125, at vol.II, p.147, subsequent references to the 'Autobiographical Letter' are in-line.

the poet refers to the West Indies in general, and to his Jamaican plan in particular (if vague) terms, as we saw in Chapter Three above. The following five excerpts are the important quotations concerning Jamaica:

PASSAGE A:
My vicinity to Ayr was of great advantage to me. — [...] I formed many connections with other Youngkers who possessed superior advantages [...] — Parting with these, my young friends and benefactors, as they dropped off for the east or west Indies, was often to me a sore affliction [...] [p.136.]

PASSAGE B:
We lived very poorly. [...] This kind of life, the cheerless gloom of a hermit with the unceasing moil of a galley-slave, brought me to my sixteenth year [...] [p.137.]

PASSAGE C:
My knowledge of ancient story was gathered from Salmon's and Guthrie's geographical grammars [...] [p.138.]

PASSAGE D:
[I] made what little preparation was in my power for Jamaica. — Before leaving my native country for ever, I resolved to publish my poems. — [...] I thought they had merit; and 'twas a delicious idea that I would be called a clever fellow, even though it should never reach my ears a poor Negro-driver, or perhaps a victim to that inhospitable climate gone to the world of Spirits. — I was pretty sure my Poems would meet with some applause; but at the worst, the roar of the Atlantic would deafen the voice of Censure, and the novelty of West-Indian scenes make me forget Neglect. — [pp.144-145.]

PASSAGE E:
My vanity was highly gratified by the reception I met with from the Publick; besides pocketing, all expences deducted, near twenty pounds. — This last came very seasonable, as I was about to indent myself for want of money to pay my freight. — So soon as I was master of nine guineas, the price of wafting me to the torrid zone, I bespoke a passage in the very first ship that was to sail [...] [p.145.]

ANALYSIS

In his letters, Burns is a chameleon correspondent, tuning his voice to suit the ear of the recipient (and, no doubt, their acquaintances to whom these literary pieces would probably be circulated), so the modern reader should be on guard in reading what can be a varnished (and often highly polished) truth. This letter deals with Burns's early life until his arrival in Edinburgh in late 1786 to find a publisher for his second edition and reveals several points about his perception of the West Indies.

As has been discussed above, the growing British Empire (especially the West- and East-Indies) provided jobs for many young Scotsmen. In 'Passage A' above, Burns notes that the lads whom he knew in the town of Ayr regularly 'dropped off for the west- or east Indies' which confirms the assumption that Burns had been aware of that potential career path, were the right patronage in place.

'Passage B' includes the often-quoted self-reference as a 'galley-slave.' The metaphor is plain: a young man 'chained' to the never-ending and repetitive cycle of farm labour. It seems crass of Burns to use 'slave' for his own position, compared to the Black slaves he will allude to in a few lines, but compare 'Glenriddell's Fox' [K.527] (discussed below), where Burns distinguishes a 'galley-slave' who is being judicially (and deservedly) punished. That might be too fine a point of distinction, for Burns, in mentioning his familiarity with Guthrie and Salmon's two volumes in 'Passage C', tells that he was well aware of the intertwining economics of trade and enslavement.[86] That being said, the conservative literary critic John Wilson (1784–1854) sympathised with the young Burns in a passage from 1817:

> While yet a boy [...] we see him laden with incessant toil — I might almost say, working the work of a slave. [...] The fields and the hills were first known to him as the scenes of bodily labour and endurance. And the very clouds of heaven agitated him with the hopes and fears connected even with the bare means of existence. But 'chill penury repressed not his noble rage.' Freedom sprang out of slavery, glory out of gloom, and light out of darkness.[87]

---

86 This is more fully discussed in Chapter 5 looking at treatments of slavery in Burns's wider readings.
87 [John Wilson], 'Vindication of Mr Wordsworth's Letter to Mr Gray, On a New Edition of Burns,' *Blackwood's Magazine* (October 1817), p.71. 'Chill penury' is quoting from Gray's 'Elegy Written

While not diluting the insensitivity of the phase, this shows that it was an opinion carried by others rather than Burns himself, so we should not treat him over-harshly here.

'Passage D' is another example of his self-absorption at that period. As a self-identified 'poor Negro-driver', it is Burns that is 'poor' and unfortunate, not the Black men, women and children that he will oversee and over-work. It is not their sufferings and death that affects him, but the fact that he might be one of the high percentage of White men who succumbed at a rate which 'could kill as many as four out of five new arrivals in their first year before their "seasoning" was complete.'[88]

The end of that passage with the 'roar of the Atlantic' and 'West Indian scenes' echo the tropes in several of his farewell poems (as discussed above), but it is hard not to feel chilled by the idea of the 'novelty' of 'scenes' distracting him from care: certainly the landscape might entertain, but could it compensate for the 'novelty' of beating a man near to death? Charles Douglas had made the role plain: Burns, should he arrive, would occupy a lowly and unrevered position in Jamaican society. How much pity (or even self-pity) does that deserve?

Finally, 'Passage E', brings his *deus ex machina*: the financial (and of course literary) success of *The Kilmarnock Edition*. The story in the telling here elides Gavin Hamilton's initial encouragement into print which was specifically to avoid having to indenture himself to Charles Douglas (there is no extant evidence of this being discussed with the Douglases, so it might be assumed that this is another mechanism to engender sympathy for Burns in his 'plight'). The inference here is that by bonding himself, albeit for a fixed period with legal protections, Burns's position would have been closer (in terms of calling for sympathy) to that of the enslaved than to his 'master.' This is a variant of what might be called 'the Redshanks Myth' where some commentators assert that the position of defeated Scottish prisoners of war who were transported and judicially indentured in the colonies by

---

in a Country Churchyard' at line 51.
88 TM Devine, 'Introduction. Scotland and Slavery,' in *RSSP*, ed TM Devine, p.14. 'It was reckoned in the 1750s that a quarter of all slaves died within three years of arrival, though mortality rates could often be significantly higher [...] in Barbados between 1741 and 1746, for instance, 43 per cent of all Africans died within three years of arrival.' *ibid*, p.9. Burnard estimates that the crude percentage mortality rate for enslaved people at this period on the island was in the 'mid thirties': the comparable adult mortality rate in England at that time as 25–30 per 1,000 (0.25 per cent), ie, a hundred times less. Burnard, 'Countrie Continues Sicklie', pp.70–71, and p.50.

Oliver Cromwell (after the Battle of Dunbar in 1650) or King George II (following Culloden, 1746) were 'white slaves.' As the indentured person retained personal legal rights and would become completely free at the end of the indenture, this argument is fallacious.[89]

EVALUATION: NEGATIVE
Burns shows that for a young man in Ayrshire, colonialism was a well-trodden path (sometimes to fortune, sometimes to death). He appears to accept that life in the West Indies involved slavery, showing a slightly dramatised self-pity, confusing the reader with references to his own 'slavery' and 'indent[ure].' These deliberately seek to narrow the divide between the poet and the enslaved people under his control, introducing a false equivalency in the mind of the reader.

No 14: [1787] [K.175] 'Castle Gordon. – Intended to be sung to Morag —[90]

After the success of the *First Edinburgh Edition,* Burns engaged in several jaunts around Scotland on what might be thought of as a stock-take of his Bardic domains. His 'Highland Tour' included paying visit to the Duke and Duchess of Gordon at Castle Gordon in Moray on 7 September 1787. Due to the intransigence of his travelling companion, William Nicol, the visit did not go completely to plan with Burns having to decline a dinner invitation with their Graces. In expiation, he sent the following poem.[91]

I

STREAMS that glide in orient plains,
Never bound by Winter's chains;
Glowing here on golden sands,
There immixed with foulest stains
From Tyranny's empurpled hands: 5
These, their richly gleaming waves,
I leave to tyrants and their slaves,
Give me the stream that sweetly laves
   The banks by CASTLE GORDON. —

---

89 See Stephen Mullen, 'The Myth of Scottish Slaves,' in *The Sceptical Scot*, March 2016, sceptical.scot/2016/03/the-myth-of-scottish-slaves/ (accessed 1 September 2024). An analogous legal status would be a mariner pressed into service with the Royal Navy in the Napoleonic Wars, a status no-one would ever define as 'slavery.'
90 *Oxford Burns*, vol.I, pp.97–98: *Second Commonplace Book*, pp.27–28.
91 *Letters*: to Mr [James] Hoy [Librarian at Castle Gordon], 20 October 1787 [L.145].

2
Torrid forests, ever gay, 10
Shading from the burning ray
Hapless wretches sold to toil;
Or the ruthless Native's way,
Bent on slaughter, blood, and spoil:
Woods that ever verdant wave, 15
I leave the tyrant and the slave,
Give me the groves that lofty brave
  The storms by CASTLE GORDON. —

ANALYSIS
These verses were written almost a year after the third boat had sailed for Jamaica without the poet. Kinsley describes lines 1 to 18 as 'common to Augustan Poetry,' citing Addison, Thompson and Goldsmith as exemplars, so this is rather more a poetical exercise than a real comparison of the enjoyment of Scotland's gloomy climate by freemen against the 'tyrant and the slave' and their exotic locales in sand, sunshine and jungle.[92]

Line 12 certainly has a positive reference to chattel slaves ('hapless wretches sold to toil') which, although brief, is unambiguously aligned with the misery of the enslaved, but then that is set against the racial caricature of the bloodthirsty 'Native' which diminishes its force. The wretched 'Slave', his 'Tyrant' master and the predatory 'Native' are mere stock characters in this poem.[93] While utilising a standard trope, Burns was probably unaware that his host, Alexander, 4th Duke of Gordon (1743–1827) had personally owned an enslaved Black servant, a 'black boy Harry', some 25 years before.[94]

---

92 *Poems*, vol.III, p.1248.
93 (It should be noted that Burns is not always as graceless to 'natives' – take the first draft of 'Poortith Cauld,' [K.398, 1793, ll.21-24] where the trope of the 'noble savage' is kindly, but paternalistically, used:
  How blest the wild-wood Indian's fate,
   He woos his simple Dearie;
  The silly bogles, Wealth and State,
   Did never make them eerie.)
94 Whyte, *Scotland and the Abolition*, p.13, p.16, and Paul Edwards, and James Walvin, *Personalities in the Era of the Slave Trade* (London/Basingstoke: The Macmillan Press, 1983), p.64, recording costs of the boy's clothing and schooling.

EVALUATION: POSITIVE (ON BALANCE)
This is a stock use of common tropes, so does not evidence any deep thought or true feeling on the slave question, although a level of sympathy for the 'hapless wretches' is glancingly mentioned. From 1788, the tenor and volume of the Abolition debate starts to rise, so that sympathetic statement in line 12 may have arisen from an early glimpse of that movement.

No 15: [1788] [K.243] 'Ode, Sacred to the Memory of Mrs [Oswald] of [Auchincruive].'

One stormy night, Burns was evicted from the comfort of the inn at Sanquhar upon the arrival of the funeral cortège of Mrs Oswald of Auchincruive, being forced to travel 12 miles 'through dub and mire' to the next inn. He immediately sought his revenge in verse on 'that venerable votary of iron avarice and sordid pride.'

>DWELLER in yon dungeon dark,
>Hangman of creation, mark!
>Who in widow weeds appears,
>Laden with unhonour'd years,
>Noosing with care a bursting purse,   5
>Baited with many a deadly curse?
>
>   STROPHE
>View the wither'd beldam's face —
>Can thy keen inspection trace
>Aught of Humanity's sweet, melting grace?
>Note that eye, 'tis rheum o'erflows,   10
>Pity's flood there never rose,
>See these hands, ne'er stretched to save,
>Hands that took, but never gave.
>[The Great despised her and her wealth,
>The Poor-man breathed a curse by stealth.]⁹⁵
>Keeper of Mammon's iron chest,
>Lo, there she goes, unpitied and unblest,   15
>She goes, but not to realms of everlasting rest!

---
95 *Additional couplet in the Don MS*

ANTISTROPHE

Plunderer of Armies, lift thine eyes,
(A while forbear, ye torturing fiends),
Seest thou whose step, unwilling, hither bends?
No fallen angel, hurled from upper skies;   20
'Tis thy trusty *quondam Mate*,
Doomed to share thy fiery fate;
She, tardy, hell-ward plies.

EPODE

And are they of no more avail,
Ten thousand glittering pounds a year?   25
In other worlds can Mammon fail,
Omnipotent as he is here?
O, bitter mockery of the *pompous bier*,
While down the wretched *vital part* is driven!
The cave-lodged beggar, with a conscience clear,   30
Expires in rags, unknown, and goes to Heaven.

ANALYSIS

Mary Ramsay or Oswald (1716–1788) was the daughter of an Aberdeenshire merchant and his wife who spent her early years in Jamaica, returning with her mother to London at her father's death in 1738. She married Richard Oswald (1705–1784) in 1750, bringing an inheritance of some £20,000 from her father's Jamaican and American colonial interests.[96] Oswald had started life as an apprentice in a family counting-house in Glasgow in the Virginia trade, and spent some time in America and Jamaica as the firm's factor. He built a fortune based on military supply contracts and slave-trading, notably through the enslaver fort called Bance Island in Sierra Leone (which had a golf course for the Scots overseers, caddied by young Black men dressed in tartan).[97]

---

96 At Alexander Ramsay's death in 1738, his estate included 51 adult male and 50 adult female slaves in Jamaica, valued at J£3,727. 'Alexander Ramsay' *UCL Legacies Database*: Alexander Ramsay (accessed 1 September 2024). That dowry would be worth ca £4million in 2024 prices.
97 Whyte, *Scotland and the Abolition*, p.46. June Evans relates an ironic story: 'When the tartan was banned "Oronoce, a black servant of the Laird of Appin, Dugald Stewart" was arrested on 25 July 1750, and apprehended by the Commanding Officer of the forces stationed in Rannoch district "for wearing the Highland garb or being dressed in Tartan livery and was forthwith committed to prison." [...] The irony of this was that an African-slave servant in Scotland should be imprisoned for wearing a tartan while in the colonies African slaves were being compelled to wear Scottish plaids

Between 1748 and 1784, 12,929 chattel slaves passed through its gates (the peak year being 1765, with 1,956) in such a profitable venture that Whyte describes him as one of '"the commanding heights" of the triangular trade, amassing £500,000 for himself.'[98]

In 1763 he acquired the Auchincruive estate near Ayr and spent considerable amounts in rebuilding and improvements under the guidance of influential Scottish architect Robert Adam (1728–1792) with fittings and furnishings to match, including a portrait of his wife by Zoffany.[99] He also paid for the reconstruction of the parish church, St Quivox, in 1767 and the solid silver Communion-ware still used to celebrate the Lord's Supper in the church was of his donation.[100] Towards the end of his life, upon the recommendation to HM Government by the economist Adam Smith (1723–1790), he was appointed as commissioner to negotiate peace terms in Paris with the Americans in 1783, gaining the soubriquet 'Oswald the Peacemaker' (somewhat ironically as he was felt to have given up too much to the Americans). Although even here, the interests of the slave-holders were preserved. Towards the end of the negotiations Henry Laurens (1724–1792) of Charleston, SC joined the meeting. Before the war, Laurens had been Oswald's largest receiving agent for chattel slaves in America and when he was captured by the Royal Navy during the war, his release on bail from the Tower of London was obtained by Oswald who stood surety for £2,000.[101] Laurens prompted Oswald to add a final, handwritten amendment to the peace treaty prohibiting the British from 'carrying away any Negroes or other property of the American Inhabitants' in a final act of loyalty to the slaveowner class (regardless of citizenship).[102]

---

manufactured in Scotland [...] as it made them conspicuous.' June Evans, *African/Caribbeans in Scotland. A Socio-Geographical Study* (Edinburgh: University of Edinburgh PhD Thesis, 1995), p.57.
98 Ibid, p.45; Hancock, *SST*, p.76. £85 million at 2024 prices.
99 Pevsner, *Ayrshire*, pp.107–111; Johann Zoffany (1733–1810), 'Mrs Oswald,' [ca 1760], National Gallery, London: Inventory No NG4931. Mary Oswald's links to slavery are summarised in the National Gallery's 2021 Report: *Phases I and II of the National Gallery and Legacies of British Slave-holdership Research Project*, at www.nationalgallery.org.uk/people/mary-oswald (accessed 1 September 2024).
100 www.ayrstquivox.com/oswald-family.html (accessed 1 September 2024).
101 W Stitt Robinson, Jr, 'Richard Oswald the Peacemaker,' *Ayrshire Archaeological and Natural History Society Collection*, 2nd series, 3 (1955), pp.119–132. Approximately £300,000 in 2024 values.
102 Hunter Miller, ed, *Treaties and Other International Acts of the United States of America*, 6 vols (Washington: Government Printing Office, 1931), vol.II, p.155. However, almost immediately there was a definitional dispute (as the British held that those already freed were no longer 'property' and

Richard died at Auchincruive in 1784, and Mary in 1788 at their London residence and they were, in turn, laid to rest in the new Oswald Vault at St Quivox kirk.[103] Burns's last meeting with her is recorded in a letter to Dr John Moore:

> In January last, on my road to Ayrshire, I had put up at Bailie Whigham's in Sanquhar, the only tolerable inn in the place. The frost was keen, and the grim evening and howling wind were ushering in a night of snow and drift. My horse and I were both much fatigued with the labors of the day, and just as my friend the Bailie and I, were bidding defiance to the storm over a smoking bowl [sc: punch], in wheels the funeral pageantry of the late great Mrs Oswald, and poor I am forced to brave all the horrors of the tempestuous night, and jade my horse, my young favorite horse, whom I had just christened Pegasus, twelve miles farther on, through the wildest moors and hills of Ayrshire, to New Cumnock, the next Inn. The powers of Poesy and Prose sink under me, when I would describe what I felt. Suffice it to say, that when a good fire at New Cumnock had so far recovered my frozen sinews, I sat down and wrote the enclosed Ode.[104]

He sent this poem to Peter Stuart (1760–1812), the newspaper editor of the *Star* in London, where it was published under the pseudonym 'Tim Nettle,' along with a covering letter:

> I dislike partial respect of persons and am hurt to see the public make such a fuss when a poor pennyless gipsey [sic] is consigned over to Jack Ketch[(a)] and yet scarce take any notice when a purse-proud

---

so fell outwith the terms of the clause). The arguments over settlement continued until the War of 1812, where more enslaved people fled to the British lines, exacerbating the situation. Resolution of the issues only occurred after both sides submitted to arbitration by Tsar Alexander I of Russia (1877 – r 1801–1825) in 1822. In 1826, US Commissioners received USD 1,204,960 in recompense for 3,601 formerly enslaved persons (an average of USD 335 or GBP 76 per person). See Steven J Brady, *Chained to History: Slavery and US Foreign Relations to 1865* (Ithaca, NY: Cornell University Press, 2022), pp.2–22.

103 UCL Legacies Database: 'Richard Alexander Oswald' (accessed 1 September 2024).
104 *Letters*: to Dr Moore, 23 March 1789 [L.322]: he had previously sent to this poem to Mrs Dunlop, (Jan[uary] 1789, L.305), who replied 'Are you not a sad wicked creature to send a poor old wife straight to the Devil, because she gave you a ride in a cold night?' 22 January 1789, in *RB & Mrs D*, p.137.

Priestess of Mammon is, by the inexorable hand of death, pinioned in everlasting fetters of illgotten gold, and delivered up to that arch-brother among the finishers of the law, emphatically called, by our Bard, the Hangman of Creation[(b)].[105]

As Thomas Crawford rightly describes this work '[i]n spite of the rhetorical energy which it generates [it] is really little more than a pompous overflow of personal spleen.'[106] For the purposes of this study, the interesting point about this poem and the accompanying commentaries is that it attacks Mary Oswald for being avaricious, purse-proud and lacking in humanity ('the venerable votary of iron avarice and sordid pride,') and it excoriates her late husband Richard as the 'plunderer of armies' for profiteering on his army contracts, but neither is criticised for the source of their amazing ('illgotten') wealth: her inheritance of a substantial investment in Black chattel slavery, and its ruthless industrialisation in Oswald's enslaving entrepôt, Bance Island.[107]

In Burns's satirical works, he rarely misses the opportunity to hit upon the subject's true human weakness. Several commentators maintain with Sally Beattie that this is 'a critical poem on Mrs Oswald of Auchincruive, on her late husband's slaving activities and her benefit of them.'[108] Yet here, in either the poem itself or in its covering letters, there is no mention of Black chattel slavery at all, and no direct critique of enslavement and trafficking being the source of her dowry, her inheritance and his fortune. (If the 'cave-lodged beggar' in the penultimate line had been a 'toil-worn slave', that would have been a different matter. This clearly implies that in 1788 and 1789 Burns did not see that making a fortune out of chattel slavery was either particularly noteworthy, nor, in fact, as attracting opprobrium.[109]

---

105 *Letters*: 'Tim Nettle' to [Peter Stuart], the Editor of the *Morning Star*, London, [May 1789], [L.338]. Burns's references: (a) Jack Ketch was the executioner of London (appointed ca 1663, died 1686) becoming an eponym. (b) Burns, in 'Address to the Diel,' [K.76] calls the Devil '*Auld Hangie*' (l.7).
106 Thomas Crawford, *Burns: A Study of the Poems and Songs* (Edinburgh: James Thin, 1978), p.205.
107 White, *Scotland and the Abolition*, p.45.
108 Melville, *Facing Our Past*, p.51.
109 The Oswalds died childless, and their estates passed to a nephew, the already wealthy Glasgow merchant George Oswald of Scotstoun (1735–1819) and thence his son Richard Alexander Oswald (1771–1841). Burns knew the latter, and his first wife Louisa ('Lucy,' ?–1797), for whom he wrote one of the versions of his 'O wat's Ye was in Yon Toun,' [K.488]. He commended young Oswald in 'The Election — A New Song,' [K.492]:

EVALUATION: NEGATIVE
The increased awareness of the Abolition debate in 1789, although not yet at its peak, should have been enough, if Burns had cared about it, to add another lash to his scurrilous denunciation of the Oswalds. Limiting their sins to their wealth and avarice, without condemning its origins, strongly implies that slavery was not (yet) a motivating influence for Burns, morally, socially, economically or poetically.

No 16: [1789] [L.353B] 'Letter: To Helen Maria Williams, [late July, early August] 1789.'

Helen Maria Williams acted as Dr Moore's amanuensis for several years, and through him forged a connection with Burns. Her radical political beliefs embraced Abolitionism and following the passage of *Dolben's Act* she published a long polemical poem on the slave trade in 1788, which she sent to Burns for criticism.¹¹⁰

> And there will be wealthy young RICHARD —
> Dame Fortune should hing by the neck
> For prodigal thriftless bestowing —
> His merit had won him respect. ll.49–52.

Burns praised Oswald to others: 'an independent-minded Country *Gentleman*,' *(Letters*, to Patrick Miller, Jr 8 March [1795] [L.659]) and in writing to John Syme, he says he now has 'the honor to call my acquaintances, the OSWALD FAMILY' calling her 'an incomparable woman' and him the possessor 'of a fine fortune, a pleasing, engaging exterior; self-evident amiable dispositions, with an ingenious, upright mind, & that too informed much beyond the usual run of young fellows of his rank & fortune [...]' [Letters, to John Syme, [May? 1795] [L.669]. Burns sent Oswald copies of the Heron Ballads (see L.662) as Oswald was an important ally to the Heron interest. In 1802 he would chair the General Election ballot which voted for Heron, but which was overturned by the Commons on petition due to Oswald's partiality. See William Thomas Roe, *An Appendix to a Treatise on the Law of Elections, Concerning the Scots and Irish Statutes* (London: Charles Hunter, 1818), pp.ccclxx–ccclxxiv. Oswald would be elected MP for Ayrshire in Liberal interest in 1832, being re-elected in 1835, though accepting the Chiltern Hundreds later that year, quitting politics through ill-health following the death of his only child, Richard Alexander Oswald, younger (1797–1834), who died while visiting Rozelle after marrying Lady Mary Kennedy of Culzean (1799–1866) the previous month.

It would appear that the Oswald/Ramsay plantations had been sold by the mid-1790s, so when Burns knew him RA Oswald Sr was not a slave-holder, however, following his wife's death in 1797, he remarried Lady Lilias Montgomerie or McQueen (?–1845) the daughter of the 12th Earl of Eglinton and widow of Lord Braxfield, the 'hanging judge', in 1817, who, through her maternal line had inherited a share of the Hamilton plantation Rozelle in Jamaica. In 1836 compensation was paid of £4,580 8s 3d (in respect of 255 enslaved person on Pemberton Valley) with a further £856 10s 3d (for Boscobelle Pen, and 42 enslaved people). *University College London. UCL Legacies Database* (accessed 1 September 2024). At Burns's death it was Oswald who organised the Ayrshire charitable donations for the poet's family. Richard and Lucy lived on the same fortune as old Mrs Oswald, but the poet found no need to excoriate them for those ill-gotten proceeds. Graham, *Plantocracy*, p.70.

110 28 Geo III, c. 54 (1778), 'An Act to regulate, for a limited Time, the shipping and carrying of Slaves in British Vessels from the Coast of Africa,' (known as 'Dolben's Act') which introduced

Burns opens his reply by thanking her for her 'excellent poem on the slave-trade' and then adding his literary thoughts on her work. For ease, the poem is given in full on the left, with Burns's comments from his letter, on the right, aligned with the appropriate passages in the poem, noting that where Burns refers to 'verses' he means to individual lines in the poem.

Helen Maria Williams,
A Poem on the Bill Lately Passed in England for Regulating the Slave Trade
(London: T Cadell, 1788), pp. 1–23.

Robert Burns
Letter to Helen Maria Williams, [late July or early August] 1789, [L.353B],
Letters, vol.1, pp.428–431.

A few strictures on Miss Williams Poem on the Slave trade — I know very little of scientific criticism, so all I can pretend to [do] in that intricate art is merely to note, as I read along, what passages strike me as being uncommonly beautiful, & where the expression seems to perplexed or faulty.

THE hollow winds of Night, no more
In wild, unequal cadence pour,
On musing Fancy's wakeful ear,
The groan of agony severe
From yon dark vessel, which contains
The wretch new bound in hopeless chains;
Whose soul with keener anguish bleeds,
As AFRIC'S less'ning shore recedes —

The Poem opens finely. There are none of these idle prefatory lines which one may skip over before one comes to the subject. —

No more where Ocean's unseen bound
Leaves a drear world of waters round,   10
Between the howling gust, shall rise
The stifled Captive's latest sighs; —
No more shall suffocating death
Seize the pent victim's sinking breath;
The pang of that convulsive hour,
Reproaching Man's insatiate power;
Man! who to AFRIC'S shore has past
Relentless, as the annual blast
That sweeps the Western Isles, and flings
Destruction from its furious wings—   20

Verses ninth and tenth in particular. 'Where ocean's unseen bound/ Leaves a drear world of waters round,' are truly beautiful. —

The simile of the hurricane is likewise fine; & indeed, beautiful as the Poem is, almost all the similes rise decidedly above it. —

---

limits on the number of enslaved to be carried on slave-ships proportionate to their size; mandated that masters have prior experience, and that a surgeon should be on each voyage with a register of deaths, and required adequate insurance.

And Woman, she, too weak to bear
The galling chain, the tainted air;
Of mind too feeble to sustain
The vast, accumulated pain;
No more, in desperation wild,
Shall madly strain her gasping child;
With all the mother at her soul,
With eyes where tears have ceas'd to roll,
Shall catch the livid infant's breath;
Then sink in agonizing death.   30

   BRITAIN! the noble, blest decree
That soothes despair, is fram'd by Thee!
Thy powerful arm has interpos'd,
And one dire scene for ever clos'd;
Its horror shall no more belong
To that foul drama, deep with wrong.

Oh, first of EUROPE'S polish'd lands
To ease the Captive's iron bands;
Long, as thy glorious annals shine,
This proud distinction shall be thine!   40
Not first alone when Valour leads
To rush on Danger's noblest deeds;
When Mercy calls thee to explore
A gloomy path, untrod before,
Thy ardent spirit springs to heal,

And, greatly gen'rous, dares to feel! —
Valour is like the meteor's light,
Whose partial flash leaves deeper night;
While Mercy, like the lunar ray,
Gilds the thick shade with softer day.   50

   For this, in Fame's immortal shrine,
A double wreathe, O PITT, is thine!
For this! while distant ages hear
With Admiration's sacred tear,
Of powers, whose energy sublime
Disdain'd to borrow force from Time,
With no gradations mark'd their flight,
But rose, at once, to Glory's height;
The deeds of Mercy, that embrace
A distant sphere, an alien-race,   60
Shall Virtue's lips record, and claim
The fairest honors of thy name!
'Tis ever Nature's gen'rous view;
Great minds, should noble ends pursue;

From verse 31st to verse 50th, is a pretty eulogy on Britain. —

Verse 36th, that foul drama deep with wrong, is nobly expressive. —

Verse 46th, I am afraid, is rather unworthy of the rest: 'to dare to feel,' is an idea that I do not altogether like.
The contrast of valour & mercy, from the 46th verse to the 50th, is admirable. —

Either my apprehension is dull, or there is something a little confused in the apostrophe to Mr Pit [sic]. — Verse 55th is the antecedent to verses 57th and 58th, but in verse 58th the connection seems ungrammatical: — Powers, [...]/ [...]/With no gradations mark'd their flight, /But *rose* at once to glory's height.
ris'n should surely be the word instead of *rose*.
Try it in Prose: Powers — their flight marked by no gradations, but these same powers [risen/rose] at once to the height of glory. —
Likewise, verse 58th, 'For this' is evidently meant to lead on the sense of verses 59th, 60th, 61st, and 62d; but let us try how the thread of connection runs. For this [...]/ [...]/ The deeds of mercy, that embrace/ A distant sphere, an alien race, / Shall Virtue's lips record, and claim/ The fairest honours of thy name.
I beg pardon if I misapprehend the matter, but this appears to me the most [if not] the only imperfect passage in the Poem. —

As the clear sun-beam, when most bright,
Warms, in proportion to its light. —
And RICHMOND, he! who, high in birth,
Adds the unfading rays of worth;
Who stoops, from scenes in radiance drest,
To ease the mourner's aching breast; 70
The tale of private woe to hear,
And wipe the friendless orphan's tear! —
His bosom for the Captive bleeds,
He, Guardian of the injur'd! pleads
With all the force that Genius gives,
And warmth that but with Virtue lives;

For Virtue, with divine controul,
Collects the various powers of soul;
And lends, from her unsullied source,
The gems of thought their purest force. 80

 OH blest decree! whose lustre seems
Like the sweet Morn's reviving beams,
That chase the hideous forms of night,
And promise day more richly bright;
Great deed! that met consenting minds
In all but those whom Av'rice binds;
Who creep in Interest's crooked ways,

Nor ever pass her narrow maze;
Or those, whom hard Indiff'rence steels
To every pang another feels. 90
For *Them* has Fortune, round their bowers
Twin'd (partial nymph)! her lavish flowers;
For *Them*, from unsunn'd caves, she brings
Her summer ice; for she springs
To climes, where hotter suns produce
The richer fruit's delicious juice;
While *They*, whom wasted blessings tire,
Nor leave *one* want, to feed desire;
With cool, insulting ease demand
Why for yon hopeless, Captive Band, 100
Is ask'd, to mitigate despair,
The mercy of the common air?
The boon of larger space to breathe,
While coop'd that hollow deck beneath?
A lengthen'd plank, on which to throw
Their shackled limbs, while fiercely glow
The beams direct, that on each head
The fury of contagion shed? —

The comparison of the sunbeam is fine. —

The compliment to the Duke of Richmond is, I hope, as just as it is certainly elegant.[111]

The thought — 'Virtue [...]/ [...]/— lends, from her unsullied source,/ The gems of thought their purest force,' — is exceedingly beautiful. —

The idea from verse 81st to the 85th, that the 'blest decree' is like the beams morning ushering in the glorious day of liberty, ought not to pass unnoticed, nor unapplauded. —

From verse 85th to verse 108th, is an animated contrast between the unfeeling selfishness of the Oppressor, on the one hand, & the misery of the captive on the other. —

Verse 88th might perhaps be amended thus — 'Nor ever *quit* her narrow maze.' — We are said to *pass* a bound, but we *quit* a maze.

Verse 100th [sic] is exquisitely beautiful. — They, whom wasted blessings tire —

---

111 Charles, 3rd Duke of Richmond, of Lennox and of Aubigny (1735–1806) piloted Dolben's Bill through the House of Lords. Interestingly, Zoffany painted the Duke's portrait in 1765, depicting him out shooting, accompanied by a young Black servant.

And dare presumptuous, guilty man,
Load with offence his fleeting span?   110
Deform Creation with the gloom
Of crimes, that blot its cheerful bloom;
Darken a work so perfect made,
And cast the Universe in shade? —
Alas, to AFRIC'S fetter'd race
Creation wears no form of grace!
To Them, Earth's pleasant vales are found
A blasted waste, a sterile bound;
Where the poor wand'rer must sustain
The load of unremitted pain!   120
A region, in whose ample scope
His eye discerns no gleam of hope;
Where Thought no kind asylum knows,
On which its anguish may repose,
But Death, that to the ravag'd breast
Comes not in shapes of terror drest,
Points to green hills where Freedom roves,
And minds renew their former loves;
Or, low'ring in the troubled air,
Hangs the fierce spectre of Despair,   130
Whose soul abhors the gift of life,
Who stedfast grasps the reeking knife,
Bids the charg'd heart in torrents bleed,
And smiles in frenzy at the deed.
So, when rude winds the sailor urge
On polar seas, near Earth's last verge;
Long with the blast he struggles hard,
To save his bark, in ice imbarr'd;
But finds at length, o'ercome with pain,
But The conflict with his fate is vain;   140
Then heaves no more the useless groan,
But hardens like the wave to stone.

 Ye noble minds! who o'er a sky
Where clouds are roll'd, and tempests fly,
Have bid the lambent lustre play
Of *one* pure, lovely, azure ray;
O, far diffuse its op'ning bloom,
And the wide hemisphere illume!
Ye, who *one* bitter drop have drain'd
From Slav'ry's cup, with horror stain'd;   150
Oh, let no fatal dregs be found,
But dash her chalice on the ground:

Verse 110th is, I doubt, a clashing of metaphors; to load a span is, I afraid, an unwarrantable expression.

In verse 114th, 'Cast the universe in shade,' is a fine idea. —

From the 115th verse to the 142d is a striking description of the wrongs of the poor African. —

Verse 120th, 'the load of unremitted pain,' is a remarkable strong expression.

The address to the advocates for abolishing the slave-trade, from verse 143d to verse 208th, is animated with the true life of Genius. —

Oh, while still she links her impious chain,
And calculates the price of pain;
Weighs Agony in sordid scales,
And marks if Death or Life prevails;
In one short moment, seals the doom
Of years, which anguish shall consume;
Decides how near the mangling scourge
May to the grave its victim urge,   160
Yet for awhile, with prudent care
The half-worn wretch, if useful, spare;
And speculates, with skill refin'd,
How deep a wound will stab the mind;
How far the spirit can endure
Calamity, that hopes no cure; —
Ye! who can selfish cares forego,
To pity those which others know;
As Light, that from its centre strays,
To glad all nature with its rays;   170
Oh! ease the pangs ye stoop to share,
And rescue millions from despair! —
For you, while Morn in graces gay,
Wakes the fresh bloom of op'ning Day;
Gilds with her purple light your dome,
Renewing all the joys of home;
Of home! dear scene, whose ties can bind
With sacred force the human mind;
That feels each little absence pain,
And lives but to return again;   180
To that lov'd spot, however far,
Points, like the needle to its star;
That native shed which first we knew,
Where first the sweet affections grew;
Alike the willing heart can draw,
If fram'd of marble, or of straw;
Whether the voice of pleasure calls,
And gladness echoes thro' its walls;
Or, to its hallow'd roof we fly,
With those we love to pour the sigh;   190
The load of mingled pain to bear,
And soften every pang we share! —

Ah, think how desolate *His* state,
How *He* the cheerful light must hate,
Whom, sever'd from his native soil,
The Morning wakes to fruitless toil;
To labours, hope shall never chear,
Or fond domestic joy endear;
Poor wretch! on whose despairing eyes
His cherish'd home shall never rise!   200
Condemn'd, severe extreme, to live
When all is fled that life can give! —
And ah! the blessings valued most
By human minds, are blessings lost!

The picture of Oppression, 'While she links her impious chain,/ And calculates the price of pain;/ Weighs Agony in sordid scales,/ And marks if Death or Life prevails,' is nobly execu[ted.]

What a tender idea is in verse 180th! indeed, that whole description of Home may vie with Thomson's description of Home, somewhere in the beginning of his Autumn. —

I do not remember to have seen a stronger expression of misery than is contained in these verses 'Condemn'd, severe extreme, to live/ When all is fled that life can give!' —

Unlike the objects of the eye,
Enlarging as we bring them nigh;
Our joys at distance strike the breast,
And seem diminish'd when possest.

Who from his far-divided shore
The half-expiring captive bore?   210
Those whom the traffic of their race
Has robb'd of every human grace;
Whose harden'd souls no more retain
Impressions Nature stamp'd in vain;
All that distinguishes their *kind*,
For ever blotted from their mind;
As streams, that once the landscape gave
Reflected on the trembling wave,
Their substance change when lock'd in frost,
And rest, in dead contraction lost; —   220
Who view unmoved, the look, that tells
The pang that in the bosom dwells;
Heed not the nerves that terror shakes,
The heart convulsive anguish breaks;
The shriek that would their crimes upbraid,
But deem despair a part of trade. —
Such only for detested gain,
The barb'rous commerce would maintain;
The gen'rous sailor, he who dares
All forms of danger, while he bears   230
The BRITISH flag o'er sultry seas,
And spreads it on the polar breeze;
He, who in Glory's high career,
Finds agony, and death are dear;
To whose protecting arm we owe
Each blessing that the happy know;
Whatever charms the soften'd heart,
Each cultur'd grace, each finer art,
E'en thine, most lovely of the train!
Sweet Poetry, thy heav'n-taught strain — 240
His breast, where nobler passions burn,
In honest poverty, would spurn
The wealth, Oppression can bestow,
And scorn to wound a fetter'd foe.
True courage in the unconquer'd soul
Yields to Compassion's mild control;
As, the refining frame of steel
The magnet's secret force can feel.

The comparison of our distant joys to distant objects, is equally original and striking.

The character & manners of the dealer in this infernal traffic is a well done, though a horrid picture. —

Verse 224th is a nervous [MISSING WORD] expressive — 'The heart convulsive anguish breaks.'

I am not sure how far introducing the Sailor was right; for, though the Sailor's common characteristic is generosity, yet, in this case, he is certainly not only an unconcerned witness, but in some degree an efficient agent in the business. —

WHEN borne at length to Western lands,
Chain'd on the beach the Captive stands, 250
Where Man, dire merchandize! is sold,
And barter'd life is paid for gold;
In mute affliction, see him try
To read his new possessor's eye;
If one blest glance of mercy there,
One half-form'd tear may check despair! —
Ah, if that eye with sorrow sees
His languid look, his quiv'ring knees,
Those limbs which scarce their load sustain,
That form, consum'd in wasting pain; 260
Such sorrow fills his ruthless eye
Who sees the lamb, he doom'd to die;
In pining sickness yield his life,
And thus elude the sharpen'd knife. —
Or, if where savage habit steels
The vulgar mind, one bosom feels
The sacred claim of helpless woe —
If Pity in that soil can grow;
Pity! Whose tender impulse darts
With keenest force on nobler hearts; 270
As flames that purest essence boast,
Rise highest when they tremble most. —
Yet *why* on one poor chance must rest
The int'rests of a kindred breast?
Humanity's devoted cause
Recline on Humour's wayward laws?
To Passion's rules must Justice bend,
And life upon Caprice depend? —

AH ye, who one fix'd purpose own,
Whose untir'd aim is *Self* alone; 280
Who think in gold the essence lies
From which extracted bliss shall rise;
To whose dull sense, no charm appears
In social smiles, or social tears;

As mists that o'er the landscape sail,
Its beauteous variations veil;
Or, if in some relenting hour,
When Nature re-assumes her power,

Your alms to Penury ye lend,
Or serve, for once, a suff'ring friend; 290
Whom no weak impulse e'er betray'd
To give that friend incautious aid;
Who with exact precision, pause
At that nice point which Int'rest draws;
Your watchful footsteps never found
To stray beyond that guarded bound; —

The description of the captive wretch when he arrives in the West Indies, is carried on with equal spirit. —

The thought that the Oppressor's sorrow on seeing his slave pine, is like the butcher's regret when his destined lamb dies a natural death, is exceedingly fine. —

I am got so much into the cant of criticism, that I begin to be afraid lest I have nothing except the cant of it; and, instead of elucidating my Author, am only benighting myself. — For this reason, I will not pretend to go through the whole poem. Some few remaining beautiful lines, however, I cannot pass over. —

Verse 280, is the strongest description of selfishness I ever saw;

the comparison in verses 285th & 286th is new and fine;

and the line, 'Your alms to Penury ye lend,' is excellent. —

Does fleeting Life proportion bear
To all the wealth ye heap with care?
When soon your days in measur'd flight
Shall sink in Death's terrific night;   300
Then seize the moments in your power,
To Mercy consecrate the hour!
Risque something in her cause at last,
Break the hard fetters of the Slave;
And learn the luxury to save!
And thus atone for all the past.
Does Avarice, your god, delight
With agony to feast his sight?
Does he require that victims slain,
And human blood, his altars stain?   310
Ah, not alone of power possest
To check each *virtue* of the breast:
As when the numbing frosts arise,
The charm of vegetation dies;

His sway the harden'd bosom leads
To Cruelty's remorseless deeds;
Like the blue lightning when it springs
With fury on its livid wings,
Darts to its goal with baleful force,
Nor heeds that ruin marks its course. —   320

OH Eloquence, prevailing art!
Whose force can chain the list'ning heart;
The throb of Sympathy inspire,
And kindle every great desire;
With magic energy controul
And reign the sov'reign of the soul!

That dreams while all its passions swell,
It shares the power it feels so well;
As visual objects seem possest
Of those clear hues by light imprest;   330
Oh, skill'd in every grace to charm,
To soften, to appal, to warm;
Fill with thy noblest rage the breast,
Bid on those lips thy spirit rest,
That shall, in BRITAIN'S Senate, trace
The wrongs of AFRIC'S Captive Race! —
But Fancy o'er the tale of woe
In vain one heighten'd tint would throw;
For ah, the Truth is all we guess
Of anguish in its last excess: 340

In verse 317, Like should surely be As, or, So: for instance, —
'His sway the hardened bosom leads/ To Cruelty's remorseless deeds;/ As (or So) the blue lightning, when it springs/ With fury on its livid wings,/ Darts to the goal with rapid force,/ Nor heeds that ruin marks its course.' —
If you insert the word Like where have placed As, you must alter, Darts, to, Darting, & Heeds, to, Heeding, in order to make it grammar.

Fancy may dress in deeper shade
The storm that hangs along the glade;
Spreads o'er the ruffled stream its wing,
And chills awhile the flowers of Spring;
But, where the wintry tempests sweep
In madness, o'er the darken'd deep;
Where the wild surge, the raging wave,
Point to the hopeless wretch a grave;
And Death surrounds the threat'ning shore —
Can Fancy add one horror more?   350

    LOV'D BRITAIN! whose protecting hand
Stretch'd o'er the Globe, on AFRIC'S strand
The honour'd base of Freedom lays,
Soon, soon the finish'd fabric raise!
And when surrounding realms would frame,
Touch'd with a spark of gen'rous flame,
Some pure, ennobling, great design,
Some lofty act, almost divine;
Which Earth may hail with rapture high,
And Heav'n may view with fav'ring eye;   360
Teach them to make all Nature free,
And shine by emulating Thee!

    THE END.

Indeed, that last Simile, beginning with 'Fancy may dress,' &c, and ending with the 350th verse, is, in my opinion, the most beautiful passage in the whole Poem. — it would honour to the greatest names that ever graced our Profession. —
A Tempest, is a favourite subject with the Poets, but I do not remember any thing even in Thomson's Winter, superior to your verses from the 344th to the 351st.

I will not beg your pardon, Madam, for these strictures, as my conscience tells me, that for once in my life I have acted up to the duties of a Christian in doing as I would be done by. —

ANALYSIS

Helen Maria Williams (1759–1827) was raised in Berwick-upon-Tweed by her widowed Scots mother, returning to London in 1781 to embark on a literary career (while assisting Dr Moore). Her views were entirely radical, with early poems celebrating the end of the American War (which was praised by Dr Johnson) and deploring Spanish colonisation of Peru. She was quickly attracted to the cause of Abolition (Wordsworth's earliest published work was his 'Sonnet on Seeing Miss Helen Maria Williams Weep at a Tale of Distress').[112] She had an early appreciation of Burns's genius, sending a sonnet to Burns praising his 'Mountain Daisy' in January 1787.[113] The French Revolution appeared to open up new political and literary vistas and she moved to Paris in 1790, publishing a series of *Letters from France*. Her extreme attachment to the relatively moderate *Girondists*, and later her criticisms of Napoleon found her imprisoned from

---

112 [William Wordsworth] 'Axilogus,' 'Sonnet on Seeing Miss Helen Maria Williams Weep at a Tale of Distress,' *European Magazine* (1787), p.202. (Wordsworth did not meet Miss Williams until 1820.)
113 Helen Maria Williams, 'Sonnet. On Reading Mr Burns' Poem upon the Mountain Daisy,' *Edinburgh Magazine* (January 1787), p.120.

time-to-time. From the Bourbon restoration of 1815 to her death, she suffered personal and financial stresses with repeated character attacks from the conservative element of English Society.[114]

This study will not analyse the qualities of the poems itself, although it is worth noting that its style as well as its message was well received on its publication:

> In easy harmonious verse, she pours forth the sentiments of an amiable mind and [shows] the pure medium of virtuous pity, unmixed with those political, commercial, and selfish considerations which operated in steeling the hearts of some men against the pleadings of humanity.[115]

While Leask's modern assessment says of it: '[j]udged by the poetic standards of its age, *The Slave Trade* makes its case with considerable rhetorical power and moral persuasion.'[116] Its influence on Burns's writing will be discussed below, where the passage around line 180 has a potential connection with 'The Slave's Lament,' while, as Nigel Leask notices, Williams's use of the phrase 'honest poverty' in line 242 has obvious implications for that famous poem of Burns's.[117]

Given her relationship to Dr Moore, Burns had to reply with a cogent critical analysis. Corey Andrews, in his wider study of 'Burns as a Critic,' describes the care and detail he sees Burns giving to a 'colleague poet's' draft:

> While polite, Burns's criticisms in the letter are exceedingly detailed in their attention to syntax, imagery and metre. He professes to 'know very little of scientific criticism' [...], yet what emerges is Burns's profound, teacherly awareness of the tools of his craft.[118]

Although that assessment is rather weakened as Burns appears to become bored of the task in the last hundred lines, saying 'I will not pretend to go through the whole poem,' which discourtesy may be the reason that Williams, when revising the poem, did not adopt any of Burns's suggestions (which further undermines Andrews's point on

---

114 *DNB*: 'Helen Maria Williams.'
115 *Monthly Review*, March 1789, p.237.
116 Leask, *Poetics*, p.53.
117 Discussed below, at p.213.
118 Corey E Andrews, 'Burns the Critic', in *Edinburgh Companion*, pp.119–121.

the quality of his criticisms.) [119]

The issue is that his critique of her poem is heavily literary, rather than openly addressing the polemical subject of Abolition. True, his language is consistently critical of the 'unfeeling selfishness' of the trafficker and sympathetic to 'the misery of the captive' enslaved (around line 85), and he is clear about 'the wrongs of the poor African' (around line 115) at the hands of 'the dealer in this infernal traffic' which creates in his mind 'a horrid picture. —' (around line 120), but one does not feel that Burns fully 'feels/ the sacred claim of helpless woe' (lines 266–267). He may appreciate the poem in private correspondence, but he does not heed its clarion call and take that message into his own public sphere. This sympathetic absence was recognised by Thomas Pringle (1789–1834), the Scots poet, admirer of Burns, South African sojourner and himself a leading Abolitionist, who first printed this letter in 1817, long after Burns's death, with the editorial opinion that

> The Critique, though not without some traits of the poet's usual sound judgement and discrimination, appears on the whole to be much in the strain of those gallant and flattering responses which men of genius sometimes find it incumbent to issue when consulted upon the productions of their female admirers.[120]

EVALUATION: POSITIVE

This appears to be almost an entirely literary critique on Burns's part rather than a confirmation of his support for the poem's polemic. On balance, while Burns is not spurred into action by the poem and adds

---

119 Miss Williams replied on 7 August, 'I do not lose a moment in returning you my sincere acknowledgements for your letter, and your criticism of my poem, which is very flattering proof that you have read it with attention. I think your observations are perfectly just except in one instance [where] [y]ou have, indeed been very profuse of panegyric on my little performance.' The poem was not included in her *Poems, Second Edition*, 2 vols (London: T Cadell, 1791) but was later revised as 'On the Bill which was Passed in England for Regulating the Slave-Trade; A Short Time before its Abolition,' in Helen Maria Williams, *Poems on Various Subjects* (London: G and WB Whittaker, 1823), pp.166–180. However, while the political passages about Pitt and Richmond are dropped and the poem updated, not a single one of Burns's literary suggestions were incorporated, and one line he specifically admired was dropped.

120 [Thomas Pringle], *Edinburgh Magazine*, September 1817. For a brief assessment of Pringle's poetry see Nigel Leask, '"Their Groves o' Sweet Myrtles": Robert Burns and the Scottish Colonial Experience,' in *Robert Burns in Global Culture*, ed by Murray Pittock (Lewisburg, PA: Bucknell University Press, 2011), pp.184–185; McGinn, *Comprehensive*, p.124.

little personal disapprobation of the 'infernal traffic,' his comments show that he is opposed to it, and several of his observations around the feelings of the 'Captive band' exhibit the kindness often found in his non-satirical poems. Overall, though, it is hard not to agree with Pringle, as the composition shows that Burns is clearly not engaged in any depth with the Abolition movement.

No 17: [1789] [K.269] 'The Five Carlins — A Ballad — Tune, Chevy Chase'; [1789] [K.270] 'The Laddies by the Banks o' Nith ('Election Ballad for Westerha')'; and [1790] [K.318] 'Epistle to Rob[er[t Graham Esq[uire] of Fintry on the Election for the Dumfries String of Boroughs, Anno 1790 —.'[121]

Burns was poetically involved in the contest for the seat of Dumfries Burghs in the 1790 General Election in support of the sitting MP, Sir James Johnstone, Baronet of Westerhall.

> The first ane was a belted knight,
>   Bred of a Border band,
> And he was gae to London town,
>   Might nae man him withstand. —   K.269, lines 29–32

> But wha is he, his country's boast?
>   Like him there is na twa, Jamie;
> There's no a callant tents the kye,
>   But kens o' Westerha', Jamie.   K.270, lines 13–16

> What Whig but melts for good SIR JAMES!
> Dear to his Country, by the names,
>   Friend, Patron, Benefactor!   K.318, lines 102–105

ANALYSIS

Burns (like many) had an antipathy to the rakish Duke of Queensbury known as 'Old Q' (1724–1810) to such an extent that, on his Grace proposing Patrick Millar, Younger of Dalswinton (1769–1845) as his candidate in the Whig interest for Dumfries Burghs in 1789, Burns turned from Miller, the son of his Ellisland landlord, to support the

---

121 These three poems will be assessed as one connected work.

sitting MP, Sir James Johnstone, 4th Baronet of Westerhall (1726–1794), whose family had been traditional opponents of the Queensbury interest and who had held the seat in the previous parliament as an independent Tory.[122]

The poet penned three election poems in support of Johnstone's unsuccessful (and extravagantly corrupt) campaign to keep his seat.[123] The poems themselves have no connection to slavery or Abolition, but the context is important as Sir James and two of his brothers were plantation owners on Grenada, Tobago and Dominica. Another brother, John (1734–1795), was a successful nabob who owned the unfortunate enslaved Bengali woman Bel (or Belinda) and Johnstone's niece was the wife of John Wedderburn, Joseph Knight's quondam 'master.'[124] Of the plantocrats, Sir William (1729–1805) (who had changed his surname to that of his heiress wife, Pultney) and Alexander (1727–1783) were both paternalist pro-slavers and Sir James, who inherited Alexander's Westerhall plantation (including its 263 enslaved people) in 1783, was an early ameliorist, who moved towards Abolition (although not prepared to adopt it unilaterally).[125]

It was Sir James who transmitted the petition of the Dumfries Synod to the Commons in April 1788 and, the following year, William Dickson dedicated his hard-hitting *Letters on Slavery* to him, apostrophising him '[w]ith the respect due, not only to an honest man, and to a virtuous Senator, but to a *humane, disinterested Planter.*'[126]

---

122 Sir James was the third of that name to serve as MP for the Dumfries Burghs at Westminster, following his father and grandfather. The latter and his father had sat for Dumfries in the old Scots Parliament.

123 Following the Union of the Parliaments in 1707, Scotland sent Members of Parliament to Westminster representing Counties (directly elected) and Groups of Burghs (indirectly elected by Town Councils). The Dumfries Burghs Constituency comprised Dumfries, Lochmaben, Annan, Sanquhar in Dumfriesshire and Kirkcudbright in the Stewartry. Each Town Council (itself a self-selected oligarchy) would vote individually, and appoint a delegate to vote on behalf of that burgh on Election Day for the candidate supported by the majority on Council. The five delegates met at the 'head burgh' (which rotated at every election) and each had a single vote (like the Electoral College of the USA), with the delegate of the head burgh having an additional casting vote. Burns, in K.269, shows a lack of knowledge on how the votes were influenced, suggesting that Lochmaben, Annan and Kirkcudbright were inclined to Johnstone whereas it was only by bribery (and kidnapping) that he won the first two on the Provost's casting vote.

124 Emma Rothschild, *The Inner Life of Empires* (Princeton: Princeton University Press, 2011), p.2.

125 Westerhall, Grenada was 'an extremely valuable estate and was reckoned to be "one of the best properties in the Islands", annually producing crops worth £10,000 in the years before 1795.' Hamilton, SCAW, p.74.

126 Wilkins, p.85; Whyte, *Scotland and the Abolition*, p.71. National Records of Scotland: *Synod of Dumfries Minutes*, (1787–1805), 15, 16 April 1788, CH2/98/5, pp.22–24; William Dickson, *Letters*

He spoke in the Commons debate of 25 April 1792 (having been returned by his brother William's pocket borough of Weymouth & Melcome Regis in 1791 after his defeat at Dumfries), calling for

> immediate abolition of the trade. He had introduced the plough into his own plantations in the West-Indies, and he found the land produced more sugar than when cultivated in the ordinary way by slaves. Even for the sake of the planters, he hoped the abolition would not be long delayed.[127]

On the deaths of Sir James and his widow, the estate passed to his brother Sir William Pultney, Bart (1729–1805), by then reputedly the richest commoner in England and 'the plough was abandoned, because, on that Estate, it was found to accomplish no saving of expense, no acceleration of labour, and because it added nothing to the crop.'[128] In 1837, Sir Frederick Johnstone (1810–1841), Pultney's grand-nephew and the seventh baronet, received government compensation of £4,867 18s 1d in respect of the emancipation of 176 enslaved people on the Westerhall plantation.[129]

EVALUATION: NEGATIVE

The slavery question was not a plank in either campaign for the parliamentary seat in 1790, and though the source of the Johnstone brothers' wealth would have been well known, and Sir James was reputed an Ameliorist and later Abolitionist, Burns did not consider it germane to the political events of the day either to condemn the plantations, nor praise Johnstone's humanity. It is interesting, however, that his dislike of Queensbury could outweigh both Burns's then Foxite tendencies and the personal relationships which the poet had with Captain Miller's father (his landlord) and his uncle (Lord Barskimming).[130]

---

on *Slavery* (London: J Phillips [and others], 1789), p.[1].
127 Clarkson, *History*, vol.II, p.458.
128 Rothschild, p.166; It would appear that Sir James's innovations were not particularly successful (or that the debts of the estate were simply too great), and to redeem borrowings from Alexander's ownership, Sir William returned to the traditional model of full enslaved labour. See Douglas Hall, 'Incalculability as a Feature of Sugar Production during the Eighteenth Century,' *Social and Economic Studies,* September 1961, pp.340–352.
129 'Sir Frederick Johnstone,' *UCL Legacies Database* (accessed 1 September 2024).
130 *Letters*: To Robert Graham of Fintry, 9 December 1789 [L.373]. Equally quixotically, Burns

No 18: [?1791 or 1793?] [K.527] 'A Fragment — On Glenriddell's Fox Breaking His Chain —' [131]

In this (fragmentary) example of Burns's later, political poetry, he reflects on his friend Captain Robert Riddell of Glenriddell's alignment with the ideals of the Foxite Whigs, including what Leask calls 'the paradox of Riddell being at once a member of Scotland's landed elite and a proselytizer for the rights of man,' through the double metaphor of Riddell's pet fox. The vulpine subject not only reminds us of the great, but controversial, Whig statesman Charles James Fox (1749–1806) in name, but makes the reader wonder about Riddell, seeking freedom for man, but enchaining a wild animal as a pet.[132]

>   THOU, Liberty, thou art my theme;
>   Not such as idle Poets dream,
>   Who trick thee up a Heathen goddess
>   That a fantastic cap and rod has:
>   Such stale conceits are poor and silly;   5
>   I paint thee out, a Highland filly,
>   A sturdy, stubborn, handsome dapple,
>   As sleek's a mouse, as round's an apple,
>   That when thou pleasest can do wonders;
>   But when thy luckless rider blunders,   10
>   Or if thy fancy should demur there,
>   Wilt break thy neck ere thou go further. —
>   These things premised, I sing a fox,
>   Was caught among his native rocks,
>   And to a dirty kennel chain'd,   15
>   How he his liberty regained. —
>
>   Glenriddell, a Whig without a stain,
>   A Whig in principle and grain,
>   Couldst thou enslave a free-born creature,

---

send His Grace a copy of 'The Whistle' with a fairly grovelling letter in 1791 [L.471], after which they were introduced. Burns covered his bases (for Riddell and Cragendarroch were political allies of Old Q) in GRM 2 by writing 'Though I am afraid His Grace's character as a man of worth is very equivocal, yet he is certainly a Nobleman of the first taste, & a Gentleman of the first manners —' *Oxford Burns*, vol.I, p281, *Glenriddell Ms*, vol.II, p.89.

131 *Oxford Burns*, vol.I, pp.237–239: *Glenriddell Ms*, vol.I, pp.146–149.
132 *Oxford Burns*, vol.I p.396.

A native denizen of Nature? 20
How couldst thou with a heart so good,
(A better ne'er was sluice'd with blood!)
Nail a poor devil to a tree,
That ne'er did harm to thine or thee?

   The staunchest Whig Glenriddell was, 25
Quite frantic in his Country's cause;
And oft was Reynard's prison passing,
And with his brother-Whigs canvassing
The Rights of Men, the Powers of Women,
With all the dignity of Freemen. — 30
   Sir Reynard daily heard debates
Of Princes', kings' and Nations' fates;
With many rueful, bloody stories
Of tyrants, Jacobites, and tories:
From liberty how angels fell, 35
That now are galley-slaves in hell;
How Nimrod first the trade began
Of binding Slavery's chains on Man;
How fell Semiramis G[o]d d[a]mn her!
Did first, with sacrilegious hammer, 40
(All ills till then were trivial matters)
For Man dethron'd forge hen-peck fetters;
How Xerxes, that abandoned tory,
Thought cutting throats was reaping glory,
Until the stubborn Whigs of Sparta 45
Taught him great Nature's Magna Charta;
How mighty Rome her fiat hurl'd,
Resistless o'er a bowing world,
And kinder than they did desire,
Polish'd mankind with sword and fire: 50
With much too tedious to relate,
Of Ancient and of Modern date,
But ending still how Billy Pit[t],
(Unlucky boy!) with wicked wit,
Has gagg'd old Britain, drain'd her coffer, 55
As butchers bind and bleed a heifer. —

>   Thus wily Reynard by degrees,
>   In kennel listening at his ease,
>   Suck'd in a mighty stock of knowledge,
>   As much as some folks at a college. —   60
>   Knew Britain's rights and constitution,
>   Her aggrandisement, diminution,
>   How fortune wrought us good from evil;
>   Let no man then despise the devil,
>   As who should say, I ne'er can need him;   65
>   Since we to scoundrels owe our freedom. —

ANALYSIS

This poem is primarily a broad allegory on the Foxite Whig politics of the day.[133] However, it strays into the question of slavery through Charles James Fox's early commitment to the Abolitionist cause. Lord John Russell (later defined the political legacy of Fox who 'vindicate[d], with partial success, but with brilliant ability, the cause of freedom and the interests of mankind. [...] He denounced the slave trade.'[134] In fact, after moving the Commons' motion for Abolition in June 1806, although he would die before the Bill passed in 1807, Fox said:

> If, during the almost forty years I have now had the honour of a seat in Parliament, I had been so fortunate as to accomplish [Abolition], and that only, I should think I had done enough [with] conscious satisfaction that I had done my duty.[135]

Turning to the poem: in lines 35–38, (once again) Burns reflects on Milton's *Paradise Lost*. The first allusion 'From liberty how angels fell,/ That now are galley-slaves in hell' is to the fall of Satan and his rebellious angels who were

---

[133] The Whig party were then in Opposition to the Government of William Pitt the Younger and had two factions, the Portland Whigs and the more radical Foxite Whigs, named after their leaders.
[134] Lord John Russell, *The Life and Times of Charles James Fox*, 2 vols (London: Richard Berkeley, 1859), vol.i, p26. Lord John (1792–1878), Earl Russell after 1861, in a long political career served twice as Prime Minister.
[135] 'A Barrister' [J Wright], ed, *The Speeches of the Right Honourable Charles James Fox in the House of Commons*, 6 vols (London: Longman, Hurst, Rees, Orme and Brown, and J Ridgeway, 1815), vol.VII, p.659.

> Hurled headlong flaming from the ethereal sky
> With hideous ruin and combustion down
> To bottomless perdition, there to dwell
> In adamantine chains and penal fire.[136]

Burns famously used 'galley-slave' in reference to his own predicament in the *Autobiographical Letter* (as discussed above), and here Milton seeks to inspire horror at the fate of the impious angels, cast from the light of liberty, enslaved penally and perpetually under the just wrath of God.[137]

However, of more interest are lines 37–38: 'How Nimrod first the trade began/ Of binding Slavery's chains on Man;' which give one of his few explicit references to chattel slavery (as opposed to the punishment enslavement just mentioned). 'Nimrod the mighty hunter before the LORD,' and Biblical King of Babylon was the grandson of Ham, and nephew of Canaan (Genesis, x, 8–10). The Biblical references to him are slight, but Rabbinistical exegesis developed a back-story which was well-known to Christian commentators, including a belief that Nimrod was the first man to enslave others. Milton addresses this in Book XII of *Paradise Lost*:

>   till one shall rise
> Of proud ambitious heart; who, not content
> With fair equality, fraternal state,
> Will arrogate dominion undeserved
> Over his brethren, and quite dispossess
> Concord and law of nature from the earth;
> Hunting (and men not beasts shall be his game)

---

136 John Milton, *Paradise Lost*, Bk.I, ll.45–48, alluding to Isaiah, xiv, 14–18.
137 Remembering that Burns mentions Satan 'at least, as Milton describes him,' with some admiration to Mrs Dunlop: *Letters*, 7 March 1788 [L.219], or to Agnes McLehose, 'My favorite feature in Milton's Satan is, his manly fortitude in supporting what cannot be remedied [...]', *Letters*, January 1788, [L.171]. That latter conception bears comparison with Olaudah Equiano (1745?–1797) in his influential slave-narrative *The Interesting Narrative of the Life of Olaudah Equiano, or Gustavus Vassa, The African. Written By Himself* (London: For the Author, 1789). Here, this same passage was used (with three other Miltonic quotations). Equiano's Miltonic descriptions of Hell and the sufferings of the fallen angels to illustrate the horrors of the West Indies and the privations and fates of the enslaved Black population. For Milton, God's revocation of the liberty enjoyed by the fallen angelic horde was just and awesome, for Equiano, slavery's depriving of liberty from the enslaved Black people was unjust and awful, using the same words but re-positioning the original trope. See Mary Nyquist, 'Equiano, Satanism, and Slavery,' in *Milton Now. Alternative Approaches and Contexts*, ed by Catharine Gray and Erin Murphy (New York: Palgrave Macmillan, 2014), pp.215–245.

> With war, and hostile snare, such as refuse
> Subjection to his empire tyrannous:
> A mighty hunter thence he shall be styled
> Before the Lord; as in despite of Heaven,
> Or from Heaven, claiming second sovranty;
> And from rebellion shall derive his name,
> Though of rebellion others he accuse.
> He with a crew, whom like ambition joins
> With him or under him to tyrannize,
> Marching from Eden towards the west, shall find
> The plain, wherein a black bituminous gurge
> Boils out from under ground, the mouth of Hell:
> Of brick, and of that stuff, they cast to build
> A city and tower, whose top may reach to Heaven;
> And get themselves a name; lest, far dispersed
> In foreign lands, their memory be lost;
> Regardless whether good or evil fame.[138]

That Nimrod, the mythological creator of chattel slavery, should be ranked with the enemies of liberty, and of the Foxite Whigs, is the clearest statement yet of Burns's developing position: that chattel slavery is a subset of the deprivations of freedom and equality which he has consistently denounced in domestic circumstances.

Again, this poem was a private, personal communication (the poem was first published in 1874) which may be why Burns feels able to write in a more controversial and anti-slavery way, knowing that its tone chimed with the views of his friend, the recipient.[139]

EVALUATION: POSITIVE

It is clear that Burns numbers Black chattel slavery with a range of other attempts to remove liberty from the individual. Again, it must be noted that it is a subtle, not overt, private, not public denunciation, but it is sufficient that he recognises many affronts to freedom that we would take for granted today.

---

138 Milton, *Paradise Lost*, XII, ll.24–47.
139 Henry A Bright, ed, *Some Account of the Glenriddell MSS of Burns's Poems* (Liverpool: Gilbert G Walmsey, 1874), p.47.

No 19: [L.508] [1792], Letter to William Corbet, [February 1792]. [140]
In February 1792, Burns wrote to William Corbet (1755–1811), one of two Supervisors General of the Excise Service in Scotland, angling for promotion to the Dumfries Port Division [see L.494]. Corbet's wife was a friend of Mrs Dunlop, who added her patronage to Burns's hopes. Corbet acquiesced to this request in August or early September. The poet sent his formal but belated thanks, promising to send Mrs Corbet a set of the two-volume *Second Edinburgh Edition*, then in press. In apologising for his late reply, Burns adds some witty (and self-serving) observations on how hard he has been working, but that:

> [n]ever did my poor back suffer such scarification from the scourge of Conscience, as during these three weeks your kind epistle has lain by me unanswered. — A negro wench under the rod of a West-Indian Mistress; a nurse under the caprice of a spoiled child, the only son & heir of a booby Squire; nay, a hen-peckt Husband under the displeasure of his virago wife — were enviable predicaments to mine. —

ANALYSIS
In corresponding with social superiors who could engage patronage influence on his behalf, Burns often adopted an engaging, chatty, witty, multi-metaphoric tone. Corbet (pushed by Mrs Dunlop) was an important potential patron, and this letter is Burns's thanks for Corbet's facilitating a transfer to the higher remuneration of the Excise's Dumfries Third Foot Walk. Here, the poet had been dilatory in his thanks, hence 'the scourge of Conscience,' which he partially (and self-servingly) attributed to his heavy hours on the Excise rounds. He looks to list several amusing stock figures who suffer daily punishment under a capricious other in a Smollett-like list, including (uncomfortably) '[a] negro wench under the rod of a West-Indian Mistress.'

House-slaves had, in a number of ways, better conditions than their fellow enslaved in the fields and boiling houses. However, neither male nor female were exempt from arbitrary and cruel punishment for perceived transgressions. As an example, take Mary Prince (1788–after 1833) who was born into enslavement on Bermuda and who was 'sold off' as a house-servant in 1800 to a Mrs Inghams where she was

---

140 *Oxford Burns*, VOL.I, pp.279–280: *Glenriddell Ms*, VOL.II, pp.85–86.

licked and flogged, and pinched by her [mistress's] pitiless fingers in the neck and arms [...] To strip me naked — to hang me by my wrists and lay my flesh open with the cow-skin [sc: whip], was an ordinary punishment for even a slight offence. [...] There was no end to my toils — no end to my blows.[141]

The others in Burns's list, the 'nurse,' 'son & heir' and 'hen-peckt' husband have some agency: the enslaved maid has virtually none. The Black housekeeper/cook/servant trope was (and to an extent still is) one of the most enduring around the enslaved: think of the servant characters in *Gone with the Wind*, or *Tom and Jerry*, while it took until 2020 for Mars to rebrand 'Uncle Ben's Rice', marketed since 1946, and for Quaker Oats to remove the 'Aunt Jemima' branding for a range of syrups and pancakes which had been sold since 1890.[142]

So, perhaps Burns should not be treated too harshly here.

EVALUATION: NEGATIVE
Like 'Uncle Ben' and 'Aunt Jemima', here Burns uses a careless trope. Furthermore, that any Black chattel-slave could be considered to have had an 'enviable predicament to mine,' is an utterly unwarranted and untrue statement, although it is a throw-away line. In 1792 the Abolition debate was significant across the country, and Dumfries (though no hotbed of Abolitionism) would hear Dickson lecture, would see Kemble perform as Yarico and then, through its leading citizens, present two petitions for Abolition to the House of Commons. Burns was more aware of the position of enslaved people and of the increasing pressure for reform, where the egregious ill-treatment of the Black enslaved was an increasing focus of the Abolitionist argument. So here, in making jest of her predicament, Burns belittles the enslaved woman.

No 20: [1792] [K.378] 'The Slave's Lament.'[143]
At face value, this song is a clear, unequivocal denunciation of Black enslavement. However, it has raised a level of controversy around

---

[141] Mary Prince, *The History of Mary Prince: A West Indian Slave, Related by Herself*, ed by Thomas Pringle (London/Edinburgh: F Wesley and A H Davis/Waugh & Innes, 1831), p.8.
[142] *Fortune*, 11 February 2021.
[143] *Scots Musical Museum*, IV.384, in *Oxford Burns* vol.ii, p.465, vol.III, pp.141–142. NB the title in *Museum* is the 'Slaves [sic] Lament.'

a number of points: its authorship by Burns; where he received his inspiration for the work; and whether it is merely passively sentimental or is an active part of 1792's growing awareness of, and opposition to, Black chattel slavery.

> IT was in sweet Senegal that my foes did me enthrall
>   For the lands of Virginia-ginia, O;
> Torn from that lovely shore, and must never see it more,
>   And alas! I am weary, weary O!
>   Torn from that lovely shore, and must never see it more;   5
>   And alas! I am weary, weary O!
>
> All on that charming coast is no bitter snow and frost,
>   Like the lands of Virginia-ginia, O;
> There streams for ever flow, and there flowers for ever blow,
>   And alas! I am weary, weary O!   10
>   There streams for ever flow, and there flowers for ever blow,
>   And alas! I am weary, weary O!
>
> The burden I must bear, while the cruel scourge I fear,
>   In the lands of Virginia-ginia, O;
> And I think on friends most dear with the bitter, bitter tear,   15
>   And alas! I am weary, weary O!
>   And I think on friends most dear, with the bitter, bitter tear,
>   And alas! I am weary, weary O!

ANALYSIS

First published in the fourth volume of Johnston's *Scots Musical Museum*, this is the song that is very often used as a 'get-out-of-jail-free card' for Burns by his supporters and commentators.

As can be seen from this chapter, Corey Andrews is not quite correct in calling this '[t]he single work in Burns's oeuvre with an overt reference to slavery', but it is fair to say that it is the sole work where its reception in 1792 would have been seen as avowedly Abolitionist.[144] Or as Gerry Carruthers trenchantly puts it, '[it] provide[s] an otherwise disappointed politically correct readership for the Scottish Bard with

---

144 Corey Andrews, '"Ev'ry Heart Can Feel": Scottish Poetic Responses to Slavery in the West Indies, from Blair to Burns', *International Journal of Scottish Literature*, 4 (2008).

a slender thread to tie him to the Abolitionist cause.'[145]

On the positive side, it was written in 1792 at the time of the heightened awareness of the Abolition Cause after William Dickson's tour around Scotland sparked a significant number of petitions and remonstrances against slavery from Kirk bodies and parishes, burgh councils, tradesmen's incorporations and others (as discussed above), including two from Burns's neighbours in and around Dumfries (although it should not be forgotten that Dickson found the town of Dumfries not particularly warm in its actual support).[146] Those efforts, combined with Burns's sentimental encounters on the page with Helen Maria Williams's 'Poem on the Slave Trade' (see above) and *Julia de Roubigné,* and on the stage with *Inkle and Yarico* (see below) make it possible to advance the proposition that this was a work written by Burns with a growing understanding of, and in direct opposition to, Black chattel slavery. It would be easy to concur with Sir Geoff Palmer that 'the "Slave's Lament" of the Burns of 1792 was written by a wiser Burns that the Burns of 1786, who was about to sail for Jamaica to be, in his own words, a "slave driver."'[147]

First of all, its authorship needs confirmation. On its first appearance in the *Scots Musical Museum,* it was signed with the cypher 'R', which is one of the codes Burns used for his own compositions, and there is a holograph copy of the song included in the collection of Burns papers bequeathed to the British Museum by Archibald Hastie, MP.[148] It was Allan Cunningham in 1825 who started the confusion by including the song in a collection he had edited, but remarking that '[o]f the author of this sweet song I can give no account.'[149] This ran on, through Kinsley (who wrote that 'Burns's part in this song is uncertain. It is ascribed to him only on the evidence of the Hastie MS,') into the recent essays by Carruthers and Leask.[150] That position has been turned around in the new Oxford Edition of the Works of

---

145 Carruthers, *Robert Burns and Slavery,* p.167.
146 Whyte, *Scotland and the Abolition,* p.79.
147 Geoff Palmer, 'Postscript: Jamaican Scottish Connections', in *Africa in Scotland, Scotland in Africa: Historical Legacies and Contemporary Hybridities,* ed by Afe Adogame and Andrew Lawrence (Leiden: Brill, 2014), p.358.
148 See *Oxford Burns,* vol.II, p.21. British Museum: Hastie MS, MS 22307.
149 Allan Cunningham, *Songs of Scotland, Ancient and Modern,* 4 vols (London: John Taylor, 1825), vol.II, p.223.
150 *Poems,* vol.III, p.1404; Carruthers, *Robert Burns and Slavery,* p.23; Leask, 'Sweet Myrtles', p.178.

Burns's *Scots Musical Museum*, edited by Murray Pittock, with a re-assessment of the song as 'Category I [A song wholly by Burns, with no prior antecedents identified, or suspected] or Category III [A song significantly by Burns, with only isolated lines or a combination of phrases, subject matter, and tune evident from earlier evidence.]'[151] That part of the controversy is now laid to rest.

An aligned critique is that, if 'The Slave's Lament' is by Burns, it is not an original work, but a reworking of a tale of a kidnapped White girl, 'The Trapann'd Maid,' which (from Kinsley to Pittock) is widely agreed by scholars to be the structural inspiration for the song:

Give ear unto a Maid,
That lately was betray'd,
    And sent into Virginny O:
In brief I shall declare,
What I have suffered there,
When that I was weary,
    Weary, weary, weary, O.[152]

Again, this criticism is not particularly valid, as Burns's main literary activity at that date was exactly that: finding shards of songs and fragments of ballads, and re-forging them on the anvil of his skill. While 'The Trappan'd Maid' provides the template and rhyme scheme, the lyric adopts the weariness of the kidnapped, but transferred to the mouth of a Black enslaved person (the lyric being unclear whether the singer is male or female). As can be seen in both *Scots Musical Museum* and Thomson's *Select Airs*, Burns repeatedly finds an old song and reworks it to produce a new finished work, so 'The Slave's Lament' cannot be dismissed on the grounds of being a mere copy, though that analysis (if accepted) nudges it slightly more towards Pittock's 'Category III.'[153]

---

151 With Pittock also seeing the influence of 'The Virginia Maid's Lament,' from Buchan's *Ancient Ballads*.
152 *Poems*, vol.III, p.1405.
153 That reworking appears to have been possibly prompted, at least in part, by a passage in Helen Maria Williams's poem, which was discussed above:
  Poor wretch! on whose despairing eyes
  His cherish'd home shall never rise!
  Condemn'd, severe extreme, to live
  When all is fled that life can give! —
  And ah! the blessings valued most

Next, two myths around the composition need confirmatory demolition. The first is that Burns witnessed a slave ship in the port of Dundee in 1787 during his Highland Tour which later inspired this song. This can be firmly denied from extant contemporary documents.[154] Neither Burns's *Journal of his Highland Tour*, nor his letter about it to Gilbert make a mention of visiting Dundee's docks, let alone encountering a slave ship (which in the triangular trade, would not have enslaved men and women on board in Dundee in any case). While there are records of Dundee to Caribbean trading in goods and materials, there is no evidence of a fully-fledged 'slaver' operating out of Dundee at that time.[155] Also, a few days later, after visiting Castle Gordon, he wrote a poem (see above) which mentions slavery in poetical tropes rather than hard reality, which appears unlikely were he burning from the shame or indignation of having seen (and smelled) a slave ship in the flesh.

The second myth is that the tune is a traditional air from Africa. Like so many Burns fantasies, this canard arises from 'honest Allan' Cunningham, who glossed 'The Slave's Lament' thus, in his 1825 song book:

> It is generally believed to be expressed in something like the simple language of that hapless race who were for so many centuries condemned by European avarice to perpetual slavery. The air too is supposed to be of African extraction. Indeed, the slaves in the West Indies have a remarkable taste for music; and every step they take, and every task they perform, is accompanied by song.[156]

This thread was picked up by the Scots antiquarian and musicologist William Stenhouse (ca 1773–1827) in his notes to an edition of the *Scots Musical Museum*, which were copied in his later work *Illustrations* (a Victorian companion to the *collection*), both published posthumously,

---

By human minds, are blessings lost!
Helen Maria Williams, *A Poem on the Bill Lately Passed in England for Regulating the Slave Trade*, ll.199–204.

154 'There are no known voyages from Dundee to Africa to transport enslaved people, although records are incomplete.' Matthew, Jarron, Erin Farley and Dolina Mechan, eds, *Breaking the Chains* (Dundee: University of Dundee, 2022), p.11.

155 *Oxford Burns*, vol.I, pp.141, 153.

156 Cunningham, *Songs*, vol.II, pp.223–224.

opining that '[t]he Slave's Lament [...] [t]he air, it is said, is an original African melody,' a supposition roundly (and quite correctly) classed as 'nonsense' by the noted scholars James C Dick, Kinsley and all subsequent commentators, including Pittock.[157]

The next question must be, is it an Abolitionist text? There are negatives in its construction, the biggest drawback being the historicisation contained in the song's geographies: the 'Slave' is captured in Senegal (which was a territory which had been ceded by Britain back to France in 1783) and transported for sale in Virginia (again, no longer under British suzerainty, *de facto* from 1776 and *de jure* from 1783). He may, however, have been influenced by Guthrie's *Geographical Grammar*, a book from his youth (see L.125) a revised edition of which he bought for the Monklands Friendly Society [see L.430). The earlier 1776 edition of Guthrie contains the following passage that may have stuck in his mind when composing this song:

> The acquisitions which the English have made upon the coast of Guinea, particularly their settlement at Senegal, have opened new forces of commerce with Africa. [...] At present England [...] supplies her American colonies with negro slaves, amounting in number to above 100,000 annually.[158]

The 1790 edition places that in the past tense (at p.278), as 'Senegal is now delivered up to France by the late treaty of peace.' Had Burns wanted to hit a blow against the contemporary British slave trade, surely he would have called out the British Guinea coast and the British West Indies rather than the French colony and the independent USA, and, in doing so, fitted the song firmly in the Abolitionist's debate in Britain?

Which encourages some to doubt the connection with chattel slavery: as Corey Andrews puts it '[t]he poem offers no explicit denunciations of slavery, instead focusing on the sorrows of departure

---

157 James Johnson and William Stenhouse, ed, *The Scottish Musical Museum*, 4 vols (Edinburgh/London: William Blackwood and Sons/Thomas Cadell, 1839), vol.IV, p.353; William Stenhouse, *Illustrations of the Lyric Poetry and Music of Scotland* (Edinburgh: William Blackwood and Sons, 1853), p.353; James C Dick, ed, *The Songs of Robert Burns Now First Printed with the Melodies for which They were Written; A Study in Tone-Poetry with Bibliography, Historical Notes, and Glossary* (London/Glasgow/Edinburgh/New York: Henry Frowde, 1903), p.479; *Poems* vol.III, p.1405.
158 Guthrie, [1776], p.231.

felt by the slave.'¹⁵⁹ When he felt strongly on an injustice, we know how hard Burns could kick back: so there is an argument that the muted tone of this song does not strike true in Burns taking up the cudgels for oppressed Black people.

However, the counter-argument to that is plain: it is obvious what the song is about, and it is the singer's enunciation of the enslaved speaker's woe that drives the sympathetic response of the auditor. Clarkson records an episode in his *History*:

> With respect to [the enslaved in the Middle passage] singing, it consisted of songs of lamentation for the loss of their country. While they sung they were in tears: so that one of the captains, more humane probably than the rest, threatened a woman with a flogging because the mournfulness was too painful for his feelings.¹⁶⁰

Just as a painting is not (and maybe should not aspire to be) a photograph, poetry (and especially song-writing) perhaps should *not* be explicit. In both, there is a medium of inspiration involved. This point was raised in a recent review of a comprehensive collection of Abolitionist poetry:

> With a few minor exceptions these works of imaginative literature devoted to the cause of abolition make depressing reading. Philanthropic indignation does not guarantee literary brilliance. Reading these selections, with their repetitive allusions to 'the Sable race,' 'Afric's sorrows,' the 'tortur'd bosoms' of 'Afric's sons,' not to mention plays with Black characters who say things like 'O Massa — You make poor black free,' one wonders whether there was not a massive, collective failure of imagination here; whether British writers were not so thrilled with the opportunity to exploit

---

159 Andrews, 'Ev'ry Heart'. Other commentators find the sentimental tone difficult. Michael Morris sums up that concern: 'Marcus Wood has importantly critiqued the sentimental construction of enslaved persons, as found in this song ['The Slave's Lament,' K.378] largely as passive, mournful victims. Despite the constant resistance to their condition, performed in a variety of ways, sentimental literature preferred them to be pitifully subject to "the middle passage, domestic and plantation tortures, rape, [and] slave auction." This critique "warns that there is often little to distinguish between representations of Africans in either pro- or anti-slavery verse [in terms of this] sentimental construction."' Michael Morris, *Scotland and the Caribbean, c.1740—1833: Atlantic Archipelagos* (Abingdon/New York: Routledge, 2015), quoting Marcus Wood, ed, *The Poetry of Slavery: An Anglo-American Anthology, 1764–1865* (Oxford: OUP, 2003), p.xvii.
160 Clarkson, vol.I, p.51.

the emotive, tear-jerking possibilities of such a subject — and serve a good cause into the bargain — that they abandoned every attempt at self-criticism.[161]

Given its importance in the analysis of Burns's opinions on slavery, this short song has received much critical attention over the last decade. In terms of its merit as a literary work, it has divided opinion: Dick (in 1903) judged it 'sentimental, but by no means a bad tune,' while in recent years Carruthers deemed it 'rather insipid' and 'fairly pallid stuff'; for Leask it was 'beautiful'; Valentina Bold found it 'personal and empathetic,' while Whyte called it 'whimsical' in 2006, revising his view to 'poignant' in 2015.[162] It is fair to say that the lyric does not jump off the page, which may influence some scholars, but when the song is sung (without undue sentimentality) a better appreciation of both its qualities today, and – more importantly – its intended effect on listeners then, can be gauged.[163] It is that tone in the work which inspired Maya Angelou's heartfelt opinion that in this song Burns goes 'beyond his race, his class, his culture, so deep into what a slave must have felt.'[164]

Burns arguably avoids that 'failure of imagination', and the song must be adjudged the better for it.

Going beyond its geographical settings, the negative case for the song would define it as a sentimental, historical ballad based on extant tropes of 'betrayal' and 'transhipment' which set up no overt denunciation of the Black chattel slave trade as a greater moral evil than, say, kidnapping, or the perceived injustices perpetrated on

---

161 Anthony John Harding, 'Review of [...], *Slavery, Abolition and Emancipation: Writings in the British Romantic Period*, (8 vols), (London: Pickering and Chatto, 1999),' *BARS Review & Bulletin no 17*.
162 James C Dick, ed, *The Songs of Robert Burns* (London/New York: Henry Frowde, 1903), p.479; Carruthers, *Slavery*, p.167; Leask, 'Sweet Myrtles,' p.178; White *Scotland and the Abolition*, p.57; Valentina Bold, *Robert Burns & 'The Slave's Lament' [Talk delivered at Wigtown Book Town Festival, 2007]*; Iain Whyte, '"The Upas Tree: Beneath whose pestiferous shade all intellect languishes and all virtue dies": Scottish Public Perceptions on the Slave Trade and Slavery, 1756–1833,' in *Recovering Scotland's Slavery Past*, ed Devine, p.187.
163 This song has been recorded many times since 2007. Its quality can be judged in this rendition by the Scots soprano Davidona Pittock for the Centre for Robert Burns Studies: burnsc21.glasgow.ac.uk/the-slaves-lament-davina-pittock/ (accessed 1 September 2024). It was earlier set to music by Joseph Haydn (1732–1809), 'The slave's lament,' Hob. XXXIa no 137.
164 Maya Angelou, speaking in the documentary film *Angelou on Burns*, directed by Ellie M Taylor in 1996.

White people judicially punished through transportation as indentured labour (first to the American colonies and now, as Burns could see, to Botany Bay in New South Wales).

Six substantive lines of 'The Slave's Lament' (shown in Table 6 below) have clear parallels with how Burns portrayed his own situation six years previously. The sentimentality of the song echoes the very self-pity exhibited in (and criticised in) 'The Farewell' [K.122] above: Burns's perception that he was being torn from his home by foes, never to look on his homeland again, while facing risk and pain in the absence of all his friends.

Table 6: Comparison of Sentiments – 'The Slave's Lament' and 'The Farewell'	
1792 – The Slave	1786 – The Bard
IT was in sweet Senegal that my foes did me enthrall	[...] farewell, my foes! My peace with these, [...]
Torn from that lovely shore, and must never see it more,	These bleed afresh, those ties I tear, To leave the bonie banks of *Ayr*.
All on that charming coast is no snow and frost,	The scenes where wretched Fancy roves
There streams for ever flow, and flowers for ever blow,	Farewell, old *Coila's* hills and dales Her heathy moors and winding vales
The burden I must bear, while the cruel scourge I fear,	I think upon the stormy wave, Where many a danger I must dare
And I think on friends most dear, with the bitter, bitter tear,	Farewell, my friends! [...] The bursting tears my heart declare

This is not to say that Burns's position in 1786 *en route* to Jamaica to become a plantation enforcer is equivalent in any way to the enslaved singer's Middle Passage journey (although Burns wrongly thought so in 1786), but, rather, it shows how Burns used sentimentality (in both works) to evoke an auditor's response using similar literary mechanics.

Certainly, the song has resonated with modern Reggae artists: Brina, initially in the 'Jamaica Sings Burns' project, recorded 'The Slave's

Lament' several times and added personal lines and content.[165] Ghetto Priest sang it as part of a Graham Fagen multi-media installation for the 2015 Venice Biennale (and since reprised) to become, in his words, 'the voice, to represent over 800 million souls.' Fagen also expressed a generous view of Burns in this context:

> In 1792 Burns wrote that song about a woman taken from Senegal to endure inhumane treatment in Virginia. This was at a time when people began to petition against slavery. Burns was a smart man and he knew plenty about slavery, its benefits and its evils. He used the arts to send monumental messages the whole world o'er of the brotherhood, and the meaning of the essence of unity, among humanity. That side of Burns is worth upholding.[166]

While the historicity of part of that statement is challenged elsewhere in this book, the overall thrust rings true, so perhaps academics are too literally critical of a song which reaches out with appeal to the non-literary-critical auditor. In 1792, the proponents of Abolition used every available medium to spread the truth: not just formal petitions, meetings and lectures, but cheap broadsides, newspaper letters, and popular songs and ballads, too, a point touched on by Andrews, who imagines Burns's inspiration around 'its melancholic refrain' with Burns 'clearly hoping that it would be taken up and sung across the nation.'[167] Having a singable sentimental song (in the right place and time) could easily persuade a listener more than a long polemic by Williams or Marjoribanks. This is shown by the almost uniformly welcoming responses from Black writers, artists and campaigners, epitomised by the South African diplomatist and poet Dr Lindiwe

---

165 'The Slave's Lament.' (Jamaica Sings Robert Burns: Brina 2015): a sample of her extra lyrics:
It was in sweet Senegal that my foes did me entrap
For the isle of Jamaica O.
Torn from that lovely shore, Mama Africa,
Oh alas! I am weary, weary O!
Torn from that lovely coast, Mama Africa,
O ah ya, ya ya ya.
166 'British Council interview with Graham Fagen,' 22 March 2018, www.britishcouncil.org/voices-magazine/how-two-artists-interpret-their-shared-history (accessed 1 September 2024.) *Herald* [Glasgow], 21 January 2018. See also, Graham Fagen, Douglas Gordon, Jackie Kay, *The Slave's Lament/Black Burns* (Edinburgh: National Galleries of Scotland, 2017).
167 Brycchan Carey, *British Abolitionism and the Rhetoric of Sensibility: Writing, Sentiment and Slavery, 1760–1807* (Basingstoke, Hants: Palgrave Macmillan, 2005), p.97.

Mabusa (1938–2021) who read this poem at a Burns Night at South Africa House in 2002 while serving as High Commissioner:

> I was completely overwhelmed by some emotional turmoil on reading this poem ['The Slave's Lament.'] Here was Burns, a white man, jumping out of his privileged white skin to figuratively and emotionally enter the body, mind and soul and sensibilities of an African slave 'torn from that lovely shore' of Senegal.
>
> The word 'torn' cut deep inside the womb. That tearing works on several levels — the physical separation, being geographically uprooted from one's country; alienation from all that is familiar and normal culture [...] an imposed new identity; chains cutting into the flesh; the whip; the sizzling of the branding iron; the meticulously orchestrated 'breaking' of who you are, because all fundamental elements that define African's humaneness must rupture. The anguish was total.[168]

So, while 'The Slave's Lament' is in no respect a clarion call for Abolition, as 'Scots Wha Hae' and 'Honest Poverty' trumpeted national independence and human brotherhood respectively, this analysis suggests that by 1792 Burns was able to see the anguish and unfairness of the Black chattel slave's situation, albeit through a rather selfish, or at least self-referential analogy. The very fact that a pro-Abolition song is included in the *Museum* 'bears witness, in any case, to the widespread interest in and support for the Abolition movement.'[169]

This poem marks a change in Burns's thoughts for the better. In many ways, its reception and analysis by the Academy is less important than its poetical and emotional effect on Black artists and audiences today.

EVALUATION: VERY POSITIVE

This work gives a clear, direct comment on the human iniquity of the slave trade. Its weaknesses as an argument are its essential slightness as a work and its historical setting (Senegal, by then a French colony, and Virginia, by then independent and American), both of which could distance the reader/listener of Burns's day such that the 'Lament'

---

168 Dr Lindiwe Mabuza, in *Touched by Burns: Images and Insights*, ed by Andy Hall (Edinburgh: Birlinn, 2008), p.137.
169 Alan Richardson, ed, *Slavery, Abolition and Emancipation: Writings in the British Romantic Period, Volume 4: Verse* (Abingdon/New York: Routledge, 1999), p.218.

fails to reach the trumpet heights of Burns's great works. Its arguable redemption comes from the equality of sympathetic narration between the slave here, and Burns himself in 'The Gloomy Night' which creates a sympathetic linkage across the two works. Its championing in recent years by significant members of the Black literary and artistic community underscores its worth. It is a song that should be sung and heard, and not perhaps clinically dissected, for its poignant worth to be appreciated.

No 21: [1794] [K.452] 'Epitaph for Mr Walter Riddell.'
Burns's epigrams on those he wished to put down, are often extremely sharp and funny. Occasionally, as here, the gall is overpowering.

> So vile was poor Wat, such a miscreant slave,
> That the worms even damn'd him when laid in his grave.
> 'In his scull there's a famine!' a starved reptile cries;
> 'And his heart it is rank poison!' another replies.

ANALYSIS

Walter Riddell (1764–1802) was second son of Walter Riddell of Newhouse and brother to Captain Robert Riddell of Glenriddell (see above). Lieutenant Riddell was serving in Antigua in 1795 when he married Ann Doig, life tenant of her late father's Rendezvous Estate, with its 207 enslaved persons. Ann died a year later, and Walter remained in Jamaica investing in another plantation. In 1790 he married Maria Banks Woodley (1772–1808), daughter of the former MP, colonial administrator and slave-holder William Woodley.[170] The Walter Riddells moved to London soon after, having two daughters before Walter put down a deposit for the purchase of Goldilea, an

---

170 William Woodley (1728–1793): slave-holder on St Kitts, where he inherited estates from his father (also William, husband of Ann Payne). He served as MP for Great Bedwyn 1761 to 1766, until appointed as Governor of Leeward Islands between 1766 and 1771. He returned to parliament for Marlborough in 1780 for four years. After some years of lobbying, he was re-appointed Governor of the Leeward Islands in 1792, dying there, in office, the following year. His will provided for his widow, younger sons and daughters (Maria receiving £6,000) with his estate passing to his son William Woodley III. In 1836, William Woodley IV received £2,770 17s 3d in compensation for 174 enslaved persons on the Needsmust Estate on St Kitts with a second, mortgaged estate yielding compensation of £2,925 4s 2d in respect of 172 enslaved persons for the benefit of creditors. www.historyofparliamentonline.org/volume/1754-1790/member/woodley-william-1728-93; wwwdepts-live.ucl.ac.uk/lbs/person/view/2146644865 (accessed 1 September 2024).

estate near his brother Glenriddell in Dumfries, renaming it Woodley Park and moving there in 1792. He returned to Antigua (to raise the balance of the purchase monies) and Maria became a firm friend of Burns until the Riddells broke with Burns over a drunken fracas which occurred in December 1783 (although Maria and Burns would be reconciled in his last months). Walter returned to Scotland having failed in his attempts to raise cash, and sold back the estate (at a loss) to its previous proprietor, as described by Burns:

> Wattie has sold his Woodley Park to Colon[e]l Goldie, the last Proprietor. Wattie gave 16000 £ for it; laid out better than 2000 £ more on it; and has sold it for 15000 £. So much for Master Wattie's sense and management, which, entre nous, are about the same pitch as his worth.[171]

The Walter Riddells moved twice to smaller houses in Dumfriesshire, and Walter returned to visit to his Antigua properties in late 1796, dying there in 1802, with his estate falling to his creditors. Maria moved to London with her surviving daughter, living in a grace-and-favour apartment at Hampton Court Palace until she remarried in 1807, dying the following year.

The use of the word 'slave' in line 1 is merely a derogatory epithet, and is very unlikely to be a transferred epithet applied to a slave-holder, so again Burns, when venting spleen on 'poor Wat' for being stupid, unkind and no businessman, does not use his ownership of enslaved people against him, even though Burns knew that Maria had developed Abolitionist views.

EVALUATION: NEGATIVE

As with Mrs Oswald of Auchincruive, Burns's invective against Walter does not use his slave-holding as a stick to beat the man. As the Abolition debate was in full swing in 1794, and given Burns's antipathy to Walter Riddell, if the poet viewed both slavery and Riddell in abhorrence, then there would have been a direct statement of condemnation, even in such a short pasquinade.

---

171 *Letters:* To John McLeod of Colbecks, 18 June 1794, [L.626].

No 22: [1794] [K.451] 'Ode for General Washington's Birthday.'[172]
In recent studies, more attention has been given to the complexity of assessing the history and legacy of the first president of the United States of America, George Washington (1732–1799), who was simultaneously the liberator of his country and the owner of enslaved Black men and women. No doubt the enslaved peoples in America rejoiced at being now in thrall to a Republican, and not a Monarchical, constitution.

Burns sent a first draft of the last section of this poem (in this form) to Mrs Dunlop, telling her 'The Subject is LIBERTY: you know, my honored Friend, how dear the theme is to me. —'[173]

> NO Spartan tube, no Attic shell,
>   No lyre Eolian I awake;
> 'Tis Liberty's bold note I swell,
>   Thy harp, Columbia, let me take.
> See gathering thousands, while I sing,   5
> A broken chain, exulting, bring,
>   And dash it in a tyrant's face!
> And dare him to his very beard,
> And tell him he no more is feared,
>   No more the Despot of Columbia's race.   10
>   A tyrant's proudest insults brav'd,
> They shout, a People freed! They hail an Empire saved.
>   Where is Man's godlike form?
>   Where is that brow erect and bold,
>   That eye that can, unmov'd behold   15
>   The wildest rage, the loudest storm
> That e'er created fury dared to raise?
>   Avaunt! thou caitiff, servile, base,
>   That tremblest at a Despot's nod,
>   Yet, crouching under th' iron rod,   20

---

172 Unbeknown to Burns, Washington owned a copy of his poems in his library at Mount Vernon: Robert Burns, *Poems, Chiefly in the Scottish Dialect, To which are Added, Scots Poems selected from the Works of Robert Ferguson*, (New-York: J and A McLean, 1788) [Egerer §11]. Appleton PC Griffin and William Coolidge Lane, *A Catalogue of the Washington Collection in the Boston Athenæum* (Boston: Boston Athenæum, 1897), no.116, p.432.

173 *Letters*: To Mrs Dunlop, 25 June 1794, [L.628], at vol.II, p.297. The poem's subsequent complex and late publishing is of no concern in this analysis.

Canst laud the hand that struck th' insulting blow!
   Art thou of man's Imperial line?
   Dost boast that countenance divine?
   Each sculking feature answers, No!
   But come, ye sons of Liberty,   25
   Columbia's offspring, brave as free,
In danger's hour still flaming in the van,
Ye know, and dare maintain, the Royalty of Man.

   Alfred! on thy starry throne,
   Surrounded by the tuneful choir,   30
The Bards that erst have struck the patriot lyre,
And rous'd the freeborn Briton's soul of fire,
   No more thy England own. —
Dare injured nations form the great design,
   To make detested tyrants bleed?   35
Thy England execrates the glorious deed!
   Beneath her hostile banners waving,
   Every pang of honour braving,
England in thunders calls — 'The Tyrant's cause is mine!'
   That hour accurst how did the fiends rejoice   40
And hell thro' all her confines, raise th' exulting voice,
   That hour which saw the generous English name
Linkt with such damned deeds of everlasting shame!
   Thee, Caledonia, thy wild heaths among,
   Fam'd for the martial deed, the heaven-taught song,   45
   To thee I turn with swimming eyes. —
   Where is that soul of Freedom fled?
   Immingled with the mighty Dead!
Beneath that hallow'd turf where WALLACE lies
Hear it not, Wallace! in thy bed of death!   50
   Ye babbling winds! in silence sweep;
   Disturb not ye the hero's sleep,
   Nor give the coward secret breath. —
Is this the ancient Caledonian form,
   Firm as her rock, resistless as her storm?   55
Shew me that eye which shot immortal hate,
   Blasting the Despot's proudest bearing:

> Shew me that arm which, nerved with thundering fate,
>   Braved Usurpation's boldest daring!
>   Dark-quench'd as yonder sinking star,   60
>   No more that glance lightens afar;
>   That palsied arm no more whirls on the waste of war.

ANALYSIS

This poem is, on the face of it, an example of the metaphorical/political sense of slavery as used by Burns. It was likely prompted by the dedication page of Paine's *Rights of Man,* which Burns had been reading, where Paine apostrophises Washington thus:

> I PRESENT you a small Treatise in defence of those Principles of Freedom which your exemplary Virtue hath so eminently contributed to establish. — That the Rights of Man may become as universal as your Benevolence can wish, and that you may enjoy the Happiness of seeing the New World regenerate the Old [...][174]

So, while Burns's words do not directly contemplate Black chattel slavery neither do they address the inconvenient fact that Washington, the hero and victor of the American War of Independence, held people in enslavement from the age of 11 until his death in 1799, thus rather diminishing the 'universality' of the 'Rights of Man' espoused by Paine.

For Washington, enslaved labour was the engine which enabled his estate and provided him income for his entire life. In 1743, upon his father's death, Washington inherited the family farm at Fredericksburg, VA with its ten enslaved people, and between 1750 and 1775 he 'bought' over 60 more on the open market, inherited a further 22 and 'rented' from other slave-holders around a dozen more on short fixed-term contracts. On his marriage to Martha Dandridge Custis (1731–1803) in the month of Burns's birth, she brought a further 84 enslaved people to Mount Vernon under a life interest from her first husband's intestate estate. To be fair, Washington would appear to have been a relatively moderate slave-holder for that period, particularly in his last years where he stopped buying and selling slaves in the market.[175]

---

174 Thomas Paine, *Rights of Man: Being an Answer to Mr Burke's Attack on the French Revolution* (London: HD Symonds, 1792), Part I, p.ii.
175 Mary V Thompson, '*The Only Unavoidable Subject of Regret*' *George Washington, Slavery,*

When Washington left Mount Vernon for the war, he took as his body-servant an enslaved man, William 'Billy' Lee (1758–1810), whom he had bought for £61 15s 0d in 1768, but initially resisted suggestions that Black men could take up arms in the revolutionary cause.[176] However, when the British issued a proclamation in December 1775 'declaring Freedom to All Indentured Serv[an]ts or Slaves (the property of Rebels) that will repair to His Majesty[']s standard', Washington's plantation manager reported this to the General and expressed his concerns: '[t]here is not a man of them [sc: the enslaved workers], but would leave us, if they believed that could make there [sic] Escape [...] & yet they have no fault to find[.] Liberty is sweet.'[177]

The estate manager was proved right on two occasions when enslaved people fled the plantation to find freedom on Royal Navy vessels. In July 1776, three of Washington's enslaved men rowed out to HMS *Roebuck* while she was cruising in the Potomac, and again in April 1781, a larger group of 17 men and women made their way on board HMS *Savage* to freedom (although it was characterised as the British 'carrying them off' to save the General's blushes).[178] Eight of them were recaptured as the tide of war turned against the British, but three embarked for Nova Scotia at the evacuation of New York.[179] As was his legal right under Oswald's Treaty of Paris, Washington repeatedly pressed his manager to sue for the compensation for those fugitives from the British Government.[180]

After the war, Washington's views on slavery continued to soften: he had long been averse to selling enslaved people on the public market and in 1786 he confirmed that 'it is [not] my wish to hold the[se] unhappy people [...] in slavery.'[181] He also resolved (with some equivocal wording) that 'I never mean (unless some particular circumstances should

---

and the Enslaved Community at Mount Vernon (Charlottesville, VA: University of Virginia Press, 2019), pp.332–336.
176 Ibid, p.278.
177 Ibid.
178 Ibid, pp.279–281. The sources are contradictory. The 1776 fugitives were Henry Washington and two others. The 1781 fugitives were: Peter, Lewis, Frank, Frederick, Gunner, Harry, Tom, Sambo, Thomas, Peter, Stephen, James, Watty/Wally, Daniel, Lucy, Esther and Deborah. The three who travelled to Nova Scotia were Henry, Daniel and Deborah.
179 Ibid, p.439, fn.143.
180 Although payments were not made until 1826: Brady, *Chained to History*. See also, Arnett G Lindsay, 'Diplomatic Relations between the United States and England bearing on the Return of Negro Slaves, 1788–1828', in *Journal of Negro History* (October 1920), pp.391–419.
181 Thompson, *Regret*, p.70, quoting letter: George Washington to Robert Morris, 12 April 1786.

compel me to it) to possess another slave by purchase.'[182] In both these letters, however, he confirmed that he would take no independent, unilateral move to manumission, believing that '[t]here is only one proper and effectual mode by which [emancipation] can be accomplished, & that is by Legislative authority.'[182] Washington's statement 'it [was] among my first wishes to see some plan adopted by the Legislature by which Slavery in this Country many be abolished by slow, sure, & imperceptible degrees' sounds rather like Sir James Johnstone (as discussed above), who failed to act unilaterally on his feelings of what was right, instead approaching Abolition with glacial Dundas-ian caution.

The radical Welsh Baptist minister Revd Morgan John Rhees (1760–1804) visited Mount Vernon in January 1795 (in Washington's absence) and excoriated the General:

> Thou great man Washington! What meaneth the ble[a]ting of these black sheep and the lowing of these Negro oxen that till thy ground? [...] The great defender of Liberty should give an example to his neighbours, worthy of himself. [...] How difficult it is for slaveholders to enter the Kingdom of Heaven.[183]

Two years later, the blind Liverpool poet, former enslaved trafficker and radical Abolition activist Edward Rushton (1756–1814) wrote an open letter to the General along the same lines:

> Oh reflect — that your rights are the rights of mankind,
>   That to all they were bounteously given,
> And that he who in chains would his fellow-man bind,
>   Uplifts his proud arm against Heaven.
>   [...]
> Oh! Washington, Ages to come will read with Astonishment that the man who was foremost to wrench the rights of America from

---

182 George Washington 10 September 1786. Founders Online, National Archives, founders.archives.gov/documents/Washington/04-04-02-0232. [Original source: The Papers of George Washington, Confederation Series, vol. 4, 2 April 1786–31 January 1787, ed. WW Abbot. Charlottesville: University Press of Virginia, 1995, pp. 243–244.]

183 Thompson, *Regret*, p.70. Rhees is echoing the words of Jesus in Matthew XIX, 24: 'And again I say unto you, It is easier for a camel to go through the eye of a needle, than for a rich man to enter into the kingdom of God.' (Also see Mark x, 25.)

the tyrannical grasp of Britain was among the last to relinquish his own oppressive hold of poor unoffending negroes.[184]

Neither appeal changed Washington's paternalist and gradualist philosophy. At Washington's death in 1799, his will immediately manumitted 'my Mulatto man William (calling himself William Lee)' with a £30 annuity 'as a testimony of my sense of his attachment to me, and for his faithful services during the Revolutionary War.'[185] (Although it is an interesting point that, had Billy Lee fled to serve a British General, he would have been a freeman for over 20 years already.) Of the other 316 enslaved people living and working at Mount Vernon, 123 people were enslaved to Washington in his own right and were to be freed upon the death of his widow, along with 33 people he had inherited on another plantation on the demise of a female relative living there. Martha chose to release them all in January 1801, perhaps in fear that she might be murdered as a way of hastening the manumissions.[186] The remaining 200 enslaved people at Mount Vernon were entailed to the four heirs of the Custis family and so could not be set free by the Washingtons, without incurring ruinous compensation to the heirs. Those poor people were never freed.[187]

Thus, at the end of his life, George Washington belatedly resolved what he had once called his 'only unavoidable subject of regret' by giving those people whom he had held enslaved 'a destiny different from that in which they were born,' a grant that Washington 'hoped

---

184 Edward Rushton, Expostulatory *Letter to George Washington, of Mount Vernon, in Virginia, On His continuing to be a Proprietor of Slaves* (Liverpool: np, 1797), title page epigram, and pp.22–23.
185 George Washington's Last Will and Testament, 9 July 1799 at Founders Online, National Archives, founders.archives.gov/documents/Washington/06-04-02-0404-0001. (accessed 1 September 2024). One of these people was West Ford (ca 1785–1863) who is the subject of an interesting controversy: 'West Ford [...] lived and worked at Mount Vernon for nearly sixty years, first as an enslaved teen-ager and continuing after he was freed. Following Washington's death, in 1799, Ford helped to manage the estate, and he maintained an unusually warm relationship with the extended Washington family. [...] His descendants have demanded that Mount Vernon recognise Ford for his contributions to the estate, which was near collapse during the decades after Washington's death. They also argue — citing oral histories from two branches of the family — that Ford was Washington's unacknowledged son, a claim that Mount Vernon officials have consistently denied.' Jill Abramson, 'Far from the Tree,' *The New Yorker*, 14 March 2022, p.20. Thompson makes the counter-argument for the father being the General's nephew, William Augustine Washington (1757–1810). Thompson, *Regret*, pp.146–151.
186 Thompson, *Regret*, pp.309–311.
187 Ibid, p.313–314.

[not to] be displeasing to the justice of the Creator.'[188] His gradualism, in retrospect, seems unbelievably passive.

This poem of Burns's embodies what later critics would name 'the Whig Interpretation of History', a view that liberal democracy (here 'freedom') was a consistent process of human development. Therefore, America's fight for independence from the British Crown is a natural progression from Wallace's fight for Scotland's independence and, in turn, both derive from Alfred the Great's codification granting 'freedom under the Law' as an essential Anglophone right. So, the overall thrust of the piece falls squarely in the ambit of political slavery.

However, there are hidden issues around chattel slavery. Burns's positioning of Alfred the Great has a flaw: for while King Alfred is rightly considered as a purposeful contributor to the rule of law and hence the unwritten constitution of the United Kingdom, his legal text, the *Domboc,* clearly sets out the parameters for the legality of slavery which existed in Anglo-Saxon England as penal enslavement (imposed as judicial punishment), voluntary enslavement (self-bonding through economic necessity) and involuntary enslavement (through military capture).[189] So two of the three men Burns apostrophises, Alfred and Washington, divided their societies by internal laws to codify chattel slavery. It may well be that both men had higher, enlightened thoughts

---

188 Rosemarie Zagarri, ed, *David Humphreys' 'Life of General Washington' with George Washington's 'Remarks'* (Athens, GA: The University of Georgia Press, 1981). The original, David Humphreys, Manuscript Biography of George Washington, [1778], is held in the American Manuscript Collection of the Rosenbach Museum and Library, Philadelphia, AMS 1079/6. Note that this museum also holds the MS of this subject ode, bound as 'The American War by Robert Burns,' Catalogue no: *Ems 462/26.63 (Burns). Colonel David Humphreys (1752–1818): soldier, diplomat, entrepreneur and poet. One of the Hartford Wits poets, he served as Washington's Aide de Camp. His commitment to anti-slavery appears stronger than his commander's, with his 1802 work 'A Poem on the Industry of the United States of America' strongly favouring emancipation. However, at Washington's death, he saluted his albeit gradualist, care in a poem of 1800:
  Where that foul stain of manhood, slavery, flow'd
  Through Afric's sons transmitted in the blood;;
  Hereditary slaves his kindness shar'd,
  For manumission by degrees prepar'd:
  Return'd from war, I saw them round him press,*
  And all their speechless glee by artless signs express. [ll.625–630]
[*Original Footnote:] General Washington, by his will, liberated all his negroes, making an ample provision: for the support of the old, and the education of the young. The interesting scene of is return home, at which the author was present, is described exactly as it existed.
David Humphreys, *The Miscellaneous Works of David Humphreys* (New York: T & J Swords, 1804), at p.180.
189 Stefan Jurasinski and Lisi Oliver, *The Laws of Alfred: The Domboc and the Making of Anglo-Saxon Lawbooks* (Cambridge: Cambridge University Press, 2021).

than many of their slave-holding peers, but they did not regard all those who lived within the boundaries of their new laws as 'a People freed!' or 'freeborn', as in the poem.

There was, of course, before, during and after the American War of Independence a significant interest in finding an accommodation with the colonies, and it was easy to mythologise Washington, the British-army-trained farmer who, like the Roman Dictator Cincinnatus (ca 519BC–ca 430BC), forsook his plough for war when his nation was imperilled, then after securing military victory over its enemies, retired again to wear the coat of a simple landowner. Yet that old plough of Washington's was operated by enslaved workers, as Rushton clearly shows. Interestingly, Burns probably saw a performance of a Comic Opera by the Scots playwright Archibald Maclaren (1755–1826) entitled *The American Slaves, or Love and Liberty*, as it was performed in the Dumfries Theatre in late 1792. The script is lost, but the local paper points us to its abolitionist stance and its inclusion of a cameo role of 'General Washington in his camp.'[190]

However, one wonders how the enslaved people on Mount Vernon would respond to 'liberty's bold note', for the free nation's new constitution enshrined slavery and its concepts for decades yet to come, following Washington's 'slow, sure, & imperceptible degrees.' Were any of those men and women working the Mount Vernon crops to 'tell him he no more is feared' and to free themselves, take a 'broken chain [...]/ And dash it in a tyrant's face' (ll.6–7) then they would face the death penalty (judicially or extra-judicially.)[191] Where does the poem call that out?

---

190 Crawford, *Bard*, p.372. Archibald McLaren or Maclaren (1755–1826): Scottish soldier and playwright of over 80 short plays between 1781 and 1826. He fought in the American War of Independence and in the Irish insurrection of 1798, after which he returned to civilian life in London. See [John Maidment, William Hugh Logan, eds], *Memoir of Archibald Maclaren, Dramatist: With a list of His Works* (Edinburgh: np, 1835).
191 *Acts of the Assembly of Virginia*, 4 *Anne c.XLIX*, An Act Concerning Servants and Slaves, [1705]: 'Article XXXIV. And if any slave resist his master, or owner, or other person, by his or her order, correcting such slave, and shall happen to be killed in such correction, it shall not be accounted felony; but the master, owner, and every such other person so giving correction, shall be free and acquit of all punishment and accusation for the same, as if such incident had never happened: And also, if any negro, mulatto, or Indian, bond or free, shall at any time, lift his or her hand, in opposition against any [C]hristian, not being negro, mulatto, or Indian, he or she so offending shall, for every such offence, proved by the oath of the party, receive on his or her bare back, thirty lashes, well laid on; cognizable by a justice of the peace for that county wherein such offence shall be committed.'

EVALUATION: NEUTRAL
Recognising the heroic efforts of Washington *quâ* military leader while ignoring him *quâ* slave-holder is understandable at both a political and hagiographic level. Burns knew well that the Virginia economy was underpinned by the economics of chattel slavery and turned a blind eye to what Washington, to his credit late in life, called his 'only unavoidable subject of regret': his ownership of hundreds of enslaved Black people.

No 23: [1794] [K.463] 'On Seeing Mrs Kemble in Yarico.'

Burns was a great supporter of the theatre, including helping to found the Theatre Royal, Dumfries in 1792 (which is the oldest working theatre in Scotland today.)[192] In October 1794, captivated by watching the leading lady's performance as a wronged woman facing enslavement, he dashed off an epigram to her, expressing his sympathy and praise:

> KEMBLE, thou cur'st my unbelief
> Of Moses and his rod:
> At Yarico's sweet notes of grief
> The rock with *tears* had flow'd. —

ANALYSIS

Elizabeth Kemble, née Satchell (1763–1841) was a popular actress and soprano whose acting was noted for its 'sweetness' in representing romantic heroines. In 1783, after several successful seasons at Covent Garden, she married fellow actor Stephen Kemble (1755–1822) and, on his leaving the company at the end of that season, she joined him as he built a career as actor-manager in provincial theatre.[193] She returned to the London stage to star in the play *Inkle and Yarico* in 1787 as the female lead, Yarico, an indigenous Native princess.[194] In it, she saves a stranded Englishman and, upon returning to the trading port, she is betrayed by him as he decides to traffic her into enslavement, but

---

192 Crawford, *Bard*, p.341.
193 *DNB*. The Kembles were evidently taken with Burns. At his death in 1796 Stephen wrote a 'Monody on the Death of Burns' which first appeared in chapbook form and he later worked up into a performance to music for two voices. See Thomas Park, ed, *The Poetical Works of Robert Burns. Collated with the Best Editions*, 2 vols (London: J Sharpe, 1807), vol.I, pp.vii–viii.
194 By George Colman the younger (1762–1836). Please see below at p.246.

her tears result in his change of mind and he marries her.[195]

The play is an odd mixture of early Abolitionist thought and crude racial (and sexual) stereotype. *The Cambridge Guide to Literature in English* describes it as a 'deserved success [...] humanely if uninsistently critical of the slave trade.'[196] It played around the country for many years on the back of both the growing calls for Abolition and Mrs Kemble's ability to reduce the house to tears, which was remarked upon in the notices of its first performance in London:

> Those sweet and pathetic tones and that exquisite plaintiveness by which Mrs Kemble, in Yarico, brought tears into the eyes of the audience, defy the powers of panegyric.[197]

Kemble's company performed the play in Dumfries in October 1794, with the opening night being reported in the local press:

> On Friday last, our theatre received a great acquisition in the favourite opera of Inkle and Yarico, by the first appearance of Mrs Kemble, in the amiable and interesting character of Yarico. Her excellent performance of that character has been the subject of high panegyric. We can only join our tribute to her established reputation, by observing that her delineations were striking, natural, and affecting, and commanded the attention and applause of an elegant audience.[198]

Burns attended the performance on Monday 25th. Is this epigram merely a gallantry from Burns to a beautiful and accomplished actress who had given him the pleasure of a sympathetic or sentimental portrayal of a tragic heroine? If, say, Mrs Kemble had played Dido, or Cleopatra, or maybe Cordelia, would her skill in drawing tears have equally affected Burns? Or was this anti-slavery text brought to life by her acting, such that stony-hearted Burns was struck by the rod of her acting skill, himself to open in floods of emotion? The

---

195 Burns bought a copy of George Coleman's *Works* from Hill for the Monklands Friendly Society: *Letters*: To Peter Hill, 2 March 1790, [L.395, at vol.ii, p.20].
196 Ian Ouseby, ed, *The Cambridge Guide to Literature in English* (Cambridge: Cambridge University Press, 1991), p.207.
197 *General Magazine, and Impartial Review*, August 1787.
198 *Dumfries Journal*, 21 October 1794.

quatrain's trope founds on the Biblical story of Moses miraculously finding water (through God's gift) in the desert wilderness in the mist of the squabbling Israelites – now Burns says that his hard heart sheds real tears towards the enslaved heroine.[199]

In 2013, a previously unknown letter from Burns to Mrs Kemble was discovered. It is a reply to her letter and is only partially dated 'Tuesday morn', so it might be imagined that, on receiving the epigram, she replied to Burns requesting a copy of his book. Instead, he offered

> to send you a Manuscript of mine which has very little other value than its being a private thing. – 'Tis a Collection of some of your humble servant and devout Admirer's Letters, which he began Collecting, for as a boon of Friendship to a much valued Character [...], as giving a faithful picture of the Author whose Work you wished to peruse.[200]

This 'Collection' was the *Glenriddell Manuscript*. The Poet asked the Actress to 'keep the book under lock & key, when you go out,' given its highly personal nature. This was quite a personal compliment to Kemble, however, the *Daily Record*, which led the news of the finding, wrote (completely incorrectly) that the manuscript 'was a further collection of his letters to his friend Robert Riddell on the anti-slavery topic' which was taken up by several commentators as proof of Burns's Abolitionist stance, being unaware that it was a collection of his poetry and general insights.[201]

---

199 *Exodus*: XVII, 5–6: '5 And the Lord said unto Moses, Go on before the people, and take with thee of the elders of Israel; and thy rod, wherewith thou smotest the river, take in thine hand, and go. 6. Behold, I will stand before thee there upon the rock in Horeb; and thou shalt smite the rock, and there shall come water out of it, that the people may drink. And Moses did so in the sight of the elders of Israel.'
200 Helena Anderson-Wright, 'A Secret of No Importance?', *Burns Chronicle* (Spring 2013), pp.10–12. The letter was discovered in an autograph album compiled by Mrs Frances Crawford Arkwright (1786–1849, Mrs Kemble's daughter) and held at the Derbyshire Record Office: Catalogue no: D2387/1/1.
201 'Letter from Robert Burns to be Unveiled Today, 254 Years After His Birth,' *Daily Record* [Scotland], 25 January 2013. As an example of the hyperbole, see this passage from 'The Portsmouth Poetry Blog': 'that he wrote poems against slavery at home and abroad and helped the actress Elizabeth Kemble to raise funds for the anti-slavery movement before Wilberforce!'

EVALUATION: POSITIVE[202]

Despite Yarico being not an African, but an indigenous Native, her enslavement was shocking for audiences in its challenging the 'out of sight, out of mind' approach to West Indian chattel slavery, and the tone of the play was clearly recognised as Abolitionist. That the audience could be turned to tears by Kemble's skill in conjuring the dignity and morality of Yarico's accusation of Inkle is both a validation of her art and of the unjustness of chattel slavery. Burns's sensibility and emotions are clearly engaged with the about-to-be enslaved Yarico, and although it is hard to see that as Burns's ringing endorsement of Abolition in the Caribbean, his engagement against slavery here seems genuine (if perhaps not motiveless), and echoes his donation of Henry McKenzie's *Julia de Roubigné*, with its anti-slavery subplot, to the Dumfries Library the previous year.[203]

**No 24: [1795] [K.482] 'Song — For a' that and a' that —';
'[A Man's a Man for a' that]'; or ['Honest Poverty'].**

The greatest difficulty in analysing Burns's protean qualities as a writer and thinker is how to remove the generations of anaphoric gloss added by all modes and manners of men and women who have found solace and inspiration from Burns's poems and songs, but have contributed suppositive interpretations that have become lodged as definitive exegesis. The thrust of this song – which Robert Crawford calls 'his best known poem of egalitarian *fraternitié*,' – is clear but it has complex depths.[204] Does it have a place in the sub-canon of Burns's works on slavery or is it in the 'political/coward slave' category?

    Is there for honest Poverty
       That hings his head, and a' that;
    The coward-slave, we pass him by,
       We dare be poor for a' that!
    For a' that, an' a' that.   5
       Our toils obscure and a' that,
    The rank is but the guinea's stamp,

---

202 This would be STRONG POSITIVE, but for doubts about Burns's motive being a response to Elizabeth Kemble's charms, rather than to the play's message.
203 See p. 279 below.
204 Crawford, *Bard*, p.383.

> The Man's the gowd for a' that. —
> [...]
> Then let us pray that come it may,
>   As come it will for a' that,
> That Sense and Worth, o'er a' the earth   35
>   Shall bear the gree, and a' that.
>   For a' that, and a' that,
>   It's coming yet for a' that,
>   That Man to Man the warld o'er,
>   Shall brothers be for a' that. —   40

ANALYSIS

Most commentators interpret this song in one of two ways: in the complicated context of Burns's overall politics and his initial response to the French Revolution, or as an embodiment of his Freemasonic beliefs. This study will not delve into that contested territory. In either of those analyses, 'coward-slave' has typically been assigned to the raft of 'political slave' metaphors (as discussed at the beginning of this chapter) and offers no direct view on Black chattel slavery.

It is obvious, but worth re-stating, that Burns does not define 'Man' in any limiting sense (such as male, or White, or Christian) so there is a simple argument that this is an inter-racial call to world brotherhood. Nigel Leask, in 2009, noted an intertextuality between this song and Helen Maria William's poem on *Dolben's Bill*, which was critiqued by Burns (as discussed above.) There, she introduces the character of the 'generous sailor' [emphasis added]:

> *His* breast, where nobler passions burn,
> In **honest poverty**, would spurn
> The wealth, Oppression can bestow,
> And scorn to wound a fetter'd foe.   ll. 241–244

Leask posits it is no coincidence that 'honest poverty' appears in both poems, but is that connecton sufficient to 'read down' (as the lawyers would say) the concept of Abolition from Williams's verses into this song of Burns's? Leask's argument is bolstered by the textual observation that line 40 of 'Honest Poverty' was first sent to Thomson as 'Shall equals be for a' that. —' the correction to 'brothers' clearly connotes the Wedgwood medal, first cast in 1787, and its famous motto, 'Am I not a Man and a Brother?'[205]

So far, so good. Leask adds a final element to the argument for including this in the Burns Abolition sub-canon around lines 7–8:

> Ostensibly of course Burns means that social rank is no gauge of intrinsic human value. But in 1794, 'guinea stamp' had another meaning, namely the branding of slaves from the Guinea Coast of West Africa (British slavery was often known as 'the Guinea Trade' given the importance of the region as a source of slaves).[206]

A weaker version of that thesis could also be posited: the gold minted into guineas first came from Guinea. Just as the gold was exported, so were the enslaved men, just as the gold was passed through the furnace and stamped into coinage, so were the enslaved forced through the middle passage, the survivors being brutalised into labouring gangs. Burns would have known that these are common trades out of Guinea from his reading of Guthrie's *Geographical Grammar*, whose 1790 edition talks about the 'Guinea Trade':

> At present England sends to the coast of Guinea, sundry sorts of coarse woollen and linen, iron, pewter, brass and hardware manufactures, lead, shot, swords, knives, fire-arms, gunpowder, and glass manufactures. And, besides its drawing no money out of the kingdom, it lately supplied the American colonies with negro slaves, amounting in number to above 100,000 annually. The other returns are in gold dust, gum, dying and other drugs, red wood, Guinea grains, and ivory.[207]

It should be remembered, as Leask says, that it has long been understood that Burns took the conceit from a play he was familiar with: William Wycherley's *The Plain Dealer*, which has no slavery connotations at all.[208] That is not to say that Burns was incapable of taking a prior expression and making it pregnant with a second

---

205 L.651, at vol.II, p.336; Thomson mangled the text as 'The Honest Man the Best of Men,' STI12 (T163), *Oxford Burns*, vol.IV, pp.204–205 and pp.537–539.
206 Leask, *Poetics*, p.57.
207 Guthrie, [1790], p.232.
208 *Poems*, vol.III, pp.1467–1468.

meaning. However, the counter-argument to Leak's thesis (and its weaker version) is quite simple: if that had been Burns's intent, would he not have written 'the Guinea stamp,' (or 'Guinea's stamp) rather that 'the guinea's stamp' where the construction favours a reading about the coin, not the region? Although that might be countered by suggesting Burns sought connotation, avoiding, as a government employee, outright denotation (although the poem as a whole had the potential to make a placeman author rather uncomfortable under any hierarchical scrutiny).

This argument is also slightly weakened by Leask's earlier analysis of the song's first (anonymous) printing in *The Glasgow Magazine* in August 1795. In it, the first verse (including 'the coward slave' line) was omitted, which he suggests 'may have deferred to the editors' stance on the issue of African chattel slavery, views of course widely shared in Scottish radical circles in the 1790s.'[209] One point comes to mind to counter that: this song is so famous today that we tend to accept or ignore its slightly unusual grammatical opening 'Is there, for honest poverty/ that hings his head, an a' that,' which George Thomson commented was 'obscurely worded and therefore I think the Song sh[ould] begin with [the]2[n]d verse.'[210] It is more likely, on balance, that editors of the *Glasgow Magazine* shared that view.

Leask's proposition is interesting and challenges discussion, although, at the end of the day, if this is a coded Abolitionist sentiment it has taken so much analysis to find this meaning (and some 200 years for it to appear) that it is a poor piece of propaganda for the Abolitionist cause if that had been Burns's intent.

An alternative argument for inclusion in the slavery sub-canon is its obvious chime with Thomas Paine and his *Rights of Man*, a book Burns knew (and which by legend) he disposed of in February 1794 by giving them over to his friend George Haugh, a Dumfries tinsmith.[211] The Painite echoes in the words of 'Honest Poverty' have been drawn in detail by John MacCunn and Thomas Crawford in

---

209 Nigel Leask, '"The Pith o' Sense and Pride o' Worth,": Robert Burns and the *Glasgow Magazine* (1795),' in *Before Blackwood's: Scottish Journalism in the Age of Enlightenment*, ed by Alex Benchimol, Rhona Brown and David Shuttleton (London: Pickering & Chatto, 2015), p.84. 'Did newspaper editors with an abolitionist agenda [...] deliberately omit the "coward slave" stanza because it was offensive to the humanitarian sensibilities of their readers in 1795–6?' Leask, *Poetics*, p.49.
210 George Thomson, annotation on the Dalhousie Mss, *Poems*, vol.III, p.1467.
211 Mackay, p.541.

terms of radical politics – but does that carry on into Abolition?[212] There is a single mention of chattel slavery in *The Rights of Man*, but only as an analogy for hereditary monarchy:

> It is no relief, but an aggravation to a person in slavery, to reflect that he was sold by his parent; and as that which heightens the criminality of an act cannot be produced to prove the legality of it, hereditary succession cannot be established as a legal thing.[213]

This omission was called out by the radical Abolitionist Edward Rushton who wrote to Paine around 1800:

> As the clear and energetic champion for broad and general liberty, you have no a superior in the annals of mankind; yet through the whole of your writings, I do not recollect a single passage that is particularly pointed against the slavery of the negros.[214]

Many commentators and biographers commend Paine as an early and influential Abolitionist, but as one trenchantly suggests while '[i]ntellectually, Paine was antislavery, [...] he rarely transformed his thought into visible and public action,' which appears not unlike Washington's own position.[215] The addressable Paine for Burns, therefore, appears to go no further than advocation of 'brotherhood' amongst White (perhaps White, Christian) men. Perhaps the leap to all mankind was Burns's own; he certainly achieves that transference for women in 'The Rights of Woman — Spoken by Miss Fontenelle on her Benefit Night,' [K.390] (although the rights claimed are 'Protection', 'Decorum' and 'Admiration' which hardly squares with a radical political agenda – even with a provocative *ça ira!* tossed into the last line).[216]

There is one further line of thought, in seeking a parallel with

---

212 John MacCunn, *Ethics of Citizenship* (Glasgow: James MacLehose, 1895), pp.65–68; T Crawford, p.365.
213 Paine, Part I, p.62.
214 'Edward Rushton's Letter to T Paine, on the Slave-Trade,' *Belfast Monthly Magazine* (31 December 1809).
215 James V Lynch, 'The Limits of Revolutionary Radicalism: Tom Paine and Slavery,' *The Pennsylvania Magazine of History and Biography* (July 1999), p.180.
216 Although Burns does affirm feminist credentials in another work from around the same period: 'English Song. [My Spouse Nancy]' [K.441] ('Husband, Husband, Cease Your Strife,' (see above, p.113.)

William Wordsworth (1770–1850), which Leask also touches on.[217] Wordsworth spent a year in France, returning around December 1792 after Wilberforce's latest Abolition bill had failed. Even more than Burns, Wordsworth makes no poetry on the slave-trade at this point, as Marcus Wood puts it:

> Even in the 1790s Wordsworth felt detached from the slave-trade as a general political issue [...] While figures as diverse as Cowper, Coleridge, and Hazlett saw the Middle Passage as a site of horror which reaches beyond the resources of the poetical imagination, Wordsworth simply is not interested in thinking about the subject as raw material for his art.[218]

A decade later, he wrote two poems about free Black people, Touissant L'Ouverture and a nameless Black Frenchwoman, on her being exiled from mainland France.[219] In 1807, after the passing of the Abolition Act, he wrote a congratulatory sonnet to Thomas Clarkson, a friend, praising his 'unabating effort' in this 'pilgrimage sublime.'[220] These are tangential poems. Many years later, Wordsworth sought to justify this passivity, writing that 'Tho' from the first I took a lively interest in the Abolition of Slavery, [...] I was too Little of a Man of Business to have an active part in the Work – Besides my place of Abode would have prevented it, had I been so inclined.'[221]

While like Burns, there is no evidence of such a 'lively interest' in the 1790s, as Leask points out, Wordsworth's autobiographical poem *The Prelude,* substantially written in 1805, with an edited version published soon after his death (in 1850), while the original manuscript was only published in 1926.

Here are the relevant sections from Book X in each version:

---

217 Leask, *Poetics*, p.58.
218 Wood, *Anthology*, p.231.
219 William Wordsworth, *Poems in Two Volumes,* 2 vols (London: Longman, Hurst, Rees and Orme, 1807), 'Touissant L'Ouverture,' vol.I, p.134; 'September 1st, 1802,' vol.I, p.135.
220 William Wordsworth, *Poems,* 2 vols (London: Longman, Hurst, Rees, Orme and Brown, 1815), 'To Thomas Clarkson, On the final passing of the Bill for the Abolition of the Slave Trade, March, 1807,' vol.ii, p.229.
221 'Letter to Benjamin Robert Haydon, 10 September 1840,' in William Wordsworth and Dorothy Wordsworth, *The Letters of William and Dorothy Wordsworth Volume VII. The Later Years, 1840–1853, Part IV,* Second Edition, ed by Alan G Hill, and Ernest de Selincourt (Oxford: OUP: 1988), pp.605–606.

The Prelude, or Growth of a Poet's Mind: An Autobiographical Poem

From the 1850 Text, published 1850: Book X, lines 245–262.[222]	From the 1805 Text, published 1926: Book X, lines 205–227.[223]

It pleased me more
To abide in the City, where I found
The general air still busy with the stir
Of that first memorable onset made
By a strong levy of humanity
Upon the traffickers in Negro blood;
Effort which, though defeated, had recalled
To notice old forgotten principles,
And through the nation spread a novel heat
Of virtuous feeling.
                   For myself, I own
That this particular strife had wanted power
To rivet my affections; nor did now
Its unsuccessful issue much excite
My sorrow; for I brought with me the faith
That, if France prospered, good men would
    not long
 	
Pay fruitless worship to humanity,
And this most rotten branch of human shame,
Object, so seemed it, of superfluous pains
Would fall together with its parent tree.
	I found the air yet busy with the stir
	Of a contention which had been raised up
	Against the Traffickers in Negro blood,
	An effort, which though baffled, nevertheless
	Had call'd back old forgotten principles
	Dismiss'd from service, had diffus'd some truths,
	And more of virtuous feeling through the heart
	Of the English people. And no few of those
	So numerous (little less in verity
	Than a whole Nation crying with one voice)
	Who had been cross'd in this their just intent
	And righteous hope, thereby were well prepared
	To let that journey sleep awhile, and join
	Whatever other Caravan appear'd
	To travel forward towards Liberty
	With more success. For me that strife had ne'er
	Fasten'd on my affections, nor did now
	Its unsuccessful issue much excite
	My sorrow, having laid this faith to heart,
	That. if France prosper'd, good Men would not
	    long
	Pay fruitless worship to humanity,
	And this most rotten branch of human shame
	Object, as seemed, of superfluous pains
	Would fall together with its parent tree.

As can be seen from these passages, the campaign against 'the traffickers in Negro blood' who promoted 'this most rotten branch of human shame' had failed 'to rivet' Wordsworth's 'affections', such that the Bill's failure brought the poet no 'sorrow.' His mind and affections were on a higher, radical plain: the principles of the French Revolution would change all of society, and slavery 'would fall together' with the entire structures of the *anciens régimes*.[224]

Could Burns have taken a similar position? Like Wordsworth to

---

[222] William Wordsworth, *The Prelude or, Growth of a Poet's Mind; An Autobiographical Poem* (London: Edward Moxon, 1850).
[223] William Wordsworth, *The Prelude. Or Growth of a Poet's Mind, Edited From The Manuscripts With Introduction Textual and Critical Notes*, ed by Ernest De Sélincourt (Oxford: The Clarendon Press, 1926).
[224] Wordsworth's later views on slavery are not of concern here.

Haydon, would he say the few positively anti-slavery poems showed his 'lively interest', however, he was too much an Excise officer 'to have an active part in the work' and besides the lack of support in Dumfries 'would have prevented it, had I been so inclined.' Similarly, given 'Honest Poverty's' 'central place in the psalmody of radicalism' (as Kinsley describes it), is Burns looking at the problem through the same lens as Wordsworth?[225] This new world will resolve class, power and inequality so why not slavery, too? Formerly enslaved people will join this new radical world, not just as free human beings, but as equal human beings.

It is an appealing analysis. Once again, the poem can be read as embracing all humanity (blind to class, colour, religion or gender) but a critic could as easily construct a more restricted case.

EVALUATION: POSITIVE
The fundamental problem is that if Abolition and the rights of Black People are being called to our attention in this poem, it is so oblique that it has taken two centuries to decode the message. On balance, it can be said that this poem is inspired by 'basic' Paine radicalism, with the message that all human beings have equal rights. While Burns, in a way like Wordsworth, may not have thought through the consequences of 'the world o'er' in terms of extending this to Africans and Black chattel slaves, however, that is an extension easily made by the reader without having to resort to coded messages, and is in line with Burns's early thinking in 'The Ordination' with its belief in humanity over race. Burns predicts (or prays) 'That Man to Man the world o'er/ Shall Brothers be for a' that.' In writing that, he makes no qualifications, adds no footnotes, hedges not with 'ifs' nor 'buts,' and speaks to us with no equivocation around a common humanity such that any form of imposed inequality must be opposed.

No 25: [1795] [K.505] 'Poetical Inscription, for an Altar to Independence at Kerrouchtry, the Seat of Mr Heron, Written in Summer 1795.'
This short poem is addressed to Patrick Heron of Heron and Kerroughtrie (1736–1803) who was Member of Parliament for the Stewartry of Kirkcudbright, for whom Burns wrote the spirited series

---
225 *Poems*, vol.III, p.1467.

of 'Heron Election Ballads.'[226] After winning the seat unopposed, Burns sent him this complimentary verse:

> Thou of an independent mind,
> With soul resolv'd, with soul resign'd;[227]
> Prepar'd pow'rs proudest frown to brave,
> Who wilt not be, nor have, a slave;
> Virtue alone who dost revere,
> Thy own reproach alone dost fear,
> Approach this shrine, and worship here.[228]

ANALYSIS
At first glance, this appears to be a 'political slavery' trope, not one linked to chattel slavery, but there is an underlying link which warrants further investigation.

For some generations, the Whig Heron family had opposed the Tory interest in the Stewartry which was led by the Earls of Galloway. Heron's grandfather, Patrick Heron (I) (1727–1761), served as MP for the Stewartry between 1727 and 1741 and family allies held the seat until 1768, after which the Tories prevailed until the death of the Earl's kinsman, Major General Alexander Stewart (1739–1794) in December 1794. Lord Galloway struggled to find a successor candidate for the by-election, finally settling on Thomas Gordon of Balmaghie (?–1806) who had made his fortune in the Madeira wine trade. However, the combination of the late General having voted occasionally with the Opposition, and the Earl's earnest importuning Dundas for an English peerage (with its seat in the Lords) made 'King Henry IX' look elsewhere in the dispense of his government patronage. His eye was caught by Patrick (III) Heron who, despite failing in the 1774 General Election, had continued to support the mainstream Portland Whigs, not the radical Foxites, and had given his stalwart

---

226 'The Stewartry' was a species of county, the last being Kirkcudbright, dissolved in 1975. 'Shires' were overseen on behalf of the Crown by sheriffs, and stewartries by stewards.
227 Note that in the forthcoming *Oxford Burns*, vol.v, *Poems*, the text is refined, the first two lines reading 'If thine be an independent mind,/ A soul resolved, a soul resigned;' with a number of minor alterations in the subsequent lines. See Gerard Carruthers and Elizabeth Ingham, 'Robert Burns, Patrick Heron and an Annotated 1793 Poems at Mount Stuart,' *Burns Chronicle*, 133.1 (2024), p.87.
228 For a discussion of the context of 'the altar', see Patrick Scott, 'Burns and the Altar of Independence: A Question of Authenticity,' *Studies in Scottish Literature*, 48.2, pp.199–206.

opposition to Scottish reform in 1792.

With Dundas's influence behind him, Heron was in too strong a position in the poll and so, after some electoral shadow boxing, the Tories did not press on to a vote and Heron took the seat unopposed. Dundas continued to support Heron in the 1796 General Election saying that 'there is not a more respectable gentleman or friend of government in the House of Commons,' allowing his unopposed re-election. However, Heron fell at his third election in 1802, winning the vote but being disqualified because of electoral irregularities (to the chagrin of Dundas), with the seat awarded to Hon Montgomery Stewart (1780–1860), the Earl's fourth son. Heron died on his return journey from Westminster.[229]

In 1793 Burns had penned, for John Syme, several epigrams against the 7th Earl of Galloway (1736–1806) who held office in London as a Lord of the Bedchamber and while travelling with Syme around the south-west, Burns met Heron in 1794. That combination encouraged Burns to write the 'Election Ballads'.[230] Burns and Heron seem an odd friendship: Heron had been one of founders of what Burns had called 'that miserable job of a Douglas, Heron & Co's bank' whose collapse had impoverished many whom Burns knew.[231] Furthermore, Heron's patron was 'slee Dundas' and his politics were of the establishment wing of the Whig party.[232] Finally, the late MP General Stewart's widow, Mrs Catherine Gordon Stewart of Afton (ca 1745–1818), was described by Burns as 'the first person of her sex and rank who patronised his humble lays.'[233] Of course, as a sitting MP, Heron's influence could be brought into promotions within the Excise, bolstering Graham of Fintry and Corbet's efforts,

---

229 www.historyofparliamentonline.org/volume/1790-1820/member/heron-patrick-1735-1803. (accessed 1 September 2024). As Heron was returned unopposed, Burns's 'Election Ballads' (KK.491, 492, 493 from 1795 and 494 in 1796) were actually irrelevant to the political process, which was probably as well, as Burns's poetical politics is significantly more radical than that of the Heron interest. See Kinsley, vol.III, pp.1474–1475.
230 ['Epigrams on Lord Galloway'], K.415 A,B,C and D, although Galloway was not thought of well in political circles, Kinsley calls the Earl 'the undeserving victim of Burns's ill-temper.' *Poems*, vol.III, p.1434.
231 *Letters*, To James Burness, 21 June 1783, [L.14].
232 History of Parliament Online, 'Heron' (accessed 1 September 2024).
233 *Letters*, to Mrs Stewart of Stair, [September 1786], [L.47] and *Letters*, [Mrs Catherine Gordon Stewart] [Note and Dedication], October 1791 [L.477]. The first of these enclosed the 'Stair Manuscript' and the second, the 'Afton Lodge Manuscript' of Burns's poems, both now in the collection of the Robert Burns Birthplace Museum.

which appears to have been more important to Burns than Heron's antecedents or principles.[234]

The specific problem with this poem is that Heron was a committed anti-abolitionist, supporting his Heron cousins and Cochrane in-laws who were Jamaican plantation owners and voting against Abolition in the Commons debate on March 1796.[235] Recent research on the *Second Edinburgh Edition* in the Mount Stuart library of the Marquess of Bute suggests that Burns was aware of Heron's interests in the West Indies in 1794.[236] When the poet presented Heron with these two volumes, in addition to filling in the asterisk-elided names of people and places in his poems, he made three longer holograph notes (in italic below), each on poems connected with the Caribbean:

- 'To Ja[s] *Smith, Mauchline now in Grenada or Barbados.*
- 'On a Scotch Bard Gone to the West Indies.' *This was written when I was preparing for Jamaica —*
- 'Along the Lonely Bank of Ayr,' *I composed this song on the way to Greenock, to embark for the West Indies — I meant it as the last voice of Coila, in Caledonia —*[237]

As no other poem is contextualised in this fashion, it carries the strong implication that Burns was seeking to foster a connection with his potential patron through a common link with Jamaica. Even if Burns was unaware of Heron's position, he would have recognised Heron's stance after reading about the Abolition debate which was lost by the narrow margin of four votes. Yet he still wrote a final poem in support of Heron. Heron was happy for *others* to 'be, or have, a slave.'

Even allowing for the Poet's declining health, and the possibility raised by Carruthers and Ingham that here Burns 'was perhaps

---

234 'A life of literary leisure with a decent competence, is the summit of my wishes. It would be the prudish affection of silly pride in me to say that I do not need, or would not be indebted to a political friend [...]' *Letters*, to Patrick Heron of Heron, [March 1795], (L.660).
235 *UCL Legacies Database*: 'Heron' and 'Cochrane' (accessed 1 September 2024).
236 Robert Burns, *Poems, Chiefly in the Scottish Dialect*, 2 vols (Edinburgh/London: William Creech/T Cadell, 1793) ['The Second Edinburgh Edition'], in the Bute Collection at Mount Stuart, Rothesay.
237 Carruthers and Ingham, pp.89–90. The pages in the *Second Edinburgh Edition* being vol.I, p.116, vol.II. p.57 and vol.II, p.148.

characteristically guided in his personal preferences'[238], Burns's political support for this man is hard to fathom.[239]

EVALUATION: NEGATIVE
Burns, in all likelihood, knew of Heron's anti-Abolitionist stance at the point of writing this specific poem, and definitely continued to support Heron poetically in the 1796 election, which occurred after the MP's vote against Abolition. While allowance must be made for a dying man anxious to bolster his limited patronage, his annotations show an unhappy appreciation of Heron's interests.

No 26: [1796] [K.496] 'Their Groves O' Sweet Myrtle. Tune: Humours of Glen.'[240]

Currie said of this song that Burns wrote not just for the residents of Scotland, but also for 'a numerous class of the natives of Scotland [...] [e]stranged from their native soil, and spread over foreign lands'; he estimated that these 'one hundred and fifty thousand [...] expatriated

Countrymen' will sing it 'with equal or superior interest, on the banks of the Ganges or of the Mississippi, as on those of the Tay or the Tweed.'[241]

> THEIR groves o' sweet myrtle let Foreign Lands reckon,
>   Where bright-beaming summers exalt the perfume;
> Far dearer to me yon lone glen o' green breckan
>   Wi' th' burn stealing under the lang, yellow broom:
> Far dearer to me are yon humble broom bowers,   5
>   Where the blue-bell and gowan lurk, lowly, unseen;
> For there, lightly tripping, among the wild flowers,
>   A listening the linnet, oft wanders my JEAN.

---

238 Carruthers and Ingham, p.85.
239 Earlier in 1784-1785, 'The Vision' [K.62] had passed poetical encomia on various Ayrshire grandees involved in the economy of enslavement either as plantocrats, MPs who would go on to support the West Indian Interest, or polemical opponents of Abolition: James Boswell of Auchinleck, George Dempster, Sir Adam Fergusson of Kilkerran, John Hamilton of Sundrum and Hugh Mongomerie of Coilsfield. Colonel William Fullerton of Fullerton is also mentioned, who made his name through military operations in India, publishing a booklet on his return encouraging more positive engagement with the local population. While Fullerton's views on slavery are ill defined, he led the 1803 prosecution of fellow commissioner for Trinidad, Sir Thomas Picton for the torture of Luisa Calderon.
240 *Oxford Burns*, vol.IV, pp.126-127 and pp.456-457: ST69 (T95).
241 *Currie Edition*, vol.I, pp.333-334.

Tho' rich is the breeze in their gay, sunny valleys,
   And cauld, CALEDONIA'S blast on the wave;   10
Their sweet-scented woodlands that skirt the proud palace,
   What are they? The haunt of the TYRANT and SLAVE.
The SLAVE'S spicy forests, and gold-bubbling fountains,[242]
   The brave CALEDONIAN views wi' disdain;
He wanders as free as the winds of his mountains,   15
   Save LOVE'S willing fetters, the chains of his JEAN.

ANALYSIS

Written towards the end of the poet's life, this pleasant poem sets the natural wanderlust of the Scots diaspora in exotic (and increasingly imperial) lands against the magnetic pull of love of home, and of one's life-partner. Leask rightly identifies the core trope:

> In accordance with Montesquieu's theory of climate determinism, Scotland is a land of liberty precisely on account of her bracing climate and untamed mountains, so that the Caledonian's only fetters are the metaphorical chains of the lover, in contrast to the literal chains of chattel slavery associated with less well favo[u]red tropical lands.[243]

By this light, Scotland, or at least each and every Scot, is constitutionally (in both senses) immune from slavery, so this veers towards 'Political Slavery' yet its setting 'furth of Scotland' does connect it with chattel slavery as well. Given the deeper understanding that Burns had shown the year before in 'The Slave's Lament', or 'Kemble in Yarico,' it is simply disappointing to have Burns fall back on stock poetic tropes around 'slaves' in their 'spicy forests' opposed to Scots as free as the wind, echoing his 'Castle Gordon' of the previous decade. Here, Burns appears to be reverting to Stair's dictum on slavery, resulting in the poet regarding both 'Tyrant and Slave' with equal 'disdain,' with the unfortunate trope of 'Love's willing fetters' compounding the problem.[244]

---

242 [See K.105 above].
243 Leask, *Groves*, p.172. Burns re-uses part of this in 'Song' [K.499], of Chloris: 'In Love's delightful fetters, she chains the willing soul!' l.19.
244 Remembering (once again) Stair's dictum: '[T]hough *Slavery* be against the Natural Law of Liberty, yet it is received for conveniency by the Nations, being more willing to lose Liberty than

EVALUATION: NEUTRAL
While this is a relatively common poetical trope, by 1795 from the change in public perception, and from his own experience, more attention to the humanity of the enslaved in their 'spicy forest' should have been expected. The attitude shown to slavery in this work of 1796 is on a par with his writings of 1787, which shows but little engagement with the growing debate since 1792.

No 27: [1796] [K.519] 'Complimentary Versicles to Jessie Lewars: The Menagerie.'

As Burns lay dying in Dumfries with Jean Armour Burns heavily pregnant, Jessie Lewars (1778–1855), the younger sister of an Excise colleague, helped with Burns's care. One day, one of his attending physicians, Dr Alexander Brown (dates uncertain), brought a handbill for a travelling menagerie which had just arrived in town: Burns took it and wrote two extempore verses for her on its back, including this:

> Talk not to me of savages,
>   From Afric's burning sun;
> No savage e'er could rend my heart,
>   As Jessie, thou hast done:

ANALYSIS
This short poem (written while the poet was dying) is a simple effusion, written on the spur of the moment by a seriously ill man to impress the young girl nursing him. However, even in sickness, Burns was almost always a careful wordsmith, so this poem shows that he had not completely adopted the understanding of the humanity of 'savages' (and by little extension, of 'slaves') but still, at core here again, the poet sees Black people as a literary trope (or perhaps part of the menagerie itself, which would be worse) and certainly not as 'a man and a brother.'

His levity here can be contrasted with a similar passage from Helen Maria Williams,

---

Life.' Stair, *Institutions*, Lib.I, §1,11, at p.6.

> Alas, to AFRIC'S fetter'd race
> Creation wears no form of grace!
> To Them, Earth's pleasant vales are found
> A blasted waste, a sterile bound;
> Where the poor wand'rer must sustain
> The load of unremitted pain!   ll.115–120

Which is particularly noticeable as these were lines where Burns made specific comments touching on the Abolitionist sentiment to Miss Williams, calling this passage 'a striking description of the wrongs of the poor African', and specifically noting that '"the load of unremitted pain," is a remarkable strong expression.'[245] Here, calling the indigenous peoples of Africa 'savages' echoes the dehumanising rhetoric of the enslaver and the trafficker in a multitude of pamphlets, poems and expostulations, for example James Boswell's footnote to his poetic diatribe in support of enslavement:

> That the Africans are in a state of savage wretchedness, appears from the most authentic accounts. Such being the fact, an abolition of the slave trade would in truth be precluding them from the first step towards progressive civilization, and consequently of happiness, which it is proved by the most respectable evidence they enjoy in a great degree in our West-Indian Islands, though under well-regulated restraint.[246]

Here we have a failure of imagination again by Burns which makes us understand how alienating language can be, even in the hands of a consummate wordsmith. The contemporary American poet Shara McCallum, reflecting on her relationship with Burns and his works has said:

> I had to square myself against the fact that men who wrote (and write) some of the literary works I hold closest never imagined the likes of me. Or if they had, worse at times has been reckoning with how their vision of someone like me bears little resemblance to how I see myself.[247]

---

245 See above, p.171.
246 [James Boswell], *No Abolition of Slavery; Or the Universal Empire of Love; A Poem* (London: R Faulder, 1791), p.7.
247 McCallum, 'Inhumanity', p.79.

Table 7: Transcription of the Dumfries Menagerie Handbill

Now exhibiting in a large and commodious Caravan in the Market-Place, for a few Days, and positively no longer, from 10 in the morning till 8 in the evening.

A GRAND MENAGERIE OF
Wild Beasts Alive
From the FOUR QUARTERS of the WORLD
The Curious in General will find, in this Collection, the most charming Variety of the
BRUTE CREATION [...]

THE ROYAL BENGAL STRIPED TIGER [...]
The striped Laughing HYÆNAS, Male and Female [...]
THE MALE PANTHER
The Mountain LIONESS [...]
The beautiful spotted LEOPARD from India
THE LARGE POLAR MONSTER [...]
A beautiful ZEBRA CAT [...]
THREE MANDARINS,
Or Wild Men of the Wood [...]

The Real KANGAROO RAT from Botany Bay. —
FEMALE ORAN-OUTANG.
The Goat of MUNDO from the Brazils. The CIVIT CATS, Male and Female. Who are striped like a Tiger, spotted like a Leopard, and are the only two in England.
A White-faced FEMALE FAIRY, from the East-indies [...]

There are a Variety of other Animals, such as different species of Monkies, Jackalls, &c.
They are all well secured in Iron Dens, so that the most timorous may approach with the greatest safety. [...]

Admittance, Ladies and Gentlemen 1s Tradesmen, Servants &c 6d.[248]

---

248 *Burns Chronicle* (1940), plate following p.32.

EVALUATION: NEGATIVE
While this is a slight work, on a day where Burns could have had little mental concentration, the trope of the Black 'savage' is so far away from the presentation of the Slave in the 'Slave's Lament' and the recognition of Miss Williams's sentiment that this seems unfortunately retrograde.

[[Considered But Rejected]: [1785] [K.84] 'Love & Liberty — A Cantata.' ['The Jolly Beggars. A Cantata.']
Sir Walter Scott praised Burns's cantata 'for humorous description and nice discrimination of character,' calling it 'inferior to no poem of the same length in the whole range of English poetry.'[249] However, thanks to Revd Hugh Blair's sensibilities, it was neither published in the poet's lifetime, nor in the *Currie Edition*. Its first outings were printed by the Glasgow pirate bookseller Thomas Stewart, but its first 'authorised' printing is in Cromek's *Select Scottish Songs* of 1810.[250]

One of the key characters in the tale is the Fiddler, whose amorous attempts to win the Raucle Carlin brings him into confrontation with the Tinker. He is first properly introduced in a Recitativo passage:

> A pigmy scraper wi' his fiddle,
> Wha us'd at trystes an' fairs to driddle.
> Her strappin limb and gausy middle
>   (He reach'd nae higher)
> Had hol'd his HEARTIE like a riddle,
>   An' blawn 't on fire.   ll.117–121

The Tinker puts him down, telling the doxy to

> Despise that SHRIMP, that wither'd IMP,
>   With a' his noise an' cap'rin;   ll.173–174

---

[249] [Walter Scott], 'Review of Cromek's Reliques of Robert Burns,' *The Quarterly Review* (February 1809), pp.19–36.
[250] *Poems*, vol.III, pp.1148–1152; RH Cromek, ed, *Select Scottish Songs. Ancient and Modern*, 2 vols (London: T Cadell and W Davies, 1810), vol.II, p.245. Cromek gives no citation for the derivation of this variant. For the complexities around the definitive text, see *Poems*, vol.III, pp.1148–1152 and John C Weston, Jr, 'The Text of Burns' "The Jolly Beggars"', in *Studies in Bibliography*, vol 3 (1960), pp.239–247.

as he is a fine figure of a man, not a puny one like the Fiddler. The musician's height is alluded to on several occasions, he is called a 'fairy fiddler' (l.53) and 'the wee Apollo' (l.126) and he reaches no higher than the doxy's 'gausy middle' (l.120), which sets up the humorous comparison between the two rivals. However, Cromek prints an alternative variation to lines 173–174, as follows:

> That monkey face, despise the race,
>   Wi' a' their noise and cap'ring,[251]

In other contexts, 'monkey face', 'their race' and 'a' their noise and cap'ring' could be offensive, racist terms relating to Black people, such as the awful passage in Long's *Jamaica* describing the enslaved 'as libidinous or shameless as monkies [*sic*] or baboons', or in the makar William Dunbar's flyting poem of around 1508, 'Of ane Blak-Moir' also know as 'My ladye with the mekle lippis' ['To a Blackamoore Lady'] who is described (unflatteringly, in Standard Habbies) as 'tute mowitt lyk an aip,' ['her jaw juts forward like an ape's'].[252] The edition of Dunbar recorded in Burns's Library at his death is the third volume of Morison of Perth's *Ancient Scottish Poets* (of 1787) which does not contain this poem. However, the year before, Creech published a more extensive collection which did include it. While the core text of the cantata was written prior to either of these editions of Dunbar, it is a possibility that Burns wrote the Cromek variant words after reading 'My ladye with the mekle lippis' and in being influenced in his perception of Black people by Dunbar's flyting. So is the 'pigmy' in 'pigmy scraper' a transference for height, or is it an indication that the Fiddler is literally a 'pigmy' – a small Black man.

Remembering Burns's use of the word 'niger' in 'The Ordination,'

---

251 Ibid.
252 Long, *Jamaica*, vol.ii, p.383. *Ancient Scottish Poets*, 3 vols (Perth: R Morison & Son, 1787); [John Pinkerton, ed], *Ancient Scotish Poems: Never Before in Print, But Now Published from the Ms Collections of Sir Richard Maitland, of Lethington, Knight [...] Comprising Pieces Written from about 1420 till 1586*, 2 vols (London/Edinburgh: Charles Dilly/William Creech, 1786), vol.i, pp.97–98. See also, Mary L Bellhouse, 'Candide shoots the Monkey Lovers: Representing Black Men in Eighteenth-Century French Visual Culture,' in *Political Theory* (December 2006), pp.741–784 who discerns 'a metonymic link contiguity between the monkey and the African. In the course of the 18th century the figure of the monkey was increasingly connected to Black males in French codes of signification. The practice of inferiorizing servants by associating them with animals was extended to blacks, who were often likened to monkeys' at pp.74–75.

[K.85] and following the assumption that was a word he heard from Richard Brown, the West Indiaman sailor, could Brown have talked of Black musicians, or Black people in general in equally ungenerous terms using the racist monkey trope which Burns then adopted?

Given the absence of a verified source from Cromek, there is too much uncertainty here to be definitive one way or the other, so this poem will not be included in the slavery sub-canon (at this time, at least.)[253]

Burns's Writings on Black Chattel Slavery – a Summary

There are 27 poems, songs or letters reviewed as having some connection with Black chattel slavery (excluding the conjecture around 'The Jolly Beggars'). They fall into four recognisable groups:

- Nine DIRECT REFERENCES to Black enslavement; [if 'Honest Poverty' is included];
- Nine FAREWELL poems preceding his proposed departure for Jamaica;
- Six poems addressed to SLAVE-HOLDERS or ANTI-ABOLITIONISTS; and
- Three POETICAL TROPES of Black enslavement.

Broadly speaking, the analyses above show that the 'Slave-holder' poems completely ignore the immorality of the subjects as direct investors in, or political supporters of, chattel slavery; that the 'Farewell' poems exhibit poetic self-pity with no reflection of the life faced by the enslaved; and that the 'Poetical Tropes' appear more like machinery inserted into the poem, than considered statements on slavery.

---

253 One final poem was reviewed, considered and rejected as being connected to chattel slavery: [A Toast] ['Extempore Toast on the anniversary of Rodney's Victory'], [K.402]. This 1793 work a toast given at a dinner for the Dumfries Volunteers commemorates the 1782 naval victory of Admiral Rodney (and Hood) at the Battle of the Saintes in 1782 which re-established British Naval supremacy in the Caribbean. Some commentators add this as a significant event in the history of chattel slavery, allowing increased investment in the British West Indian enslaved economy and given Rodney's life-long advocacy of it, eg *Slavery and Colonialism in Edinburgh: An Independent Review* (Edinburgh: Edinburgh City Council, 2022): p.3. 'Rodney Street: Named after Admiral Sir George Rodney (1718-1792), commander of British naval forces at the Battle of the Saintes which took place on 12 April 1782 and preserved British rule and control of slavery in Jamaica. Robert Burns famously referenced the event in his 1793 poem 'Lines on the Commemoration of Rodney's Victory'. This toast by Burns is focused on the anti-French sentiment rather than a direct link to the maintenance of the slave economy of the Caribbean.

A number of commentators have been harsh on Burns in terms of what are called here the 'Direct References.' First, many of these nine works have been overlooked (notably 'On Seeing Mrs Kemble in Yarico' and 'On Glenriddell's Fox breaking his Chains'), and secondly, there has been too much concentration on 'The Slave's Lament.'

In evaluating Burns's overall position on the question of slavery, it must be remembered that the whole question of Abolition was developing in the public and political spheres contemporaneously with his writings; as Whyte generously says, '[in] the mid-eighteenth century the idea that Britain should abandon the slave trade, let alone plantation slavery, would have been all but unthinkable.'[254] From 1788 that proposition was in active debate, with William Dickson's lecture tour of Scotland in 1792 generating a wider wave of protest and petitions. Of course, it has to be borne in mind that after Burns's early death in 1796, 11 more long years would be needed for Abolition (of the slave trade alone, not the hateful institution itself) to pass the King, Lords and Commons. That being said, in perusing the newspapers from 1792 onwards, Burns must have read of the increasing controversy: even in his hometown of Dumfries, which was no hotbed for Abolition, Dickson lectured, and both the Presbytery and the Heritors submitted petitions to Parliament in 1792, while many friends and correspondents of Burns in Ayrshire and Edinburgh assumed prominent, public Abolitionary stances.

---

254 Whyte, *Scotland and the Abolition*, p.95.

Table 8: Burns's Writings on Slavery – Summary

#	YEAR	TITLE	GENRE	PRE '87	'87–'91	'92–'96
1	1784	Epistle to J[ohn] R[ankine]	*Direct*	V NEG		
2	1785	The Mauchline Wedding	*Slave-holder*	NEGATIVE		
3	1785/6	The Ordination	*Direct*	POSITIVE		
4	1786	Extempore — To Gavin Hamilton	*Farewell*	NEUTRAL		
5	1786	On a Scotch Bard, […]	*Farewell*	V NEG		
6	1786	Lines Written on a Bank-note	*Farewell*	V NEG		
7	1786	Lines to an Old Sweetheart	*Farewell*	NEGATIVE		
8	1786	The Gloomy Night is gath'ring Fast	*Farewell*	NEGATIVE		
9	[1786]	Will Ye Go to the Indies, My Mary?	*Farewell*	NEGATIVE		
10	1786	Highland Lassie, O —	*Farewell*	NEGATIVE		
11	1786	The Farewell, To the Brethren […]	*Farewell*	NEGATIVE		
12	1786	Epistle to Capt William Logan, Park	*Farewell*	NEGATIVE		
13	1786	'Autobiographical Letter'	*Direct*	NEGATIVE		
14	1787	Castle Gordon	*Trope*	POSITIVE		
15	1789	Ode, to the Memory of Mrs O[swald]	*Slave-holder*		NEGATIVE	
16	1789	Letter to Miss Helen Maria Williams	*Direct*		POSITIVE	
17	1789	Three Election Ballads	*Slave-holder*		NEGATIVE	
18	1791	On Glenriddell's Fox	*Direct*		POSITIVE	
19	1792	Letter to William Corbet	*Direct*		NEGATIVE	
20	1792	The Slave's Lament	*Direct*			V POS

#	YEAR	TITLE	GENRE	PRE '87	'87–'91	'92–'96
21	1794	Epitaph for Mr W[alter] R[iddell]	Slave-holder			NEGATIVE
22	1794	Ode for Washington's Birthday	Slave-holder			NEUTRAL
23	1794	On Seeing Mrs Kemble in Yarico	Direct			POSITIVE
24	1795	Song — For a' that and a' that	Direct [?]			POSITIVE
25	1795	Poetical Inscription	Slave-holder			NEGATIVE
26	1796	Their Groves o' Sweet Myrtle	Trope			NEUTRAL
27	1796	The Menagerie	Trope			NEGATIVE

To attempt to quantify what the effect of growing public awareness means, the next table shows each work, ranked by its evaluation, in two periods: the earlier is up to Burns failing to board the *Roselle* at Leith in December 1787, and the later is the rest of his life, with 1792 as a watershed in terms of public Abolitionist support.

Table 8a: Burns's Writings on Slavery – Evaluation by Period						
DATE WRITTEN	VERY NEGATIVE	NEGATIVE	NEUTRAL	POSITIVE	VERY POSITIVE	Total
1784–1785	1	1	0	0	0	2
1786	2	7	1	1	0	11
Before the Roselle	3	8	1	1	0	13
1787–1791	0	2	0	3	0	5
1792–1796	0	4	2	2	1	9
The rest of Burns's life	0	6	2	5	1	14
TOTAL	3	14	3	6	1	27
BROAD TOTALS	17		3	7		27

This is not the picture of someone committed to a firm view on the topic. It is hard not to agree with Basker in saying that '[t]he famous Scottish poet's response to slavery was muted and contradictory. [...] Burns was not consistent or extensive in his expression of sympathy for African slaves.'[255] An argument in his defence could be that any 1784 to 1786 poem should not be judged against Society's more developed thoughts of 1792. Yet even if those early evaluations were adjusted one place to the right, Burns remains at the lower end of the spectrum of active support for, let alone active participation in, Abolition, as shown below:

Table 8b: Burns's Writings on Slavery – Adjusted Evaluation by Period						
DATE WRITTEN	VERY NEGATIVE	NEGATIVE	NEUTRAL	POSITIVE	VERY POSITIVE	Total
1784–1786 adjusted[256]	0	3	8	1	1	13
The rest of Burns's life	0	6	2	5	1	14
SUBTOTALS	0	9	10	6	2	27
OVERALL		9	10	8		27

This study has shown that Burns's writings did engage with Black chattel slavery more than just in his 'The Slave's Lament,' but his inconsistency is frustratingly disappointing and is typified by looking at numbers 12 to 15: positive anti-slavery sentiment is actively shown to Helen Maria Williams, and in 'Glenriddell's Fox', but before he writes 'The Slave's Lament' he makes the 'negro-wench' comment in the letter to Corbet. It is not enough of an excuse to say that in his Dumfries years, he was wary of further admonition from the Excise Board for dabbling in politics, nor that his last years were wracked by illness and money worries: if he could write 'Honest Poverty' in 1795, he could have written a barnstorming justification for Abolition showing truly and universally that 'a man's a man for a' that.'

But, as we know, he did not.

---

255 James Basker, ed, *Amazing Grace: An Anthology of Poems about Slavery, 1660–1810* (New Haven: Yale University Press, 2002), p.445.
256 This moves 'VERY NEGATIVE' to 'NEGATIVE', 'NEGATIVE' to 'POSITIVE' etc.

CHAPTER FIVE

Slavery and Burns's Reading

THE YOUNG ROBERT BURNS was noted as a voracious reader within the limitations of his family's relative poverty. James Mackay captured the ethos of the Burnes family:

> He may have lacked material things, but he came from a home where learning was highly regarded, and where books, like Chaucer's poor clerk of Oxford, were more highly prized than furniture. The story that visitors to the Burnes home at meal-times invariably found the whole family (including the girls) seated at the table with a horn-spoon in one hand and a book in the other is apocryphal but probably not far short of the mark for all that.[1]

As a boy, his father's friends, Andrew Urquhart the gardener at Bourtreehill, John Murdoch the tutor and Alexander Paterson the Grammar School master (and subsequently his widow) all lent books to their friend's son. His reading was supplemented by the few books William Burnes could afford to buy, and several odd volumes lent or given by boys he knew at the school in Ayr.[2] Burns later included a description of his development as a reader in his 'Autobiographical Letter' and he regularly mentioned books he had read with his correspondents.[3] His poems are replete with quotations and literary allusions, attesting to his familiarity with the major English and Scots poets in particular. While he was not a member of the prestigious

---

[1] Mackay, *Burns*, p.65. This story originated with Willie Patrick, who worked on Mossgiel, many years after the event. 'The whole of this numerous household were accustomed to take their food in the kitchen, and Patrick mentioned that he never saw the poet at any meal except when he was reading, spoon in the one hand, book in the other.' William Jolly, *Robert Burns at Mossgiel: with Reminiscences by his Herd-boy* (Paisley: Alexander Gardner, 1881), p.26.

[2] 'I recollect indeed my father borrowed a volume of English history from Mr Hamilton of Bourtreehill's gardener. It treated of the reign of James the First, and his unfortunate son, Charles, but I do not know who was the author; all that I remember of it is something of Charles's conversation with his children.' 'Gilbert's Narrative', p.66.

[3] From the 'Autobiographical Letter.'

Ayr Library Society, he did found the Monklands Friendly Society (the 'MFS') with his friend Glenriddell and the Dumfries Library was one of many different associations which elected him to honorary membership in recognition of his poetic genius.[4] At his intestate death, his personal library of books was valued at an impressive £90 (not many people today have books worth £5,000 at home) and some years later his sons reconstructed (as far as they could recall) its contents for Robert Chambers.[5] A 20th-century reconstruction of his reading was undertaken by John S Robotham, based on literary references within the Burns canon (while noting that Robotham appears not to have seen the Chambers list).[6]

Using both these lists, and various volumes owned by Burns (and often annotated by him) now housed in various library special collections, it is possible to find the various books he read which mentioned slavery on either side of the debate, in fiction, poetry, philosophy, history and what we would now call economics. This catalogue, arranged alphabetically by author, shows particular passages which Burns read (and in some cases, commented upon) which gives an overview of the discussion of the rights and wrongs of chattel slavery that he encountered in his personal reading. Of course, he also had access to newspapers, which kept him current in the debates in Parliament and across the Nation.

The breadth of his reading is quite amazing for a man of his social class, and bears witness to his father's ambitions and the pedagogical

---

[4] A number of commentators have stated that William Burness was a member of the Air Library Society (founded by Dr Dalrymple and others in 1761) but he is not found as a member in the Society's minutes. Ayr Carnegie Library: *Air Library Society Minutes: 1776–1830*, Local Collection 670/QMC. For Monklands see *Letters*: To Sir John Sinclair of Ulbster, Bart, [August or September 1791], [L.469]. For Dumfries: Mackay, pp.527–528, quoting *Minutes of the Dumfries Library Society*, 3 March 1793.

[5] 'On the decease of Burns, the Books in his Library were numerous and well-selected; and an Edinburgh Bookseller valued them at £90, a large sum for a miscellaneous collection of volumes brought at once to peremptory sale. The following list has been furnished to the Publishers, by the sons of the Poet; and although it comprises a portion only of their father's Library, it will be accepted by his admirers as a most interesting memorial.' Robert Burns, *The Works of Robert Burns*, 2 vols, ed by Robert Chambers (Glasgow: Blackie & Son, 1857), vol.I, pp.ccxlvii–ccxlviii. It is likely that the bookseller here was Burns's friend and correspondent, Peter Hill.
Using the 'Bank of England Inflation Calculator,' £90 in 1796 would be the equivalent of £8,600 in 2024 values.

[6] John S Robotham, 'The Reading of Robert Burns,' *Bulletin of the New York Public Library*, vol. XXIV (1970), pp.561–576. Reprinted in Carol McGuirk, ed, *Critical Essays on Robert Burns* (London/New York Prentice Hall/GK Hall, 1998), pp.281–297.

efforts of Hugh Rodger and John Murdoch. For the purposes of this enquiry, some 50 books we know he read by about 40 authors mention slavery: some (like Gibbon) historically, some in novels and plays, in economics or in Enlightenment philosophy. There are many passages identified below which are clear in their denunciation of slavery and its particularly brutal manifestation in Jamaica and the Caribbean; eight of the authors on Burns's shelves were specifically noted as 'coadjutors and forerunners' of the Abolition movement by Clarkson in his *History*. A few writers sit on the fence, and a very few are positive supporters of the *status quo* to some extent or other.

In an early letter to his former schoolmaster John Murdoch he had described his favoured reading:

> My favourite authors are of the sentim[enta]l kind, such as Shenstone, particularly his Elegies, Thomson, Man of feeling, a book I prize next to the Bible, Man of the World, Sterne, especially his Sentimental journey, Mcpherson's Ossian, &c these are the glorious models after which I endeavour to form my conduct [...]

He continues that 'the man whose mind glows with sentiments lighted at their sacred flame' would be one 'whose heart distends with benevolence to all the human race.'[7] He tells Dr Moore that he had read two *Geographical Grammars*, which were critical of slavery, prior to his acceptance of the overseer's position with the Douglases. Ten years later he told Mrs Dunlop that Cowper's *The Task* contained 'the religion that exalts, that ennobles man.'[8] The six authors he cites in these two letters were unequivocally against Black chattel slavery and these themes were common. Carey describes the artistic response in the Romantic period:

> In Britain, antislavery sentiment was widespread between 1780 and 1833, particularly in the 1780s and early 90s, and again in the 1820s and 30s. As such, antislavery can be identified as one of the key movements of the Romantic era. This centrality is reflected in the cultural productions of the period: poets, novelists, philosophers and political writers joined hands with dramatists,

---
7 *Letters*: To John Murdoch, 15 January 1783, [L.13], at vol.I, p.17.
8 *Letters*: To Mrs Dunlop, 15 December 1793, [L.605], at vol.II, p.269.

artists, printmakers and musicians both to reflect and to influence public opinion, and in many cases writers and artists were the leaders of local and national antislavery organisations.[9]

But the beliefs of all these authors, though finely written and appealing to Burns, were not sufficient to dissuade him from the Jamaica job in 1786 nor, more worryingly, to maintain any sustained interest in Abolition. This is a key part of the paradox of Burns and Slavery.

A List of Burns's Books Relating to, or Discussing, Slavery[10]

1. JAMES BEATTIE (1735–1803)

Scottish philosopher and poet whose career was as Professor of Moral Philosophy and Logic at Marischal College in Aberdeen. He also assisted Johnson and Thomson in their song collections. Burns named him (to Revd John Skinner) 'the immortal author of the *Minstrel*,' [L.203] and Burns quotes him (directly or indirectly) in his poems 19 times.

Clarkson says of Beattie, that he 'took the opportunity, in [*Essay on Truth*], of vindicating the intellectual powers of the Africans from the aspersions of Hume, and of condemning their slavery as a barbarous piece of policy, and as inconsistent with the free and generous spirit of the British nation.' [vol.I, p.83].

From *The Minstrel; Or, the Progress of Genius. A Poem* (2 vols) (London: E & C Dilly, 1771–1774).

> Sweet were your shades, O ye primeval groves,
> Whose boughs to man his food and shelter lent,
> Pure in his pleasures, happy in his loves,
> His eye still smiling, and his heart content.

---

9 Brycchan Carey, 'Slavery and Romanticism,' *Literature Compass* (May 2006), p.397.
10 The specific editions of the books Burns mentions are rarely given (some gifts, and the MFS purchases can be accurately assigned) so for this purpose an edition has been chosen as close as possible to the date Burns mentions it. His reading list has been compiled through (a) the list of Burns's library at his death, furnished to Robert Chambers by the poet's sons, (b) books related in Burns's 'Autobiographical Letter,' and 'Murdoch Letter', (c) books acquired for Monklands Friendly Society, (d) other books and authors mentioned by Burns in his letters (or in 'Gilbert's Narrative'), (e) books quoted as epigraphs or otherwise mentioned in his poems. Note that the brief biographies of authors are based on Margaret Drabble, ed, *The Oxford Companion to English Literature* (Oxford: OUP, 1985).

> Then, hand in hand, Health, Sport, and Labour went.
> Nature supply'd the wish she taught to crave.
> None prowl'd for prey, none watch'd to circumvent.
> To all an equal lot heaven's bounty gave
>   No vassal fear'd his lord, no tyrant fear'd his slave.
>
>   vol.1, p.19.

From *An Essay on the Nature and Immutability of Truth: In Opposition to Sophistry and Scepticism* (Edinburgh/London: A Kincaid and J Bell/E and C Dilly, 1771).[11]

> These assertions [of Hume's] are strong; but I know not whether they have any thing else to recommend them. For, first, though true, they would not prove the point in question, except it were also proved, that the Africans and Americans, even though arts and sciences were introduced among them would still remain unsusceptible of cultivation. The inhabitants of Great Britain and France were as savage two thousand years ago, as those of Africa and America are at this day. To civilize a nation, is a work which it requires long time to accomplish. And one may as well say of an infant, that he can never become a man, as of a nation now barbarous, that it never can be civilized. [...]
>
>   It is easy to see, with what views some modem authors throw out these hints to prove the natural inferiority of negroes. But let every friend to humanity pray, that they may be disappointed. Britons are famous for generosity; a virtue in which it is easy for them to excel both the Romans and the Greeks. Never let it never be said, that slavery is countenanced by the bravest and most generous people on earth; by a people who are animated with that heroic pallium, the love of liberty beyond all nations ancient or modern; and the fame of whose toilsome, but unwearied, perseverance, in vindicating, at the expense of life and fortune, the sacred rights of mankind, will strike terror into the hearts of sycophants and tyrants, and excite the admiration and gratitude of all good men [...]   pp.511–512.

---

11 In this essay, Beattie rebuts Hume's views on race, qv. Burns refers to this in 'The Vision' [K.62]
  'Hence, sweet harmonious BEATTIE sung
    'His "Minstrel lays;"
  'Or tore. With noble ardour stung,
    'The *Sceptic's* bays.   ll.171–174.

Burns's interest in Beattie may have led him to read other works not listed in his Library, including: 'The Triumph of Melancholy,' in *Original Poems and Translations* (London: A Millar, 1760):

> Will ye one transient ray of gladness dart
> Cross the dark cell where hopeless Slavery lies?
> To ease tir'd Disappointment's bleeding heart,
> Will all your stores of softening balm avail?   p.28

Or his *Elements of Moral Science* (2 vols) (London/Edinburgh: T Cadell/William Creech, 1790/1793) which has a concerted argument against Slavery encapsulated in this paragraph:

> So repugnant is slavery to the British genius, [...] now every slave, of whatever colour, from the moment of his arrival in Great Britain, and as long as he remains in it, is a free man, and a British subject, whether baptized or not; the law protects his person and his property; he has no more to fear from his master, than any other free servant has; he cannot be bought or sold; but if he has bound himself by contract to serve his master for a certain length of time, that contract, like those entered into by apprentices, and some other servants, will be valid. — I wish I were warranted to add, that the same regard is had to the rights of human nature in all the British dominions. But I must confess, with anguish of heart, that it is not so; for that almost all the products of the West Indies, and some too of the East, are procured for us, by the sweat, the tears, and the blood of miserable slaves. [...]: vol.II, p.31.

2. DR JAMES ANDERSON FRSE, FSA (SCOT) (1739–1808)

A farmer and agricultural reformer, and editor of *The Bee* between December 1790 and January 1794. Dr Blacklock introduced him to Burns who subscribed to *The Bee* (and encouraged others to do so), however, he did not contribute any works to the enterprise.[12]

The Bee carried a weekly digest of news and politics, which included reports on Abolitionary activity both in terms of petitions, and business in Parliament, which is not recorded here. It also published

---

12 *Letters*: To Dr Anderson, 1 November 1790 [L.427].

factual articles, poetry and prose fiction almost entirely Abolitionist in sympathy. Firstly, some documentary articles:

'Sugar Raised in Britain. Intelligence Respecting Arts. Plan for Moderating the Price of Sugar', February 1792, pp.330–333.

> [...] Many plants, that are natives of Britain, can be made to yield sugar in considerable quantities [...] Thus might the slave trade be annihilated, even without the intervention of law; and without the convulsive struggle that may be dreaded, should that measure be pushed forward in spite of the opposition to be expected from those who believe their interest would be affected by any alteration in the law respecting this article. [...]

'Extracts from Coxe's Travels [to Russia]', July 1792, p.80.

> [...] The example she [the Emperess Catherine] has set the nobles by franchising the peasants who were her own property, is amiable; and it is to be hoped the nobles will soon be convinced that it is their interest to imitate her. [...] it would appear that the lords of such peasants are strangers to the sweets of liberty, since they are not more anxious that their fellow men should enjoy them; or are under the most, selfish prejudiced, and depraved principles. But this is not peculiar to Russian lords; many among ourselves, notwithstanding our boasted superior knowledge, are no strangers to these principles, witness the African slave trade.

'Regulations of the Spaniards for the Gradual Enfranchisement of Slaves', December 1792, pp.263–264.

> [...] [T]he master is obliged by law to allow him one working day in the course of the week to himself, besides Sunday; so that if he chooses to work for his master on that day, he receives for the same the wages of a free man; as whatever he earns by such labour, is so secured to him by law, that the master cannot deprive him of it. This is certainly a step towards abolishing absolute slavery; for as soon as the slave is able to purchase another working day, the master is obliged to sell it him at one-fifth part of its original

cost, and so, likewise, the remaining four days, at the same rate, whenever the slave is able to redeem them; after which he is entirely free. This is such an incentive to industry, that even the most supine are tempted to exert themselves.

'Account of Benjamin Banneker a Negro Calculator', February 1793, pp.251–253.[13]

Benjamin Banneker, a free negro, has calculated an almanack for the ensuing year 1792; [...]
[...] I consider this negro as a fresh proof that the powers of the mind are disconnected with the colour of the skin, or, in other words, a striking contradiction to Mr Hume's doctrine, that the negroes are naturally inferior to the whites, and unsusceptible of attainments, in arts and sciences. In every civilized country, we shall find thousands of whites liberally educated, and who have enjoyed greater opportunities of instruction than this negro, his inferiors in those intellectual acquirements and capacities, that form the most characteristic feature of the human race. But the system that would assign to these degraded blacks an origin different from the whites, if it is not ready to be deserted by philosophers, must be relinquished, as similar instances multiply; and that such must frequently happen, cannot well be doubted, should no check impede the progress of humanity, which, meliorating the condition of slavery, necessarily leads to its final extinction. [...]

---

13 Benjamin Banneker (1731–1806): son of a freed enslaved man and his wife, the daughter of an English transportee mother and a formerly enslaved man. After a limited education at the Quaker School in Baltimore, he worked as a farmhand on his parents' farm. Aged 22 he made a working clock of wood and entertained neighbours with mathematical puzzles. In 1772 he made friends with George Ellicot who introduced him to astronomy. When a relative, Andrew Ellicott, was appointed to mark the boundaries of Washington DC in 1791, he employed Banneker as his assistant. Banneker met and corresponded with Thomas Jefferson who forwarded his first Almanac to Condorcet in Paris. After several years of his almanacs, Banneker retired, selling his farmland to the Ellicots, living in the farmhouse and working on astronomy and mathematics. Virtually all of his papers and models were destroyed in a fire on the day of his funeral. A Silvio Bedini, *The Life of Benjamin Banneker* (New York: Landmark, 1972).

'The King v Stephen Devereux', May 1793, pp.109–112.[14]

[...] Edward Willams was called on the part of the defendant; and having been very properly cautioned by Lord Kenyon, deponed, that the negro girl was so weak, that she frequently fouled herself, for which Captain Kimber flogged her 'sometimes with a bit of a rope, sometimes with a horse whip, when lying upon deck, and not able to stand; and that he had seen her flogged for a week every day by the captain; that one day he and another, by the captain's order, fastened her by one hand to the mizen stay, and boused her up as quick as they could; then by both hands with her feet about three inches off the deck ; then for about ten minutes by one leg, her hands touching the deck, but her head three or four inches above it, the captain walking the deck, and giving her about six strokes with his whip while so suspended, the girl both moaning inwardly, and crying out in her own language; and that after the was taken down and washed, not before, she was rubbed with palm oil. [...]'.

'From the Editor', July 1793, pp.38–39.

A very respectable correspondent, who signs himself *Humanitas*, has taken the trouble to transcribe a very long extract from Mr Clarkson's book on slavery, giving some shocking instances of cruelty to negro slaves, [...] The instances narrated in the paper here quoted are shocking to humanity indeed.

Abolitionist poetry is frequently printed, often in the voice of the enslaved captive themselves.

---

14 Captain John Kimber commanded the slaver *Recovery* in the triangular trade. On a voyage in late 1791 he tortured and whipped to death a young woman who could not exercise ('dance' as the argot put it). This was cited by Wilberforce in the House of Commons on 2 April 1792, resulting in Kimber's arrest a few days later, but was acquitted by an Old Bailey jury the following June. Kimber campaigned for two of the prosecution witnesses to be tried for perjury including Devereux, who was found not guilty. See 'A Student of the Temple,' *The Trial of Captain John Kimber, for the Murder of Two Female Negro Slaves on Board the Recovery, African Slave Ship* (London: C Stalker, [1792]).

'The Poor Negro Beggar's Petition and Complaint',
By 'A Country Reader', May 1791, pp.63–65

O MASSA, poor negro! God Almighty you bless:
O Massa, poor negro! in utmost distress.
[...]
Death shall release me from sorrow and pain;
Then my dear native home I'll revisit again.

'The Negro's Complaint',
[Anon, but Dr James Currie/William Roscoe.]
June 1792, pp.249–250.15

WIDE over the tremulous sea,
  The moon spread her mantle of light,
[...]
Ah, wretch! in wild anguish he cried,
  From country and liberty torn!
Ah Maraton! would thou hadst died
Ere o'er the salt seas thou wast borne!

'Mungo's Address',
[Anon.], February 1793, pp.215–216[16]

[...] O! sons of freedom, equalise your laws,
Be all consistent, plead a negro's cause;
That all the nations, in your code may see
The British negro, like the Briton, free.
But, should he supplicate your laws in vain,
To break for ever this disgraceful chain,
At least let gentle usage so abate
The galling terrors of its passing state,
That he may share the great Creator's plan,
For though no Briton still Mungo is a man!

---

15 Published anonymously (originally in 1788 as 'The African'), but by Dr James Currie and William Roscoe.
16 This is better known as 'The Epilogue to "The Padlock"', *Gentleman's Magazine* (October 1787), pp.913–914. See entry for Isaac Bickerstaffe (below).

Samples of prose fiction highlighting Abolition include the following two pieces:

'Copy of a Letter from an English Slave-driver at Algiers to his Friend in England', February 1791, pp.229–233.

> l have now got into a very good birth [...] driving the slaves to the field, and keeping them to their work when they are there. To be sure it went hard with me at first to whip my country-folks; but custom, as the saying is, is second nature. So I whip them now without minding it, just for all the world as if they were a parcel of horses; [...] For one white slave that we have here, the English have ten black ones in the West Indies, and they use their slaves much more cruelly than we do ours. [...] our dealings are mercy, compared with your treatment of the poor nigers, which both you and I have seen at Kingston, and which you will remember, by this same token, that when we got a-board again, we wished they would rise and cut all the white men's throats. So you must take care of taking up wrong notions to my disadvantage; for we just do here to the whites what the whites do to the blacks in the West Indies; only we use them more mercifully...

'Zimeo, A Tale', March 1792, pp.28–31; pp.69–75; pp.108–111.[17]

[*Précis*] Zimeo, a prince of Benin, was enslaved with his lover and her father, taken to Jamaica where they were sold apart. Retaining his nobility even in enslavement, he leads a revolt on the Island, slaughtering the White community, but saving Wilmont, an English Quaker, whose slaves plead for their beneficent master's life. Amongst those slaves are Zimeo's lover, their infant son, and her father. Zimeo, with his army and his family, retreats to the hills until Wilmot brokers a peace between the White and Black communities.

---

17 [Jean-François de Saint-Lambert], *Les Saisons, Poëme* (Amsterdam: np: 1769), 'Ziméo. Par George Filmer, né primitive,' pp.245–282. Condensed and translated into English for the *Edinburgh Magazine* pp.271–276 then (without authorial attribution) in *The American Museum* ed by Matthew Carey [Philadelphia] as 'Zimeo. — A West Indian Tale' (November 1789), pp.371–373; (December 1789), pp.472–475 and subsequently copied here. Jean-François [soi-disant Marquis] de Saint-Lambert (1716–1803): Soldier, poet and Academician of the Encyclopédie circle. A friend of Voltaire (qv) and Diderot.

However, not every article printed was critical of chattel slavery, with two notices propagating the 'kind master trope':

'Notes', November 1791, p.xiv.

> In the month of August died in Jamaica, an old Negro woman, named Cooba, at the very advanced age of 110. She belonged to the Hon Thomas Chambers, from whom, and a numerous family of descendants, down to the fourth generation, she had every comfort and convenience of life; besides which, having been at liberty to come as she pleased.[18]

'Obituary of the Learned Right Honourable Robert Lord Romley', December 1793, p.312.[19]

> [...] Finally, I cannot stop without recording, that when a slave, on lord Romney's plantations in the West Indies, was asked by one who met him, in the field if he was a slave of lord Romney's. 'No Massah,' replied he, 'lord Romaey, de good lord Romney have no slaves, I be his child and servant. lord Romney be de father of his people.'

3. ISAAC BICKERSTAFFE (1733–?1808)

Irish playwright, a child page to the Earl of Chesterfield, then, after service as in the 5th Foot and as an officer in the Royal Marines, he wrote the first comic opera for the London stage, *Love in a Village* (with music by Arne), in 1762. He continued to write (with varying degrees of success) including a version of Coleman's *Inkle and Yarico* until his implication in a homosexual act caused him to flee to Paris in 1772.

Burns quotes Bickerstaffe's *Love in a Village* in a 1788 letter to

---

18 Hon Thomas Chalmers (?–1794): English plantocrat, Custos of St Elizabeth, Jamaica, Colonel of the local Militia and owner of the Cabbage Valley plantation. His heirs received compensation for 342 enslaved people amounting to £5,983/18/3. *UCL Legacies Database*: 'Thomas Calmers' (accessed 1 September 2024).

19 Robert, 2nd Baron Romley FRS FSA (1712–1793): a founder of the Society for the Encouragement of Arts, Manufacturers and Commerce in 1758. He married the only daughter of a major St Kitts planter, whose plantations were inherited by his eldest son and then his son (2nd Earl Romsey) received around £7,500 compensation for 432 slaves. *UCL Legacies Database*: 'Earl Romsey' (accessed 1 September 2024).

Agnes McLehose, and he requests that Miss Fontenelle performs Bickerstaffe's *The Spoilt Child* at Dumfries in November 1792.[20] So it is not impossible that he was also acquainted with *The Padlock*.

From *The Padlock: A Comic Opera* (Dublin: W and W Smith [and others], [1768]).

This popular play introduced the first black-face comic to the British stage, 'Mungo,' (which would become a stock name for this invented Black enslaved character). The *Oxford Companion to English Literature* suggests that '[a]s feeling for the oppressed Negro grew, the role appears to have been played with increasing stress on sentiment.'[21] A sample of Mungo's lines follows:

> Dear heart, what a terrible life am I led,
>   A dog has a better, that's shelter'd and fed;
> Night and day, 'tis de same,
>   My pain is dere game:
> Me wish to de Lord me was dead.   Act 1, Sc VI, p.11

4. HUGH BLAIR (1718–1800)

Scottish minister of religion, rhetorician and litterateur. Burns met Revd Dr Blair, Minister of St Giles and first Professor of Rhetoric and Belles Lettres at the University of Edinburgh, in late 1786, describing him as one of his 'very warm friends in the Literati' to Dr John Mackenzie, 6 Dec[ember] 1786 [L.61A]. Blair made several comments on the poet's draft for the *First Edinburgh Edition*, leading Burns to thank him (not entirely sincerely) 'for that kindness, that patronage, that friendship you have shown me' and referred to him as 'Scotia's sacred Demosthenes', although his private assessment of Blair in CPB2 is more equivocal.[22] 'Dr [Blair] is merely an astonishing proof of what industry and application can do – [...] his vanity is proverbial.'[23] Blair was a noted Abolitionist.

---

20 *Letters*, to Agnes McLehose, 19 January 1788 [L.181], and [to Miss Louisa Fontenelle], [November 1792], [L.520].
21 *Oxford Companion to English Literature*, 'Padlock, The' at p.730.
22 *Letters*, [L.101]: to Dr Hugh Blair, [4 May 1787]; 'Extempore Verses on Dining with Lord Daer,' [K.127], l.26.
23 *Oxford Burns*, vol.1, p.84; *Second Commonplace Book*, pp.5–6.

From *Lectures on Rhetoric and Belles Lettres* (3 vols) (London/Edinburgh: A Strahan and T Cadell/W Creech, 1787).

> It is an observation made by several writers, that Eloquence is to be looked for only in free states. All other qualifications, [...] you may find among those who are deprived of liberty; but never did a slave become an orator; he can only be a pompous flatterer. vol.1, p.281.

From *Sermons* (4 vols) (London/Edinburgh: A Strahan and T Cadell/W Creech, 1790–1794).

> Wherever Christianity prevails, it has discouraged, and in some degree, abolished slavery. It has rescued human nature from that ignominious yoke, under which, in former days, the one half of mankind groaned. vol.1, p.85

5. ROBERT BLAIR (1669–1746)

Scots Minister of Athelstaneford, East Lothian. Blair's poem *The Grave* provided the epigraph for 'To J S[mith],' [K.79] and (in Kinsley's belief) at least seven lines of inspiration in Burns's poems.

From *The Grave, a Poem* (London: G Robinson, 1776).

> (As if a slave was not a shred of nature,
> Of the same common nature with his lord:)   p.14

> The very turf on which we tread, once liv'd;
> And we that live must lend our carcases
> To cover our own offspring: in their turns
> They too must cover theirs. 'Tis here all meet
> The shiv'ring Icelander, and sun-burnt Moor;
> Men of climes that never met before;
> [...]
> Here the o'er-loaded Slave flings down his Burthen
> From his gall'd Shoulders,
>   pp.26–27

6. NICHOLAS BOILEAU (1636–1711)

An influential French poet and critic. Burns quotes Boileau's *L'Art Poetic* ('le vrai n'est toujours le vraisemble') to Mrs Dunlop [L.238, 28 April 1788] and to Revd Thomas Smith [L.462A, 4 July 1791].

From *The Works of Mons[ieu]r Boileau Despereaux* (2 vols) (London: E Sanger and E Curll, 1711).

> [...] [without Liberty] we commonly, instead of Orators become Pompous Flatterers. [...] no Slave can ever be an Orator; since when the mind is deprest and broken by Slavery, it will never dare to think or say anything Bold: All its Vigour evaporates of itself, and it remains always as in a Prison. In short, to make use of Homer's expression
>   The Day that makes a Free-born Man a Slave,
>   Robs him of half his Virtue, &c.
>
> vol.II, p.85

7. SAMUEL BUTLER (1613–1680)

English clerk and secretary to noblemen. A noted satirist, pensioned by Charles II. (Kinsley suggests that Butler's poetry influenced Burns on three occasions, however, none appears particularly convincing.)

From *Hudibras. A Poem in Three Cantos* (3 vols) (London: J Edwards, 1793).

> Others to prostitute their great hearts,
> To be baboons' and monkeys' sweet-hearts:
> Come with the dev'l himself in league grow
> By's representative a negro.
>
> Canto I, Part II, ll.387–400

8. MIGUEL DE CERVANTES SAAVEDRA (1547–1616)

The great Spanish novelist, wounded at the Battle of Lepanto (1571) and later captured and enslaved at Algiers. See Smollett below.

From Tobias Smollett, trans and ed, *The History and Adventures of the Renowned Don Quixote* (4 vols) (London: Printed for Harrison & Co, 1782).

> In the year 1574, [Cervantes] was unfortunately taken by a Barbary corsair, and conveyed to Algiers, where he was fold to a Moor, and remained a slave for the space of five, years and a half: during, which, he exhibited repeated proofs of the most enterprizing genius and heroick generosity. Though we know not on what occasion he fell into the hands of the Barbarians, he himself gives us to understand, in the history of the Captive, that he resided at Algiers in the reign of Hassan Aga, whose cruelty he describes.
>
> vol.I, p.vii

9. MARCUS TULLIUS CICERO (106BC–43BC)

The greatest Roman orator and Consul during the Catiline Conspiracy, latterly murdered by order of the First Triumvirate. His freedman, Tiro, discussed above is traditionally credited with inventing the ampersand.

From William Melmoth, ed, *The Letters of Marcus Tullius Cicero to Several of His Friends* (3 vols) (London: J Dodsley, 1778).

> I protest to you, my dear brother, you have performed an act extremely agreeable to me in giving Tiro his freedom: as a slate of servitude was a situation far unworthy of his merit. [...] If I receive much satisfaction from the services of my freedman Statius: how much more valuable must the fame good qualities appear in Tiro, as they have the additional advantages of his learning, his wit and his politeness to recommend them?
>
> vol.II, p.466

> But if the peace you propose, is to re-establish a most oppressive tyranny, be well assured there is not a man in his senses who will not rather renounce his life than thus suffer himself to be made a slave.
>
> vol.III, p.226

10. THOMAS COOPER (1759–1839)

English barrister, writer and scientist. Emigrated to Pennsylvania with Joseph Priestly in 1794. Imprisoned for radical sedition for 6 months in 1800. He taught at Dickinson College and UPenn, moving to South Carolina College (now USC, home of the G Ross Roy Collection) in 1820, serving as its President from 1821 to 1834. He was an ardent Abolitionist.

From *Some Information Respecting America* (London: J Johnson, 1794).

I know that your fortune is moderate; that you have political objections to many parts of the present government in England; and you have been an opponent also of the slave-trade. What then will probably be the conditions you would seek in the situation you are finally to adopt? [...] Being opposed to the system of Negro slavery, you will have very strong, if not insuperable objections, to those parts of the continent where slaves are the only servants to be procured; and where the law and the practice of the country tends to support this humiliating distinction between man and man.   pp.3–4

The southern states of Georgia, and North and South Carolina, seem quite out of the question, from the extreme heat of the climate and the prevalence of Negro slavery. About one-third of the gross number of the inhabitants of the southern provinces (Maryland, Virginia, the Carolinas, Georgia, and Kentucky) are slaves. The whole number of slaves in the United States of America is about 700,000.   p.7

To the state of Delaware, to which also there is a farther objection arising from [...] the present prevalence of Negro slavery in that portion of the Continent.   p.11

The objections to Maryland and Virginia relate to climate and slave-labour. These States are very unpleasantly warm in the summer season to an English constitution, (particularly the former) and the impossibility of procuring any Servants but Negro-slaves   p.20

The climate is full as hot in Kentucky as in Maryland and the atmosphere is moist. There is scarcely any labour to be hired but that of slaves, let out for the purpose by their owners. These slaves form about one-fifth of the whole number of inhabitants. p.24

Virginia, Rappahannock Labour. Slaves only, either purchased or rented. They are hired at from 6 to 9L a year, the master finding provisions and cloathing, and paying the tax. The usual allowance to a slave is a peck and half of the meal of Indian corn, per week j sometimes pickled and faked herrings or mackarel. The cloathing is very trifling. [...] Virginia Near the South West Mountains: Labour 9L to 12L a year for a slave, with food and cloathing. The very few white servants that are to be procured, cost from 12L to 16L a year, and board, and are worth but little; for it being customary for all labour to be done by slaves, the whites thinking it degrading, will not work with the blacks. [...] pp.87–90

The separate American states have, (with one small exception) abolished the slave trade, and they have in some instances abolished negro slavery; in others they have adopted efficacious measures for its certain, but gradual abolition. The importation of slaves is discontinued, and can never be renewed, so as to interrupt the repose of Africa, or endanger the tranquillity of the United States. p.218

11. WILLIAM COWPER (1731–1800)

English poet. Burns was lent or gifted Cowper's poems, which he called 'the best Poet out of sight since Thomson,' by William Dunbar [L.274: To William Dunbar, 25 September 1788] and later commented to Mrs Dunlop, 'Is not *The Task* a glorious poem? The religion of *The Task*, bating a few scraps of Calvinistic divinity, is the religion of God and Nature: the religion that exalts, that ennobles man.' [L.605: To Mrs Dunlop, 15 December 1793, at vol.II, p.269.]

Additionally, it is assumed that Burns also read Cowper's 1788 two-volume edition, adding 'Charity' and 'Table Talk' to his reading. Additionally, of the poems not published in book form in Burns's lifetime, it is assumed that he saw the two poems 'The Negro's Complaint' and 'The Morning Dream' when printed in the *Scots Magazine* in 1792. It is less certain that he would have seen Cowper's pamphlets, such as 'Pity for the Poor Africans' or 'Sweet Meat has Sour Sauce' but as they were widely circulated, it is not impossible and they are included in his reading list. Less likely are the two poems 'Sonnet Addressed to William Wilberforce Esq' and 'Epigram' which were printed in the *Northampton Mercury* in 1792, and these are not included.[24] It is important to stress how valued Cowper was by the Abolitionist movement:

> The last of the necessary forerunners and coadjutors [of Abolition] was our much-admired poet, Cowper; and a great coadjutor he, was when we consider what value was put upon his sentiments, and the extraordinary circulation of his works. There are few persons, who have not been properly impressed by [Book II of *The Task*.] [Clarkson, vol.I, p.108]

> The amiable poet Cowper had frequently made the Slave-trade the subject of his contemplation. He had already condemned it in his valuable poem The Task. But now he had written three fugitive pieces upon it. Of these the most impressive was that, which he called The Negro's Complaint [...] This little piece, Cowper presented in manuscript to some of his friends in London; and these, conceiving it to contain a powerful appeal in behalf of the injured Africans, joined in printing it. [...] From one it spread to another, till it travelled almost over the whole island. Falling at length into the hands of the musician, it was set to music; and it the found its way into the streets both of the metropolis and the country, where it was sung as a ballad; and where it gave a plain account of the subject, with an appropriate feeling, to those who heard it. [Clarkson, vol.I, pp.188–191]

From *The Task: A Poem, in Six Books* (London: J Johnson, 1785).

[...] My ear is pain'd,
My soul is sick, with every day's report
Of wrong and outrage, with which Earth is fill'd.
There is no flesh in man's obdurate heart,

---

[24] These last two poems can be found in Basker, pp.301–302.

It does not feel for man; the natural bond
Of brotherhood is sever'd as the flax,
That falls asunder at the touch of fire.
He finds his fellow guilty of a skin
Not colour'd like his own; and having power
To' enforce the wrong, for such a worthy cause
Dooms and devotes him as a lawful prey.
Lands intersected by a narrow frith
[...]
And, worse than all, and most to be deplored
As human nature's broadest, foulest blot,
Chains him, and tasks him, and exacts his sweat
With stripes, that Mercy with a bleeding heart
Weeps, when she sees inflicted on a beast.
Then what is man? And what man, seeing this,
And having human feelings, does not blush,
And hang his head, to think himself a man?
I would not have a slave to till my ground,
To carry me, to fan me while I sleep,
And tremble when I wake, for all the wealth
That sinews bought and sold have ever earn'd
No: dear as freedom is, and in my heart's
Just estimation prized above all price,

I had much rather be myself the slave;
And wear the bonds, than fasten them on him.
We have no slaves at home — Then why abroad?
And they themselves once ferried o'er the wave
That parts us are emancipate and loosed.
Slaves cannot breathe in England; if their lungs
Receive our air, that moment they are free;
They touch our country, and their shackles fall.
That's noble, and bespeaks a nation proud
And jealous of the blessing. Spread it then,
And let it circulate through every vein
Of all your empire; that, where Britain's power
Is felt, mankind may feel her mercy too.

Book II, vol. II, pp. 53–55

Grace that makes the slave a freeman.
                                    Book v, vol.II, p.227

'The Negro's Complaint By Mr Cowper, author of the Task &c.,'
Scots Magazine, 1 January 1792, p.32.
   [*To the tune of 'Hosier's Ghost' or 'As near Porto Bello lying'*]

FORC'D from home and all its pleasures
        Afric's coast I left forlorn;
To increase a stranger's treasures,
        O'er the raging billows borne.

Men from England bought and sold me,
        Paid my price in paltry gold;
But tho' their's they have inroll'd me,
        Minds are never to be sold.

Still in thought as free as ever,
        What are Europe's rights, I ask,
Me from my delights to sever,
        Me to torture, me to task?

Fleecy locks and black complexion
        Cannot forfeit nature's claim:
Skins may differ, but affection
        Dwells in White and Black the same.

Why did all-creating Nature
        Make the plant for which we toil?
Sighs must fan it, tears must water,
        Sweat of ours must dress the soil.

Think, ye Masters iron-hearted,
        Sitting at your jovial boards,
Think how many Blacks have smarted
        For the sweets your cane affords.

Is there, as ye sometimes tell us,

Is there one who reigns on high?
Has he bid you buy and sell us,
    Speaking from his throne the sky?

Ask him, if your knotted scourges,
    Matches, blood-extorting screws,
Are the means that duty urges
    Agents of his will to use?

Hark! He answers! — Wild Tornados
    Strewing yonder sea with wrecks,
Wasting towns, plantations, meadows,
    Is the voice with which he speaks.

He, foreseeing what vexations
    Afric's sons should undergo,
Fixed their Tyrants habitations
    Where his whirlwinds answer — No.

By our blood in Afric wasted,
    E're our necks received the chain;
By the miseries that we tasted,
    Crossing in your barks the main;

By our sufferings, since ye brought us
    To the Man-degrading smart,
All sustain'd by patience, taught us
    Only by a broken heart;

Deem our nation brutes no longer,
    Till some reason ye shall find
Worthier of regard, and stronger
    Than the colour of our kind.

Slaves to Gold, — whose sordid dealings
    Tarnish all your boasted powers,
Prove that you have human feelings,
    E're you proudly question ours!

Pity for the Poor Africans (London: Thomas Dicey, 1788).

— Video meliora, proboque,
Deteriora sequor.

My Mind far better Things approves,
My Heart far worse, in Practice loves.

I own I am shock'd at the purchase of slaves,
And fear those who buy them and sell them are knaves:
What I hear of their hardships, their tortures, and groans,
Is almost enough to draw pity from stones.

I pity them greatly, but I must be mum,
For how could we do without sugar and rum?
Especially sugar, so needful we see?
What, give up our desserts, our coffee, and tea!

Besides, if we do, the French, Dutch, and Danes,
Will heartily thank us, no doubt, for our pains;
If we do not buy the poor creatures, they will,
And tortures and groans will be multiplied still.

If foreigners likewise would give up the trade,
Much more in behalf of your wish might be said;
But, while they get riches by purchasing blacks,
Pray tell me why we may not also go snacks?

Your scruples and arguments bring to my mind
A story, so pat, you may think it is coin'd,
On purpose to answer you, out of my mint;
But I can assure you I saw it in print.

Once a youngster at school, more sedate than the rest,
Had his integrity put to the test;
His comrades had plotted an orchard to rob,
And ask'd him to go and assist in the job.

He was shock'd, sir, like you, and answer'd 'Oh no!
What! rob our good neighbour! I pray you don't go;
Besides, the man's poor, his orchard's his bread,
Then think of his children, for they must be fed.'

You speak very fine, and you look very grave,
But apples we want, and apples we'll have;
If you will go with us, you shall have a share,
If not, you shall have neither apple nor pear.

They spoke, and Tom ponder'd 'I see they will go;
Poor man! what a pity to injure him so!
Poor man! I would save him his fruit if I could,
But staying behind will do him no good.

If the matter depended alone upon me,
His apples might hang, till they dropp'd from the tree;
But, since they will take them, I think I'll go too,
He will lose none by me, though I get a few.'

His scruples thus silenc'd, Tom felt more at ease,
And went with his comrades the apples to seize;
He blam'd and protested, but join'd in the plan:
He shard in the plunder, but pitied the man.

From **'Charity'**, in *Poems* (2 vols) (London: J Johnson, 1788).

God, working ever on a social plan.
By various ties attaches man to man:
He made at first, though free and unconfin'd,
One man the common father of the kind;
That ev'ry tribe, though plac'd as he sees best,
Where seas or deserts part them from the rest,
Diff'ring in language, manners, or in face,
Might feel themselves allied to all the race [...]
   Again — the band of commerce was design'd
T'associate all the branches of mankind; [...]
But ah! what wish can prosper, or what pray'r,

For merchants rich in cargoes of despair.
Who drive a loathsome traffic, gauge, and span,
And buy the muscles and the bones of man!
The tender ties of father, husband, friend,
All bonds of nature in that moment end;
And each endures, while yet he draws his breath,
A stroke as fatal as the scythe of Death.
The sable warrior, frantic with regret
Of her he loves, and never can forget,
Loses in tears the fast-receding shore,
But not the thought, that they must meet no more:
Depriv'd of her and freedom at a blow,
What has he left that he can yet forego?
Yes, to deep sadness sullenly resign'd,
He feels his body's bondage in his mind;
Puts off his gen'rous nature; and, to suit
His manners with his fate, puts on the brute.
   O most degrading of all ills, that wait
On many a mourner in his best estate!
All other sorrows Virtue may endure,
And find submission more than half a care;
Grief is itself a med'cine, and bestow'd
T'improve the fortitude that bears the load.
To teach the wand'rer, as his woes increase,
The path of Wisdom, all whose paths are peace;
But slav'ry! — Virtue dreads it as her grave:
Patience itself is meanness in a slave:
Or if the will and sov'reignty of God
Bid suffer it a while, and kiss the rod,
Wait for the dawning of a brighter day
And snap the chain the moment when you may.
Nature imprints upon whate'er we see
That has a heart and life in it, Be free
[...]
Canst thou, and honor'd with a Christian names
Buy what is woman-born, and feel no shame;
Trade in the blood of innocence, and plead
Expedience as a warrant for the deed?

So may the wolf, whom famine has made bold,
To quit the forest and invade the fold:
So may the ruffian, who, with ghostly glide,
Dagger in hand, steals close to your bed-side;
Not he, hut his emergence forc'd the door,
He found it inconvenient to be poor.
Has God then given its sweetness to the cane,
Unless his laws be trampled on — in vain?
Built a brave world, which cannot yet subsist.
Unless his right to rule it be dismiss'd?
Impudent blasphemy! So Folly pleads,
And, Avrice being judge, with ease succeeds.
But grants the plea, and let it stand for just,
That man make man his prey, because he must;
Still there is room for pity to abate.
And soothe the sorrows of so sad a state.
A Briton knows, or if he knows it not,
The Scripture plac'd within his reach, he ought.
That souls have no discriminating hue.
Alike important in their Maker's view;
That none are free from blemish since the fall,
And Love divine has paid one price for all.
The wretch, that works and weeps without relief
Has one that notices his silent grief.
He from whose hands alone all pow'r proceeds,
Ranks its abuse among the foulest deeds,
Considers all injustice with a frown;
But marks the man that treads his fellow down.
Begone — the whip and bell in that hard hand
Are hateful ensigns of usurp'd command.
Not Mexico could purchase kings a claim
To scourge him, weariness his only blame.
Remember Heav'n has an avenging rod:
To smite the poor is treason against God.

Trouble is grudgingly and hardly brook'd,
While life's sublimest joys are overlook'd:
We wander o'er a sunburnt thirsty soil,

Murm'ring and weary of our daily toil,
Forget t'enjoy the palm-tree's offer'd shade,
Or taste the fountain in the neighbouring glade:
Else who would lose, that had the pow'r t' implorer
Th' occasion of transmuting fear to love?
O 'tis a godlike privilege to save.
And he that scorns it is himself a slave.
Inform his mind; one flash of heav'nly day
Would heal his heart, and melt his chains away.
Beauty for ashes is a gift indeed,
And slaves, by truth enlarg'd, are doubly freed.
Then would he pay, submissive at thy feet,
While gratitude and love made service sweet,
My dear deliv'rer out of hopeless night,
Whose bounty bought me but to give me light,
I was a bondman on my native plain,
Sin urg'd, and Ignorance made fast, the chain;
Thy lips have shed instruction as the dew,
Taught me what path to shun, and what pursue;
Farewell my former joys! I sigh no more
For Africa's once loved, benighted shore;
Serving a benefactor I am free;
At my best home, if not exil'd from thee.

vol.I, pp.181–191

From **'Table Talk'**, Poems (2 vols) (London: J Johnson, 1788).

To him that fights with justice on his side.
Let laurels, drench'd in pure Parnassian dews,
Reward his mem'ry, dear to ev'ry muse,
Who, with a courage of unshaken root
In honour's field advancing his firm foot,
Plants it upon the line that justice draws,
And will prevail or perish in her cause.
Tis to the virtues of such men, man owes
His portion in the good that heav'n bestows,
And when recording history displays
Feats of renown, though wrought in antient days,

Tells of a few stout hearts that fought and dy'd
Where duty plac'd them, at their country's side;
The man that is not mov'd with what he reads,
That takes not fire at their heroic deeds,
Unworthy of the blessings of the brave,
Is base in kind and born to be a slave.
>> vol.I, pp.2–3

'Sweet Meat has Sour Sauce; or, The Slave-Trader in the Dumps' [pamphlet, 1788].

A TRADER I am to the African shore,
But since that my trading is like to be o'er,
I'll sing you a song that you ne'er heard before,
Which nobody can deny, deny,
>> Which nobody can deny.

When I first heard the news it gave me a shock,
Much like what they call an electrical knock,
And now I am going to sell off my stock,
>> Which nobody can deny.

'Tis a curious assortment of dainty regales,
To tickle the negroes with when the ship sails,
Fine chains for the neck, and a cat with nine tails
>> Which nobody can deny.

Here's supple-jack plenty, and store of rat-tan,
That will wind itself round the sides of a man,
As close as a hoop round a bucket or can,
>> Which nobody can deny.

Here's padlocks and bolts, and screws for the thumbs,
That squeeze them so lovingly till the blood comes;
They sweeten the temper like comfits or plums,
>> Which nobody can deny.

When a negro his head from his victuals withdraws,
And clenches his teeth and thrusts out his paws,
Here's a notable engine to open his jaws,
    Which nobody can deny.

Thus, going to market, we kindly prepare
A pretty black cargo of African ware,
For what they must meet with when they get there,
    Which nobody can deny.

'Would do your heart good to see 'me below
Lie flat on their backs all the way as we go,
Like sprats on a gridiron, scores in a row,
    Which nobody can deny.

But ah! if in vain I have studied an art
So gainful to me, all boasting apart,
I think it will break my compassionate heart,
    Which nobody can deny.

For oh! how it enters my soul like an awl!
This pity, which some people self-pity call,
Is sure the most heart-piercing pity of all,
    Which nobody can deny.

So this is my song, as I told you before;
Come, buy off my stock, for I must no more
Carry Cæsars and Pompeys to Sugar-cane shore,
Which nobody can deny, deny,
    Which nobody can deny.

12. WILLIAM DUNBAR (?1456–?1513 [dates disputed])

Scottish priest, diplomatist and makar to the court of James IV of Scots and Queen Margaret Tudor who perhaps fell on Flodden Field. The greatest of the Scottish Chaucerians. This poem was likely inspired by one of the earliest Black people who lived in Scotland: 'Bla[c]k Ellen', who, with 'Bla[c]k Margaret were maids to Queen Margaret

Tudor, consort of James IV, King of Scots from their capture in 1506.[25] Scholars dispute whether this poem is merely an extreme 'flyting' or if it exhibits crude racism. Burns was acquainted with Dunbar's works both through Ramsay's *The Evergreen* (edition unknown) and the third volume of *Ancient Scottish Poets* (Perth: R Morrison, 1788) and, although this poem is in neither, he may have read wider, especially Creech's 1787 edition which does carry this poem. Kinsley records 15 references to Dunbar in Burns's works.

'Of Ane Blak-Moir Ladye', John Pinkerton, ed, *Ancient Scotish Poems: [...] Comprising Pieces Written from about 1420 till 1586* (2 vols) (London/Edinburgh: Charles Dilly/William Creech, 1786).

LANG heff I maed of ladyis quhytt;
Now of ane black I will indytt,
That landet furth of the last schippis;
How fain wald I descryve perfytt
My ladye with the mekle lippis!

How scho is tute-mowitt lyk ane aep;
And lyk a gangarel unto graep.
And how hir schort catt-nois up skippis.
And how scho schynes lyk ony saep.
My ladye with the mekle lippis.

Quhen scho is clad in reche apparrall,
Scho blinkis as brycht as ane tar-barrell.
Quhen scho was born, the sone tholit clippis;
The nycht be fain faucht in hir quarrel.
My ladye with the mekle lippis.

---

25 'It is uncertain who were the first Africans to arrive in 16th century Scotland but the Accounts of the Lord High Treasurer of Scotland show a presence of men, women and children. The two African women captured from a Portuguese ship by the Bartons of Leith in 1506 caused a sensation upon their arrival in Leith and Edinburgh. [... and] were presented to King James IV. The two women were later converted to [C]hristianity and were baptised as Margaret and Ellen [...] with [the latter] becoming the lady of the tournament of the black knight, with King James IV overcoming opponents to win her hand.' June Evans, *African/Caribbeans in Scotland. A Socio-Geographical Study* (Edinburgh: University of Edinburgh PHD Thesis, 1995), p.43.

Quha for hir saik, with speir and scheld,
Pressis maist mychtely in the feld,
Sall kiss, and with hir go in grippis;
And fra thynefurth hir luiff sall weld:
My ladye with the mekle lippis.

And quhai in felde receavis schaem,
And tynis thair his knychtl naem,
Sall cum behind and kis hir hippis;
And nevir to other confort claem.
My ladye with the mekle lippis.

 Quod Dunbar of ane blak-moir.

To a Black Lady
[Author's modern verse translation]

Long have I writ of ladies white,
Now of one black I will indite,
 That landed off the latest ships;
Who fain would I describe aright,
 My lady with the great big lips.

Her jaw sticks out like any chimp,
And waddles, grabbing like a toddler imp,
 And how her short cat's nose up-tips,
With soap and water now she'll pimp
 My lady with the great big lips.

When she is clad in rich apparel,
She gleams as bright as a big tar barrel;
 When she was born the sun fell in eclipse,
The [k]night so glad to fight in her quarrel:
 My lady with the great big lips.

Who for her sake with spear and shield
Proves himself most mightily in the field,
 Shall kiss her and embrace her as each grips;

And thenceforth to him her love shall yield,
   My lady with the great big lips.

And who in the field falls in shame,
And loses there his knightly name,
   Shall come behind and kiss her hips,
And never to other comfort claim,
   My lady with the great big lips.

13. REVD JOHN DYER (1699–1757)
Welsh poet, painter and clergyman. Dyer receives the following praise from Clarkson:

> Dyer, in his poem called The Fleece, expresses his sorrow on account of this barbarous trade, and looks forward to a day of retributive justice on account of the introduction of such an evil.
> [Clarkson, vol.1, pp.58–59]

From 'The Fleece,' ***The Poetical Works of John Dyer*** (Edinburgh: The Apollo Press, 1779).

But cheerful are the labours of the loom,
By health and ease accompany'd: they bring
Superior treasures speedier to the state
Than those of deep Peruvian mines, where slaves
(Wretched requital!) drink, with trembling hand,
Pale Palsy's baneful cup. [...]
                    Book III, ll.361–366, at pp.104–105

On Guinea's sultry strand the drapery light
Of Manchester or Norwich is bestow'd —
For clear transparent gums and ductile wax,
And snow-white ivory; yet the valued trade
Along this barbarous coast in telling wounds
The generous heart, the sale of wretched slaves:
Slaves by their tribes condemn'd, exchanging death
For life-long servitude; severe exchange!
These till our fertile colonies, which yield

The sugar-cane and the Tobago leaf,
And various new productions, that invite
Increasing navies to their crowded wharfs.
   But let the man whose rough tempestuous hours
In this advent'rous traffic are involv'd,
With just humanity of heart pursue
The gainful commerce: wickedness is blind:
Their sable chieftains may in future times
Burst their frail bonds, and vengeance execute
On cruel unrelenting pride of heart
And avarice. There are ills to come for crimes. [...]
Book IV, ll.189–108, at pp.122–123

14. JOHN GAY (1685–1732)

English poet, satirist and playwright, Gay was an (unsuccessful) investor in the South Sea Company which owned the Asiento contract for carrying enslaved people to the Spanish New World. However, it should be borne in mind that investors, such as Gay, were motivated by speculation and not by the underlying business of the company itself, so owning shares in this enterprise, taken alone, does not imply a positive adherence to the slave-trade.

From *The Poetical Works of John Gay. Including his Fables* (3 vols) (Edinburgh: At the Apollo Press, by the Martins, 1777).

Fables. 'I. The Tiger, the Lion and the Traveller':

Forced to forgo their native home,
My starving slaves at distance roam.
Within these woods I reign alone,
The boundless forest is my own.
vol.III, p.11, ll.51–54

From *The Beggar's Opera*:

Macheath] Were I laid on Greenland's coast,
And in my arms embraced my lass,
Warm amidst eternal frost,

> Too soon the half-year's night would pass.
> Polly] Were I sold on Indian soil,
> Soon as the burning day was closed,
> I could mock the sultry toil
> When on my charmer's breast reposed.
> Mac] And I would love you all the day,
> Polly] Every night would kiss and play,
> Mac] If with me you'd fondly stray
> Polly] Over the hills, and far away.
>   Act I, Scene XIII, Air XVI—'Over the Hills, and Far Away.'

Themes of slavery also occur in Gay's *The Captives* (which is indebted to Aphra Behn, through Southerne, see below) and in *Polly*, his sequel to *The Beggar's Opera*. As one commentator summarises:

> The two plays have much in common, and with respect to slavery, they share three important characteristics. First, the slavery that is the main precondition of the plot has clear connections with contemporary slavery [...]. Second, the liberation of a slave-hero that is the central action of the plot implies sympathy with slaves and dislike of slavery. Third, there are other elements of the plots that work against this to justify enslavement. In short, the plays at once turn upon a slave's liberation and implicitly endorse the institution of slavery.[26]

15. EDWARD GIBBON (1737–1794)

English historian and Member of Parliament. His letters in 1790–1792 further show his opposition to the slave-trade.

From ***The History of the Decline and Fall of the Roman Empire*** (12 vols) (London: W Strahan and W Cadell, 1783).

> [T]here still remained, in the centre of every province and of every family, an unhappy condition of men who endured the weight, without sharing the benefits, of society. In the free states of antiquity the domestic slaves were exposed to the wanton rigour

---

[26] John Richardson, *Slavery and Augustan Literature, Swift, Pope, Gray* (London: Routledge, 2004), p.113.

of despotism. The perfect settlement of the Roman empire was preceded by ages of violence and rapine. The slaves consisted, for the most part, of barbarian captives, taken in thousands by the chance of war, purchased at a vile price, accustomed to a life of independence, and impatient to break and to revenge their fetters. [...] The progress of manners was accelerated by the virtue or policy of the emperors; and by the edicts of Hadrian and the Antonines the protection of the laws was extended to the most abject part of mankind. The jurisdiction of life and death over the slaves, a power long exercised and often abused, was taken out of private hands, and reserved to the magistrates alone. The subterranean prisons were abolished; and, upon a just complaint of intolerable treatment, the injured slave obtained either his deliverance or a less cruel master.
vol. VI p.82.note39

16. RICHARD GLOVER (1712–1785)

English merchant and financier in the City of London who served as Member of Parliament for Weymouth (1760–1768), being noted for his opposition to Walpole. This quotation is more likely to be about 'political' slavery rather than chattel slavery, as Glover supported the petition of the West Indian Merchants to Parliament in 1775.

From *Leonidas, A Poem* (2 vols) (London: T Cadell and Richardson and Urquhart, 1770).

> For never yet was an epic poem wrote with so noble and useful a design: the whole plan and purpose of it being to shew the superiority of freedom over slavery; and how much virtue, public spirit, and the love of liberty, are preferable, both in their nature and effects, to riches, luxury, and the insolence of power.
> vol.I, pp.xi–xii

17. WILLIAM GUTHRIE (1708–1770)

Scottish journalist and historian. Burns first mentions this book in 'the Autobiographical Letter': 'My knowledge of ancient story was gathered from Salmon's and Guthrie's geographical grammars,' [L.125: to Dr Moore, August 1787, at vol.I, p.138] and then buys later editions for the Monklands Friendly Society in April 1789 and

January 1791 [L.325: to Peter Hill, 2 April 1789, at vol.I, p.392; L.430: to same, 17 January 1791, at vol.II, p.66].

From *A New Geographical, Historical, and Commercial Grammar, and Present State of the Several Kingdoms of the World* (London: Charles Dilley and George Robinson, 1772) and (London: Charles Dilley and GGJ and J Robinson, 1790).

> 1772 edition: The acquisitions which the English have made upon the coast of Guinea, particularly their settlement at Senegal, have opened new forces of commerce with Africa. [...] At present England [...] supplies her American colonies with negro slaves, amounting in number to above 100,000 annually. p.231

> 1790 edition: The acquisitions which the English made upon the coast of Guinea, particularly their settlements at Senegal, opened new forces of commerce with Africa. [...] Senegal is now delivered up to France by the late treaty of peace. [...] it lately supplied the American colonies with negro slaves, amounting in number to above 100,000 annually. p.252

The misery and hardships of the negroes is truly moving; and though great care is taken to make them propagate, the ill treatment they receive so shortens their lives, that instead of increasing by the course of nature, many thousands are annually imported to the West Indies, to supply the place of those who pine and die by the hardships they receive. They are indeed, stubborn and untradable for the most part, and they must be ruled with a rod of iron; but they ought not to be crushed with it, or to be thought a sort of beasts without souls, as some of their overseers do at present, though some of these tyrants are themselves the dregs of this nation, and the refuse of the jails of Europe. Many of the negroes, however, who fall into the hands of gentlemen of humanity, find their situations easy and comfortable; and it has been observed, that in North America, where in general these poor wretches are better used, there is less waste of negroes, they live longer, and propagate better. And it seems clear, from the whole course of history, that those nations which have behaved with the greatest humanity to their slaves, were always well served, and run the lead hazard from their rebellions. The slaves, on their first arrival from the coast of Guinea, are exposed naked to sale; they are then generally very simple and innocent creatures, but they soon become roguish enough; and when they come to be whipped, excuse their faults by the example of the whites. They believe every negroe returns to his native country after death. This thought is so agreeable, that it cheers the poor creatures, and renders the burden of life easy, which would otherwise to many of them be quite intolerable. They look on death as a blessing, and it is surprising to see with what courage and intrepidity some of them meet it; they are quite transported to think their slavery is near at an end, that they shall revisit their native shores, and see their old friends and acquaintance. When a negro is about to expire, his fellow slaves kiss him, and wish him a good journey, and fend their hearty good wishes to their relations in Guinea. They make no lamentations; but with a great deal of joy inter his body, believing he is gone home and happy.

pp.659–660 [1772]; pp.832–833 [1790]

The negroes, except those who attend gentlemen, who have them dressed in their own livery, have once a year Osnaburghs, and a blanket for clothing, with a cap or handkerchief for the head.

p.658 [1772]; pp.832 [1790]

The negroes in the plantations are subsisted at a very easy rate. This is generally by allotting to each family of them a small portion of land, and allowing them two days in the week, Saturday and Sunday, to cultivate it: some are subsisted in this manner, but others find their negroes with a certain portion of Guinea or Indian corn, and to some a salt herring, or small portion of bacon or fat pork a day. All the rest of the charge consists in a cap, a shirt, a pair of breeches, stockings and shoes; the whole not exceeding 40s a year, and the profit of their labour yields 10 or 15L. [1789: 10 or 12L annually.] The price of men negroes, upon their first arrival, is from 33–36L. [1789: 30 to 36L.] women and grown boys about 50s less; but such negro families as are acquainted with the business of the islands, generally bring about 40L upon an average, one with another; and there are instances of a single negro man, expert in business, bringing 150 guineas, [1789: 156 guineas,] and the wealth of a planter is generally computed from the number of slaves he possesses.

p.684 [1772]; p.827 [1790]

Before the late war, there were allowed to be in our West Indies at lead 230,000 negro slaves; and, upon the highest calculation, the whites there did not amount to 90,000 souls. [...] That the disposition of the West Indians themselves, who for cheapness choose to do every thing by negroes which can possibly be done by them, contributes greatly to the small number of whites of the lower stations. Such indeed is the powerful influence of avarice, that though the whites are kept in constant terror of insurrections and plots, many families employ 25 or 30 negroes as menial servants, who are infinitely the most dangerous of the slaves, and in cafe of any insurrection, they have it more in their power to deliver a sudden and fatal blow.   p.684 [1772]; p.827 [1790]

18. [HENRY HOME,] LORD KAMES (1696–1782)

Scottish judge, philosopher and agricultural improver. Philosophically (as seen above) he was a polygenist, yet by *Knight v Wedderburn*, his opinion was 'Slavery is a forced state, — for we are all naturally equal.'[27]

From *Sketches of the History of Man* (4 vols) (Edinburgh/London: William Creech/A Strahan and T Cadell, 1788).

The black colour of Negroes, thick lips, flat nose, crisp wooly hair, and rank smell distinguish them from every other race of Men.

vol.I, pp.12–13

If the only rule afforded by nature for classing animals can be depended upon, there are different species of men as well as of dogs: a mastiff differs not more from a spaniel, than a white man from a negro, or a Laplander from a Dane. And if we have any belief in

---

27 See Table 1 above.

Providence, it ought to be so. Plants were created of different kinds to fit them for different climates, and so were brute animals. Certain it is, that all men are not fitted equally for every climate. Is there not then reason to conclude, that as there are different climates, so there are different species of men fitted for these different climates?

vol.I, p.19

The colour of the Negroes, as above observed, affords a strong presumption of their being a different species from the Whites; and I once thought, that the presumption was supported by inferiority of understanding in the former. But it appears to me doubtful, upon fecund thoughts, whether that inferiority may not be occasioned by their condition. A man never ripens in judgment nor in prudence but by exercising these powers. At home, the negroes have little occasion to exercise either they live upon fruits and roots, which grow without culture: they need little clothing: and they erect houses without trouble or art*. Abroad, they are miserable slaves, having no encouragement either to think or to act. Who can say how far they might improve in a place of freedom, were they obliged, like Europeans, to procure bread with the sweat of their brows? Some nations in Negroland, particularly that of Whidah, have made great improvements in government, in police, and in manners. The negroes on the Gold coast are naturally gay: they apprehend readily what is said to them, have a good judgment, are equitable in their dealings, and accommodate themselves readily to the manners of strangers.

[* The negro slaves in Jamaica, who have Sunday only at command for raising food to themselves, live as well, if not better, than the free negroes who command every day of the week. Such, in the latter, is the effect of indolence from want of occupation.]

vol.I, pp.64–65

Whence the rough and harsh manners of our West-Indian planters, but from the unrestrained licence of venting ill humour upon their negro slaves? Why are carters a rugged set of men? Plainly because horses, their slaves, submit without resistance. An ingenious writer, describing Guiana in the southern continent of America, observes, that the negroes, who are more numerous than the whites, must be kept in awe by severity of discipline. [...] I am inclined however to believe, that the harsh treatment of these poor people is more owing to the avarice of their masters, than to their own perverseness. That slaves in all ages have been harshly treated, is a melancholy truth. vol.I, p.368

In all the West-India colonies, the slaves continually decrease so as to make frequent recruits from Africa necessary. 'This decrease' says the author of a late account of Guiana, 'is commonly attributed to oppression and hard labour; tho' with little reason, as the slaves are much more robust, healthy, and vigorous, than their masters. The true cause is, the commerce of white men with young Negro wenches, who, to support that commerce, use every mean to avoid conception and even to procure abortion. By such practices they are incapacitated to bear children when they settle in marriage with their own countrymen. That this is the true cause, will be evident, from considering, that in Virginia and Maryland, the stock of slaves is kept up without any importation because in these countries commerce with Negro women is detested, as infamous and unnatural.' [...] but there is a stronger cause of depopulation, viz. the culture of sugar, laborious in the field, and unhealthy in the house by boiling, &c. The Negroes employ'd in the culture of cotton, coffee, and ginger, seldom need to be recruited. Add, that where tobacco and rice are cultivated, the flock of Negroes is kept up by procreation, without necessity of recruits, Because there, a certain portion of work is allotted to the Negroes in every plantation; and when that is performed, they are at liberty to work for themselves. The management in Jamaica is very different: no task is there assigned, and the poor slaves know no end of labour: they are followed all day long by the lower overseers with whips. And hence it is, that a plantation in Jamaica, which employs a hundred slaves, requires an annual recruit of no fewer than seven. vol.III, pp.155-156

19. HOMER (*fl*: c 8th BC)

The ancient Greek poet was translated by James Macpherson (1736–1796): Scottish writer and historian, famed for his 'Ossian' which was an early book Burns read and enjoyed [L.54], the use of 'duan' in 'The Vision' [K.62] being one direct influence.

From James Macpherson, trans, *The Poems of Homer* (2 vols) (London: Becket & de Hondt, 1773).

Slavery features in several of the tales within *The Iliad* and *The Odyssey*. Note, for example:

> 'Timid I ought to be called: Of spirit destitute and vile; —
> should I yield in ALL to thee.
> Reign o'er other slaves: Presume not ME to command [...]'
> vol.I, p.15

In *Odyssey* Book XIII, the return of Odysseus to Ithaca, a key part of the plot is a comparison of the 'good slaves', principally Eumaeus, and the 'bad slaves' who will be hanged after the attack on the Suitors.

20. REVD JAMES HURDIS (1763–1801)
English clergyman and minor poet. Educated at Oxford after a fellowship at Magdalen, he served in Sussex parishes. He was elected 11th Professor of Poetry at Oxford in 1793. An ardent Abolitionist, he was a friend and correspondent of William Cowper (qv). Burns bought this volume from Hill in 1790 (see L.387).

From *The Village Curate, A Poem*, Second Edition (London: J Johnson, 1790).

> My eye is cast on Britain's western isles,
> And I behold a patient slave grown faint
> Under the lash. Inhuman dog, forbear.
> The man who now lies bleeding at thy feet
> Was once a monarch [...]
> Cross not again the proud Atlantic wave,
> With hellish purpose to enslave the free,
> Or load the pris'ner with eternal chains,
> For he is Man as thou art. Not for thee,
> And only thee did God's creative Word
> Call into being this vast work, the world.
> Nor yet for thee that Word incarnate shed
> His precious blood. [...],

For Adam was his sire, and Adam thine;
And he shall share redemption too with thee,
With thee, and me, and all this Gentile world, [...]

pp.102–104

21. DAVID HUME (1711–1776)

Scottish historian and philosopher. His position as the philosophical genius of the Scottish Enlightenment has been thrown into debate due to a single footnote comment on race. Burns applauded Beattie's response to Hume's sceptical views on religion (see above).

From *Essays and Treatises on Several Subjects* (4 vols) (London/Edinburgh: A Millar/A Kincaid and A Donaldson, 1753–1756) and from *Essays and Treatises on Several Subjects* (2 vols) (London/Edinburgh: T Cadell [and others]/C Elliot, 1788).

From 'On the Liberty of the Press'.

> 'Tis seldom that liberty of any kind is lost all at once. Slavery has so frightful an aspect to men accustom'd to freedom that it must steal in upon them by degrees, and must disguise itself in a thousand shapes, in order to be receiv'd.
>
> [1753], vol.I, p.13; [1788] deleted

From 'On the Populousness of Ancient Nations'.

> The chief difference between the *domestic* œconomy of the ancients and that of the moderns consists in the practice of slavery, which prevailed among the former, and which has been abolished for some centuries throughout the greater part of Europe. [...] The remains which are found of domestic slavery, in the American colonies, and among some European nations, would never surely create a desire of rendering it more universal. The little humanity, commonly observed in persons, accustomed, from their infancy, to exercise so great authority over their fellow-creatures, and to trample upon human nature, were sufficient alone to disgust us with that unbounded dominion.
>
> [1753] vol.IV, pp.140–141; [1788] vol.I, pp.342–343

I shall add, that, from the experience of our planters, slavery is as little advantageous to the master as to the slave, wherever hired servants can be procured. A man is obliged to cloath and feed his slave; and he does no more for his servant: The price of the first purchase is, therefore, so much loss to him: not to mention, that the fear of punishment will never draw so much labour from a slave, as the dread of being turned off, and not getting another service, will from a free-man. [1788] vol.I, p.348

'Tis computed in the West Indies, that a stock of slaves grow worse five per cent every year, unless new slaves be brought to recruit them. They are not able to keep up their own number, even in those warm countries, where cloaths and provisions are so easily got. How much more must this happen in European countries, and in or near great cities?

All I pretend to infer from these reasonings is, that slavery is in general disadvantageous both to the happiness and populousness of mankind, and that its place is much better supplied by the practice of hired servants. [1753] vol.IV, pp.149; [1788] vol.I, p.353

From 'Of National Characters' 1753.

I am apt to suspect the negroes and in general all other species of men (for there are four or five different kinds) to be naturally inferior to the whites. There never was a civiliz'd nation of any other complexion than white, nor even any individual eminent either in action or speculation. No ingenious manufactures amongst them, no arts, no sciences. On the other hand, the most rude and barbarous of the whites, such as the ancient GERMANS, the present TARTARS, have still something eminent about them, in their valour, form of government, or some other particular. Such a uniform and constant difference could not happen, in so many countries and ages, if nature had not made an original distinction between these breeds of men. Not to mention our colonies, there are NEGROE slaves dispersed all over EUROPE, of whom none ever discovered any symptoms of ingenuity; though low people, without education, will start up amongst us, and distinguish themselves in every profession. In JAMAICA, indeed, they talk of one negro as a man of parts and learning; but it is likely he is admired for slender accomplishments, like a parrot who speaks a few words plainly.

[1753] vol.1, p.291

Variant first paragraph, from **'Of National Characters'** 1788.

I am apt to suspect the negroes to be naturally inferior to the whites. There scarcely ever was a civilized nation of that complexion,

[1788] vol.1, p.484

22. JOHN LOCKE (1632–1704)

The great English philosopher, educated at Westminster and Christ Church, Oxford. Modern scholarship finds Locke a conflicted figure given his administrative roles in companies concerned with the slave trade, and his drafting of a constitution for Carolina which codified enslavement. Burns would not have been aware of that controversy, although he confirms (in the 'Autobiographical Letter') that he read the *Essay Concerning Human Understanding*, but there is no record of his reading the *Two Treatises*, although he does quote a letter of Locke's to 'Clarinda' (*Letters*, [L.182]) which could indicate a wider familiarity with Locke's works.

From *An Essay Concerning Human Understanding in Four Books* (3 vols) (Edinburgh: J Dickson and C Elliot, 1777).

> This [rational consideration] is so far from being a restraint or diminution of freedom, that it is the very improvement and benefit of it; it is not an abridgement, it is the end and use of our liberty; and the farther we are removed from such a determination, the nearer we are to misery and slavery. vol.1, p.365

From *Two Treatises on Government* (London: J Whiston [and others], 1772).

> Slavery is so vile and miserable an Estate of Man, and so directly opposed to the generous Temper and Courage of our Nation; than it is hardly to be conceived that an Englishman, much less a Gentleman, should plead for it. p.1

23. HENRY MACKENZIE (1745–1831)

Scottish lawyer and writer, known as a sentimental novelist. He was Comptroller of the Taxes for Scotland and a leading litterateur at Edinburgh. He was an important part of Burns's early reading and helped the poet's literary career both through his influential review in *The Lounger* in December 1786, and in negotiating the sale of Burns's copyright to Creech the following year. Burns had told his former tutor, Murdoch, that *The Man of Feeling* was 'a book I prize next to the bible,' [*Letters*: 15 January 1783, K.13] while he calls it one of 'my bosom favourites' in the 'Autobiographical Letter'. Burns wrote to Mackenzie saying that 'whatever is good about my heart is much indebted to Mr Harley [the 'Man of Feeling.'] *Letters*: 4 May 1787 [L.101]. It is important to remember that Burns thought so much of this writer that he donated a copy of *Julia de Roubigné* (along with *Humphrey Clinker* and two volumes of non-fiction) to the Dumfries Library in September 1793.

From *The Man of Feeling* (London: A Strahan, and T Cadell, 1783).

> This, said he, is a young lady, who was born to ride in her coach and six, She was beloved, if the story I have heard is true, by a young gentleman, her equal in birth, though by no means her match in fortune: but love, they say, is blind, and so she fancied him as much as he did her. Her father, it seems, would not hear of their marriage, and threatened to turn her out of doors, if ever she saw him again. Upon this the young gentleman took a voyage to the West Indies, in hopes of bettering his fortune, and obtaining his mistress; but he was scarce landed, when he was seized with one of the fevers which are common in those islands, and died in a few days, lamented by every one that knew him. This news soon reached his mistress, who was at the same time prodded by her father to marry a rich miserly fellow, who was old enough to be her grandfather. pp.61–62

From *Julia de Roubigné: A Tale in a Series of Letters* (2 vols) (London: W Strahan and T Cadell, 1777).

> [*Savillion writes from the French West-Indies*] To a man not callous from habit, the treatment of the negroes, in the plantations here,

is shocking. I felt it strongly, and could not forbear expressing my sentiments to my uncle. He allowed them to be natural, but pleaded necessity, in justification of those severities which his overseers sometimes used towards his slaves. [...]

Next morning I called those negroes who had formerly been in his service together, and told them that, while they continued in the plantation, Yambu [*an enslaved man who was formerly a prince in Guinea*] was to superintend their work: that if they chose to leave him and me, they were at liberty to go; and that, if found idle or unworthy, they should not be allowed to stay. He has, accordingly, ever since had the command of his former subjects, and superintends their work in a particular quarter of the plantation; and having been declared free, according to the mode prescribed by the laws of the island, has a certain portion of ground allotted him, the produce of which is his property. I have had the satisfaction of observing those men, under the feeling of good treatment, and the idea of liberty, do more than almost double their number subject to the whip of an overseer. I am under no apprehension of desertion or mutiny; they work with the willingness of freedom, yet are mine with more than the obligation of slavery.

I have been often tempted to doubt, whether there is not an error in the whole plan of negro servitude, and whether whites, or Creoles born in the West Indies, or perhaps cattle, after the manner of European husbandry, would not do the business better and cheaper than the slaves do. The money which the latter cost at first, the sickness (often owing to despondency of mind) to which they are liable after their arrival, and the proportion that die in consequence of it, make the machine, if it may be so called, of a plantation, extremely expensive in its operations. In the list of slaves belonging to a wealthy planter, it would astonish you to see the number unfit for service, pining under disease, a burden on their master. I am talking only as a merchant; — but as a man — good heavens! when I think of the many thousands of my fellow creatures groaning under servitude and misery! — Great God! hast thou peopled those regions of thy world for the purpose of casting out their inhabitants to chains and torture? — No; thou gavest them a land teeming with good things, and lightedst up thy sun to bring forth spontaneous plenty; but the refinements of man, ever at war with thy works, have changed this scene of profusion and luxuriance, into a theatre of rapine, of slavery, and of murder! [...] Habit, the tyrant of nature and of reason, is deaf to the voice of either; here she stifles humanity, and debases the species — for the master of slaves has seldom he soul of a man.

Among the legends of an European nursery, are stories of captives delivered, of slaves released, who had pined for years in the durance of unmerciful enemies. Could we suppose its infant audience transported to the seashore, where a ship laden with slaves is just landing: the question would be universal, 'Who shall set these poor people free? — The young West Indian asks his father to buy a boy for him, that he may have something to vent his spite on when he is peevish.

'Letter XXVIII: Savillion to Beauvarais,' vol.II, pp.28–41

24. JOHN MILTON (1608–1674)

English poet, writer and Latin Secretary to the Lord Protector. Burns writes of approvingly of Milton's Satan on several occasions, notably praising 'the dauntless magnanimity; the intrepid, unyielding independence; the desperate daring, and the hobble defiance of hardship, in that great Personage. Satan' to William Nicol, 18 June 1787, [L.114].

From 'Paradise Lost', *The Poetical Works of John Milton* (2 vols) (Edinburgh: A Kincaid and A Donaldson, 1755).[28]

> till one shall rise
> Of proud ambitious heart, who not content
> With fair equalitie, fraternal state,
> Will arrogate Dominion undeserv'd
> Over his brethren, and quite dispossess
> Concord and law of Nature from the Earth;
> Hunting (and Men not Beasts shall be his game)
> With Warr and hostile snare such as refuse
> Subjection to his Empire tyrannous:

---

28 Burns's copy, with his autograph on each title page, is held by the Library of St Paul's School, London.

A mightie Hunter thence he shall be styl'd
Before the Lord, as in despite of Heav'n,
Or from Heav'n claming second Sovrantie;
And from Rebellion shall derive his name,
Though of Rebellion others he accuse.
Hee with a crew, whom like Ambition joyns
With him or under him to tyrannize,
Marching from Eden towards the West, shall finde
The Plain, wherein a black bituminous gurge
Boiles out from under ground, the mouth of Hell;
Of Brick, and of that stuff they cast to build
A Citie and Towre, whose top may reach to Heav'n;
And get themselves a name, least far disperst
In foraign Lands thir memorie be lost
Regardless whether good or evil fame.
[...]
O execrable Son so to aspire
Above his Brethren, to himself assuming
Authoritie usurpt, from God not giv'n:
He gave us onely over Beast, Fish, Fowl
Dominion absolute; that right we hold
By his donation; but Man over men
He made not Lord; such title to himself
Reserving, human left from human free.
[...]
Since thy original lapse, true Libertie
Is lost, which always with right Reason dwells
Twinn'd, and from her hath no dividual being:
Reason in man obscur'd, or not obeyd,
Immediately inordinate desires
And upstart Passions catch the Government
From Reason, and to servitude reduce
Man till then free. Therefore since hee permits
Within himself unworthie Powers to reign
Over free Reason, God in judgement just
Subjects him from without to violent Lords;
Who oft as undeservedly enthrall
His outward freedom: Tyrannie must be,

Though to the Tyrant thereby no excuse.
Yet somtimes Nations will decline so low
From vertue, which is reason, that no wrong,
But Justice, and some fatal curse annext
Deprives them of thir outward libertie,
Thir inward lost: Witness th' irreverent Son
Of him who built the Ark, who for the shame
Don to his Father, heard this heavie curse,
Servant of Servants, on his vitious Race.
                Book XII, ll.24-47, 64-72, 83-104

25. MICHEL DE MONTAIGNE (1533–1592)
French moralist and the inventor of the 'essay' as a literary form. However, he appears to have had no direct literary influence on Burns's writings.

From *The Essays of Michael Seigneur de Montaigne, Translated into English* (3 vols) (London: S and E Ballard, 1759).

> Such as are in immediate fear of a losing their estates, of banishment, or of slavery, live in perpetual anguish, and lose all appetite and repose; whereas such as are actually poor, slaves, or exiles, ofttimes live as merrily as other folk.   vol.I, p.63

> We do not know where death awaits us: so let us wait for it everywhere. To practice death is to practice freedom. A man who has learned how to die has unlearned how to be a slave.
>   vol.I, p.76

26. DR JOHN MOORE (1729–1802)
Scots medic, Abolitionist and writer whose interest in Burns arose when Mrs Dunlop sent him a *Kilmarnock Edition* in 1786. From that introduction followed 'The Autobiographical Letter' and a sustained correspondence. In return, Moore sent Burns a copy of his *Zeluco*, which the poet said he had 'read over [...] many times' *(Letters:* To Dr Moore, 28 February 1791, [L.437]).

From *Zeluco, Various Views of Human Nature, Taken from Life and Manners, Foreign and Domestic* (2 vols) (London: A Strahan and T Cadell, 1789).

[Précis] Zeluco, an Italian nobleman, is the personification of vice. The novel traces his gothic career from the slave-plantations of the West Indies to the fashionable society of Italy, as he connives, steal and murders until his own untimely death.

The first part is an early and detailed Abolition tract: Zeluco, recognising the honourable nature of Hanno, an enslaved man, and in debate with The Doctor, teases out the key Abolitionist points:

- That the enslavers' self-interest is insufficient to ensure humane treatment of the enslaved, as evidenced by cruel punishments and murder;
- That the unlimited power of the enslaver diminishes both him and the enslaved;
- That, although enslavement is discussed in the Old Testament of the Bible, the message of Christ was universal love and respect;
- That the situation of the poor, common labourer in England is not comparable with that of the enslaved in the West Indies.

The character of the Doctor sums up the Abolitionist view to Zeluco:

> how infinitely more pleasing is it to be considered as the distributor of happiness, than the inflictor of pain? What man, who has it in his power to be loved as a benefactor, would choose to be detested as an executioner, and see sorrow, terror, and abhorrence, in the countenances he daily beholds?' [...] My advice is this: Alter intirely your conduct towards your slaves; scorn not those who demand justice and mercy; treat them with much more indulgence, and sometimes with kind-ness; for certainly that man is in a most miserable as well as dangerous situation, who lives among those who rejoice in his sickness, howl with despair at his recovery, and whose only hope of tranquillity lies in their own death or in his.'. The physician having made this remonstrance, took his leave. Zeluco remained musing for a considerable time after he was gone; the result of his reflections was a determination to behave

with more indulgence to his slaves, being alarmed by what was suggested, and convinced that such conduct in future was highly expedient for his own personal security. Those resolutions were however very imperfectly kept. vol.i, pp.150–158

27. REVD JOHN NEWTON DD (1725–1807)
An Englishman who went to sea as a boy and his involvement in the slave-trade led, in time, to his religious conversion and an Abolitionist stance. In 1764 he took Holy Orders in the Church of England at Olney, where he befriended Cowper (see above) working jointly on the *Onley Hymns* (including 'Amazing Grace.') In 1772 he became rector of St Mary Woolnoth in London where he preached until his death a few months after the passage of the Abolition Bill in 1807. Burns purchased Newton's *Letters* for Monklands, describing it to Peter Hill as 'damned trash,' [L.430], so it is assumed that, despite Burns's fondness for Cowper, he did not rate Newton.

From ***Letters, Sermons, and a Review of Ecclesiastical History, and Hymns*** (6 vols) (Edinburgh: Murray and Cochrane, 1787).

> The ship I went on board was bound to Sierra Leon, and the adjacent parts of what is called *the windward coast of Africa.* [...] I determined to remain in Africa; and amused myself with many golden dreams that I should find an opportunity of improving my fortune. [...] There are still upon that part of the coast a few white men settled, (and there were many more at the time I was first there), whose business it was to purchase slaves &c in the rivers and country adjacent, and sell them to the ships at an advanced price. vol.i, p.36

> During the time I was engaged in the slave-trade, I never had the least scruple as to its lawfulness. I was on the whole satisfied with it, as the appointment Providence had marked out for me; yet it was in many respects, far from eligible. It is indeed accounted a genteel employment, and is usually very profitable, though to me it did not prove so, the Lord feeling that a large increase of wealth would not be good for me. However, I considered myself a sort of *gaoler* or *turnkey*, and I was sometimes shocked with an

employment that was perpetually conversant with chains, bolts and shackles. In this view I had often petitioned in my prayers, that the Lord, in his own time, would be pleased to fix me in a more humane calling [...] vol.I, p.95

HYMN 41.
Amazing grace! (how sweet the sound!)
   That sav'd a wretch like me!
I once was lost, but now am found,
   Was blind, but now I see. vol.VI, p.43, ll. 1–4

28. 'PETER PINDAR' (Pseudonym of DR JOHN WOLCOT) (1738–1819)

Born in Devon, qualified MD at Aberdeen University, travelled to Jamaica as the new governor's physician. He briefly took Holy Orders, having been offered patronage by the governor, but returned to Cornwall on the latter's death, taking up physic again. In 1778 he came to London, developing a career as a writer of satirical verse. He contributed English songs to Thomson's *Select Airs* (including 'Lord Gregory'). Wolcot/Pindar was referred to on many occasions by Burns, who called him 'a delightful fellow, & a first favourite of mine.' (*Letters:* To George Thomson, [February 1796], [L.689]).

From 'Azid, Or the Song of the Captive Negro' *The Scots Magazine*, August 1795, pp.517–518.

   POOR Mora eye wet wid tear,
      And heart like lead sink down wid wo;
   She seem her mournful friends to hear,
      And see der eye like fountain flow.
   No more she give me song so gay,
   But sigh, 'Adieu, dear Domahay.' [...]

   But why do Azid live a slave,
      And see a slave his Mora dear?
   Come, let we seek at once de grave —
      No chain, no tyrant den we fear.
   Ah, me! I hear a spirit say,
   'Come, Azid, come to Domahay.' [...]

29. ALEXANDER POPE (1688–1744)

English poet and satirist. An investor in the South Sea Company bubble, as speculation rather than an investment in chattel slavery. Burns's very early 'Now Westlin' Winds' [K.2] shows influences from Pope's 'Windsor-Forest', while 'A Prayer, In the Prospect of Death' [K.13] is modelled on Pope's 'Universal Prayer' with multiple other references (direct or allusive) throughout Kinsley.[29] Pope is also quoted 17 times in Burns's *Letters*. Clarkson alludes to him thus:

> Pope, in his Essay on Man, where he endeavours to show that happiness in the present depends, among other things, upon the hope of a future state, takes an opportunity of exciting compassion in behalf of the poor African, while he censures the avarice and cruelty of his master: 'Lo, the poor Indian! [...]'
>
> [Clarkson vol.I, p.52]

From William Warburton, ed, *The Works of Alexander Pope* (6 vols) (London: C Bathurst [and others], 1787).

From '**Windsor-Forest**'.

> Oh stretch thy reign, fair Peace! from shore to shore,
> Till Conquest cease, and Slav'ry be no more;
> Till the freed Indians in their native groves
> Reap their own fruits, and woo their sable loves,
> Peru once more a race of Kings behold,
> And other Mexico's be roof'd with gold.
> There purple Vengeance bath'd in gore retires,
>
> ll.397–422, at vol.I, p.55

From '**An Essay on Man**'.

> Lo, the poor Indian! whose untutor'd mind
> Sees God in clouds, or hears him in the wind;
> His soul, proud Science never taught to stray
> Far as the solar walk or milky way;

---

29 Burns, *Poems*, vol.III, pp.1005–1006, 1012–1013.

Yet simple nature to his hope has giv'n,
Behind the cloud-topt hill, an humbler heav'n,
Some safer world in depth of woods embrac'd,
Some happier island in the watry waste,
Where slaves once more their native land behold,
No fiends torment, no Christians thirst for gold.

vol.II, pp.46–47

30. ALLAN RAMSAY (1686–1758)

Scottish poet, wigmaker and bookseller, whose song collections contributed to the revival of Scots vernacular poetry. 'Immortal Allan' Ramsay, as Burns calls him in L.346, is an important influence on Burns (as he says in the 'Autobiographical Letter'), who quotes Ramsay some 20 times in his correspondence. There are 85 references to Ramsay in Kinsley's index. This song is the marching song of the Royal Company of Archers, the volunteer regiment which is the Monarch's bodyguard in Scotland, which elected Burns a member in April 1792.

From 'The Archers' Song,' *The Tea-table Miscellany: Or, a Collection of Choice Songs, Scots and English. Twelfth Edition* (4 vols) (London: A Millar, 1763).

'Tis now the archers royal,
An hearty band and loyal,
An hearty band and loyal,
That in just thought agree,
Appear in ancient bravery,
Despising all base knavery,
Which tends to bring in slavery,
Souls worthy to live free.

Penultimate verse, at vol.I, p.198

31. DAVID RAMSAY (1749–1815)

Son of a Scots immigrant to America, physician, historian and politician. His second and third wives were the daughters of Revd John Witherspoon and Henry Laurens, both slave-holders, however, he favoured Abolition.

From *History of the American Revolution* (2 vols) (London: np, 1790).

> An adherent to independence was now considered as one who courted exile, poverty and ruin. Many yielded to the temptation, and became British subjects. The mischievous effects of slavery, in facilitating the conquest of the country, now became apparent. As the slaves had no interest at stake, the subjugation of the state [sc: South Carolina] was a matter of no consequence to them. Instead of aiding in its defence, they by a variety of means threw the weight of their little influence into the opposite scale. vol.II, p.223

32. MARIA RIDDELL (1772–1808)

English Daughter of the Governor of the Leeward Islands and wife of Walter Riddell, a plantation owner on Antigua. Friend and obituarist of Burns. Melissa Bailes correctly reminds us that 'Riddell's selective elisions of well-known aspects of West Indian society, such as slavery, register her efforts to reconcile these colonies with British values' in as species of 'self-censorship.'[30] Absent a period of estrangement, she and Burns shared each other's writings and correspondence, so it is possible that Burns read the Letter above or talked with her about her views on Black chattel slavery, which were not addressed in her travelogue.[31]

From *Voyages to the Madeira, and Leeward Caribbean Isles: With Sketches of the Natural History of These Islands* (Edinburgh/London: Peter Hill/T Cadell, 1792).

> The inhabitants [of Barbuda] are black, mostly slaves to Sir William Codrington; their employment is husbandry. The sugar cane does not flourish here in any perfection. The chief commodity, from which the owner derives any benefit, is the cattle, which breed wild among the woods. 'Antigua and Barbuda', p.37

> The *saccharum arundo*, or sugar-cane, is a species of reed, divided into joints two or three inches long, and filled with a pith that

---

30 Melissa Bailes, 'Hybrid Britons: West Indian Colonial Identity and Maria Riddell's Natural History,' *European Romantic Review* (April 2009), p.207.
31 *Burns Encyclopaedia*, pp.266–270.

yields the sweet juice or syrup, which is afterwards (by a long and tedious process) converted into sugar.

'Natural History of Antigua', p.103

From Robert Kerr, *The Memoirs of the Life, Writings, & Correspondence of William Smellie* (2 vols) (Edinburgh: J Anderson, 1811).

Our ancestors, when they instituted the accursed traffic of the slave trade, brought over a nation, who, though long patient and submissive to servitude, seem now to have nearly touched, by the decree of Providence, the term of their bondage, and have already begun to retaliate the injuries imposed upon them by their persecuting masters. The negroes of St Domingo, as you have probably seen by the papers, have massacred, in a general insurrection, 152,000 of the French whites; and the rest having escaped to America, the former remain in the undisputed possession and sovereignty of the island, wherein they had so long mourned their captivity. But we must deplore, however zealous in the cause of liberty and justice, that the laws of humanity should thus be violated, before the rights of half mankind can be firmly established, which I fear they will not be yet without the effusion of more blood. Would to heaven this dreadful example of reprisals might expiate the guilt of the infatuated Europeans, whose avarice and rapine first dragged them reluctant from their native soil, and deprived them at once of their country, their families, and their freedom, to gratify their own superfluous luxuries: 'Car c'est a ce prix qu'on vend le sucre en Europe.' — Vide VOLTAIRE'S Candide.[32]

Letter: Riddell to Smellie, 17 November 1793, vol.II, pp.375-376

33. THOMAS SALMON (1679–1767)
English historian and geographer, who circumnavigated the world with George Anson in 1739–40. Burns mentions this book in the 'Autobiographical Letter': 'My knowledge of ancient story was gathered from Salmon's and Guthrie's geographical grammars.'

---

32 See entry for Voltaire below.

From *A New Geographical and Historical Grammar* (London: W Johnston, 1766).

> It were to be wished also, that the *English* would forbear to treat their Negroes with that Cruelty they have formerly done, which, no Doubt, occasioned many of them to desert; for though Torture be abolished in *England*, it was exercised upon the Negroes here [in Jamaica] with the greatest Barbarity: They were almost whipped to Death without any Trial, by the arbitrary Commands of a private Planter, for the smallest Offences; and for greater Crimes were fastened to the Ground and burnt by Inches, till they expired in Torments. The Crime, perhaps, was no other than an Attempt to gain that Freedom they had been injuriously deprived of, which would be looked upon as an heroic Action in a *Christian* Slave, taken Captive by the Turks. p.591

34. IGNATIUS SANCHO (1729?–1780)

Born on a slave ship on the Middle Passage and brought enslaved to England aged around three. Through the Duke of Montague he obtained an education and employment. He was the first Black person to vote in a British parliamentary election, and the first Black person to have an obituary in the British press. This book was recommended to Burns by Agnes McLehose at the height of the Sylvander/Clarinda correspondence in January 1788: 'Did you ever read Sancho's Letters? They would hit your taste,' but the volume is not mentioned in his replies.[33] Given the intensity of their epistolary affair, it would seem likely that Burns would take his 'mistress's' advice. Also, he did read 'Sterne's Works' (see below) and depending on which edition he owned, the correspondence between Sterne and Sancho may have been included.

Miss Crewe and J Jekyll, eds, *Letters of the late Ignatius Sancho, an African* (2 vols) (London: J Dodsley J Robson, J Walter, R Baldwin, and J Sewell, 1782).

> Look round upon the miserable fate of almost all of our unfortunate

---

[33] 'Letter: Clarinda to Sylvander, 10 January 1788 in *The Correspondence Between Burns and Clarinda*, ed by WC McLehose (Edinburgh: William Tait, 1843), p.137.

colour — superadded to ignorance, — see slavery, and the contempt of those very wretches who roll in affluence from our labours superadded to this woeful catalogue — hear the ill-bred and heart-racking abuse of the foolish vulgar. vol.I, p.42

I am one of those people whom the vulgar and illiberal call 'Negurs.' — The first part of my life was rather unlucky, as I was placed in a family who judged ignorance as the best and only security for obedience. [...] Consider slavery — what it is — how bitter a draught, and how many millions are made to drink it. vol.I, pp.95–96
Commerce was meant by the goodness of the Deity to diffuse the various goods of the Earth to every part — to unite mankind in the blessed chains of brotherly love — society — and mutual dependence. [...] In Africa, the poor wretched natives — blessed with the most fertile and luxuriant soil — are rendered so much the more miserable for what Providence meant as a blessing: — the Christians' abominable traffic for slaves — and the cruelty of the petty Kings — encouraged by their Christian customers — who carry them strong liquors, to enflame their national madness — and powder — and bad fire-arms — to furnish them with the hellish means of killing and kidnapping — But enough — it is a subject that sours my blood. vol.I, pp.4–5

35. WILLIAM SHAKESPEARE (1564–1616)
The great English playwright and poet. Burns misquotes the passage 'Rude am I' in a letter to the bookseller James Sibbald in 1787 [L.71] and to Mrs Dunlop [L.264] the following year. Burns makes frequent use of Shakespeare in his works.

From *The Tragedy of Othello, The Moor of Venice*:

> RODERIGO: What a full fortune does the thick-lips owe
> If he can carry 't thus! Act 1, Scene 1, Lines 72–73

> IAGO: Zounds, sir, you're robbed. For shame, put on your gown!
> Your heart is burst. You have lost half your soul.
> Even now, now, very now, an old black ram
> Is tupping your white ewe. Arise, arise!

Awake the snorting citizens with the bell,
Or else the devil will make a grandsire of you. [...]
I am one, sir, that comes to tell you your daughter
and the Moor are now making the beast with two backs.
>   Act I, Scene I, ll.95–100, 130–131

OTHELLO: Rude am I in my speech,
And little bless'd with the soft phrase of peace:
For since these arms of mine had seven years' pith,
Till now some nine moons wasted, they have used
Their dearest action in the tented field, [...]
And therefore little shall I grace my cause
In speaking for myself. [...]
Wherein I spoke of most disastrous chances:
Of moving accidents by flood and field,
Of hairbreadth 'scapes i' th' imminent deadly breach,
Of being taken by the insolent foe
And sold to slavery, of my redemption thence,
>   Act I, Scene III, ll. 96–104, 155–160

From *The Tempest*:

FERDINAND: I am in my condition
A prince, Miranda — I do think, a king;
I would, not so! — and would no more endure
This wooden slavery than to suffer
The flesh-fly blow my mouth. Hear my soul speak.
>   Act III, Scene I, lines 70–74

36. WILLIAM SHENSTONE (1714–1763)

English poet, essayist and a notable early landscape gardener. He was an important inspiration for Burns in his early writings: '[m]y favorite authors are of the sentimental kind, such as Shenstone, particularly his elegies [...]' is one of several mentions in *CPB1*. Shenstone is quoted in the preface to *The Kilmarnock Edition,* and 'Man was made to Mourn,' [K.64] and 'The Twa Dogs' [K. 71] each contain one quoted phrase from Shenstone, as do several letters, for example, the first two lines of the quote above, are slightly misquoted to Mrs Dunlop, 16 August 1788, [L.264].

He is also noticed by Clarkson: '[t]he poet Shenstone, [...] seems to have written an Elegy on purpose to stigmatise the trade.' [Clarkson, vol.1, p.57.]

From 'Elegy xx,' *The Poetical Works of Will[iam] Shenstone* (2 vols) (London: Joseph Wenman, 1780), pp.102–104.

[He compares his humble fortune with the distress of others, and his subjection to Delia with the miserable servitude of an African slave.] [34]

> [...] Slave tho' I be, to Delia's eyes a slave,
> My Delia's eyes endear the bands I wear;
> The sigh she causes well becomes the brave,
> The pang she causes 'tis even bliss to bear.
>
> See the poor native quit the Libyan shores,
> Ah! not in Love's delightful fetters bound!
> No radiant smile his dying peace restores,
> Nor love, nor fame, nor friendship, heals his wound.
>
> Let vacant bards display their boasted woes;
> Shall I the mockery of grief display?
> No; let the Muse his piercing pangs disclose,
> Who bleeds and weeps his sum of life away! [...]

37. ADAM SMITH (1723–1790)

Scots philosopher and Professor. He held the office of Commissioner for the Customs, Scotland. Burns had a letter of introduction to Smith (who was keen to find patronage for the poet) from Mrs Dunlop, but Smith had left on his final journey to London [L.94: To Mrs Dunlop. 15 April 1787, at vol.1, p.105]. 'Remorse,' [K.26], 'Address to the Unco Guid,' [K.39], 'To a Mouse,' [K.69] and 'To a Louse', [K.83] all show clear influence of Smith's philosophy, Burns having read *Theory of Moral Sentiments*. Later, Graham of Fintry lent Smith's *Wealth of Nations* to Burns (who then bought his own copy):

---

34 *First Commonplace Book*, p.7, quoted in *Oxford Burns*, vol.1, p.43. 'But stain'd with blood, and crimson'd o'er with crimes'.

That extraordinary man, Smith, in his Wealth of Nations, find[s] my leisure employment enough. — I could not have given and mere *man* credit for half the intelligence Mr Smith discovers in his book. I would covet much to have his ideas respecting the present state of some quarters of the world that are or have been the scenes of considerable revolutions since his book was written. —
To Robert Graham, 13 May 1789, [L.341]

Clarkson's admiring comments on Smith are:

Dr Adam Smith, in his Theory of Moral Sentiments, had, so early as the held them up in an honourable, and their tyrants in a degrading light. There is not a Negro from the coast of Africa, who does not, in this respect, possess a degree of magnanimity, which the soul of his sordid master is too often scarce capable of conceiving Fortune, never exerted more cruelly her empire over mankind, than when she subjected those nations of heroes to the refuse of the gaols of Europe, to wretches who possess the virtue neither of the countries they came from, nor of those they go to, and whose levity, brutality, and baseness so justly expose them to the contempt of the vanquished. And now, in 1770, in his Wealth of Nations, he showed in a forcible manner (for he appealed to the interest of those concerned) the dearness of African labour, or the impolicy of employing slaves. [Clarkson, vol.1, pp.85–87.]

From *The Theory of Moral Sentiments, Third Edition* (2 vols) (London/Edinburgh: A Millar, A Kincaid and J Bell/T Cadell, 1790).[35]

There is not a negro from the coast of Africa who does not, in this respect, possess a degree of magnanimity which the soul of his sordid master is too scarce capable of conceiving. Fortune never exerted more cruelly her empire over mankind, than when she subjected those nations of heroes to the refuse of the jails of Europe, to wretches who possess the virtues neither of the countries which they come from, nor of those which they go to, and whose levity, brutality, and baseness, so justly expose them to the contempt of the vanquished.   vol.II, p.37

---

35 Burns's copy of this work is held at Smith's *alma mater*, University of Glasgow at Sp Coll RB 2905–2906.

From *An Inquiry into the Nature and Causes of the Wealth of Nations, Fourth Edition* (3 vols) (London: T Cadell and W Davies, 1786).[36]

The wear and tear of a slave, it has been said, is at the expense of his master; but that of a free servant is at his own expense. The wear and tear of the latter, however, is, in reality, as much at the expense of his master as that of the former. The wages paid to journeymen and servants of every kind must be such as may enable them, one with another, to continue the rage of journeymen and servants, according as the increasing, diminishing, or stationary demand of the society may happen to require. But though the wear and tear of a free servant be equally at the expense of his master, it generally costs him much less than that of a slave. The fund destined for replacing or repairing, if I may say so, the wear and tear of the slave, is commonly managed by a negligent master or careless overseer. That destined for performing the same office with regard to the free man, is managed by the free man himself. [...] It appears, accordingly, from the experience of all ages and nations, I believe, that the work done by freemen comes cheaper in the end than that performed by slaves. It is found to do so even at Boston, New York, and Philadelphia, where the wages of common labour are so very high.   vol.I, p.122

In the ancient state of Europe, the occupiers of land were all tenants at will. They were all or almost all slaves; but their slavery was of a milder kind than that known among the ancient Greeks and Romans, or even in our West Indian colonies. [...] This species of slavery still subsists in Russia, Poland, Hungary, Bohemia, Moravia, and other parts of Germany. It is only in the western and south-western provinces of Europe that it has gradually been abolished altogether.[...] But if great improvements are seldom to be expected from great proprietors, they are least of all to be expected when they employ slaves for their workmen. The experience of all ages and nations, I believe, demonstrates that the work done by slaves, though it appears to cost only their maintenance, is in the end the dearest of any. [...] The late resolution of the Quakers in Pennsylvania to set at liberty all their negro slaves, may satisfy

---

36 Also at Glasgow, Sp Coll RB 2942–2944.

us that their number cannot be very great. Had they made any considerable part of their property, such a resolution could never have been agreed to. In our sugar colonies, on the contrary, the whole work is done by slaves, and in our tobacco colonies a very great part of it. The profits of a sugar-plantation in any of our West Indian colonies are generally much greater than those of any other cultivation that is known either in Europe or America; and the profits of a tobacco plantation, though inferior to those of sugar, are superior to those of corn, as has already been observed. Both can afford the expense of slave-cultivation, but sugar can afford it still better than tobacco. The number of negroes accordingly is much greater, in proportion to that of whites, in our sugar than in our tobacco colonies. vol.II, pp.86–89

Land occupied by tenants is properly cultivated at the expence of the proprietor, as much as that occupied by slaves. There is, however, one very essential difference between them. Such tenants, being freemen, are capable of acquiring property, and having a certain proportion of the produce of the land, they have a plain interest that the whole produce should be as great as possible, in order that their own proportion may be so. A slave, on the contrary, who can acquire nothing but his maintenance, consults his own ease by making the land produce as little as possible over and above that maintenance. vol.II, p.90

In all European colonies the culture of the sugar-cane is carried on by negro slaves. The constitution of those who have been born in the temperate climate of Europe could not, it is supposed, support the labour of digging the ground under the burning sun of the West Indies; and the culture of the sugar-cane, as it is managed at present, is all hand labour, though, in the opinion of many, the drill plough might be introduced into it with great advantage. But, as the profit and success of the cultivation which is carried on by means of cattle, depend very much upon the good management of those cattle, so the profit and success of that which is carried on by slaves must depend equally upon the good management of those slaves; and in the good management of their slaves the French planters, I think it is generally allowed, are superior to the English.

The law, so far as it gives some weak protection to the slave against the violence of his master, is likely to be better executed in a colony where the government is in a great measure arbitrary than in one where it is altogether free. [...] The protection of the magistrate renders the slave less contemptible in the eyes of his master, who is thereby induced to consider him with more regard, and to treat him with more gentleness. Gentle usage renders the slave not only more faithful, but more intelligent, and therefore, upon a double account, more useful. He approaches more to the condition of a free servant, and may possess some degree of integrity and attachment to his master's interest, virtues which frequently belong to free servants, but which never can belong to a slave who is treated as slaves commonly are in countries where the master is perfectly free and secure.

vol.II, pp.394–396

Slaves, however, are very seldom inventive; and all the most important improvements, either in machinery, or in the arrangement and distribution of work which facilitate and abridge labour, have been the discoveries of freemen. [...] In the manufactures carried on by slaves, therefore, more labour must generally have been employed to execute the same quantity of work than in those carried on by freemen. The work of the former must, upon that account, generally have been dearer than that of the latter. vol.III, pp.37–38

38. WILLIAM SMELLIE (1740–1795)

As well as being a prominent Edinburgh printer (who set Burns's *First* and *Second Edinburgh Editions* for Creech in 1787 and 1793), he was the first editor of the *Encyclopaedia Britannica* and a founder of the Crochallan Fencibles.

When Burns introduced Maria Riddell to Smellie (who would go on to publish her travelogue, see above) he said that 'she is a great admirer of your book.' [L.494: To William Smellie, 22 January 1792, at vol. II, p.130]. Burns lent his first volume to Findlater [L.606: to William Stewart,? December ?1793] and asked Hill when the second volume of 'old sinful Smellie' would be out [L.614: to Peter Hill, February 1794, at vol.II, p.278] while referring to 'Elliot's pompous Encyclopaedia Britannica' to Mrs Dunlop, 13 November 1788, [L.285].

A Philosophy of Natural History (2 vols) (Edinburgh/London: Heirs of Charles Elliot/C Elliot and T Kay, T Cadell, and GGJ & J Robinson, 1790).

There are several distinct races of mankind inhabiting different portions of the earth, which differ one from another more or less in form, in features, in complexion, and in character. The cause of these varieties have never been satisfactorily pointed out. They have been attributed to climate, to situation, to manner of life, &c.; but none of these circumstances appear sufficient to produce them, and we therefore still remain in ignorance on the subject. These distinct races may be considered as five in number. 1. The Caucasian. 2. The Mongolian or Tartar. 3. The American. 4. The Negro or African. 5. The Malay. [...]

4. The African, or Negro, is remarkable for his narrow and depressed forehead; his flat and broad nose; his thick lip: his projecting jaws; black, crisped, and curled hair or wool, black skin and eyes; and some other differences in bodily shape, which it is not necessary to enumerate. These characteristics are confined to Africans, and their descendants in different parts of the world. The individuals belonging to this race have seldom been distinguished for their mental faculties or moral endowments. They have always remained in a barbarous state, and are with difficulty induced to adopt the customs and habits of civilized life. [...]

But notwithstanding all these differences in man, he maintains every where a decided rank, far above that of any other animal.

vol.I, pp.32-33

[William Smellie (contributor)], *Encyclopaedia Britannica* (Second Edition) (10 vols) (Edinburgh: for J Balfour [and others], 1777-1784).[37]

<u>LIBERTY, denotes a date of freedom, in contradistinction to slavery</u> or restraint; and may be considered as either natural or civil. [...] The idea and practice of this political or civil liberty flourishes in their highest vigour in these kingdoms, where it falls little short of

---

[37] Smellie effectively wrote the whole of the first edition of the encyclopaedia in 1771. The expanded Second Edition involved a number of writers. In the extracts above (from the Second Edition), text carried forward from the First Edition (ie, Smellie's writing) is underlined. First Edition text deleted is shown in square brackets and underlined.

perfection, [...] And this spirit of liberty is so deeply implanted in our constitution, and rooted even in our very soil, that a slave or a negro, the moment he lands in Britain, falls under the protection of the laws, and so far becomes a freeman; though the matter's right to his service may possibly still continue.

[1771] vol.II, p.973; [1778] vol.VI, p.4205

NEGROES, properly the inhabitants of Nigritia or Negroland in Africa, called also *Blacks* and *Moors*; but this name is now given to all the Blacks. [...] Negroes are brought from Guinea, and other coasts of Africa, and sent to the colonies in America, to cultivate tobacco, sugar, indigo, &c and in Mexico and Peru to dig in the mines; and this commerce, however indefensible on the foot of religion or humanity, is now carried on by all the nations that have settlements in the West Indies. Those Negroes make the best slaves who are brought from Angola, Senegal, Cape Verd[e], the river Gambia, the kingdoms of Joloffes, &c. There are various ways of procuring them: some, to avoid famine, sell themselves, their wives and children, to their princes or other great men; others are made prisoners of war; and great numbers are seized in excursions made for that very purpose by the petty princes into one another's territories, in which it is usual to sweep away all, without distinction of age or sex.

[1771] vol.III, pp.395–396; [1778] vol.VII, pp.5374–5375

SERVANT, [...] As to the several sorts of servants: it was observed under the article LIBERTY, that pure and proper slavery does not, nay cannot, subsist in Britain: such we mean, whereby an absolute and unlimited power is given to the master over the life and fortune of the slave. And indeed, it is repugnant to reason, and the principles of natural law, that such a state should subsist anywhere. The three origins of the right of slavery, assigned by Justinian, are all of them built upon false foundations [...] Upon these principles the law of England abhors, and will not endure the existence of slavery within this nation [...] And now it is laid down, that a slave or negro, the instant he lands in Britain, becomes a freeman; that is, the law will protect him in the enjoyment of his person, and his property. Yet, with regard to any right which the matter may have lawfully acquired to the perpetual service of John or Thomas, this will remain exactly in the same state as before: for this is no more than the same state of subjection for life, which every apprentice submits to for the space of seven years, or sometimes for a longer term. Hence, too, it follows, that the infamous and unchristian practice of with-holding baptism from negro-servants, lest they should thereby gain their liberty, is totally without foundation, as well as without excuse. The law of England as upon general and extensive principles it gives liberty, rightly understood, that is, protection, to a Jew, a Turk, or a Heathen, as well as to those who profess the true religion of Christ; and it will not dissolve a civil obligation between master and servant, on account of the alteration of faith in either of the parties: but the slave is entitled to the same protection in England before, as after baptism; and, whatever service the Heathen negro owed of right to his American master, by general, not by local law, is the same (whatever it be) is he bound to render when if brought to England and made a Christian. [...]

[1771] vol.III, p.5890; [1778] vol.x, pp.8105–8106

SLAVE, a person in the absolute power of a master, either by war or conquest. [...]

We find no mention of slaves before the deluge; but immediately after, viz in the curse of Canaan, Gen. IX, 25: whence it is easily inferred, that servitude commenced soon after that time; for in Abraham's days we find it generally established. Some will have it to have commenced under Nimrod, because it was he who first began to make war, and of consequence to make captives; and to bring such as he took, either in his battles or irruptions, into slavery.

Among the Romans, [...] slaves were esteemed the proper goods of their matters, and all they got belonged to them; but if the master was too cruel in his correction, he was obliged to sell his slave at a moderate price. [...] Slavery is absolutely abolished in Britain and France, as to personal servitude. [Slaves make a considerable article of the traffick in America. The British south-sea company have, by treaty, the sole privilege of furnishing the Spanish West Indies with slaves.]

[1771] vol.III, pp.605–606; [1778] vol.x, p.8180

39. TOBIAS SMOLLETT (1721–1771)

A Scottish surgeon, firstly with the Royal Navy, then in practice in London. A writer of picaresque novels, histories and journalism. He married, in Jamaica, an heiress who had an enslaved workforce on her plantation.[38] Burns read many of his novels (including the two above) saying 'I want Smollet[t]'s works for the sake of his incomparable humour', Letter: To Peter Hill 18 July 1788 [l.255]. Burns thought so much of *Humphrey Clinker* that he donated a copy of it, (along with *Julia de Roubigné*) and two other volumes) to the Dumfries Library in September 1793.

From *The Adventures of Roderick Random* (2 vols) (London: Harrison and Co, 1780).

The Slave-Trade features in several of the episodes of this novel, too long to quote here, but in précis:

- Roderick is apprenticed to a surgeon, Mr Crab who tells him 'before I was of your age, I was broiling on the coast of Guinea' (as surgeon on a slave ship). (p.26)
- He meets Thomson, who 'had offered his service, in the quality of mate, to the surgeon of a merchant's ship bound to Guinea on the slaving trade' but secured a Naval warrant instead. (p.93)
- While visiting Jamaica he met his old friend Thomson, now a plantation surgeon overseer. Roderick is invited to stay overnight while 'a couple of stout negroes' are ordered to escort his colleague back to his ship. Roderick spent ten days with Thomson on the plantation, as 'by far the most agreeable period of my life.' (p.127)
- Roderick takes part in a slaving voyage to Guinea, selling trade goods for 'slaves and gold dust' to see in the markets of Buenos Aires. Over a six-month period, the slavers gather 400 enslaved people (although Roderick's 'adventure' was invested in gold dust, not slaves which they sell quickly. (pp.246–247)
- 'Our ship being freed from the disagreeable lading of negroes, to whom indeed I had been a miserable slave, since our leaving the coast of Guinea, I began to enjoy myself.' (p.248)

---

38 *UCL Legacies Database*: 'Tobias Smollett' (accessed 1 September 2024).

From ***The Expedition of Humphry Clinker*** (3 vols) London/Salisbury: W Johnston/B Collins, 1771).

> Two negroes belonging to a Creole gentleman, who lodged in the same house, taking their station at a window in the stair-case, about ten feet from our dining-room door, began to practice upon the french-horn; and being in the very first rudiments of execution, produced such discordant sounds, as might have discomposed the organs of an ass. — [Bramble] sent his man to silence those blasts [...] The sable performers, far from taking the hint and withdrawing, treated the messenger with great insolence; bidding him carry his compliments to their master, colonel Rigworm, who would give him a proper answer, and a good dubbing into the bargain; in the mean time they continued their noise, and even endeavoured to make it more disagreeable; — laughing between whiles, at the thoughts of being able to torment their betters with impunity.
>
> [Squire Bramble thrashes the musicians with his cane and sends them back to Colonel Rigworm then] he retired to his apartment in expectation of hearing from the West Indian; but the colonel prudently declined any farther prosecution of the dispute.
>
> vol.I, pp.48–49

> The ball was opened by a Scotch lord, with a mulatto heiress from St Christopher's;
> vol.I, p.74

> I am not yet Scotchman enough to relish their singed sheep's-head and haggice, which were provided at our request, one day at Mr Mitchelson's, where we dined. The first put me in mind of the history of Congo, in which I had read of negroes heads sold publickly in the markets;
> vol.III, p.232

From ***The Present State of all Nations. Containing a Geographical, Natural, Commercial and Political History of all Countries in the Known World*** (8 vols) (London, 1769).

> The traffic for slaves, however, is barbarous, inhuman and a reproach to a free country. It is not to be doubted that the trade to Africa might be extended and improved to much greater advantage,

without this scandalous commerce in human flesh; and it might be easily proved, that the plantations in America could be sufficiently laboured by hired servants. vol.II, p.236

Whether, instead of making slaves of these people, it would not be more becoming those nations that assume to themselves the name and character of Christians, to give them a relish for the blessings of life, by extending traffic into the country in the largest degree it will admit of, and introducing among them a more civilized way of life, we submit to the reader's consideration [...] But, it is to be feared, this can never be brought about while the slave-trade continues to be the great object of the Europeans; for that will ever spirit up wars and hostilities among the negro princes and chiefs, for the sake of making captives of each other for sale, and thereby obstruct civilizing the natives, and extending trade into the interior parts of their country, which otherwise might be very practicable. vol.VIII, pp.61–62

40. THOMAS SOUTHERNE (1659–1746)

Irish poet and dramatist in London who contributed prologues and epilogues to Dryden's plays. He wrote the successful tragedy *Oroonoko*, a staging of Aphra Behn's novel, in 1695 and it remained popular throughout the 18th century. This early anti-slavery work places the enslaved Africans and the indigenous Indians as the more moral and decent beings, compared to the treacherous white Christian enslavers and officials. Burns slightly misquotes Southerne's 'The Fatal Marriage' to Agnes McLehose [L.176] and mentions him in 'Prologue, Spoken by Mr Woods,' [K.151]. Clarkson includes him in his Pantheon:

In the year 1696, Southern [*sic*] brought forward his celebrated tragedy of Oronooko, by means of which many became enlightened upon the subject, and interested in it. For this tragedy was not a representation of fictitious circumstances, but of such as had occurred in the colonies, and as had been communicated in a publication by Mrs Behn. [Clarkson, vol.I, p.48]

From 'Oroonoko: A Tragedy,' in *Plays, with an Account of the Life and Writings of the Author* (3 vols) (London: Evans & Becket, 1774), vol.II, pp.286–358.

[*Précis*] The plot concerns Oroonoko, an African king's grandson and heir. Both men love a white woman called Imoinda, and when the younger wins her affections, the elder has her sold and enslaved. By chance Oronooko himself is captured by English traders, and is trafficked to a Caribbean colony where he is reunited with Imoinda. His princely virtue makes him leader of the enslaved, who rise in revolt. The English deputy-governor, who lusts for Imoinda himself, tricks Oroonoko into surrender then barbarically punishes him. To control their fates, Oroonoko enters a suicide pact with Imoinda, killing her, then himself.[39]

41. SIR RICHARD STEELE (1672–1729)

Born in Dublin, educated at Charterhouse and Merton, Oxford. After a brief military career, he became involved in Whig politics and in writing, notably editing *The Spectator* with Addison; he is considered to have been highly influential in establishing polite norms for the 18th century. Burns says, in the 'Autobiographical Letter', 'my knowledge of modern manners, and of literature and criticism, I got from The Spectator.' (*Letters*, [L.125] at vol.I. p.138.) In 1789 he bought a set for Monklands (*Letters*, To Peter Hill, 2 April 1789, [L.325] at vol.I. p.389.) *The Spectator* (mainly Addison's work) is quoted regularly in both his Poems and Letters. On 'Inkle and Yarico,' see p.209 above.

From *The Spectator*, No.XI, 13 March 1711.

> I was the other Day amusing myself with Ligon's Account of Barbadoes; and, in Answer to your well-wrought Tale, I will give you (as it dwells upon my Memory) Out of that honest Traveller, in his fifty fifth page, the History of Inkle and Yarico.[...]

[*Précis*] Thomas Inkle, an English merchant lands with a ship's crew on the shores of America, where they are ambushed by Native Americans,

---

39 Southerne makes several important changes to Behn's original. Imoinda becomes a White European (not the daughter of an African general), the Deputy-Governor's passion for her is elevated in a sub-plot, and Oroonoko takes his own life rather than being executed by the English.

with the sailors killed and only Inkle is saved by the Native American princess, Yarico. They become lovers, however when rescued by an English ship at the end of the story, 'the prudent and frugal young Man [Inkle] sold Yarico to a Barbadian Merchant; notwithstanding that the poor Girl, to incline him to commiserate her Condition, told him that she was with Child by him. But he only made use of that Information, to rise in his Demands upon the Purchaser.'

42. REVD LAURENCE STERNE (1713–1768)

English Anglican parson and writer. Another early influence in Burns's reading: *Tristram Shandy* was 'a bosom favorite' and 'Sterne, especially his Sentimental Journey' is called out in Letter to John Murdoch [L.13]. Clarkson recognised Sterne's contribution:

> Sterne, in his account of the Negro girl in his *Life of Tristram Shandy*, took decidedly the part of the oppressed Africans. The pathetic, witty, and sentimental manner, in which he handled this subject, occasioned many to remember it, and procured a certain portion of feeling in their favour. [Clarkson, vol.1, pp.60–61]

The Works of Laurence Sterne, With a Life of the Author, Written by Himself (10 vols) (London: W Strahan, [and others], 1780).

From 'Sermon X. Job's Account of the Shortness and Troubles of Life, Considered', *The Sermons of Mr Yorick*:

> Consider how great a part of our species — in all ages down to this — have been trod under the feet of cruel and capricious tyrants, who would neither hear their cries, nor pity their distresses. — Consider slavery — what it is — how bitter a draught — and how many millions are made to drink it![40]   vol.VI, pp.202–203

From *The Life and Opinions of Tristram Shandy, Gentleman*:

> When *Tom*, an' please your honour, got to the shop, there was nobody in it, but a poor negro girl, with a bunch of white feathers

---

40 Quoted by Sancho (qv).

slightly tied to the end of a long cane, flapping away flies — not killing them. — 'Tis a pretty picture! said my uncle *Toby* — she had suffered persecution, *Trim*, and had learnt mercy —

She was good, an' please your honour, from nature, as well as from hardships; and there are circumstances in the story of that poor friendless slut, that would melt a heart of stone, said *Trim*; and some dismal winter's evening, when your honour is in the humour, they shall be told you with the rest of Tom's story, for it makes a part of it —

Then do not forget, *Trim*, said my uncle *Toby*.

A negro has a soul? an' please your honour, said the corporal (doubtingly).

I am not much versed, corporal, quoth my uncle *Toby*, in things of that kind; but I suppose, God would not leave him without one, any more than thee or me —

It would be putting one sadly over the head of another, quoth the corporal.

It would so; said my uncle *Toby*. Why then, an' please your honour, is a black wench to be used worse than a white one?

I can give no reason, said my uncle *Toby* —

— Only, cried the corporal, shaking his head, because she has no one to stand up for her—

— 'Tis that very thing, *Trim*, quoth my uncle *Toby*, — which recommends her to protection — and her brethren with her; 'tis the fortune of war which has put the whip into our hands *now* — where it may be hereafter, heaven knows! — but be it where it will, the brave, Trim! will not use it unkindly.

God forbid, said the corporal.

Amen, responded my uncle Toby, laying his hand upon his heart. vol.IV, pp.189–191

Letters of the Late Laurence Sterne to His Intimate Friends:[41]
From 'LETTER LXXVI. From Mr Sterne, To Ignatius Sancho. Coxwould, July 27, 1766,'

> THERE is a strange coincidence, Sancho, in the little events (as well as in the great ones) of this world: for I had been writing a tender tale of the sorrows of a friendless poor negro-girl, and my eyes had scarce done smarting with it, when your letter of recommendation, in behalf of so many of her brethren, and sisters, came to me — but why *her brethren*? or yours, Sancho! any more than mine? It is by the finest tints, and most insensible gradations, that nature descends from the fairest face about St James's, to the sootiest complexion in Africa: — at which tint of these is it, that the ties of blood are to cease? and how many shades must we descend lower still in the scale, ere mercy is to vanish with them? But 'tis no uncommon thing, my good Sancho, for one half of the world to use the other half of it like brutes, and then endeavour to make 'em so. — For my own part, I never look *westward* (when I am in a pensive mood at least) but I think of the burthens which our brothers and sisters are *there* carrying, and could I ease their shoulders from one ounce of them, I declare I would set out this hour upon a pilgrimage to Mecca for their sakes, [...]   vol.IX, pp.199–201

43. REVD JAMES STERLING (1701–1763)

Irish poet, playwright and clergyman. A graduate of Trinity College Dublin, while living in London he took Holy Orders and emigrated to the USA to minister a parish in Maryland.

Poems by the Revd James Sterling (London: GGJ and J Robinson, 1789). From 'Epistle to Mrs Meares':

> Lo one, the friend of arbitrary sway,
> Affirms, whole millions must a king obey;
> Must bow their necks beneath his iron rod,
> And pray to Cæsar, as they pray to God.

---

[41] See Ignatius Sancho above at p.291.

By tenets base, which but the base can bear,
He heaps up thousands for his worthless heir;
His country's curse attends him to the grave;
His prince, in secret, shall despise the slave.

pp.204–208

44. DUGALD STEWART (1753–1828)

Scots mathematician and philosopher. Followed his father into the mathematics chair at Edinburgh in 1755, exchanging into the Chair of Moral Philosophy in 1785. As an Ayrshireman in Edinburgh, he was an early patron of Burns's and was much struck with the poet's abilities. That respect was reciprocated, as Burns alluded to him as 'that plain, honest, worthy man, the Professor [...] I think his character, divided into ten parts, stands thus — four parts Socrates — four parts Nathaniel — and two parts Shakespeare's Brutus.' [L. 53A: to Dr John McKenzie, 25 October 1786.] Stewart and his father feature in 'The Vision' [K.62, at ll.121–126] and in 'The Brigs of Ayr,' [K.121, at ll.229–230] while the Professor appears in 'Extempore Verses on Dining with Lord Daer,' [K.127, at l.25] and in '[To William Creech],' [K.154, at l.39].

From *Elements of the Philosophy of the Human Mind* (3 vols) (London/Edinburgh: A Strahan and T Cadell/W Creech, 1792).

> so the good citizen of the world, whatever may be the political aspect of his own times will never despair of the fortunes of the human race; but will act upon the condition, that prejudice, slavery, and corruption, must gradually give way to truth, liberty, and virtue; and that, in the moral world, as well as in the material, the farther our observations extend, and the longer they are continued, the more we shall perceive of order and of benevolent design in the universe. vol.I, p.269

> the labour of slaves never can be as productive as that of freemen. vol.II, p.367

45. JAMES THOMSON (1700–1748)

Scottish poet and tragedian, whose innovative *Seasons* captured public opinion and remains highly influential. He was an early inspiration for Burns, as outlined to Murdoch, CPB1 and the 'Autobiographical Letter'. Kinsley's Index lists 56 references to Thomson. In the Letters, Thomson is frequently mentioned, and often quoted: 13 quotes from *The Seasons*, eight from *Alfred* and six others. On *Alfred*, Burns calls this a 'favorite' quotation: 'What proves the heroe truly Great/ Is never, never to despair.' Clarkson cites one of the above passages:

> Thomson also, in his Seasons, marks this traffic as destructive and cruel, introducing the well-known fact of sharks following the vessels employed in it. [Clarkson, vol.1, p.17.]

The Works of James Thomson. With His Last Corrections and Improvements. To Which is Prefixed, the Life of the Author (3 vols) (London: J Rivington [and others], 1788).

From **'The Seasons: Summer'**.

> What all that Afric's golden rivers roll,
> Her odorous woods, and shining ivory stores?
> Ill-fated race! the softening arts of Peace,
> Whate'er the humanizing Muses teach;
> The godlike wisdom of the temper'd breast;
> Progressive truth, the patient force of thought;
> Investigation calm, whose silent powers
> Command the world; the LIGHT that leads to HEAVEN;
> Kind equal rule, the government of laws,
> And all-protecting FREEDOM, which alone
> Sustains the name and dignity of Man:
> These are not theirs. [...]
>   Increasing still the terrors of these storms,
> His jaws horrific arm'd with threefold fate,
> Here dwells the direful shark. Lur'd by the scent
> Of steaming crowds, of rank disease, and death,
> Behold! he rushing cuts the briny flood,
> Swift as the gale can bear the ship along;

And, from the partners of that cruel trade,
Which spoils unhappy Guinea of her sons,
Demands his share of prey; demands themselves.
The stormy fates descend: one death involves
Tyrants and slaves; when strait, their mangled limbs
Crashing at once, he dyes the purple seas
With gore, and riots in the vengeful meal.   vol.I, p.67–72

From 'Liberty'.

At the throng'd levee bends the venal tribe:
With fair but faithless smiles, each varnish'd o'er,
Each smooth as those that mutually deceive,
And for their falsehood each despising each;
Till shook their patron by the wintry winds,
Wide flies the withered shower, and leaves him bare.
O far superior Afric's sable sons,
By merchant pilfer'd, to these willing Slaves!
And, rich, as unsqueez'd favourite, to them,
Is he who can his Virtue boast alone!
    v, ll.190–199 at vol.II, p.121

From 'Alfred'.

When Britain first, at Heaven's command
    Arose from out the azure main;
This was the charter of the land,
    And guardian angels sang this strain:
      'Rule, Britannia, rule the waves;
      'Britons never will be slaves.'   vol.III, p.130

46. VOLTAIRE (pseudonym of Francois-Marie Arouet) (1694–1778)

'Voltaire was the universal genius of the Enlightenment.'[42] His position on the question of Black chattel slavery is complex: although he wrote against slavery, he was a confirmed polygenesist and also a long-term investor in the Compagnie des Indes when it traded in enslaved people. (It is possible, that he was also a direct investor in other enslaving

---

[42] *Oxford Companion to English Literature*, p.1034.

ventures, but the evidence is unclear.) Burns ordered a set of Voltaire's works (in French) from Peter Hill in 1790 (see L.395).[43]

Voltaire, ***The Works of Voltaire: A Contemporary Version*** (40 vols) ed by John Morley and Tobias Smollett, trans by William F Fleming (Paris: ER DuMont, 1901).

From '**Candide: or the Optimist**', *The Works*, vol.1.

As they drew near to the town, they saw a negro stretched out on the ground with only one half of his habit, which was a kind of linen-frock; for the poor man had lost his left leg and his right hand.

'Good God!' said Candide in Dutch, 'what dost thou there, friend, in this deplorable condition?'

'I am waiting for my master, Mynheer Vanderdendur, the famous trader,' answered the negro.

'Was it Mynheer Vanderdendur that used you in this cruel manner?'

'Yes, sir,' said the negro; 'it is the custom here. They give a linen-garment twice a year, and that is all our covering. When we labour in the sugar works, and the mill happens to snatch hold of a finger, they instantly chop off our hand; and when we attempt to run away, they cut off a leg. Both of these cases have happened to me, and it is at this expense that you eat sugar in Europe; and yet when my mother sold me for ten patacoons on the coast of Guinea, she said to me: 'My dear child, bless our fetiches; adore them forever; they will make thee live happy; thou hast the honour to be a slave to our lords the whites, by which thou will make the fortune of us thy parents.' Alas! I know not whether I have made their fortunes; but they have not made mine: dogs, monkeys, and parrots are a thousand times less wretched than I. The Dutch fetiches who converted me tell me every Sunday, that the blacks and whites are all children of one father, whom they call Adam. As for me, I do not understand any thing of genealogies; but if what these preachers say is true, we are all second cousins; and you must allow that it

---

43 We do not know the specific edition acquired by Burns, so the specific passages he read are conjecture. Burns was proud of the French he had learned from John Murdoch, but his accent appears questionable as evidenced in the following rhyme: 'Faites mes BAISEMAINS respectueuse,/ To sentimental Sister Susie,' 'Epistle to Capt[ain] Will[ia]m Logan at Park' [K.129], ll.73–74.

is impossible to be worse treated by our relations than we are.'

'O Pangloss!' cried out Candide, 'such horrid doings never entered thy imagination. Here is an end to the matter; I find myself, after all, bound to renounce thy Optimism.'

'Optimism,' said Cacambo, 'what is that?'

'Alas!' replied Candid, 'it is the obstinacy of maintaining that everything is best when it is worst.' And so saying, he turned his eyes to the poor negro and shed a flood of tears; and in that weeping mood he entered the town of Surinam. pp.139–140

From 'The Philosophical Dictionary', *The Works*, vol.XI.

Different Races of Men

We have elsewhere seen how many different races of men this globe contains, and to what degrees the first negro; and the first white who met were astonished at one another. p.174

From 'The Philosophical Dictionary', *The Works*, vol.XIII.

Those who call themselves whites and Christians proceed to purchase negroes at a good market, in order to sell them dear in America, The Pennsylvanians alone have renounced this traffic, which they account flagitious. [...]

Interrogate the lowest labourer covered with rags, fed upon black bread, and sleeping on straw, in a hut half open to the elements; ask this man whether he will be a slave, better fed, clothes, and bedded; not only will he recoil with horror at the proposal, but regard you with horror for making the proposal. Ask a slave if he is willing to be free, and you will hear his answer. That alone ought to decide the question. [...]
[Footnote: It is certainly possible that a man might prefer enslavement over misery; but this alternative is not a necessary condition of human life. Besides, one is often a slave and miserable at the same time.]

Puffendorf says, that slavery has been established 'by the free consent of the opposing parties.' I will believe Puffendorf when he shows me the original contract. pp.212–222

From 'The Travels of Scarmentado', *The Works*, vol. III.

The ship in which I embarked was taken by the negro corsairs. The master of the vessel complained loudly, and asked why they thus violated the laws of nations. The captain of the negroes thus replied: 'You have a long nose and we have a short one. Your hair is straight and ours is curled: your skin is ash-coloured and ours is of the colour of ebon; and therefore we ought, by the sacred laws of nature, to be always at enmity. You buy us in the public markets on the coast of Guinea like beasts of burden, to make us labor in I don't know what kind of drudgery, equally hard and ridiculous. With the whip held over our heads, you make us dig in mines for a kind of yellow earth, which in itself is good for nothing, and is not so valuable as an Egyptian onion. In like manner, wherever we meet you, and are superior to you in strength, we make you slaves, and oblige you to cultivate our fields, or in case of refusal cut off your nose and ears.'

To such a learned discourse it was impossible to make any answer. I went to labour in the ground of an old negress, in order to save my nose and ears. After continuing in slavery for a whole year, I was at length happily ransomed. pp.62–63

From 'Short Studies on English and American Subjects', *The Works*, vol. XXXIX

In 1757 they reckoned thirty thousand persons in that part of San Domingo belonging to the French, besides one hundred thousand slaves, blacks and mulattoes, who worked in the several plantations of sugar, cocoa, and indigo; and who sacrificed their lives and healths to please those newly-acquired wants and appetites, which were unknown to our forefathers. We send for these negroes to the coast of Guinea, and to the Gold and Ivory coasts. I do not know what the present price may be; but about thirty years ago a good negro could be bought for fifty livres, which is about five times less than what we pay for a fat ox. We tell them with one breath that they are men like us, and that they are re-deemed by the blood of a God, who was crucified for them; and the next we set them to work like beasts of burden, and feed them worse. If they attempt to make their escape, we cut off one of their legs, and after having supplied its place with a wooden one, we make them turn a sugar-mill by hand; and yet shall we pretend, after all this, to talk of the law of nations?

The little islands of Martinique and Guadeloupe yield the same commodities as San Domingo. These islands, and the events that have happened in them, are mere points in the history of the universe; but, after all, these countries, though hardly perceptible in a map of the world, produced in France an annual circulation of nearly sixty millions in merchandise. This trade does not enrich a country; far from it, for it is the cause of many shipwrecks, and the loss of a number of lives. Therefore it certainly cannot be looked on as a real good; but as mankind have made new wants for themselves, it prevents the kingdom from purchasing at a dear rate from foreigners, a superfluity that has, by this means, become a necessity. pp.258–259

From 'Short Studies on English and American Subjects', *The Works*, vol. 39.

THE NEGRO race is a species of men as different from ours as the breed of spaniels is from that of greyhounds. The mucous membrane, or network, which nature has spread between the muscles and the skin, is white in us and black or copper-coloured in them. [...]

Their eyes are not formed like ours. The black wool on their heads and other parts has no resemblance to our hair; and it may be said that if their understanding is not of a different nature from ours, it is at least greatly inferior. They are not capable of any great application or association of ideas, and seem formed neither for the advantages nor abuses of our philosophy. They are a race peculiar to that part of Africa, the same as elephants and monkeys. [...] p.241

47. HELEN MARIA WILLIAMS (1759–1827)
A Poem on the Bill Lately Passed in England for Regulating the Slave Trade (London: T Cadell, 1788).

An important poetical work, commemorating the passage of Dolben's Act. See its analysis (and her biography) in 'Slavery and Burns's Writings,' at p.213 above.

48. REVD EDWARD YOUNG (1683–1765)

English cleric and writer, educated at Winchester and Oxford. He embarked on a career as a playwright and satirist, taking holy orders in 1730 as rector of Welwyn. He married in 1731, and after his wife's death in 1740 wrote *Night-Thoughts*, a bestseller in the 'graveyard genre' which was widely read across Europe. Kinsley cites Young some 15 times in his Index, while Burns frequently quotes Young in his letters, with 16 quotes from *Night-Thoughts*, and four from other poems by Young.

From *The Complaint: or, Night-Thoughts on Life, Death, and Immortality* (Glasgow: Robert Smith, Junior, 1764).[44]

> Immortal! ages past, yet nothing gone!
> Morn without eve! a race without a goal!
> Unshorten'd by progression infinite!
> Futurity for ever future! life
> Beginning still, where computation ends!
> 'Tis the description of a Deity!
> 'Tis the description of the meanest slave:
> The meanest slave dares then Lorenzo scorn?
> The meanest slave thy sov'reign glory shares
> Proud youth! fastidious of the lower world!
> Man's lawful pride includes humility;
> Stoops to the lowest; is too great to find
> Inferiors; all immortal! brothers all!
> Proprietors eternal of thy love.   Night 6, pp.142–143

Conclusion

For a man of his station and time, Burns was extremely well read. His knowledge of the novel, poetry, philosophy and political economy is impressive and the influence of what he read can be found in his writings. So, when it comes to the debate around slavery the list above shows that Burns was familiar with many of the key texts – primarily those on the side of Abolition.

---

44 Burns's copy is held at Dumfries & Galloway Museums Service, Ref: DUMFM:1936.2.15. Another edition, inscribed by Burns to 'Clarinda', is in the library of the Duke of Buccleuch at Dalkeith.

Prior to accepting the Douglas job, while he had laughed along with Roderick Random on the coast of Guinea and with Matthew Bramble silencing the Black musicians, he had equally read non-fiction works, notably Guthrie and Salmon, which laid forth the bleak truths of the Jamaican economy's operation through enslaved labour. His reading of Adam Smith, for example, could cast his mind in sympathy with the mouse, but not encourage its extension to the Black enslaved (at least, not with any sustained conviction). Burns had read virtually all of the list of authors Clarkson named his 'co-adjutors' for Abolition, and several of them Burns openly called his favourite writers. How could a man of Burns's sensibility read Cowper's *Task* with such relish, yet miss the Abolitionist underpinning of it (even if he did not read his later explicit anti-slavery works)? If one assumed that his literary interaction with Dr Moore and Miss Williams was driven by loyalty to Mrs Dunlop rather than an engagement with the subject, it is surprising (to say the least) that his often-expressed love of Henry Mackenzie's novels, particularly the later *Julia de Roubigné*, did not engender some greater, even merely sentimental, response in favour of the horrid lot of the Black chattel slave.

The paradox is clear: there is an abundance of 'input' from anti-Slavery writers who were important literary influences on Burns, but very, very little of that is translated into 'output' in his poems, songs or prose writings. He had said to John Murdoch (as discussed above) '[m]y favourite authors are of the sentim[enta]l kind, [...] these are the glorious models after which I endeavour to form my conduct,' yet in terms of his engagement with the questions of slavery and Abolition, this hardly seems to be true. As the *Financial Times* journalist Tony Barbour said on reviewing a volume about the books read by Stalin, 'yet, to be well-read is in itself no guarantee of an humane approach to politics and life.'[45]

So, while, in fiction, *Zeluco* and *Julia* probably stimulated a line of creative, sentimental thought which produced 'The Slave's Lament,' and watching Mrs Kemble in *Inkle and Yarico* engendered sympathetic response to the plight of the enslaved, his wider reading appears to have prompted no lasting adherence to the cause of Abolition. Is this another failure of imagination or it a sign of something more reprehensible?

---

45 *Financial Times*, 5/6 February 2022.

CHAPTER SIX

Slavery in Burns's Counterfactual Caribbean

WHEN GERRY CARRUTHERS called Burns's acceptance of the slave-driver's job 'a failure of sympathy, a failure in imagination' on the poet's part, he does not touch on how our imaginations, the imaginations of ranks of Burns's readers, singers, listeners, whistlers, even academics, shudder at the thought that the Burns, widely admired for his humanity, had volunteered to become instrumental in 'the Black Holocaust.'[1] This is a vexed question, important to get right, but hard to work out how. At the simplest level, we all share Jackie Kay's hope:

> I like to think that had he ever gone, he would have turned straight back once he'd realised what it involved, I can't reconcile my version of Burns in my head with a man that would have comfortably been an overseer.[2]

But it is the empathy we, the reader, have for Burns that takes that hope and assumes that Burns could 'do no wrong.' Nigel Leask is correct in his approach in saying

> There is always a danger, however, given the scanty evidence available concerning Burns and slavery, of resorting to postcolonial blame, or at least special pleading, based largely on speculation as to 'what would have happened' had Burns travelled to Jamaica in 1786.[3]

However, Kay's heartfelt hope is not certain, for perhaps on arrival Burns might have found that he had spent the remaining profits from the *Kilmarnock Edition* and could not afford an immediate passage home (as the return ticket would cost him a year's cash salary). Another

---
1 Carruthers, *Robert Burns and Slavery*, p.166.
2 Jackie Kay, *Inside the Mind of Robert Burns*, directed by Les Wilson and broadcast on 21 January 2021 by BBC Scotland.
3 Leask, *Poetics*, p.47.

potential scenario could be that Burns's streak of stubborn pride would see him stick to his last rather than return to Ayrshire as an even poorer failure, avoiding the Armours' added vengeful scorn on top of their moral and legal wrath. How can we work out what would have become of him in those inhospitable climes?

There are five principal ways to construct a valuable counterfactual history for Robert Burns and Jamaica: one is to recognise the serious risks to Burns's life in travelling to, and working in, the tropics; a second and third would be to take our concept of Burns, the man and poet, and fictionalise his experiences in Jamaica (one scenario where he revolts against the society, the other where he, in pain, acquiesces more or less), with the fourth finding a real historical figure who shared social characteristics with Burns, who did take up a 'slave-driver's' job, and follow that man's career as it developed. The fifth, and final, imagines the unthinkable, where Burns becomes an active member of plantocrat society.

For this study, the first scenario will use a short essay by Robert Crawford combined with research into Caribbean mortality rates in that period, the second will review the 2005 book *Illustrious Exile* by Andrew O Lindsay. The third scenario is based on Shara McCallum's 2021 poem sequence *No Ruined Stone*. The fourth scenario will look at the life of Burns's slightly younger contemporary, the Scottish slave-driver turned Abolitionist leader Zachary Macaulay, with the final scenario imagined from scratch.

COUNTERFACTUAL ONE: Death

We know from his series of 'Farewell' poems that Burns understood (to an extent) the dangers of his move across 'the surging billow's roar' to 'that fatal, deadly shore' where 'Death in ev'ry shape appears.'[4] The shortest counterfactual scenario is that he, like so many of the cadre of young unseasoned White men, would die within the first year of landing in Jamaica. In his detailed analysis of mortality rates on the island at this period, which was discussed above, Trevor Burnard summarised the very present risk to health:

---

4 *Poems*, 'The Gloomy Night is gath'ring Fast,' [K.122], ll.17–19.

In Jamaica [...] harsh work regimes, poor nutrition, and epidemic and endemic disease, were disastrous for African health. [...] The health of the hundreds of thousands of Europeans who moved to the British West Indies in pursuit of the legendary wealth that this region offered [...] was even worse than the African's demography.[5]

Given Burns's existing health problems (particularly considering his mental and physical breakdown in Irvine in 1781), he may not even have survived the sea voyage. It is not an impossible notion that he could have been one of the 3–5 per cent of unlucky passengers who died while crossing the Atlantic.[6] If Burns survived the journey certainly he would be at high risk at his disembarkation at Jamaica. Mortality was highly seasonal, rising in the third quarter each year and peaking between October and December as Yellow Fever spread. Burns's chances would not have been helped as both the *Nancy* and the *Bell* would have dropped him off at exactly the most dangerous time.[7]

Even once a man had been 'seasoned' and lived through the perilous first year or two, Burnard's calculations show an average White mortality rate (in late 18th century Jamaica) for 20- to 30-year-olds at 368 per 1,000, with the average life expectancy at 30 to be 15 years.[8] This compares to mortality rates in Scotland where that same man's life expectancy would have been 25.8 years.[9] Burns, of course, at age 30, had less than one-third of that (only eight years), so, on a crude assumption that he had one-third of the average Jamaican life expectancy of 15 years remaining, he would die in about five years' time, in mid-1791, aged 32.

Robert Crawford has penned a short counterfactual with this end, imagining Burns dying of fever on his 28th birthday shortly after disembarking at Savanna-la-Mar. His essay concludes (rather poignantly):

---

5 Burnard, 'Countrie Continues Sicklie,' p.54.
6 Ibid.
7 Ibid, p.57. Remember Burns's discussion with Mr & Mrs Whyte of Jamaica at the home of Dr Douglas. See *Letters*, To James Smith, 14 August 1786, [L.40].
8 Ibid, pp.60, 61.
9 As of 1755, from RA Houston, *The Population History of Britain and Ireland 1500–1750* (Cambridge: Cambridge University Press, 1995), p.41.

Although there were calls in Scotland for a second edition of [Burns's] poems, these soon petered out. It was not until the 20th century that a few scholars called attention to the remarkable promise of some of the verse which Burns had published in Kilmarnock. In 1987, to mark the bicentenary of the poet's death, Professor David Daiches, to whom Burns's modern reputation owes so much, arranged for a stone obelisk to be placed close to what is believed to be the site of this obscure poet's last resting place. It is inscribed simply, 'Robert Burns, poet and assistant overseer, born Alloway, Scotland, 25th January 1759; died Savanna la Mar, 25th January 1787.'[10]

Crawford appears to have forgotten that Burns was told by Dr Douglas not to travel via Savanna-la-Mar, but this story could as easily end in a Caribbean grave on the north coast of the island. The problem with this scenario is that death releases the Poet from making any moral choice over the enslavement underpinning plantation life; it therefore fails to come to terms with how we might imagine Burns interacting with the Jamaican economy and its voluntary White and involuntary Black participants, which is what this counterfactual exercise seeks to achieve.

COUNTERFACTUAL TWO: Illustrious Exile

In 2006, Andrew O Lindsay completed another kind of Burnsian Caribbean counterfactual in his novel *Illustrious Exile*.[11] Using the conceit of a trove of discovered manuscripts (as in Margaret Atwood's *A Handmaid's Tale* or *The Flashman Papers* series by George Macdonald Fraser), Lindsay provides us with a 'transcript' of a lost manuscript by the poet, only 'discovered' in the late 20th century.

---

10 Robert Crawford, 'What if ... Robert Burns had left Scotland?', *Prospect Magazine* (October 2014). Professor David Daiches (1912–2005): academic, critic and author of many books, including *Robert Burns* (New York: Rinehart & Co, 1950) and *Robert Burns and His World* (London: Thames & Hudson, 1971).
11 Andrew O Lindsay, *Illustrious Exile: A Novel* (Leeds: Peepal Tree Press, 2006).

Journal
of my Sojourn
In the
West Indies
Comprising an Account of the Island
of Jamaica; its Inhabitants; the Workings
of its Plantations, and other Observations
Relating to Life in the Tropics.
by
Robt Burns, Esq
Erstwhile Poet, and Farmer at Mossgiel, Ayrshire

Commenced on the first day of
July 1786

Oh, fond attempt to give a deathless lot
To names ignoble, born to be forgot!
Wm Cowper.[12]

Lindsay starts Burns from an even poorer place than his historical position: Wilson, the Kilmarnock printer, having turned down his poems, his passage has had to be raised in a 'whip round' by the poet's patrons and friends: Aiken, Hamilton, McMath and Richmond. The book opens as Burns and new wife Mary Campbell are being transported across the Atlantic by Captain Cathcart on the *Bell*.

There are three problems with this scenario. One is that he travels with Mary Campbell as his wife, which has been shown above to have been impossible. However, as she dies after 50 pages into the book, this error does not damage the overall quality of the imagined scenario. As the overwrought Robert banally confides in his journal: 'What a transient business is life! What is there here for me now?'[13]

The second, greater, problem is that we really get no feel for the raw stench of slavery. The Jamaican episode opens with Burns and Mary ensconced in a little cottage (with a Black house servant) on the plantation of Charles Douglas, who is drawn as a committed (if

---

12 Ibid, p.iv. The quotation is from Cowper's 'On Observing some Names of little Note recorded in the Biographia Britannica,' ll.1–2.
13 Ibid, p.52.

ill-tempered) ameliorist. This *gemütlich* life does not throw Burns or the reader into the mess that an independent observer (such as, say, Zachary Macaulay, see below) felt on arrival. The picture of his life as a 'bookie' is quite false, as previously described: 'Bookkeepers were not expected to marry, and were often forbidden to do so.'[14]

Similarly unlikely, as a young widower, he is shown as being caring and courteous to Adah, his Black, enslaved housekeeper, avoiding imposing himself sexually until she initiates their intimate relationship. This hardly tallies with the historical Robert and his congress with White servants in Scotland: Meg Cameron, Jenny Clow and Anna Park.

The overarching problem, however, is that there is little feel for the true, daily horror of the lives of the enslaved. Yes, the book is peppered with references to the egregious planter Thomas Thistlewood (1721-1786) and has several stock White 'villains' (most of whom get a verbal or physical drubbing from Burns), although Burns is employed by a man who does defend slavery, but who seeks to protect his investment in human stock by being a 'good master' to his enslaved workers. In contrast, Robert is presented as an almost saintly figure through the evident presumption that Burns is governed by an innate (and unswerving) belief in the indivisible unity of man ('that man to man,' etc) or, as Lindsay writes elsewhere, Burns was invariably directed by this internal maxim: 'Whatever mitigates the woes, or increases the happiness of others, this is my criterion of goodness; and whatever injures society at large, or an individual in it, this is my measure of iniquity.'[15] This removes all dramatic tension over how the scenario will develop.

Lindsay shows this by having Burns be generally friendly and considerate to almost everyone (except the caricatures of the upper-class or hard-core slave-holders). What goes awry is that Burns starts off with a pro-Abolition inclination that, in researching his writing and reading prior to 1787, just cannot be found to exist in the historical Burns. Take these two examples:

---

14 Anon, 'Burns Jamaica Connexons,' *Burns Chronicle* (1903), p.81.
15 Andrew O Lindsay, '"Negro-driver" or "Illustrious Exile": Revisiting Illustrious Exile: Journal of my Sojourn in the West Indies (2006),' *International Journal of Scottish Literature*, 4 (2008), quoting *Letters*: to Mrs Dunlop, 21/22 June 1789, [L.350], vol.I, p.419.

> I remember when I was a lad of fifteen or so, when I had first begun to commit the sin of rhyme, there was much talk about a Joseph Knight [...] [p.19]
>
> I have obtained a copy of Equiano's book [...] I read it with great interest, amazement and joy [...] [p.151]

To be true, any counterfactual experiment has to use only historical evidence prior to the inflexion point; Lindsay breaks that rule in the first quote above as there is no historical evidence that young Burns heard any 'talk' about Knight, while the second passage seems unlikely: a White bookie buying Equiano from Jamaican bookshop – what bookseller would stock it, and what would the community think of a man who read it?

Because of this, the counterfactual experiment is not effective, for it is obvious that Burns has been programmed to revolt against the plantocrat society, which effectively guarantees the outcome. The counterfactual fails on its own premise. In the early part of the book Burns asks himself (for the reader's benefit) 'why do I go to be a poor Negro-driver?' His response is that 'I take refuge in the hope that the trade may soon cease, and I shall not find the situation of the slaves as terrible as some would have us believe.' [p.19.] Which, *pace* Iain Whyte, is unbelievable in almost any man's mouth in 1786, and does not reflect the way he mainly approached (or failed to approach) the fate of those whom he called 'the buckskin kye' under 'the poor Negro-driver's' lash.

(Not to spoil the plot) but the novel and Burns's life end in Guyana after Burns is forced from Jamaica in a scandal: his downfall coming not through opposing slavery or promoting equality, but through the *hamartia* of his sex-drive. Lindsay tells us 'My Robert Burns is compelled to question himself deeply on questions of race, slavery and empire and then act', yet the book (at least in the Jamaican part) does not bring Burns close to touching the pitch. It is easy to agree with Michael Morris's view that

> Burns in this novel moves from naivety to outright abolitionism, expressing spotlessly politically correct attitudes. The famous philanderer here forsakes the practice of concubinage prevalent

amongst his companions [...] Burns' impeccable anti-racism and anti-sexism comments constrains much of the impact the novel might have made in probing comfortable constructions of Burns's memory.[16]

Lindsay, by assuming that Burns's fellow feeling would immediately embrace the lot of the enslaved under him, removes any moral discovery on the part of the poet. There is no peril in this tale, as Burns is predestined to the Good, his shortbread-tin icon unblemished without a spot of rust.

COUNTERFACTUAL THREE: No Ruined Stone

The third counterfactual is based on Shara McCallum's *No Ruined Stone,* a 2021 volume of 38 modern poems outlining, in her words,

> [a]n account of an alternate past, given voice primarily by a fictive Burns and his fictional granddaughter, a white-skinned black woman, a mulatta who is 'passing.'[17]

The series opens as Burns is on board the *Bell,* sailing 'towards the fettered horizon,' arriving in Kingston to face a life-threating 'seasoning,' which comes close to driving him mad.[18] He meets Charles Douglas at Ayr Mount, reflecting that 'the Ayr I knew, another life/ corrodes inside of this one' as he sets to work and 'watch the children of affliction/ [...]/ curved against the arc of the whip' having become 'the detested Negro driver I feared.'[19] [M]isery clings to the hem of his clothes' as he contemplates the 'Faustian bargain' he and his fellows have made.[20] Sex, and in time love, with the enslaved Nancy is not enough, nor is his growing status as 'Bard:' 'in Jamaica, if they bid me sing/ am I not all I wanted to be?'[21]

Nancy falls pregnant by Burns, and Charles Douglas ridicules his subordinate for wanting to buy her and their daughter Agnes's

---

16 Morris, *Archipelagos,* p.101.
17 Shara McCallum, *No Ruined Stone* (Leeds: Peepal Tree Press, 2021), p.74.
18 Ibid, 'Ae Fond Kiss,' p.19, l.14; 'Voyage,' p.20.
19 Ibid, 'Another Life,' p.20, ll.14–15; 'Landscape,' p.21, ll.3,4,22.
20 Ibid, 'Dear Gilbert,' p.23, l.11; 'Dear Gilbert,' p.26, l.8.
21 Ibid, 'The Hour of Dream,' p.25; 'Bard,' p.28, ll.16–17.

freedom by appealing to Dr Patrick who 'warms/ to the notion these Africans have souls.'[22] Robert writes to Gilbert to say that '[o]ur Mason brothers have taken up the cause of this poor poet;/ there is talk of a second printing.'[23] Which spurs him to write 'Tam o'Shanter' '[in] the wee hours returning from a Mason/ gathering where I'd been bousing,' and to rework the songs of his mother. However, he recognises that his fate is cast: 'whatever danger may be in plunging/ forward, there is ever more in turning back.'[24] His writing takes up more time in an escape from his diurnal life and his poems have become 'my sole, my only/ faithful companion' as 'they are all/ I have and all that stays bedlam/ from overtaking me.'[25] Burns's health, both mental and physical, and his relationship with 'Douglas, ever drunk, daily curses/ *this idiot poet* his brother sent,/ *this idiot loathe to use the whip*,' decline proportionally until Burns succumbs to fever, dying in July 1796.[26] A posthumous second edition in Edinburgh in 1797 secures his fame.

In 1806 the 'fou and foul-tempered' Charles Douglas, with his soul 'shrunken by the whip' rapes Agnes, who dies bearing his daughter, Isabella.[27] Her grandmother, Burns's Nancy, raises her at Mount Ayr, where as an Obeah-woman, 'Miss Nancy' has developed a parallel influence to Douglas's on the plantation.[28] Before Douglas's (unspecified) violent death in 1815, for (unexplained) expediency, he frees Nancy and Agnes, sending them of 'with just enough/ of a purse' and a fabricated back-story that Douglas had married a dark-complexioned Spanish woman, who (like Agnes) died in childbirth.[29] They arrive in Kingston, with Nancy assumed to be Isabella's enslaved servant and then the women sail for Scotland that year as young mistress and her old retainer.[30] Agnes goes to school in Glasgow, becoming an exotic but accepted playmate while maintaining her cover-story.[31] In

---

22 Ibid, 'Douglas's Reply,' pp.29–30, ll.25–26.
23 Ibid, 'Dear Gilbert,' p.31, ll.10–12.
24 Ibid, 'Tam o' Shanter,' p.32, ll.1–2, 24–25.
25 Ibid, 'Dear Gilbert,' p.31, ll.21–23; 'Crumbo-Jingle,' p.34, ll.18–20.
26 Ibid, 'Fate,' ll.18–20; *[Family Tree]*, p.38.
27 Ibid, 'Story, The First,' p.45, ll. 4, 18.
28 Ibid, 'Augur,' p.33, l.22.
29 Ibid, 'Springbank,' p.46, ll.23–24; 'Passing,' pp.49–50, ll.12–13; 46–47. Which echoes the parentage story of Dido Belle (see p.55 above).
30 Ibid, 'Springbank,' p.46, ll.14–16.
31 Ibid, 'Passing,' pp.49–50, ll.26–34.

1825 she visits Edinburgh where she thinks of her grandfather: '[e]verywhere I turn, you ghost this city', admiring his statue (positioned outside Canongate Kirk, as Fergusson's is in actuality today).[32] That year she marries a Scots doctor, meets Zachary Macaulay and mourns the death of her grandmother.[33]

As she reads her grandfather's poems and contemplates her grandmother's death she finds the paradox that sits at the heart of these poems, and indeed of this present book:

[...]   How
Do I claim you as kin and bear knowing —
Even you, who glimpsed divinity
In the smallest of creatures, lit
The animal soul, spoke
Nothing of her suffering?[34]

That Isabella, Burns's private, genetic posterity, cannot combine with Burns's public literary posterity to provide the whole Burns in the round is the direct result of his 1786 engagement with Black chattel slavery, meaning that Isabella ('his unclaimed kin') cannot 'perform the impossible/ to return the past whole.'[35]

While attempting to ignore the greater literary quality of *No Ruined Stone* compared to *Illustrious Exile*, this counterfactual has a greater balance between what Burns might have to do out of economic necessity, while not entirely sinking to the level of planters' society in the slave economy. Here Burns is no plaster saint in his struggles within Jamaican society: he is always aware of that struggle and its physical, mental and moral cost, and the failure to break free kills him. However, the moral voice of his poems will be his posterity.

COUNTERFACTUAL FOUR: Zachary Macaulay (1768–1838)

Zachary Macaulay is the chosen analogy of a young man of the time who went through almost exactly the same change of life as Burns was

---

32 Ibid, 'The Bard, Edinburgh, 1825,' p.44, ll.1, 17–19.
33 Ibid, 'Woman in an Edinburgh Drawing Room,' p.47, ll.19–24; 'Chance,' p.51.
34 Ibid, 'To a Mouse,' p.58, ll.28–33.
35 Ibid, 'The Bard, Edinburgh, 1825,' p.44, ll.29–31.

planning in 1786 and who recorded his life-changing experiences for history. Like Burns, his biographers have verged on the hagiographic, but Iain Whyte's recent book is a more balanced review and is informed by Whyte's work on the wider story of Scotland and Abolition.[36] It is no coincidence that McCallum uses the historical Macaulay in developing the story of the fictional Isabella [Burns] Douglas.[37] The key document used in creating this counterfactual is a letter Macaulay sent to his future wife Selina Mills (1767–1831) in 1797, two years prior to their marriage. This is what might be called Zachary's own 'Autobiographical Letter,' another chime with Burns's history.[38]

He was the son of Revd John Macaulay MA (1720–1789), himself a son of the manse of Harris, by his second wife and the eighth of their 12 children (plus a half-brother). Macaulay Senior was a noted moderate in the controversies of the Kirk, which did not always sit well with his congregation. Having served the parishes of South Uist, then Lismore and Appin in Argyll, Revd John was minister at Inverary when Zachary was born. He was translated to Cardross in Dunbartonshire when Zachary was six, and led that parish until his death when he was succeeded by his son Revd Alexander Macaulay (1769–1800), who was a member of the Synod of Glasgow and Ayr when it approved its anti-slavery petition in 1788.[39]

Raising a family of 13 on a minister's stipend was a challenge, but was achieved by home schooling and then by sending the boys off to a career as soon as possible. In Zachary's case, having evidenced some mathematical ability, he was sent to a merchant's counting house in Glasgow. The firm is not mentioned, but it would likely be in either the sugar or the tobacco trade, and so Macaulay's connection to slavery started as soon as he left home, before he sailed for his five-year sojourn in Jamaica in 1784.

---

36 Iain Whyte, *Zachary Macaulay 1768–1838: The Steadfast Scot in the British Anti-Slavery Movement* (Liverpool: Liverpool University Press, 2011).
37 Although, in a recent essay, McCallum calls Macaulay 'a study in contrast to Burns.' Shara McCallum, '"Man's Inhumanity to Man": Burns, Jamaica, and *No Ruined Stone*,' *Burns Chronicle*, 133.1 (2024), p.80. This study sees closer parallels.
38 Knutsford, *Macaulay*, pp.3–11.
39 'Cardross and Kilmahew: John McAulay,' in *Fasti Ecclesiæ Scoticanæ. (New Edition)*, vol.III: *Synod of Glasgow and Ayr*, ed by Hew Scott (Edinburgh: Oliver & Boyd, 1920), p.336. The children were high achievers: two MPs (and the wife of a third), a lieutenant general, and a minister in each of the Churches of Scotland and of England. *Minutes of the Synod of Glasgow and Ayr* (1761–1802), 8 April 1788, NRS: CH2/464/4, p.226.

Zachary Macaulay's 'Autobiographical Letter.'

This has been divided into two parts (slightly edited for extraneous religious statements). The first part, covering Macaulay's early life and education, is highly reminiscent of Burns's letter to Dr Moore; the Macaulay letter is set on the left-hand side with comparable passages from Burns on the right.

The second section tells, again in Macaulay's own private words to his fiancée, of his tribulations in Jamaica and the horrors he experienced as a slave-driver, before good fortune brought him home to Britain.

ZACHARY MACAULAY	ROBERT BURNS
Soon after I reached the age of fourteen, I became in a great measure my own master, by being removed from the control of my father and mother, and placed in a merchant's counting-house in Glasgow. This was a line of life which I entered upon with great regret, for I had at that time a strong passion for literature; but I acquiesced readily in my father's determination, from perceiving that his stipend could not well afford the expense of a literary education.	I was born a very poor man's son

ZACHARY MACAULAY

I felt the disappointment, however, very acutely, and thought I lost by this arrangement all my past labour to which I had been greatly stimulated by the hope of academical honours. I had already acquired a pretty general knowledge of the Latin language, and had also such a tincture of Grecian learning as enabled me to read Homer without much difficulty. I read French with tolerable ease, and had besides made considerable progress in mathematics. What made me prize all this the more was that it had been acquired mainly by my own exertions, for I had the misfortune never to have been under any regular system of tuition. It was only at times that I had any other instructor besides my father, and his avocations were so numerous as to render it altogether impossible for him to pay me the requisite attention. Being the oldest son at home, the care of instructing the others devolved on me; and though by this circumstance I was a good deal aided in my learning, yet I think I can trace to it the rise of several tempers which have caused me no small trouble in after life, particularly my impatience and self-confidence, my imposing tone, and dogmatical, magisterial style as well in writing as speaking.

ROBERT BURNS

Though it cost the schoolmaster some thrashings, I made an excellent English scholar; and by the time I was ten or eleven years of age, I was a critic in substantives, verbs, and particles.

I spent my nineteenth summer on a smuggling coast, a good distance from home, at a noted school, to learn mensuration, surveying, dialling, &c., in which I made a pretty good progress.

ZACHARY MACAULAY

But my reading was by no means confined to the dead languages. My father had a large collection of books, and my appetite for them was quite insatiable. There were few of the English classics that I had not read. The great poets were quite familiar to me. I was, besides, an eager hunter after that sort of anecdote wherewith ephemeral publications abound.

What stimulated me to this, in addition to the pleasure they afforded myself, was, I remember, an eager desire of shining in conversation. I much affected the company of men; and having a good memory, though very little judgment, and a great share of conceit and assumption, I was in the habit of obtruding my remarks whatever the subject of conversation was. I was much encouraged to this by the notice and ill-timed commendation which was occasionally bestowed upon me when I ought rather to have been repressed. […]

I had at this time some religious impressions on my mind, the effect of education. I liked to hear sermons, I thought it wrong not to say my prayers, and I felt a salutary check of conscience when I perceived myself flying directly in the face of a divine mandate. […]

ROBERT BURNS

[Burns lists many books, fiction, non-fiction and poetry, along with several periodicals.]

Polemical divinity about this time was putting the country half mad, and I, ambitious of shining in conversation parties on Sundays between sermons, at funerals, &c, used a few years afterwards, to puzzle Calvinism with so much heat and indiscretion, that I raised a hue and cry of heresy against me, which has not ceased to this hour.

I was a good deal noted for a retentive memory, a stubborn sturdy something in my disposition, and an enthusiastic ideot piety. — I say ideot piety, because I was then but a child.

ZACHARY MACAULAY

I remained in Glasgow upwards of two years; and during those two years I improved indeed in the knowledge of useful learning, but I made much more rapid progress in the knowledge of evil. The people with whom I chiefly associated were of two classes. Those whose society I most eagerly coveted were students in the University, and many of those who stood high in point of talents flattered me with their particular regard. I was admitted to all their convivial meetings, and made one of their society on all occasions.

As they were much more advanced in years than I was, I naturally looked up to them for information; and as many of them were really men of wit and taste, I gladly received the law from their mouths. But some of them, who, with I am sorry to say sentiments little altered, are at this day invested with the sacred names of ambassadors for God, made a cruel use of their influence. They employed it in eradicating from my mind every trace of religious belief I recoiled at first with a kind of horror from the propositions they advanced with respect to the Bible and the existence of a God. But my scruples soon yielded to the united efforts of arguments whose fallacy I was unable to detect, of wit whose brilliancy dazzled me, and of sharp and pointed raillery which served to silence me.

ROBERT BURNS

My vicinity to Ayr was of some advantage to me. My social disposition, when not checked by some modification of spited pride, was, like our catechism definition of infinitude, without bounds or limits. I formed several connexions with other younkers who possessed superior advantages; the youngling actors who were busy in the rehearsal of parts in which they were shortly to appear on the stage of life, where alas, I was destined to drudge behind the scenes.

Thus abandoned of aim or view in life, with a strong appetite for sociability, as well from native hilarity, as from a pride of observation and remark; a constitutional melancholy or hypochondriasm that made me fly solitude; add to these incentives to social life, my reputation for bookish knowledge, a certain wild logical talent, and a strength of thought, something like the rudiments of good sense, and it will not seem surprising that I was generally a welcome guest where I visited, or any great wonder that always where two or three met together, there was I among them.

ZACHARY MACAULAY	ROBERT BURNS
Nor were temptations wanting, for the other class of persons with whom I associated were as profligate in their practice as the students were in their principles. My immediate superiors in the counting-house were of this class, as well as many others in the mercantile line of life with whom I necessarily became acquainted. Taught by them, I began to think excess in wine, so far from being a sin, to be a ground for glorying; and it became one of the objects of my ambition to be able to see all my companions under the table. And this was the more surprising as I really disliked, nay even loathed, excessive drinking.	The contraband trade was at that time very successful, and it sometimes happened to me to fall in with those who carried it on. Scenes of swaggering riot and roaring dissipation were till this time new to me, but I was no enemy to social life. Here, though I learnt to fill my glass, and to mix without fear in a drunken squabble,
This same principle of ambition, however, operated in some respects as a check upon me, for I had access, through introductions from my father, to many respectable families in the town whose civilities I was anxious not to forfeit. I was therefore careful in preserving at least appearances, and also in avoiding that notoriety which would have exposed me to my father's displeasure. The domestic society which I thus enjoyed was not of a nature to counteract in any considerable degree the pernicious effects of the above-mentioned associations.	In my seventeenth year, to give my manners a brush, I went to a country dancing-school. — My father had an unaccountable antipathy against these meetings, and my going was what to this moment I repent, in opposition to his wishes. My father, as I said before, was subject to strong passions; from that instance of disobedience in me, he took a sort of dislike to me, which, I believe was one cause of the dissipation which marked my succeeding years. I say dissipation, comparatively with the strictness, and sobriety, and regularity of presbyterian country life; for though the will-o-wisp meteors of thoughtless whim were almost the sole lights of my path, yet early ingrained piety and virtue, kept me for several years afterwards within the line of innocence.

ZACHARY MACAULAY

Being tolerably accommodating, I fell into the predilections of the ladies of the family, which were entirely for new plays and marble-covered books.

When I was not draining the midnight bowl, I was employed in wasting the midnight oil by poring over such abominable, but fascinating works as are to be found under the head of novels in the catalogue of every circulating library. There are some few, however, of the immensity of books of this nature which I perused at that period of my life that still afford me pleasure when I recollect them. The characteristic conversations of Miss Burney's *Evelina* and *Cecilia*, the humour of Smollett, and the native manners-painting style of Fielding have still their charm for me.

To my other defects I now accordingly added something of the romantic and extravagant. I was continually laying the plan of wonderful adventures, conning speeches to repeat to ladies delivered from the hands of robbers and assassins, or adjusting the particulars of some affair of honour. With all this, however, I was exceedingly attentive to business; and my employers, when I left them, presented me with a considerable gratuity to mark their approbation of my conduct.

ROBERT BURNS

Vive l'amour et vive la bagatelle, were my sole principles of action. The addition of two more authors to my library gave me great pleasure; Sterne and McKenzie — *Tristram Shandy* and *The Man of Feeling* were my bosom favourites.

My reading only increased while in this town by two stray volumes of *Pamela*, and one of Ferdinand Count Fathom which gave me some idea of novels.

and the ideas I had formed of modern manners, of literature, and criticism I got from the *Spectator*.

My reading was enlarged with the very important addition of Thompson's and Shenstone's *Works*; I had seen human nature in a new phasis; and I engaged several of my school-fellows to keep up a literary correspondence with me. This improved me in composition. I had met with a collection of letters by the wits of Queen Anne's reign, and I pored over them most devoutly. I kept copies of any of my own letters that pleased me, and a comparison between them and the composition of most of my correspondents, flattered my vanity. I carried this whim so far, that though I had not three farthings worth of business in the world, yet almost every post brought me as many letters as if I had been a broad plodding son of day-book and ledger.

ZACHARY MACAULAY

Towards the end of the year 1784 a circumstance happened which gave a temporary suspension to my career, and led to a few sober reflections. I then saw that the only way that remained to extricate myself from the labyrinth in which I was involved was going abroad. I made known my wish to my father, and it was determined that I should try my fortunes in the East Indies.

Just as this determination had been taken, Sir Archibald Campbell, who was related to us, persuaded my father to alter it, and to suffer me to go out under his patronage to Jamaica, where he had been Governor, and where his influence was of course supposed able to effect any views of aggrandisement, however large, which I might form. What reason Sir Archibald could have had for persuading us to this step I have never been able to fathom, for the letters of recommendation he gave me were so far from yielding me any essential service, that not one of them even procured me an ordinary invitation.[40]

ROBERT BURNS

This was a most melancholy affair, which I cannot yet bear to reflect on, and had very nearly given me one or two of the principal qualifications for a place among those who have lost the chart, and mistaken the reckoning of Rationality. I gave up my part of the farm to my brother; in truth it was only nominally mine; and made what little preparation was in my power for Jamaica. But, before leaving my native country for ever, I resolved to publish my poems. I weighed my productions as impartially as was in my power; I thought they had merit; and it was a delicious idea that I should be called a clever fellow, even though it should never reach my ears — a poor negro-driver — or perhaps a victim to that inhospitable clime, and gone to the world of spirits [...] I was pretty confident my poems would meet with some applause; but at the worst, the roar of the Atlantic would deafen the voice of censure, and the novelty of West-Indian scenes make me forget neglect. I threw off six hundred copies, [...] As soon as I was master of nine guineas, the price of wafting me to the torrid zone, I took a steerage passage in the first ship that was to sail from the Clyde.

---

40 Major-General Sir Archibald Cambell of Inverneil (1739–1791): military engineer, colonial administrator and MP for Stirling Burghs. A protégé of his kinsman, Argyll, and of Dundas, he served in several colonial positions including Jamaica as Lieutenant Governor (1779–1781) and Governor (to 1784). He was responsible for upgrading the island's defences against the French. He married Alan Ramsay Jr's daughter, a cousin of Dido Belle. After a distinguished career he was buried in Westminster Abbey (close to where Zachary would be interred). One assumes that Zachary arrived after his kinsman had departed, with local patronage in the hands of his replacement, although granting a favour to 'yesterday's man' who still had Dundas's ear would not seem a bad idea. www.historyofparliamentonline.org/volume/1754-1790/member/campbell-archibald-1739-91

These look like two very similar men in terms of upbringing, education and intellect. Both face a crisis as a young man – we know Burns's well; Macaulay gives no detail of the 'labyrinth' he had fallen into but that it necessitated emigration, like Burns. Whyte discounts debt and drunken brawling, and posits 'a sexual relationship that led to a pregnancy,' which seems a worthy supposition (although it could be an entanglement of a 'breach of promise' with a girl).[41] Whatever the reason, we find them both packing their bags, Zachary in 1784 and Burns in 1786, for a new life in Jamaica.

The parallels up to now are strong enough to accept a counterfactual experiment that Burns could well respond to the challenges of the Caribbean the same way as the similar-minded Macaulay. Here is the second part of his 'Autobiographical Letter,' with emphasis added:

> During the voyage to Jamaica I had a good deal of time for reflection, and I endeavoured to fortify myself, by previous resolutions, against the evils to which I felt myself prone. **Company I had found my greatest snare, and I resolved to guard against it; and though every reformation proceeding on such grounds as mine then did must be partial and inadequate, yet one good effect arising from it was a resolution of abstaining from all excess in drinking, which I afterwards adhered to.**
>
> At this time I had not yet reached the age of seventeen, and found myself, on landing at Jamaica, without money, or without a single friend to whom I could turn for assistance. The letters of recommendation to persons in high position, with which I had been provided by Sir Archibald Campbell, were entirely neglected. The visions which had been presented to me of rapidly increasing wealth and honours now vanished entirely, but the disappointment did not seriously affect my spirits. I felt certainly indignation and resentment at the coldness and indifference shown me by men, from whom I thought I had a right to expect different treatment. But I recollect feeling a degree of self-complacency in finding myself able to reconcile my mind to very considerable hardships, rather than submit to repeat the humiliating applications which I had already made to those persons.

(accessed 1 September 2024).
41 Whyte, *Macaulay*, pp.10–11.

My trials, however, were not of long duration. One or two private gentlemen to whom a friend of mine had written to introduce me, soon found me out, and showed me great kindness. Through their exertions I obtained the situation of under-manager or book-keeper on a sugar plantation.

Here I entered upon a new mode of life which waged war with all my tastes and feelings. My position was laborious, irksome, and degrading, to a degree of which I could have formed no previous conception, and which none can imagine fully who have not, like me, experienced the vexatious, capricious, tyrannical, and pitiless conduct of a Jamaica overseer. To this, however, I made it a point of honour to reconcile my mind. Indeed I saw there was no medium for me, under the circumstances, between doing so and starving.

While my health remained good, **I therefore submitted with cheerfulness to all the severe toil and painful watchings which were required of me. What chiefly affected me at first was, that by my situation I was exposed not only to the sight, but also to the practice of severities over others, the very recollection of which makes my blood run cold. My mind was at first feelingly alive to the miseries of the poor slaves, and I not only revolted from the thought of myself inflicting punishment upon them, but the very sight of punishment sickened me.**

The die, however, was now cast; there was no retreating. I should gladly indeed have returned to Europe, but I had not the means. I had no friend at home to whom I could apply except my father, **[For Burns, his brother Gilbert] and I would almost sooner have died than have added any more to the pressure of that anxiety which a numerous family necessarily caused him.** In the West Indies, I was bound, if I would not forfeit the regard of all who were disposed to serve me, even to give no vent to those feelings which would have seemed to reproach them with cruelty. As the only alternative, therefore, I resolved to get rid of my squeamishness as soon as I could, as a thing which was very inconvenient and in this I had a success beyond my expectations.

Virgil's expression, 'Easy is the descent to Hell,' is a bold, but perfectly just representation of the rapidity with which we move downwards in the scale of moral rectitude when once we have made a voluntary declension from the path of duty. I soon satisfied myself that the duty which I owed to my employers, for I used still to moralise, required the exact fulfilment of their orders; and that the duty which I owed to myself, my father, and my friends, required that I should throw no obstacles, which the voice of all in the world whom I had hitherto known was so far from sanctioning, that it condemned them as foolish, childish, and ridiculous, in the way of my fortune.

At this time, that is in the year 1785, I find myself writing thus to a friend at home: — 'But far other is now my lot, doomed by my own folly to toil for a scanty subsistence in an inhospitable clime. The air of this island must have some peculiar quality in it, for no sooner does a person set foot on it than his former ways of thinking are entirely changed. The contagion of an universal example must indeed have its effect. You would hardly know your friend, with whom you have spent so many hours in more peaceful and more pleasant scenes, were you to view me in a field of canes, amidst perhaps a hundred of the sable race, cursing and bawling, while the noise of the whip resounding on their shoulders, and the cries of the poor wretches, would make you imagine that some unlucky accident had carried you to the doleful shades.'

This picture, shocking as it is, owes nothing to fancy; but my mind was now steeled, and though some months before this period, **in writing to the same friend I had had a heart to draw in very lively colours, and with pathetic touches which I really felt, the miseries of the negroes, yet now I was callous and indifferent, and could allude to them with a levity which sufficiently marked my depravity. I had indeed raised for myself an imaginary standard of justice in my dealings with them, to which I thought it right to conform.**

But the hour of retribution seemed to be at hand. Dangerous, and repeated, and long-continued attacks of illness brought me frequently to the very borders of the grave. My sufferings were extreme; and they were aggravated by the most cruel neglect and the most hard-hearted unkindness. There was a kind of high-mindedness about me which kept me from complaining even in my lowest extremity of wretchedness, nor did the hope of better days ever forsake me. Nay, when stretched upon a straw mattress, with 'tape-tied curtains, never meant to draw,' burning with fever, pining under the want of every necessary comfort, shut out from the sight or converse of any one whom I could call a friend, unable to procure even a cup of cold water for which I did not myself crawl to the neighbouring rivulet, **I maintained an unbroken spirit. [...]**

When health returned my sufferings were soon forgotten; and better prospects opening upon me, and friends rising up daily who showed a willingness to serve me as soon as I was master of my business, I began to like my situation. 'I even began to be wretch enough to think myself happy.'

My outward conduct indeed, for a West Indian planter, was sober and decorous, for I affected superiority to the grossly vulgar manners and practices which disgrace almost every rank of men in the West Indies, but my habits and dispositions were now fundamentally the same. In these I was quite assimilated to my neighbours, and this is a part of my life of which I scarce like either to speak or think. It was a period of most degrading servitude to the worst of masters.

While I was in this state of mind I received a letter from an uncle in London, containing an advantageous offer if I chose to return to England. After much hesitation and debate I resolved to accept the offer. I took my passage for London, and arrived there just as I had completed my twenty-first year. [*1789*]

During my stay abroad, degraded as I became in some respects, **I by no means lost my taste for reading. I had very few books, it is true, and very little time to peruse them, but I eagerly employed the little time I had in keeping alive my acquaintance with the French and Latin languages.** Horace was my constant companion, and served to amuse many a tedious hour. I liked his philosophy, and I thought that I derived from it, as well as from Voltaire's poem on the equality of human conditions, motives to support me from sinking under my trials. I pleased myself with thinking so; although I apprehend that I owed more to a constitutional firmness of nerve and to vanity, than to the plausible reasoning of Voltaire, or the justly conceived in many instances, and elegantly expressed sentiments of the Roman poet.

I read very little during this period. **Thomson, I think, was the only English poet I had with me, but his beauties were quite inexhaustible. [...]**

My vanity, which the low situation to which I was reduced at times, it may have been supposed, would have tended to mortify, was on the contrary increased. **The state of information among my brother book-keepers and overseers, and even among planters and merchants in Jamaica, is, generally speaking, very low. I was among them a kind of prodigy, and I was referred to on disputed points as an oracle. [...]**

I found when I returned to England, that I had contracted a boorishness of manner, arising doubtless from the nature of my employment and associations, which proved a dreadful mortification to my vanity when I came to perceive it, as I soon did. While absent from Europe I had scarce seen a white lady; and among men in the West Indies, whatever be their rank, there is a total emancipation not only from the trammels of ceremony, but, notwithstanding a great deal of hospitality and even kindness, from the more necessary forms of good-breeding. I am content to bear the occasional uneasiness still flowing from this source as a memento of the greater punishment I at that time of my return to England incurred, and as some check to my too prevalent passion for appearing well in the eyes of others.

Like Burns, Macaulay 'obtained the situation of under-manager or book-keeper on a sugar plantation.' No doubt thinking of the kind of tasks he had performed on the books back in Glasgow, he turned up to his new post to be met with a radically different prospect of the duties required of him. However unpleasant this was, Macaulay was trapped with no money for the passage home and no other way of sustaining himself, so he took that unhappy compromise that many have done: adopting the option of participating in the tyranny but oiling his conscience by trying to be a 'fair' master and 'shelter' the enslaved people from the worst excesses of his brother enforcers. But, time, heat, drink and moral compromise wore Macaulay down and soon he was adopting the cast of mind of the society around him, even beginning to enjoy a fairly dissipated life on the island. Simply put, the industry based on the slave trade was inhuman, so it was no surprise that the White 'society' built on it was brutalised too, and facing the dichotomy of trying to get rich quicker than quickly dying of fever, the 'cosie' 'Jamaica bodies' as Burns pictured them in his verses, were a fiction. As Shara McCallum recently wrote: 'of all the colonies, Jamaica was one of the plainest expressions of "man's inhumanity to man."'[42]

On top of the uniform inhumanity and the appalling social mores, there was, of course, a genuine risk of death in service. After a serious bout of illness had renewed Macaulay's Christian introspection, by chance his uncle in London wrote offering a free passage home and place of work. After deliberation, Macaulay took the chance to escape from 'a period of most degrading servitude to the worst of masters', and returned to England in 1789, but did not leave the 'thick cloud of evils' behind, or forgotten. His Abolitionist brother-in-law, Thomas Babington (1758–1837) introduced him to Wilberforce and after a period in Sierra Leone, Macaulay became one of the leaders of the Abolition movement, working tirelessly to promote the causes of Abolition and Emancipation until his death. He was commemorated in 1842 in Westminster Abbey with a life-sized bust bearing Wedgwood's medallion which sits only a few yards away from Burns's bust in Poet's Corner.[43]

When Burns was considering fleeing Scotland for Jamaica two years later than Zachary's departure, he had published his poems with the aim of realising enough cash to pay his passage out, but the unexpected financial success allowed him to stay in Scotland and so he never met the hard truths which were faced by Macaulay. Macaulay's experience is a fair representation of what Burns would have known ahead of leaving and what he would have found life like 'as a poor Negro driver' had he actually landed on the Caribbean shore. There was not yet a widespread debate about, let alone a broad condemnation of, slavery, and the harsh truths were likely to have been understated or hidden from the folks at home, who were happy to let sleeping dogs lie in return for a consistent supply of sugar. A young man, like Zachary, was unlikely to have a realistic appreciation of the inherent

---

42 McCallum, *Man's Inhumanity*, p.80.
43 www.westminster-abbey.org/abbey-commemorations/commemorations/zachary-macaulay (accessed 1 September 2024). Lisa Williams blogs that Zachary 'returned to Britain in a state of torment after witnessing the brutality of the slave system in his job on a Jamaican plantation, [...] However, this didn't prevent Macaulay from going on to make a fortune from selling seized slaving vessels after 1807,' which is a *non sequitur* as the policy of prize money was a deliberate (and broadly successful) government policy to incentivise the Royal Navy and other actors in the suppression of the transatlantic slave trade by rewarding the captors with defined shares in the forfeited vessels' value. 'Remaking our Histories: Scotland, Slavery and Empire' at www.nationalgalleries.org/art-and-artists/features/remaking-our-histories-scotland-slavery-and-empire (accessed 1 September 2024).

and omnipresent cruelty underlying every part of the slave economy.

In this counterfactual experiment, Macaulay's journey (physical, mental and moral) seems a good tool to use to interpret Burns's mindset in 1786 and to draw out what might have happened to the poet after sailing. Neither man had a clear vision or comprehension of the Kurtzian horrors they would starkly face across the sea. We cannot know for certain that Burns would follow Macaulay's path, but considering Burns's temperament it is not an unfair counterfactual. Just as he and Macaulay travelled similar roads before Jamaica, (and others could be included, John Newton, Edward Rushton or James Currie), this experiment gives hope that Burns, if he lived, would come back fighting against this particularly unpleasant example of 'man's inhumanity to man.'

COUNTERFACTUAL FIVE: The Unthinkable (That Needs to be Thought of)

The final counterfactual to be considered is that Robert actively accepts his fate and the facts of Jamaican plantation life. Here, by analogy with his historical career in the Excise, he becomes a diligent slave-driver and hardens as Macaulay did initially. As Moreton, the Jamaican commentator, put it '[l]ike wax softened by heat [men] melt into Jamaican manners and customs.'[44] As with the Excise, despite his reservations about the job, he actively seeks promotion on the plantation, first to become a 'bookie' then to the overseer's role (which would require him to show initiative, energy and 'skill' in handling the enslaved workforce): all with a view of bettering his lot through the significantly higher salary (and the potential to 'invest' in one or two enslaved persons).[45] With more comfortable bed and board, and an assumption that Robert could save half of his 250-Jamaican-Pounds salary, he could plan to amass at least twice the 'Jamaican siller' that Sandy Bell brought home. At the end of five years' overseeing, he would have saved 625 Jamaican Pounds (equivalent to £875 Sterling) plus any profits if there were to be a second edition of his poems.

Although hard to quantify, there may have been a route for Burns to escape from the direct role of management of the enslaved. Long

---
44 Moreton, p.73.
45 See p.101 above.

records that, due to the difficulties in terrain (and early incompetence), there were regular disputes over boundaries between the various estates on the island and, in consequence, '[Scotland] has likewise furnished some of the most able surveyors known here. [...] This business was formerly very profitable, and remains so in the hands of able draughtsmen, the charges of making plans being very high.'[46] Burns was trained in 'dialling and mensuration' and so, if he could raise the indemnity bond of 300 Jamaican Pounds needed to be certified by the governor, he had the skills needed to pass from the direct arm of the plantocracy to an indirect role as a surveyor, without loss of earning power.[47]

Does that much money (even if partly earned indirectly) allow him to buy back his conscience? Perhaps this gives him a final chance for a Macaulay trigger. Or perhaps the iron has entered his soul, and rusted it, and escaping the tropical miasmata, he returns to Ayrshire with the plantocrat's swagger, where some new rustic poet might satirise him in his own 'Mauchline Wedding.' It is impossible to say that that was impossible.

Evaluation of These Possible Counterfactuals

Which of these imagined histories is the most likely? To assess the overall probabilities of outcome, the process flow in Table 9 has been created to evaluate the above five counterfactuals. The date of Burns's death remains fixed as 21 July 1796 in all cases. DEATH: Crawford's counterfactual death at Savanna-la-Mar ('C1') could not have occurred, so it has been adapted to imagine his death on arrival at Port Antonio ('C2'), all else being equal. Further sub-scenarios have been added to assume that: he dies on board ship ('D0'), or within the 'seasoning period' of the year of arrival ('D1') or after four years, reflecting Burnard's estimates of life expectancy ('D3').

- EXILE (REJECTION): Lindsay's novelisation is followed, but without the marriage to Mary Campbell who dies in 1786.

---

46 *Long*, vol.II, p.292.
47 In 2012, the Royal Institution of Chartered Surveyors awarded Burns a posthumous, honorary membership 'to acknowledge Burns' professional training as a land surveyor.' *Herald* [Glasgow], 20 November 2012.

Burns breaks down, leaves the plantation and dies in poverty ('L1') with a slight variant where he flees the island early, attempting some form of escape but again dies poor on the far side of the Atlantic ('L2').
- EXILE (ACQUIESENCE): the first half of McCallum's poem cycle forms the basis for this scenario. When Burns dies in Jamaica in 1796, his Masonic friends facilitate a 1797 *First Edinburgh Edition* which propels the late poet to Bard-dom ('M1').
- CONVERSION AND RETURN: which follows the pattern of Zachary Macaulay's life in Jamaica. He passes through his 'moment of understanding' and, with the profits of his Second Edition being remitted, he returns home as a committed abolitionist ('Z1') or scrapes together enough to return to Scotland anyway ('Z2'). A third scenario is that, after making his fortune by 1794, he has a change of heart and adopts abolition ('Z3').
- ACCEPTANCE: he sees the job as a means to an end, accepting the injustice and immorality and returns home as a typical plantocrat with a small pot of 'Jamaica siller.'

SLAVERY IN BURNS'S COUNTERFACTUAL CARIBBEAN

Table 9: Burns in a Counterfactual Caribbean — Process Chart

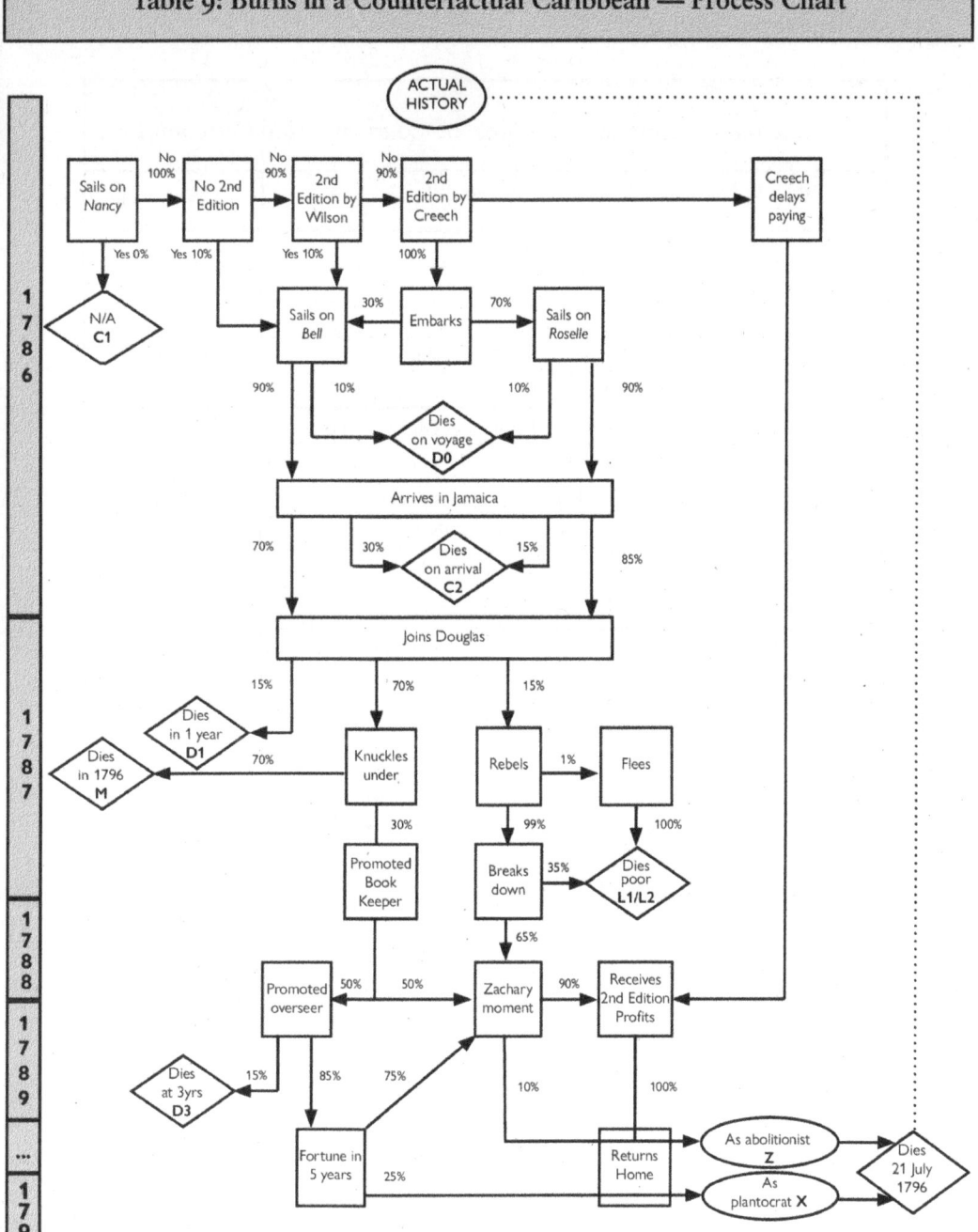

Assigning probabilities to each step in the process results in these statistical outcomes:

Table 9a: Percentage Evaluation of Counterfactual Outcomes

OUTCOME	SCENARIO	SCENARIO DESCRIPTION	LIKELIHOOD	
DEATH	D0	Dies on the voyage	10%	50%
	D1	Dies within one year	11%	
	D3	Dies after four years	9%	
	C1	Crawford: dies at Savanna-la-Mar	0%	
	C2	Adjusted Crawford: dies at Port Antonio	20%	
CONVERSION	Z1	Zachary: before 2nd Edition profits	7%	40%
	Z2	Zachary: with 2nd Edition profits	20%	
	Z3	Zachary: after 5 years as overseer	13%	
EXILE	L1	Lindsay: *Illustrious Exile*	2%	7%
	L2	Adjusted Lindsay: Flees	1%	
	M	McCallum: *Ruined Stone*	4%	
ACCEPTANCE	X	Becomes a successful plantocrat	3%	3%
TOTAL			100%	100%

Of course, one can assign different percentage probabilities in the process chart, which could make slight differences with no overall change in outcomes, so the overall evaluation appears robust. The probable outcomes are ranked below by likelihood:

Table 9b: Ranked Evaluation of Counterfactual Outcomes

RANKING	SCENARIO	SCENARIO DESCRIPTION	LIKELIHOOD
1	C2	Crawford: dies at Port Antonio	20%
2	Z2	Zachary: with 2nd Edition profits	20%
3	Z3	Zachary: after 5 years as overseer	13%
4	D1	Dies within one year	11%
5	D0	Dies on the voyage	10%
6	D3	Dies after three years	9%
7	Z1	Zachary: before 2nd Edition profits	7%
8	M	McCallum: unhappy acquiescence	4%
9	X	Becomes a successful plantocrat	3%
10	L1	Lindsay: *Illustrious Exile*	2%
11	L2	Adjusted Lindsay: Flees	1%
12	C1	Crawford: dies at Savanna-la-Mar	0%
TOTAL			100%

The most likely outcome, in exactly half of the counterfactual scenarios, results in Burns's death in Jamaica (a rational outcome given the overall picture of White mortality set against Burns's inherently poor health). Just under that, at 40 per cent, is his conversion as an independent spectator of the horrors of a Jamaican economy predicated on enslaved labour. The two outliers, his life falling apart while in exile or falling into acceptance of the plantocrats' code, are both very unlikely and in the single digit percentages.

Conclusion

Robert Burns, of course, did not go to Jamaica, and thus he avoided personal responsibility for 'driving' enslaved people in the plantation economy, as Morris puts it:

> Soon the 'plough driver' was able to avoid the post of 'negro driver' by pursuing literary fame as a 'quill driver' in Enlightenment Edinburgh. As a result of the episode, the figure of Robert Burns has

provided a focal point for modern attempts to recover the memory of Scottish connections with slavery and the black Atlantic.[48]

Had he gone there, what would he have lost? In all likelihood, our esteem today and, with his weak heart, his life in rather short order, as shown in the analysis above in Table 9a, with a 50 per cent probability of Burns dying at some point in his Jamaican foray. However, the numbers show that the next most likely scenario (at 20 per cent, and overall, 40 per cent) would be emulating Macaulay, returning home probably on the back of the profits of his second edition, joining the Excise service and actively supporting abolition until his early death in Scotland in 1796.

Lord Rosebery (1847–1929), the greatest Burns orator of the Victorian and Edwardian eras, put his thoughts to 'an imaginative sketch of what would have happened if Burns had really gone to Jamaica'.

> I think myself that his genius would have evaporated under those conditions; that he probably would not have lived long, and that we should only have known him by his first volume, but, of course, he might have taken a different line and risen to wealth in the West Indies, as many West Country people did in those days, and he might have come back and strutted on the Broomielaw as a rum lord, a sugar lord, or a tobacco lord, and even then he would have been a totally different Burns from the one whom we hallow and remember.[49]

Had Burns lived, would he have collapsed morally and adopted the mores and habit of his fellow bookie community (self-medicating with rum *ad libitum*)? Or would he have become outspoken (and ultimately crushed by the system), or achieved an *éclaircissement* like Zachary Macaulay's and actually followed the maxim that Andrew Lindsay quoted, to mitigate the woes of an injured society by returning home and using his poetical genius to bolster the progress of Abolition?

That last is the most likely outcome if his fragile health held up in the geographical and moral swamp in which he found himself.

---

48 Ibid, p.98.
49 Earl of Rosebury quoted in Anon, 'The Auld Brig of Ayr: Re-Opening Ceremony,' *Burns Chronicle* (1911), pp.34–49, at p.42.

CHAPTER SEVEN

Slavery in Burns's Afterlife

SO, IN THE poet's youth (perhaps, on balance, for understandable reasons) and in his later life (rather more surprisingly), Robert Burns seems to have had little direct engagement with the growing movement to secure freedom for Black chattel slaves compared with other social issues of the day such as the governance of the Kirk, the constitution of the State or the 'Rights of Women.' However, the tone of his work and its underlying themes of independence, equality and respect for each other, outwith the bounds of sex, or wealth or class, allowed many in the years after his death to adopt his poetry in support of the abolition of this form of chattel slavery, and subsequently seeking to promote equality and civil rights.

An early example, marking the termination of the controversial 'apprenticeship' provisions of Britain's abolition of the slave trade, is this Irish paraphrase of one of Burns's most potent works:

Paraphrase of Burns's Song, *Scots, Wha Hae Wi' Wallace Bled*.
Written for the First of August, 1838.[1]

Injured men! who long have bled,
'Neath the yoke of despots led,
Your bonds are burst, your foes are fled;
    Hail! blest Victory!

Now's the day, and now's the hour,
See the front of Freedom's tower,

---

[1] *Newry Examiner and Louth Advertiser*, 15 August 1838. The Slavery Abolition Act *1833* (3 & 4 Will IV c 73) abolished slavery within the British Empire (save for possessions in the control of the Honourable East India Company) from 1 August 1834, however, those persons manumitted under the Act were obliged to serve as 'apprentices' for varying terms, no later than 1 August 1840. Peaceful protests by the 'apprentice' community brought forward that end date, and Abolition was completed on freeing all 'apprentices' under the Act on 1 August 1838.

> See retire before her power —
>   Chains and Slavery!
>
> Who would be a traitor knave?
> Who would fill a coward's grave?
> 'Tis who left the wretched Slave
>   In hopeless misery!
>
> Who, for Freedom's rights and law,
> Freedom's sword would strongly draw?
> 'Tis who in that poor Slave saw
>   The trace of Deity!
>
> 'Tis he who drain'd his dearest veins
> To heal oppression's woes and pains;
> To free the Slave from servile chains,
>   That *all* should happy be.
>
> Proud usurpers low are found,
> Tyrants prostrate strew the ground;
> Liberty's in every sound; —
>   Yes! — To-day they're free!

The power of Burns's words was not confined to British advocates of abolition and emancipation, as will be seen in the next two sections looking at, first, the Emancipation movement in the USA before and after the American Civil War, and secondly the Civil Rights movement in the 20th century, in particular the leadership rhetoric of Dr Martin Luther King, Jr.

The 19th Century: Antebellum Advocacy and Action

Early Black leaders in the American Abolition movement regularly looked to Burns and his poems for inspiration, Dr James McCune Smith (1813–1865) being one of them. Born into slavery in New York City, he and his family were freed under the blanket New York State Emancipation Act of 1827. In his youth, while working as a blacksmith's apprentice, he concurrently received an education through the African Free School No 2, where the schoolmaster noticed his pupil's intellectual abilities were suitable for a medical school training. After a rejection by Columbia College (now University) in New York, McCune Smith was offered a place at University of Glasgow and, on being funded by the US abolitionist community, he sailed for Scotland in 1832.

> When he reached Scotland, he breathed a pure atmosphere. The land of Knox, Wallace, Bruce, and Burns, extended her arms while the thistle waved on her breast, and welcomed the youthful child of genius. [...] He entered Glasgow University, and made way for himself among his fellow students. In that school he met with no peculiar advantages or disadvantages, on account of complexion. He was received on terms of equality, and this was all that he desired.[2]

He matriculated in 1832 as is recorded in the Latin enrolment lists of the ancient university: '*12983 JACOBUS McCUNE SMITH filius natu maximus Samuelis, Mercatoris apud New York,*' graduating with a BA in 1835, an MA the following year, and in 1837 he became the first Black person in the world to earn the degree of doctor of medicine.[3] At each degree examination, the university class records show that he was top or nearly top of the class. McCune Smith was clever and industrious, and he was supported financially by the Glasgow Emancipation Society, for whom he spoke at rallies and meetings during his Scottish sojourn. After a spell of further training at Paris, and a contretemps over whether, as a qualified physician, he should be allowed to cross the Atlantic in the comforts of cabin class or, as a Black man, be exiled to steerage, Dr McCune Smith returned to New York, when 'the colored citizens of his native New York tendered him a public welcome.' Ransom F Wake, his old schoolmaster, speaking on their behalf, honoured McCune's Scottish hosts, who were

---

2 [Revd] H[enry] H[ighland] G[arnet], *Emancipator and Republican* [Boston, MA], 15 September 1847. Henry Highland Garnet (1815–1882): Born a slave, after escaping to New York was educated at the African Free School and then high school. He became a Presbyterian minister and prominent abolitionist. He was the first Black clergyman to preach to the US Congress and died in Monrovia as the US Minister to Liberia.
3 W Innes Addison, *The Matriculation Albums of the University of Glasgow. From 1728 to 1858* (Glasgow: James MacLehose, 1913), p.392. ('JAMES McCUNE SMITH eldest-born son of Samuel, Merchant in New York.')

Characterised by that nobleness of feeling and benevolence of heart so peculiar to Scotia's gifted sons, who regard a man from real worth and not for the fortuitous circumstances of color; with them no matter what may be the complexion of an individual 'whether an Indian or African sun may have burned upon him,' they would still exclaim with their own poet
'A man's a man for a' that.'[4]

For the next 27 years he practised medicine and ran his own pharmacy, firstly in Manhattan, and latterly in Brooklyn, where he treated patients without discrimination while additionally serving as the physician to the New York Colored Asylum (until it was burned down in a riot). He remained interested in language and literature, and maintained lifelong support for abolition, often using the words of Robert Burns as illustration or exhortation.[5] One of his friends and coadjutors said of Glasgow and his own welcome there:

[My Glasgow host] conferred upon me one of the highest favours a Scotchman could confer or a Negro could appreciate — *he gave*

---

4 *Colored American*, 26 September 1837. Ransome F Wake (?–1883): teacher (later head teacher) of African Free School No 2 in New York City. Active in the Episcopal Church (as a vestryman 1843–1854) and as a Prince Hall Mason. The quotation 'whether [...] him' is from John Philip Curran's defence speech at the trial of the United Irishman Archibald Rowan Hamilton in January 1794 where he cited Somerset's case as supporting Catholic Emancipation in Ireland:
I speak in the spirit of the British Law, which makes liberty commensurate with, and inseparable from, the British soil — which proclaims, even to the stranger and the sojourner, the moment he sets his foot upon British earth, that the ground on which he treads is holy, and consecrated by the genius of UNIVERSAL EMANCIPATION. No matter in what language his doom may have been pronounced; no matter what complexion incompatible with freedom, an Indian or an African sun may have burnt upon him; no matter in what disastrous battle his liberty may have been cloven down; no matter with what solemnities he may have been devoted upon the altar of slavery; the first moment he touches the sacred soil of Britain, the altar and the god sink together in the dus ; his soul walks abroad in her own majesty; his body swells beyond the measure of his chains, that burst from around him, and he stands redeemed, regenerated, and disenthralled, by the irresistible Genius of UNIVERSAL EMANCIPATION!
John Philip Curran, *Speeches*, 2 vols (New York: Isaac Riley, 1809), vol.I, pp.49–124, at p.83. See also the report of this meeting in William Cooper Nell, *The Colored Patriots of the American Revolution* (Boston: Robert F Wallcutt, 1855), p.353. William Cooper Nell (1816–1874): Abolitionist, journalist and editor, he was the first Black employee of the Federal civil service in 1861. He too used Burns on occasion, notably during the dispute in September 1839 between Garrison and others as to whether women should be allowed to be full members of the Abolition movement when he transcribed a Robert Burns's poem 'The Rights of Woman' into an album owned by a young Black girl. Mary Anne Dickerson, *Album*, Library Company of Philadelphia, [13860.Q].
5 J Stauffer, ed, *The Works of James McCune Smith* (Cambridge, MA: Harvard University Press, 2007).

me a copy of Burns' poems, from his own library. That was almost equal to proffering me the freedom of Glasgow, or making me a Scotchman. Well did I use that volume while sojourning in the country that gave birth to it and its immortal author!⁶

In 2018, Dr McCune Smith's *alma mater* announced that a new £90 million educational facility for 2,500 students would be built on campus named The James McCune Smith Learning Hub, with the twin purposes of marking 'pride in our association with his legacy' while providing 'reparative justice due to the University's historical links with racial slavery, and emphasis[ing] our commitment to that programme.'⁷ This magnificent facility opened (quietly due to COVID) in June 2021.

Burns was already widely read (and celebrated) across the USA by the late 1830s. In fact, his poems were pirated by the *Pennsylvanian Packet* newspaper almost as soon as a copy of his *First Edinburgh Edition* crossed the Atlantic in 1787. Here Burns was displayed as a poet who was 'a friend to American ideology,' with pirate editions of his work being published that year in both Philadelphia and New York, and regularly thereafter.⁸ In 1816 the first Burns Supper in the Americas was held in Philadelphia, with similar clubs being formed in Baltimore, New Jersey and New York soon after, and the phenomenon spread throughout the States. The first identified Black playwright in America, William Brown (1790–1849), opened a new theatre, The African Grove, in Mercer Street, Greenwich Village in 1821 and the following January put on a show entitled 'Scots Wha Hae' with the Black actor/singer James Hewlett (?–1849) in the starring role singing Burns songs.⁹

---

6 Samuel Ringgold Ward, *Autobiography of a Fugitive Negro* (London: John Snow, 1855), p.332. Samuel Ringgold Ward (1817–1866): Born into slavery, fled north to freedom. After education at the African Free School, he was a prominent abolitionist, newspaper editor, the first Black trade union leader and a congregationalist minister. Ward added a caveat to the quote: 'O that I liked *oaten cakes, haggis, cockie-leekie* or BAGPIPES, as much as Burns!'
7 *Press Release*: University of Glasgow, 7 October 2018, www.gla.ac.uk/news/archiveofnews/2018/october/headline_615335_en.html (accessed 1 September 2024). For the details of the University's research and programme of restitution, see Stephen Mullen and Simon Newman, *Slavery, Abolition and the University of Glasgow* (Glasgow: University of Glasgow, 2018).
8 For a detailed study of the early reception of Burns in North America, see Rhona Brown, '"Guid Black Prent": Robert Burns and the Contemporary Scottish and American Periodical Press,' in *Robert Burns and Transatlantic Culture*, ed by Sharon Alker, Leith Davis and Holly Nelson (Farnham: Ashgate, 2012), pp.71–98.
9 Marvin McAllister, 'Transnational Balladeering: "Scots Wha Hae wi' Wallace Bled" in 1820s

Of the tropes used in toasting and commemorating 'Scotia's Bard' and in commending his poems and songs, one of the most repeated is the 'man o' independent mind' who follows the desire for freedom won by Bruce and Wallace (and often Knox), contributing and receiving recognition regardless of his wealth or class. Burns's perceived universality was an important part of his adoption by Black abolitionists in the US:

> In every region where the English language is known the songs of Burns give rapture; and from every land, and from climes the most remote, comes the praise of Burns as a poet.[10]

This reading of Burns was a keynote for the Abolition movement, particularly in the use of the quotation 'a man's a man' as they drew out the logic of that phrase by extending it to race and colour.

There are many papers, books and pamphlets on the adoption of Burns's 'A Man's a Man' as a liberal, radical, socialist or even Marxist slogan (and not just in English, considering the importance of Feiligrath's translation 'Trotz Alledem') around the brotherhood of man – or, as might be phrased now, the existence of inalienable human equality.[11] Burns was enthusiastically adopted by William Lloyd Garrison (1805–1879) who has been described as:

> [a] printer, newspaper publisher, radical abolitionist, suffragist, civil rights activist [who] spent his life disturbing the peace of the nation in the cause of justice. In his later years, he reminded listeners of his fundamental creed: 'I am still for immediate, unconditional, everlasting emancipation from oppression of everyone on the face of the earth.'[12]

Afro-New-York,' *Studies in Scottish Literature*, 38.3 (2012), pp.108–118.
10 William Wells Brown, *The American Fugitive in Europe: Sketches of Places and People Abroad* (Boston/Cleveland, OH/New York: John P Jewett and Company/Jewett. Proctor & Worthington/ Sheldon, Lamport & Blakeman, 1855), p.253. William Wells Brown (ca 1814–1884): American fugitive slave, writer and abolitionist orator.
11 Murray Pittock, 'Introduction: "The mair they talk, I'm kend the better": Burns and Europe,' in *The Reception of Robert Burns in Europe*, ed by Murray Pittock (London: Bloomsbury, 2014), p.3.
12 Anon, 'To the New England Women's Tea Party,' *The Woman's Journal* [Boston, MA] (20 December 1873), p.405. Garrison invoked Burns in other campaigns for human rights and equality, for example, for Women: he wrote 'HUMAN EQUALITY: A SUPPLEMENT TO "A MAN'S A MAN",' of which this is the final verse:

One of his obituaries captured his philosophy in a way he would have appreciated: '[f]ew abolitionists believed so completely as he did in the complete humanity of the negro [...] "A man's a man for a' that" expressed his innermost conviction and feeling.'[13] Garrison is first recorded as having used the quotation in the context of abolition and emancipation when visiting England in May 1833, stressing then how he sympathised with the poverty of the English industrial poor as well as for the oppressed enslaved people in America, two groups who both needed relief.[14]

However, for the Abolitionists, equality was not the sole message within the iconic wording: the Wedgwood image, 'am I not a man and a brother,' carries connotations of the Burns song, and the *Massachusetts Abolitionist* prominently featured 'Honest Poverty' on its front page in early 1839 under the title 'Manhood by Robert Burns'; the use of its most famous line as a slogan grew from there.[15] For the American Abolitionist, the key message in the song was in the repeated use of the word 'man', the essential quality that the pro-slavery lobby denied in Black chattel slaves; for the enslavers, the slave-holders and their

---

Then hail the day, come when it may,
As come it will, for a' that,
When woman's worth, oer all the earth,
Shall honored be, for a' that!
For a' that, and a that,
Co-equal, free, and a' that;
Through her enfranchisement our race
Shall nobly rise, for a' that.

(Monographic. Retrieved from the Library of Congress, www.loc.gov/item/amss.as105600 (accessed 1 September 2024).) Or, '[i]n the discussion of fundamental principles and the rights of our common humanity, what have we to do with sex? If "a man's a man, for a' that," so is a woman a woman.' (Letter: William Lloyd Garrison to the Editor of the New York *Tribune*, 15 February 1879, in *Garrison's Letters,* vol.VI, p.454.)
Or for the rights of the Chinese community:
'We have allowed all other peoples to take up their abode with us [...] We must either drive out these, or keep the barrier down and let the Chinese find an equal entrance, and be protected in the enjoyment of equal rights and privileges. "A man's a man for a' that".' (Letter: William Lloyd Garrison to Sarah Maria Parsons, 6 February 1877, in *Garrison's Letters,* vol.VI p.558.)
And even for animal rights:
If it be true that 'Man's inhumanity to man makes countless thousands mourn,' it is equally true that his barbarity to fish, and fowl, and cattle, mightily augments the sum of mortal agony.
(Letter: William Lloyd Garrison to John S Rarey, 20 March 1861, in *Garrison's Letters,* vol.V, p.15).
13 Oliver Johnson, 'Death of Garrison,' *The Index,* 12 June 1879.
14 Letter: William Lloyd Garrison to *The Liberator,* 9 May 1833, in *The Letters of William Lloyd Garrison, Volume I (1822–1835),* ed by Walter M Merrill (Cambridge, MA: Belknap Press, 1971), p.229.
15 *Massachusetts Abolitionist* (14 March 1839).

enforcers, enslaved workers were not 'men, women and children', but 'things' they owned. Burns's words vigorously challenged that racist assumption.

The question of slavery in the US Constitution and its laws is too complex a topic to develop here, however, the key in this context is that the freedoms exalted by Burns and praised by his (White) American republican readers were often described as flowing from Jefferson's *Declaration of Independence*. Yet, the US Constitution accepted the existence of slavery, even, for one purpose, evaluating a slave as three-fifths of a person.[16] This two-faced approach, or 'Liberty Paradox,' was born of the compromise needed to build unanimity between the Northern and Southern States in the belligerent face of the British Crown and its armies, but in doing so created a dilemma that would have to be resolved sometime in the future.

> The country's founding document written by Thomas Jefferson declared that 'all men are created equal,' and it was based on Locke's philosophy that no human being was naturally subordinated to anyone else. Jefferson also followed Locke in supposing that subordination could be legitimate only with the consent of all

---

16 *Constitution of the Unites States of America*,
Representatives and direct Taxes shall be apportioned among the several States which may be included within this Union, according to their respective Numbers, which shall be determined by adding to the whole Number of free Persons, including those bound to Service for a Term of Years, and excluding Indians not taxed, three fifths of all other Persons. *Article 1, Section 2, Clause 3* (Repealed by the 14th Amendment of 1868).
In the first draft of the *Declaration of Independence*, Jefferson (although a slave-holder himself) included the following denunciation of King George III:
> he has waged cruel war against human nature itself, violating its most sacred rights of life & liberty in the persons of a distant people who never offended him, captivating & carrying them into slavery in another hemisphere, or to incur miserable death in their transportation thither. This piratical warfare, the opprobrium of infidel powers, is the warfare of the CHRISTIAN king of Great Britain, determined to keep open a market where MEN should be bought & sold, he has prostituted his negative for suppressing every legislative attempt to prohibit or to restrain this execrable commerce: and that this assemblage of horrors might want no fact of distinguished die, he is now exciting those very people to rise in arms among us, and to purchase that liberty of which he has deprived them, & murdering the people upon whom he also obtruded them; thus paying off former crimes committed against the liberties of one people, with crimes which he urges them to commit against the lives of another.

In one of the many compromises the American Republic made over slavery, this passage was dropped from the final draft after pressure from not just Georgia and North Carolina, but from Northern men active in the transatlantic trade.
Julian P Boyd, ed, *The Papers of Thomas Jefferson, Volume 1* (Princeton: Princeton University Press, 1950), pp.423–428.

concerted parties, and no one could consent to the subordination of slavery. Given these assumptions and the legality of black slavery in America it followed that whites believed they were superior to blacks in the sense that they were human beings and blacks were not. [...] For example, according to one writer for the *Richmond Examiner,* a 'respectable public journal' **the Negro is justifiably enslaved 'because he is not a man.'**[17]

This was directly countered by Abraham Lincoln in his speech at Peoria, IL, in 1854 during 'the Lincoln-Douglas Debates':

If the negro is a *man*, why then my ancient faith teaches me that 'all men are created equal.' And that there can be no moral right in connection with one man's making a slave of another.[18]

Or as William Lloyd Garrison trenchantly espoused that argument just before the war by quoting Burns in support of Lincoln's argument: 'Thus do I test the nation by its own revolutionary standard, taking Bunker Hill Monument for my measuring line. No matter for race or complexion – "a man's a man for a' that."'[19]

The use of that famous line of Burns's is not just a statement about equality between 'men', it is a purposeful declaration that the Black speaker or writer is a 'man', too. So, without what some commentators felt was the passivity of the striking Wedgwood image, the American Abolitionists stood to assert both their man-hood (person-hood) and therefore their equality as a fact, as equal members of the same species, *homo sapiens*. The power of Burns's conception and words became a rhetorical lightning-bolt for the cause: simultaneously illuminating and powerful.

The interesting point for this analysis is the frequency of the use of the phrase 'a man's a man' in Abolitionist papers, speeches and letters of the time. It was not just McCune Smith and Garrison who invoked Burns, but a roster including most of the leading anti-slavery

---

17 Bernard R Boxill, 'A Man's a Man for All That,' *The Monist* (April 2010), pp.188–207. [Emphasis added.]
18 Abraham Lincoln, *The Collected Works of Abraham Lincoln*, 10 vols, ed by Roy Prentice Basler (Brunswick: Rutgers University Press, 1953), vol.II, p.266.
19 William Lloyd Garrison, 'Letter marking the Anniversary of the Martyrdom of John Brown,' *Douglass's Monthly* (January 1861), p.398.

speakers (both Black and White) associated with the movement. As can be seen from the following selection, the specific quotation is used to first remind the audience that the enslaved person is a 'man' (in the sense of a member of 'mankind,' not a male) and, on that basis, the enslaved person is an equal.

Table 10: 'A Man's a Man' in the Rhetorical Lexicon of Abolition, 1836–66	
It is vain for gentlemen to deny the fact, that the feelings of society are fast becoming adversed to slavery. [...] The noble sentiment of Burns: 'Then let us pray that come it may, As come it will for a' that, That man to man, the warld o'er, **Shall brothers be for a' that'** is rapidly spreading. The day-star of human liberty has risen above the dark horizon of slavery, and will continue its bright career, until it smiles alike on all men. PA Bolling, 1832* One cannot be ashamed to think it should be necessary [in this century ...] to repeat, justify, and defend such a plain proposition, as that man if free, and that his fellow-man has, and can have, no right of property in him. [...] **Is not rank merely the guinea stamp?** and is not the moral and accountable nature of man the gold on which it is impressed? Revd Archibald Bennie, 1836[a] My fellow Abolitionists disregarded all national distinctions in carrying out the abolition work: they acted on the principle that **'a man's a man for a' that.'** William Lloyd Garrison, 1840[b] Galleries of Paintings, are as free to the Black as the white man in London. There is no distinction on account of color. The white man gains nothing by being white, and the Black man loses nothing by being Black. **'A man's a man for a' that.'** Frederick Douglass, 1846[c]	I have only to ask your sympathy for the American abolitionists. Let me assure you that they are a most remarkable body of men and women, as remarkable as can be found in the world. They are those who have been tried in the fire – those whom you ought to admire, and to whom you ought to give the right hand of fellowship. Let us pray for the freedom of the slave. It is coming, it is coming. 'Then let us pray that come it may, As come it will for a' that – That sense and worth o'er a' the earth May bear the gree and a' that. For a' that and a' that, It's coming yet for a' that – That man to man the to man the warld o'er, **Shall brothers be for a' that.'** William Lloyd Garrison, 1846[d] My visit to [London] has been exceedingly gratifying, on account of the freedom I have enjoyed in visiting such places of instruction and amusement as those from which I have been carefully excluded by the inveterate prejudice against color in the United States. Botanic and Zoological gardens, Museums and Panoramas, Halls of Statuary and Blush to behold the light of day — blush to look into any mirror — until you are prepared to endorse the glorious sentiment, that, whatever may be his origins, complexion or estate, **'A MAN'S A MAN'S A MAN FOR A' THAT.'** William Lloyd Garrison, 1847[e]

Table 10: 'A Man's a Man' in the Rhetorical Lexicon of Abolition, 1836–66

But the Bard of Scotia has higher claims on our sympathies than any we have yet emulated. His soul was full of deep, earnest devotion to the cause of freedom, liberty of thought and speech; and his noble song **'A Man's a Man'**, will be to still future generations a watchword and a spell against slavery.
Mrs S T Martyn, 1848[f]

W[ilia]m G Allen favored the meeting with an instructive speech on the mental powers and abilities of the colored man, showing, in a peculiarly happy manner, 'that **a man's a man, black or white**'
William G Allen, 1849[g]

THE SLAVE'S A MAN, FOR A' THAT.
Though stripped of all the dearest rights
 Which nature claims, and a' that,
There's that which in the slave unites
 To make the man, for a' that:
For a' that, and a' that,
 Though dark his skin, and a' that,
We cannot rob him of his kind,
The slave 's a man, for a' that.

Though by his brother bought and sold,
 And beat and scourged, and a' that,
His wrongs can ne'er be felt or told, —
 Yet he's a man, for a' that:
For a' that, and a' that,
 His body chained, and a' that,
The image of his God remains,-
The slave's a man, for a' that.
William Wells Brown, 1849[h]

'A man's a man for a' that.' God counts every man a unit. And let us beware how we count a man less than his maker counts him.
Gerrit Smith, 1850[i]

We loath and detest all laws which give or withhold political rights on account of color. **'A man's a man for a' that'**, and ought to have the full rights of manhood, whether his ancestors were Celts, Goths, or Hottentots, whether his complexion be ebony or ivory.
Horace Greeley, 1851[j]

I have no faith in the permanent inferiority of nations! I think all history proves the opposite. Virtue, patience, energy, self-denial and an eternal purpose to improve, may place the African where the Saxon now is! whilst the opposite vices may degrade the Saxon below the African! [...] treating with contempt, all those false teachers of Christ, who recognize caste among nations, let us take more to our hearts those followers of our Savior, who honor God by the recognition of the Brotherhood of men! [...] But then, as Burns has it, **'a man's a man for all that'**.
Cassius Marcellus Clay, 1851[k]

We drew up and published [...] a preamble and resolutions protesting against being disenfranchised and denied the right to oath, and our determination to use all moral means to secure legal claim to all the rights and privileges of American citizens [...] our earnest but feeble protest contributed its humble share in the rebuilding of a commonwealth [in California] where **'a man's a man for all that'**.
Mifflin Wistar Gibbs, 1851[l]

But with me, all men are men. Are the skin and the mind of my fellow men dark? **'A man's a man for a' that!'** I still recognize him as a man. He is my brother: and I still have a brother's heart for him.
Gerrit Smith, 1854[m]

[T]he idea she wished to advance was, that in the sight of God, each man was just as great as another, [...] that, abstractly, whatever his position, **'A man's a man for a' that'**.
Elizabeth C Wright, 1853[n]

Table 10: 'A Man's a Man' in the Rhetorical Lexicon of Abolition, 1836–66

'All men are created equal, and are endowed by their Creator with certain inalienable rights, among which are *life, liberty, and the pursuit of happiness*.' [...] ALL MEN — *not* all men of the Colonies, not all Anglo-Saxon men — not all white men, not all rich men, not all men of royal blood, not all American born [men]; but ALL MEN. It was no matter whether the cold, oblique rays of the north had paled a man's face into the standard of Anglo-Saxon beauty, or whether the vertical rays of the South had darkened it to the hue of the raven's wing; **'a man's a man for a' that.'** This was the spirit of '76, the spirit that inspired the revolution.
Revd Ichabod Codding, 1854.[o]

American slavery [...] by its operation brings down the noblest work of God to a level of the beasts that perish. As far as it can do, it dehumanizes man, and treats him as a thing without a soul. It may be remarked, however, in passing, **'A man's a man, for a' that.'**
Revd AC Baldwin, 1857[p]

I say, what of all this? **'A man's a man for a' that.'** I sincerely believe that the weight of the argument is in favor of the unity of origin of the human race, or species — that the arguments on the other side are partial, superficial, utterly subversive of the happiness of man, and insulting to the wisdom of God.
Frederick Douglass, 1854[q]

Again – take these slaveholding pleas to Scotland, from the graves of the dead and the homes of the living they shall be replied to in thunder-tones, in the living words of BURNS:
   'A man's a man, for a' that.'
   'Who would be a traitor knave?
   [...] Let him turn and flee!'
William Lloyd Garrison, 1854[r]

No matter what physical difference may exist among men; no matter whether an African, an Asiatic, a European, or an American sun may have shone upon them; no matter whether the human soul be enshrined in ebony, bronze, or ivory, **'a man's a man for a' that'**, equal in rights before God and the Constitution of the country.
Francis Gillette, 1854[s]

AN IMPROMPTU.
 'E'en the poor slave we pass not by,
   A man's a man for all that!'

Suggested by seeing the never-ending series of pictures illustrating Southern life in *Harpers' Magazine*, which seem intended to show the slave content with his degradation, and to familiarize the North with it.

1.
Clothe him in mean and dirty rags,
 In soleless shoes and crownless hat,
And sketch him thus for magazines;
 'A man's a man for all that!'

2.
Feed him on corn, call him a brute;
 Draw his dull face, his feet so flat;
Give him contented words to suit;
 'A man's a man for all that!'

3.
Starve out his mind, make him like those
 Who once in thickest darkness sat; — .
Call him a chattel, a machine,
 'A man's a man for all that!'

4.
Teach him to sin, then hunt him down,
 Tear quivering flesh with rod and cat;
Burn him for crimes yourselves have taught
 'A man's a man for all that!'

5.
Then picture Southern chivalry,
 With broadcloth fine and white cravat,
With polished manners, shining wit;
 'A man's a man for all that!'

6.
O, deadly sin! that presses out
 The soul's life-blood in Slavery's vat.
'Where is thy brother?' God shall say;
 How will the South reply to that?
LLAV, 1858[t]

Table 10: 'A Man's a Man' in the Rhetorical Lexicon of Abolition, 1836–66

'A man's a man' — it seems to us a very simple, very obvious, altogether indisputable proposition — of course 'a man's a man'; but it was long before the world learned this simple truth, in fact, the world has not well learned it yet. 'A man's a man' — it was only in the present century that the legislature of Great Britain assented to this principle. In the United States of America it is not yet assented to, and probably will not be for many a year to come. In many of those states, which glory in their freedom, a man is not held to be a man; if he be of negro descent, if he be the purchased possession of a planter, then, although he is an intelligent being, though he is clever in his work, though he may be superior to his owner in all physical, mental, and moral properties, the man's a beast for a' that. Burns's words must be altered to suit the climate of the Southern States. [...] And it is only because we have the Gospel of Jesus Christ, with all its manly and noble truths, that we can hope with the poet, that

> 'For a' that and a' that,
> It's coming yet for a' that,
> That man to man, the world o'er
> Shall brothers be, for a' that.'

Revd Hugh Stowell Brown, 1859[u]

That they [the Democratic Party] should appeal to the prejudices of low people against the rights of colored men is to be expected. We shall honor the Republican party if they stand up and say boldly yes: we do abominate slavery and all of its progeny of treasons against liberty! We believe **a man's a man**, and that elsewhere than on this doctrine, Republicanism can never have any enduring foundations.
Editorial, *Oberlin Evangelist*, 1857[v]

The American people will outlive this mean prejudice against complexion. Sooner or later they will learn **'a man's a man for a' that'**.
Harriet Jacobs & Louisa Jacobs, 1864[w]

Chief-Justice Taney was much censured for favoring the sentiment that black men have no rights which white men are bound to respect. [...] Within a few weeks the Chief-Justice has left our world. There is a world (and maybe he has gone to it) where to condemn a man for his skin is held to be a mistake; and where those few words of dear Robert Burns, **'A man's a man for a' that,'** infinitely outweigh all the nonsense and blasphemy which pro-slavery courts and pro-slavery parties and pro-slavery churches have uttered to the contrary.
Gerrit Smith, 1864[x]

We shall realise the truth that 'all men are endowed by their Creator with inalienable rights,' and that on the American continent this is the right of all, whether he come from east, west, north or south; and, although complexions may differ, **'a man's a man for a' that'**.
The State Convention of the Colored People of South Carolina, 1865[y]

When, sir, with my own eyes I saw the negro — for the sake of the government that had protected him and defended me — bare his breast to the rebel steel and stand in his line for the sake of Old Glory, the flag of my country —amid the rain of rebel shot and shell — when the dreaded Minie [bullet] struck him, he fell; and his life's blood was ebbing out. I noticed it was red, and I felt that it was eloquent, for it moved me; and I turned away, sir, and with Burns, the Scottish poet, I said in my heart **'A man's a man for a' that.'**
Lieutenant Colonel John Anderson Danks, 1866[z]

Notes on Table 10: 'A Man's a Man' in the Rhetorical Lexicon of Abolition, 1836–1866

*George W[ashington] Williams, *History of the Negro Race in America from 1619 to 1880*, 2 vols (New York/London: G P Putnam's Sons, 1882), vol.II, p.34. Philip Archelaus Bolling (ca 1806–1876): Virginian landowner and lawyer. Served in the Virginia Legislature 1831–1832 where he was, although a slave-holder himself, a leading proponent of gradual emancipation. A Revd Archibald Bennie, 'Speech Seconding the Resolution,' Public Meeting, 8 February, 1836, in Anon, *A Voice to the United States of America, from the Metropolis of Scotland* (Edinburgh: William Oliphant and Son, 1836), p.21.*
Revd Archibald Bennie (1797–1846): A divinity graduate of Glasgow, he served parishes in Glasgow and Stirling before being called to Lady Yester's Kirk, Edinburgh in 1835. In 1841 he was appointed Chaplain in Ordinary to the Queen and Dean of the Chapel Royal.[a] Anon, *Report of the Speeches and Reception of the American Delegates at the Great Public Meeting of the Glasgow Emancipation Society* (Glasgow: George Gallie, 1840), p.19.[b] Letter: Frederick Douglass to William Lloyd Garrison May 23, 1846, in Philip Foner, ed, *Life and Writings of Frederick Douglas: Early Years 1817–1849* (New York: International Publishers, 1950), p.165[c] 'Speech at Paisley,' *Renfrewshire Advertiser* (26 September 1846).[d] Letter: William Lloyd Garrison to Heman Humphrey, 9 July 1847, in *Garrison's Letters*, vol. III, p.491.[e] Mrs ST Martyn, 'Burns and His Monument on the Banks of the Doon,' *The Lady's Wreath, 1848–1849* [New York], p.209. Sarah Towne Smith Martyn (1805–1879): American writer, magazine editor and social reformer, noted for her work in Temperance and the Anti-Slavery movement.[f] W[illiam] C[ooper] N[ell], 'Meetings of the Friends of Equal School Rights,' *Liberator* (9 November 1849). Professor William Gustavus Allen (ca 1820–1888): US Educator and Abolition activist. Born free, he was the second Black college professor in the US, and, in 1853, became the first Black man to marry a White woman (Mary King) in the USA, which led to his near lynching and their exile in the UK, where they continued to campaign and lecture.[g] William Wells Brown, *The Anti-Slavery Harp* (Boston: Bela Marsh, 1849), pp.44–45, first two of six stanzas, at p.44. William Wells Brown (1814–1884): Born into slavery, he escaped aged 19 although not legally free until 1854. Author and playwright, a campaigner for Abolition and other social reform. In this work, Brown also adapted other Burns songs, such as 'I'll Be Free, I'll be Free,' to 'Sweet Afton,' (pp.19–20), 'Fling Out the Anti-Slavery Flag,' to 'Auld Lang Syne' (p.22), 'On to Victory,' to the tune of 'Scots Wha' Hae,' (p.32).[h] Gerrit Smith (1797–1874): philanthropist social reformer (including abolition). He briefly served as a congressman in 1853–1854. In 1859 he financed John Brown's raid on Harper's Ferry, and in 1867 (with Horace Greeley and Cornelius Vanderbilt) paid Jefferson Davies's bail. Gerrit Smith, *Substance of the Speech made by Gerrit Smith, in the Capitol of the State of New York, March 11th and 12th, 1850* (Albany: Jacob T Hazen, 1850), p.14.[i] *New-York Tribune*, 17 January 1851. Horace Greeley (1811–1872): New York journalist and editor who founded the *New-York Tribune*.[j] Cassius Marcellus Clay quoted in Anon, *Proceedings of the Convention, of the Colored Freemen of Ohio, Held in Cincinnati, [...] 1852* (Cincinnati: Dumas & Lawyer, 1852), p.285. Cassius Marcellus Clay (1810–1903), Yale-educated son of a prominent slave-holder in Kentucky who converted to abolition, publishing the *True American*, an antislavery journal. During the Civil War, Clay was a friend of and advisor to Lincoln.[k] Mifflin Wistar Gibbs, *Light and Shade* (Little Rock, AK: for the Author, 1902), p.36. Mifflin Wistar Gibbs (1823–1915): Lawyer, judge and activist. Born in Philadelphia, went to California in the Gold Rush and campaigned against race laws there. He emigrated to British Columbia in Canada, where he became the first Black person elected to public office in the province in 1861. He returned to the USA after the Civil War, and was involved in Reconstruction at Little Rock, AR. Later, he served as US Consul in Madagascar.[l] Gerrit Smith, *Speeches of Gerrit Smith in Congress* (New York: Mason Brothers, 1865),' Speech on the Nebraska Bill,' p.203.[m] Anon, *Proceedings of the American Anti-slavery Society at its Second Decade [...] December 1853* (New York: American Anti-Slavery Society, 1854), p.37. Elizabeth Clendenon Wright (later Mrs Lyman Jewell) (1826–1882): Teacher and naturalist, active in social reform temperance, women's rights and suffrage, and anti-slavery.[n] Mark Hubbard, ed, *Illinois's War. The Civil War in Documents* (Athens, OH: Ohio University Press, 2013), p.21. Revd Ichabod Codding (1810–1866): Educated at New York and in Vermont, from 1836 he toured the mid-West in the cause of abolition.[o] Revd A C Baldwin, 'Letters to a Christian Slaveholder,' in *Three Prize Essays on American Slavery*, [ed by Sewell Harding] (Boston: Congregational Board for Publishing,

1857), p.63. Revd Abraham Chittenden Baldwin (1804–1887): Congregationalist pastor, poet and early telegraphist.[p] 'The Claims of the Negro Ethnographically Considered, Address Delivered at Western Reserve College, July 12, 1854,' in *Life and Writings of Frederick Douglass: Pre-Civil War decade, 1850–1860*, ed by Philip Foner (New York: International Publishers, 1950), p.307.[q] *New York Times*, 15 February 1854; Garrison, *No Compromise on Slavery: An Address* (New York: American Anti-Slavery Society, 1854), p.12.[r] Speech on 'The Execution of United States Laws,' US Senate 23 February 1854, in *Congressional Globe, New Series XXXI*, ed by John C Rives (City of Washington [DC]: John C Rives, 1855), p.322. Francis Gillette (1807–1879): Connecticut agriculturalist, abolitionist and newspaperman. Despite failing to be elected Governor on ten occasions, he filled a US Senate vacancy as a Free Soiler for just under one year from 1854.[s] *The Liberator*, 25 June 1858.[t] Hugh Stowell Brown, *Twelve Lectures to the Men of Liverpool, Volume Second* (Liverpool: Gabriel Thomson, 1859), pp.3, 14. Revd Hugh Stowell Brown (1823–1886): Manx-born, he trained as a surveyor before being called to the Baptist ministry in Liverpool. At his peak, his working men's lectures drew crowds of over 1,000.[u] *The Oberlin Evangelist*, 16 September 1857.[v] Harriet A Jacobs and Lisa [sic] Jacobs, 'Letter from Teachers of the Freedmen,' *National Anti-Slavery Standard*, 16 April 1864. Harriet A Jacobs (1813/15–1897) and her daughter Louisa Matilda Jacobs (1833–1917): Harriet, born into slavery, was the illegitimate daughter of a North Carolina politician. She escaped north and, with her daughter, was an active abolitionist and educator. She published an important autobiography in 1861.[w] Smith, *Speeches*, p.50.[x] Anon, *Proceedings of The State Convention of the Colored People of South Carolina, [...] November 1865* (Charleston, SC: South Carolina Leader Office, 1865), p.26.[y] Speech in the 'Debate in the House of Representatives, Thursday March 29, 1866 [...] Relative to the Reconstruction of the Rebellious States,' in *The Legislative Record: Containing the Debates and Proceedings of the Pennsylvania Legislature for the Session of 1866*, ed by George Bergner [Harrisburg [PA]: Telegraph Steam Book and Job Office, 1866), p.xc. John Anderson Danks (1826–1896): a grocer to trade and a pastor in the Methodist Episcopal Church. Served 1861-1864 in the 63rd Pennsylvanian Volunteer Infantry and was elected on the Republican ticket for a single session in the Pennsylvania House of Representatives.[z] [Emphasis added.]

The range of use of Burns's shibboleth is extraordinary, so much so that even the anti-Abolitionists recognised its potent ubiquity. In an argument that could inevitably only be determined through the blood of the American Civil War, the pro-slavery lobby was every bit as vocal and trenchant as the Abolitionists. At least one of them recognised the effective use that Robert Burns (himself an icon of the Southern states, as will be discussed below) was being put to by their opponents.

An abolition meeting is held at some town in Ohio, New York, or Pennsylvania; speeches are made, negro wrongs are dwelt upon, Burns is quoted, 'A man's a man for a that,' and Terence also, '*Homo sum et nihil a me alienum puto*,' 'My black brother,' and 'All men are born free and equal.' The meeting terminates; an impression is made, and frequently even upon strong minds. There are no libraries within reach; the different authors' works are too expensive, and the abolition poison runs through the mental system, as hydrophobia through the physical, until the patient becomes a rabid, raving fanatic.[20]

20 John Campbell, *Negro-mania: Being an Examination of the Falsely-Assumed Equality of the Various Races of Men* (Philadelphia: Campbell & Power, 1851), p.546. Publius Terentius Afer

While this was the most prominent use of Burns in promoting Abolition/Emancipation, other works were called into service too. Garrison, being of an inherently combative nature, also often quoted from 'Scots wha hae' with its belligerent – for a pacifist – rejoinder to the foreboding threat of 'chains and slaverie'. His general rhetorical use of Burns can be seen in two of his speeches in 1836 and 1837:

> The spirit of southern slavery is a spirit of EXTERMINATION against all who dare represent it as a dishonor to our country, rebellion against God, and treason against the liberties of mankind. [...] As Christian warriors, whose weapons are not carnal but spiritual, from man to man, and from rank to rank, the interrogation shall pass —
>
>   'Who would be a traitor-knave?
>   [...]   Let him turn and flee!' [21]

> It is an established doctrine among us, that British oppression, Russian oppression, Turkish oppression, and indeed all other oppression excepting that of our southern States, — the most detestable and intolerable of them all! — may be rightly resisted unto blood. [...] let them not presume to arraign any man, or body of men, who shall shout in the ears of our slaves —
>
>   'Lay the proud usurpers low!
>   [...]   But they shall be free!' [22]

Or, here, in the cause célèbre of the 1854 arrest of Anthony Burns (1834–1862) in Boston under the terms of the Fugitive Slave Act:[23]

(?185BC–?159BC), or 'Terence' to English readers, was a playwright and slave in Rome. This quotation translates as 'I am human, and I think nothing human is alien to me.' Terence, *The Woman of Andros. The Self-Tormentor. The Eunuch* [Loeb Classical Library 22], ed and trans by John Barsby (Cambridge, MA: Harvard University Press, 2001), pp.174–175. John Campbell (1810–1874) was an Irish Chartist who fled Manchester for Philadelphia in 1843. A bookseller, he founded the Social Reform Society in 1844. As a radical Ulsterman, it is highly likely that Campbell knew Burns's works well.

21 Letter: Garrison to Henry E Benson, 26 January 1836, *Garrison's Letters*, vol.II, p.33.
22 Letter: Garrison to The Editor of the *Boston Courier*, 11 March 1837, *Garrison's Letters*, vol. II, pp.226–227. [The misquotation is Garrison's.]
23 *An Act to Amend, and Supplementary to the Act entitled 'An Act respecting Fugitives from Justice, and Persons escaping from the Service of their Masters,'* Pub Law 31—60 (1850), which required citizens to cooperate in the return of enslaved people who had escaped their bondage under

His surname of Burns — did not the spirit of Robert Burns seem to have risen from his grave at Dumfries, Scotland, crossed the Atlantic, and now to have pleaded in Boston streets his imprisoned and about-to-sacrifice colored namesake's behalf, in his own world-wide known words, with a slight alteration of them for better adaptation to this new Boston kidnapping case; — as that multitude stood there, surrounding the court-house — filling the streets — thronging the Melodeon — gathered in from all parts of the country — burning with shame and indignation, and only restrained by the utter hopelessness of the attempt against such odds of powder and ball, from an effort to rescue the prisoner: —

> Who would be a traitor knave?
> Now's the day and now's the hour,
> See the front of battle lower,
> See approach proud PIERCE'S power,
>   Chains and slavery!
> Who would be a traitor knave?
> Who so base as be a slave?
> Who would fill a coward's grave?
>   Let him turn and flee!
> Lay the proud oppressor low!
> Tyrants fall in every foe!
> Liberty's in every blow!
>   Let us do or die!

And yet, in spite of [this] inspiration in his very name, we must send him back to the hell of slavery![24]

Garrison also wrote a powerful anti-slavery anthem to the tune of 'Auld Lang Syne' which became the abolitionist movement's theme

---

penalty of heavy fines.
24 *Liberator*, 21 July 1854. Anthony Burns (1834–1862): born into slavery in Virginia, he escaped to Boston in 1853, where in time he was denounced, captured and tried. The people of Boston objected (some violently in riot) and President Franklin D Pierce (1804–1869, president 1853–1857) sent a detachment of US Marines to ensure that Burns was delivered to a Virginia-bound ship in Boston harbour. In time, Abolitionists raised money and bought him out of slavery, after which he studied for the Baptist ministry, serving a parish in Ontario in the years up to his death. The Melodeon was a large concert hall on Washington Street, Boston.

song, 'I am an Abolitionist.' While other works of Burns were played in aid of the Movement for Abolition, however, it was 'a man's a man' that remained the touchstone and watch-word of their aims.[25] In some ways, it reached its apogee when used by Harriet Tubman, also known as Moses, the most famous of the 'conductors' of the Underground Railway in the 1850s. This volunteer network saved thousands of escaping Black people by spiriting them from house to house in the United States until they reached safety and undisputed freedom in Canada. She is reported as singing this song while she and her escapees crossed the iron railway bridge to Canada and to liberty:

> De hounds are baying on my track,
> Ole Master comes behind,
> Resolved that he will bring me back,
> Before I cross the line;
> I'm now embarked for yonder shore,
> Where a man's a man by law,
> De iron horse will bear me o'er,
> To 'shake de lion's paw;'
> Oh, righteous Father, wilt thou not pity me
> But carry me to Canada where the slaves are free.[26]

---

[25] 'Song of the Abolitionist.' Words by WL Garrison. Tune – 'Old Lang Syne.'
1. I am an Abolitionist! I glory in the name;
Though now by slavery's minions hissed, And covered o'er with shame;
It is a spell of light and power, The watch-word of the free;
Who spurns it in the trial-hour, A craven soul is he.
2. I am an Abolitionist! Then urge me not to pause,
For joyfully do I enlist In Freedom's sacred cause;
A nobler strife the world ne'er saw, Th'enslaved to disenthral;
I am a soldier for the war, Whatever may befall.
3. I am an Abolitionist! Oppression's deadly foe;
In God's great strength will I resist, And lay the monster low;
In God's great name do I demand, To all be freedom given,
That peace and joy may fill the land, And songs go up to heaven.
4. I am an Abolitionist! No threats shall awe my soul;
No perils cause me to desist, No bribes my acts control;
A freeman will I live and die, In sunshine and in shade,
And raise my voice for liberty, Of nought on earth afraid.

[26] Sarah H Bradford, *Harriet: The Moses of Her People* (New York: George Lockwood & Sons, 1886), p.50. Harriet Tubman (née Araminta Ross ca 1822–1913). She escaped slavery herself and rescued over 70 slaves through the network of the Underground Railway and prepared the intelligence for a major raid which freed some 700 more. At the end of her life, she was active as a Suffragist. She will feature on the USA's proposed redesign of the $20 bill in 2030.

During the long period of debate and campaign against slavery in the run-up to the Civil War and its consequential Emancipation, Burns was used repeatedly and forcefully to bolster Abolitionist rhetoric by Garrisson and others, but amongst all those voices, one man in particular cleaved to Burns and his words as a beacon of freedom: Frederick Douglass.

The 19th Century: A Hero For Our Time – the Black Douglass

The leader in quoting Burns as inspiration for Emancipation was the great Black orator and transatlantic campaigner: the once enslaved Frederick Douglass, who travelled the length and breadth of the USA and the British Isles in his quest to free his fellow human beings.

> In Scotland, too, renowned in her struggles for liberty by the heroic deeds of Wallace and Bruce, and his own great prototype Douglass, a land illustrious in poetic associations with Burns the ploughman poet, and Walter Scott of Abbotsford – there from the elite of Edinburgh and Glasgow, as also the peasantry of Loch Katrine, 'O'er hill and dale,/ By the bonnie highland heather,' in contrast with the awards of Republican America, Frederick Douglass was honored, as the language of Scotia's own bard proclaimed, 'A man for a' that.'[27]

It is hard to précis such an eventful life as Douglass's: born into enslavement in 1818 in Maryland and named Frederick Bailey, he first worked as a house servant and was briefly taught the alphabet by his slave-holder's wife before her husband forbad any further education as likely to cause future 'trouble.' So, Frederick secretly taught himself to read and write, and was able in time to study an anthology of essays and speeches called *The Columbian Orator*.[28] He was sub-hired to a generous plantation owner who held a Sabbath School for his enslaved workers, but his slave-holder disapproved of these ameliorist policies and in time took him back, hiring him out in 1833 to a more typical

---

27 William Cooper Nell, 'Reception of Frederick Douglass at the Belknap-street Church, Boston, 3 May 1847,' in *Liberator* (21 May 1847).
28 Caleb Bingham, ed, *The Columbian Orator: Containing a Variety of Original and Selected Pieces, Together with Rules, Calculated to Improve Youth and Others in the Ornamental and Useful Art of Eloquence* (Boston: JHA Frost, 1832). Around the same time, Abraham Lincoln was also studying this volume.

and violent farmer named Edward Covey (1806–1875) who sought to 'break' Douglass through overwork and repeated heavy whippings. One day Frederick turned on Covey and in a lengthy brawl, knocked him down, giving him hope that escape might be possible. In 1838, with the help of a free Black woman called Anna Murray (1813–1882), he fled on a circuitous route to New York where Anna joined him and where they married.

The next year they moved to New Bedford, Massachusetts, meeting the Black Abolitionist Nathan Johnston (1797–1880) who enjoyed Scottish literature and introduced Frederick to the poetry of Burns and Walter Scott. Bedford had been reading *The Lady of the Lake*, and suggested Frederick and Anna adopt the surname 'Douglass' after one of the poem's heroes (and Bruce's lieutenant, 'Guid Sir James,' or 'The Black Douglas') to help hide them from his legal slave-holder.

In 1839 Douglass was licensed to preach in the American Methodist Episcopalian Zion Church, and in 1841 his association with William Lloyd Garrison started when he took up a position as an anti-slavery advocate travelling around the Free States lecturing on Abolition. His physical presence, rhetorical flourish and argumentative skill soon made him both prominent and newsworthy, and stood to disprove the racist statement that all Black people were intellectually inferior to their White 'masters.'[29]

Robert Burns's life and his poetry were inspirational to the young, free Douglass. In fact, the first book he bought after fleeing the South was a copy of Burns's poems. It is a copy of the one-volume Philadelphia edition and it became his talisman. This book can be seen today in the collection of the University of Rochester Library. It bears these inscriptions in Douglass's handwriting:

recto	verso
To Lewis H Douglass from his affectionate Father – Fred^k Douglass Oct 15, 1867.	This book was the first bought by me after my escape from slavery. I have owned it for thirty-one years and now give it to my son as a keep sake. F D.

---

[29] Pettinger, pp.7–15.

Burns's poems, being an expression of the love of liberty penned by an ordinary man with his ups-and-downs of fate, captured Douglass, and as he read more about the poet and his life he became, in his own words, 'an enthusiastic admirer of Rob[er]t Burns.'[30] John Stauffer captures the symbiosis between Douglass and Burns: '[b]oth men had been born poor, were oppressed by elite Whites and treated like brutes, and found in language a way to remake themselves and build a vision of humanity.'[31] This admiration had a strongly practical aspect, too, as increasingly he adopted quotations from the poet within his core rhetoric, echoing and amplifying the poet's use within the wider movement (as shown in the quotations above).

Douglass became a prominent speaker in the broad alliance of Abolitionist groups, and this led Douglass to write the first of his biographies, *The Narrative of the Life of Frederick Douglass, An American Slave*, in 1845. Its success was such that his friends were nervous of his re-capture (under the Fugitive Slave Act) and so he was sent on a mission to the British Isles between August 1845 and November 1846 in order both to distance himself from bounty-hunters and to campaign against the new Free Church of Scotland's funding by Southern slave-holders. This opportunity had a particular resonance for Douglass as it would enable him to visit Scotland and, more particularly, to see for himself the birthplace of Robert Burns.

It is his generous welcome across Scotland that adds to our understanding of Douglass in relation to Burns. Not only did he quote Burns on a regular basis, but others called out the visitor's rational affection for Scotland's national poet. Revd George Gilfillan of Dundee (1813–1878), himself a Burns scholar and minor poet, called his guest 'the most powerful of natural orators, the self-taught, the Burns of the African race,' and gifted him a volume of the Bard's works.[32] In terms of his admiration for Burns, the highlight of the

---

30 Frederick Douglass, 'A Fugitive Slave Visiting the Birthplace of Robert Burns,' *Albany Evening Journal* (13 June 1846).

31 John Stauffer, *Giants: The Parallel Lives of Frederick Douglass and Abraham Lincoln* (New York: Twelve Books, 2008), p.125.

32 Quoted in Pettinger, pp.139, 143. Douglass's library is preserved at his final home, Cedar Hill, Anacostia, MD, now the Frederick Douglass National Historic Site. It holds two further copies of Burns's works owned by Douglass: Revd George Gilfillan, ed, *The Poetical Works of Robert Burns, With Memoir, Critical Dissertation and Explanatory Notes*, 2 vols (Edinburgh/London/Dublin: James Nicol/James Nisbet/W Robertson, 1856) [Egerer §595] and *The Complete Poetical Works of Robert Burns with Explanatory and Glossarial Notes and a Life of the Author*, by James Currie MD (New

speaking tour was surely his visit to Ayr. He addressed two rallies at the Relief Church ('Cathcart Church') and took time to not only visit Burns Cottage and Burns Monument, but to call on Isabella Burns Begg (Burns's 80-year-old sister) (1771–1858) and her daughters at their home in Alloway.[33]

The church was full for both of his addresses, and the audience heard Douglass praise Burns in his homeland:

> he was proud of having been in the land of him who had spoken out so nobly against the oppressions and wrongs of slavery – he alluded, of course, to Robert Burns.[34]

He wrote feelingly about Burns afterwards to his Quaker friend, Abigail Mott.[35] This letter was printed in the Albany papers and widely copied. He used this open letter to make a thinly coded attack on contemporary slave-holding society in the States:

> I have ever esteemed Robert Burns a true soul [...] Burns lived in the midst of a bigoted and besotted clergy — a pious, but corrupt generation — a proud, ambitious, and contemptuous aristocracy, who, esteemed a little more than a man, and looked upon the plowman, such as was the noble Burns, as being little better than a brute. He became disgusted with the pious frauds, indignant at the bigotry, filled with contempt for the hollow pretensions set up by the shallow-brained aristocracy. He broke loose from the moorings which society had thrown around him. [...] The elements of character which urge him on are in us all, and influencing our conduct every day of our lives. We may pity him, but we can't despise him. We may condemn his faults, but only as we condemn our own. His very weakness was an index of his strength. Full of faults of a grievous nature, yet far

---

York: D Appleton, 1842) [Not in Egerer, though the second edition of this printing is at §455]. A print of 'Tam o'Shanter' is still hung in his bedroom. www.nps.gov/frdo/learn/historyculture/upload/Books-in-FDS-library.pdf (accessed 1 September 2024).
33 Frederick Douglass, 'A Few Facts and Personal Observations of Slavery: An Address Delivered in Ayr, Scotland on March 24, 1846,' from *Ayr Advertiser*, 26 March 1846, in John Blassingame et al, eds, *The Frederick Douglass Papers: Series One — Speeches, Debates, and Interviews* (New Haven: Yale University Press, 1979), vol.I, p.195.
34 Relief Church, Cathcart Street, Ayr, 23 March 1846, reported in *Ayr Observer*, 31 March 1846.
35 Abigail Lydia Motte Moore (1795–1846): American educator who founded the Rochester Anti-Slavery Society in 1838 and was an active Abolitionist for the rest of her life.

more faultless than many who have come down to us in the pages of history as saints.[36]

Here we see the image of Scotia, not Columbia, as being 'the sweet land of liberty' emanating from the pen of Burns, the ordinary ploughman poet. This was a classic image used extensively both in the US and in the UK by prominent Abolitionists, but which Douglass had now made into a personal trope. The speaking tour was a success on many levels and cemented the view of Douglass in the public mind, with his quotations from Burns being particularly noted. As Douglass (appropriately) wrote to a friend about his emotions on returning to the US from Scotland, 'Kings may be blest, but I was glorious/ O'er all the ills of life victorious.'[37]

Douglass quoted many writers, poets and thinkers in his speeches and lectures, but Burns is ubiquitous: from Douglass's early platform performances up to his death through a heart attack in 1895 after speaking to a meeting on Women's rights, Burns is both inspiration and exemplar for him. Burns spoke to Douglass about what the essentials of humanity were, not just in individual silos such as slavery or women's rights, but overarchingly and philosophically in common humanity as well. This can be best seen on reading one of his most repeated general lectures called 'Self-made Men,' which he first gave in 1859 and delivered on many occasions, as late as 1893.[38] In this long address, he looks to a world where neither race nor birth defines a person's advancement in civil society. In drawing out his argument, he uses four quotations from Burns, and additionally apostrophises him as 'Scotia's matchless son of song.' His argument is captured in the following passage towards the end of his lecture:

> But the respectability of labor is not, as already intimated, the only or the most powerful cause of the facility with which men rise from humble conditions to affluence and importance in the United States. A more subtle and powerful influence is exerted by

---

36 Douglass, *Birthplace*.
37 Quoted in Pettinger, p.142 (note 1).
38 Frederick Douglass, 'Self-Made Men,' in John Blassingame and John McKivigan IV, eds, *The Frederick Douglass Papers, Series One, Vol. 5* (New Haven: Yale University Press, 1992), pp.545–575. There are two quotations from 'The Twa Dogs', and one each from 'Tam o'Shanter' and 'Honest Poverty.' An edited text can be found at Appendix IIC.

the fact that the principle of measuring and valuing men according to their respective merits and without regard to their antecedents, is better established and more generally enforced here than in any other country. In Europe, greatness is often thrust upon men. They are made legislators by birth.

> A king can make a belted knight,
> A marquis, duke and a' that.

But here, wealth and greatness are forced by no such capricious and arbitrary power. Equality of rights brings equality of positions and dignities.[39]

It can be no coincidence that he gathered these thoughts first in Burns's centenary year. For Frederick Douglass, his own journey echoed his (slightly romanticised) recollection of Burns's short life, guided by their common view that 'a man's man, for a' that,' a sentiment he would continue to use until the end of his campaigning life. However, before that day, America must fall into the carnage of its Civil War.

The 19th Century: In Word and Deed – the American Civil War[40]

It is commonplace, when thinking of Scotland and the American Civil War of 1861 to 1865, to make reference to Mark Twain's observation that the war between the North and the South reflected a conflict between the philosophies of Robert Burns and Sir Walter Scott, pitting modern, progressive equality against antiquated, reactionary chivalry. However, neat as this soundbite is, the facts around the reception and use of Burns within that war is significantly more complex.[41]

As discussed, Burns's poems were avidly read in the USA in newspapers and the pirate editions which followed some few months after each legitimate printing, so by the Burns Centenary, the celebration of Scotland's poet had been firmly embedded in American

---

39 Ibid, p.574.
40 This section is an expanded discussion of a topic first approached in the author's article 'Early Burns Suppers in the USA,' *Burns Chronicle* (Summer 2010), pp.19–24.
41 Twain did attack Scott, but did not formulate the exact conceit of North vs South equals Burns vs Scott. Mark Twain, *Life on the Mississippi* (Boston: James A Osgood and Company, 1883), p.469.

culture for nearly 50 years, both through reading and singing his works, and also by the convivial toasting of his memory at Burns Suppers.[42] The secular worship of Burns extended to over 70 Burns events in January 1859, spanning east to west across 23 of the 33 admitted states, along with Nevada Territory and Washington, DC.

Table 11: Burns Centenary Celebrations Across the Antebellum USA, 1859			
CELEBRATIONS IN SLAVE STATES/DISTRICTS		CELEBRATIONS IN FREE STATES/TERRITORIES	
Alabama	1	California	3
Texas	1	New Hampshire	1
Georgia	1	Connecticut	3
Virginia	1	New Jersey	2
Louisiana	1	Illinois	5
Washington, DC	2	New York	17
Maryland	2	Iowa	2
Mississippi	1	Ohio	2
Missouri	1	Massachusetts	10
South Carolina	1	Pennsylvania	6
		Michigan	3
		Rhode Island	3
		Minnesota	1
		Wisconsin	2
		Nevada	1
9 States (plus DC) with 12 Celebrations		15 States with 61 Celebrations	
TOTAL: 24 States (plus DC) with 73 Celebrations			

As the chairman of the St Louis, MO dinner described the international reception of Burns:

> It was not left to Scotchmen alone to commemorate the man. Burns belongs to no nation. Humanity claims and loves him. The hundreds of Americans assembled, if a correct analysis of their estimate of Burns could be made, would find that deeper than their admiration of the unrivalled genius of the poet lay a home-like affection for the loving-hearted manly Robert Burns.[43]

---

42 McGinn, *Comprehensive*, pp.80–101; Arun Sood, *Robert Burns and the United States of America. Poetry, Print and Memory 1786–1866* (London: Palgrave Macmillan, 2018).
43 James Ballantine, *Chronicle of the Hundredth Birthday of Robert Burns* (Edinburgh/London: A

But, of course, at Missouri's dinner, that 'humanity' did not extend across the barriers of race. Burns's open humanity was vouchsafed in other contexts, perhaps most memorably by the abolitionist clergyman (and brother of Harriet Beecher Stowe) Revd Henry Ward Beecher, who addressed Burns's Jamaica chapter forthrightly in New York:

> He had got into great trouble. [...] and he had determined, as the last resort of a broken-down and discouraged man, to go to Jamaica as the overseer of a plantation. I think I see Robert Burns on a plantation, with a whip under his arm. I think I see Robert Burns following a gang of slaves, and chanting 'A man's a man for a' that.' Poor Burns was in a very bad way, but he was not as bad as that.[44]

Here, Beecher captures the easiest of the Apologies for Burns: with his back to the wall, and without understanding the ground rules, he would have emigrated but on arrival and in seeing the horror, like Zachary Macauley, he would have been revolted.

The American participants in the Burns Centennial reflected the politics and fault lines that would break the country apart two years later. The New York Burns Club, at dinner after Beecher's address, read a letter from President Buchanan (who remains, even with contemporary competition, one of the weakest US presidents).[45] The President sent his warm admiration in words rather clearer than his political messages:

> Poor Burns! I have always deplored his hard fate. He has ever been a favorite of mine. The child of genius and of misfortune, he is read every where and by all classes throughout the extent of our country, and his natural pathos has reached all hearts.[46]

Fullerton & Co, 1859), pp.549–605.
44 Henry Ward Beecher, 'Robert Burns: A Centennial Oration at the Cooper Union,' in Ballantine, *Chronicle*, p.580. Revd Henry Ward Beecher (1813–1887): Congregationalist minister, orator and campaigner.
45 James Buchanan Jr (1791–1868), 15th President of the USA (1857–1861). A Democrat, but strong on 'States Rights.'
46 J Cunningham, ed, *The Centennial Birth-day of Robert Burns, as Celebrated by the Burns Club of the City of New York* (New York: Lang & Lang, 1860), p.48.

He also telegraphed the dinner at Washington DC, honouring 'Robert Burns, the child of impulse, and of genius.'[47] For those politicians who had not joined the President on the fence, the Immortal Memory speech in Springfield, IL was pronounced by his successor-to-be, Abraham Lincoln while, with no apparent irony after having been served dinner by Black chattel slaves in Washington DC, the slave-holding Senator James Pearce of Maryland called on Speaker James Lawrence Orr of the House of Representatives, another leading pro-slavery politician and slave-holder, to speak 'for America and the devotion of her sons to Burns in that fervid strain characteristic of South Carolina orators,' and later lead the company in singing 'Auld Lang Syne.'[48] From the highest to the lowest citizen, across the states and territories, Burns was praised and loved. During 1859 and in the Januaries of 1860 and 1861 there was no appreciable adoption of Burns as an exclusive spokesman for either side of the impending war. As Professor Nairne of Columbia College speaking in New York avowed, 'The South is quite as enthusiastic for Burns as the North.'[49]

The election of Lincoln as President in November 1860 brought a lover of Burns and his egalitarian ideas to the White House and to the brink of War. However, the firing on Fort Sumter, which opened the conflict, did not result in a monopoly of Burns's readers, singers and dinners being north of the Mason-Dixon line. Much has been written about Burns's influence on Lincoln as a great poet inspiring a great orator, or as two like-minded men of humble birth seeking to promote the brotherhood of man. His love of Burns was longstanding: as a circuit lawyer in Illinois, 'a copy of Burns was his constant companion,' while White House evenings were enlivened by the President's readings and recitations.[50] Lincoln was regularly invited to Burns Suppers, but after

---

47 Anon, *Celebration of the Centennial Anniversary of the Birth of Robert Burns, by the Burns Club of Washington City, DC* (Washington DC: Joseph Shillington, 1859), p.7.
48 'The Centennial Anniversary of the Birth of Robert Burns, Celebrated in Springfield, January 25, 1859,' *Journal of the Illinois State Historical Society*, vol.17 (April–July 1924), pp.205–210; Ballantine, pp.604, 605. Speaker Orr's portrait was removed in 2020 on the orders of Speaker Pelosi (along with three others) as '[t]here is no room in the hallowed halls of Congress or in any place of honor for memorializing men who embody the violent bigotry and grotesque racism of the Confederacy.'
49 Ballantine, *Chronicle*, p.591. Charles Murray Nairne (1808–1882): Born in Perth, graduated from St Andrews and emigrated to New York in 1847, marrying a wealthy lady from Virginia. From 1857 to 1881 he was Professor of Moral and Intellectual Philosophy and Literature at Columbia College (Columbia University from 1896), NY.
50 Ferenc Morton Szasz, *Abraham Lincoln and Robert Burns: Connected Lives and Legends*

toasting the Immortal Memory at Springfield, IL in 1859 he usually declined to speak at these events. The last and most poignant was a request to toast Burns at the Washington Burns Club in January 1865; the President sent his apologies, in the often-anthologised sentiment, saying that 'I can say nothing worthy of his [Burns's] generous heart and transcending genius.'[51] Eighty days later he was dead.

But just as the Federal President could recite the Ayrshire bard from memory, so too, could the Confederates' President, Jefferson Davis.[52] Despite his opposite politics, he found equal comfort in the Ayrshireman's words and works as a young law student and later as a statesman, saying years later, 'what dear old memories rise at the names intimately associated with Scotland's and nature's sweet singer.'[53]

The unfolding events of 1861 drew many men from the companionship of the Burns Supper to the colours of their respective States. Amongst those who took up arms, the Union army had the 79th New York Volunteer Highlanders and the 12th Illinois Volunteers ('The First Scotch'), who had marched in New York's and Chicago's Burns Centenary celebrations respectively; meanwhile the Confederacy deployed the Union Light Infantry and the 1st South Carolina Battalion's Highland Guard who had provided honor guards at Charleston's Burns Centenary.[54] Notable Burnsians took commanding military roles, such as Speaker Orr, now Colonel Orr of 1st South Carolina (or 'Orr's') Rifles, and Colonel Robert G 'Bob' Ingersoll, the freethinking Burns aficionado, at the head of his 11th Illinois Volunteer

---

(Carbondale: Southern Illinois University Press, 2008), p.63, quoting William Dean Howells. Milton Hay, a clerk to Lincoln's practice in Springfield, IL, said that Lincoln could recite, from memory, 'Tam o'Shanter,' 'Holy Willie's Prayer,' 'most of The Cottar's Saturday Night,' 'Death and Doctor Hornbook,' 'The Address to the Deil,' 'Highland Mary,' and 'Bonnie Jean,' ibid.

51 *Washington Evening Star*, 26 January 1865; Abraham Lincoln, *The Collected Works of Abraham Lincoln*, 10 vols, ed by Roy Prentice Basler (Brunswick: Rutgers University Press, 1959), vol.VIII, p.237. Burns and Lincoln are magnets for myth. James Duff Law (1865–1928), a Scots emigrant, entrepreneur and writer claimed in his memoir of Scots influence in the USA that 'The late Tom Donaldson, of Philadelphia, told the writer that Lincoln told Donaldson that Lincoln got the idea of negro emancipation from "A Man's a Man for a' That."' James D Law, *Here and There in Two Hemispheres* (Lancaster, PA: The Home Publishing Company, 1903), p.251.

52 Jefferson F Davis (1808–1889): American politician, being the first and only President of the Confederate States of America (1861–1865).

53 Jefferson Davis, *Scotland & the Scottish People: An Address Delivered in the City of Memphis, Tennessee on St Andrew's-Day, 1875* (Glasgow: Anderson and Mackay, 1876), p.15.

54 Ballantine, *Chronicle*, pp.564, 560.

Cavalry.[55] As the country split in conflict, the works of Burns could be found in both grey and in blue pockets: if brothers could fight each other, so could Burnsians.[56] In the early days of the war, many described the *casus belli* as 'State's Rights' under the Constitution, but the reason behind those States seceding was clearly the question of Slavery. Garrison was (as ever) blunt:

> WHAT THE WAR IS: — Let it be clearly understood by men of all parties that the war is—not a war of aggression, or of its own seeking, on the part of the National Government, but purely of self-defence, and for SELF-PRESERVATION — a war not to subjugate THE PEOPLE of the South, but to crush a desperate and traitorous SLAVE OLIGARCHY, who despise popular rights, and who have not dared to submit the Constitution of their New Confederacy to the verdict of Southern votes; a war for the illimitable extension and unenduring existence of a system which turns millions of God's rational creatures into beasts and merchandise, and for the overthrow of all free institutions, and the subversion of the Declaration of Independence on the part of the conspirators. Surely all honest, upright, patriotic citizens, can have but one opinion about it. Surely never before could a people, in taking up arms to defend all that is dear to them, and put down a tyrannical usurpation, more appropriately use the words of Burns:
>
> Who would be a traitor knave? [...]
> Let us do or die.[57]

Of course, one constituency favoured the Union: the enslaved men themselves were actors in the war, with Douglass exhorting them, in Burns's tone, to 'go and be a sodger,'

---

[55] JW Mattison, 'Orr's South Carolina Rifles,' *Southern Historical Society Papers*, 27 (1899), pp.157–165. Ingersoll visited Burns Cottage in 1878, writing his frequently anthologised 'The Birthplace of Robert Burns.' Robert G Ingersoll, *The Works of Robert G Ingersoll*, 13 vols, ed by CP Farrell (New York: CP Farrell, 1900), vol.III, pp.119–120.

[56] There are many contemporary references to soldiers in the field reading or singing Burns, for example Lloyd A Hunter, ed, *For Duty and Destiny: The Life and Civil War Diary of William Taylor Stott, Hoosier Soldier and Educator* (Indianapolis: Indiana Historical Society Press, 2010), pp.266–268.

[57] Quoted in Peter Sinclair, *Freedom or Slavery in the United States* (London: J Cauldwell, 1861), pp.39–40.

If you are sound in body and mind, there is nothing in your color to excuse you from enlisting in the service of the Republic against its enemies. If color should not be a criterion of rights, neither should it be a standard of duty. The whole duty of a man, belongs alike to white and Black. 'A man's a man for a' that'. [...] So much for insisting that, both on the ground of principle and consistency, the 'self-evident truths' contained in the Declaration of Independence ought to be reduced to practice, and that, whatever may be the color of his skin, 'a man's a man for a' that'![58]

Over the four years of attrition, the works of Robert Burns brought solace to the fighting men of both sides. A Scots engineer, Sir William Allan (1837–1903), had a particularly conflicted interaction with the war, being captured and imprisoned by Federal troops in 1861 as one of the many Scots blockade runners supporting the South (purely for financial gain), yet later writing poetically and supportively about emancipation. In later life, he recalled hearing 'soldiers of the Union, and Confederate, armies singing our Scotch songs.'[59] Some years later he captured that in one of his own poems:

> Where far Columbia's lonely forests wave,
> I've seen thy spirit brooding o'er the brave,
> Then every breast was filled with courage high,
> And every heart felt but to 'do or die,'
> Inspired to battle-deeds which shook the world
> Till Slavery's flag low in the dust was hurled;
> Oft by the Potomac's dark-rolling streams, —
> Columbia's patriot sons beheld thy dreams,
> And felt the sacred fire of Freedom glow,
> Which conquering laid 'the proud usurpers low,'
> And swept away 'Oppression's woes and pains,'
> While freemen's hands struck off all 'servile chains.' [60]

---

58 Frederick Douglass, 'Why Should the Colored Man Enlist?', *FD Douglass's Monthly*, April 1863. His son Lewis H Douglass (1840–1908), who had received his father's *Burns's Works* two years before, enlisted in the 54th Massachusetts Infantry in March 1863, was promoted to Sergeant-major and was discharged due to serious injury incurred at the Second Battle of Fort Wagner that July.
59 See 'Sir William Allan MP' in Catherine W Reilly, *Mid-Victorian Poetry 1860–1879* (London: Mansell, 2000), p.10.
60 William Allan, *A Book of Poems: Democratic Chants and Songs in English and Scottish*

Letters home and journals of officers and men in both armies often contained quotations or references to Burns and his works, sometimes comforting, sometimes to emphasise their just cause, or all-to-often to recognise 'man's inhumanity to man.' Indeed, that particular quotation (which will be picked up a century later, as discussed below) is one of the few literary digressions of General Ulysses S Grant, who was overheard reciting it while watching a column of wounded men after the battle of Fort Donelson.[61] Also, the Burns Supper tradition was maintained in the field: the New York Highlanders celebrated 'the anniversary of Burnes [sic] birth day' at Fredericksburg in January 1863, and in Tennessee the following year where:

> down yonder in Eastern Tennessee amongst the serried hosts of warriors, [is] the camp of the 79th Highlanders, [...] engaged with us in celebrating the natal day of the favorite Poet by the light of their camp fires — and surrounded by all the paraphernalia of war.[62]

Certainly, Burns Suppers continued at home both in the North and the South, although those at table remembered their 'absent friends,' such as the Burns Club No 1 of Schuylkill County, PA whose dinner numbers were depleted by the absent members 'serving their adopted country in the army of the Union,' in January 1862.[63] That same year Lieutenant-Colonel Patrick of the 5th Ohio Volunteer Infantry telegraphed his friends at the Cincinnati Burns Club with the traditional greeting of 'gude night an' joy be wi' ye all' on the night of their supper, and their Poet Laureate, John Proudfoot, responded with an 'updated' 'Scots Wha Hae'.[64] Again, we find both sides appealing to Burns equally (as they would each pray to God, steadfast in their beliefs of righteous support for their respective causes). Below are two reworkings of the great 'Battle Hymn of the Scots' each catching the frisson of the defender against tyrannical might, proving that the same raw materials can be used to create antithetical products.

(Sunderland: Hills, 1891), pp.67–68.
61 Ron Chernow, *Grant* (London: Head of Zeus, 2017), p.181.
62 Terry A Johnston, Jr, ed, *Him on the One Side and Me on the Other: The Civil War Letters of Alexander Campbell, 79th New York Infantry Regiment, and James Campbell, 1st South Carolina Battalion* (Columbia: USC Press, 1999), pp.124–125. These brothers left Crieff for the USA; enlisting in the opposing armies, they faced each other in battle at Secessionville in June 1862. *Scottish American Journal* [New York, NY], 30 January 1864.
63 *Weekly Miners' Journal* (Pottsville, PA), 1 February 1862.
64 *Cincinnati Commercial Tribune*, 27 January 1862.

The South
A Parody on 'Scots Wha Ha'e.'
[by] 'C': Feb'y 1st, 1862[65]

Sons of SECESSIA glorious *land*!
Sons of The South — noble band;
Proudly keep your gallant stand,
    On to Victory.

Now's the day, and now's the hour;
See the front of battle lower;
See approach fanatic Lincoln's power,
    Chains and Slavery.

By the dearest human ties,
By the starving ORPHAN'S cries,
We must strike for Freedom, and rise —
    And they shall be Free.

Lay those Vandal hordes low;
Tyrants fall in every foe;
Liberty's in every blow —
    Strike for Victory!

Who, will be a TRAITOR knave?
Who, will fill a COWARD'S grave?
Who, so base as be a Yankee's slave?
    Let him turn and flee!

Who, in this STRUGGLE would pause?
Let him read *Our Righteous Laws* —
Let him join our Southern Cause,
    For we SHALL be Free!

Scots Wha Hae
John Proudfoot[66]

Scots wha hae come here to bide!
Scots whase sires for freedom died!
Up! and in your country's pride
    Strike for Libertie!

Now the South rebellious rears!
See! its servile army dares!
Hark! the traitor Davis swears,
    'Long live Slaverie!'

Wha can neutral stand a fool?
Wha submit to sic misrule?
Wha wink at or be the tool
    Of base Tyrannie?

Wha's for Union, order, law?
Wha's for freedom gi'en to a'?
Let him glorious stand or fa',
    Ranked with braverie!

By Fort Sumter, by our slain.
By oppression's cruel chain,
We shall frae our flag the stain
    Wipe eternallie!

Lay the proud enslavers low!
Rebels fall in every foe!
Heaven and justice nerve the blow!
    On to victorie!

After four gruelling years of internecine combat, Lincoln and the North prevailed and General Lee met General Grant at Appomattox Courthouse to accept the Confederate surrender on 9 April 1865. Afterwards, as the South's generalissimo mounted his horse Traveler to leave the field, Grant instructed the Union Army band to strike up 'Auld Lang Syne.'[67] Again, both sides sought solace in Burns, now more sombrely recalling the cost, his words 'Man's inhumanity to man/ Makes countless thousands mourn!' remembering a staggering

---
65 Anon, *Broadside*, (np: np, [1862]), Duke University Libraries, Conf Pam 12mo #803.
66 John Proudfoot, *The Scotchman in America* (Cleveland: Fairbanks, Benedict, 1873), pp.214-215. John Proudfoot (1802-1888): a housepainter who emigrated from Dumfries to Cleveland, OH in the late 1830s. Founder and poet-laureate of the Cleveland St Andrew's Society (1840) and the Cleveland Burns Club (1849).
67 Grant, p.510.

620,000 casualties in four years.[68] And then, weeks later, one final tragic death – the assassination of the Burns-quoting President, Lincoln himself.

Jefferson Davis was captured (ironically by one Captain Robert Burns) and held in military prison while the Federal Government debated whether he should face murder or treason charges in court. When asked about his fate, Davis calmly quoted from Burns's 'Address to the Unco Guid,' beginning '[w]ho knows the heart — it's He alone,/ Decidedly can try us'.[69] It is said that Lincoln had planned to visit Scotland and the Burns shrines after stepping down from his office and it was left to his widow, Mary Todd Lincoln (1818–1882), to perform that pilgrimage to Alloway in 1869. She was followed in 1874 by Jefferson Davis, who found that the poet's nieces, the Misses Begg, had put his portrait up in the Cottage and invited him to stay for tea. President Grant, three years later, had to make do with the Freedom of the Burgh.[70]

Joseph DuRant, in an interesting article on the use of Burns by both sides in the Civil War, pondered:

> Looking back at these uses of Burns and seeing the differences in the North and South of a nation on the cusp of a terribly bloody conflict holds a special resonance. Today's readers of Burns hold many different pictures of the poet in their minds. This is one of the most fascinating characteristics of Burns: his ability to speak to a wide range of people. Clearly the readers of the *Daily Dispatch* and the *Anti-Slavery Bugle* gravitated towards different aspects of the same man. Their reasons clearly seem to justify their different ways of life. Burnsian might, upon seeing this, ask themselves what aspects of Burns they see that are reflected in their own values. Is our own Burns the 'true Burns' or is he simply the Burns that is true to us?[71]

---

68 Amanda Foreman, *World on Fire: Britain's Crucial Role in the American Civil War* (London: Random House, 2010), pp.791–792. This figure is the formally accepted number of fatalities, however, there are views that the total could have been much higher at 750,000–800,000. In context, the 620K is higher than the combined casualty list of US forces in the 20th century: WWI (117k), WWII (405k), Korea (37k) and Vietnam (58k).
69 John J Craven, *The Prison Life of Jefferson Davis* (New York: Carleton Publisher, 1867), p.297.
70 Davis, p.16. His tour guide was the noted Burnsian journalist and editor Charles Mackay (1814–1889), who had been the vocal pro-South correspondent for *The Times* during the war.
71 Joseph DuRant, 'Robert Burns in Mid-Nineteenth Century American Newspapers,' *Burns Chronicle* (2016), p.33.

After the Civil War and the period of 'Reconstruction', a wider global political and social consensus formed: first, slavery became completely unimaginable as a concept (then, in turn, the Walter Scott 'chivalry' of 'Dixie' (the Confederacy) became equally unsupportable, a process which is reaching its culmination today in the US with the removal of many contested Confederate memorials and the renaming of streets which had honoured slave-holders. Therefore, the support and love that the Confederates had for Burns started to be airbrushed out (as was the significant level of support from Scotland for the South during the hostilities) and the conceit of Burns and Lincoln as brothers in philosophy, poetry, and a tragically shortened life became the understood truth. The Union rightly won the war and with it, the argument against slavery, and Burns's 'Honest Poverty' was its theme. General Matthew Trumbull (1826–1894) of the 9th Iowa Cavalry was a Scottish Chartist who had abandoned Britain as a young man to find the political life in the New World that he could not achieve in the Old. He described this arc of history in 1889:

> 'A man's a man for a' that,' is the American Declaration of Independence condensed into the poetry of Scotland. The inspiration and the doctrine of both productions is the equality of man. I have seen the Declaration of Independence criticized not only for its diction but for its politics too. I have seen fifty thousand critics in a line criticizing it with shot and shell and musketry. What of it? When their criticism ended, the flag born of the declaration streamed above their speechless cannon, and from every star in its brilliant constellation there shone upon the world the gospel of the new political testament: 'All men are created equal;' 'A man's a man for a' that.'[72]

Thus the 'Star o' Rabbie Burns' joined the constellation of the 'Star Spangled Banner' and as the late-Victorian trend of simplification of Burns worship smoothed out dangerous inconsistencies in the Bard's story (around Highland Mary, his adultery and his finances as well as the Jamaica plan) it was natural that his life and works were remembered as solely buttressing Lincoln's memory and legacy.

---

[72] Kenneth L Lyftogt, *Iowa's Forgotten General: Matthew Mark Trumbull and the Civil War* (Iowa City: University of Iowa Press, 2005), p.xi.

However, this chapter again shows that the life of Burns and his global reception is often significantly more complex than we remember, as both sides in the Civil War had used Burns as their inspiration. That being said, the enthusiastic use of Burns as an icon of freedom and humanity by so many Black and White anti-slavery advocates shows how his words inspired others to seek, and ultimately achieve, freedom.

Postbellum to the World War: Winning the Wars, Losing the Peace

The postbellum United States saw the end of slavery, yet failed to find equal justice across racial lines. Douglass and the next generation of activists still had a litany of wrongs and abuses to overcome: 'Jim Crow' laws, segregation and the horrors of lynching each affected the lives of every Black person (and other minorities in other ways) virtually every day regardless of their new-gained constitutional freedom.

Again, their advocacy and oratory found solace and power in the words of Burns. Douglass remained active until the day of his death in 1895, but he was joined again by many others whose names are recorded in the history of the fight for equality, with Burns's 'a man's a man' remaining a prominent slogan. In the six decades following the Civil War, virtually every prominent leader in the Civil Rights movement continued to use Robert Burns's words to communicate the simple message of equality.[73]

---

[73] Although not exclusively, as Sood reminds us, the Ku Kux Klan ('KKK') used Burnsian elements (and influences from Sir Walter Scott) in their initiation and other ceremonies. Sood, pp.160, 180. However, this was true of a number of fraternal organisations at that period, see McGinn, *Comprehensive*, pp.156–157.

Table 12: Further Rhetorical Use of 'A Man's a Man', 1871–1920

In conclusion the speaker quoted the lines of Burns, so expressive of brotherly humanity, terminating with
'When man to man, the
    world o'er,
Shall brothers be for a' that.'
William Lloyd Garrison, 1865[a]

We hope and trust that the boundary lines of color and race shall be obliterated from the map of common sense, and that every man shall stand on his own merits as a man, and the world shall behold the consummation of the poet's highest hope, that
'Man to man the world o'er
Shall brothers be, an' a' that.'
JT Shuten, 1865[b]

What a commentary on our 'obscure citizens,' who know what it is to be gentlemen in something else besides the name — gentlemen in practice, not only in theory — and who can say with Burns that **'a man's a man for a' that,'** whether his face be as black as midnight or as white as the driven snow.
Lieutenant Henry Ossian Flipper, 1871[c]

Although I am not Robert Burns (laughter) I have always believed with our grand man and poet Burns, whose memory would live, live, live for ages to come, **'The rank is but the guinea stamp, The man's the gowd for a' that.'** (Applause).
Revd Josiah Henson, 1877[cc]

There is but one destiny, it seems to me, left for us, and that is to make ourselves and be made by others a part of the American people in every sense of the word. [...] The American people have their prejudices, but they have other qualities as well. They easily adapt themselves to inevitable conditions, and all their tendency is to progress, enlightenment and to the universal.
  It's comin' yet for a' that,
    That man to man the world   o'er
  Shall brothers be for a' that.
Frederick Douglass, 1883[d]

Races and varieties of the human family appear and disappear, but humanity remains and will remain forever. The American people will one day be truer to this idea than now, and will say with Scotia's inspired son:
  A man's a man for a' that.
Frederick Douglass, 1886[e]

We propose to accomplish our purposes by the peaceful methods of agitation, through the ballot and the courts, but if others use the weapons of violence to combat our peaceful arguments, it is not for us to run away from violence. **A man's a man**, and what is worth having is worth fighting for.
T Thomas Fortune, 1890[f]

The well-rounded college man heeded the principles of true democracy and believed that **'a man's a man for a' that.'** Merit — not wealth or color — is the test of influence and honor.
William H Lewis, 1891[g]

[...] And I do not think it was all blasphemy in Renan when he said Jesus Christ was first of democrats, i.e., a believer in the royalty of the individual, a preacher of the brotherhood of man through the fatherhood of God, a teacher who proved that the lines on which worlds are said to revolve are imaginary, that for all the distinctions of blue blood and black blood and red blood — **a man's a man for a' that.** [...] And the last monster to be throttled forever methinks is race prejudice [...] That the principles of true democracy are founded in universal reciprocity, and that **'a man's a man'** was written when God first stamped His own image and superscription on His child and breathed in his nostrils the breath of life. [....] The slave brother, however, from the land of oppression once saw the celestial beacon and dreamed not that it ever deviated from due North. He believed that somewhere under its beckoning light, lay a far away country where **a man's a man.**
Anna Julia Cooper, 1892[h]

Table 12: Further Rhetorical Use of 'A Man's a Man', 1871–1920	

Let every negro with one spark of love for his race and its future, who believe **'a man's a man for all that and a' that,'** and who, above all, loves its country and its laws, attend the Indignation Meeting.
Wilson B Woodford, 1893[i]
 	
THE JAMAICA ADVOCATE
'A man's a man for a' that.'
Joseph Robert Love, 1894[j]
 	
The fathers of the Reformation had no idea [… that] the broad foundation stone of all human rights, the great democratic principle **'A man's a man, and his own sovereign for a' that'** they did not dare enunciate. They were incapable of drawing up a Declaration of Independence for humanity. Liverpool was the center of slave interests from the days of good Queen Bess to the Abolition of slaves by the British in 1807. […] In 1862, 55 years later, the strongest sympathy evinced for the pro-slavery party in the United States was found in Liverpool. […] But Liverpool has learned that she can prosper without the slave trade or slave labor. […] Here a 'colored' person can ride in any sort of conveyance in any part of the country without being insulted; stop in any hotel or be accommodated in any restaurant one wishes without being refused with contempt; wander into any picture gallery, lecture room, concert hall, theatre or church and receive only the most courteous treatment from officials and fellow sightseers. The privilege of being once in a country where **'A man's a man for a' that,'** is one which can best be appreciated by those Americans whose black skins are a bar to their receiving genuine kindness at home.
Ida B Wells, 1894[k]
 	
I thank God that I have grown to the point where I can sympathize with a white man as much as I can sympathize with a black man. […] To me **'a man's a man for a' that and a' that.'**
Booker T Washington, 1896[l]
	Here in France no one judges a man by his color. The color of the face neither helps nor hinders. **'A man's a man for a' that and a' that.'**
	Booker T Washington, 1899[m]
	
	It was the problem of the privileged class — the question as to whether the state existed for the sole privilege of the king and the king's friends; whether after all ordinary people not well born were really men in the broader meaning of the term. We who were born to sing with Burns, 'The rank is but the guineas stand [sic], **the man's the gawd [sic] for a' that,'** have faint conception of the marvellous hold which the idea of rank, of high birth once held on earth.
	WEB Du Bois, 1900[n]
	
	The caste way of thinking in the South, both as applied to poor whites and to Negroes, he simply could not understand. The weak and the ignorant of all races he despised and had no patience with them. 'But others — **a man's a man,** isn't he?' […] Cresswell replied: 'No, never if he's black, and not always when he's white,' and he stalked away.
	WEB Du Bois, 1911[o]
	
	Mr Scott spoke of the patriotic sacrifices are making to win the war […] God grant that when the battle has been won, […] we will realize the prayer and dream of the sainted Scotch poet **'when man to man the world o'er shall brothers be, for a' that.**
	A W Scott, 1918[p]
	
	Listen to the poet, Robert Burns:
	  For a' that and a' that
	  It's coming yet for a' that,
	  That man to man the world o'er
	  Shall brothers be for a' that.'
	And I believe it.
	Revd H Mickens, 1920[q]

Notes on Table 12: Further Rhetorical Use of 'A Man's a Man', 1871–1920

[a]William Lloyd Garrison, 'Lecture to the Young Men's Association, Chicago,' *Chicago Tribune*, 17 November 1865; [b]J T Shuften (dates uncertain): Black newspaper editor in Atlanta, GA. 'What is a Man?', *The Colored American* [Atlanta, GA], 30 December 1865; [c]Henry Ossian Flipper, *The Colored Cadet at West Point. Autobiography of Lieut[enant] Henry Ossian Flipper, USA, First Graduate of Color from the US Military Academy* (New York: H. Lee & Co, 1878), p.303. Henry Ossian Flipper (1856–1940): Born into slavery in Georgia, after school he became the fifth black cadet at West Point. He persevered against the racism that forced out the other four men, and was commissioned into the 10th US Cavalry, a 'buffalo soldier' unit. In 1881 he was unjustly dismissed from his commission. He worked as an engineer in Latin America, with a brief spell as assistant to the Secretary of the Interior. Posthumously pardoned by President Clinton in 1999, his bust is on display at West Point; [cc]Josiah Henson, Speech at the Mechanics Institute, Dumfries, *Dumfries and Galloway Standard & Advertiser*, 25 April 1877. Revd Josiah Henson (1789–1883): His parents were enslaved in America, and he and his wife fled in 1830 to Canada and freedom. They established a community for fugitives and he was ordained a Methodist Minister and made a notable fundraising tour of the UK in 1877, meeting Queen Victoria. Harriet Beecher Stowe said that he was in part the inspiration for the character 'Uncle Tom'; [d]Frederick Douglass, 'The United States Cannot Remain Half-Slave and Half-Free, Address delivered in the Congregational Church, Washington, DC, on the Twenty-first Anniversary of Emancipation in the District of Columbia, 16 April 1883,' *Frederick Douglass Papers* IV, p.356. [e] Frederick Douglass, 'The Future of the Colored Race,' *Frederick Douglass Papers* IV, p.356. [f]T Thomas Fortune, 'It is Time to Call a Halt,' *New York Age*, 25 January 1890. Timothy Thomas Fortune (1856–1928): Born into slavery in Florida, after limited formal education he became a journalist. On moving to New York, he founded the leading Black newspaper *The New York Age* in 1881, editing it until 1907. From 1923 until his death he was editor of Marcus Garvey's *Negro World*. A prominent activist, he founded the National Afro-American league in 1887 and latterly was a speechwriter for Booker T Washington; [g]William Henry Lewis (1868–1949): the son of a free Black couple, studied at Virginia State, Amherst College and then Harvard Law School. Played football at both, being the first Black man selected as an 'All American.' After graduating, he served 12 years as Harvard's football coach before becoming the first Black US Attorney (1903) and Assistant US Attorney General (1910). He resumed private practice in 1913 and maintained a profile in the pressing for civil rights. 'Class Oration, Amherst Graduation 1892' in Gregory Bond, 'The Strange Career of William Henry Lewis,' in *Out of the Shadows: A Biographical History of African American Athletes*, ed by David K Wiggins (Fayetteville, AR: University of Arkansas Press, 2006), p.45; [h][Anna J Cooper], *A Voice from the South, By a Black Woman from the South* (Xenia, OH: The Aldine Press, 1892), pp.118, 154, 168, 303. Dr Anna J Cooper (1858–1964): American educator and campaigner for civil rights and feminism. Educated at Oberlin College (BA, MA) and later awarded a PhD by the Sorbonne. [i]Wilson B Woodford (ca 1871–1902): the only Black lawyer in Decatur, IL in 1893. 'An Open Letter to Decatur's Colored Citizens [on the Lynching of Samuel J Bush,]' *Decatur Daily Republican*, 3 June 1893. [j]Masthead of the newspaper, Dr Robert Love (1838–1914): Born and educated in the Bahamas, he became a teacher, emigrating to New York in his late 20s. There he was ordained at Trinity Church and served parishes in Savanna, GA and Buffalo, NY where he passed his medical career. His ministry ended in Haiti, and he took up medicine full-time until expelled for political activity. In 1894 he arrived in Jamaica, founding the *Jamaica Advocate* as a workingman's newspaper. He was active in local politics, as a Justice of the Peace and parochial board member. [k]*Inter-Ocean*, 9 April 1894. Ida B Wells (1862–1931): born into slavery, she trained as a teacher then became a journalist noted for writing about lynching and campaigning against extra-judicial murders. [l]Booker T Washington, 'An Address before the National Educational Association [Buffalo, NY]', in *The Booker T Washington Papers, Volume 4: 1895–98*, ed by Louis R Harlan et al (Urbana/Chicago/London: University of Illinois Press, 1975), p.197. See also, 'A Speech at the Institute of Arts and Sciences [Brooklyn, NY]', ibid, p.218. Booker T Washington (1856–1915): Born into slavery in Virginia, after the Civil War he worked his way through college, becoming the first director of the

Tuskegee Institute in Alabama. His work in education for the Black community, with his writings on civil rights, found him advising Presidents Theodore Roosevelt and Taft, although his approach was perceived by some as too non-confrontational. ᵐBooker T Washington: 'To the Editor of the Washington Colored American,' in *The Booker T Washington Papers. Volume 5: 1899–1900*, ed by Louis R Harlan and Raymond W Smock (Urbana/Chicago/London: University of Illinois Press, 1976), p.142; ⁿWEB Du Bois, 'The Present Outlook for the Darker Races on Mankind, An Address to the Third Annual Meeting of the American Negro Academy,' *A M E Church Review*, October 1900. [The misquotation is believed to be a printer's error.] W[illiam] E[dward] B[urghart] Du Bois (1868-1963): sociologist, historian, author, editor and activist. After education at Fisk, Berlin and Harvard (where he was the first Black person awarded a PhD). He taught at Atlanta University and was one of the founders of The National Association for the Advancement of Colored People (NAACP) in 1909 and edited its magazine, *The Crisis*, between 1910 and 1934. Widely considered the leader of the African American community, towards the end of his life he formally embraced Communism and emigrated to Ghana, where he died. ᵒW E B Du Bois, *The Quest of the Silver Fleece: A Novel* (Chicago: A C McClurg, 1911), p.407. ᵖArmond Wendell Scott (1873 - 1960): Grandson of enslaved people, he was called to he Bar and practised at Wilmington, DE until he was run out of town by White supremacists in 1898. After a struggle, he resumed practice in Washington, DC being appointed Municipal Judge in 1935. ᑫRevd H M Mickens, 'Introducing Mr Marcus Garvey, 23 March 1920,' in The *Marcus Garvey and Universal Negro Improvement Association Papers*, Vol II, ed by Robert A Hill et al (Berkeley/Los Angeles/London: University of California Press, 1983), p.266. Revd HM Mickens (dates uncertain): Methodist preacher and civil rights activist.

Thus, this Burns quotation was a cornerstone of the campaign for true equality and was not solely used in the context of Black Emancipation and Civil Rights. A good example of its other uses is 'The Red Man's Pledge of Peace Marker' at the Chickasaw National Capital at Tishomingo, OK. This tall stone obelisk bears The Great Seal of the Chickasaw Nation and beneath it, four quotations over a peace pipe crossed over a war axe and two hands grasped in peace. Its first quotation is from 'The Red Man's Pledge of Peace' by Alexander L Posey (1873–1908), a noted Creek Indian poet, the third is by Theodore Roosevelt (1858–1919), 26th President of the USA (1901–1909) and Nobel Peace Laureate, and the fourth is by Haskell Paul (1907–1987), a Chickasaw Judge and cultural historian. The second inscription appears thus:

'It's comin' yet for a' that
that man to man the world o'er
shall brothers be for a' that.'
     Robert Burns
     Scottish Poet[74]

---

74 Posey had been introduced to Burns as a child and claimed him as a favourite poet. Like several other poets of the time, Burns's use of 'dialect' encouraged him to develop a poetic voice which echoed his Muskagee ancestry.

Man's Continuing Inhumanity to Man

A third poem of Burns's was quoted, albeit less regularly: 'Man was Made to Mourn.' Its influence in the context of the immorality of enslavement first appears in print as a footnote to a long didactic Abolitionist poem by Thomas Branagan (1774–1843), an Irish-born Methodist preacher in Philadelphia, in 1805:

'Written in Imitation of Burns.'

If he's designed that lordling's slave,
   By nature's law design'd;
Why was an independent wish
   E'er planted in his mind?

If not, why is he subject to
   His cruelty and scorn?
And why has man the power and will
   To make his fellow mourn?

But this, even this should not disturb
   The honest negro's breast;
This partial view of human kind
   Is surely not the last.

The poor oppressed virtuous slave
   Had never sure been born,
Had there not been some recompense
   To comfort them that mourn.[75]

Of course, Frederick Douglass, too, was aware of this work of Burns's:

In the old slave times, the colored people were expected to work without thinking. They were commanded to do as they were told.

---

[75] Thomas Branagan, *The Penitential Tyrant, or, Slave Trader Reformed: A Pathetic Poem, in Four Cantos* (New York: Samuel Wood, 1807), pp.77–78, imitating 'Man was made to Mourn,' [K.64]. Thomas Branagan (1774–1843): Born in Dublin, he ran away to sea working on a slaver. While an overseer on an Antiguan plantation he converted to Methodism and, moving to Philadelphia, preached and prolifically wrote poetry and prose in favour of Abolition.

They were to be hands — only hands, not heads. Thought was the prerogative of the master. Obedience was the duty of the slave. I, in my ignorance, once told my old master I thought a certain way of doing some work I had in hand was the best way to do it. He promptly demanded, 'Who gave you the right to think?' I might have answered in the language of Robert Burns,

> Were I designed yon lordling's slave,
> By Nature's law designed,
> Why was an independent thought
> E'er planted in my mind?

But I had not then read Robert Burns. Burns had high ideas of the dignity of simple manhood. [76]

This poem was regularly printed in the press, as well as in the myriad editions of Burns's Works (see, for example *The Massachusetts Abolitionist*, October 1838). Writers and speakers, however, focused on one particular couplet from this poem which would feature prominently (often without attribution) in the lexicon of Abolitionist (and Black rights) rhetoric: 'man's inhumanity to man, makes countless thousands mourn.' These words of Burns were regularly used in the Antebellum times:

> I took leave of Mr Armfield and of his establishment [Messrs Franklin & Armfield, Slave Traders of Alexandria, VA] and returned to my lodgings in the city, ruminating as I went, on the countless evils, which 'man's inhumanity to man,' has occasioned in this world of sin and misery.   Ethan Allen Andrews, 1836[77]

> Alas! I had not then learned the measure of 'man's inhumanity to man,' nor to what limitless extent of wickedness he will go for the love of gain.   Solomon Northup, 1853[78]

---

76 Speech: 'The Blessings of Liberty and Education,' 3 September 1894, *Frederick Douglass Papers*, vol.5, p.622.
77 Ethan Allen Andrews, *Slavery and the Domestic Slave Trade in the United States* (Boston: Light & Stearns, 1836), pp.135–136. Ethan Allen Andrews (1787–1858): Lexicographer and university professor.
78 Solomon Northup, *Twelve Years a Slave. Narrative of Solomon Northup, a Citizen of New-York, Kidnapped in Washington City in 1841, and Rescued in 1853, from a Cotton Plantation near the*

As the post-Civil War politics played out, this third quotation from Burns gained currency. Following the 13th Amendment, on the face of the US Constitution, Black people were now 'men, for a' that,' but the divisions had not been healed. Speakers for Black rights now began to use a different tenor of Burns, 'that man's inhumanity to man/ Makes countless thousands mourn.' Both the oppressor and the oppressed are now recognised as 'men,' yet the oppressor still responds inhumanly. Looking back, it is horrific that so much blood and energy was shed in the American Civil War, but without truly resolving the question.

Perhaps because of that slow pace of change, the optimism of 'it's coming yet, for a' that' seemed misplaced and so the most quoted poem shifted from 'Honest Poverty' to 'Man was made to Mourn,' and in particular those two memorable lines. Although typically used negatively, a rare and early positive use was in the funeral oration over the body of Frederick Douglass in 1896, summing up his labours:

> It is said that 'man's inhumanity to man makes countless thousands mourn.' The opposite is equally true, that man's humanity makes countless thousands glad. None deserve more the laurel wreath than he who wins it through his sympathies for the human race. The broader the circle of those sympathies the brighter should shine the crown of reward. Judged by the most severe standard Mr Douglass, because of the catholicity of his sympathies, has now and will ever wear a victor's adornment, undimmed by the dust of ages, and unharmed by the ravages of time.[79]

However, in the 20th century, the quote assumes a more sombre tone. Following the traumas of the First and Second World Wars, many felt that there should be established a supra-national treaty defining and guaranteeing human rights for all humanity, which led to *The Universal Declaration of Human Rights* being proclaimed by the United Nations General Assembly in Paris on 10 December 1948 (as General Assembly Resolution 217A). The wider context of this

---

Red River, in Louisiana (Auburn/Buffalo/London: Derby and Miller/Derby, Orton and Mulligan/ Sampson Low, Son & Company, 1853), p.48. Solomon Northup (ca 1807–ca 1864): A free black man of New York who gave up farming to become a travelling musician. In Washington DC he was kidnapped and forced into slavery in Louisiana, until rescued and released in 1853.

79 George W Cook, 'Eulogy on the Life and Services of Honorable Frederick Douglass,' in *In Memoriam: Frederick Douglass*, [ed by Helen Douglass] (Philadelphia: JC Yorston & Co, 1897), p.276.

document lies without the scope of this discussion, however, the issue of enslavement was not forgotten in two of its final articles:

> Article 1: All human beings are born free and equal in dignity and rights. They are endowed with reason and conscience and should act towards one another in a spirit of brotherhood.
>
> Article 4: No one shall be held in slavery or servitude; slavery and the slave trade shall be prohibited in all their forms.

Reading 'Article 1' feels like a 30-word prose summary of 'A Man's a Man' and it is no coincidence. The drafting committee, chaired by Eleanor Roosevelt (1884–1962), included China's delegate, the academic and diplomatist PC Chang (1892–1957). He was a man of wide reading and application, spending much of his time counselling the drafting committee to remember non-Western philosophies, such as the teachings of Confucius, when defining human rights. He also knew and valued the works of Burns. His son, who attended many drafting sessions, later remembered:

> Day after day, they debated what would constitute basic human rights, and how it should be clearly stated in the document so that there would not be any misunderstanding or misinterpretation. My father repeated many times the phrase 'Man's inhumanity to man.'[80]

Here again, we find Robert Burns guiding us towards the better. Yet, these words would become core to one of the greatest Civil Rights campaigners a decade later, receiving wide currency in the speeches of Dr Martin Luther King, Jr (1929–1968).

Thirty-five years after Douglass's interment, the young Martin Luther King, Jr was born. This man, without doubt one of the greatest public speakers in history, understood the cadence of positive rhetoric with uncanny skill. It is fair to assume that an unconsidered phrase never entered his speeches or his prose. So, it is interesting to see how this Burns quotation, 'man's inhumanity to man', is a repeated text of his, from his first use of it in 1955 to his last, in his final year of life.

---

80 Y Chang, 'Thoughts on My Beloved Father,' in *Peng Chun Chang, 1892–1957: Biography and Collected Works*, ed by HC Ruth and S-C Cheng ([San Jose, CA]: S-C Cheng, 1995), p.179.

Dr King often quoted secular poets in his writings, speeches and sermons: classical English writers such as Donne and Cowper, or the American 'fireside poets' Ralph Waldo Emerson or James Russell Lowell, sometimes with attribution, sometimes without. Nowhere in his voluminous writings does King mention Robert Burns by name, so an open question remains: was he knowingly quoting from Burns's 'Man was made to Mourn'? Had he come across the phrase in the writings of the previous generations of abolitionists? Perhaps he found it in that common reference book for sermons and speeches, *Bartlett's Quotations*? Or did he see the phase as a quasi-proverbial stock quotation whose source (be it the Bible, Shakespeare or Burns) had been eclipsed by the phrase's ubiquity? This phrase is so common in his writings that it obviously meant a great deal to him and as an effective use of language for his audience, it became one of his rhetorical tropes.

His earliest uses of the quotation were tentative, present in the original sermons of July 1955 and January 1956, but it was later excised from the printed versions of both:

> The New Testament is right when it affirms: 'No chastening for the present seemeth to be joyous, but grievous: nevertheless, afterward it yieldeth the peaceable fruit of righteousness.' Pharaoh exploits the children of Israel until they are relegated to the status of things rather than persons — nevertheless afterward! Pilate yields to the crowd and crucifies Christ on a cross between two thieves — nevertheless afterward. **The early Christians are thrown to the lions and carried to the chopping blocks until man's inhumanity to man becomes barbaric and unbelievable — nevertheless afterward.**[81]

> There are other forces that at a times cause all of us to question the ableness of God. When we notice the stark and colossal reality of evil in the world — that something that Keats calls 'the giant agony of the world;' — when we notice the long ruthlessness of flash floods and tornadoes wiping away people as if they were weeds in an open field; when we behold ills like insanity falling on some individuals at birth leaving them living their days in a tragic cycles of meaninglessness; **when we experience the madness of war and the barbarity of man's**

---

[81] 'Death of Evil Upon the Seashore,' Sermon at Dexter Avenue Baptist Church, 24 July 1955. [Emphasis added.]

inhumanity to man; we find ourselves asking why do all of these things occur if God is able to prevent them. Can a God who is both all-powerful and all-loving allow such glaring evils to exist?[82]

However, the phrase forms into a fully formed trope within Dr King's core rhetoric a few months later in a sermon and repeated later that day at a dinner in New York City on 17 May 1955 where he called for his audience, and wider society, to become 'maladjusted' to segregation and racial oppression:

> The world is in desperate need of such maladjusted persons. It is only through such maladjustment that we will emerge from the bleak and desolate midnight of 'man's inhumanity to man' to the bright and glittering daybreak of freedom and justice.[83]

Jason Miller has studied the influence of the poetry of Langston Hughes on King's rhetoric, believing that 'the bright and glittering daybreak of freedom and justice' was inspired by Hughes's poem 'Youth.' In his researches he explored the King Archives, reporting that

> It is unclear how King came into contact with this line from Burns's poem. No reference to this poem appears in any of King's index cards located at the Robert Woodruff Library at Atlanta University, it does not appear to be in any of the books he owned, and no clear connection to another preacher's sermon has yet been noted.[84]

Miller also makes the important point that, in the manuscript and the printed copy, Burns's words were in quotation marks for the first, and only time. That flags that Dr King new he was using another's

---

82 'Our God Is Able,' Sermon at Dexter Avenue Baptist Church, 1 January 1956, Martin Luther King, Jr, *The Papers of Martin Luther King, Jr: Volumes II to VII*, ed by Clayborne Carson, et al (Berkeley, Los Angeles CA: University of California Press, 1994–2014) ['*MLK Papers*'], vol VI, p.245. [Emphasis added.]
83 'Sermon, Cathedral of St John the Divine, New York City,' *MLK Papers* III, p.262 and 'Speech, The Annual Dinner of the NCAAP Legal Defense and Education Fund, Waldorf-Astoria, New York City,' *MLK Papers*, vol III, p.286.
84 Jason Miller, 'Langston Hughes and Martin Luther King, Jr: Together in Nigeria,' *South Atlantic Review: Special Issue, The Global Hughes* (Spring 2018), p.26, later expanded in W Jason Miller, *Origins of the Dream: Hughes's Poetry and King's Rhetoric* (Gainesville, FL: University of Florida Press, 2015), pp.125–126.

direct words, but it is now impossible to tell if he knew they were by Burns. It is worth noting that the 17 May sermon and speech were in honour of the second anniversary of the Supreme Court's ruling in *Brown v Board of Education*, which overthrew racial segregation in schools. It is not beyond belief to expect that Dr King followed that case through the courts in detail, and may have read the oral arguments before the Bench, finding the passage where Justice Felix Frankfurter questioned Robert L Carter (attorney for Oliver Brown in the Supreme Court Appeal) on 9 December 1952:

> Now unless you say that this legislation [on racial segregation] merely represents man's inhumanity to man, what is the root of this legislation? [...] But I want to know why this legislation, the sole basis for which is race — is there just some wilfulness of man in some states, or some, as I say, of man's inhumanity to man, some ruthless disregard of the facts of life?[85]

While incapable of confirmation, this hypothesis is the closest connection between the phrase and Dr King yet posited. However, he found it, and whether knowingly or unknowingly used, this quotation from Burns was important both to King as a speaker and to his auditors. King's potential awareness of the authorship of the phrase need not be a stumbling block, however, in assessing Burns's influence in the history of anti-slavery movements. As Carol McGuirk rightly encapsulates the question:

> Burns's poetic career itself — is linked, as in [Frederick] Douglass, to Burns's name or remains, as in King, unspoken is not as important today as it must have been for Burns in his lifetime. For like the lovers he depicts in 'Corn Rigs,' his words are at this point fully embedded in the general landscape of literary and colloquial speech. [...] the essence of Burns's 'immortal memory' [is] not in his life or works per se but rather in the *memory of mortals*, the interactive matrix of living cultural exchange.[86]

---

85 Philip B Kurland and Gerhard Casper, eds, *Landmark Briefs and Arguments of the Supreme Court of the United States: Constitutional Law. Volume 49: Brown v Board of Education (1954 & 1955)* (Arlington, VA: University Publications of American, Inc, 1975), p.16. [Emphasis added.]
86 Carol McGuirk, 'Burns and Aphorism; Or, Poetry into Proverb: His Persistence in Cultural Memory Beyond Scotland,' in *Robert Burns and Transatlantic Culture*, ed Alker, p.186.

'Man's inhumanity to Man' is a vibrant phrase, and the point that this quotation underscores for King is that despite the Emancipation victory which enshrined the principle of 'a man's a man,' the watchword of the 19th-century abolitionists, there remained, socially, practically and legally, a gulf between White people and Black people, imposed by the former. So, while both were now constitutionally and legally recognised as 'a man', the '[White] man's inhumanity to [the Black] man' remained the blight on Civil Rights.

Dr King used 'man's inhumanity to man' in two distinct rhetorical tropes. The first is in the formulation of May 1956: 'we will emerge from the bleak and desolate midnight of man's inhumanity to man to the bright and glittering daybreak of freedom and justice,' ['the Grand Trope']. The second uses simpler language around the short phrase 'man's inhumanity to man,' ['the Simple Trope']. The Grand Trope featured in around 40 speeches and articles, the Simple Trope in another two dozen.[87] (Some readers might be surprised at this level of 'repetition' by a major public orator, but remember that even as recently at the 1960s, the US print and broadcast media were local in nature with no 'national newspapers', so a speaker on tour, very much like Frederick Douglas, or Oscar Wilde and Charles Dickens in the previous century, would have a core speech delivered serially on tour, typically with local or topical additions.)

The Grand Trope featured prominently in his speeches and writing throughout 1956 and 1957, and he repeatedly used it in public sermons and in private letters to supporters and politicians between 1958 and 1961 and as late as 1965 and 1966.[88] It appears in pivotal speeches; for instance, he repeatedly invokes it in his eulogy to the four Black children who were killed in the white-supremacist bombings of a Black Baptist Church in Birmingham, Alabama in 1963, and in his

---

[87] Given the voluminous nature of the King Archives and the contemporary press coverage, it is highly likely that these numbers are understatements. McGuirk (in 2015) was the first commentator to flag King's use of the quotation, albeit only in the Kirk 'Autobiography': 'Over a century later, The Autobiography of Martin Luther King, Jr [...] used the phrase 'Man's inhumanity to Man' [...] no fewer that six times.' Carol McGuirk, *Reading Robert Burns: Texts, Contexts, Transformations* (London: Pickering & Chatto, 2015), p.190. Note, however, that the six times related to two separate speeches, and a statement. Martin Luther King, Jr, *The Autobiography of Martin Luther King, Jr*, ed by Clayborne Carson (London: Abacus, 2000), (a) 'Statement on Ending the Bus Boycott,' 20 December 1956, p.97 and (b) 'Eulogy for the Martyred Children, 18 September 1963, pp.227, 232 and (c) 'Man's inhumanity to man is not only perpetrated by the vitriolic actions of those who are bad. It is also perpetrated by the vitiating inaction of those who are good.' p.223.

[88] Letter: to Clarence L Jordan, 8 February 1957, *MLK Papers*, vol IV, p.123.

acceptance speech for the Nobel Peace Prize the following year.[89] The Simple Trope also features in his condemnation of international incidents, from colonialism to the Sharpeville Massacre and the Vietnam War.[90] He continued to use the Simple Trope several times a year until early 1968, when he used both tropes for a final time. In January, he used the Grand Trope in his peroration at Ohio State:

> Through such maladjustment I believe that we can emerge from the bleak and desolate midnight of man's inhumanity to man into the bright and glittering daybreak of freedom and justice. I haven't lost faith in the future. I still feel that we can develop a kind of coalition of conscience, and with this coalition move on into a brighter tomorrow. With this faith we will be able to do it [...] With this faith, we will be able to hew out of the mountain of despair a stone of hope. We will be able to transform the jangling discords of our nation into a beautiful symphony of brotherhood. We will be able to speed up the day when all of God's children — black men and white men, Jews and Gentiles, Protestants and Catholics — will be able to join hands and sing in the words of the old Negro spiritual 'Free at last, free at last, thank God Almighty we're free at last.'[91]

And weeks later, in his own pulpit at Ebenezer Baptist Church, he used the Simple Trope in his 'Drum Major' sermon: 'And think of what has happened in history as a result of this perverted use of the drum major instinct. It has led to the most tragic prejudice, the most tragic expressions of man's inhumanity to man.'[92]

Exactly two months later he was assassinated in Memphis, Tennessee.

---

89 'Eulogy for the Martyred Children, Birmingham, AL, 22 September 1963,' in Martin Luther King, Jr, *A Call to Conscience: The Landmark Speeches of Martin Luther King, Jr*, ed by Clayborne Carson (New York: IPM/Warner Books, 2001), pp.81–83. 'Acceptance Speech, on the Occasion of the Award of the Nobel Peace Prize in Oslo, 10 December 1964,' ibid, pp.105–109.
90 'Sermon Notes: Faith in Man. 25 February 1956,' *MLK Papers*, vol.VI, p253; 'Telegram to Claude Barnett, 24 March 1960,' *MLK Papers*, vol.V, p.400; 'Speech: 'The Casualties of the War in Viet Nam, 25 February 1967,' reprinted in *The Atlantic*, 'MLK Special Edition,' February 2018.
91 Speech at Ohio Northern University, 11 January 1968: www.onu.edu/mlk/mlk-speech-transcript (accessed 1 September 2024).
92 'Sermon: The Drum Major Instinct, Ebenezer Baptist Church, Atlanta, GA, 4 February 1968,' in Martin Luther King, Jr, *A Knock at Midnight*, ed by Clayborn Carson and Peter Holloran (New York: Warner Books, 1998, pp.186–196.

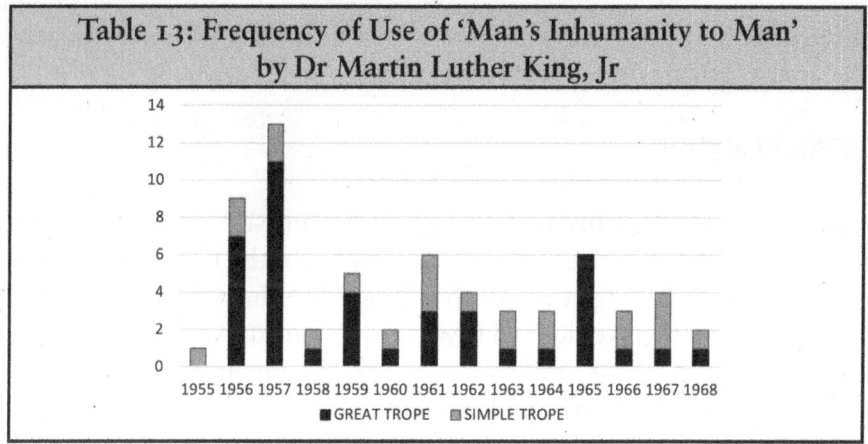

Table 13: Frequency of Use of 'Man's Inhumanity to Man' by Dr Martin Luther King, Jr

It is only appropriate that in giving the Funeral Elegy, Dr King's former teacher, Revd Dr Benjamin E Mays (1894–1984), said of him:

> He was convinced also that people could not be moved to abolish voluntarily the inhumanity of man to man by mere persuasion and pleading, but that they could be so moved to do so by dramatizing the evil through massive nonviolent resistance.[93]

The importance of those words, 'man's inhumanity to man', to King has been recognised since the creation of Martin Luther King, Jr Day as a Federal holiday in the USA. This quotation regularly appears in connection with the day's remembrance, as in this 2008 Martin Luther King Day Message from President Obama:

> For most of this country's history, we in the African-American community have been at the receiving end of man's inhumanity to man. And all of us understand intimately the insidious role that race still sometimes plays – on the job, in the schools, in our health care system, and in our criminal justice system.[94]

The phrase 'man's inhumanity to man' inspired Dr King and his

---

[93] Benjamin E Mays, *Born to Rebel: An Autobiography* (Athens, GA/London: University of Georgia Press, 2003), 'Eulogy at the Funeral Services of Martin Luther King, Jr, at Morehouse College, Atlanta, Georgia, April 9, 1986,' p.357.
[94] President Barack Obama, 'Speech at Ebenezer Baptist Church, Atlanta GA,' 20 January 2008, *The Guardian*, 21 January 2008.

audiences and yet it came from the pen of a man who very nearly became a 'Negro driver,' Robert Burns.

A Poetical Coda

The effect of the words of Burns over almost two centuries of debate about racial equality and civil rights in the USA chimes with Shelley's (overquoted) dictum that 'poets are the unacknowledged legislators of the world.'[95] However, it is in danger of eclipsing an equally important and poetic legacy: the inspiration Burns has given to generations of Black poets.

The effect of 'The Slave's Lament' on contemporary Black artists has been discussed above, but Burns as a model, put simplistically as an 'outsider' poet – perceived as an 'ordinary working man' writing in 'non-standard English' – is a key strand in the development of Black Anglophone poetry. Here, rather than quoting Burns, writers channel his work, developing new poetry bearing the stamp of Burns. The 1898 poem 'Color' by the poet and activist Katherine D Tillman (1870–1923) is a simple, but striking, example:

> There is a silent majesty which speaks
>   From lives of noble men
> Of every nation, tongue and clime,
>   That's beyond malicious ken.
>
> And men with countenance as black
>   As skies of midnight hue
> May yet be men of courage great
>   Of manhood tried and true.
>
> Then believe the Ploughman Poet
>   Manhood depends on worth,
> And scorn the prejudice that adorns
>   The dark faced men of earth.[96]

---

95 Percy Bysshe Shelley, 'The Defence of Poetry,' in *Essays, Letters from Abroad, Translations and Fragments*, 2 vols, ed by Mrs [Mary Wollstonecraft] Shelley (London: Edward Moxton, 1840), vol.I, p.57.
96 *State Bystander* [Des Moines, IA], 25 February 1898; and amended slightly in Katherine D Tillman, *Recitations*, (Philadelphia: AME Book Concern, [1902]), p.32.

The first, sustained identification of this theme was in the works of the Black American poet Paul Laurence Dunbar (1872–1906). He was the son of formerly enslaved parents and as a schoolboy he repeatedly read Burns amongst other poets. Dunbar's use of dialect, his ordinary themes and his status as a labouring-class poet (his early employment was as an elevator operator) led to him being called 'The Robert Burns of Negro Poetry.'[97] The highly regarded critic William Dean Howells (1837–1920) first drew attention to the similarities between the two poets when he reviewed Dunbar's second collection of verse in 1896:

> Burns has long had the consecration of the world's love and honor, and I shall not do this unknown but not ungifted poet the injury of comparing him to Burns, yet I do not think that one can read his negro poems without thinking that they are of like impulse and inspiration with the work of Burns, when he was most Scotch, when he was most peasant.[98]

A few times, Dunbar goes further, and actively echoes a specific poem by Burns, as in 'My Sort o' Man' which is clearly his response to 'Honest Poverty':

> I don't believe in 'ristercrats;
>   I like the honest tan
> That lies upon the healthful cheek
>   An' speaks the honest man;
> [...]
> What though the thousands sneer an' scoff,
>   An' scorn yore humble birth?
> Kings are but puppets; you are king
>   By right o' royal worth.   ll.33–36 and 45–48.[99]

Or his short poem 'Confirmation' which (although unsignposted) clearly reads as a biography, and appreciation, of Burns:

---

97 First coined by the US poet James Whitcombe Riley (1849–1916), himself a dialect poet of the Mid-West who loved Burns. It was taken up as the rubric to his biographical essay by Langston Hughes (see below) in his *Famous American Negroes* (New York: Dodd, Mead, 1954), p.71.
98 WD Howells, 'Life and Letters,' *Harper's Weekly*, 27 June 1896, p.630.
99 Paul [Laurence] Dunbar, *Oak and Ivy* (Dayton, OH: Press of the United Brethren Publishing House, 1893), pp.39–40.

He was a poet who wrote clever verses,
  And folks said he had fine poetical taste;
But his father, a practical farmer, accused him
  Of letting the strength of his arm go to waste.

He called on his sweetheart each Saturday evening,
  As pretty a maiden as ever man faced,
And there he confirmed the old man's accusation
  By letting the strength of his arm go to *waist*.[100]

While Dunbar's prose and poetry are much more complex than a simple or exclusive relationship with Burns, the connection lived on after his death, which occurred at an even younger age than Burns, with WEB Du Bois saying of him, '[a]s a poet, he means as much to America's Negroes what Robert Burns means to Scotchmen.'[101] Shortly after Dunbar's death, a close friend outlined why this was so:

> Nature [...] took Burns from a plow, and Paul from an elevator, and Paul has done for his own people what Burns did for the peasants of Scotland — he has expressed them in their own way and in their own words. There are many analogies between the two poets [...].[102]

The next generation of Black poets in the USA were part of the wider cultural movement in the 1920s and '30s now known as 'the Harlem Renaissance' where, again, the influence of the politics and poetry of Robert Burns can be found. An early poet associated with this was Claude McKay (1890–1948). McKay was born in Jamaica, with its myriad Scottish connotations, and the local reception of his early poems brought him the soubriquet 'Jamaica's Burns,' which was indeed apposite, as he wrote in later life: 'I chose Burns as my model, as he was so strong, sweet and amorous of abundant life, and I was writing in the Jamaican dialect.'[103] A clear example of this self-identification

---

100 Ibid, p.54.
101 [WEB DuBois], 'Negere Som Digtere, af Carl Kjersmeier [Book Review],' *The Crisis* (August 1925), p.188.
102 Letter, Brand Whitlock (1869–1934) to HA Tobey, 11 February 1906, quoted in Langston Hughes (see below) in his *Famous American Negroes* (New York: Dodd, Mead, 1954), p.74.
103 Claude McKay, 'On Becoming a Catholic,' quoted in Geta J LeSeur, 'Claude McKay's

can be found in his first collection of verse, which includes the poem 'Rise and Fall. (Thoughts of Burns — With Apologies to His Immortal Spirit for making Him speak in the Jamaican Dialect)'

> DEY read 'em again an' again,
>   An' laugh an' cry at 'em in turn;
> I felt I was gettin' quite vain,
>   But dere was a lesson fe learn.
> [...]
> Te-day I am back in me lan',
>   Forgotten by all de gay throng,
> A poorer but far wiser man,
>   An' knowin' de right from de wrong.[104]

Others in and alongside the movement also found inspiration in the Scots poet. One, Jean Toomer (1894–1967), an American whose father had been born into enslavement, made his name with his first novel, *Cane*, in 1923. In it, a short poem, 'Reapers', was inspired by Burns's 'To a Mouse'.[105] The Burnsian inspiration was more sustained through the writings of Langston Hughes (1901–1967) who was one of the most prominent writers identified with the Harlem Renaissance. A few years after Hughes's death, one commentator observed that:

> underlying the poetical principle of both Burns and Hughes is a fondness for the common man and a romantic belief in his goodness. [...] Both poets emphasise so fully with the downtrodden, that they frequently allow their persona to speak directly.[106]

While both Sterling Allen Brown (1901–1989) and Julia Fields (born 1938) were each encouraged by their parents to learn the poems of major Romantic poets, notably Burns's (in Fields's case leading to a stint at Edinburgh University). In an interview, Brown recalled:

Romanticism,' *CLA Journal* (March 1989), p.296.
104 Claude McKay, *Songs of Jamaica* (Kingston, Jamaica/London: Aston W Garner & Co/Jamaica Agency, 1912), p.37, ll.1–4 and 25–28.
105 Jean Toomer, *Cane* (New York: Boni & Liveright, 1923), p.6; see also Justin Mellette, 'Jean Toomer's "Reapers" and Robert Burns,' *The Drouth*, www.thedrouth.org/jean-toomers-reapers-and-robert-burns-justin-mellette/ (accessed 1 September 2024).
106 Aaron Kramer, 'Robert Burns and Langston Hughes,' *Freedomways* 8 (1968), pp.160, 162.

My mother was a great reader of poetry. My mother read. I remember her sweeping the floor, standing over the broom, reciting to me Robert Burns, Paul Laurence Dunbar. You see Burns is important to me. Burns is very important, what he did with the language, how he turned away from the neo-classic high flown.[107]

For two years, from 1926, Brown taught at Lincoln University, Jefferson City, MO. After classes, he invited his students to his home, where they explored jazz and writers beyond the curriculum:

In our in-home gatherings, some of us learned about poems of Robert Burns that don't appear in college textbooks — at any rate, they didn't appear in the textbooks of the day. And they were the sort that would have had Brown railroaded out of town if he had read them in class.[108]

This is an area which deserves greater research as there may well be more authors inspired directly or indirectly by Burns. What can be seen is that each of the important Black writers lister here found analogies and strength in appreciating the life and works of Robert Burns, and did so, importantly, without cavil over his acceptance of a job as a 'slave-driver' in Jamaica, or his failure to stand foursquare with the Abolitionists on the 1790s. Burns's wider 'dialect' voice, his championing of 'the honest man' and decrying 'man's inhumanity to man' has proved to be a more important and enduring memorial in Black culture.[109]

---

107 Grace Cavalieri, 'Interview with Sterling Brown, (1977),' *Beltway Poetry Quarterly*, www.beltwaypoetry.com/cavalieri-interviews-brown/ (accessed 1 September 2024).
108 Black History Museum Committee, eds, *Sterling A Brown, A UMUM Tribute* (Philadelphia: Black History Museum UMUM Publishers, 1982), p.47.
109 Which extends through to today's poets such as Jackie Kay and Shara McCallum, who are discussed elsewhere.

Conclusion

Despite nearly becoming a functioning part of the tyranny of Black slavery in the Caribbean, Burns was fervently adopted by the Abolitionist movement in the United States as the exemplar poet of our common humanity. That thoughtful and committed campaigners such as Frederick Douglass, who freed himself from enslavement, or William Lloyd Garrison, the White man who campaigned pugnaciously for equal rights for Black people, as well as other racially oppressed groups (such as the Chinese immigrant population) and women should adopt Burns as their icon is striking. For, as Douglass rightly said in his letter to Abigail Mott, Burns was a 'true soul,' who was '[f]ull of faults of a grievous nature, yet far more faultless than many who have come down to us on the page of history as saints.' Those qualities not only gave positive inspiration to politicians and activists but also gave momentum to a distinct Black voice in literature.

Equally, Burns cannot be condemned for the support the Confederates, enslavers, slave-holders, enforcers and even the Ku Klux Klan took from his writings, but should be recognised as inspiring the important moral change that Black people had equal human rights, as equal men (and women and children) 'for a' that.' Even during the disappointing century after the Civil War when civil rights were traduced in many communities (particularly, but in no wise exclusively) in the southern USA, campaigners, most notably Dr Martin Luther King, Jr, built on Burns's prophecy by underscoring 'that man's inhumanity to man' still made 'countless thousands mourn.' King carried on the tradition and practice of using Burns's imagery to change perceptions.

So, while Burns was not perfect (and which human being has no fault?) the changes wrought by many through using his words to better the lives and rights of countless people are demonstrable proof of the power and genius of his poetry, fitly electing him as one of Shelley's 'unacknowledged legislators of the world,' or as Douglass aptly summed it: 'so let us separate his good from his evil deeds – thus may we make him a blessing rather than a curse to the world.'[110]

---

110 Frederick Douglass, *Albany Evening Journal*, 13 June 1846.

CHAPTER EIGHT

Conclusion: Should Burns 'Fall'?

THIS BOOK HAS, for the first time, sought to lay out all the connections, direct and indirect, personal and societal, in philosophy and in practice, between our national poet, Robert Burns, and what many might call our 'National Disgrace', the involvement of Scots (as participants, enablers, investors or consumers) in Black chattel slavery. Black enslaved people were forcibly torn from homes in Africa and trafficked to the gulag, or 'killing fields' in Trevor Burnard's words, of the Caribbean.[1] There, through inhuman force, they toiled to death to produce goods for consumption in Scotland. What is the ultimate verdict on Burns the poet and the man in terms of his stance on Black chattel slavery? Should his 60 statues face the fate of the slave-traders Edward Coulston in Bristol or Dumfries-born Robert Milligan at London's West India Docks? Or will they be defaced in outrage, as actually happened to his statues in Dunedin and Brisbane?[2] Is his snow-white, domed mausoleum a whited sepulchre which should be painted black? Should his birthplace and his monuments carry prominent plaques warning of his complicity with Black chattel slavery? In a time where once-revered benefactors are now recognised as outed outcast malefactors, how should we deal with this contentious part of the complex life of Scotland's National Poet?[3]

This is a difficult topic, and one ill-served by hasty or ahistorical judgements. 'The past is another country; they do things differently there' is LP Hartley's noted aphorism. That 'other country' does issue

---

1 Burnard, 'Plantation Slavery', p.396.
2 Burns is often said to be the non-religious figure with the largest number of statues in the world. He is more likely to be fifth after Mao Zedong, Christopher Columbus, Vladimir Ilyich Ulyanov Lenin and HM Queen Victoria. Joseph Vissarionovich Stalin, prior to the wholesale removal of his statues, would have ranked fourth, which is quite apposite in this discussion.
3 The Dunedin statue had placards attached reading 'complicit in slavery' and 'rapist': *NZ Herald*, 14 June 2020 (see cover illustration). It is ironic that this was one of the only two Burns statues attacked as the city of Dunedin was founded by Burns's nephew Revd Thomas Burns (1796–1871). At Brisbane, the text on the plinth was crossed out and the word 'genocide' written in spray paint, with 'Genocide occurred here' and 'Black Lives Matter' and '#BLM: Racists' added on other faces: *Courier-Mail*, 21 April 2021.

visas for us to visit and learn, but like all travel, one must be conscious of how much baggage one carries from home to the destination. Chattel slavery is, and always has been, immoral. It was, however, in many places and for many centuries, legal. So, as we look on our forebears and their involvements with enslavement, think awhile on how our grandchildren will look on us and our parents, and our custodianship of Earth in the face of Global Warming. As a number of commentators now stress in the wider field of Scotland and slavery, the collective amnesia (or in Mullen's striking phrase, the 'it wisnae us' factor) for a long, long time sheltered the Scots from the recognition of how involved our whole nation was in the extraction of profit (and the consumption of goods) from Black chattel slavery on the one hand, and the repatriation of that capital to invest in the twin pillars of Scots pride: the Enlightenment and the Industrial Revolution, on the other. An 1878 study of country houses in and around Glasgow, many built on tobacco-lord, plantocrat or nabob wealth, talked about the then-owner of Auchencruive, Richard Alexander Oswald (III), noting without any embarrassment that '[t]here is hardly one left [alive] of our old West Indians, probably not one Glasgow man that ever owned a slave.'[4] Even later, in the Author's youth in Burns's Ayr in the 1960s, the town council were still naming new streets after plantations once owned by the Hamilton family and worked by enslaved men and women – and it is a short step from that to Dr Celeste-Marie Bernier's view that 'slavery bleeds in every building, in every brick, in every town across Scotland.'[5] Certainly, the Chinese conglomerate which acquired the ancestral Hunter Blair estate of Blairquhan in Ayrshire, unaware that it had been built on the Rozelle plantation's sugar profits, expressed complete surprise when the *Financial Times* informed them of its history:

---

[4] John Guthrie Smith and John Oswald Mitchell, *The Old Country Houses of the Old Glasgow Gentry* (Glasgow: James Maclehose & Sons, 1878), 'Moore Park,' LXXIV, fn 4.

[5] In 1967, when Ayr Town Council was contemplating building housing on the outskirts of the Rozelle Estate (which was in the process of being donated to the burgh by Lieutenant Commander John Hamilton RN), the minutes record the decision that 'because of the association of the Hamiltons of Rozelle with the West Indies the names of the islands be listed by the Burgh Surveyor so that those which are suitable might be used for streets to be formed on Rozelle Estate,' and duly named one street 'Pemberton Valley,' after the largest slaveholding plantation the Hamiltons controlled. Rob Close, the architectural historian, states that '[i]n May 1969 the Council decided to drop this policy, perhaps due to a perceived lack of suitable names,' and not because of the association with slavery. It still exits, as do Leeward Park, St Vincent Crescent and Windward Park. See *Ayr Town Council Minutes 1966–1967*: Works Committee, 20th February 1967, quoted in Rob Close, *The Street Names of Ayr* (Ayr: Ayrshire Archaeological and Natural History Society, 2001). *Herald*, 4 November 2018.

it had 'no idea' about the castle's history when it bought the property from the Hunter Blairs in 2012. It said that any reference could damage its 'hard-earned business reputation' and expose the property to vandalism.[6]

Even two centuries ago, it was hard to disentangle the posthumous Burns from the slaving community. The first Burns Supper at Burns Cottage in July 1801 had nine guests: Dr Douglas was an absentee slave-holder, and Captain Ferguson had owned enslaved people on his wife's estate in Pennsylvania before fleeing as a loyalist and introduced his nephew John as Overseer on the Rozelle plantation.[7] Two were members of Hunter's Bank (Provost Ballantine and David Scott) which had built an unsuccessful refinery at Ayr harbour to process sugar from Jamaican plantations and were subsequently active in financing in the West Indies, while Captain Primrose Kennedy of Drummellan had been a comrade-in-arms with, and had fought against, George Washington. Finally, the Revd Hamilton Paul would be presented to his first parish by the slave-holder Richard Alexander Oswald (II) of Auchincruive.[8] Likewise, of the five-man committee for the Alloway Burns Monument in 1814, two (Hunter Blair and Hamilton of Pinmore) were active plantocrats, while one of the largest donations for its construction was £70 remitted by 'the Scotsmen of Tobago.' In a similar vein, the Dumfries Mausoleum Committee membership included 'Wm Taylor Esq, of Jamaica,' with the third largest contribution to the fund being a 'Trinidad Subscription' of £96.[9] We know that Burns Suppers were held in Jamaica as early as 1806, and it is likely that the Trinidad and the Tobago fundraising arose out of Burns dinners, too.[10] The early Burns Supper celebrants, or participants in the Monument or Mausoleum fundraising dinners would have enjoyed, as their Bard

---

6 Henry Mance, 'A Reckoning with History,' *Financial Times*, 26/27 September 2020.
7 Renton, *Blood Legacy*, pp.190–191. 'In a story not short of monstrous people, John Fergusson joins the first rank.'
8 McGinn, *Comprehensive*, p.41.
9 *First Minute Book of the Trustees of Burns Monument*, RBBM Collection, p.1. William Taylor senior of Troqueerholm (1763–1831): West Indian merchant, partner in Hibbert, Taylors and Simpson at Kingston, Jamaica and London until retiring around 1816. A wealthy man, his personal, moveable estate at death was some £50,000 (ca £4.25 million in 2023). Philip Sully, *Robert Burns and Dumfries* (Dumfries: Thos Hunter & Co, 'Standard' Office, 1896), pp.23, 27, and *UCL Legacies Database*: 'William Taylor, Sr' (accessed 1 September 2024).
10 McGinn, *Comprehensive*, p.79.

had, steaming bowls of punch brewed out of Scots water, but using West Indian rum, West Indian lemons, West Indian spices and (of course) West Indian sugar, all produced by enslaved Black labour.[11] That is a pattern of consumption that echoes today, with millions of unthinking purchases of £2 tee-shirts every year: again, from the *Financial Times*: '[c]otton has always been associated with human rights abuse, from slavery on 19th-century US plantations to recent child labour in Uzbekistan.' Those issues touch on so many consumer goods that we, as a society, crave: phones as much as fabrics. The desire for (cheap, cheaper or cheapest) gratification so often trumps the duties of care and respect due to invisible 'others' who toil to provide it to us.[12]

In any assessment of Burns's potential culpability, the first step (as in Chapter One) is to view slavery in his lifetime. It is not an exaggeration to say that the enslaved economy of the West Indies touched much, if not all, life in Britain. In Georgian society, there was a hierarchy of involvement: at the top, the 'slave traders' of the Triangular Passage and the plantocrats and their myrmidons (not forgetting the Black African and Arab communities who were the 'first enslavers');[13] then the enablers, by hand (manufacturing and transporting goods for colonial use and shipping colonial produce back), and by mind (the bankers, lawyers, insurers and others who facilitated that transatlantic commerce and the investment of colonial profits); then the largest group, the home consumers of sugar, rum, cotton, spices and other commodities all produced (out of sight) at the cost of the human rights and dignity of the enslaved populace (out of mind). However, that hierarchy was, as fact, all legal and in the early 18th century; it would even have been rare to find a voice denouncing it as immoral. What would happen, however, is akin to Thomas Kuhn's 'Paradigm Shift' in the philosophy of science: the change in received opinion from 'slavery is normal' to 'slavery is abnormal' was not a

---

11 Burns mentions to Cunningham that his toddy is made of 'damn'd generous Antigua [rum].' *Letters*, to Alexander Cunningham, 10 September 1792, [L.506] at p.147.
12 John Gapper, 'Forced labour is the price of a cheap cotton T-shirt,' *Financial Times*, 19/20 September 2020.
13 As an example of the complexities around this debate, it has been shown by metallurgical testing that some of the Benin Bronzes were cast from bracelet-shaped ingots of bronze used by Portuguese traffickers to trade with the enslavers of Benin. Hence some of their repatriations may be returning the profits of enslavers to their descendants.

linear, predictable progression. So, for much of Burns's life, slavery was simply not questioned, but accepted as something happening 'yonder awa'.' The Paradigm Shift took until 1807 to win out, by which time Burns had been dead and buried for a decade.

Chapter Two sought to match those societal issues against the chronology of Burns's short life. Evidence shows that he had seen (at least one) Black person, and several Biracial people, in the communities of his youth. He was, briefly, one of those enablers-by-hand in growing flax and learning to heckle rough linen, and he narrowly avoided becoming one of the enforcers on the front line of inhumanity. His poetic ascent brought him into the salons of Edinburgh and the dining rooms of Dumfriesshire where he formed acquaintanceship with many plantocrats and politicians who voted against Abolition, alongside a smaller group of people who were more disposed to question enslavement on moral grounds. Despite two Abolition petitions, as William Dickson ruefully noted, Dumfries was hardly fertile ground for the growth of Abolition. Burns, having been called out for 'disaffection' by his Excise masters, could be forgiven for not being part of the Abolitionist minority active around him, particularly as his heath failed and his finances worsened.

That social silence echoes through his works. A crucial point is that Burns was not racist, as 'The Ordination' shows. However, some early poems see 'herding the buckskin kye' as a perfectly normal outcome for a Scots lad, as indeed it probably was in the 1780s. The poetry around his proposed emigration to Jamaica is more about self-pity for his position, and never about the enslaved workforce whose brutal conditions would be violently enforced by Burns. His famed satirical whip never lashed an enslaver specifically for their enslaving actions and profits, either before or after the great years of petitions in 1788 and 1792, and he wrote political ballads supporting Members of Parliament who voted in the 'West Indian Interest.' That being said, when engaged by Helen Maria Williams's poem or Elizabeth Kemble's acting, he responded with some (modest) moral force against Black chattel slavery, and, of course, he wrote 'The Slave's Lament.' In his final three years, his health, his finances and the wider society's interest in Abolition were at low points. It would take a decade after the poet's death for Abolition to re-appear and be enacted.

Perhaps the biggest concern about Burns's understanding of Black chattel slavery is found in his library where most of the important literary or philosophical discussions against enslavement sat on his shelves. From the high sensibility of Mackenzie's *Julia de Roubigne* or Moore's *Zeluco* to the Enlightenment philosophies of Adam Smith or Dugald Stewart, or the activist poetry of Cowper and others, Burns read most of, if not all, the core texts of Abolitionist thought. Yet that brought little to no sustained reaction from him – not in letters, nor in poems or nor in actions. Burns was well aware of the inherent cruelty of the plantation system, as the specifics of his role under Charles Douglas, using a dog and a whip, had been explained to him with independent verification from his reading of Guthrie and Salmon, who described the punishments inflicted on the enslaved who 'were almost whipped to Death [...] for the smallest offences.'[14] This is a paradox of the highest order.

Which leads us to the second possibility: he knew but simply did not care. We know that he had some (limited) connections with Black and mixed-race people, so the defence that it was a problem out of sight is hard to sustain. In any case, the reading advanced above for 'The Ordination' (and, maybe, 'Honest Poverty') posits that Burns was not a racist, or one who sought to justify enslavement on the basis of a fundamental racial superiority. So, what had created a barrier between his humanity and an outright opposition to the inhumanity of chattel slavery?

One answer to that could be distance. Just as Burns makes no mention of the lot of the industrial poor in his poems but is keenly attuned to the hardships of rural poverty, is it the distance from slavery that promotes his near silence? The modern analogy might be questioning the foreign aid budget in the face of NHS cutbacks, an argument fairly regularly heard: sort out our problems at home, and once 'our people' are provided for, look beyond our shores. However, given the depth of Burns's reading and the range of anti-slavery and Abolitionist themes he encountered on the written page, even if Dumfries society were tacitly silent on the subject, there is a resounding gap between the poet's reading and his writing that is hard to bridge, even on this supposition.[15]

---

14 Salmon, p.591.
15 It would be pushing this argument too far to assume that Burns would have supported Hume's provocative dictum that 'it is not irrational for me to prefer the destruction of the entire world to

The next possible answer is built around the fact that the Black people Burns saw in Ayrshire were servants to the wealthy. In 'The Twa Dogs,' he sees the lot of the servant class as almost parasitical on their rich masters, living (in his view) a pampered life compared to his own cottar class. So that could create a 'fire break' to his sympathies, as the suffering of the 'ha' folk' was cloaked in livery. Of course, the lot of the plantation enslaved was significantly worse than that of an enslaved personal maid or valet in Scotland, but Burns had the servants in front of him, not the labouring enslaved. Burns had his own problems to face, so it might have been easy to position chattel slavery as something 'yonder awa'' as, indeed, the majority of the British public did in the mid-1790s.

To answer the often-asked question, 'what would Burns have done if he had gone to Jamaica,' a set of five counterfactual scenarios were created and ranked by probability of outcome. The most likely outcome (in half of the scenarios) was that the Poet would succumb to the dreaded Yellow Fever (or possibly on die board, while crossing the Atlantic). That of course, resolves nothing in terms of his culpability in accepting the enforcer's role, although it does mitigate his abundant self-pity in several of his 'Farewell' poems of 1786. The second most likely gives greater comfort in that his life would follow the arc of fellow-Scot Zachary Macaulay, falling into acquiescence until a shock awakening to the horrors of enslavement.

In Burns's short life, his sporadic sympathy for the Black chattel slave was far less than his sustained sympathy for the common working folk of Scotland. After his death, his works, 'Honest Poverty' and 'Man was made to Mourn' which eloquently and emotionally captured that engagement with the 'common folk', were full-throatedly adopted by Black and White campaigners seeking to end slavery and expand universal human rights. It is important to remember that not one of those ardent campaigners criticised him, either for Jamaica or for the relative absence of condemnation of enslavement in his works. His words, 'A man's a man', 'Let us do or die', 'Man's inhumanity to man/ Makes countless thousands mourn', were clarion calls which inspired countless tens of thousands to agitate to remove the blight

---

the merest scratching of my little finger' (*Treatise on Human Nature*, II,ii, 3) rather than Adam Smith's more benevolent approach over the 'Chinese Earthquake' thought experiment (*Theory of Moral Sentiments*, III, 3.4).

of enslavement, changing the world for the better.

Another possible answer to his apparent disengagement is often suggested: that having sailed too close to the political wind already, the danger of losing his Excise position (and his only income, which was in any case, insufficient to cover his family's household expenditure) pressed him into silence. There was no purposeful ban on government placemen campaigning for Abolition, as shown by the fact that the treasurer and deputy-treasurer of the Edinburgh committee for Abolition were serving Excise officers. Even if Burns felt that his 'card was marked' and so he had to be publicly cautious (which could well be a fair point, as Dumfries was not particularly Abolitionist and there were people who would happily speak against Burns either in malicious gossip or in formal complaint), there is no connection with the growing call for ending slavery in his private letters which could often be outspoken on other political and social issues. A good example is the letter which caused the breach with Mrs Dunlop, over 'a certain pair of personages [...] a perjured Blockhead & an unprincipled Prostitute' (the executed King Louis XVI and Queen Marie Antoinette) where he quotes 'my friend Roscoe' approvingly for a pro-Revolutionary poem. Why did he never mention Roscoe's pioneering Abolitionism, nor his popular anti-slavery poem *The Wrongs of Africa*?[16] Such a political statement against monarchy tends to diminish the defence that Burns could not speak out (even in private correspondence) against slavery because of his Excise commission (and his reprimand for political thought). These comments on France, albeit in a private letter, are many times more incendiary than anything he could have said about chattel slavery, which is never mentioned in his correspondence.

Thinking of revolutionary France does give another explanation for Burns's silence: what might be called the 'Wordsworth Gambit,' where a reliance on a whole new world order about to be created through a top-down revolution, which started with the Fall of the Bastille in 1789, would lead to the freedom of the ordinary man and the enslaved together. As the Lake poet described in *The Prelude*, 'if France prosper'd' the branch of slavery 'would fall with the parent tree.' Given Burns's sympathies in the early 1790s, this is not too much of a stretch to believe as possible, but there is no hint of an argument

---

16 *Letters*: To Mrs Dunlop, 20 December 1794–1 January 1795, [L.649] at vol.II, p.334.

like this in his works. The corollary to that thought is, of course, that the abolition of slavery by the French revolutionaries compromised the British agenda, for we know that many proponents of Abolition fell silent between the execution of Louis XVI and the Battle of Trafalgar as every policy of Republican, and in turn Imperial, France became defined as 'anti-British,' allowing the powerful West India Interest to define an anti-slavery stance as unpatriotic in wartime.

The last solution, and probably the most likely, comes back to the 'coward slave problem.' His two openly Abolitionist poems, 'The Slave's Lament' and 'Mrs Kemble', both concern female slaves. (While the gender of the 'Slave' is not mentioned in the former, the song being rooted from 'The Trapann'd Maid' along with its sentimentalism makes a female connotation more intuitive). The female slave is given no option to die in combat and, assuming suicide a sin, she has to face her fate – *vae victæ* – when the battle is lost. This chimes with Burns's awareness of the female condition in his society (thinking of his enumerated 'Rights of Women'). Could it be that Burns considers the enslaved Black man to be, as Lord Stair had cast it, 'being more willing to lose Liberty than Life' and hence he is in fact a 'coward slave' in having voluntary chosen an ignominious life over a valiant death? This suggestion is supported by Frederick Douglass's remembrance of beating his enslaver/enforcer, Covey, and afterwards feeling that he 'was no longer a servile coward,' becoming 'a freeman in fact, albeit still 'a slave in form.'

However, there is not a shred of contemporary evidence which could guide us to conclude that one or other of these options explained the poet's mindset in his last years.

He simply appears to be disengaged, and we cannot truly know not why. The apophthegm (erroneously) attributed to Burke comes to mind: 'the only thing necessary for the triumph of evil is for good men to do nothing.' And Burns did virtually nothing.

That is maybe too harsh a judgement, but the gaping gap in his sympathy hurts us. Perhaps it hurts so much because many of us have made similar mental reservations when faced with the endemic issues around race and slavery. Gerry Carruthers puts it well:

> That Burns, a man of undoubtedly genuine humanitarian spirit, is largely silent or maybe even confused on the Abolitionist issue

should be a sober lesson to us all in how, for various potential reasons, we can lose sight of the big socio-moral questions that face us. We should not be complacent. We live in a world where United Nations figures show us that slavery of one kind or another [...] is at least as endemic and virulent as in the time of Robert Burns. If Burns, arguably, did not do enough, too few of us who have come after him have done anything effective either.[17]

Yet that clashes with the near-universal and long-held view of Burns being a caring man, typified in a Burns Night poem written by the working-class, Anglo-Scot Robert McLean Calder (1841–1885) in the 1870s:

An' sympathy thou didna lack
Where stern oppression bowed the back
For serf or slave, or white or black,
    Thy heart did yearn.
An curst the tyrant wha could mak'
    'A brither mourn.'[18]

Or, as Kofi Annan described him a century later, 'a poet of the poor, an advocate of social and political change, and an opponent of slavery, pomposity and greed.'[19] Why was he inactive in caring for the victims of one of the greatest crimes against the humanity he otherwise championed? A passage that Dr Martin Luther King, Jr wrote in 1960 after meeting Senator John F Kennedy for the first time strikes a chord here:

John Kennedy did not have the grasp and comprehension of the depths of the problem at that time [June 1960], as he later did. He knew that segregation was morally wrong and he certainly intellectually committed himself to integration, but I could see that he didn't have the emotional involvement then. He had not

---

17 Carruthers, *Slavery*, p.174.
18 'Robert Burns. (Written for a Caledonian Society Gathering)', in Robert McLean Calder, *A Berwickshire Bard: The Songs and Poems of Robert McLean Calder*, ed by WS Crockett (Paisley: J and R Parlane, 1897), pp.17–25, lines 49–54.
19 Kofi Annan, 'Inaugural Robert Burns Memorial Lecture', United Nations Building, New York, 13 January 2004. Text from UN Information services: www.unis.unvienna.org/unis/pressrels/2004/sgsm9112.html (accessed 1 September 2024).

really been involved in and with the problem. He didn't know too many Negroes personally. He never had the personal experience of knowing the deep groans and passionate yearnings of the Negro for freedom, because he just didn't know Negroes generally and he hadn't any experience in the civil rights struggle [...] but I had no doubt he would do the right thing on the civil rights issue, if he were elected President.[20]

On balance, that seems to capture the position where we find Robert Burns: a man who exhibited moral and intellectual strength on other injustices, but was not as yet emotionally engaged with the specifics of Black chattel slavery. Like Dr King's judgement on the future president, considering Burns, we 'have no doubt he would do the right thing' in time. Unfortunately, he was not to be given that time.

The answer to the conundrum is not inside Burns's head, asleep in Dumfries, but in his voice, which is with us still. That voice has been used extensively in promoting the advance of Abolition, Emancipation and the Civil Rights movement by people of different countries, different decades and different skin colours. Those men and women who have been effective in calling out and combatting the injustices of slavery have embraced the poetry of Burns gladly, and have used his words for the last 200 years to exemplify our common humanity in opposition to the concepts and practices of enslavement in all its forms. No-one could rationally oppose the sentiment of 'a man's a man' today, and we combat 'man's inhumanity to man' formally in the United Nations Declaration of Human Rights, and informally by recognising the good and the strong insights in Burns's poems and songs. For while there is little in them specifically about Black chattel slavery, there is much about our inner humanity and how we should respond to wrong. Let the last word fall to Frederick Douglass, as the final verdict on Robert Burns and Slavery:

> The hope of the world is in human brotherhood; in the union of mankind, not in exclusive nationalities; in bringing the ends of the earth together, not in widening the distance between them; in world-wide co-operation, not in barren and fruitless isolation; and

---

20 King, *Autobiography*, pp.143-144.

until I give up the belief in the essential identity of human nature and human destiny, and shall adopt the belief that color is more than manhood, that progress is merely a fiction of the brain, that men were created to hate and destroy each other, and not to love, bless and improve each other, I shall continue to hope

> 'It's coming yet for a' that, —
> That man to man, the world all o'er,
> Shall brothers be' &c.[21]

Burns could have done more, but so could we, particularly when we are inspired by his words. Let us keep honouring his memory and his statues while actively using his words to continue to move society towards his dream of common, universal equality.

---

21 Frederick Douglass, 'The Haytian Emigration Movement,' *FDP*, Four, 1, p.88.

APPENDIX I

Original Article: 'Burns and Slavery'
(first posted on Scotland.org in December 2006)

ROBERT BURNS, SCOTLAND'S national poet, is loved the world over as the bard of freedom, liberty and the common good of humankind. So it comes as a great shock to many that he once accepted a job to help manage a slave plantation in the West Indies. What is the real story here? How could our Burns, the people's poet, look to become an instrument in what many now call 'The Black Holocaust'?

Hard Times and Difficult Choices

Burns's life had many turns of fate and in many ways, the year 1786 saw him at the lowest of them. Financially, he faced ruin as a combination of his father's death and the poor soil on the farm he worked with his brother had reduced them to near starvation. His love life was even more troubled. He had been nearly married to his first love Jean (to the horror of her parents and the Church) but they had agreed to separate (without knowing that Jean was pregnant with twins); then Robert had fallen in love with another, 'Highland Mary', who died suddenly while waiting for him to come to her. Jean's vindictive father sought court proceedings to arrest him so, like a fox with the hounds snapping at his heels, Robert needed to escape.

Patrick Douglas was a doctor and friend of Burns with investments in an estate in Jamaica. This made him wealthy through the sugar which was so much in demand in Scotland (We still retain a sweet tooth today!). His brother was the resident manager and had a vacancy on the small white staff of overseers. Burns accepted the position, although some friends worried about his health in the climate, and he planned his emigration from the woes around him.

But the fact that hurts is that, like all West Indian plantations, the Douglas enterprise was firmly built on black slave labour. Some commentators play the 'get-out-of-jail-free card' to RB here. He was 'only to be the bookkeeper'.

It is true that the appellation sounds quite dull; but being 'bookkeeper' was as much about managing the assets as the numbers. He would have a daily interface with the truth of slavery – from assisting in purchases, through recording punishments and deaths and an ambitious young man might seek advancement by volunteering to be more 'hands-on'. Certainly, in a letter, Burns described his role as 'a poor Negro driver' which puts him more on the executive than the administrative arm.

History intervened though as, in a last defiance of his enemies, he published his *Poems* to instant acclaim and Robert turned from the ports towards the City of Edinburgh, fame and marriage with Jean. But the worry remains: our poet had voluntarily contracted to become a manager of enslaved human beings – does this harm our view of him?

Burns and Slavery

The obvious irony is that 'slavery' is an important word in many of Burns's poems. His great national poem, based on Bruce's speech to the army before Bannockburn, 'Scots Wha Hae', reflects blood-firing sentiments that are still active in Scotland today. Throughout he contrasts the importance of freedom with the outrageously unacceptable 'Chains and Slaverie'.

The only directly relevant poem is 'The Slave's Lament' (of 1792) which, while not in the first rank of his talent, at least reinforces our view of Burns as the friend of humanity and an enemy of injustice or oppression.

> It was in sweet Senegal that my foes did me enthral,
>   For the lands of Virginia, –ginia, O:
> Torn from that lovely shore, and must never see it more;
>   And alas! I am weary, weary O:
>   Torn from that lovely shore, and must never see it more;
>   And alas! I am weary, weary O.
> All on that charming coast is no bitter snow and frost,
>   Like the lands of Virginia, –ginia, O:
> There streams for ever flow, and there flowers for ever blow,
>   And alas! I am weary, weary O:
>   There streams for ever flow, and there flowers for ever blow,

>   And alas! I am weary, weary O:
>   The burden I must bear, while the cruel scourge I fear,
>   In the lands of Virginia, –ginia, O;
>   And I think on friends most dear, with the bitter, bitter tear,
>   And alas! I am weary, weary O:
>   And I think on friends most dear, with the bitter, bitter tear,
>   And alas! I am weary, weary O.

So we have a definitively Abolitionist poem, but how do we reconcile those sentiments with Burns's contract to serve the slave masters?

Injustice at Home

The first step is to recognise Burns's total hatred of injustice. In his 'Address to Beelzebub' he attacks the chieftains who 'own' the Highland peasant folk trying to escape to a new life in Canada; while in 'The 'Twa Dogs', he pictures the poor Lowland tenants badgered by the laird's factor (an overseer in another context) when they are hard pressed to pay the rent. This reflects some cruel realities in Scotland at that time. Until 1799, coalminers and salters were legally bound for life as serfs to the pits and pans they worked – the master could legally sell mine and men as one going concern! So Burns had seen forms of slavery – legal in the case of miners and social in terms of the poor tenant farmers – in his native Ayrshire.

Many believed (either innocently or to hide their shame) that white serfdom and the black slavery were similar. Shortly after Burns's 1786 crisis, William Wilberforce made his first speech against the Slave trade, a call which particularly appealed to Scots and which grew into a popular Scottish movement for freedom, peaking in 1792. I think we see here the development of Robert's understanding of the iniquity of black slavery over those six years.

Injustice Abroad

The second element was in being a West Coast man. The economic foundation of Glasgow was the riches of the families who farmed – or had slaves to do it for them – the great Virginian tobacco fields. These entrepreneurs (whose names still grace the streets in Glasgow) created the wealth that allowed a commercial rivalry to Edinburgh. The 'Tobacco Lords' were astute and like the butcher who never shows how sausages are made, they held quiet on the true human costs. Sad to say that many were – or chose to be – fooled into accepting that pitiless proverb: 'you can't make an omelette without breaking eggs'.

Scots were prominent in the West Indies, representing over a third of the white Jamaican population. Advancement was possible, if you didn't focus on the morality. To make it easier, a salary of £30 a year looked quite tempting compared to an average labouring wage of £23 or the subsistence existence of a smallholder. Robert would have seen many lads leave in similar straits, only to return after a decade: weathered brown in skin, but golden in pocket.

I love Burns, but he was no saint (that's both a compliment and a criticism). He is a mix of passion and pragmatism, and in June 1786 he was in a right hard fix. Without reading his mind, did he see oppression and poverty in Scotland in a similar light to the oppression of Jamaica?

The Abolition Debate

Burns's growing awareness echoes the development of thought in Scotland arguing for Abolition. The arguments were strong, as some of us can understand from watching the apartheid regime collapse slowly, and that growing conviction would have been an influence on many.

In terms of the active debate, Burns would have seen the slave-holders championed by people that he despised: from Richard Oswald who bought the estate of Auchincruive near Robert's farm in Ayrshire from his profits as one of the few active Scots slave traders, to the noxious James McLehose (the feckless husband of 'Clarinda', his great Edinburgh love) – all people whom Burns reviled.

On the side of emancipation stood 'Dalrymple mild' of Ayr Auld Kirk who had baptised the infant Robert Burns in 1759, William Robertson and Hugh Blair in whose Edinburgh salons he was lionised and even that hard businessman Creech, the publisher of Burns's later editions. We know which people Burns would side with in this argument.

But in 1786, the position was less clear, voices were still gathering, evidence was remote and disguised; so it's not too hard to imagine a young man with no prospects grabbing at a lifeline and venturing abroad without too many questions. Upon arrival, we can only guess at his horror as the depravity and barbarism unfolded.

Thank heavens, the publication of his *Poems* meant that the sloop left for the Indies without Burns. I am certain that whatever the rationale for accepting the passage initially, the man who shared his fears with the mouse in the field, who consistently defied oppression and who understood 'man's inhumanity to man' could not have been complicit.

It seems too coincidental that the abolitionist's badge of the period, with Wedgwood's iconic design of the kneeling slave, carried the slogan:

'Am I not a man and a brother?'
Or as we sing with our Burns,
'that man to man the world o'er, shall brothers be for a' that.'
That is his true belief. Let it be so.

APPENDIX II

Frederick Douglass

A) Burns Anniversary Festival
Frederick Douglass' Paper [Rochester, NY], 2 February 1849.[1]

FREDERICK DOUGLASS, WHO was present as an invited guest, being called upon by a number of voices, rose and said — Mr Chairman: I regard it as a pleasure, not less than a privilege, to mingle my humble voice with the festivities of this occasion. Although I am not a Scotchman, nor the son of a Scotchman, (perhaps you will say 'it needs no ghost to tell us that,' [a laugh,] but if a warm love of Scotch character — a high appreciation of; Scotch genius — constitute any of the qualities of a true Scotch heart, then indeed does a Scotch heart throb beneath these ribs. From my earliest acquaintance with Scotland, I have held that country in the highest admiration. As I travelled through that land two years since, and became acquainted with its people, and realized their warmth of heart, steadiness of purpose, and learned that every stream, hill, glen and valley, had been rendered classic by heroic deeds in behalf of Freedom, that admiration was increased. That you may know that I have some appreciation of the genius of the bard whose birth-day you are here to celebrate, I went a pilgrimage to see the cottage in which he was born; and had the pleasure of seeing and conversing with a sister of the noble poet Io whose memory we have met to do honor. I can truly say that it was one of the most gratifying visits I made during my stay in Scotland. I saw', or thought l saw, some lingering sparks in the eyes of this sister, that raised to mind the fire that ever warmed the bosom of Burns. But, ladies and gentlemen, this is not a time for long speeches I do not

---

1 A number of Scottish Newspapers carried the following short report (or a version of it):
A MAN'S A MAN FOR A' THAT. —At the conclusion of a short speech at a Burns' anniversary festival, in Rochester (US), Mr Frederick Douglass said: — 'Though I am not a Scotchman, and I have a coloured skin, I am proud to be among you this evening. And if any think me out of my place on this occasion (pointing at the picture of Burns) , I beg that the blame may be laid at the door of him who taught me that "a man's a man for a' that."' *Scotsman*, 10 March 1849.

wish to detain you from the social pleasures that await you. I repeat again, that though I am not a Scotchman. and have a colored skin, I am proud to be among you this evening. — And if any think me out of my place on this occasion: [pointing at the picture of Burns,] I beg that the blame may be laid at the door of him who taught me that 'a man's a man for a' that.' [Mr D sat down amid loud cries of 'go on!' from the audience.] Mr Dempster, the Scottish vocalist, very opportunely happened to be in the city on this evening, and as became a true Scotchman and admirer of the Scotch poet, hastened to lend the aid of his eloquent voice to add to the interest of the occasion. [Dempster sang] that song of Burns' which is, and will always be, the admiration of all men: 'A man's a man for a' that,' which brought raptures of applause from the audience. It was after the singing of this song, that the call for Mr Douglass arose, and that 'man for a' that,' got upon the platform, and delivered a short speech, of which a sketch will be found above.

B) A Fugitive Slave Visiting the Birthplace of Robert Burns
Albany Evening Journal, 13 June 1846.

The following is an extract from a Letter of FREDERICK DOUGLASS, to a Friend, dated April 23, 1846. The writer, be it remembered, is a 'Runaway Slave,' who, during his eight years of stolen Freedom, in defiance of all the disadvantages under which his class labor, has qualified himself to think and write thus: –

I am now in the town of Ayr. It is famous for being the birth-place of Robert Burns, the poet, by whose brilliant genius every stream, hill, glen and valley in the neighborhood have been made classic. I have felt more intense in visiting this place than any other in Scotland, for, as you are aware, (painfully perhaps) I am an enthusiastic admirer of Rob[er]t Burns.
    Immediately on our arrival, Friend Buffum and myself were joined by the Rev. Mr Renwick, the Minister in whose meeting house we are to lecture during our stay, and proceeded forthwith to see Burns' Monument. It is about three miles from town, and situated on the south bank of the river 'Doon,' and within hearing of its gentle steps

as it winds its way over its pebbled path to the Ocean.

The place of the Monument is well chosen, being in full view of all the places mentioned and referred to in the Poet's famous poem called 'Tam O'Shanter,' as well as several others of his most popular poems. From the Monument (which I have not time to describe,) may be seen the Cottage where Burns was born – the old and new bridge across the Doon – 'Kirk Alloway,' called by Burns the 'Haunted Kirk.' The banks of 'Doon' rising majestically from the sea toward the sky, and the Clyde stretching off to the highlands of Arran, whose dim out-line is scarcely discernible through the fog by which it is almost constantly overhung, makes the spot admirably and beautifully adapted to the monument of Scotland's noble bard.

In the Monument there is a finely executed marble bust of Burns – the finest thing of the kind I ever saw. I never before, looking upon it, realized the power of man to make the marble speak. The expression is so fine, and the face is so lit up, as to cause one to forget the form in gazing upon the spirit.

In another room, there are two statues carved out of free-stone – the one of Souter Johnny and the other of Tam O'Shanter, two characters named in his most famous poem. These were also finely executed and shared my attention, but I was drawn to Burns. In a glass case near his bust there was a bible, given by Burns to his 'sweet Highland Mary' – there is also in the same case a lock of her hair neatly fastened to a card.

As I gazed on the hair of her he so dearly loved, and who by death was snatched from his bosom, and up to his bust glowing with expression, I received a vivid impression, and shared with him the deep melancholy pourtrayed in the following lines –

> Ye banks and braes of bonnie Doon,
> How can ye bloom sae fresh and fair;
> How can ye chant, ye little birds,
> And I sea weary, fu' o' care!
> Thou'll break my heart, thou warbling bird,
> That wantons thro' the flowering thorn:
> Thou minds me o' departed joys,
> Departed never to return.

Oft hae I rov'd by a bonnie Doon
To see the rose and woodbine twine.
And ilka bird sang o' its luve,
And fondly sae did I o' mine.
Wi' lightsome heart I pu'd a rose,
Fu' sweet upon its thorny tree,
And my fause luver stole my rose,
But ah! She left the thorn wi' me.

On our way to the Monument we enjoyed a pleasure and a privilege I shall never forget. It was that of seeing and conversing with Mrs. Beggs, an own sister of Robert Burns, and also seeing and talking with the poet's two nieces, daughters of Mrs Beggs. They live by the road side in a small thatched cottage, humble but comfortable. When Mr. Renwick made them acquainted with the fact that we were from America they received us warmly. One of the nieces said her uncle was more highly esteemed in America than in Scotland. –

Mrs Beggs [sic] is the youngest sister of Robert Burns, and though now approaching 80, she does not look to be more than sixty. She enjoys good health, is a spirited looking woman, and bids fair to live yet many days. The two daughters are truly fine looking women. Coal black hair, full, high foreheads, and yet black eyes, sparkling with the poetic fire which illumined the breast of their brilliant uncle.

Their deportment was warm and free, yet dignified and lady-like. They did every thing to make our call agreeable, and they were not ignorant as to the means of putting us fully at ease. Two letters in their uncle's own hand writing was early put into our hands. An original portrait, said to be excellent, was discoursed upon. I thought it much like those we usually see in his works.

We sat fifteen or twenty minutes. It might have been longer, as happy moments pass rapidly. Too leave – bade farewell. I saw in them so much of what I love in every body else. I felt as if leaving old and dear friends. I have ever esteemed Robert Burns a true soul but never could I have had the high opinion of the man or his genius, which I now entertain, without my present knowledge of the country to which he belonged – the times in which he lived, and the broad Scotch tongue in which he wrote.

Burns lived in the midst of a bigoted and besotted clergy – a pious but corrupt generation – a proud, ambitious, and contemptuous aristocracy, who, esteemed a little more than a man, and looked upon the ploughman, such as was the noble Burns, as being little better than a brute. He became disgusted with the pious frauds, indignant at the bigotry, filled with contempt for the hollow pretensions set up by the shallow-brained aristocracy.

He broke loose from the moorings which society had thrown around him. Spurning all restraint, he sought a path for his feet, and, like all bold pioneers, he made crooked paths. We may lament it, we may weep over it, but in the language of another, we shall lament and weep with him. The elements of character which urged him on are in us all, and influencing our conduct every day of our lives. We may pity him but we can't despise him. WE may condemn his faults, but only as we condemn our own. His very weakness was an index of his strength. Full of faults of a grievous nature, yet far more faultless than many who have come down to us on the page of history as saints. He was a brilliant genius and like all of his class, did much good and much evil. Let us take the good and leave the evil – let us pursue his wisdom but shun his folly; and as death as separated his noble spirit from the corrupt and corruptible dust with which it was encumbered, so let us separate his good from his evil deeds – thus may we make him a blessing rather than a curse to the world.

Read his 'Tam O'Shanter,' 'Cottar's Saturday Night,' 'Man was Made to Mourn,' 'To my Mary in heaven.' Indeed, dear A, read his poems, and, as I know you are no admirer of Burns, read it to gratify your friend Frederick. So much for Burns.'

c) Self-made Men
in John Blassingame and John McKivigan IV, eds,
The Frederick Douglass Papers, Series One, Volume 5
(New Haven: Yale University Press, 1992), pp.545–575

The subject announced for this evening's entertainment is not new. Man in one form or another, has been a frequent and fruitful subject for the press, the pulpit and the platform. This subject has come up for consideration under a variety of attractive titles, such as 'Great Men,' 'Representative Men,' 'Peculiar Men,' 'Scientific Men,' 'Literary

Men,' 'Successful Men,' 'Men of Genius,' and 'Men of the World'; but under whatever name or designation, the vital point of interest in the discussion has ever been the same, and that is, manhood itself, and this in its broadest and most comprehensive sense. [...]

But it is not my purpose to attempt here any comprehensive and exhaustive theory or philosophy or the nature of manhood in all the range I have indicated. I am here to speak to you of a peculiar type of manhood under the title of Self-Made Men. [...]

My first [question] is, 'Who are self-made men?' My second is, 'What is the true theory of their success?' My third is, 'The advantages which self-made men derive from the manners and institutions of their surroundings,' and my fourth is, 'The grounds of the criticism to which they are, as a class, especially exposed.'

On the first point I may say that, by the term 'self-made men,' I mean especially what, to the popular mind, the term itself imports. Self-made men are the men who, under peculiar difficulties and without the ordinary helps of favoring circumstances, have attained knowledge, usefulness, power and position and have learned from themselves the best uses to which life can be put in this world, and in the exercises of these uses to build up worthy character. They are the men who owe little or nothing to birth, relationship, friendly surroundings; to wealth inherited or to early approved means of education; who are what they are, without the aid of any of the favoring conditions by which other men usually rise in the world and achieve great results. In fact they are the men who are not brought up but who are obliged to come up, not only without the voluntary assistance or friendly co-operation of society, but often in open and derisive defiance of all the efforts of society and the tendency of circumstances to repress, retard and keep them down. They are the men who, in a world of schools, academies, colleges and other institutions of learning, are often compelled by unfriendly circumstances to acquire their education elsewhere and, amidst unfavorable conditions, to hew out for themselves a way to success, and thus to become the architects of their own good fortunes. They are in a peculiar sense, indebted to themselves for themselves. If they have traveled far, they have made the road on which they have travelled. If they have ascended high, they have built their own ladder. From the depths of poverty such as these have often come. From the heartless pavements of large and crowded cities; barefooted, homeless, and friendless, they have come. From hunger, rags and destitution, they have come; motherless and fatherless, they have come, and may come. Flung overboard in the midnight storm on the broad and tempest-tossed ocean of life; left without ropes, planks, oars or life-preservers, they have bravely buffeted the frowning billows and have risen in safety and life where others, supplied with the best appliances for safety and success, have fainted, despaired and gone down forever.

Such men as these, whether found in one position or another, whether in the college or in the factory; whether professors or plowmen; whether Caucasian or Indian; whether Anglo-Saxon or Anglo-African, are self-made men and are entitled to a certain measure of respect for their success and for proving to the world the grandest possibilities of human nature, of whatever variety of race or color. [...]

But I come at once to the second part of my subject, which respects the Theory of Self-Made Men.

'Upon what meat doth this, our Caesar, feed, he hath grown so great?' How happens it that the cottager is often found equal to the lord, and that, in the race of life, the sons of the poor often get even with, and surpass even, the sons of the rich? How happens it from the field often come statesmen equal to those from the college? I am sorry to say that, upon this interesting point, I can promise nothing absolute nor anything which will be entirely satisfactory and conclusive. Burns says:

> I see how folks live that hae riches,
> But surely poor folks maun be witches

The various conditions of men and the different uses they make of their powers and opportunities in life, are full of puzzling contrasts and contradictions. Here, as elsewhere, it is easy to dogmatize, but it is not so easy to define, explain and demonstrate. The natural laws for the government, well-being and progress of mankind, seem to be equal and are equal; but the subjects of these laws everywhere abound in inequalities, discords and contrasts. We cannot have fruit without flowers, but we often have flowers without fruit. The promise of youth often breaks down in manhood, and real excellence often comes unheralded and from unexpected quarters. [...]

My theory of self-made men is, then, simply this: that they are men of work. Whether or not such men have acquired material, moral or intellectual excellence, honest labor faithfully, steadily and persistently pursued, is the best, if not the only, explanation of their success. But in thus awarding praise to industry, as the main agency in the production and culture of self-made men, I do not exclude other factors of the problem. I only make them subordinate. Other agencies co-operate, but this is the principal one and the one without which all others would fail. [...]

I do not desire my lecture to become a sermon; but, were this allowable, I would rebuke the growing tendency to sport and pleasure. The time, money and strength devoted to these phantoms, would banish darkness and hunger from every hearthstone in our land. Multitudes, unconscious of any controlling object in life, flit, like birds, from point to point; now here, now there; and so accomplish nothing, either here or there.

> For pleasures are like poppies spread,
> You seize the flower, its bloom is shed!
> Or like the snow-falls in the river,
> A moment white — then melts forever;
> Or like the borealis race,
> That flit ere you can point their place;
> Or like the rainbow's lovely form
> Evanishing amid the storm.

They know most of pleasure who seek it least, and they least who seek it most. The cushion is soft to him who sits on it but seldom. The men behind the chairs at Saratoga and Newport, get better dinners than the men in them. We cannot serve two masters. When here, we cannot be there. If we accept ease, we must part with appetite. A pound of feathers is as heavy as a pound of iron, —and about as hard, if you sit on it long enough. Music is delightful, but too much of it wounds the ear like the filing of a saw. The lounge, to the lazy, becomes like flint; and to him, the most savory dishes lose their flavor.

> It's true, they need na starve or sweat,
> Thro' winter's cauld or simmer's heat;
> But human bodies are sic fools,
> For all their colleges an' schools,

> That when na real ills perplex them,
> They mak enow, themselves to vex them.

But the industrious man does find real pleasure. He finds it in qualities and quantities to which the baffled pleasure seeker is a perpetual stranger. He finds it in the house well built, in the farm well tilled, in the books well kept, in the page well written, in the thought well expressed, in all the improved conditions of life around him and in whatsoever useful work may, for the moment, engage his time and energies. [...]

Examples of successful self-culture and self-help under great difficulties and discouragements, are abundant, and they vindicate the theory of success thus feebly and with homely common sense, presented. For example: Hugh Miller, whose lamented death mantled the mountains and valleys of his native land with a broad shadow of sorrow, scarcely yet lifted, was a grand example of the success of persistent devotion, under great difficulties, to work and to the acquisition of knowledge. In a country justly distinguished for its schools and colleges, he, like Robert Burns, Scotia's matchless son of song, was the true child of science, as Burns was of song. He was his own college. The earth was his school and the rocks were his school master. Outside of all the learned institutions of his country, and while employed with his chisel and hammer, as a stone mason, this man literally killed two birds with one stone; for he earned his daily bread and at the same time made himself an eminent geologist, and gave to the world books which are found in all public libraries and which are full of inspiration to the truth seeker. [...]

A word now upon the third point suggested at the beginning of this paper; namely, The friendly relation and influence of American ideas and institutions to this class of men. [...]

America is said, and not without reason, to be preeminently the home and patron of self-made men. Here, all doors fly open to them. [...]

Of course these remarks are not intended to apply to the states where slavery has but recently existed. That system was the extreme degradation of labor, and though happily now abolished its consequences still linger and may not disappear for a century. To-day, in the presence of the capitalist, the Southern black laborer stands abashed, confused and intimidated. He is compelled to beg his fellow worm to give him leave to toil. Labor can never be respected where the laborer is despised. This is today, the great trouble at the South. [...]

But the respectability of labor is not, as already intimated, the only or the most powerful cause of the facility with which men rise from humble conditions to affluence and importance in the United States. A more subtle and powerful influence is exerted by the fact that the principle of measuring and valuing men according to their respective merits and without regard to their antecedents, is better established and more generally enforced here than in any other country. In Europe, greatness is often thrust upon men. They are made legislators by birth.

> A king can make a belted knight,
> A marquis, duke and a' that.

But here, wealth and greatness are forced by no such capricious and arbitrary power. Equality of rights brings equality of positions and dignities. Here society very properly saves itself the trouble of looking up a man's kinfolks in order to determine his grade in life and the measure of respect due him. It cares very little who was his father or grandfather. [...]

Ladies and gentlemen: Accept my thanks for your patient attention. I will detain you no longer. If, by statement, argument, sentiment or example, I have awakened in any, a sense of the dignity of labor or the value of manhood, or have stirred in any mind, a courageous resolution to make one more effort towards self-improvement and higher usefulness, I have not spoken altogether in vain, and your patience is justified.

Bibliography

Manuscripts

Ayr Carnegie Library: *Air Library Society Minutes: 1776–1830,* Local Collection 670/QMC.

Beinecke Rare Book & Manuscript Library, Yale Library General Collection of Rare Books and Manuscripts, Boswell Collection Addition, MS GEN 150, Box 3, folders 111–113. *Correspondence between Charles Douglas and Patrick Douglas.*

'Inventories of the Estate of Charles Douglas, with Copies of His Will,' GEN MSS 150: Box 21/Folder 621.

Patrick Charles Douglas Boswell Family Papers 1653–1807, MS GEN 972, Box 1, Folder 2471/10, *Patrick Douglas, Journals, 1799–1804.*

Folder 2479, *Indenture Between Mr Robert Johnston and Patrick Douglas, Whitsunday 1746.*

Folders 2474/1–11, *Patrick Douglas, Journals and Day Books, 1778–1807.*

Thomas Thistlewood Papers, OSB MSS 176, Series I. Diaries. Diaries of Thomas Thistlewood.

British Museum, 'Hastie Manuscript,' MS 22307.

Friends' Library, London, William Dickson, 'Diary of a Visit to Scotland for the Abolition Committee, January – March 1792.' TEMP MSS 10/14/2.

Library Company of Philadelphia, Mary Anne Dickerson, *Album,* [13860.Q].

Mount Stuart, Rothesay, Bute Collection, Robert Burns, *Poems, Chiefly in the Scottish Dialect,* 2 vols (Edinburgh/London: William Creech/T Cadell, 1793).

National Archives [of the USA], George Washington's Last Will and Testament, 9 July 1799 at Founders Online, National Archives, founders.archives.gov/documents/Washington/06-04-02-0404-0001 (last accessed 1 September 2024.)

National Records of Scotland, *Ailsa Muniments,* GD25/9/72/9, 'Contract Betwixt Sir John Kennedy & Scipio Kennedy his servant for 19 years, 6 February 1725.'

Ayr Kirk Session Minutes (1781–1793), CH2/751/14.

Kirkoswald Kirk Session Minutes (1617–1660, 1694–1758), CH2/562/1.

Old Parish Registers, Ayr, Births, 578/40.

Canongate, Deaths, 658/3.
Kirkoswald, Births, 601/20.
Kirkoswald, Marriages, 601/20.
Mauchline, Births, 604/20.

Synod of Dumfries Minutes (1787–1805), CH2/98/5.

Synod of Glasgow and Ayr, Minutes (1761–1802), CH2/464/4.

Male Servant Tax Rolls, volume 1 (1777–1778, counties) E326/5/1/20; volume 2 (1778–1779, counties) E326/5/3/20.

Robert Burns Birthplace Museum, *Letter, Charles Douglas to Patrick Douglas, 19 June 1786,* Object Number 3.6138.

Letter, Charles Douglas to Patrick Douglas, 8 August 1786, Object Number 3.6139.

First Minute Book of the Trustees of Burns Monument.

Robert Burns, *The Stair Manuscript*.

The Afton Lodge Manuscript.

Rosenbach Museum and Library, Philadelphia, David Humphreys, *Manuscript Biography of George Washington, [1778]*, American Manuscript Collection, AMS 1079/6.

University of Rochester Library, Rare Books and Special Collections, Robert Burns, *The Works of Robert Burns: With an Account of his Life, And Criticism on his Writings: To Which are Prefixed, Some Observations on the Character and Condition of the Scottish Peasantry by James Currie, MD; Including Additional Poems, Extracted from the Late Edition Edited by Allan Cunningham* (Philadelphia: J. Crissy, 1841), as inscribed by Frederick Douglass.

The University of Michigan, William L Clements Library, *James Stothert Papers (1784–1807)*: Acquisition 1974. M-1650.

Legislation and Law Cases

Acts of the Parliament of Scotland, iv, 286 [1606], c.10: 'An Act anent Coalyers and Salters, 1606.'

Acts of the Parliament of Scotland, iv, 535, [1617] c.8, 'Regarding the Justices for Keeping of the King's Majesty's Peace and their Constables, 1617.'

Acts of the Assembly of Virginia, 4 Anne c.XLIX, An Act Concerning Servants and Slaves, [1705].

12 William II, c6 The Criminal Procedure Act, 1701 (APSX 272 c6).

10 Ann, c.12, 'The Church Patronage (Scotland) Act, 1711.'

15 Geo III, c.58, 'An Act [...] respecting Colliers, Coal-bearers, and Salters, 1775.'

25 Geo III, c.37, 'Bridge of Ayr Act, 1785.'

28 Geo III, c.54, 'An Act to regulate, for a Limited Time, the Shipping and Carrying of Slaves in British Vessels from the Coast of Africa, 1788.'

34 Geo III, c.59, 'Ayr Harbour Act 1794.'

39 Geo III, c.55, 'An Act to Explain and Amend the Laws Relative to Colliers in that Part of Great Britain called Scotland, 1799.'

3 & 4 Will IV c.73, 'Slavery Abolition Act, 1833.'

Reid against Scot[t] of Harden and his Lady, (1687) MOR 9505; Fountainhalls, I.439.

Sir William Wallace of Craigie v William Cunningham of Brownhill, (1708) MOR 2349.

The Burgesses of Rutherglen v Andrew Leitch, (1747) MOR 1841.

Robert Sheddan against a Negro, (1757), MOR, 14545; 5 Brn 324.

David Dalrymple against David Spens [Spence], a Negro, Court of Session: Unextracted processes, 1st arrangement, McNeill office (1574–1861), NRS, CS236/D/4/3 box 104 and NRS, CS236/S/3/13.

HM Advocate v Bel[l] alias Belinda; NRS, JC26/193 and NRS, JC11/28.

Mrs Margaret Porterfield v Houston Stewart Nicolson of Carnock (1770); Hailes Decisions, vol.I, pp.371–378.

Mrs Margaret Houston Stewart Nicolson v Houston Stewart Nicolson, Esq, House of Lords, upon Appeal from The Courts of Scotland, (1771) 3 Paton 655.

Lieutenant William Stewart v James Graham (1782) [unreported, at scos.law.virginia.edu/node/54751], (accessed 1 September 2024).

Somerset v Stewart (1772), English Reports vol. 98, pp.499–510.
Joseph Knight, a Negro, against John Wedderburn, Esq, (1774), *Hailes Decisions*, vol.I, pp.776–780.
'Corporations (Scotland): General Report and Local Reports,' *Parliamentary Papers: Session 19 February – 10 September 1835*, vol.XXIX.

Books and Articles

'A Student of the Temple,' The Trial of Captain John Kimber, for the Murder of Two Female Negro Slaves on Board the Recovery, African Slave Ship (London: C Stalker, [1792]).
Abramson, Jill, 'Far from the Tree,' *The New Yorker*, 14 March 2022, pp.20–26.
Adair, James M, *Unanswerable Arguments Against the Abolition of the Slave Trade, With a Defence of the Proprietors of the British Sugar Colonies* (London: J P Bateman, [1790]).
Addison, W Innes, *The Matriculation Albums of the University of Glasgow. From 1728 to 1858* (Glasgow: James McLehose, 1913).
Aitcheson, Jean, 'Servants in Ayrshire 1750 – 1914' in *Ayrshire Monographs No 26* (Ayr: AANHS, 2001).
Alibhai-Brown, Yasmin, 'LKJ: As Good as His Words,' *The Independent* [London], 19 June 2003.
Allan, William, *A Book of Poems: Democratic Chants and Songs in English and Scottish* (Sunderland: Hills, 1891).
Anderson-Wright, Helena, 'A Secret of No Importance?', *Burns Chronicle* (Spring 2013), pp.10–12.
Andrews, Corey, '"Ev'ry Heart Can Feel": Scottish Poetic Responses to Slavery in the West Indies, from Blair to Burns', *International Journal of Scottish Literature*, 4, (Spring/Summer, 2008).
  'Burns the Critic' in *The Edinburgh Companion to Robert Burns*, ed by Gerard Carruthers (Edinburgh: Edinburgh University Press, 2009), pp.110–124.
Andrews, Ethan Allen, *Slavery and the Domestic Slave Trade in the United States* (Boston: Light & Stearns, 1836).
Annan, Kofi, 'Inaugural Robert Burns Memorial Lecture, United Nations Building, New York, 13 January 2004' (New York: UN Information Services, 2004).
Anon, *Lloyds Register of Shipping for 1786* (London: Lloyds Register, 1786).
Anon, *Lloyds Register of Shipping for 1787* (London: Lloyds Register, 1787).
Anon, 'The Epilogue to "The Padlock"', *Gentleman's Magazine* (October 1787), pp.913–914.
Anon, *Strictures on an Address to the People of Great Britain on the Propriety of Abstaining from West Indies Sugar and Rum* (London: T Boosey, 1792).
Anon, *A Voice to the United States of America, from the Metropolis of Scotland* (Edinburgh: William Oliphant and Son, 1836).
Anon, *Report of the Speeches and Reception of the American Delegates at the Great Public Meeting of the Glasgow Emancipation Society* (Glasgow: George Gallie, 1840).
Anon, *Celebration of the Centennial Anniversary of the Birth of Robert Burns, by the Burns Club of Washington City, DC* (Washington DC: Joseph Shillington, 1859).

Anon, 'The Centennial Anniversary of the Birth of Robert Burns, Celebrated in Springfield, January 25, 1859,' *Journal of the Illinois State Historical Society*, vol. 17 (April–July 1924), pp.205–210.

Anon, *Proceedings of the American Anti-slavery Society at its Second Decade [...] December 1853* (New York: American Anti-Slavery Society, 1854).

Anon, *Proceedings of the Convention, of the Colored Freemen of Ohio, Held in Cincinnati, January 14, 15, 16, 17 and 19, 1852* (Cincinnati: Dumas & Lawyer, 1852).

Anon, *Proceedings of The State Convention of the Colored People of South Carolina, Held in Zion Church, Charleston, November 1865* (Charleston, SC: South Carolina Leader Office, 1865).

Anon, 'Burns' Jamaica Connections,' *Burns Chronicle* (1903), pp.79–83.

Anon, 'Enterprise and Refinement: James Hunter and the Ayr Sugar House,' www.southayrshirehistory.wordpress.com/2013/08/05/enterprise-and-refinement-james-hunter-and-the-ayr-sugar-house/ [accessed 1 September 2024.]

Aristotle, *Politics*, Loeb Classical Library 264, trans by H Rackham (Cambridge, MA: Harvard University Press, 1932).

Bailes, Melissa, 'Hybrid Britons: West Indian Colonial Identity and Maria Riddell's "Natural History",' *European Romantic Review*, April 2009, pp.207–217.

Baldwin, Revd AC, 'Letters to a Christian Slaveholder,' in *Three Prize Essays on American Slavery* [ed by Sewell Harding] (Boston: Congregational Board for Publishing, 1857).

Ballantine, James, *Chronicle of the Hundredth Birthday of Robert Burns* (Edinburgh/London: A Fullerton & Co, 1859).

Barclay, Tom, *Report: Monuments in Council Care, Council Property and Street Names in South Ayrshire with Possible Connections to Slavery and Other Negative Aspects of Britain's Colonial Past, and to Racism* (Ayr: South Ayrshire Council, [2021]).

Basker, James, ed, *Amazing Grace: An Anthology of Poems about Slavery, 1660–1810* (New Haven: Yale University Press, 2002).

Beattie, James, *The Minstrel; Or, the Progress of Genius. A Poem*, 2 vols (London: E & C Dilly, 1771–1774).

Original Poems and Translations (London: A Millar, 1760).

An Essay on the Nature and Immutability of Truth: In Opposition to Sophistry and Scepticism (Edinburgh/London: A Kincaid and J Bell/E and C Dilly, 1771).

Elements of Moral Science, 2 vols (London/Edinburgh: T Cadell/William Creech, 1790/1793).

Bedini, A Silvio, *The Life of Benjamin Banneker* (New York: Landmark, 1972).

Bellhouse, Mary L, 'Candide shoots the Monkey Lovers: Representing Black Men in Eighteenth-Century French Visual Culture,' in *Political Theory*, December 2006, pp.741–784.

Bennie, Revd Archibald, 'Speech Seconding the Resolution,' Public Meeting, 8 February, 1836', in Anon, *A Voice to the United States of America, from the Metropolis of Scotland* (Edinburgh: William Oliphant and Son, 1836), p.21.

Bergner, George, ed, *The Legislative Record: Containing the Debates and Proceedings of the Pennsylvania Legislature for the Session of 1866* (Harrisburg, [PA]: Telegraph Steam Book and Job Office, 1866).

Biagetti, Samuel, '"What Virtue Unites, Death Cannot Separate": The Trials of Early Freemasonry in Jamaica, 1739–1800,' *The Journal of Caribbean History*, 51.1 (2017), pp.1–27.

The Holy Bible (Authorised King James Version).

Bingham, Caleb, ed, *The Columbian Orator: Containing a Variety of Original and Selected Pieces, Together with Rules, Calculated to Improve Youth and Others in the Ornamental and Useful Art of Eloquence* (Boston: J H A Frost, 1832).

Black History Museum Committee, eds, *Sterling A Brown, A UMUM Tribute* (Philadelphia: Black History Museum UMUM Publishers, 1982).

Blair, Hugh, *Lectures on Rhetoric and Belles Lettres*, 3 vols (London/Edinburgh: A Strahan and T Cadell/W Creech, 1787).

Sermons, 4 vols (London/Edinburgh: A Strahan and T Cadell/W Creech, 1790–1794).

Blair, Robert, *The Grave, a Poem* (London: G Robinson, 1776).

Boileau-Despréaux, Nicolas, *The Works of Mons[ieu]r Boileau Despereaux*, 2 vols (London: E Sanger and E Curll, 1711).

Bold, Valentina, *Robert Burns & 'The Slave's Lament'* [Talk delivered at Wigtown Book Town Festival, 2007].

Bond, Gregory, 'The Strange Career of William Henry Lewis,' in David K Wiggins, ed, *Out of the Shadows: A Biographical History of African American Athletes* (Fayetteville, AR: University of Arkansas Press, 2006), pp.39–58.

Boswell, James, *The Journal of a Tour to the Hebrides, with Samuel Johnson, LLD* (London: Charles Dilly, 1785).

[Anonymously], *No Abolition of Slavery; Or the Universal Empire of Love; A Poem* (London: R Faulder, 1791).

Boxill, Bernard R, 'A Man's a Man for All That,' *The Monist*, April 2010, pp.188–207.

Bradford, Sarah H, *Harriet: The Moses of Her People* (New York: George Lockwood & Sons, 1886).

Brady, Steven J, *Chained to History: Slavery and US Foreign Relations to 1865* (Ithaca, NY: Cornell University Press, 2022).

Branagan, Thomas, *The Penitential Tyrant, or, Slave Trader Reformed: A pathetic poem, in four cantos* (New York: Samuel Wood, 1807).

Bright, Henry A, ed, *Some Account of the Glenriddell MSS of Burns's Poems: With Several Poems never before Published* (Liverpool: Gilbert G Walmsey, 1874).

Brown, Hugh Stowell, *Twelve Lectures to the Men of Liverpool, Volume Second* (Liverpool: Gabriel Thomson, 1859).

Brown, MP, ed, *Decisions of the Lords of Council and Session, Reported by Sir David Dalrymple, Bart, Lord Hailes*, 2 vols (Edinburgh: Wm Tait, 1826).

Brown, Rhona, '"Guid Black Prent": Robert Burns and the Contemporary Scottish and American Periodical Press,' in Sharon Alker, Leith Davis and Holly Nelson, eds, Robert *Burns and Transatlantic Culture* (Farnham: Ashgate, 2012), pp.71–98.

Brown, William Wells, *The Anti-Slavery Harp: A Collection of Songs for Antislavery Meetings* (Boston: Bela Marsh, 1849).

The American Fugitive in Europe: Sketches of Places and People Abroad (Boston/Cleveland, OH/New York: John P Jewett and Company/Jewett, Proctor & Worthington/Sheldon, Lamport & Blakeman, 1855).

Burnard, Trevor, '"The Countrie Continues Sicklie": White Mortality in Jamaica, 1655–1780,' *Social History of Medicine*, 12.1 (1999), pp.45–72.

'Plantation Slavery in the British Caribbean,' in Damien A Pargas and Juliane Schiel, eds, *The Palgrave Handbook of Global Slavery Throughout History* (London: Palgrave Macmillan, 2023), pp.395–412.

Burnard, Trevor, Laura Panza and Jeffrey G Williamson, *The Social Implications of Sugar: Living Costs, Real Incomes and Inequality in Jamaica c. 1744* (Cambridge, MA: National Bureau of Economic Research, 2017).

Burns, Robert, *Poems, Chiefly in the Scottish Dialect* (Kilmarnock: John Wilson, 1786).

Poems, Chiefly in the Scottish Dialect, To which are added, Scots Poems selected from the works of Robert Fergusson (New York: J and A McLean, 1788).

Poems, Chiefly in the Scottish Dialect, 2 vols (Edinburgh/London: William Creech/T Cadell, 1793).

The Works of Robert Burns. With an Account of his Life, and a Criticism on His Writings, to which are Prefixed, Some Observations on the Character and Conditions of Scottish Peasantry, 4 vols, ed by James Currie (London/Edinburgh: Cadell & Davies/Creech, 1800).

The Works of Robert Burns. With an Account of his Life, and a Criticism on His Writings, to which are Prefixed, Some Observations on the Character and Conditions of Scottish Peasantry [Second Edition], 4 vols, ed by James Currie (London/Edinburgh: Cadell & Davies/Creech, 1801).

The Poetical Works of Robert Burns. Collated with the Best Editions, 2 vols ed by Thomas Park (London: J Sharpe, 1807).

The Poems & Songs of Robert Burns, With a Life of the Author, ed by Revd Hamilton Paul (Air: Wilson and McCormick, 1819).

The Works of Robert Burns, [...] (Philadelphia: J Crissy, 1841).

The Complete Poetical Works of Robert Burns with Explanatory and Glossarial Notes and a Life of the Author, by James Currie MD (New York: D Appleton, 1842).

The Life and Works of Robert Burns, 4 vols, ed by Robert Chambers (London/Edinburgh: W&R Chambers, 1851–1854).

The Poetical Works of Robert Burns, With Memoir, Critical Dissertation and Explanatory Notes, 2 vols, ed by Revd George Gilfillan (Edinburgh/London/Dublin: James Nicol/James Nisbet/W Robertson, 1856).

The Works of Robert Burns, 2 vols (Glasgow: Blackie & Son, 1857).

The Songs of Robert Burns, ed by James C Dick (London/New York: Henry Frowde, 1903).

The Poems and Songs of Robert Burns, 3 vols, ed by James Kinsley (Oxford: Clarendon Press, 1968).

The Letters of Robert Burns (Second Edition), 2 vols, ed by J De Lancey Ferguson and G Ross Roy (Oxford: OUP, 1985).

The Oxford Edition of the Works of Robert Burns: Volume I: Commonplace Books, Tour Journals, and Miscellaneous Prose, ed by Nigel Leask (Oxford: OUP, 2014).

The Oxford Edition of the Works of Robert Burns: Volumes II and III: The Scots Musical Museum, ed by Murray Pittock (Oxford: OUP, 2018).

The Oxford Edition of the Works of Robert Burns: Volume IV: Robert Burns's Songs for George Thomson, ed by Kirsteen McCue (Oxford: OUP, 2021).

Burns, Robert and Mrs Frances Anna Wallace Dunlop of Dunlop, ed by William Wallace, *Robert Burns and Mrs Dunlop* (London: Hodder & Stoughton, 1896).

Burns, Robert and Agnes McLehose, ed by W C McLehose, *The Correspondence Between Burns and Clarinda* (Edinburgh: William Tait, 1843).

Butler, Samuel, *Hudibras. A Poem in Three Cantos*, 3 vols (London: J Edwards, 1793).

Buxton, Thomas Fowell, *The African Slave Trade and its Remedy* (London: John Murray, 1840).

Byron, Lord [George Gordon], *Works of Lord Byron*, 6 vols, ed by RE Protheroe (London, John Murray; 1898–1901).

'C', *The South. A Parody on 'Scots Wha Ha'e.'* [Broadside], (np: np, [1862]), Duke University Libraries, Conf Pam 12mo #803.

Cairns, JW, 'After Somerset: The Scottish Experience,' *Journal of Legal History*, 33.3 (2012), pp.291–321.

'Enforced Sojourners: Enslaved Apprentices in Eighteenth-Century Scotland,' in *Ad Fontes: Liber Amicorum Prof Beatrix van Erp-Jacobs*, ed by EJMFC Broers & RMH Kubben (Oisterwijk [NL]: Wolf Legal Publishers, 2014), pp.67–81.

Calder, Robert McLean, *A Berwickshire Bard: The Songs and Poems of Robert McLean Calder*, ed by WS Crockett (Paisley: J and R Parlane, 1897).

Campbell, Alexander and James Campbell, *Him on the One Side and Me on the Other: The Civil War Letters of Alexander Campbell, 79th New York Infantry Regiment, and James Campbell, 1st South Carolina Battalion*, ed by Terry A Johnston, Jr (Columbia: USC Press, 1999).

Campbell, John, *Negro-mania: Being an Examination of the Falsely-Assumed Equality of the Various Races of Men* (Philadelphia: Campbell & Power, 1851).

Carey, Brycchan, *British Abolitionism and the Rhetoric of Sensibility: Writing, Sentiment and Slavery, 1760–1807* (Basingstoke, Hants: Palgrave Macmillan, 2005).

'Slavery and Romanticism,' *Literature Compass*, (2006), pp.397–408.

Carruthers, Gerard, 'Burns and Slavery', *The Drouth*, 26 (2007), pp.21–26.

'Robert Burns and Slavery,' in *Fickle Man: Robert Burns in the 21st Century*, ed by Johnny Roger and Gerard Carruthers (Dingwall: Sandstone Press, 2009), pp.163–175.

et al, 'Some Recent Discoveries in Robert Burns Studies', *Scottish Literary Review*, 2.1 (2010), pp.143–147.

Carruthers, Gerard and Elizabeth Ingham, 'Robert Burns, Patrick Heron and an Annotated 1793 Poems at Mount Stuart,' *Burns Chronicle*, 133.1 (2024), pp.82–91.

Carswell, Catherine, *The Life of Robert Burns* (Glasgow: William Collins, 1930).

Cavalieri, Grace, 'Interview with Sterling Brown, (1977),' *Beltway Poetry Quarterly*, www.beltwaypoetry.com/cavalieri-interviews-brown/ (accessed 1 September 2024).

Cervantes Saavedra, Miguel de, *The History and Adventures of the Renowned Don Quixote*, 4 vols, ed and trans by Tobias Smollett (London: Harrison & Co, 1782).

Chang, Y, 'Thoughts on My Beloved Father,' in *Peng Chun Chang, 1892–1957: Biography and Collected Works*, ed by HC Ruth and S-C Cheng ([San Jose, CA]: S-C Chenge, 1995).

Chase, Salmon P, 'Reclamation of Fugitives from Service. An Argument for the Defendant in Jones v Van Zandt,' in *Fugitive Slaves and American Courts: The Pamphlet Literature. Series II, Volume I*, ed by Paul Finkelman (New York/London: Garland Publishing, 1988), pp.341-448.

Chernow, Ron, *Grant* (London: Head of Zeus, 2017).

Cicero, Marcus Tullius, *The Letters of Marcus Tullius Cicero to Several of His Friends*, 3 vols, ed by William Melmoth (London: J Dodsley, 1778).

Clarkson, Thomas, *The History of the Rise, Progress and Accomplishment of the Abolition of the African Slave-trade by the British Parliament*, 2 vols (London: Longman, Hurst, Rees, and Orme, 1808).

Close, Rob and Ann Riches, *The Buildings of Scotland: Ayrshire and Arran* (New Haven/London: Yale University Press, 2012).

Cobbett's Parliamentary History of England, Volume XXVIII, [1789-1791] (London: Longman, Hurst, Rees, Orme & Brown [and others], 1816).
    Volume XXX, [1792-1794] (London: Longman, Hurst, Rees, Orme & Brown [and others], 1817).

[Cooper, Anna J], *A Voice from the South, By a Black Woman from the South* (Xenia, OH: The Aldine Press, 1892).

Cooper, Thomas, *Some Information Respecting America* (London: J Johnson, 1794).

Cowper, William, *The Task: A Poem, in Six Books* (London: J Johnson, 1785).
    Poems, 2 vols (London: J Johnson, 1788).

Craton, Michael, *Empire, Enslavement and Freedom in the Caribbean* (Kingston: Ian Randle, 1997).

Craven, John J, *The Prison Life of Jefferson Davis* (New York: Carleton Publisher, 1867).

Crawford, Robert, *The Bard* (London: Julian Cape, 2009).
    'What if ... Robert Burns had left Scotland?', *Prospect Magazine* (October 2014).

Crawford, Thomas, *Burns: A Study of the Poems and Songs* (Edinburgh: James Thin, The Mercat Press, 1978).

Cromek, RH, *Reliques of Robert Burns* (London: T Cadell, and W Davies, 1808).
    ed, *Select Scottish Songs. Ancient and Modern, With Critical Observations and Biographical Notices by Robert Burns*, 2 vols (London: T Cadell and W Davies, 1810).

Cross, Thom, 'Robert Burns's Planned Journey to Jamaica may have been merely a Cri de coeur,' *Herald* [Glasgow], 30th April 2013.

Cunningham, Allan, *Songs of Scotland, Ancient and Modern*, 4 vols (London: John Taylor, 1825).

Cunningham, J[oseph], ed, *The Centennial Birth-day of Robert Burns, as Celebrated by the Burns Club of the City of New York* (New York: Lang & Lang, 1860).

Cunninghame Graham, RB, *Doughty Deeds, An Account of the Life of Robert Graham of Gartmore, Poet & Politician, 1735-1797* (London: W. Heinemann, Ltd, 1925).

Curran, John Philip, *Speeches*, 2 vols (New York: Isaac Riley, 1809).

Daiches, David, *Robert Burns* (New York: Rinehart & Co, 1950).
    Robert Burns and His World (London: Thames & Hudson, 1971).

Davis, Jefferson, *Scotland & the Scottish People: An Address Delivered in the City of Memphis, Tennessee on St Andrew's-Day, 1875* (Glasgow: Anderson and Mackay, 1876).

[Defoe, Daniel], *A Tour Thro' the Whole Island of Great Britain, Third Edition* (London: J Osborn [and others], 1742).

[de Saint-Lambert, Jean-François], *Les Saisons, Poëme* (Amsterdam: np: 1769).

Devine, TM, *Scotland's Empire, The Origins of the Global Diaspora* (London: Penguin, 2004).

'Did Slavery Make Scotia Great?', *Britain and the World*, 4.1 (2011), pp.40–64.

ed, *Recovering Scotland's Slavery Past. The Caribbean Connection* (Edinburgh: EUP, 2015).

'Introduction. Scotland and Slavery,' in *Scotland's Slavery Past: The Caribbean Connection*, ed by TM Devine (Edinburgh: EUP, 2015), pp.1–20.

'Lost to History,' in *Recovering Scotland's Slavery Past. The Caribbean Connection*, ed by TM Devine (Edinburgh: EUP, 2015), pp.21–40.

'Conclusion: History, Scotland and Slavery,' in *Recovering Scotland's Slavery Past: the Caribbean Connection*, ed by TM Devine (Edinburgh: Edinburgh University Press, 2015), pp. 246–251.

and Philipp R Rössner, 'Scots in the Atlantic Economy, 1600–1800,' in *Scotland and the British Empire*, ed by John M MacKenzie and TM Devine (Oxford: OUP, 2011), pp.30–53.

Dick, James C, ed, *The Songs of Robert Burns Now First Printed with the Melodies for which They were Written; A Study in Tone-Poetry with Bibliography, Historical Notes, and Glossary* (London/Glasgow/Edinburgh/New York: Henry Frowde, 1903).

Dickson, William, *Letters on Slavery* (London: J Phillips [and others], 1789).

Dirks, Robert, 'Resource Fluctuations and Competitive Transformation in West Indian Slave Societies', in *Extinction and Survival in Human Populations*, ed by Charles D Laughlin and Ivan A Brady (New York: 1978).

Douglass, Frederick, 'A Fugitive Slave Visiting the Birthplace of Robert Burns,' *Albany Evening Journal*, 13 June 1846.

My Bondage and My Freedom (New York/Auburn: Miller, Orton & Co, 1857).

'Why Should the Colored Man Enlist?', FD Douglass's Monthly, April 1863.

The Frederick Douglass Papers: Series One — Speeches, Debates, and Interviews, ed by John Blassingame, et al (New Haven: Yale University Press, 1979).

Life and Writings of Frederick Douglas: Early Years 1817–1849, ed by Philip Foner (New York: International Publishers, 1950).

Life and Writings of Frederick Douglas: Pre-Civil War decade, 1850–1860, ed by Philip Foner (New York: International Publishers, 1950).

The Frederick Douglass Papers series 3, vol 1, ed by John M McKivigan (New Haven: Yale University Press, 2009).

[Douglass, Helen, ed], *In Memoriam: Frederick Douglass* (Philadelphia: JC Yorston & Co, 1897).

'DR', 'Burns and Jamaica,' *Burns Chronicle* (1911), pp.77–79.

Drabble, Margaret, ed, *The Oxford Companion to English Literature* (Oxford: OUP, 1985).

Draffen of Newington, George, 'Masonic Etiquette and Scottish Usage,' *Grand Lodge of Scotland Year Book 1966* (Edinburgh: Grand Lodge of Scotland, 1966).

Draper, Nicholas, 'Scotland and Colonial Slave Ownership: The Evidence of the Slave Compensation Records,' in *Recovering Scotland's Slavery Past. The Caribbean Connection*, ed by TM Devine (Edinburgh: EUP, 2015), pp.166–186.

Du Bois, WEB, 'The Present Outlook for the Darker Races on Mankind, An Address to the Third Annual Meeting of the American Negro Academy,' *AME Church Review*, October 1900.

The Quest of the Silver Fleece: A Novel (Chicago: AC McClurg, 1911).

'Negere Som Digtere, af Carl Kjersmeier [Book Review],' *The Crisis* (August 1925), p.188.

Dunbar, Paul [Laurence], *Oak and Ivy* (Dayton, OH: Press of the United Brethren Publishing House, 1893).

DuRant, Joseph, 'Robert Burns in Mid-Nineteenth Century American Newspapers,' *Burns Chronicle* (2016), pp.26–33.

Dyer, John, *The Poetical Works of John Dyer. With the Life of the Author* (Edinburgh: The Apollo Press, by the Martins, 1779).

[Edinburgh City Council], *Slavery and Colonialism in Edinburgh: An Independent Review* (Edinburgh: Edinburgh City Council, 2022).

Edwards, Paul, and James Walvin, *Personalities in the Era of the Slave Trade* (London/Basingstoke: The Macmillan Press, 1983).

Equiano, Olaudah, *The Interesting Narrative of the Life of Olaudah Equiano, or Gustavus Vassa, The African. Written By Himself* (London: For the Author, 1789).

Evans, June, *African/Caribbeans in Scotland. A Socio-Geographical Study* (Edinburgh: University of Edinburgh PhD Thesis, 1995).

Ewing, JC, ed, *Robert Burns's Literary Correspondents, 1786–1796: A Chronological List of Letters Addressed to the Poet, with Precises of their Contents* (Alloway: Burns Monument Trustees, 1938).

Fagen, Graham, Douglas Gordon and Jackie Kay, *The Slave's Lament/Black Burns* (Edinburgh: National Galleries of Scotland, 2017).

'British Council interview with Graham Fagen,' 22 March 2018, www.britishcouncil.org/voices-magazine/how-two-artists-interpret-their-shared-history (accessed 1 September 2024).

Ferguson, J De Lancey, 'Burns and Hugh Blair,' *Modern Language Notes*, 45.7 (1930), pp.440–446.

Flipper, Henry Ossian, *The Colored Cadet at West Point. Autobiography of Lieut[enant] Henry Ossian Flipper, USA, First Graduate of Color from the US Military Academy* (New York: H. Lee & Co, 1878).

Forbes, Sir William, *An Account of the Life and Writings of James Beattie LL.D*, 2 Vols (London: E Roper, 1824).

Foreman, Amanda, *World on Fire: Britain's Crucial Role in the American Civil War* (London: Random House, 2010).

Fortune, T Thomas, 'It's Time to Call a Halt,' *New York Age*, 25 January 1890.

Fox, Charles James, *The Speeches of the Right Honourable Charles James Fox in the House of Commons*, 6 vols, ed by 'A Barrister' (London: Longman, Hurst, Rees, Orme and Brown, and J Ridgeway, 1815).

Fryer, Linda G, Marjory Harper, and Allan I Macinnes, eds, *Scotland and the Americas, c 1650–c 1939: A Documentary Source Book* (Edinburgh: Scottish History Society, 2002).

[Galt, John], *Annals of the Parish or, The Chronicles of Dalmailing* (Edinburgh: William Blackwood, 1821).

Gapper, John, 'Forced labour is the price of a cheap cotton T-shirt,' *Financial Times*, 19/20 September 2020, p.13.

Garrison, William Lloyd, 'Speech at Paisley,' *Renfrewshire Advertiser*, 26 September 1846.

— *No Compromise on Slavery: An Address* (New York: American Anti-Slavery Society, 1854).

— 'Letter marking the Anniversary of the Martyrdom of John Brown,' *Douglass's Monthly* (January 1861), p.398.

— 'Lecture to the Young Men's Association, Chicago,' *Chicago Tribune*, 17 November 1865.

— 'Human Equality: A Supplement to "A Man's a Man,"' Monographic. Retrieved from the Library of Congress, www.loc.gov/item/amss.as105600 (accessed 1 September 2024.).

— *The Letters of William Lloyd Garrison, Volume I (1822–1835)*, ed by Walter M Merrill (Cambridge, MA: Belknap Press, 1971).

— *The Letters of William Lloyd Garrison, Volume III (1841–1849)*, ed by Walter M Merrill (Cambridge, MA: Belknap Press, 1973).

Garvey, Marcus, Robert A Hill, and Barbara Bair, eds, *The Marcus Garvey and Universal Negro Improvement Association Papers, Vol. VII: November 1927–August 1940* (Berkeley: University of California Press, 1991).

Gay, John, *The Poetical Works of John Gay. Including his Fables*, 3 vols (Edinburgh: At the Apollo Press, by the Martins, 1777).

Gerzina, Gretchen H, 'Georgian Life and Modern Afterlife of Dido Elisabeth Belle,' in *Britain's Black Past*, ed by Gretchen H Gerzina (Liverpool: Liverpool University Press, 2020), pp.161–178.

Gibbon, Edward, *The History of the Decline and Fall of the Roman Empire*, 12 vols (London: W Strahan and W Cadell, 1783).

Gibbs, Mifflin Wistar, *Light and Shade, An Autobiography with Reminiscences of the Last and Present Century* (Little Rock, AK: for the Author, 1902).

Gillen, Vincent P, *Sugar, Ships & Slavery: An Illustrated History of Georgian & Victorian Greenock*, 2 vols (Greenock: Cartsburn Publishing, 2022).

Gillette, Francis, Speech on 'The Execution of United States Laws,' US Senate 23 February 1854, in *Congressional Globe*, New Series XXXI, ed by John C Rives (City of Washington [DC]: John C Rives, 1855), p.322.

Gladstone, Hugh S, 'Maria Riddell; Friend of Burns,' in *Dumfriesshire and Galloway Natural History & Antiquarian Society Transactions and Journal of Proceedings, 1914-15*, ed by GW Shirley (Dumfries: By the Council of the Society, 1915), pp.16–56.

Glover, Richard, *Leonidas, A Poem*, 2 vols (London: T Cadell and Richardson and Urquhart, 1770).

Graham, Eric J, and Mark Duffill, 'Black People in Scotland during the Slavery Era,' *Scottish Local History*, Winter 2007, pp.11–16.

Graham, Eric J, *The Shipping Trade of Ayrshire, 1689–1791, Ayrshire Monographs No 8* (Darvel: Ayrshire Archaeology and Natural History Society, 1991).

Burns & the Sugar Plantocracy of Ayrshire (Ayr: Ayrshire Archaeology and Natural History Society, 2009).

'The Scots Penetration of the Jamaican Plantation Business,' in *Recovering Scotland's Slavery Past. The Caribbean Connection*, ed by TM Devine (Edinburgh: EUP, 2015), pp.82–98.

Gregory, James M, ed, *Frederick Douglass the Orator* (Springfield MA: Willey & Co, 1893).

Griffin, Appleton PC, and William Coolidge Lane, *A Catalogue of the Washington Collection in the Boston Athenæum*, (Boston: Boston Athenæum, 1897).

Guthrie, William, *A New Geographical, Historical, and Commercial Grammar, and Present State of the Several Kingdoms of the World* (London: Charles Dilley and George Robinson, 1772).

(London: Charles Dilley and GGJ and J Robinson, 1790).

Hague, William, *William Wilberforce: The Life of the Great Anti-Slave Trade Campaigner* (London: Harper Collins Publishers, 2007).

Hall, Andy, ed, *Touched by Burns: Images and Insights* (Edinburgh: Birlinn, 2008).

Hall, Douglas, 'Incalculability as a Feature of Sugar Production during the Eighteenth Century,' *Social and Economic Studies,* September 1961, pp.340–352.

Halliday, RT, 'Burns and Freemasonry in Dumfriesshire', *Burns Chronicle,* 1947, pp.26–31.

Hamilton, Douglas J, *Scotland, the Caribbean and the Atlantic World, 1750–1820* (Manchester: Manchester University Press, 2005).

Hancock, David, 'Scots in the Slave Trade', in *Nation and Province in the First British Empire: Scotland and the Americas, 1600–1800*, ed by Ned C Landsman (Lewisburg, PA: Bucknell University Press, 2001), pp.60–93.

Harding, Anthony John, 'Review of Peter J Kitson and Debbie Lee, (gen eds), *Slavery, Abolition and Emancipation: Writings in the British Romantic Period* (8 vols), (London: Pickering and Chatto, 1999),' *BARS Review & Bulletin,* 17.

Harris Bob, and Charles McKean, *The Scottish Town in the Age of the Enlightenment 1740–1820* (Edinburgh: Edinburgh University Press, 2014).

Haynes, Stephen R, *Noah's Curse: The Biblical Justification of American Slavery* (Oxford: OUP, 2002).

Hempstead, James L, 'David Sillar,' *Burns Chronicle* (May 1994), pp.107–118.

Henderson, Lizanne, 'Scotland and the Slave Trade: Some South West Connections,' *Scottish Local History,* Spring 2008, pp.47–53.

Henson, Josiah, 'Speech at the Mechanics Institute, Dumfries,' *Dumfries and Galloway Standard & Advertiser,* 25 April 1877.

Heron, Robert, *A Letter to William Wilberforce [etc.]* (London: Jordan and Maxwell, 1806).

Hill, Robert A, et al, eds, *The Marcus Garvey and Universal Negro Improvement Association Papers,* Vol II (Berkeley/Los Angeles/London: University of California Press, 1983).

Hinks, Peter P, and Stephen David Kantrowitz, eds, *All Men Free and Brethren: Essays on the History of African American Freemasonry* (Ithaca, NY: Cornell University Press, 2013).

[Home, Henry] Lord Kames, *Elements of Criticism*, 2 vols (Edinburgh/London: A Kincaid & W Creech and John Bell/T Cadell, 1774).

Sketches of the History of Man, 4 vols (Edinburgh/London: William Creech/A Strahan and T Cadell, 1788).

Homer, *The Poems of Homer*, 2 vols, trans by James Macpherson (London: T Becket & PA de Hondt, 1773).

Houston, RA, *The Population History of Britain and Ireland 1500–1750* (Cambridge: Cambridge University Press, 1995).

Howells, WD, 'Life and Letters,' *Harper's Weekly*, 27 June 1896, p.630.

Hubbard, Mark, ed, *Illinois's War. The Cicil War in Documents* (Athens, OH: Ohio University Press, 2013).

Hughes, Langston, *Famous American Negroes* (New York: Dodd, Mead, 1954).

Hume, David, *A Treatise on Human Nature* (London: John Noon, 1739).

Essays and Treatises on Several Subjects, 2 vols (London/Edinburgh: T Cadell [and others]/C Elliot, 1788).

Humphreys, David, *The Miscellaneous Works of David Humphreys* (New York: T & J Swords, 1804).

Hunter, Lloyd A, ed, *For Duty and Destiny: The Life and Civil War Diary of William Taylor Stott, Hoosier Soldier and Educator* (Indianapolis: Indiana Historical Society Press, 2010).

Hutcheson, Francis, *A System of Moral Philosophy in Three Books*, 2 vols, ed by Francis Hutcheson MD (Glasgow/London: R and A Foulis/A Miller, T Longman, 1755).

Ingersoll, Robert G, 'The Birthplace of Robert Burns,' in *The Works of Robert G Ingersoll*, 13 vols, ed by CP Farrell (New York: CP Farrell, 1900), vol.III, pp.119–120.

Innes, William, *The Slave Trade Indispensable: In Answer to the Speech of William Wilberforce Esq on 13 March, 1789*, (London: np, 1789).

Jacobs, Harriet A, and Lisa [sic] Jacobs, 'Letter from Teachers of the Freedmen,' *National Anti-Slavery Standard*, 16 April 1864.

Jamieson, John, *Etymological Dictionary of the Scottish Language*, 4 vols (Edinburgh: W Creech [and others], 1808).

Jarron, Matthew, Erin Farley, and Dolina Mechan, eds, *Breaking the Chains* (Dundee: University of Dundee, 2022).

Jefferson, Thomas, *The Papers of Thomas Jefferson, Volume 1, 1760–1776*, ed by Julian P Boyd (Princeton: Princeton University Press, 1950).

Johnson, James, and William Stenhouse, eds, *The Scotish Musical Museum*, 4 vols (Edinburgh/London: William Blackwood and Sons/Thomas Cadell, 1839).

Johnson, Oliver, 'Death of Garrison,' *The Index*, 12 June 1879.

Jolly, William, *Robert Burns at Mossgiel: with Reminiscences by his Herd-boy* (Paisley: Alexander Gardner, 1881).

Jurasinski, Stefan, and Lisi Oliver, *The Laws of Alfred: The Domboc and the Making of Anglo-Saxon Lawbooks* (Cambridge: Cambridge University Press, 2021).

Karras, Alan L, *Sojourners in the Sun: Scottish Migrants in Jamaica and the Chesapeake, 1740–1800* (London/Ithaca: Cornell University Press, 1992).

Kay, Jackie, 'Missing Faces,' *The Guardian* [London], 24 March 2007.

'Let Poetry Raise Our Spirits, Let Poetry Give Us Hope,' *Sunday Post*, [Dundee] 22 March 2020.

Kemble, Stephen George, *Odes, Lyrical Ballads, and Poems on Various Occasions* (Edinburgh: For the Author, by J Ballantine and Co, 1807).

Kerr, Robert, *The Memoirs of the Life, Writings, & Correspondence of William Smellie*, 2 vols (Edinburgh: J Anderson, 1811).

King, Jr Martin Luther, *The Papers of Martin Luther King, Jr.* Volume II: *Rediscovering Precious Values, July 1951 – November 1955*, ed by Clayborne Carson, et al (Berkeley, Los Angeles CA: University of California Press, 1994).

Volume III: *Birth of a New Age, December 1955 – December 1956*, ed by Clayborne Carson, et al (Berkeley, Los Angeles CA/London: University of California Press, 1999).

Volume IV: *Symbol of the Movement, January 1957 – December 1958*, ed by Clayborne Carson, et al (Berkeley, Los Angeles CA: University of California Press, 2000).

Volume V: *Threshold of a New Decade, January 1959 – December 1960*, ed by Clayborne Carson, et al (Berkeley, Los Angeles CA: University of California Press, 2005).

Volume VI: *Advocate of the Social Gospel, September 1948 – March 1963*, ed by Clayborne Carson, et al (Berkeley, Los Angeles CA: University of California Press, 2007).

Volume VII: *To Save The Soul of America, January 1961 – August 1962*, ed by Clayborne Carson, et al (Berkeley, Los Angeles CA: University of California Press, 2014).

A Knock at Midnight, ed by Clayborn Carson and Peter Holloran (New York: Warner Books, 1998).

The Autobiography of Martin Luther King, Jr, ed by Clayborne Carson (London: Abacus, 2000).

A Call to Conscience: The Landmark Speeches of Martin Luther King, Jr, ed by Clayborne Carson (New York: IPM/Warner Books, 2001).

Kinghorn, AM, 'Robert Burns and Jamaica', *A Review of English Literature*, July 1967, pp.70–80.

'Burns's "Clarinda" in Jamaica', *Burns Chronicle* (1975), pp.2–13.

Kitching, Paula, *Scotland and the Slave Trade: 2007 Bicentenary of the Abolition of the Slave Trade Act* (Edinburgh: Scottish Executive, 2007).

Klein, Herbert S, Stanley L Engerman, Robin Haines, and Ralph Shlomowitz, 'Transoceanic Mortality: The Slave Trade in Comparative Perspective,' *William & Mary Quarterly* (January 2001), pp.93–118.

Knutsford, Viscountess, *Life and Letters of Zachary Macaulay* (London: E Arnold, 1900).

Kramer, Aaron, 'Robert Burns and Langston Hughes,' *Freedomways* 8 (1968), pp.159–166.

Kurland, Philip B, and Gerhard Casper, eds, *Landmark Briefs and Arguments of the Supreme Court of the United States: Constitutional Law. Volume 49: Brown v Board of Education (1954 & 1955)* (Arlington, VA: University Publications of American, Inc, 1975).

Law, James D, *Here and There in Two Hemispheres* (Lancaster, PA: The Home Publishing Company, 1903).

Leask, Nigel, 'Burns and the Poetics of Abolition', in *The Edinburgh Companion to Robert Burns*, ed by Gerard Carruthers (Edinburgh: Edinburgh University Press, 2009), pp.47–60.

Robert Burns and Pastoral, Poetry and Improvement in Eighteenth Century Scotland (Oxford: Oxford University Press, 2010).

'"Their Groves o' Sweet Myrtles": Robert Burns and the Scottish Colonial Experience,' in *Robert Burns in Global Culture*, ed by Murray Pittock (Lewisburg, PA: Bucknell University Press, 2011), pp.172–188.

'"The Pith o' Sense and Pride o' Worth": Robert Burns and the Glasgow Magazine (1795),' in *Before* Blackwood's: *Scottish Journalism in the Age of Enlightenment*, ed by Alex Benchimol, Rhona Brown and David Shuttleton (London: Pickering & Chatto, 2015), pp.73–87.

LeSeur, Geta J, 'Claude McKay's Romanticism,' *CLA Journal* (March 1989), pp.296–308.

Lewis, William Henry, 'Class Oration, Amherst Graduation 1892' in Gregory Bond, 'The Strange Career of William Henry Lewis,' in *Out of the Shadows: A Biographical History of African American Athletes*, ed by David K Wiggins (Fayatteville, AR: University of Arkansas Press, 2006).

Lincoln, Abraham, *The Collected Works of Abraham Lincoln*, 10 vols, ed by Roy Prentice Basler (Brunswick: Rutgers University Press, 1953–1959).

Lindsay, Andrew O, *Illustrious Exile: Journal of My Sojourn in the West Indies* (Leeds: Peepal Tree, 2006).

'"Negro-driver" or "Illustrious Exile": Revisiting Illustrious Exile: Journal of my Sojourn in the West Indies', *International Journal of Scottish Literature*, Spring/Summer (2008).

Lindsay, Arnett G, 'Diplomatic Relations between the United States and England bearing on the Return of Negro Slaves, 1788–1828', *Journal of Negro History*, October (1920), pp.391–419.

Lindsay, Maurice, *Robert Burns* (London: MacGibbon & Key, 1954).

The Burns Encyclopaedia, rev and ed by David Purdie, Kirsteen McCue and Gerard Carruthers (London: Robert Hale, 2013).

Locke, John, *An Essay Concerning Human Understanding in Four Books*, 3 vols (Edinburgh: J Dickson and C Elliot, 1777).

Two Treatises on Government (London: J Whiston [and others], 1772).

Lockhart, J[ohn] G[ibson], *Life of Robert Burns* (Edinburgh/London: Constable & Co/ Hurst, Chance, and Co, 1828).

[Long, Edward], *The History of Jamaica*, 3 vols (London: T Lowndes, 1774).

Low, Donald A, ed, *Robert Burns: The Critical Heritage* (London: Routledge & Kegan Paul, 1974).

Lyftogt, Kenneth L, *Iowa's Forgotten General: Matthew Mark Trumbull and the Civil War* (Iowa City: University of Iowa Press, 2005).

Lynch, James v, 'The Limits of Revolutionary Radicalism: Tom Paine and Slavery,' *The Pennsylvania Magazine of History and Biography*, July 1999, pp.177–199.

Mabuza, HE Dr Lindiwe, in *Touched by Robert Burns: Images and Insights*, ed by Andy Hall (Edinburgh: Birlinn, 2008), pp.134–138.

MacCunn, John, *Ethics of Citizenship* (Glasgow: James MacLehose, 1895).

Mackay, James, *Burns: A Biography of Robert Burns* (Edinburgh: Mainstream Publishing, 1992).

Mackenzie, Henry, *Julia de Roubigné: A Tale in a Series of Letters*, 2 vols (London: W Strahan and T Cadell, 1777).

The Man of Feeling (London: A Strahan, and T Cadell, 1783).

'Surprising Effects of Original Genius, Exemplified in the Poetical Productions of Robert Burns, an Ayrshire Ploughman,' *Lounger*, 97.9 (1786), pp.385–388.

MacMillan, Ian, 'The Coward Slave,' *Burns Chronicle* (Autumn, 2009), p.22.

[Maidment, John and William Hugh Logan, eds], *Memoir of Archibald Maclaren, Dramatist: With a list of His Works*, (Edinburgh: np, 1835).

Mance, Henry, 'A Reckoning with History,' *Financial Times*, 26/27 September 2020.

Marcolongo, Andrea, trans Will Schutt, *Shifting the Moon from its Orbit: A Night at the Acropolis Museum* (London: Europa Editions UK, 2024).

Martyn, Mrs ST, 'Burns and His Monument on the Banks of the Doon,' *The Lady's Wreath, 1848–1849* [New York], p.209.

Mattison, JW, 'Orr's South Carolina Rifles,' *Southern Historical Society Papers*, 27 (1899).

Mayes, Benjamin E, *Born to Rebel: An Autobiography* (Athens, GA/London: University of Georgia Press, 2003).

McAllister, Marvin, 'Transnational Balladeering: "Scots Wha Hae wi' Wallace Bled" in 1820s Afro-New-York,' *Studies in Scottish Literature*, 38.3 (2012), pp.108–118.

McCallum, Shara, *No Ruined Stone* (Leeds: Peepal Tree Press, 2021).

'"Man's Inhumanity to Man": Burns, Jamaica, and *No Ruined Stone*,' *Burns Chronicle*, 133.1 (2024), pp.77–81.

McClure, David, 'Records and Functions of the Ayrshire Commissioners of Supply', *Scottish Local History Journal* (1997).

McGinn, Clark, 'Burns and Slavery,' *Scotland Now*, 6 (2006), www.friendsofscotland.gov.uk/scotlandnow/issue-06/history/burns-and-slavery.html (accessed 1 September 2024).

'Burns and Slavery. Robert Burns: Face to Face with Slavery – 1780s,' *Burns Chronicle* (Spring 2010), pp.6–14.

'Burns and Slavery. Other Voices, Other Evidence – the 1790s,' *Burns Chronicle* (Spring 2010), pp.14–19.

'Burns and Slavery. "A Man's a Man for a' that": Burns and the Abolition of Slavery in the US,' *Burns Chronicle* (Spring 2010), pp.19–24.

'Early Burns Suppers in the USA,' *Burns Chronicle* (Spring 2010), pp.19–24.

'The Scotch Bard and "The Planting Line": New Documents on Burns and Jamaica,' *Studies in Scottish Literature*, 43.2 (2017), pp.255–266.

The Burns Supper: A Comprehensive History (Edinburgh: Luath Press, 2019).

'Robert Burns's Black Neighbours in Ayrshire,' *Burns Chronicle* (March 2024), pp.1–18.

McGuirk, Carol, ed, *Critical Essays on Robert Burns* (London/New York: Prentice Hall/GK Hall, 1998), pp.281–297.

'Burns and Aphorism; or, Poetry into Proverb: His Persistence in Cultural Memory Beyond Scotland,' in *Robert Burns and Transatlantic Culture*, ed by Sharon Alker, Leith Davis and Holly Faith Nelson (Farnham: Ashgate, 2012), pp.169–186.

Reading Robert Burns: Texts, Contexts, Transformations (London: Pickering & Chatto, 2015).

McKay, Claude, *Songs of Jamaica* (Kingston, Jamaica/London: Aston W Garner & Co/ Jamaica Agency, 1912).

'On Becoming a Catholic,' *Phylon*, 25.3 (1964).

McVie, John, 'The Lochlie Litigation and the Sequestration of William Burnes,' *Burns Chronicle* (1935), pp.69–87.

Mellette, Justin, 'Jean Toomer's "Reapers" and Robert Burns,' *The Drouth*, www.thedrouth.org/jean-toomers-reapers-and-robert-burns-justin-mellette/ (accessed 1 September 2024).

Melville, Jennifer, ed, *Facing Our Past: Interim Report on the Connections between the Properties now in the care of the National Trust for Scotland and Historical Enslavement* (Edinburgh: National Trust for Scotland, 2011).

Mickens, Revd HM, 'Introducing Mr Marcus Garvey, 23 March 1920,' in The *Marcus Garvey and Universal Negro Improvement Association Papers*, Vol II, ed by Robert A Hill et al (Berkeley/Los Angeles/London: University of California Press, 1983), p.266.

Miller, Hunter, ed, 'The Treaty of Paris, 1783' in *Treaties and Other International Acts of the United States of America*, 6 vols (Washington: Government Printing Office, 1931), vol.II, pp.151–156.

Miller, Jason, 'Langston Hughes and Martin Luther King, Jr: Together in Nigeria,' *South Atlantic Review: Special Issue, The Global Hughes* (Spring 2018), pp.22–41.

Miller, W Jason, *Origins of the Dream: Hughes's Poetry and King's Rhetoric* (Gainesville, FL: University of Florida Press, 2015).

Milton, John, *Paradise Lost, A Poem in Twelve Books [...] with [...] Notes [...] and Various Critical Remarks and Observations [...] A New Edition*, 2 vols, ed by Elijah Fenton (London: R Bladon, T Lawes, S Crowder, C Ware, and T Payne, 1784).

The Poetical Works of John Milton, 2 vols (Edinburgh: A Kincaid and A Donaldson, 1755).

Mintz, Sidney W, *Sweetness and Power: The Place of Sugar in Modern History* (New York: Viking Penguin, 1985).

Montaigne, Michel de, *The Essays of Michael Seigneur de Montaigne, Translated into English*, 3 vols (London: S and E Ballard, 1759).

Moore, John, *Zeluco, Various Views of Human Nature, Taken from Life and Manners, Foreign and Domestic*, 2 vols (London: A Strahan and T Cadell, 1789).

Moreton, JB, *West India Manners and Customs: A New Edition* (London: J Parsons, 1793).

Morris, Michael, 'Robert Burns: Recovering Scotland's Memory of the Black Atlantic,' *Journal for Eighteenth Century Studies* (2014), pp.343–359.

Scotland and the Caribbean, c.1740–1833: Atlantic Archipelagos (Abingdon/New York: Routledge, 2015).

'Yonder Awa: Slavery and Distancing Strategies in Scottish Literature,' in *Recovering Scotland's Slavery Past: The Caribbean Connection*, ed by TM Devine (Edinburgh: EUP, 2015), pp.41–61.

'The Problem of Slavery in the Age of Improvement: David Dale, Robert Owen and New Lanark Cotton,' in *Cultures of Improvement in Scottish Romanticism, 1707–1840*, ed by Alex Benchimol and Gerard Lee McKeever (New York: Routledge, 2018), pp.111–131.

Moss, Michael, *The 'Magnificent Castle' of Culzean and the Kennedy Family* (Edinburgh: EUP, 2002).

Mullen, Stephen, *It Wisnae Us: The Truth About Glasgow and Slavery* (Edinburgh: The Royal Incorporation of Architects in Scotland, 2009).

'The Myth of Scottish Slaves,' in *The Sceptical Scot*, March 2016, sceptical. scot/2016/03/the-myth-of-scottish-slaves/ (accessed 1 September 2024.).

Robert Burns, Slavery and Abolition: Contextualising the Abandoned Jamaica Sojourn in 1786, burnsc21.glasgow.ac.uk/robert-burns-slavery-and-abolition-contextualising-the-abandoned-jamaica-sojourn-in-1786-part-1-of-2/ (accessed 1 September 2024).

Glasgow, Slavery and Atlantic Commerce: An Audit of Historic Connections and Modern Legacies (Glasgow: City of Glasgow, 2022).

Mullen, Stephen, and Simon Newman, *Slavery, Abolition and the University of Glasgow* (Glasgow: University of Glasgow, 2018).

'Scotland and Jamaican Slavery: the problem with numbers,' *Centre for the Study of the Legacies of British Slavery Blog*, 12 November 2021, lbsatucl.wordpress.com/2021/11/12/scotland-and-jamaican-slavery-the-problem-with-numbers/ (accessed 1 September 2024).

Murray Lyon, David, *History of the Lodge of Edinburgh (Mary's Chapel) No 1* (Edinburgh: William Blackwood and Sons, 1873).

Myers, Norma, *Reconstructing the Black Past: Blacks in Britain 1780–1830* (London/Portland OR: Frank Cass & Co, 1996/2006).

Nell, William Cooper, 'Reception of Frederick Douglass at the Belknap-street Church, Boston, 3 May 1847,' in *The Liberator*, 21 May 1847.

as 'WCN', 'Meetings of the Friends of Equal School Rights,' *Liberator*, 9 November 1849.

The Colored Patriots of the American Revolution, With Sketches of Several Distinguished Colored Persons to which are added a Brief Survey of the Condition and Prospects of Colored Americans (Boston: Robert F Wallcutt, 1855).

Noble, Andrew, 'Burns, Scotland, and the American Revolution,' in *Robert Burns and Transatlantic Culture*, ed by Sharon Alker, Leith Davis and Holly Faith Nelson (Farnham: Ashgate, 2012), pp.31–51.

Northup, Solomon, *Twelve Years a Slave. Narrative of Solomon Northup, a citizen of New-York, Kidnapped in Washington City in 1841, and Rescued in 1853, from a Cotton Plantation near the Red River, in Louisiana* (Auburn/Buffalo/London: Derby and Miller/Derby, Orton and Mulligan/Sampson Low, Son & Company, 1853).

Nyquist, Mary, 'Equiano, Satanism, and Slavery,' in *Milton Now. Alternative Approaches and Contexts*, ed by Catharine Gray and Erin Murphy (New York: Palgrave Macmillan, 2014), pp.215–245.

Obama, President Barack, 'Speech at Ebenezer Baptist Church, Atlanta GA,' 20 January 2008, *The Guardian*, 21 January 2008.

Ouseby, Ian, ed, *The Cambridge Guide to Literature in English* (Cambridge: Cambridge University Press, 1991).

[The] Oxford English Dictionary, Second Edition (Oxford OUP, 1989).

Paine, Thomas, *Rights of Man: Being an Answer to Mr Burke's Attack on the French Revolution* (London: HD Symonds, 1792).

Palmer, Geoff, *The Enlightenment Abolished: Citizens of Britishness* (Penicuik: Henry Publishing, 2007).

— 'Postscript: Jamaican Scottish Connections', in *Africa in Scotland, Scotland in Africa: Historical Legacies and Contemporary Hybridities*, ed by Afe Adogame and Andrew Lawrence (Leiden: Brill, 2014), pp.349–360.

Parker, Matthew, *The Sugar Barons, Family, Corruption, Empire and War* (London: Windmill, 2012).

Parkhill, John, *Sketch of the Life of Peter Burnet, a Negro, Who came to Paisley Sixty Years ago, where He still lives, a very Old and Respectable Man* (Paisley: J Neilson, 1841).

Paterson, James, *A Complete Commentary [...] on 'Paradise Lost'* (London: R Walker, 1744).

Paterson, James, *History of the County of Ayr*, 2 vols (Ayr: James Dick, 1847).

— *History of the Counties of Ayr and Wigton* (Edinburgh: James Stille, 1863).

Pettigrew, William A, *Freedom's Debt: The Royal African Company and the Politics of the Atlantic Slave Trade, 1652–1752* (Chapel Hill, NC: Omohundro Institute of Early American History and Culture, 2013).

Pettinger, Alasdair, *Frederick Douglas and Scotland, 1846: Living an Antislavery Life* (Edinburgh: EUP, 2019).

'Philomusus', *Mirth diverts all Care: Being Excellent New Songs, Compos'd by the Most Elegant Wits of the Period, On Diverse Subjects* (London: J Morphew, 1708).

Phillips, Kate, *Bought & Sold: Scotland, Jamaica and Slavery* (Edinburgh: Luath Press, 2022).

Pindar, Peter, [pseudonym of Dr John Wolcott], *A Poetical, Serious, and Possibly Impertinent, Epistle to the Pope: Also, a Pair of Odes to His Holiness, on His Keeping a Disorderly House; with a Pretty Little Ode to Innocence* (London/Edinburgh: T Evans/Robertson and Berry, 1793).

[Pinkerton, John, ed], *Ancient Scotish Poems: Never Before in Print, But Now Published from the Ms Collections of Sir Richard Maitland, of Lethington, Knight [...] Comprising Pieces Written from about 1420 till 1586*, 2 vols, (London/Edinburgh: Charles Dilly/William Creech, 1786).

Pittock, Murray, 'Slavery as a Political Metaphor in Scotland and Ireland in the Age of Burns', in *Robert Burns and Transatlantic Culture*, ed by Sharon Alker, Leith Davis and Holly Faith Nelson (Farnham: Ashgate, 2012), pp.19–31.

— 'Introduction: "The mair they talk, I'm kend the better": Burns and Europe,' in *The Reception of Robert Burns in Europe*, ed by Murray Pittock (London: Bloomsbury, 2014), pp.1–8.

Pittock, Murray, and Joel Ambrosine, *Robert Burns and the Scottish Economy: Final Report* (Glasgow: For the Scottish Government, 2019).

Pope, Alexander, *The Works of Alexander Pope*, 6 vols, ed by William Warburton (London: C Bathurst [and others], 1787).
Pottle, Frederick A, *Pride and Negligence: The History of the Boswell Papers* (New York: McGraw-Hill, 1981).
Press Complaints Commission, *Mr Andrew Morgan v The Sun about Accuracy* (28 March 2012), www.pcc.org.uk/cases/adjudicated.html?article=NzcooQ==&type= (accessed 1 September 2024).
Prince, Mary, *The History of Mary Prince: A West Indian Slave, Related by Herself*, ed by Thomas Pringle (London/Edinburgh: F Wesley and A H Davis/Waugh & Innes, 1831).
Proudfoot, John, *The Scotchman in America* (Cleveland: Fairbanks, Benedict, 1873).
Rait, Robert S, *The History of the Union Bank of Scotland* (Glasgow: John Smith, 1930).
Ramsay, Allan, *The Tea-table Miscellany: Or, a Collection of Choice Songs, Scots and English. Twelfth Edition*, 4 vols, (London: A Millar, 1763).
Ramsay, David, *History of the American Revolution*, 2 vols (London: np, 1790).
Ramsay, James, *Essay on the Treatment and Conversion of African Slaves in the British Sugar Colonies* (London: James Phillips, 1784).
Reilly, Catherine W, *Mid-Victorian Poetry 1860–1879, An Annotated Biobibliography* (London: Mansell, 2000).
Renton, Alex, *Blood Legacy: Reckoning with a Family's Story of Slavery* (Edinburgh: Canongate, 2021).
Révanger, Cécile, 'Freemasonry and Blacks,' in *Handbook of Freemasonry*, ed by Henrik Bogdan and JAM Snoek (Netherlands: Brill, 2014), pp.422–438.
Rice, Alan, *Radical Narratives of the Black Atlantic* (London/New York: Continuum, 2003).
Richardson, Alan, ed, *Slavery, Abolition and Emancipation: Writings in the British Romantic Period, Volume 4: Verse* (Abingdon/New York: Routledge, 1999).
Richardson, John, *Slavery and Augustan Literature, Swift, Pope, Gray* (London: Routledge, 2004).
R[iddell], Maria, *Voyages to the Madeira, and Leeward Caribbean Isles: with Sketches of the Natural History of These Islands* (Edinburgh/London: Peter Hill/T Cadell, 1792).
Ritchie, Daniel, '[Review] "The Bard: Robert Burns A Biography," by Robert Crawford,' *Christianity and Literature* (Summer 2011), pp.668–671.
Rives, John C, ed, *Congressional Globe, New Series XXXI* (City of Washington [DC]: John C Rives, 1855).
Robertson, James, *Joseph Knight* (London/New York: Fourth Estate, 2003).
Robinson, W Stitt, Jr, 'Richard Oswald the Peacemaker,' *Ayrshire Archaeological and Natural History Society Collection*, 2nd series, 3 (1955), pp.119–132.
Robotham, John S, 'The Reading of Robert Burns,' *Bulletin of the New York Public Library*, XXIV (1970), pp.561–576.
Roe, William Thomas, *An Appendix to a Treatise on the Law of Elections, Concerning the Scots and Irish Statutes* (London: Charles Hunter, 1818).
[Roscoe, William], *The Wrongs of Africa*, 2 vols (London: R Faulder, 1787).
Rothschild, Emma, *The Inner Life of Empires* (Princeton: Princeton University Press, 2011).
Rushton, Edward, *Expostulatory Letter to George Washington, of Mount Vernon, in Virginia, On His continuing to be a Proprietor of Slaves* (Liverpool: np, 1797).

'Edward Rushton's Letter to T Paine, on the Slave-Trade,' *Belfast Monthly Magazine* (31 December 1809).

Russell, Lord John, *The Life and Times of Charles James Fox*, 2 vols (London: Richard Berkeley, 1859).

Salmon, Thomas, *A New Geographical and Historical Grammar* (London: W Johnston, 1766).

Sancho, Ignatius, *Letters of the late Ignatius Sancho, an African*, 2 vols, ed by Miss Crewe and J Jekyll (London: J Dodsley, J Robson, J Walter, R Baldwin and J Sewell, 1782).

Sassi, Carla, 'Acts of (Un)willed Amnesia: Dis/appearing Figurations of the Caribbean in Post-Union Scottish Literature,' in *Caribbean-Scottish Relations Colonial and Contemporary Inscriptions in History, Language and Literature*, ed by Carla Sassi, Giovanna Covi, Joan Anim-Addo and Velma Pollard (London: Mango Publishing, 2007), pp.131–198.

'Sir Walter Scott and the Caribbean: Unravelling the Silences,' *The Yearbook of English Studies*, 47 (2017), pp. 224–240.

Scott, Hew, ed, *Fasti Ecclesiæ Scoticanæ (New Edition), Volume III: Synod of Glasgow and Ayr* (Edinburgh: Oliver & Boyd, 1920).

Scott, Patrick, and Gerard Carruthers, 'Burns and the Alter of Independence: A Question of Authenticity,' *Studies in Scottish Literature*, 48.2, pp.199–206.

[Scott, Sir Walter], 'Review of Cromek's Reliques of Robert Burns,' *The Quarterly Review* (February 1809), pp.19–36.

Seal-Coon, FW, *An Historical Account of Jamaican Freemasonry* (Kingston: Goulding Print, 1976).

Shakespeare, William, *The Works*, [no edition specified].

Shaw, JE, *Ayrshire, 1745–1950, A Social and Industrial History* (Edinburgh & London: Oliver & Boyd, 1953).

Shelley, Percy Bysshe, 'The Defence of Poetry,' in *Essays, Letters from Abroad, Translations and Fragments*, 2 vols, ed by Mrs [Mary Wollstonecraft] Shelley (London: Edward Moxton, 1840), vol.1, pp.1–57.

Shenstone, William, *The Poetical Works of Will[iam] Shenstone*, 2 vols (London: Joseph Wenman, 1780).

Shuften, JT, 'What is a Man?', *The Colored American* [Atlanta, GA], 30 December 1865.

Sinclair, Peter, *Freedom or Slavery in the United States, Being Facts and Testimonies for the Consideration of the British People* (London: J Cauldwell, 1861).

Smellie, William, [contributor], *Encyclopaedia Britannica* (Second Edition), 10 vols (Edinburgh: for J Balfour [and others], 1777–1784).

A Philosophy of Natural History, 2 vols (Edinburgh/London: Heirs of Charles Elliot/C Elliot and T Kay, T Cadell, and GGJ & J Robinson, 1790).

Smith, Adam, *The Theory of Moral Sentiments, Third Edition*, 2 vols (London/Edinburgh: A Millar, A Kincaid and J Bell/T Cadell, 1790).

An Inquiry into the Nature and Causes of the Wealth of Nations, Fourth Edition, 3 vols (London: T Cadell and W Davies, 1786).

Smith, Gerrit, Substance of the Speech made by Gerrit Smith, in the Capitol of the State of New York, March 11th and 12th, 1850 (Albany: Jacob T Hazen, 1850).

Speeches of Gerrit Smith in Congress (New York: Mason Brothers, 1865).
Smith, James McCune, *The Works of James McCune Smith: Black Intellectual and Abolitionist*, ed by J Stauffer (Cambridge, MA: Harvard University Press, 2007).
Smith, John Guthrie, and John Oswald Mitchell, *The Old Country Houses of the Old Glasgow Gentry, Illustrated by Permanent Photographs by Annan* (Glasgow: James Maclehose & Sons, 1878).
Smollett, Tobias, *The Adventures of Roderick Random*, 2 vols (London: Harrison and Co, 1780).
— *The Expedition of Humphry Clinker*, 3 vols (London/Salisbury: W Johnston/B Collins, 1771).
— *The Present State of all Nations. Containing a Geographical, Natural, Commercial and Political History of all Countries in the Known World*, 8 vols (London: R Baldwin and others, 1769).
Smout, TC, *A History of the Scottish People 1560–1830* (Glasgow: William Collins, 1969).
Sood, Arun, *Robert Burns and the United States of America: Poetry, Print, and Memory* (Cham: Palgrave McMillan, 2018).
Southerne, Thomas, *Plays, with an Account of the Life and Writings of the Author*, 3 vols (London: Evans & Becket, 1774).
'SRG', 'If Burns had gone to Jamaica?', *Burns Chronicle* (1911), pp.79–82.
Stenhouse, William, *Illustrations of the Lyric Poetry and Music of Scotland* (Edinburgh: W Blackwood & Sons, 1853).
Sterling, James, *Poems* (London: GGJ and J Robinson, 1789).
Sterne, Laurence, *The Works of Laurence Sterne, With a Life of the Author, Written by Himself*, 10 vols (London: W Strahan, [and others], 1780).
Stevenson, David, *The Origins of Freemasonry: Scotland's Century 1590–1710* (Cambridge: Cambridge University Press, 1988).
— *The First Freemasons: Scotland's Early Lodges and their Members* (Aberdeen: Aberdeen University Press, 1988).
Stewart, Dugald, *Elements of the Philosophy of the Human Mind*, 3 vols (London/Edinburgh: A Strahan and T Cadell/W Creech, 1792).
Stewart, John, *An Account of Jamaica [etc.]* (Kingston, Jamaica: np, 1809).
Stott, William Taylor, *For Duty and Destiny: The Life and Civil War Diary of William Taylor Stott, Hoosier Soldier and Educator*, ed by Lloyd A Hunter (Indianapolis: Indiana Historical Society Press, 2010).
Strawhorn, John, *Ayrshire in the Time of Burns* (Kilmarnock: Ayrshire Archaeological and Natural History Society, 1959).
— *Mauchline Memories of Robert Burns* (Darvel: Ayrshire Archaeological and Natural History Society, 1985).
— 'Ayrshire and the Enlightenment,' in *A Sense of Place. Studies in Scottish Local History*, ed by Graeme Cruickshank (Edinburgh: Scotland's Cultural Heritage, 1988), pp.188–201.
— *The Scotland of Robert Burns* (Darvel: Alloway Publishing, 1995).
Sully, Philip, *Robert Burns and Dumfries: 1796–1896* (Dumfries: Thos Hunter & Co, 'Standard' Office, 1896).
Szasz, Ferenc Morton, *Abraham Lincoln and Robert Burns: Connected Lives and Legends* (Carbondale: Southern Illinois University Press, 2008).

Taylor, Michael, *The Interest: How the British Establishment Resisted the Abolition of Slavery* (London: Bodley Head, 2020).

Terence, *The Woman of Andros. The Self-Tormentor. The Eunuch* [Loeb Classical Library 22], ed and trans by John Barsby (Cambridge, MA: Harvard University Press, 2001).

Thompson, Mary V, *'The Only Unavoidable Subject of Regret.' George Washington, Slavery, and the Enslaved Community at Mount Vernon* (Charlottesville, VA: University of Virginia Press, 2019).

Thomson, James, *The Works of James Thomson. With His Last Corrections and Improvements. To Which is Prefixed, the Life of the Author*, 3 vols (London: J Rivington [and others], 1788).

Thornton, RD, *James Currie, The Entire Stranger and Robert Burns* (Edinburgh/London: Oliver & Boyd, 1963).

Tillman, Katherine D, *Recitations* (Philadelphia: AME Book Concern, [1902]).

Toomer, Jean, *Cane* (New York: Boni & Liveright, 1923).

Tough, Kate, *tilt-shift* (Tarland: Tapsalteerie, 2016).

Twain, Mark, *Life on the Mississippi* (Boston: James A Osgood and Company, 1883).

Voltaire, (Francois-Marie Arouet), *Œuvres Completes de Voltaire*, 70 vols, [ed by Condorcet Decroix and Beaumarchais] ([Paris]: la Société Littéraire-typographique, 1785).

The Works of Voltaire: A Contemporary Version, 40 vols, ed by John Morley and Tobias Smollet, trans by William F Fleming (Paris: E R DuMont, 1901).

Von Tunzelmann, Alex, *Fallen Idols: Twelve Statues that made History* (London: Headline Publishing Group, 2021).

Ward, JR, *British West Indian Slavery, 1750–1834* (Oxford/New York: Clarendon Press, 1988).

Ward, Samuel Ringgold, *Autobiography of a Fugitive Negro, His Anti-slavery Labours in the Unites States, Canada, & England* (London: John Snow, 1855).

Washington, Booker T, 'An Address before the National Educational Association [Buffalo, NY]', in *The Booker T Washington Papers, Volume 4: 1895–98*, ed by Louis R Harlan et al (Urbana/Chicago/London: University of Illinois Press, 1975), p.197.

'A Speech at the Institute of Arts and Sciences [Brooklyn, NY]', ibid, p.218.

'To the Editor of the Washington Colored American,' in *The Booker T Washington Papers. Volume 5: 1899–1900*, ed by Louis R Harlan and Raymond W Smock (Urbana/Chicago/London: University of Illinois Press, 1976), p.142.

Weir, John, *Lodge St James Tarbolton, Kilwinning No 135 (the Lodge of Robert Burns): A Historical Review 1771–1976* (Cumnock, Ayrshire: A Guthrie & Sons, Ltd, [1976]).

Weld, Theodore, *The Bible Against Slavery. An Inquiry into the Patriarchal and Mosaic Systems on the Subject of Human Rights* (New York: American Anti-Slavery Society, 1838).

Weston, John C, Jr, 'The Text of Burns' "The Jolly Beggars",' in *Studies in Bibliography*, 3 (1960), pp.239–247.

Whatley, Christopher A, *The Finest Place for a Lasting Colliery. Coal Mining Enterprise in Ayrshire c.1600–1840* ([Ayr]: AANHS, 1983).

'"The Fettering Bonds of Brotherhood": Combination and Labour Relations in the Scottish Coal-Mining Industry c. 1690–1775,' *Social History* (May,1987), pp.139–154.

Whyte, Iain, *Scotland and the Abolition of Black Slavery, 1756–1838* (Edinburgh: EUP, 2006).

Zachary Macaulay 1768–1838: The Steadfast Scot in the British Anti-Slavery Movement (Liverpool: Liverpool University Press, 2011).

"The Upas Tree: Beneath whose pestiferous shade all intellect languishes and all virtue dies': Scottish Public Perceptions of the Slave Trade and Slavery, 1756–1833,' in *Recovering Scotland's Slavery Past. The Caribbean Connection*, ed by TM Devine (Edinburgh: EUP, 2015), pp.187–205.

Wilkins, Frances, *Dumfries & Galloway and the Transatlantic Slave Trade* (Kidderminster: Wyre Forest Press, 2007).

Williams, Helen Maria, 'Sonnet. On Reading Mr Burns' Poem upon the Mountain Daisy,' *Edinburgh Magazine* (January 1787), p.120.

A Poem on the Bill Lately Passed in England for Regulating the Slave Trade (London: T Cadell, 1788).

Poems on Various Subjects: With Introductory Remarks on the Present State of Science and Literature in France (London: G and W B Whittaker, 1823).

Williams, Lisa, 'Remaking our Histories: Scotland, Slavery and Empire', at www.nationalgalleries.org/art-and-artists/features/remaking-our-histories-scotland-slavery-and-empire (accessed 1 September 2024).

'African Caribbean Residents of Edinburgh in the Eighteenth and Nineteenth Centuries', *Kalfou* (Spring 2020), pp.42–49.

Williams, George W[ashington], *History of the Negro Race in America from 1619 to 1880*, 2 vols (New York/London: GP Putnam's Sons, 1882).

[Wilson, John], 'Vindication of Mr Wordsworth's Letter to Mr Gray, On a New Edition of Burns,' *Blackwood's Magazine*, (October, 1817), pp.65–74.

Wood, Marcus, ed, *The Poetry of Slavery: An Anglo-American Anthology, 1764–1865* (Oxford: OUP, 2003).

Woodford, Wilson B, 'An Open Letter to Decatur's Colored Citizens [on the Lynching of Samuel J Bush,]' *Decatur Daily Republican*, 3 June 1893.

Wordsworth, William, as 'Axilogus,' 'Sonnet on Seeing Miss Helen Maria Williams Weep at a Tale of Distress,' *European Magazine* (1787), p.202.

Poems in Two Volumes, 2 vols (London: Longman, Hurst, Rees, and Orme and Brown, 1807).

Poems, 2 vols (London: Longman, Hurst, Rees, Orme and Brown, 1815).

The Prelude, or Growth of a Poet's Mind: An Autobiographical Poem (London: Edward Moxon, 1850).

The Prelude, or Growth of a Poet's Mind: An Autobiographical Poem. Edited from the Manuscripts, with Introduction, Textual and Critical Notes, ed by Edward de Selincourt (Oxford: Clarendon Press, 1926).

Wordsworth, William, and Dorothy Wordsworth, *The Letters of William and Dorothy Wordsworth Volume VII. The Later Years, Part IV, 1840–1853*, Second Edition, ed by Alan G Hill and Ernest de Selincourt (Oxford: OUP: 1988).

Young, Allan and Patrick Scott, *The Kilmarnock Burns: A Census* (Columbia, SC:

University of South Carolina Libraries, 2017).

Young, Edward, *The Complaint: Or, Night-Thoughts on Life, Death, and Immortality* (Glasgow: Robert Smith, Junior, 1764).

Zagarri, Rosemarie, ed, *David Humphreys' 'Life of General Washington' with George Washington's 'Remarks'* (Athens, GA: The University of Georgia Press, 1981).

Newspapers and Periodicals

A M E Church Review
The American Museum [Philadelphia]
The Atlantic
Ayr Advertiser
Ayr Observer
The Bee [Edinburgh]
Belfast Monthly Magazine
Caledonian Mercury [Edinburgh]
Cincinnati Commercial Tribune
Colored American [New York, NY]
Courier Herald [Brisbane, Qld]
Dumfries Journal
Edinburgh Evening Courant
Edinburgh Magazine
Emancipator and Republican [Boston, MA]
European Magazine [London]
Daily Record [Scotland]
Douglass's Monthly [Rochester, NY]
Financial Times [London]
Fortune [New York]
General Magazine, and Impartial Review [Baltimore, MD]
The Gentleman's Magazine [London]
The Glasgow Herald/The Herald
Glasgow Mercury
Greenock Telegraph
The Guardian [London]
Irvine Herald
The Liberator [Boston, MA]
Massachusetts Abolitionist [Boston, MA]
Monthly Review
National Anti-Slavery Standard, [Boston, MA]
New-York Tribune
New York Times
New York Weekly Tribune
NZ Herald [Dunedin]
Prospect Magazine [London]
The Scotsman [Edinburgh]

Scottish American Journal [New York, NY]
State Bystander [Des Moines, IA]
Sunday Post [Dundee]
Washington Evening Star [Washington, DC]
Weekly Miners' Journal [Pottsville, PA]
The Women's Journal [Boston, MA]

Broadcasts, Films and Recordings

Bissett, Allan and Jackie Kay, *Inside the Mind of Robert Burns*, produced/directed by Les Wilson, transmitted on BBC Scotland, 21 January 2021.

Marley, Bob, 'Redemption Song,' final track on Bob Marley & the Wailers, *Uprising* (Island Records, 1980).

McQueen, Steve, dir, *Twelve Years a Slave* (2013).

Scottish Poetry Library, *The Trysting Thorns*, www.scottishpoetrylibrary.org.uk/the-trysting-thorns/ (accessed 1 September 2024).

Sumbwanyambe, May, *The Trial of Joseph Knight,* produced/directed by Bruce Young, transmitted on BBC Radio 4, 12 July 2018.

Taylor, Elly M, *Angelou on Burns*, produced/directed by Elly M Taylor, transmitted on BBC2, 21 August 1996.

Databases

History of Parliament Online, www.historyofparliamentonline.org.

National Gallery Report: *Phases I and II of the National Gallery and Legacies of British Slave-holdership Research Project,* at www.nationalgallery.org.uk/people/ (accessed 1 September 2024).

Runaway Slaves in Britain: Bondage, Freedom and Race in the Eighteenth Century, www.runaways.gla.ac.uk/ (accessed 1 September 2024).

Slave Voyages Database, www.museumoflondon.org.uk/news-room/press-releases/robert-milligan-statue-statement (accessed 1 September 2024).

University College London. *Legacies of British Slave Ownership:* www.ucl.ac.uk/lbs (accessed 1 September 2024).

Index

Abingdon Earl of 32
Abolition of Slavery Act (1807) 32, 184, 217, 285, 385, 408
Adair Dr James Mckittrick, Jr 70, 78
Adair Dr James Mckittrick, Sr 78
African Grove Theatre 353
Alexander Claude, of Ballochmyle 29, 48
Alexander, Wilhelmina 29n
Alfred King, (The Great) 202, 207, 310
Alison Alexander 82
Allan Sir William 378
Allen Professor William Gustavus 359, 361n
Alloway 24, 25, 38, 65, 85, 321, 370, 381, 423
American Civil War 350, 362nn, 363, 372-383, 386nn, 390, 403
Anderson Dr James 240-241
Anderson Morag 19
Andrews Corey 177-178, 189, 193-194, 197
Andrews Ethan Allen 389
Angelou Maya 195
Annan Kofi 413
Apprenticeship
 — Freemason 152-153
 — Post-Abolition 33, 36n, 81, 349
 — Trade 34-35, 43, 51, 240, 301
Armour or Burns Jean 45, 63, 84, 87, 92, 97, 106, 148, 154, 156, 224, 225, 416-417
Armour James 85, 319, 416,
'Articles of War' 36n
Auchincruive 50, 162, 405, 406, 419
Auld Lichts 25, 126-128, 132-134,
Ayachi Janette 19
Ayr 23-25, 43, 46, 48, 49, 63, 66-67, 74-75, 77, 92, 151, 154, 158, 235, 352, 370, 406, 422
Ayr – Street Names 405n
Ayr Bank – See Douglas, Heron & Co
Ayr Mount (Jamaica) 86, 87, 106, 325, 326
Babington Thomas 341
Baldwin Revd Abraham Chittenden 360, 363n
Ballantine John 24-25, 49, 66, 73, 85, 93
Ballantine Patrick 49, 102
Bance Island 163, 166
Banneker Benjamin 242
Barskimming Lord 57, 58-59, 77, 181
Beattie James 40, 133, 238-240
Beattie Sally 60-64, 166
Beecher Revd Henry Ward 374
Begg Isabella Burns 370, 424
Bel (or Belinda) (Indian Servant) 54, 180
Bell Alexander 'Sandy' 71, 75-76, 102, 124-126, 342

Belle Dido Elizabeth 55n, 79, 326n, 335n
Benin Bronzes 407n
Bennie Revd Archibald 358, 362n
Benson William 70
Biblical Passages
 — Curse of Ham (Genesis) 131-132
 — Moses and the Rock (Exodus) 209-211
 — Moses and Zipporah (Exodus) 130
 — Nimrod (Genesis) 183, 185-186, 301
 — Zimri And Kosbi (Numbers) 128-129
Bickerstaffe Isaac 244n, 246-247
Black Population
 Ayrshire 74
 England and Wales 43
 Scotland 51
Black Prince 47, 75
Blair David 111
Blair Revd Dr Hugh 78, 123-124, 228, 247-248, 419
Blair Revd Robert 248
Blairquhan Castle 405-406
Boileau Nicholas 249
Bolling Philip Archelaus 358, 362n
Boswell Alexander of Auchinleck, Lord Auchinleck 57, 58-59
Boswell Douglas Hamilton 86, 88n
Boswell James of Auchinleck 48, 61, 223n, 226
Boswell Jane Douglas 86, 88n
Branagan Thomas 388
Briggs Susi 19
Brown Captain Richard 62, 71, 94, 123, 132, 239
Brown Dr Alexander 225
Brown Major 47, 75
Brown Revd Hugh Stowell 361, 362n
Brown Sterling Allen 401-402
Brown William Wells 354, 360, 362n
Buchanan President James 374
Burnard Trevor 31n, 39-40, 100, 101n, 141, 159n, 319-320, 343, 404
Burnes William 62, 63, 65, 73, 235, 236n,
Burness James 65
Burns Anthony 364-365
Burns Cottage, Alloway 49, 62, 85, 370, 377, 406, 421
Burns Gilbert 38-39, 67, 73, 84, 86-87, 97, 98, 106, 192, 238n, 326-326n, 337,
Burns Mausoleum, Dumfries 404, 406
Burns Monument, Alloway 370, 406, 422-423
Burns Monument, Edinburgh 406
Burns's Letters —
 To Robert Aiken, [About 8 October] 1786 133

To Dr Anderson, 1 November 1790 240
To John Arnot, 17 April 1786 88
To John Arnot, 10 August 1786 90
To John Ballantine, [End September] 1786 92
To John Ballantine, 27 November 1786 93
To David Blair, 27 August 1789
To David Brice, 12 June 1786 89
To David Brice, 17 July 1786 90
To Gilbert Burns 22 July 1786 [Deed of Assignment] 90
To [James Burness], 21 June 1783 65, 221
To Bruce Campbell, 13 November 1788 116
To Thomas Campbell, 19 August 1786 91
To Margaret 'Peggy' Chalmers, 21 October 1787 111
To William Corbet, [February 1792] 187-188, 232, 234
To Alexander Cunningham, 10 September 1792 407
To Mrs Dunlop, 15 April 1787 294
To Mrs Dunlop, 7 March 1788 185
To Mrs Dunlop, 28 April 1788 249
To Mrs Dunlop, 10 August 1788 96
To Mrs Dunlop, 16 August 1788 293
To Mrs Dunlop, 21 August 1788 125
To Mrs Dunlop, 13 November 1788, 298
To Mrs Dunlop, Jan[uary] 1789 165
To Mrs Dunlop, 21/22 June 1789 323
To Mrs Dunlop, 15 December 1793 237, 252
To Mrs Dunlop, 25 June 1794 201
To Mrs Dunlop, 20 December 1794 – 1 January 1795 411
To Miss Rachel Dunlop, 2 August 1788 116
To [John Francis Erskine of Mar], 13 April 1793 82, 117
To Miss Louisa Fontenelle], [November 1792] 147
To Robert Graham of Fintry, 9 December 1789 25, 181
To Robert Graham of Fintry, 31 December 1792 81
To Heron Heron of Heron, [March 1795] 222
To Peter Hill, 2 February 1790 155
To Mr [James] Hoy, 20 October 1787 160
To John Hutchison, 2 January 1787 94
To John Kennedy, 10 August 1786 92, 103n
To John Kennedy, 26 September 1786 92
To Wiliam Logan, 30 October 1786 93, 154, 232
To Agnes McLehose, January 1788 185
To Agnes McLehose, 28 December 1787 111,
To Agnes McLehose, 4 January 1788 304
To Agnes Mclehose, 19 January 1788 247
To John Mcleod of Colbecks, 18 June 1794 200n
To Patrick Miller, Jr 8 March [1795] 167n

To Dr John Moore, 2 August 1788 ['The Autobiographical Letter'] 66, 67, 71, 86, 99, 123, 156-160, 185, 235, 269, 278, 279, 283, 288, 290, 305, 310,
To Dr John Moore, 23 March 1789 165
To Robert Muir, 8 September 1786 92, 94
To Robert Muir, 15 December 1786
To John Murdoch, 15 January 1783 237
To William Nicol, 18 June 1787 282
To William Nicol, [20 February] 1793 112
To William Niven, July 1780 67
To John Richmond, 30 July 1786 90
To John Richmond, 1 September 1786 91
To John Richmond, [27 September] 1786 92
To Mrs R[obert] Riddell, [December 1793] 113
To David Sillars [Sic], [Early Summer 1791] 72
To Sir John Sinclair of Ulbster, Bart, [August or September 1791] 236
To James Smith, 14 August 1786 91, 320
To James Smith, 11 June 1787 95, 107
To Revd Thomas Smith, 4 July 1791 249
To [Mrs Catherine Gordon Stewart], October 1791 221
To Mrs Stewart of Stair, September 1786 221
To Peter Stuart, [May 1789] 165
To John Syme, [May? 1795] 167
To George Thomson, 26/27 October 1792 97
To Helen Maria Williams, Dated [late July or early August] 1789
Burns's Life — Excise 63, 81-82, 87, 93, 98, 117, 187, 219, 221, 234, 342, 408, 411
— Freemasonry 62, 73, 79, 85, 150-154, 154, 212-215
— Statues 404, 415
Burns's Editions of Works
— Kilmarnock Edition 18, 63, 87, 106, 144, 159, 283, 293, 318
— Currie Edition 15, 74, 83, 86, 223, 228
— Currie Edition (1801) 39
— First Edinburgh Edition 63, 75, 123, 133, 146, 160, 247, 328, 344, 353
— Second Edinburgh Edition 63, 187, 222, 298
— George Washington's Copy 209
— Frederick Douglass's Copies 368, 369n
Burns's Poems
— Address of Beelzebub (The) 68, 69n, 418
— Annotations in Verse 118
— Answer to an Invitation 117
— Auld Lang Syne 139n, 150, 365 [Imitation], 375, 380
— Author's Earnest Cry and Prayer (The) 115
— Beware o' Bonie Ann 112
— The Brigs of Ayr 66, 309

INDEX

— Castle Gordon 63, 160-162, 193, 224, 232
— Dedication to G[avin] H[amilton] 133
— Dream (The) 68
— Election Ballads (Heron) 218, 221
— Election Ballads (Westerhall) 63, 179-181, 232
— English Song 113
— Epistle To Capt[ai]n William Logan, Park 154-156
— Epistle To J[ohn] R[ankine] 84, 99, 121-124
— Epitaph For Mr W[alter] R[iddell] 199-200
— Extempore — To Gavin Hamilton 134-136
— Farewell, to the Brethren (The) 150-154
— Highland Lassie, O — 148-150
— Honest Poverty 15, 121, 212-219, [Chapter Seven, passim]
— Humble Petition of Bruar Water (The) 116
— I Ha'e a Wife o' My Ain 117
— Jolly Beggars (The) 111, 228-230
— Kirk's Alarm (The) 117
— Kissing My Katie 112
— Letter To J[ame]s T[ennan]t of Gl[e]nc[onne]r 71
— Lines to an Old Sweetheart 144-145
— Lines Written on a Bank-Note 143-144
— Lines Written on Windows of the Globe Tavern, Dumfries 82
— Lovely Davies 112
— McPherson's Farewell 120
— Man Was Made to Mourn [Chapter Seven, passim]
— Mark Yonder Pomp 113
— Mary Morison 111
— Mauchline Wedding (The) 124-126,
— Menagerie (The) 225-227
— O Lay Thy Loof in Mine, Lass 112
— Ode For General Washington's Birthday 201-209
— Ode, Sacred to The Memory of Mrs O[swald] 162-167
— On a Scotch Bard 136-143
— On Glenriddell's Fox Breaking His Chain 182-186, 230
— On Scaring Some Water-Fowl on Loch Turit
— On Seeing Mrs Kemble in Yarico 224, 230, 412
— Oroananaoig Oo, The Song of Death 120
— Ordination (The) 124-134,
— Poetical Inscription 219-223

— Prologue, Spoken by Mr Woods 304
— Rights of Woman (The) 216
— Scots Wha Hae 15, 120, 349 [Paraphrase], 380 [Paraphrase/Parody]
— She Says She Loe's Me Best o' a' 113
— Slave's Lament (The) 15, 16, 18, 63, 80, 123, 147, 177, 188-199, 224-225, 230, 235, 317, 398, 408, 412, 417
— Solemn League and Covenant (The) 117
— Song — For a' That and a' That [see Honest Poverty]
— Song [O Poortith Cauld] 112 Sweetest May 112
— The Gloomy Night is Gath'ring Fast 145-147, 196
— Their Groves o' Sweet Myrtle 113, 223-225
— Tho' Women's Minds 112
— Twa Dogs (The)
— Verses Written on a Window at the Inn at Carron
— Will Ye Go to the Indies, My Mary? 148-150

Burns Supper – The First, in 1801 85, 406
Burns Supper – The First in the USA 363
Burns Suppers – West Indies 406
Burns Suppers – USA 1859 373-374
Burnside Revd William 81
Butler Samuel 248
Byron Lord 17
'C' (Confederate Poet) 380
Cairns John 41, 43, 51
Calder Robert Mclean 412
Calderon Louisa 223n
Cameron Meg 156, 323
Campbell John 363
Campbell Major General Sir Archibald of Inverneil 335
Campbell Mary ('Highland Mary') 84, 87, 104-105, 148-150, 322, 343-344, 382, 416, 423
Carey Brycchan 56, 197n, 237-238
Carron Ironworks 69-70
Carruthers Gerry 16, 18, 42-43, 84, 97n, 106n, 110, 190, 195, 220n, 222-223, 318, 411, 413
Carswell Catherine 141n, 146-147
Cartwright John 47-48, 63, 76, 77, 125-126,
Catherine Empress of Russia 'The Great' 241
Catrine Cotton Works 29, 71
Cayenne Mister 42-43
Cervantes Saavedra Miguel De 249-250
Chambers Robert 237, 238n
Chambers Hon Thomas 246
Chang P C 390-391

459

Church Patronage 31, 126-127
Cicero Marcus Tullius 250-251
Cincinnatus 208
Clarkson Thomas 31-32, 63, 194, 217, 237, 238, 243, 253, 266, 287, 293-294, 295, 304, 306, 310, 317
Clay Cassius Marcellus 359, 362n
Clow Jenny 156, 323
Codding Revd Ichabod 360, 362n
Colliers 35-37, 54, 59, 70-71, 81n
Cooba (Enslaved Woman) 246
Cooper Dr Anna J 384, 386n
Cooper Thomas 136n, 251-252
Copeland (Dumfries Surgeon) 81
Corbet William 187-188, 221, 232, 234
Coulston Edward 404
Coward Slavery 109, 118-121, 212-213, 412
Cowper William 217, 252-263, 275, 285, 322, 392, 409
Crawford Robert 19, 83, 86, 142, 212, 319, 320-321
Crawford Thomas 166, 215-216,
Cromek Robert H 145n, 228-230,
Culzean Castle And Kennedy Family 44-46, 74, 167n
Cunningham Allan 190, 192
Cunningham Graham of Gartmore Robert 78, 155
Dale David 29
Dalrymple Revd Dr William 25, 78, 236n, 419
Dalrymple James of Stair (Viscount Stair) 35n, 50-51, 52n, 113, 114, 118, 119n, 224, 225n, 412
Danks John Anderson 361, 363
Davis President Jefferson 376, 381,
De Saint-Lambert Jean-François 241-242
Devine Sir Tom 18n, 30n, 40, 61, 80, 159n
Dick James C 195,
Dickerson Mary Anne 352n
Dickson William 28, 60, 63, 81, 180, 188, 190, 231, 408
Dolben's Act (1778) 32, 63, 167, 170n, 213, 315
Douglas Captain Andrew 44
Douglas Charles 37, 77n, 83, 85-86, 87-96, 99, 100, 101, 102, 141, 143, 149, 156, 159, 237, 322, 325, 409
Douglas Charles – Enslaved persons 86n
Douglas Charles – Illegitimate Children 86n
Douglas Dr Patrick of Garallan 37, 41n, 85, 86, 87-96, 101, 135, 152, 154, 321, 406, 416
Douglas or Kennedy Jean 44-46
Douglas, Heron & Co ['The Ayr Bank'] 23, 65, 221
Douglass Anna Murray 368

Douglass Frederick 118-119, 120, 358, 360, 362n, 363n, 367-372, 377-378, 383, 384, 386n, 388-389, 390, 391, 394, 395, 403, 412, 414-415, 421-430
Douglass Lewis H 368, 378n,
Du Bois W[Illiam] E[dward] B[urghart] 385, 387n, 400
DuRant Joseph 381
Dunbar Paul Laurence 400-401, 402
Dunbar William 229, 263-266
Dundas Henry (Lord Melville) 80, 205, 220-221, 335n
Dundas Robert Lord President 36, 57-59, 77
Dundee 43n, 192
Dunduff Lady 46
Dunlop Anna Frances Wallace of Dunlop 63, 78, 86n, 96, 99n, 106, 124-125, 156, 165, 185n, 187, 201, 237, 249, 252, 283, 292, 293, 294, 298, 317, 323n, 411
Dyer Revd John 266-267
Equiano, Olaudah 185
Erskine, John Francis of Mar 82, 117
Fairlie, Alexander of Fairlie 65
Ferguson, Captain Hugh 406
Fields, Julia 401
Flipper, Henry Ossian 384, 386
Fortune, T Thomas 384, 386
Fox, Charles James 182, 184
Fry, Michael 18
Galloway, Earl of 220, 221
Galt, John 41, 42, 126
Gammetta 49, 75
Garnet, Revd Henry Highland 351
Garrison, William Lloyd 352, 354, 355, 357, 358, 360, 362, 364, 365, 366, 368, 377, 384, 386, 403
Garvey, Marcus 119, 386, 387
Gay, John 267, 268
Georgeson, James 79
Gibbon, Edward 257, 268
Gibbs, Mifflin Wistar 359, 362
Gillette, Francis 360, 363
Gilfillan, Revd George 369
Glencairn, James, Earl of 48, 63, 126
Global Climate Crisis 405
Glover, Richard 269
Gordon, Alexander, Duke of 160, 161
Gordon, Jane, Duchess of 160
Gory 77, 78
Graham, Robert of Gartmore 78, 155
Grant, General/President Ulysses S 379-381
Gray, Or Kennedy, Margaret 45, 74
Guthrie, William 29, 99, 100, 108, 142-143,

INDEX

157, 158, 193, 214, 269-272, 290, 317, 409
Haliburton Campbell 82
Hamilton Alexander ('Sandy') West 49-50
Hamilton, Douglas 26, 41, 67, 105, 139, 149, 155, 180
Hamilton, Gavin 73, 87, 97, 103, 134, 232, 322
Hamilton, Hugh of Pinmore and Bellisle 49-50, 406
Hamilton, Jane 49, 75
Hamilton, John of Sundrum 34, 48-49, 73, 151, 153, 223, 405
Hamilton, Robert (II) of Bourtreehill 48, 86, 235
Hartley, LP 404
Hastings, Warren 71
Haynes, Stephen R 132
Henson, Revd Josiah Henson 384, 386
Heron, Patrick of Heron 79, 167, 219-223
Hill, Peter 79, 155, 210, 236, 270, 275, 285, 289, 298, 302, 305, 312
Homer 249, 274-275, 330
Honourable East India Company 14, 29, 71, 349
Howells, William Dean 376, 399
Hughes, Langston 393, 399, 400, 401,
Hume, David 110, 238-239, 242, 276-278, 409
Humphreys, General David 207
Hunter Blair Sir David 406
Hunter's Bank, Ayr 24, 49, 86, 102, 406
Hurdis, James Revd 275
Hutcheson, Francis 51, 61
Hutchinson, John 90, 94, 95, 100
Ingersoll, Colonel Robert G 376, 377
Irvine 29, 46, 48, 62, 67, 69, 72, 73, 75, 135, 320
Jacobs, Harriet A 361, 363
Jacobs Louisa Matilda 361, 363
Jamaica
   – Enslaved Punishments 140, 141, 142, 185, 187-188, 284, 337, 409
   – Enslaved Rations 140-141
   – Enslaved Revolts 48, 245, 305
   – Marriage/Concubinage 149, 155-156,
   – Mortality 31n, 38-40, 135-136, 141, 153, 159n, 318-321
   – Scots Population 37-39, 139,
Jefferson, Thomas 242, 324-325, 356
Johnson, Linton Kwesi 7
Johnston, Nathan 368
Johnston, James 189
Johnstone, Alexander 180
Johnstone, Sir James of Westerhall 179-181, 205
Joppa (Ayrshire Village) 49, 75
Judicial Indenture & Transportation 34, 103, 159-160, 196
Kaithness, David 34
Kames, Henry Home, Lord 57, 58, 272-274

Kay, Jackie 7, 17, 197, 318, 402
Kemble, Elizabeth, Mrs 63, 188, 209-212, 224, 231, 233, 317, 408, 412
Kemble, Stephen 209
Kennedy, Captain Primrose of Drumellan 406
Kennedy, David 25
Kennedy, Douglas 46
Kennedy, President John F 413
Kennedy, Scipio 44-46, 62, 74, 77, 130
Kilkerran, Lord 53
Kimber, Captain John 243
King, Dr Martin Luther, Jr 350, 391-397, 403, 413, 414
Kinghorn, A M 37, 99, 139
Kinsley, James 25, 110, 138, 161, 190, 191, 193, 219, 221, 248, 249, 264, 287, 288, 310, 316
Kirkoswald 45, 46, 62, 74, 130, 144
Ku Klux Klan 403
L'Ouverture, General Touissant 152, 217
Latchemo 54
Lauder, Sir Harry 140
Laurens, Henry 164, 288
Law Cases (Enslavement)
   — 'The Tumbling Lassie Case' (1687) 51
   — Brown v Board of Education (1954) 394
   — Dalrymple v Spens (1771) 53, 62
   — Knight v Wedderburn (1774) 54-56, 58-60, 62, 77, 79, 126, 180, 272
   — Porterfield v Nicolson of Carnock (1770, 1771) 54
   — Rex v Stephen Devereux (1793) 243
   — Sheddan v Montgomery (1757) 48, 53, 62
   — Somerset's Case (1772) 55, 62
   — Stewart v Graham (1782) 57
Leask, Nigel 32, 105, 115, 118, 122, 129, 141, 177, 178, 182, 190, 195, 213-215, 217, 224, 318
Lee, General Robert E 380
Lee, William 'Billy' 204, 206
Lewars, Jessie 225
Lewis, William Henry 384, 386
Liddle, Rod 16, 17
Lincoln, Mary Todd, Mrs 381
Lincoln, President Abraham 357, 362, 367, 375, 376, 380-382
Lindsay, Andrew O 20, 156, 319, 321-325, 343, 346-347, 348
Lindsay, or Hill, Elisabeth 79
Locke, John 278, 356
Lochhead, Liz 19
Long, Edward 29, 37-38, 140, 229, 343-343
Love, Revd Dr Robert 385, 386

Mabuza, Lindiwe 7, 198
Macaulay, Selina, Mrs 328
Macaulay, Zachary 20, 41, 105, 139, 319, 323, 327-344, 348, 410
Mackay, Charles 381
Mackenzie, Henry 93-94, 107, 279, 317, 409
Mackinlay, Revd James 126-127
Macpherson, James 274-275
Mansfield, Earl of 54-55, 57, 79
Marley, Bob 119
Martyn, Sarah Towne Smith 359, 362
Mays, Revd Dr Benjamin E 397
McAdam, John Loudon 46, 47
McCallum, Shara 20, 226, 319, 325, 328, 340-341, 344, 346-347, 402
McCune Smith, Dr James 350-353, 357
McGill, Dr William 25
McGowan, Private 47
McKay, Claude 400-401
McLehose, Agnes ('Nancy'/'Clarinda') 78, 111, 149, 185, 247, 291, 304, 419
McNulty, Victoria 19
Melville, Jennifer 27, 44, 46, 65, 79, 166
Metaphorical Slavery 109-111
Mickens, Revd H M 385, 387,
Millar, Patrick of Dalswinton 179
Milligan, Robert 80, 404
Milly (Servant) 47, 74
Milton, John 131-132, 185-186, 281-283
Mitchell, Collector John 81
Monboddo, Lord 57, 58, 77
Montaigne, Michel de 283
Montesquieu, Chales Louis de Secondat, Baron de 224
Moore, Dr John 66, 95-96, 156, 165, 167, 176-177, 237, 269, 283, 317, 329, 409
Morgan, Andrew 16
Mott, Abigail 370, 403
Mount Vernon, VA 201, 203-206, 208,
Muirkirk Ironworks 28, 71
Mulatto Girl, Beith 48
Mullen, Stephen 26, 34, 38, 52, 160, 353
Murdoch, John 38, 62, 71, 74, 235, 237, 238, 279, 306, 310, 312, 317
Myers, Norma 43
Nairne, Professor Charles Murray 375
Napoleonic And Revolutionary Wars 32, 36, 82, 160
National Trust for Scotland 26, 27, 44, 79
Nell, William Cooper 352, 367
New Lichts 25, 127
Newman, Simon 38, 353
Newton, Revd John 285, 342
Nicol, William 63, 69, 112, 160, 281

Northup, Solomon 139, 389, 390
Orr, Speaker James 375-376
Osnaburgh [and variant spellings]
— cloth 29, 67-68, 271
— Prince Bishop 67
— town 29
Ossian 237, 274
Oswald, George of Scotstoun 166
Oswald of Auchincruive, Richard 163-165, 419
Oswald, Richard Alexander (I) of Auchencruive 165, 166, 167
Oswald Richard Alexander (II) of Auchencruive 167, 406
Oswald Richard Alexander (III) of Auchencruive 405
Othello 46, 74
Paine, Thomas 203, 215-216, 219
Palmer, Sir Geoff 190
Patrick, Lt-Col 379
Paul, Haskell 387
Paul, Revd Hamilton 126, 406
Pearce, Senator James 375
Petitions For Abolition 60, 63, 79-80, 152, 167, 180, 188, 190, 197, 231, 240, 328, 408
Pindar, Peter 286
Pitt, William (The Younger) 178, 184
Pittock, Murray 114, 118, 146, 178, 191, 193, 354
Political Slavery 109, 113-118
Pope, Alexander 287
Posey, Alexander L 387
Prince 47, 75,
Prince Hall Masonry 152, 352
Pringle, Thomas 178-179, 188
Proudfoot, John 379, 380,
Pultney, Sir William 180-181
Queensbury, Duke of ('Old Q') 179, 181
Ramsay, Allan 81, 89, 288
Ramsay, David 288
Ramsay (Dumfries Solicitor) 81
Ramsay, or Oswald, Mary, Mrs 162-167
Red Man's Pledge of Peace Marker 387
Renton, Alex 53, 155, 406
Rhees, Revd John Morgan 205
Richard (Servant) 47
Richmond, Duke of 170, 178
Riddell, Maria 70, 113, 199-200, 289, 298
Riddell, Robert of Glenriddell 182, 199, 211
Riddell, Walter 78, 199-200, 289
Rodney, Admiral 32, 230
Rodgers, Hugh 74, 237
Romley, Lord 246
Roosevelt, Colonel (President) Theodore 387
Roscoe, William 79, 81, 244, 411
Rosebery, Earl of 348

INDEX

Rozelle, Ayr 48, 167, 405
Rozelle, Jamaica 167, 405, 406
Rum Punch 31, 165, 407
Rushton, Edward 76, 205, 206, 208, 216, 342
Salmon, Thomas 99, 108, 141, 143, 157, 158, 269, 290, 317, 409
Salters – See Colliers 35-36, 54, 69, 71, 81, 418
Sancho, Ignatius 62, 78, 133, 291, 308
Scotland, Alexander 74
Scott, David 406
Scott, Patrick 83, 103, 220
Scott, Sir Walter of Abbotsford 30, 31, 228, 367, 368, 372, 382
Scottish Government
Shakespeare, William 7, 292, 392
Shelley, Percey Bysshe 398, 403
Shenstone, William 237, 293-294, 334
Ships
— Bell 87, 91, 93, 106, 320, 322, 325
— Kitty & Amelia 80
— Nancy 18, 87, 90, 91, 105, 106, 320
— Roselle 87, 94, 107, 233
Shuften, J T 386
Sillar, David 72
Smellie, William 78, 153, 290, 298-299
Smith, Dr Adam 133, 164, 294-295, 317, 409
Smith, James 91, 95, 107, 222, 320
Smith, Mungo of Drongan 36, 47, 75, 151, 153
Smollett, Tobias 187, 249-250, 302, 312, 334
Smout, T C 33, 35
Southerne, Thomas 268, 304, 305
Steele, Sir Richard 305
Stenhouse, William 192, 193
Sterling, Revd James 308
Stern, Revd Laurence 133, 237, 291, 306, 308, 334
Stewart, Professor Dugald of Catrine 78, 83, 98, 163, 309, 409
Stewart, Thomas 228
Stowe, Harriet Beecher 374, 386
Stuart, Peter 165, 166
Swinton, John 56
Syme, John 167, 221
Symington, William 47
Terence (Publius Terentius Afer) 363, 364
Thirteen Colonies – Loss 32, 40
Thompson, or Neilson, Peggy 144
Thomson, George 97, 149, 213-215, 286
Thomson, James 114, 172, 176, 191, 237, 238, 286, 310
Tiro (Freedman) 250
Tom (Servant) 78
Toomer, Jean 401
Tough, Kate 31

'Trappan'd Maid (The)' 191, 412
'Trotz Alledem' 354
Troup, Dr Jonathan 39, 40
Trumbull, General Matthew 382
Trysting Thorns (Poet Group) 19
Tubman, Harriet 'Moses' 366
'Tyler's Toast' The 151
UN Universal Declaration of Human Rights 390, 414
University of Glasgow 48, 71, 83, 295, 351, 353, 362
US Constitution 356, 377, 390
US Declaration of Independence 53, 62, 356, 377-378, 382
Voltaire (Francois-Marie Arouet) 245, 290, 311-312, 339
Wake, Ransome F 351, 352
Wanlockhead Lead Mines 47, 69, 70
Ward, Samuel Ringgold 42, 353
Washington, General George 201, 203-209, 406
Washington, Martha Dandridge Custis 203
Waters, Alexander 49
Wedderburn, 'Sir' John 55, 56, 180
Wedgwood's Anti-Slavery Medallion 63, 214, 341, 420
Wells, Ida B 385, 386
Whitefoord, Sir John 47-48, 76
Whyte, Iain 18, 28, 43, 44, 48, 50, 52, 60, 61, 74, 78, 80, 82, 98, 124, 139, 145, 161, 163, 164, 180, 190, 195, 231, 320, 324, 328, 336
Wilberforce, William 21, 28, 60, 61, 62, 136, 211, 243, 253, 341, 418
Williams, Helen Maria 16, 63, 167-168, 176-178, 190, 191, 192, 197, 213, 225-226, 228, 232, 234, 315, 317, 408
Witherspoon, Revd John 53, 288
Wolcot, Dr John – See Pindar, Peter 286
Wood, Marcus 194, 217
Woodford, Wilson B 385, 386
Wright, Elizabeth Clendenon 359, 362
Wycherley, William 214
York, Duke of – See Osnaburgh Bishop 68
Young, Revd Edward 46, 75, 316
Zoffany, Johann 29, 164

Luath Press Limited

committed to publishing well written books worth reading

LUATH PRESS takes its name from Robert Burns, whose little collie Luath (*Gael.*, swift or nimble) tripped up Jean Armour at a wedding and gave him the chance to speak to the woman who was to be his wife and the abiding love of his life. Burns called one of the 'Twa Dogs' Luath after Cuchullin's hunting dog in Ossian's *Fingal*. Luath Press was established in 1981 in the heart of Burns country, and is now based a few steps up the road from Burns' first lodgings on Edinburgh's Royal Mile. Luath offers you distinctive writing with a hint of unexpected pleasures.

Most bookshops in the UK, the US, Canada, Australia, New Zealand and parts of Europe, either carry our books in stock or can order them for you. To order direct from us, please send a £sterling cheque, postal order, international money order or your credit card details (number, address of cardholder and expiry date) to us at the address below. Please add post and packing as follows: UK – £1.00 per delivery address; overseas surface mail – £2.50 per delivery address; overseas airmail – £3.50 for the first book to each delivery address, plus £1.00 for each additional book by airmail to the same address. If your order is a gift, we will happily enclose your card or message at no extra charge.

Luath Press Limited
543/2 Castlehill
The Royal Mile
Edinburgh EH1 2ND
Scotland
Telephone: 0131 225 4326 (24 hours)
Email: sales@luath.co.uk
Website: www.luath.co.uk